Global Political Islam

This book is an accessible and comprehensive account of the international and global dimensions of political Islam in the twenty-first century. Drawing on insights from international relations and Islamic studies, it explains the complex interaction between political Islam, nationalism, and globalization and demonstrates how this transcends any simplified model of a "clash of civilizations." The book illuminates the theory with a number of detailed case studies of the Arab Middle East, Central and South Asia, Southeast Asia and Islam in Europe and North America. It also provides a detailed account of Al-Qaeda as a transnational network. Subjects covered by the book include:

- history of political Islam
- how political Islam interacts with the nation-state and the global economy
- the cultural and identity politics of Islam
- a wide variety of international case studies
- profiles of key movements and individuals

Fully illustrated throughout, featuring maps, a glossary and suggestions for further reading, this is the ideal introduction to the crucial role of political Islam in the contemporary world.

Peter Mandaville is Associate Professor of Government and Politics at George Mason University, USA. He is the author of *Transnational Muslim Politics: Re-imagining the Umma* and has also co-edited several volumes of essays. Research interests include the impact of globalization in the Muslim world, theories of cosmopolitanism, and global development.

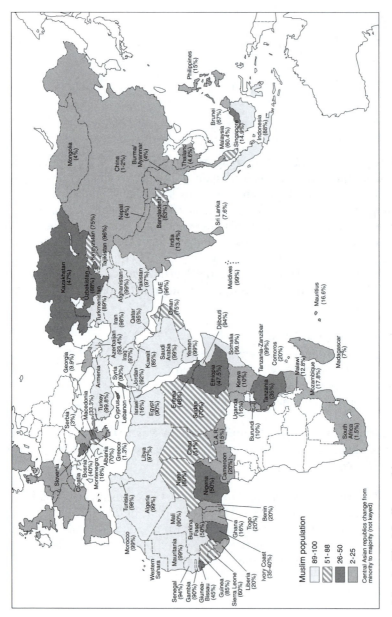

Map 1a The Muslim world

Muslim population

89–100
51–88
26–50
2–25

Central Asian republics change from
minority to majority (not keyed)

Philippines (15%)
Brunei (67%)
Indonesia (88%)
Malaysia (60.4%)
Singapore (14.9%)
Thailand (4.6%)
Mongolia (4%)
China (1–2%)
Burma/Myanmar (4%)
Kyrgyzstan (75%)
Tajikistan (96%)
Kazakhstan (47%)
Uzbekistan (88%)
Nepal (4%)
Bangladesh (83%)
Sri Lanka (7.6%)
Turkmenistan (89%)
India (13.4%)
Afghanistan (99%)
Pakistan (97%)
UAE (96%)
Maldives (99%)
Mauritius (16.6%)
Iran (98%)
Qatar (95%)
Oman (75%)
Azerbaijan (93.4%)
Iraq (97%)
Saudi Arabia (99%)
Kuwait (85%)
Yemen (99%)
Djibouti (94%)
Somalia (99.9%)
Tanzania-Zanzibar (99%)
Comoros (20%)
Madagascar (7%)
Georgia (9.9%)
Armenia
Syria (90%)
Jordan (92%)
Ethiopia (47.5%)
Kenya (10%)
Malawi (12.8%)
Mozambique (17.8%)
Turkey (99.8%)
Cyprus
Lebanon
Israel (16%)
Egypt (90%)
Eritrea (46%)
Sudan (70%)
Uganda (16%)
Tanzania (35%)
Macedonia (33.3%)
Serbia (3%)
Burundi (10%)
Albania (70%)
Greece (1.3%)
Libya (97%)
Chad (51%)
C.A.R. (15%)
South Africa (1.5%)
Slovenia
Bosnia (40%)
Croatia
Montenegro (18%)
Niger (80%)
Cameroon (20%)
Nigeria (50%)
Tunisia (98%)
Algeria (99%)
Benin (20%)
Morocco (99%)
Mali (90%)
Burkina Faso (50%)
Ghana (16%)
Togo (20%)
Western Sahara
Mauritania (99%)
Ivory Coast (35–40%)
Senegal (94%)
Gambia (90%)
Guinea-Bissau (45%)
Guinea (85%)
Sierra Leone (60%)
Liberia (20%)

Map 1b The Muslim world

Muslim distribution

Sunni

Shia

Global Political Islam

Peter Mandaville

Routledge
Taylor & Francis Group

LONDON AND NEW YORK

First published 2007
by Routledge
2 Park Square Milton Park Abingdon Oxon OX14 4RN

Simultaneously published in the USA and Canada
by Routledge
270 Madison Avenue, New York, NY 10016

Routledge is an imprint of the Taylor & Francis Group, an informa business

© 2007 Peter Mandaville

Typeset in Times New Roman by
Taylor & Francis

British Library Cataloguing in Publication Data
A catalogue record for this book is available from the British Library

Library of Congress Cataloging in Publication Data
Mandaville, Peter P., 1971-
  Global political Islam / Peter Mandaville.
    p. cm.
  Includes bibliographical references and index. [etc.]
  1. Islam and politics. 2. Islam and state. 3. Globalization–Religious
aspects–Islam. 4. Ummah (Islam) I. Title.
  JC49.M255 2007
  320.5'57–dc22
    2007006491

ISBN 10: 0-415-32606-0 (hbk)
ISBN 10: 0-415-32607-9 (pbk)
ISBN 10: 0-203-35851-1 (ebk)

ISBN 13: 978-0-415-32606-3 (hbk)
ISBN 13: 978-0-415-32607-0 (pbk)
ISBN 13: 978-0-203-35851-1 (ebk)

Contents

Illustrations

Figures

Maps

Tables

A note on transliteration and style

In order to make it accessible to a broad, non-specialist readership, this text has adopted a minimal scheme for the transliteration of Arabic, Urdu, Farsi, and Turkish terms. Very few diacritics have been used, and generally only the medial hamza or ayn of Arabic terms has been indicated. Each term is italicized upon first usage, but thereafter appears in regular style.

In rendering Muslim names, effort has been made wherever possible to adopt the English spellings preferred by the individual in question or by the standard works on them.

All dates, unless otherwise specified, are common era (CE).

Preface

This book is designed as a resource for broad audiences in the social sciences and humanities—as well as the advanced general reader—seeking to understand the emergence, evolution, and possible futures of what is commonly called political Islam. That particular terminology, however, is eschewed here in favor of an emphasis on "Muslim politics"—a framing that to my mind offers a richer account of the social relationships between actors, symbols, and structures.

In order to facilitate use of the book across multiple academic fields, disciplinary jargon has been kept to a minimum—even at the risk of rendering the text dangerously atheoretical. By providing a rich pool of case study information, however, it is hoped that readers and instructors alike will find the text a valuable empirical base from which they might examine various political and sociological theories of their choosing. Later editions are likely to include a survey of various theories (both causal and hermeneutic) of Muslim politics for those who wish to have this material immediately to hand alongside the case studies and historical overviews.

That is not to say, however, that the current addition is wholly devoid of theoretical perspective (such a thing is, of course, impossible anyway). By seeking to appreciate Muslim politics "in global perspective," this book, particularly in its later chapters, hopes to draw the reader's attention to the crucial interplay between local and global forces in shaping Muslim politics as a lived reality in today's world. To this end, we cover not only those Muslim political actors whose discourses and practices are organized transnationally, but we also look closely at how global flows—of people, images, ideas, money—inflect the conduct of Muslim politics in local settings.

Initially commissioned in the aftermath of September 11, 2001 as an overview of global political Islam, this book took quite some time to come together. Part of this was a deliberate desire on my part to get some distance from and perspective on the geopolitical aftermath of those events so as to avoid producing a reactionary "post-9/11 book." It also became increasingly clear to me that as many new observers of Muslim politics came to understand the nature of political Islam through the prism of 9/11, they were likely to bypass the complex history of mainstream (and mostly non-violent) Islamism that so transcends the narrow moment of Al-Qaeda. For this reason, it seemed to me that a comparative overview of Islamism around the world, with strong global/transnational coverage, was what was called for at this time. To those readers struck by the seemingly disproportionate amount of history in what is after all essentially a social science text, I would just say that this book was written in Washington D.C. during a time that most conversations about Muslim politics tended to proceed in a worrying dehistoricized manner.

So while this text is largely a description of events, ideas, and personalities rather than a set of claims or a "grand narrative" about the meaning and future of Muslim politics, I have not been able to resist wholly the temptation in places to integrate some of my own research interests—particularly in Chapter 9, where I look at the changing nature of Islamic authority under globalizing conditions.

Many of the countries and movements dealt with in this book (e.g. HAMAS and Hizbullah) continued to experience significant and rapid developments as it went to press. By its very nature, this is material that dates rather quickly in terms of basic chronology. As much as possible, however, I have sought to frame my coverage of these events in terms of the larger and long-term patterns and trends to be found within given countries and movements, and it is these elements that hopefully will come across most strongly to the reader.

Washington D.C.
December 2006

Acknowledgments

A work of this sort inevitably incurs a great deal of debt, and in this case so many have helped it along the way—both directly and indirectly. Conversations with numerous colleagues over the past five years have had a significant impact on the shape and content of this book and I would like to take this opportunity to thank: Bekim Agai, Steve Artner, Osman Bakar, Asma Barlas, Dale Eickelman, Greg Fealy, Graham Fuller, Yvonne Haddad, Mohammed Hafez, Sumaiya Hamdani, Shireen Hunter, Paul Lubeck, Eric McGlinchey, John Paden, Michael Peletz, Tariq Ramadan, Olivier Roy, Armando Salvatore, Meena Sharify-Funk, Steve Simon, Diane Singerman, Kathryn Spellman, John Voll, Carrie Wickham, Quintan Wiktorowicz, Hakan Yavuz, Muhammad Qasim Zaman, and Malika Zeghal. All of them influenced my thinking, made suggestions, or provided important sources as well as much appreciated support and encouragement.

I am particularly grateful to several scholars who read and offered extremely valuable feedback on draft chapters, notably Robert Hefner, Bruce Lawrence, and Vali Nasr. Todd Silverstein read the manuscript in its entirety and offered very constructive editorial and substantive feedback throughout. The insights of all those mentioned above have been reflected in the text wherever possible, but they should not be held responsible for the final product.

Valuable early research assistance was provided by Tanya Fraikin, Xander Meise, and Julia Whitelock, while Elizabeth Gramza and Eric Grynaviski helped to identify and update crucial source material. Christopher Anzalone drafted the glossary and also provided valuable input on early drafts of the main text. A special debt of gratitude is owed to Fatima Ayub and Tariq Mangru, both of whom have been involved in various aspects of the project. They provided key research assistance and offered important suggestions for the main text. Only their tireless work in the final phase of manuscript preparation made its completion possible.

At Routledge I would like to thank Nadia Seemungal and Natalja Mortensen for their valuable editorial assistance. My biggest thanks, however, goes to Craig Fowlie, who first approached me with the idea of writing the book, and helped significantly to shape its content and scope. His patience and kindness of spirit at times when altogether different dispositions on his part would have been wholly warranted should be an inspiration to us all in these trying times.

Alicia Phillips Mandaville rallied and encouraged me when my faith in the project dwindled. Her advice and support added much to the book and sustained me through its conclusion.

Some of the research contained in this book was carried out with the generous support of the Pew Charitable Trusts, the Faculty of Social Sciences at the University of Kent, and the Office of Provost at George Mason University.

Portions of Chapters 7 and 8 are reprinted with the kind permission of Princeton University Press and Cambridge University Press, respectively.

Abbreviations

AKP	Justice and Development Party (Turkey)
AMAL	Afwaj al-Muqawama al-Lubnaniyya
ARAMCO	Arabian American Oil Company
CCMTF	Le Comité de Coordination des Musulmans Turcs de France
CDLR	Committee for the Defense of Legitimate Rights
CFCM	Le Conseil Français du Culte Musulman
DP	Democratic Party
ECFR	European Council for Fatwa & Research
FIS	Front Islamique du Salut
FLN	Front de Libération Nationale
FNMF	Fédération Nationale des Musulmans de France
FSU	Former Soviet Union
GIA	Armed Islamic Group
GMP	Grande Mosquée de Paris
GSPC	Salafist Group for Preaching and Combat
HAMAS	Harakat al-Muqawama al-Islamiyya
HT	Hizb ut-Tahrir
HW	Hizb al-Wasat
IAF	Islamic Action Front
IDA	Islamic Democratic Alliance
IDF	Israeli Defense Force
IIPF	Islamic Iran Participation Front
IJT	Islami Jamiat-i-Talaba
IRM	Islamic Renaissance Movement (Algeria)
IRP	Islamic Renaissance Party (Central Asia)
IUM	Islamic Movement of Uzbekistan
JI	Jama'at-i Islami
JUI	Jamiat Ulema-e-Islam
MB	Muslim Brotherhood
MCB	Muslim Council of Britain
MINAB	Mosques and Imams National Advisory Board
MIRA	Movement for Islamic Reform in Arabia
MMA	Muttahhida Majlis-e-Amal

MRD	Movement for the Restoration of Democracy
MSP	Movement for the Society of Peace
MTI	Mouvement de la Tendence Islamique
MWL	Muslim World League
NDP	National Democratic Party
NEP	National Economic Policy
NIF	National Islamic Front
NSP	National Salvation Party
NU	Nahdlatul Ulama
OIC	Organization of the Islamic Conference
PA	Palestinian Authority
PAS	Parti Islam Se-Malaysia
PJD	Justice and Development Party
PLO	Palestinian Liberation Organization
PNA	Pakistan National Alliance
PPP	Partai Persatuan Pembangunan (Indonesia)
PPP	Pakistan People's Party
RPP	Republican People's Party
SAVAK	Sazamane Etelaat Va Amniate Kechvar
SCIRI	Supreme Council for the Islamic Revolution in Iraq
SPLA	Sudanese People's Liberation Movement
TJ	Tablighi Jamaat
UAE	United Arab Emirates
UMNO	United Malays National Organization
UNRWA	United Nations Relief Works Agency
UOIF	Union des Organisations Islamiques de France
USSR	Union of Soviet Socialist Republics
WAMY	World Assembly of Muslim Youth
WLUML	Women Living Under Muslim Law
YMMA	Young Muslim Men's Association

1 Introduction: thinking about Islam and politics in global perspective

There is little doubt today as to the importance of Muslim politics in contemporary world affairs. From the emergence of transnational networks pursuing global militant agendas in the name of Islam, to the persistence and transformation of traditional Islamic political parties, to the appearance of global media personalities claiming to speak as authoritative and authentic Islamic voices—Islam and politics seem today to be everywhere. But how well do we actually understand this phenomenon? Muslim politics are certainly much discussed today, but—arguably—little or poorly understood within most circles of debate and deliberation. How can we best make sense of this highly complex, diverse, and sometimes even contradictory world of religion and politics? How to understand the relative importance of the multiple manifestations of Muslim politics around the world and the many competing voices claiming to speak on behalf of Islam? What is the difference between those Islamist movements that emphasize *jihad* and those that pursue politics through non-violent, even democratic, means—and how do they relate to each other? What possible futures might we predict for political Islam?

These are a few of the questions that this book will address. In some cases possible answers to several of these puzzles will be offered, while in other instances the book will try to provide the reader with the background information and analytical tools necessary to reach his or her own conclusions. It should be clarified now that this book, while certainly ambitious in scope, does not attempt to provide anything like a grand, unified theory of Islam and politics. While key cross-cutting themes will certainly be identified, the primary emphasis throughout will be on the inherent pluralism and diversity of Muslim politics—that is, on the *impossibility* of a single theory to account for political Islam. It will be suggested, however, that there are better and worse explanations as to why Islamic social and political movements appear and assume the forms that they do under certain circumstances. As numerous analysts of political Islam have observed over the years, particular formulations of Islam and politics certainly do seem to suit specific social, political, and economic conditions. This text is offered, then, in the spirit of a comparative, synthetic overview: a guide to the wide-ranging global landscape of Islam, an introduction to the broad ecology of thought and practice in contemporary Muslim politics, and a critical survey of some of the key ideas advanced by leading scholars in their efforts to explain the phenomenon of political Islam. In a modest way, this book also hopes to offer the rough contours of its own distinctive analytic—one that emphasizes the importance of the interplay between global and local contexts of Muslim politics in a time of unprecedented social interconnectedness and interdependence.

The structure of the book is roughly as follows. This introductory chapter will orient the reader to some of the key themes and concepts surrounding the discussion of religion and politics more generally (e.g. the idea of religion and politics as separate domains, debates on secularism) and the specific challenges we face when dealing with this topic in the context of Islam. The reader will also be asked to reconsider some of the assumptions he or she may hold about just what counts as politics and how to recognize the presence of politics or religion in a given setting and social relationship. In other words, even though we may often be dealing with Muslim-majority countries, how do we know when Islam is actually a relevant factor in a given political situation—that is, how can we tell when Islam really has an influence? Because this book seeks to emphasize the wider global context of Islam, this first chapter will also offer some suggestions about how to approach the interplay between local and global levels of analysis in a world of intense interconnectedness. While not a text on globalization *per se*, it is nevertheless important to evaluate whether and how some of the trends and transformations commonly associated with this term may inflect our analysis of Muslim politics in distinctive new ways.

The analysis offered in this book is firmly rooted in a belief that an understanding of the interplay between Muslim societies and various local, regional and world political issues throughout history is absolutely crucial to achieving any kind of handle on contemporary Muslim politics. To this end, the next two chapters briefly explore key themes and concepts in the history of Islam and politics, while progressively introducing a new framework for understanding today's political Islam. Chapter 2 covers a broad swath of history from approximately the seventh century CE up to the late eighteenth century. It looks at Muslim politics in the time of the Prophet Muhammad and immediately after, explaining the emergence and consolidation of certain key institutions and norms in Muslim politics prior to the expansion and fragmentation of the early Muslim community. The various regional polities and Islamic empires that rose and fell over the subsequent 10 centuries are briefly surveyed before acclimatizing the reader to the onset and implications of European colonialism in the Muslim world. The chapter then analyzes a variety of Islamic responses to Western imperialism before moving on to examine the process of modern state formation in the Muslim world in the post-colonial period. The chapter concludes with an overview of the interaction between wider world politics and

Muslim politics. We will look at how what seemed initially to be a crisis for Islam in the face of widespread support for the secular nation-state model in the early twentieth century quickly evolved into the precursors of what eventually became the political project of Islamism.

Chapter 3 provides a detailed overview of the emergence of modern Islamism through an examination of postcolonial state formation in the Muslim world. It looks at major Islamic political theorists in the twentieth century, and also the key activists and scholar-activists who gave birth to the Islamist project. The conventional model of state-based Islamism is then illustrated through a detailed study of the formation and evolution of the Muslim Brotherhood in Egypt—the prototypical modern Islamist movement and model for many subsequent groups around the Muslim world. We analyze the ideology and organization of the Brotherhood, and trace its development through three generations. The chapter concludes by surveying major developments in twentieth-century Islamism in a number of other key settings.

Having identified the major animating forces behind Islam and politics today, the next section of the book seeks to provide the reader with a wealth of concrete empirical detail regarding how these trends are actually playing out in specific Muslim contexts. The next five chapters offer detailed case studies of Islam and politics across a range of national, regional, and transnational settings. The reader will find chapters that deal with topics such as Islamist participation in elections and normal political processes, the nature and evolution of Islamism in those countries that style themselves as "Islamic states," and the impact of conflict and war on Muslim politics. Obviously key countries—such as Turkey, Iran, Pakistan, Egypt, and Saudi Arabia—are covered, but in an attempt to emphasize the global context of Muslim politics, this section moves away from the conventional country-by-country case study model to include dedicated sections on important transregional and transnational movements (such as the Muslim Brotherhood and Al-Qaeda) as well as a number of less frequently covered non-governmental organizations and traditional social formations in the Muslim world such as *Sufi* brotherhoods, the Tablighi Jamaat, and the Fethullah Gülen movement. New Muslim contexts, such as Europe and North America, are also explored, as are some of the major individual scholars, activists and opinion-makers whose ideas today are making waves across multiple Muslim world locales.

The final two chapters of the book draw on the key themes identified in the first section, combining them with the subsequent case study material to offer extended reflections on several of the most important issues surrounding contemporary discussions of Islam and politics. The first of these takes up one of the most confusing questions circulating around Islam and politics today: the issue of who speaks for Islam. Without a central hierarchy of religious authority, it is often unclear who in the Muslim world counts as an "official" representative of the religion. Furthermore, with the formation of modern nation-states in the Muslim world, centralized political authorities were able to challenge the authoritative role of religious figures. This chapter explores the various contexts and circumstances that allow a given person or movement today to be granted status as a legitimate voice of Islamic authority or authenticity. The contingent interplay of local and global politics and the pluralizing effects of new media such as satellite television and the Internet are identified as particularly important factors in the new politics of Islamic authority. We will look at how radical and moderate voices alike seek to capture "market share" in these new spaces for defining Muslim identity, values, and political priorities. What is the nature of the wider ecology in which claims to authentic Islam are made today? How do these different actors compete and play off each other in the process of creating new constituents for their distinctive visions of Muslim politics?

The concluding chapter seeks to draw together the broad range of analytical threads running throughout the text. Its key argument is that Muslim politics—through the intervening effects of globalization and the emergence within certain Muslim communities of a political consciousness transcending national borders—is entering a phase in which the methods, goals, and vocabularies of Islamism are undergoing considerable transformation. It is suggested that "classic" Islamism, as a totalizing project seeking to capture state power, is increasingly forced to compete with Muslim political agendas above *and* below the state that seek, respectively, to establish transnational Islamic polities, or to open up spaces for the inclusion of religion in public life and greater recognition of Muslim identity claims within the context of broadly secular societies. The idea that the net effect of these developments is moving us towards a condition that some analysts have termed "post-Islamism" is also considered. The book concludes with some reflections on how these disparate strategies and politics will likely play out in the coming years.

Islam in the world: Some basic facts

Before getting into substantive discussion, it would be helpful to orient the reader to the subject matter at hand: Muslims and the Muslim world. Comprising approximately 1.25 billion people across almost every continent, Islam constitutes one of the great and certainly the fastest growing world religion today. Often thought of as a Middle Eastern phenomenon, it is worthwhile taking note of the fact that the four countries with the greatest number of Muslims are actually in Southeast Asia (Indonesia) and South Asia (Pakistan, Bangladesh, and India). The states of the former Soviet Union are home to large numbers of Muslims, and significant populations are to be found in West and East Africa. So it is important to immediately disabuse ourselves of the idea that the Middle East and Muslim world—despite their common overlap in contemporary discourse—are coterminous. Today we also hear much about the idea of Islam and the

West as two separate entities. As Chapter 2 will demonstrate, it actually makes much more sense in historical perspective to emphasize overlap and exchange between these world cultures rather than conflict and incompatibility. Furthermore—and as will be seen in Chapter 9—Islam is an increasingly important religion today in many of the countries that we would think of as part of the West.

It almost goes without saying that, given this size and geographical breadth, Islam is a thoroughly diverse phenomenon—a fact that makes it difficult and even dangerous to try conclusively to define what Islam has to say about a given idea or situation, or what the "Islamic" view on something might be. Inevitably, this perspective will vary significantly from context to context. As will be explained in greater detail below, then, this book uses the term "Islam" to refer to a particular tradition of discourse and practice that is variously defined across multiple social and historical settings. There is therefore no connotation of normativity implied in our usage, for example, of the term "Islamic." Islam should always be considered in relation to how it is understood and experienced in specific contexts and circumstances. That does not mean that anything and everything counts as Islam. Embodied within the very idea of a tradition is the notion that this tradition has boundaries—but these, it should be emphasized, are always open to contestation and negotiation. Likewise, there is no attempt made here to define who or what counts as Muslim. For our purposes a Muslim is anyone who identifies him or herself, at least in part, with Islam—regardless of how the latter may be understood.

Broadening our understanding of politics

It may strike the reader as slightly strange to begin with a discussion of the definition of politics, but this is necessary given the wide range of phenomena under consideration in this book, some of which we propose to treat as "political" although they would not generally be considered part of the commonplace world of politics. Conventional understandings of politics

Table 1.1 Largest Muslim populations by country

Country	Total Population	% Muslim	Total Muslims
1. Indonesia	241,973,879	88%	213,469,356
2. India	1,080,264,388	16.2%	174,755,562
3. Pakistan	165,803,560	98%	162,487,489
4. Bangladesh	147,365,352	88%	129,681,509
5. Egypt	77,505,756	91%	70,530,237
6. Turkey	69,660,559	99%	68,963,953
7. Iran	68,017,860	99%	67,337,681
8. Nigeria	128,771,988	50%	64,385,994
9. Morocco	32,725,847	99%	32,300,410
10. Algeria	32,531,853	99%	32,206,534

tend to equate it with particular sets of activities and institutions—more specifically the processes through which actors pursue governmental power in the context of the modern nation-state. We generally have a sense of the kinds of activities that count as political (e.g. elections, coups d'état, lobbying) and the relevant sorts of actors and institutions (political parties, nation-states, militaries). To be sure, many of the Muslim countries and organizations covered in this volume will correspond quite closely to this model. In Jordan and Kuwait, for example, Islamist political parties contest parliamentary elections in the hope of having a greater role in legislative processes. In the case of certain other social forces to be examined, however, we will need to recalibrate some of our assumptions in order to recognize them as properly political. For example, a few of the movements we will look at reject the very model of the nation-state and seek instead to establish forms of political community premised on very different norms and principles. It is still not difficult, however, to see such groups as political since it is clear that they are seeking to challenge prevailing institutions through which social power is exercised. More challenging, however, are the cases of certain mystical orders or movements that emphasize personal piety—many of which ostensibly eschew politics altogether. The approach advanced by this book is one that would see any rejection of politics as a particular sort of political act. Usually what is being articulated in such claims is a challenge to a specific vision of public morality that understands social order and "the good" to accrue from the direct exercise of power via the institutional channels of government. By way of an alternative, these movements seek to emphasize an understanding of the public good as something that best emerges through an emphasis on personal piety and devotion—that is, the idea that one creates the good Islamic society not by top-down legislation but rather through the collectivization of individually pious Muslims.

With this illustration in mind, we can say that for our present purposes it will be important to regard as political all actors and activities involved in the establishment, maintenance or contestation of particular visions of public morality ("the good") and of social order. There is, of course, something to be said for the analytic utility of narrow definitions. Indeed, if we widen our understanding of politics too far then everything becomes political—and hence for purposes of analysis, nothing is political. Well aware of this pitfall, it should be pointed out that in the vast majority of cases to be examined in this book, the end point of Muslim politics involves challenges to state authority via methods and tactics easily recognizable as political according to standard criteria. A broader definition of politics is being proposed primarily to enable us to recognize and include in our analyses of these processes social actors and even ideas whose political relevance might not otherwise be immediately discernible. It is an approach that permits a richer, more nuanced and more comprehensive appreciation of the relationship between Islam and politics.

Religion and politics in Europe and the Muslim world

Before we wade into the comparative analysis of Muslim politics that constitutes the central focus of this book, it would be worthwhile to dwell briefly on a number of more general issues surrounding the analysis of religion and politics in a globalizing world. The intersection of religion and politics is notoriously tricky terrain to navigate, and we would do well to examine some of the baggage we inevitably bring to the analytical table. This is not only because religion and politics are usually highly emotive and polarizing subjects unto themselves, touching on issues around which people frequently stake strong senses of identity, morality, and worldview. This is also because we often tend to hold particular views about the proper relationship between these two spheres, and feel varying levels of comfort when we encounter situations in which the two seem to be mixing. Different societies around the world inevitably have different histories, traditions and norms relating not only to the intermingling of religion and politics, but to the very definition of the boundaries that delineate and—sometimes—separate these two domains. Of particular importance here, of course, is the vexed question of secularism. Secular norms are arguably part of the foundation of the modern sovereign state model that seems to have propagated around the world during the last century. There is, however, a very strong sense in which this understanding of secularism is a legacy of the very particular historical experience of political modernity that played out in Europe over several centuries. A closer examination reveals that the rise of secularism in the West was not simply a case of the modern state eradicating the church, but rather something more resembling a process of the state reorganizing, repositioning and co-opting aspects of religious authority—a pattern we will see repeated in the Muslim world after the colonial period. As the sovereign nation-state system began to reproduce itself in parts of the world culturally and historically distinct from Europe—settings possessing their own understandings of how religion and politics do or do not fit together—it was inevitable that tensions would flare around the question of secularism. It is thus important to begin our undertaking by looking at some of the prevailing assumptions about secularism and how the terms of this debate map onto and compare with similar discussions in the Muslim world.

Secularism in the West

Secularism, as it developed in the sociocultural bloc commonly known as "the West," can be understood primarily as the product of major shifts in two aspects of European society beginning in the fifteenth century and consolidating around a number of key historical events in the seventeenth. The first of these deals with the realm of philosophy. With the advent of the period known as the Renaissance, there began in Europe a transformation over how and where people sought knowledge about the world. Where Medieval Europe had been dominated by an understanding of knowledge as a means to salvation—and hence relying on holy scripture to the exclusion of worldly knowledge—the Renaissance and eventually the Enlightenment marked a rediscovery of classical learning from antiquity and a new emphasis on the transformative capacity of human reason and rationality. No longer was worldly endeavor confined to a narrow confirmation of divine revelation, but rather the emphasis came to be on the idea that people could, through the production of knowledge and, eventually, through science, control the world around them. People were again to be the agents or makers of history rather than merely the passive components of divine schemas. Knowledge was increasingly to be based on observable, empirical facts rather than exclusively on faith, mysticism, and myth (which continued to have important roles for some time). It is important to note that this trend did not initially herald a decline in the social influence of religion—rather, people simply began to seek rational proofs for the existence of God and reason-based evidence for the truth of religious teaching.

The second shift tied to the emergence of secularism is concerned with responses to the increasingly prevalent role of the Catholic Church in Europe's political economy since at least the fourteenth century. Proto-nationalist princes found themselves at odds with efforts by Rome to protect and enforce, by increasingly political means, the universalist remit of papal authority. By the early sixteenth century, theologians and sovereigns alike had come to resent the pervasive influence of the Catholic Church. Dissident religious thinkers, such as Martin Luther—instigator of the Protestant Reformation in 1517—took issue with what he saw as the excessive commodification of spirituality through practices such as the selling of indulgences. As the Reformation gathered force, the political landscape of Europe was reorganized along political and religious fault-lines with various imperial houses allying themselves with competing religious forces that in turn sought to supplant the authority of these same princes. From the mid-sixteenth to mid-seventeenth century, Europe was mired in a series of religious wars, culminating in the Peace of Westphalia in 1648 at the conclusion of the bitter Thirty Years War, during which up to 20 percent of Germany's population was killed.

This date is conventionally cited as marking the start of the modern system of sovereign states in Western Europe. It is important to note that one of the primary aims of the treaty that finally brought an end to hostilities was to embed a principle of noninterference by the church in the affairs of sovereign princes. This was still not the idiom of secularism that eventually came to define the liberal tradition (since kings rather than individuals were still able to determine the official religion of their political domains), but it did mark a watershed moment in the reorganization of the relationship between church and state as institutions. Over the next 200 years, the advent of political liberalism in Europe—with its emphasis on individual over collective rights—combined with increasing instances of religious persecution by sovereign authorities, led to a recasting of secularism within political systems such as the modern French Republic and the new United States of America. In the religious realm, the Protestant Reformation had served to "reworld" the church by reorienting the social meaning of doctrine such that it served to link the imperatives of everyday life (work, education, etc.) with one's fate in the hereafter. This was not an individualization of religion—pressures from the church to conform certainly continued—but Protestantism questioned the logic of exceptionalism that sealed the official Church from the advent of modernity. Even this "standard" form of secularism varies significantly between national contexts in the contemporary world. The *laïcisme* of France, which empties public life and discourse entirely of anything to do with religion, contrasts with the British tradition of secularism as religious pluralism and tolerance and the American version focused on the individual right to religious freedom.

In summary, then, the received tradition of Western secularism that constitutes the default lens through which many of us view questions of religion and politics, can be understood as the cumulative outcome of several distinct but inter-related developments: (1) a philosophical shift in early modern Europe whereby human reason, rationality and empirical inquiry came to cast doubt on pure faith and the mystical aspects of religious experience as legitimate foundations for the production of knowledge; (2) the difficult and violent history whereby the institutions of church and state in Europe were decoupled; and (3) the emergence and eventual normalization of a set of political values based on liberalism that emphasized the rights of individuals above all else—most particularly the state and the church.

In addition to this "formal" mode of secularism, it is also important for us to understand a more generic, largely sociological, dimension of the secular. As we will see, this is an understanding of secularism that figures particularly prominently in many debates regarding the compatibility of Islam with secular norms. What we are alluding to here is that sense in which the idea of secularism is often taken today to refer to a constellation of similar (but by no means identical) trends, found especially in Europe and North America from the late nineteenth century onward. This includes the privatization or compartmentalization of religion as a sphere of social activity ("once a week on Sundays"), lower levels of active participation in organized religion and a general decline in the influence of religion in everyday life—in short, a turning away from religion in the West over the past century (if measured, say, according to levels of regular church attendance). Some caution is certainly merited when positing such a trend. This is not only because the prevalence of and popular participation in religion varies significantly across Western societies (with consistently higher levels, for example, in the United States than in Europe), but also because events of the past 15 years have suggested that many people, even in countries with longstanding secular norms, are once again turning to religion as a source of meaning, identity, and values. It is nonetheless important to make this point about the multiple meanings of secularism since, as we will see, part of the controversy in the Muslim world surrounding the idea of the West or of "being Western" is that a lack of religiosity and even hostility towards religion is widely understood to be one of its defining characteristics.

The religious and the political in Islam

The anthropologist of religion Talal Asad cautions us against the dangers of transplanting the very particular set of assumptions about religion and politics that derive from the preceding history of European secularism on to the history of other faith traditions.[1] Indeed, he goes so far as to argue that our commonplace understanding of the religious and the political as separate, clearly demarcated spheres of human activity is itself a product of our locatedness in the European tradition rather than a "natural" analytic distinction. "[W]hile religion is integral to modern Western history," he argues, "there are dangers in employing it as a normalizing concept when translating Islamic traditions."[2] In short, we are being warned that while it may seem obvious to Western liberals (although not all Westerners fit this bill— witness conservative Catholics, Evangelicals, Mormons, etc.) that religion and politics constitute two quite separate spaces, each with its own rules, norms, and logics, this may not be the case in other cultures and societies. It will be important for the discussions to follow that we gain some comparative insight into how the boundaries and debates between "being religious" and "being political" have played out historically in the Muslim world.

Before looking closely at the interplay between these forces in Islamic history, it might be worth making a few quick observations by way of direct comparison with what were identified above as the driving forces of secularism in the West. We are able this way to immediately throw into relief key points of similarity but also sharp contrasts that help us to understand why these issues are particularly challenging in the Muslim context. First, within the realm of philosophy, it is important to note that the Muslim world witnessed its own version of a debate regarding the status of reason versus pure revelation as sources of knowledge some five centuries before this took place in the West. Without going into the details of this period (some of which will be touched on in later chapters), suffice it to say that the net effect of these debates was to restructure the enterprise of knowledge production in the Muslim world such that an early tendency towards relatively open inquiry (inspired by Greek philosophy) gave way to a sharp distinction between knowledge concerning morality and law, seen as not amenable to reason or rational and thought, and the realms of science and technology. The importance of this distinction will become clear later when we go on to examine the meaning and nature of the political in Muslim contexts.

As regards the competition between "church" and state in the Islamic world, the first and most obvious point to make is that unlike the Christian tradition, Islam does not possess a formal church or hierarchy of religious authority—at least not in the *Sunni* tradition to which 90% of the world's Muslims adhere. This certainly does not mean, however, that voices of and claims to religious authority have been absent from the machinations of worldly power in Islam. While not organized as a centralized, institutional authority, the Muslim world has historically seen the emergence of various classes of privileged interpreters and transmitters of religious knowledge. The *alim* (pl. *ulama*; "religious scholar"), *faqih* (pl. *fuqaha*; "legal specialist"); and *imam* ("prayer leader," but also a generic term for a person in a position of religious authority) are all terms and titles that invest their holders with the ability to speak with authority in the name of Islam to state and society alike. More important than this social class, however, is the cumulative tradition of method and knowledge that it has produced and, in turn, been produced by. This perhaps is the key distinction to be drawn with Christianity. Where "official" Christianity could be found in the formal institutional hierarchy of the Church, the closest thing to "official" Islam resides in a highly diverse yet remarkably cohesive tradition of theology and jurisprudence, developed and passed down through the centuries by an elite corps of specialists in the field religious knowledge. These figures and the tradition they represent, as we will see, have at various times in Islamic history been allied with, co-opted by, and directly opposed to state power. The key point to grasp for now, though, is that the lack of formal church-like institutions in Islam renders direct comparison with Europe's early experience of secularism as a decoupling of church and state rather difficult. Likewise, when one begins to contemplate the idea of an "Islamic Reformation,"[3] we find that there exists no centralized religious authority either to lead such an effort or to serve as its target—no "church," in other words, to undertake reform or to be reformed.[4] Rather the hegemony of particular understandings of religion exists, as Talal Asad shows us, within a discursive tradition rather than within any given institution.[5] This is a theme we take up in considerably more detail in Chapter 9.

The last point of comparison to make at the outset relates to the relationship between secularism and liberalism in the European tradition. Where prevailing secular norms in Europe and North America tended to develop in parallel with the consolidation of the modern liberal state, the experience of state formation outside the West has not generally been marked by the same primary emphasis on liberal political values. In Europe the norms of political liberalism, buttressed by the emergence of a market-based capitalism premised on concomitant economic values, came to be organically intertwined with the institutional forms of the sovereign nation-state over several turbulent centuries. When this particular model of the state spread beyond Europe and North America, mainly in the post-colonial period, it entered countries with very different kinds of social orders and political histories, very few of which were premised on liberal ideals. As we will see in later chapters, this has inevitably been a major source of tension as regards both the successful consolidation of modern nation-states outside the West, but also the question of religion's role in political societies not defined by liberalism.

Islam is often represented as a "comprehensive" way of life that pervades all sectors of human activity and experience among its adherents. The idea of the divine connectedness of all things, as invoked by the central precept of *tawhid* ("oneness"), is often taken to imply that in Islam it makes no sense to speak of the separateness of religion from any other domain of life. In the realm of politics, this idea is most commonly expressed through the maxim *al-islam din wa dawla* ("Islam is [both] religion and state")—a phrasing which, while recognizing the possibility of a conceptual distinction between these two spheres, refutes the practical possibility of their disjuncture in Islam. Where Christian scripture, in the notion of rendering unto Caesar that which is Caesar's, allows for a clear division between worldly and divine authority, Islamic sources tend to emphasize the totalizing sovereignty of God. Of greatest relevance for our purposes, however, is not the fact that the Qur'an and other key scriptural sources make a case for the all-encompassing nature of Islam, but rather the fact that they offer very little by way of detail regarding the proper forms and conduct of politics—except to state that these activities should occur in accordance with the moral system of Islam. Unsurprisingly, these ambiguities and silences— as we will see later—have given rise over the centuries to vociferous debate as to the relationship between Islam and politics. On the one hand, some Muslim scholars have held that from the Qur'an and the traditions of the Prophet Muhammad can be derived a very specific and distinctively Islamic model of governance. On the other there are those who maintain that *any* system of government is acceptable so long as it is compatible with the moral principles of Islamic teaching. This ongoing effort by—and, deliberatively, *between*—believers to discern the political implications of Islam will be introduced below as a core component of what we will come to call Muslim politics. Modern Islamic political theory—as we will see in Chapter 3—gives us a sense of the wide range of perspectives within the Muslim world regarding the intersection of religion and politics. Theorists such as Rashid Rida, for example, argued that any political system must indeed be derived from the *shari'ah* of Islam, and in the absence of a caliphate Muslims should strive to create a distinctly Islamic form of the modern state. His contemporary Ali Abd al-Raziq took quite a different view, however, arguing that the separation of religion and politics was integral to Islamic history and that the Qur'an did *not* seek to establish any particular political order.[6] Later thinkers, such as Abdolkarim Soroush, writing in the wake of Iran's Islamic Revolution, would argue a position that many saw as tantamount to secularism but which reversed the logic of the Western model. For Soroush, it is not the case that the non-empirical reason of religion threatens the conduct of modern politics, but rather that the inherently corrupting dimensions of political power pose a danger to religion. So religion and politics should indeed be kept separate, but in the name of protecting the former from the latter.[7]

Aside from the theoretical relationship between Islam and politics as defined by scriptural sources, we would of course also want to look to the historical record of Muslim societies to determine whether something like a distinction between religion and politics can be found. Our survey of early Islamic political history in Chapter 2 will be particularly revealing in this regard, but the short answer is that Islamic history is replete with examples of Muslim sovereigns who seemed to operate with a very clear notion of religion and politics as quite distinct arenas, and, indeed with a highly developed sense of how manipulation of the former could prove useful in achieving political power in the name of all manner of tribal, ethnic, and imperial formations. While the institution of the caliphate (see Chapter 2) was in theory to serve as the worldly guardian of a divinely ordained moral system, fragmentation and factional competition in the rapidly expanding Muslim community meant that within a century of the Prophet's death, the caliphate had effectively become beholden to dynastic politics. Over the centuries, politics came to be recognized in the Muslim world as a distinct discipline unto itself. In the eleventh century, for example, some 500 years before Machiavelli's *The Prince*, there appeared in several Muslim languages various kingship manuals—such as Nizam al-Mulk's *Siyasatnama* ("Book of Politics")—describing techniques and tactics of governance easily recognizable to any practitioner of the modern political arts.

Despite this apparent differentiation between religious and political spheres in Islam, it is worth noting that until relatively recently, there was no formal distinction drawn between religious and secular law in most of the Muslim world. Historically, rulers of Muslim peoples derived a large measure of their legitimacy from religion and from the enforcement of religious law—which, certainly by the Middle Ages, had itself become a diverse body of jurisprudence, overlapping in significant ways with the customary laws of the various cultures and societies that came to embrace Islam. Right up to the dissolution of the Ottoman Empire after World War I, the legitimacy of the Sultan-Caliph in Istanbul ultimately rested on his executive authority as the chief enforcer of the Law. And although the Ottoman Empire recognized, through the *millet* system and the *qanun* courts, legal pluralism in relation to religious identity and customary practice, its Muslim subjects generally had little experience of court systems that were not ultimately shari'ah based—at least symbolically, if not in substance. We should not forget, however, that in a number of other Muslim-majority settings, the advent of European colonialism tended to mean the introduction of dual legal systems featuring elements of both common law (regarding civil and criminal matters) and religious law (usually with respect to issues of personal status). In the post-colonial period, the legal systems of most Muslim-majority countries have been primarily based on secular common law models (often derived from British and French cognates). In this regard, we can say that a strong measure of formal secularism has been present in Muslim countries for over a century.

What, then, are the implications here for our comparison of secularism in the Western tradition and the relationship between religion and politics in Islam? Aside from the observations made at the outset regarding certain key institutional differences between these traditions (e.g. the lack of a formal religious hierarchy in Islam, the absence of liberalism in the political societies of the Muslim world), we might now consider the following additional points. First, while Islamic scripture and theology does not formally recognize a division between religion and politics, it remains sufficiently circumspect regarding the specifics of politics under Islam as to permit considerable latitude of thought and practice in this area. Moreover, and second, Islamic history is full of many examples of Muslim rulers co-opting religious authorities and using the mantle of religion as a means by which to pursue goals better understood in terms of dynastic or proto-national agendas. Third, while the subjects of Islamic empires up until the nineteenth century (and in the central provinces of the Ottoman Empire through World War I) lived under legal systems that made no formal division between religious and secular law, most citizens of Muslim-majority nation-states today (and before that as subjects of various European colonial powers) have considerable direct experience of secular law.

Up until this point, our discussion of secularism in Islam has been largely structured around issues of law. In the absence of a formal "church," the legal system has served as the best institutional manifestation of the tradition we have equated above with "official" Islam. The aspect of secularism least examined so far in the Muslim context relates to the sociological question of the extent to which religion endures as a source of social normativity. Have Muslim societies experienced an overall decline in religiosity comparable to that in the West? This is obviously far too complex a question to be answered here in meaningful sociological terms given the problems associated with speculating as to the inner moral worlds and intentions of individuals. Two observations that we might make a little more safely, however, relate to the embeddedness of religion in wider social institutions and the presence of religion in public consciousness. In many Muslim countries, particularly those where hereditary monarchies (such as Saudi Arabia) and the influence of tribal ties remains strong (such as Pakistan), religion often plays a role in underpinning the legitimacy of these institutions. When it comes to the issue of everyday consciousness of religion, it might be useful to turn to some polling data. When we look at a selection of Muslim countries polled by the World Values Survey between 2000 and 2002, the average percentage of respondents indicating that God is very important in their lives is 91%. Compare this with 23% for a selection of Western countries on the same question, a figure that falls to 12% if we remove North America from the sample. We need to be very careful, however, in terms of what significance we impute to these figures. They tell us nothing about linkages between religious consciousness and social or political behaviors. As will be discussed below, it is not always so easy to tell when religion matters in a given situation. Indeed, there is a strong sense in which a question such as the importance of God—given the social embeddedness of religion alluded to above—functions as something like a "mom and apple pie" question in Muslim settings—that is, one that everyone rallies around, but which tells us very little about the extent to which religion actually figures in everyday decision-making. What we do get some sense of, however, is the large extent to which religion is present in the public vocabulary and readily available as a discursive resource for social mobilization, a point that will become relevant later as we examine various examples of Muslim politics.

In summary, it becomes clear that Muslim traditions—and the relationship between religion and politics within them—cannot be fully understood when approached through an analytical lens defined primarily by the Western experience of institutional secularism. The histories have been distinctive, the institutional manifestations of religion quite disparate, and the social location and role of religion rather different. Furthermore, the prevailing sentiment regarding secularism in the Muslim world is negative, equating it primarily with a lack of religiosity or "Godlessness" rather than formal separation of religion and politics. This does not mean, however, that Muslims do not in practice recognize—and, as we will see below, actually *desire*—some distance between religious authority and processes of modern state governance.

When does Islam count?

While we have now been able to say something about secularism in the West, and the comparative historical experience of religion and politics in the Muslim world, the more directly pertinent question of religion's influence on political behavior and decision-making has not yet been addressed. That is, we have not actually tackled the question of how, as analysts of Muslim politics, we are able to determine the role and relative importance played by religion in a given situation. The central purpose of this section is to sound a cautionary note regarding the danger of imputing too much significance to the role of Islam in Muslim settings. There are three main points to be made in this regard.

First, to even speak of something such as the "Muslim world" is to engage our subject matter at a very high level of abstraction, and moreover one that gives us very little sense of the social reality of Islam as a lived experience. What is at stake in describing something as part of the "Muslim world"—or in speaking of "Muslim peoples?" We always need to ask ourselves what, analytically, we seek to accomplish by framing our subject in a particular way and via specific terms or labels. To choose the Muslim world as a unit of social analysis suggests, at the very least, that we recognize all those contained within it to possess—at some level—a relationship to something called Islam. In and of itself, this is not problematic, although it is worth asking why we have chosen Islam as an organizing principle. Is it the most appropriate lens through which to view our subject matter given what we are hoping to discern? When might other categories of analysis— such as the "developing world" or "tribal-patrimonial societies"—not sometimes be more helpful when trying to explain particular forms of politics? Just to provide a brief example: the societies of Europe and North America could be considered as part of something we might call the Christian world. Yet in contemporary commentary regarding society, politics, and economics in these countries, we rarely find them referred to in this way. Indeed, for most of us it would probably seem rather strange to do so since it is not clear that Christianity has much to do with these issues. Compare this with today's discourse on Islam, where it seems to be quite commonplace and apparently not at all odd to find constant references to the "Muslim world." Why this discrepancy and what lies behind it? Is it that we feel these societies to be best understood through reference to their "Muslimness?" Do we have an assumption, tacit or otherwise, that Islam is somehow the primary determinant of outcomes in these settings? Thus where we absolutely need to be careful is when we begin to ascribe norms, behaviors and sentiments to Islam—or to a particular people as Muslims— without a more nuanced appreciation of how and where those who constitute a given society understand the role of Islam (see third point below). As studies by numerous scholars have suggested, religion does not always constitute the primary political identity assumed by Muslims—sometimes national, tribal, or ethnic claims trump the religious.[8] In short, as analysts of Muslim politics, we need to avoid prematurely projecting Islam onto a given setting, or defining it in terms of its "Muslimness" without being very clear as to why we are choosing to do so. This point is offered in a spirit of self-reflexivity given that the term "Muslim world" occurs throughout this text.

A second point, and one which only serves to re-emphasize the importance of what has just been said, relates to the vast size and diversity of the Muslim world: approximately 1.25 billion people encompassing hundreds of distinct ethnic, national and linguistic groups across multiple continents spanning the globe. Religious thought and practice in the Muslim world mirrors this enormous pluralism, with Islam often understood in very different ways from one society to another. Likewise, the social and political significance of the religion varies greatly from setting to setting. In this regard one needs to be very careful when evaluating statements that make claims about the Muslim world as a whole, or which purport to explain *the* Islamic position on a given issue. A keen appreciation of the pluralism intrinsic to the Muslim world is hence crucial to meaningful social analysis, as is an understanding of the idiosyncrasies of religion in particular Muslim settings. It is, however, also dangerous to go too far to the other extreme and assume that particular forms of Islam somehow arise *sui generis* in each distinct Muslim locale. As has been explained above, Islam refers to a religious tradition that has developed cumulatively over some 1,400 years. While it has certainly traveled far and wide over the years, picked up many local flavors, and been mediated by countless sociocultural and political contexts, Islam still endures as a distinct tradition of discourse recognizable across manifold societies and communities. It is also a dynamic tradition insofar as it is constantly and contextually interpreted and reinterpreted. The lived embodiment of Islam may vary from setting to setting, the terms and parameters of Islamic normative discourse will certainly differ, but there is also a core corpus of Islam that somehow connects all Muslims. Indeed, one of the great challenges of analyzing Islam and politics lies in achieving some understanding of how particular groups of Muslims or even individual believers, engage this tradition and understand its relevance to the situations they face on a daily basis across the Muslim world.

To make these various points more tangible, and also to better illustrate this issue of the diversity of the Muslim world, let us look for a moment at some public opinion data from the Muslim world regarding religion and politics. When asked in 2002 by the Pew Global Attitudes Project whether religion is a matter of personal faith that should be kept separate from government policy, majorities in all Muslim countries surveyed indicated that they mostly or completely agreed with this statement (ranging from highs of 90% and 88% in Lebanon and Turkey to a low of 53% for both Jordan and Pakistan). However, when subsequently asked how much of a role Islam should play in the political life of their countries, the very same respondents indicated in large majorities (with the exception of Turkey) that religion should play a fairly or very large role in politics. On the face of it, these two responses might be seen as contradictory. One reasonable interpretation of this apparent discrepancy is that people draw a clear distinction between specific, substantive matters of policy being subject to the religious beliefs of policy-makers, and politics as a general sphere of activity requiring the moral guidance provided by religious teaching. As we will see in several of the case studies later in the book, this latter view correlates strongly with support for religiously based political parties that run on a strong anti-corruption platform.

If we turn to the question of the appropriate political role for religious leaders, the results become even more interesting and varied. Asked if religious leaders should play a role in politics, an overwhelming majority (91%) in Nigeria and strong majorities (63–77%) in Jordan, Pakistan, and Bangladesh agreed; Indonesia was on the borderline with 51% agreement; and only 40% in Turkey agreed with the statement. In order to understand this variation across settings, it is necessary to examine the history of involvement in politics by religious leaders. We also need to ask questions about who is understood to count as a religious leader, and what people understand by "playing a role in politics." The strong Nigerian response, for example, does not indicate widespread desire amongst Muslims in that country for an Iranian-style theocracy, but rather indicates the important social role that religious leaders have recently played in ensuring regional identity and unity vis-à-vis other religious and political communities. In other words, it is a response that tells us more about domestic politics and the popular desire for law and order in Nigeria than it does about the political nature of Islam. When it comes to Indonesia, there is much less of a tradition of religious leaders playing a direct role in postcolonial politics, but simultaneously a keen sense that figures from some of the country's mass religious movements (see "Indonesia: a paradigmatic 'Muslim Democracy'?" in Chapter 4) have played an important role in furthering the causes of political reform and democratization. This is perhaps a counter-intuitive interpretation of what is implied by religious leaders playing a larger role in politics, but one that we would only be able to offer after delving into Indonesia's recent political history. As we can see looking across these cases, and the many more to be examined throughout this book, a sensitivity to local histories, understandings, and experience of religion and politics emerges as the crucial factor in making meaningful sense of the various Muslim politics we encounter in the world.

Which brings us to our third point: the fact that Muslims in different settings will often develop quite unique understandings (based on local histories and experience) of how and where their religion relates to everyday life and practical politics. As we have just seen, this can sometimes render direct comparison between Muslim settings very tricky, but it does not

Table 1.2 Muslim views on religion and politics

Q. 37e: Religion is a matter of personal faith and should be kept separate from government policy.

	Jordan	Pakistan	Bangladesh	Nigeria	Indonesia
Completely Agree	24	33	53	61	42
Mostly Agree	29	20	18	25	31
Mostly Disagree	29	11	12	7	20
Completely Disagree	18	15	10	6	8
Don't know/refused	0	20	7	1	0
	100	99	100	100	101

Q. 51: How much of role do you think Islam should play in the political life of our country?

	Jordan	Pakistan	Bangladesh	Nigeria	Indonesia
Very large role	46	75	42	41	47
Fairly large role	27	11	32	20	35
Fairly small role	10	1	8	12	13
Very small role	15	2	13	21	4
Don't know/refused	2	10	4	6	2
	100	100	99	100	101

Source: Pew Research Center (2003). "Views of a Changing World 2003"

mean that we should give up altogether. It may often be difficult for us to determine—and actually even dangerous, from a social analysis point of view, to speculate about—whether an individual has behaved in a particular way because of his or her religion, or because of some other factor altogether. While it is certainly dangerous, as emphasized above, to quickly impute causality to religion, it is equally problematic to discount religion altogether, or to view it in exclusively instrumentalist terms. To provide a sense of these complexities, we might consider some examples of conflict from the past 20 years. In several cases of civil war since the end of the Cold War, most notably that of Bosnia, the conflicting parties seemed to be organized along religious lines. Much has been made, and with good cause, of the ways in which religious identity was used in this conflict to mobilize political actors and to sharpen antagonisms in a dispute that was really about political autonomy, territory, and uneven access to resources. Or take the example of Northern Ireland, another example of a conflict that broke down along religious lines, but which very few observers really understood to be driven by disagreements over theology. Or consider the case of the Rushdie Affair in 1988, where thousands of disenfranchised South Asian immigrants in the UK marched in protest and burned copies of what they perceived as a blasphemous novel in Salman Rushdie's *The Satanic Verses*. Parallels can certainly be drawn between this case and the furor over the Danish newspaper cartoons of the Prophet Muhammad that erupted in early 2006. Finally, what about the case of Palestinian suicide bombers? Much is made by some of the religious motivations to be found in discourses of martyrdom and the promise of lavish rewards in the hereafter for those who die in the name of jihad. There are other analysts, however, who would interpret such an act as a relatively instrumentalist albeit extreme military tactic in the context of a political struggle for national liberation. After all, a number of suicide attacks have also been carried out by members of Fateh and other secular Palestinian factions. How then can we understand where religion figures in all of these examples? While it may be true that better explanations of the wider contexts in each of these cases are to be found in notions such as ethno-nationalism, territorial dispute, unequal access to resources on the part of minority communities, and racial discrimination, we would be wrong to discount religion from our analysis altogether. For some actors in these various events, an understanding of religion may indeed have been very important or even decisive in terms of how they behaved in given situations. In other cases, actors clearly appealed to religion in order to try and define group boundaries in particular ways and also to provoke certain responses. We might as analysts want to enquire as to the circumstances under which such appeals succeeded or failed. In short, despite the challenges entailed in trying to identify the precise role of religion, there is clearly still much of interest to be learned by looking at how and under what conditions different understandings of religion become relevant and are invoked with regard to political questions.

On Muslim politics

Up to this point, we have been using the term "Muslim politics" as if its meaning were fairly self evident. However, there is in this particular choice of terminology an important point about the distinctive analytical approach being advanced in this book. Muslim politics, on our understanding, is not the same as "political Islam" or "Islamism," two terms the reader may regard as largely synonymous. Islamism, as will be clarified in more detail in Chapter 3, refers to a particular kind of Muslim politics—one that seeks to create a political order defined in terms of Islam (usually a shari'ah-based state). Political Islam, while certainly preferable to terms such as Islamic fundamentalism, is less useful for our purposes in two respects. First, in positing "political" as a qualifier for Islam, it ends up reinforcing some of the very boundaries between spheres of thought and practice that we are trying to challenge. To say that we are dealing with an instance of political Islam would be to suggest that there are times when Islam is not political (i.e. that it is sometimes "just" religious). The term Muslim politics is useful because it allows us to keep the diversity and pluralism of Islam front and center through an emphasis on Muslims as social actors. To focus on Muslims rather than Islam is to emphasize real people in real settings facing real issues. The more we stress Islam as a unit of analysis, the more we face the dangers of abstraction and unwarranted generalization. Islam keeps us mired in debates about normativity, where an emphasis on Muslims allows us to appreciate the dynamic nature of Islam as a lived experience. The use of the adjectives Muslim and Islamic is hence significant in what follows. When we speak of, for example, Muslim thinkers and Islamic intellectuals, we are referring to two quite different things. The first includes any Muslim engaged in intellectual effort while the second points more specifically to Muslims whose intellectual projects are framed specifically in terms of Islamic normativity.

To study Muslim politics, then, is to look at the diverse ways in which people who identify themselves as Muslims in a variety of social locations—be they religious scholars, bureaucrats, intellectuals, merchants, scientists—understand, make use of, and mobilize the symbols and language of Islam around issues of social order, power, and authority. This approach tends to resist making claims about the nature and content of Islam and instead primarily concerns itself with the various ways in which people engage and draw upon religious tradition as they construct and contest social orders. It helps us both to broaden our understanding of what counts as politics (as per the appeal made above) and to appreciate how certain issues, conventionally understood as limited in their political import, can be transformed into highly politicized public symbols. The emphasis on Muslim politics rather than "Islamism" is also a more inclusive formulation that allows us to examine political actors who define their motivations and goals, at least in part, as related to Islam, but who do not pursue anything like the establishment of formal Islamic political systems. In other words, Muslim politics allows us to focus on a broader range of, and the interplay between, actors engaged in all manner and means of Muslim politics whether or not they have as their goal the establishment of an Islamic political order. So then, political parties seeking to implement political systems based on shari'ah law, such as the Muslim Brotherhood, are certainly engaged in Muslim politics—but similarly the groups that in early 2006 mobilized around the publication of cartoons in a Danish newspaper perceived as insulting to the Prophet Muhammad. Appeals to and mobilizations around the language and symbols of Islam in the pursuit of normative agendas were common to both—hence our description of them both as forms of Muslim politics.

This book is certainly not the first to advocate a Muslim politics approach. As a new and distinct analytical trope, the phrase was probably first coined and systematically elaborated by Dale Eickelman and James Piscatori in their 1996 book of the same name.[9] The reader should refer to this title for the most substantive social scientific statement to date on Muslim politics. While subsequent edited volumes have also embraced the general approach, this book constitutes the first attempt to offer in monographic form a broad, comparative, and global overview of Muslim politics with integrated case studies.[10]

Local politics in a Global world

The final set of introductory points that need to be made here concern this book's emphasis on the global nature of Muslim politics. Writers in academia and journalism tend to use the term "global" these days to mean several different things: to identify something as part and parcel of the wider phenomenon known as globalization; as a way of referring to international phenomenon while de-emphasizing the nation-state; and to contrast—or emphasize the relationship between—broader transnational social contexts, and more local ones. It will hopefully not confuse the reader too much that this book proposes to use, variously, all three meanings.

More specifically as regards Muslim political contexts, our emphasis on the global hopes to serve four central purposes:

(1) To clarify the role played by globalization in animating and enabling new forms of Muslim politics (on which we will have more to say below and again in Chapter 4).
(2) To emphasize the relationship and interplay between local instances of Muslim politics and events, trends, and ideas to be found not only in the wider Muslim world, but also within the emergent spaces of transnational culture and politics (new media, global lifestyles, increasing awareness of "global" issues—and their concomitant political vocabularies—such as human rights and the environment). The central idea here is that while all politics may indeed be local, there remain very few

spaces of local politics that are not connected in some way to other global contexts.

(3) Through an emphasis on the global/local and transnational dimensions of Islam, to find a middle space for exploring comparative politics in the Muslim world that avoids, on the one hand, treating national contexts of Muslim politics as self-contained units of analysis largely sealed off from the wider world, and, on the other, positing the existence of a monolithic global Islam or "Muslim international." The emphasis here is on exploring the *relationality* of various Muslim political contexts and not on either staking claims to the utter uniqueness of each, or seeing each as part of an undifferentiated Islamic bloc.

(4) To bring into focus the fact that there do now exist Muslim political actors and movements (moderates and radicals alike) organized and operating on a global scale, some of whose ambitions and goals are similar in scope. We can also point to various locally based actors making use of media and networks to build up global constituencies for their particular accounts of what it means to be a Muslim today.

While this is not meant primarily to be a book about Islam and globalization, it will be suggested that aspects of globalization have been important in terms of enabling new forms of Muslim politics, permitting them to reach new audiences, and—in some cases—becoming an actual target of these politics. Globalization is a complex phenomenon that in its common usage has both analytical and normative connotations depending on context. It is most commonly associated with the rise of a world political economy and the ever-closer integration of markets and regions through e.g. lower barriers to trade and transnational finance. More broadly, it can be seen as the world propagation of neoliberal economic norms. The normative discourse on globalization, then, is one that understands this process to be a route to greater prosperity for the world's nations, and is most commonly identified with advocates of the so-called "Washington Consensus" such as the World Bank, the IMF, and many of the world's leading economic power and multinational corporations. There are also to be found in the literature definitions that try to achieve a more sociological understanding of globalization, and it is primarily from these authors that the idiom of globalization employed in this book is drawn. Stated in broad terms, these approaches emphasize the unprecedented levels of interconnectedness between societies and peoples that globalization enables. Some authors such as David Harvey and Anthony Giddens have spoken of this in terms of the compression of time and space.[11] Others, such as Jan Aart Scholte, emphasizing the notion of "supraterritoriality," connect globalization with a decline in the importance of territory in the establishment and maintenance of social relations.[12] The most commonly cited manifestations of globalization give credence to aspects of all of these approaches. They include, just to cite a few examples, dramatic increases in the numbers of people traveling and moving around the world due to shifting labor markets and the relatively cheap availability of air travel; the rise of "global cities," such as London, New York, and Tokyo (not to mention Shanghai and Bangalore, India)—all of which have to some extent become disembedded from their national-territorial contexts and now serve as nodal points in the global economy referred to above; and (3) the emergence of new breeds of information and communications technologies and new media such as the Internet and satellite television, all of which have significantly reduced the barriers and costs associated with communicating across borders and getting messages in front of broad, worldwide audiences.

Indeed it is tempting to speculate, as has Roland Robertson, one of the earliest sociological theorists of globalization, about the impact of these developments on peoples' understanding of the world as a social space. He has proposed the notion of "globality" in reference to a particular type of consciousness enabled by globalization, one that refers to the idea that people are now increasingly able to imagine the world as a single space and to have a clearer sense of the complex array of cross-cutting relationships at various levels that define their place in it.[13] Following quite naturally from this, other scholars have been led to speculate about the effects of globalization on how people understand their identities and social affiliations.[14] Taking these theoretical insights into the Muslim world, some writers have speculated about the extent to which globalization might give new credence—and social reality—to the notion of the *umma*, a term with long-standing universalist connotations referring to the world community of Islam.[15] The "people flows" alluded to above have involved large numbers of Muslims traveling regionally and globally as labor migrants, and new media forums have begun to create global public spheres for Muslim discourses of all sorts.[16] While claims about a new umma may be somewhat premature at this point, it is undoubtedly the case that Muslims today have a greater awareness of the lives and predicaments of their co-religionists across diverse national settings. As a number of our case studies will demonstrate, this intensified sense of "Muslim globality" has major implications for the nature and forms of Muslim politics that we find in the world today.

2 Islam and politics: history and key concepts

This book is primarily concerned with Muslim politics in the contemporary world. It is, however, impossible for the reader to understand the nature, form, and symbols of Islamic politics today without some appreciation of their evolution through history. This chapter will offer a historical overview of politics in the Muslim world and, in the process, introduce the reader to key concepts and terms that will be necessary for understanding contemporary Muslim politics and political discourse. As is perhaps inevitable when one aspires to survey nearly 1,500 years of history over multiple continents in a single chapter, the coverage here is far more superficial than a proper historical inquiry would warrant. The aim is to allow the reader to discern the broad trajectory of Muslim politics over time, and to understand key patterns, as well as important moments of disjuncture and upheaval. In addition to covering major historical events, the narrative offered here will also incorporate an overview of the development of Islamic political thought from the time of the Prophet Muhammad up to and including Muslim responses to the formation of modern nation-states and the advent of globalization in the Muslim world.[1]

The origins of Islam

An integral component of the great monotheistic tradition, the history of Islam is inextricably intertwined with that of Judaism and Christianity. While Islamic history is conventionally dated from the time of the Prophet Muhammad in the early seventh century, Muslims, like all followers of the three great monotheistic faiths, believe the origins of their religion to lie in Adam & Eve. In Islam, particular importance is placed on the Prophet Ibrahim (the Arabic form of Abraham). Muslims believe that the *Ka'aba*, a structure in the center of Mecca's Grand Mosque and the holiest site in Islam, was built by Ibrahim and his son Ismail (Ishmael). For Muslims, the books and prophets of the Old Testament are considered sacred, and Muslims also assign a place of special significance and reverence to the figure of Jesus—who appears frequently in the Qur'an. Although differing in significant ways from the other two religions on certain matters of theology and law (as of course, do Judaism and Christianity), Muslims nevertheless worship the same God as Jews and Christians and adhere to the teachings of the same moral universe.

For our purposes it will be convenient to begin our account of Muslim political history with the emergence of the Prophet Muhammad in the Arabian peninsula in the seventh century, and the growth around him of a social movement. It is particularly important to understand accurately the significance of the Prophet Muhammad in the Islamic tradition. Muhammad is believed by Muslims to be the final prophet in the line of Abraham, specifically chosen by God to deliver his last revelation to humankind. Where Christians understand Jesus to be God, Muhammad is wholly human. Indeed, it would severely violate the basic monotheistic creedal impulse of Islam to impute to him any kind of divine significance. Muhammad is primarily God's messenger, the medium through which the Holy Qur'an—the divine text of Islam—was revealed. Beyond his role as a human conduit for the delivery of the Qur'an, however, Muhammad does have further significance for Muslims. Despite his exclusively human status, the Prophet is believed to be the living embodiment of Qur'anic teaching, an idea captured in the notion of Muhammad as *insan al-kamil* ("the perfect person"). It is for this reason that in addition to the Qur'an, the living example of the Prophet is considered as a definitive source of Islamic authority—a concept we will cover in greater detail below.

Let us familiarize ourselves with the social context of the Arabian peninsula at the time Muhammad's prophethood began. Arabia in the seventh century was primarily populated by various nomadic and semi-nomadic tribes. Western Arabia, the subregion with which we are most immediately concerned, constituted an important segment in a transnational trade route that connected Jerusalem and other cities of the Levant with Yemen and, via seafaring merchants, to points further east. The city of Mecca, about halfway up the Red Sea coast between Yemen and the Levant, was a particularly important nodal point in this trading system. Every caravan passed through Mecca, and the city had grown rich on account of its strategic location and its key role in providing all manner of goods and services relating to mercantile activity. It was into a prominent Meccan clan, the Quraysh that Muhammad was born in about 570. Orphaned early in his life, Muhammad was raised by his uncle and learned the family's trade, eventually taking up a role within the city's bustling commercial activity and earning a reputation as a particularly upstanding and judicious provider of financial services.

Muhammad's religious role does not begin until about the age of 40. In order to escape from what he had come too see as the hectic, alienating and overly materialistic commercial life of Mecca, he would sometimes hike out to an outcropping caves beyond the city walls to be with himself and think. It was during one of these excursions in 610 that, according to Islamic tradition, the archangel Gabriel appeared to Muhammad and informed him of his prophetic calling. Having confessed to his wife of the time, Khadija—herself a prominent Meccan business figure—that he feared he was going insane, Muhammad was urged by her to embrace rather than turn away from his calling and Khadija pledged to live by the revelation he brought. Ali—his young cousin (and eventual son-in-law)—followed suit, and the two of them are generally credited as being the first converts to Islam.

At this point it would be useful to say something about the nature of religion in Arabia at this time so that the reader can understand how genuinely different—and, to some, dangerously revolutionary—the message brought by Muhammad was. Mecca in the seventh century was a thoroughly polytheistic society, worshipping a complex and seemingly endless array of gods and deities—often in the form of idols—at shrines and temples throughout the city. People appealed to different deities for different purposes—so, for example, one god to seek intercession regarding the fate of a particular caravan, and another to influence the weekly price of aromatic gums. Religion was not so much a source of moral guidance as it was a way to seek control over the natural world for profit and personal gain. It is worth noting that Judaism and Christianity were not wholly foreign to this milieu given the presence of Jewish and Christian communities in Arabia.

The message that Muhammad brought could not have been more at odds with prevailing religious norms. At its very core was the notion of God's essential oneness (tawhid) and omnipotence, a strict monotheism that expressly forbade the worship of anyone or anything other than the one God of the Abrahamaic tradition. Even representations of God were considered dangerous distractions that could lead the believer back to the path of *shirk* (idolatry). The relationship between humanity and the divine was to be direct and without intercession. It is hence submission to the divine will of God that defines what it means to be a Muslim, in contrast to the instrumentalism characteristic of religious practice in Muhammad's Mecca. *Islam* in Arabic refers to the notion of submission or surrender to God, and a *Muslim*, therefore, is "one who submits." More than just a metaphysics of divine oneness, however, there was also to be found in the revelation brought by Muhammad a complete moral system. Over the years, as we will see later, this became embodied and codified as an actual body of law. Suffice it for now to summarize those aspects of the religion that eventually came to be known as the "Five Pillars of Islam":

1. The *shahada* ("bearing witness") or profession of faith as to the unique and singular nature of God and the recognition of Muhammad as his messenger. Technically, the embrace of this creed is all that is required to become a Muslim.
2. The practice of *salat*, or prayer, to be performed five times daily by believing Muslims.
3. Fasting—*sawm*—from dawn to dusk during the holy month of Ramadan.

4. The payment of *zakat*, a kind of tithe, in the form of a percentage of income dedicated to charitable purposes.
5. The requirement that once during a lifetime, all able-bodied Muslims with sufficient means make a pilgrimage (*hajj*) to the holy city of Mecca.

It is worth noting that although Islam represented a sharp theological rupture in terms of religion in Arabia, there are many elements of pre-Islamic tribal practice and customary law that came to be integrated into or at least tolerated by Islam as its influence and significance expanded. What this means in practice is that from very early on it has been sometimes difficult to definitively discern when a given norm or behavior is the result of religion, and when its origins lay in customary practices that have come to be articulated and justified in terms of religion. This is a point that will prove important later when we go on to examine some of the characteristics commonly associated with Muslim political societies.

At this point we can also identify the two primary sources of authoritative knowledge and practice in Islam. The first of these is the Holy Qur'an itself, believed by Muslims to be the literal word of God as revealed to the Prophet. The chief supplement to the Qur'an is found in Muhammad's *sunna*—that is, Prophetic tradition. The model of thinking and behavior that Muhammad provided during his lifetime is considered by Muslims to be the best example of how the divine knowledge of the Qur'an was to be translated into lived practice. In this sense, Muhammad is regarded as the worldly embodiment of Qur'anic normativity. The sunna is hence preeminent among the various "secondary" (in the sense of not being intrinsically divine) sources of Islamic authority. The collection and categorization of reports about what the Prophet said and did in various situations—known as *hadith*—emerged as a distinctive scholarly discipline in the years following his passing. More detail about the nature and uses of the *sunna* will be provided below.

The hijra and early community in Medina

Muhammad did not get a sympathetic hearing from the notables of Mecca when he began to speak publicly about, and encourage others to accept, his new religion. This is not surprising given that part and parcel of the message was a direct critique of the city's entire social order. Meccan life was castigated as ungodly and corrupt, and the prevailing religious practices denigrated as blasphemous. Muhammad and those who had accepted Islam soon found themselves the target of considerable persecution and hostility. After several difficult years, Muhammad decided that his position in Mecca was untenable. Thus in 622, when the Prophet received an invitation from the nearby city of Yathrib to move to that city along with his community of Muslims, he accepted. Yathrib was a less affluent and politically unstable city to the northeast of Mecca. So important was this migration or *hijra* to Yathrib that it marks the beginning of, and gives its name to, the Islamic calendar. More than just the movement of a people from one setting to another, it had symbolic significance as a shift in the very basis of social affiliation and polity. Many of Muhammad's followers broke with their families in order to go with the Prophet and in this sense the hijra represented a migration from a model of community premised on tribal and clan affiliations to a form of community based on a shared vision of divinely given social order.

Yathrib, soon renamed Medina (after *medinat al-nabi* – "City of the Prophet"), was a far less affluent and politically unstable city to the northeast of Mecca. Rife with sectarian and tribal factionalism, Muhammad had been hired by the Yathribi tribal authorities to act as an arbiter in public affairs. As part of the deal, his status as a Prophet was recognized, and the security of his community guaranteed. Thus begins Muhammad's career as a politician and public official. After consolidating his position in Medina, the Prophet began forming alliances with local tribes and attracting more and more followers to Islam. With these new forces he began to conduct highly successful raids against Meccan trade caravans, and this eventually brought him into direct conflict with his former home city. Over the next half decade Medina and Mecca fought a number of battles and in 630 Muhammad's forces triumphed over Mecca and returned to a city now eager to accept the new faith. One after another, the tribal leaders of Arabia swore oaths of allegiance to Muhammad over the next two years. By the time of the Prophet's death in 632 he had managed to bring all of central Arabia under his effective control.

In terms of the theory and practice of Muslim politics, the death of Muhammad is significant in two regards. As the indisputable political leader of all Muslims during his lifetime, the Prophet's death marked the first time the Muslim community had to settle questions of political leadership and the conduct of public affairs. It was also significant in that it represented the disappearance of an immanent model of Islamic normativity. While Muhammad was alive, correct and "authentic" Islam was always immediately available, embodied in the Prophet's conduct. His death thus also marks the beginning of Muslim politics in the sense of debate and contestation between multiple interpretations of the religion.

Regarding the question of who should succeed the Prophet as the community's political leader, there was initially some debate between two distinct camps. One group believed that the leadership of the community should remain vested within Muhammad's family. They favored the candidacy of Ali, the Prophet's cousin and son-in-law, citing various occasions upon which the Prophet had publicly recognized Ali as a preeminent leader of the community. This group would eventually evolve into the *Shi'i* sect of Islam (from *shi'at Ali*, "partisans of Ali"). The other camp, disputing the idea that Muhammad had ever stated unequivocal views on his successor, preferred the idea of choosing a leader according to the consensus of the community's senior figures. This latter view prevailed, and Abu Bakr, one of the Prophet's oldest and closest friends, was quickly chosen as the first caliph (from *khalifa*, "successor"). Hence was born the political institution of the caliphate, a position and office that endured in some form for 1,300 years until its abolition in 1924 by Mustapha Kemal.

The rashidun caliphs

The first four successors to the Prophet (who ruled from 632 to 661) are known as the *rashidun* ("rightly guided") caliphs, and the events and personalities of this period have carried a special normative valence throughout Islamic history. This is widely regarded as a period when the affairs of the Muslim community were conducted in very close accordance with the Qur'an and the sunna of the Prophet. In short, things are perceived as having been done correctly under the rashidun. As we will see, later social and political movements, responding to what they perceived as diversions from the path of Islam, would often call for a conscious return to the model of the Prophet's early companions.

The rashidun period also marked a time of phenomenal growth in terms of both the geographic expanse of lands under Muslim control, and the diversity of the Muslim peoples. The first caliph, Abu Bakr (632–34), spent most of his short reign reintegrating a number of recalcitrant tribes who had rebelled in the wake of Muhammad's death—a process that later became known as the Wars of Apostasy. It was during the rule of the second caliph, Umar (634–44) that Islam's amazing territorial expansion began. Muslim forces were able to gain significant lands from both the Sassanid Empire in the east and the Byzantines in the north—with the result that, within a decade, much of the Middle East from Egypt across to Palestine, Syria, and even some areas of Persia and Armenia had been integrated into the Muslim state. Umar was also responsible for establishing most of the administrative and economic practices and policies of the new Muslim polity. Rather than directly occupying newly acquired territories, the Arabian Muslims would tend to dispatch governors and revenue officials to administer through a system of garrison towns.

Religious growth was also significant during this period, with mass conversions to Islam. Very little of this involved coercion on the part of Muslims conquerors. Rather, people embraced Islam for a variety of reasons including the favorable tax status associated with being a believer, or because a local notable or tribal leader had decided to convert. In other cases, people were genuinely impressed by the successes of the Muslims or drawn to the religious message itself. Those who chose not to convert were generally left to practice their faith under Muslim rulers as protected religious minorities or *dhimmis*—which usually involved paying a higher rate of tax.[2]

The next caliph, Uthman (644–56), the first to be "elected" by a more formally constituted commission, continued many of his predecessor's policies and his general style of rule. Unlike Umar, however, Uthman tended to be more partial to members of his own family when making selections for senior regional governorships. As a member of one of the most prestigious clans of the Quraysh tribe, there is a sense in which Uthman's reign represented the beginning of a re-encroachment on Muslim politics of tribal influences. Under Uthman more of North Africa and Persia came under Muslim rule. He also oversaw the collection of the first standardized edition of the Qur'an, with the chapters (*surat*) appearing in the order with which we are familiar today. That Uthman felt the need to do this was indicative, at least in part, of discomfort at the religio-political heart of the Muslim empire with certain localized approaches to Qur'anic recitation and interpretation. In other words, the emergence of religious pluralism in this regard was seen as a threat to the political authority of the center and the cohesiveness of the faith. Indeed, Uthman's rather heavy-handed attempts to centralize religious authority were at the root of the general discontent about his rule that began to emerge, particularly among those already alarmed at his tendency toward clan favoritism.

When, at the apex of this displeasure in 656, Uthman was assassinated, Ali finally ascended to the leadership of the Muslim community. His authority was immediately challenged, however, by several prominent figures, not least of all the governor of Syria, Mu'awiya, a kinsman of Uthman who accused Ali of making insufficient efforts to identify and punish his predecessor's assassins. While this pretext was certainly part of the issue, the challenge to Ali was the natural next phase in a growing search for decentralization among the most powerful regions of the Muslim empire—exacerbated by the clan factionalism that had been reintroduced by Uthman. This and other challenges from within soon found Ali fighting the first of several civil wars that would mar his caliphate. When, on the verge of defeating Mu'awiya, Ali acceded to arbitration as a means of settling the conflict, he unwittingly created the first major political schism in Islam. A group that came to be known as the *Khawarij* ("seceders") announced that they were loyal to neither Mu'awiya (because he had dared to question the authority of the caliph) nor Ali (since he had displayed weakness by not subduing his mutinous foe). The Khawarij are important because part of their platform involved recognizing only the Qur'an and sunna as sovereign. Some analysts have pointed to the importance of their influence on later Islamist movements with secessionist tendencies. With Ali's political position fatally compromised, he soon fell prey to a Khawarij assassin, bringing an end to the rashidun period in 661.

The three decades following the death of Muhammad represented a period of phenomenal activity on the part of the new Muslim state, and also one of the most impressive and rapid empire-building exercises in human history; too rapid perhaps, since, in the end, the rate of expansion quickly overtook the ability of the political center to accommodate and integrate its new diversity and the attendant political challenges. The limits of the Medina geopolitical worldview soon revealed themselves as Islam quickly transcended its Arabian—and even Arab—roots to emerge as a thoroughly cosmopolitan religion.

The great Islamic dynasties (661–1258)

The death of Ali marked the end of the first period of Islamic political history and the point of transition into an extended era of dynastic rule. Over the next 1,300 years or so, the Muslim world would witness the rise and fall of many empires and sultanates. Some of them managed to encompass the many lands and nations of Islam within a single polity, while others were narrower in scope and coexisted simultaneously with other Muslim empires. In some cases previously subject peoples rose up to seize effective rule from their former masters and defend Islam against foreign invaders. In short, what we have termed Muslim politics were pervasive throughout this period. In the section that follows we will look at the most important of the various Islamic dynasties and sultanates. By the tenth century, if not earlier, it was also possible to recognize the constituent elements of Muslim political society in terms of various social classes and institutions, both formal and informal. We will thus also take this opportunity to outline and explain the configuration of religious and political authority in medieval Islam, a period that saw the emergence of social forces that remain important even today.

The Umayyad dynasty (661–750): the limits of Arabo-centric power

After Ali's demise, Mu'awiya was able to make a successful bid for the caliphate, and so was born the first of the great Islamic dynasties, with its capital now moved from Medina to Damascus. If the rashidun period had been defined by rapid territorial expansion, the Umayyad period could be described primarily as an attempt to consolidate and rationalize the Arab administration of foreign territories. Mu'awiya and his heirs—this was a dynasty after all, in contrast to the non-hereditary system of succession followed under the first four caliphs—went about establishing a complex administrative system and bureaucracy. The basic structures for these were often borrowed from the empires the Muslims had conquered. Much of the emphasis during this period was on fiscal policy, with the introduction of ever more complicated systems of taxation that maximized revenues from non-Muslims and, most importantly in terms of future political ramifications, non-Arab Muslims. Land revenues were also emphasized as more and more fertile territories came under Muslim control.

The Umayyad period also saw the emergence of a decisive sectarian schism with the emergence of Shi'i Islam. As has already been mentioned, the roots of Shi'ism trace back to a disagreement at the time of the Prophet's death over who should assume the political leadership of the community. This resentment festered among certain supporters of Ali ("Alids") even during the rashidun period, with some feeling that his role was consistently and deliberately marginalized—a situation that ripened into open hostility once he assumed the caliphate. Before Mu'awiya died, he named his son, Yazid, as his successor, destroying any hope on the part of those who continued to support Ali that one of his sons might come to power. Ali's younger son Husayn declined to accept Yazid's authority and traveled from Medina to the Iraqi city of Kufa to join with a group of Alids in mounting a rebellion against the Damascus caliphate. They were preempted in this by the arrival of an Umayyad army and during the ensuing Battle of Karbala (680 CE), Husayn and his family were all killed. The martyrdom of Husayn is commemorated by Shi'a each year on the anniversary of this battle, the tenth day ("*Ashura*") of the month of Muharram. This was a decisive moment in the emergence of Shi'ism as a separate sect in Islam. More details regarding the doctrinal and political differences between these two sects will be provided below.

Territorial gains under the Umayyads were significant. By the end of this first dynasty, Muslim rule extended from Spain in the West, down across all of North Africa and the Middle East and throughout Persia into parts of present day Pakistan. Despite the increased geographic and cultural diversity of the Muslim state, effective power came to be concentrated in the hands of a relatively small Arab aristocratic elite. Concern began to mount amongst those who had taken it upon themselves to be the guardians and transmitters of religious knowledge, the ulama ("religious scholars"), that the Umayyad rulers had lost sight of the egalitarianism, austerity and humility at the core of Islam and the rashidun period's model of "good governance." Although the caliph and his regional agents did create positions charged with the enforcement of religiously prescribed norms and arbitration of the same, these came to be perceived as just another extension of what looked increasingly like monarchic rule.

The final decade of Umayyad rule saw the emergence of opposition movements on a number of fronts. Resenting the decadence of the Umayyad rulers and their narrow circles of favoritism, Muslims—Arab and non-Arab alike—began to decry the failure of their rulers to properly implement an Islamic system of equitable governance. They were joined in this by other long standing detractors, such as the Khawarij and the Shi'a. Religious scholars, many of them based at centers of learning in Iraq, had begun the process of codifying Islamic morality into a legal system, the shari'ah. They were prompted to do this, at least in part, by a desire to establish a standard of conduct that would throw the policies of the present rulers into stark contrast. After a series of revolts, the Umayyads fell in 750 to the Abbasids, a clan descended from al-Abbas, one of the Prophet's uncles.

The Abbasid dynasty (750–1258): cosmopolitanism and fragmentation

Abbasid rule, which saw the capital move yet again from Damascus to Baghdad, technically lasted some 500 years, although the clan of al-Abbas lost effective power by the tenth century. Often regarded as Islam's "golden age," under the Abbasids the empire made its greatest achievements in the fields of science and philosophy. This period also saw the consolidation of the four schools of jurisprudence that would come to define the dominant Sunni ("orthodox") denomination—of which more below. Although we can wonder whether the Abbasid rulers were actually any more religious than their Umayyad forebears, it is certainly the case that they were great patrons of religion and religious learning. Many new mosques and associated centers of religious scholarship were established, and the Islamic legal sciences flourished. In the field of philosophy, the early ninth century saw the rise of the *Mu'tazili* school of thought, strongly influenced by Greek rationalism. The politicians even took an interest in these developments, adopting Mu'tazilism as the official doctrine of the empire under the caliph Ma'mun. This orientation remained dominant until challenged by the rival school of *Asharism*, which sought to uphold the superiority of revealed knowledge. The later Abbasid period also saw major contributions to philosophy (and the revisiting of certain aspects of this same debate) by figures such as al-Ghazali in Baghdad and Ibn Rushd in Cordoba.

In political terms, although the Abbasid caliphs based much of their authority on claims to greater religiosity and the "re-Islamization" of governance, they did little to alter the essentially imperial and monarchical structure of the Umayyad bureaucracy. Two areas in which important changes were made, however, related to the extensive use of non-Arab officials in various senior court positions and the reintroduction of a taxation system based on the early Islamic distinction between Muslims and non-Muslims, meaning that non-Arab Muslims were no longer taxed at a higher rate. The Abbasid period was also characterized by considerable political fragmentation. Although the "official" caliphate rested with the Abbasids through 1258 (and then, in purely symbolic terms, even until 1517), the dynasty's capacity for centralized rule had been effectively eroded by the mid-tenth century. A number of regional kingdoms and sub-dynasties began to emerge, such as the Shi'i Fatimids in North Africa. Control of the Iraqi heartland fell into the hands of another Shi'i clan, the Buyids, and eventually to the Seljuq Turks. Meanwhile, the Umayyads had reappeared in Spain, making a separate claim to the caliphate from 929, and the growing autonomy of various local governors in nominally Abbasid territories saw them acquiring more and more real political power from the late tenth century. The dynasty formally ended in 1258 when Baghdad was sacked by the Mongols and the caliph killed—although by this time the Abbasid rulers were little more than figureheads.

The rise of Muslim political society: ulama, Sufis, shari'ah, and the state

We find here a convenient spot at which to temporarily pause our historical narrative and look more closely at a number of key concepts and social roles that will emerge as relevant in our later analyses of contemporary Muslim politics. It was under the Abbasids that the various social classes and institutions that collectively compose what we might call "Muslim political society" emerged. By this term we are referring to the interwoven system of political and religious authority composed of the caliph (as Commander of the Faithful and chief enforcer of religious law), the religious scholars or ulama as repositories of religious learning who simultaneously provide a mediating layer between the state and society, and the institutions and traditions of religious law and jurisprudence. This latter subsystem, as we will see, is particularly complicated both in terms of its relationship with the state and various developments in legal thought during the Abbasid period that rendered rather ambiguous the question of the extent to which it was possible to further supplement the law once the parameters and central content of the four orthodox legal schools had consolidated. In this section we will provide an overview of the major concepts, persons, and institutions that compose this political society.

In its broad sense, the term "alim" (pl. ulama) can be applied to individuals trained in any of the various branches of religious scholarship. The ulama hence comprise specialists in fields such as *tafsir* (Qur'anic interpretation), *sira* (biographical work on the Prophet), *kalam* (theology), and the collection and verification of hadith. In a more specific sense, the term "ulama" is also commonly used in reference to those invested with the capacity to engage matters of religious law. In this sense it also encompasses the more specific titles of *mufti*, *faqih*, and *qadi* detailed below.

While it was under the Abbasids that the ulama emerged as a fully developed social and professional class, it is certainly possible to identify persons engaged in aspects of religious scholarship from the rashidun period onward. Under the caliph Uthman, in particular, efforts were made to standardize the ordering of verses in the Qur'an and to begin the systematic preservation of reports (hadith) about the Prophet's life. Hadith science evolved into a complex discipline, involving the collection and categorization of thousands of narrative accounts relating to the Prophet Muhammad. Every person within the chain of transmission (*isnad*) of each hadith, all the way back to the individual who had actually witnessed what the Prophet had done or said, was subject to scrutiny in terms of their reputation and biography. Based partly on the strength of the isnad but also partly on the presence of corroborating reports, each hadith was assigned a grade indicating its reliability. Those with the strongest and most sounds isnads received a grade of *sahih* ("genuine") in contrast with those at the other end of the spectrum graded as *da'if* ("weak").[3] The early Abbasid period saw the publication of the two major authoritative collections of sahih hadith, those of Bukhari and Muslim.

The science of jurisprudence (*fiqh*) began to emerge during the late Umayyad period. One of the earliest and still most respected sources for legal methodology is the *Muwatta* ("The Trodden Path") of Imam Malik, a

Medinan scholar whose work joined that of three other scholars working between the early eighth and mid-ninth centuries (Abu Hanifa, al-Shafi'i, and Ibn Hanbal) to create four eponymous legal schools (*madhahib*; sing. *madhhab*) of Sunni Islam. By the late ninth century, Islamic jurisprudence had become a well-developed science and the shari'ah (literally, "the path") of the Qur'an codified as a living body of law. As fiqh became a discipline in its own right, a corps of theorists and technicians—the *fuqaha* (sing. faqih, "jurists")—emerged as its chief architects. Working in tandem with other religious scholars, the jurisconsults created the *usul al-fiqh* (principles of jurisprudence), introducing important distinctions regarding various categories of law such as the division between matters of worship (*ibadat*) and issues of social normativity (*mu'amalat*).

With the completion of the great hadith collections and the legal treatises of the four great classical scholars, matters of jurisprudential deliberation came to be structured around four key sources of authority:

(1) *Qur'an* – as the literal word of God, the Qur'an was always the paramount source of authority. The discipline of Qur'anic exegesis (tafsir) emerged as particularly important in terms of debating the precise meaning of the Word and its implications for the daily lives of Muslims. Perhaps inevitably, there also ensued numerous debates regarding allegorical versus literal understandings of Qur'anic verse and the created versus eternal nature of the Qur'an.

(2) *Sunna* – second only to the Qur'an, the Prophet's tradition was regarded as a living model for the correct application of shari'ah. Certain of the hadith (the *hadith qudsi*) are assigned a status almost tantamount to that of the Qur'an insofar as they are regarded as the revelation-sourced knowledge that came to the Prophet in dreams, or which were rendered in his own words.

(3) *Ijma* – the "consensus" of the leading scholars of the age is also considered a relatively safe grounding point for legal deliberation. The Qur'an exhorts Muslims to decide matters on the basis of the community's ijma—i.e. investing this notion with significant democratic potential. In practice, however, it came to refer only to the consensus of the learned jurisconsults.

(4) *Qiyas* – a term referring to the method of analogical deduction. When neither the Qur'an nor sunna is clear on a particular point of law, a legal scholar may deduce an opinion based on examples from an analogous situation involving similar core principles.

Another key concept in legal methodology, particularly prevalent during the years in which the critical mass of the shari'ah was assembled, was *ijtihad*— or the exercise of independent judgment and interpretation regarding legal matters. Confidence in ijtihad as a method more or less paralleled the fortunes of Mu'tazili philosophy which relied in large measure on the power of reason. When Asharism began to question the dangers of rational knowledge, similar concern came to be raised about ijtihad as a basis for building the shari'ah. By the tenth century, a prevailing opinion emerged to the effect that ijtihad was no longer necessary, and, moreover, was becoming increasingly dangerous by introducing various distortions (read: personal preferences) into the canon. This event became known as the closing of the gates to ijtihad. Numerous later scholars would debate the question of whether the gates were completely or permanently closed, and also the issue of who might hold the keys that could open them again.[4] For the time being, however, the law was now Law, and subsequent jurisprudential efforts were focused on the interpretation and application of existing shari'ah rather than on expanding its content.

As Islamic jurisprudence evolved, there emerged a clearer division of labor in terms of the various roles played by figures within the legal profession. In the early years of Islamic expansion much in the way of legal interpretation and enforcement was left to the discretion of regional and local governors. As the bureaucracy expanded under the Umayyads, specialized positions were created to ensure that commerce was conducted in accordance with the shari'ah and also to enforce public virtue. The creation of an actual court system saw the appointment of the first qadis (judges). It is important to note that while the legal system was shari'ah based, religion was by no means the exclusive source of law. Considerable measures of customary law (*urf*) were incorporated into the statutes so long as they were compatible with the shari'ah. In addition to the aforementioned juristic class, it is also worth mentioning the role of the mufti. Literally this term refers to anyone possessing the credentials necessary for issuing *fatwas* (legal opinions). In many cases, however, the mufti became a quasi-official role and referred to the chief legal scholar of a given state.

Some clarification regarding the notion of the fatwa is also warranted, particularly given the confusion surrounding the meaning of this term that emerged at the time of the Rushdie Affair in the late 1980s, when it came to be understood in popular discourse as referring to a "death sentence." A fatwa (pl. *fatawa*) refers to a legal opinion as issued by a competent authority, usually an alim or faqih. Its content may be based on any of the four methodologies mentioned above, but a fatwa is often the result of an act of ijtihad. Since a fatwa is nothing more than the opinion of a scholar, the strength of its influence is generally a function of the reputation of its promulgator and his skill in situating his reasoning within the mainstream of Islamic legal discourse. Fatwas are rarely binding and can usually be abrogated by subsequent acts of ijtihad. Religious scholars over the ages have frequently debated the question of just who is authorized to issue a fatwa. While most muftis generally possess a certain modicum of formal training in the legal sciences, there have been instances of individuals with little or no formal qualification issuing fatwas that entered into mainstream political discourse—such as Usama Bin Laden's 1998 fatwa declaring war on the United States. In this regard, fatwas and their ambiguous status, have been the site of considerable Muslim politics.

The social role and position of the ulama evolved alongside the increasingly expansive and complex Muslim state throughout the medieval period and into the Middle Ages. Under the early caliphs, the ulama were nothing more than a small cadre of specialists who had dedicated their lives to the collection and elucidation of religious knowledge. As a group of "learned men," they were consulted by the authorities on various matters, but did not yet constitute a discrete social milieu. It was the advent of jurisprudential science from the late Umayyad period onward that allowed the ulama to emerge as a distinctive professional class. In terms of the question of where the ulama fit within Muslim political society, it is worth remembering that part of the impulse behind the codification of the shari'ah was the perceived failings and irreligiosity of the Umayyad rulers. In this regard, the early ulama played a quasi-civil societal role in buttressing emerging forms of opposition politics. Subsequently, the Abbasids were careful to patronize religious scholarship and to keep certain ulama very close to them as something akin to official scholars of the state. When the caliph or his deputies required religious sanction for a particular policy decision, it was of course helpful to have jurists on hand who could articulate this justification in the language of shari'ah. Thus we can say that the relationship between the ulama and the state varied over time, witnessing periods both of official co-option and also times when the ulama served as a mediating layer between the state and the concerns of popular society. Though generally hesitant to directly question the authority of the state for fear of prompting social disorder (*fitna*), many ulama did not hesitate to issue dissident fatwas when consulted by members of the public. Unsurprisingly some of them found themselves out of favor with the authorities on occasion, and even spent periods of time in prison or entered exile abroad.

Muslim imperial bureaucracies produced and soon came to rely on their own self-sufficient legal systems. And what of the authority of the caliph himself? As we have already seen above, the Commander of the Faithful, while still vested with some religious authority as the chief enforcer of the shari'ah, evolved into more of a secular authority during the dynastic period. In some cases, the political sovereigns introduced their own parallel legal systems (the *mazalim* courts) that permitted the enforcement of royal ordnances and the prosecution of various matters outside the remit of personal status law, the one area where the jurisdiction of shari'ah went unquestioned. In summary, then, we can say that whereas early caliphs had direct experience of, and were hence better able to represent, Prophetic tradition, later holders of this office were alienated from the idea of the pious sovereign. The religious component of caliphal authority was certainly invoked when politically expedient to do so, but for the most part this was largely symbolic. It is hence safe to say that those present day political movements in the Muslim world that seek to reestablish the caliphate have the rashidun rather than the late Abbasid model in mind.

Also central to the social fabric of Islam during the entire period under consideration were the various Sufi brotherhoods. Sufism, the mystical variant of Islam, has been in existence in organized form since shortly after the death of the Prophet. It emphasizes the emotive dimensions of religious experience, and the spiritual pursuit of divine love. Sufi religious practice involves a number of distinct forms of worship, the most common collective form of which is known as *dhikr* ("remembrance"), during which the attributes of God or short sections of Qur'an and hadith are meditatively intoned. In terms of its social organization, Sufism is composed of a vast array of brotherhoods (*tariqat*, "paths"), and it is generally through joining a tariqa that one embraces the Sufi path. There are often various levels of brotherhood affiliation available, but the standard model involves a disciple (*murid*) placing himself under the spiritual tutelage of a master (*sheikh*). By the twelfth century, the social significance of the Sufi brotherhoods had become undeniable. Many of the tariqat—such as the Naqshbandiyya and Qadiriyya—became thoroughly transnational, with branch lodges (*zawiyas*) in all major cities.

It is important to note that Sufism does not represent a sect or legal school. Rather, it constitutes a complementary mode of seeking religious knowledge and experience that is not in and of itself opposed to or incompatible with the shari'ah and other aspects of Islamic orthopraxis. Indeed, many of the early religious scholars admired the spiritual vitality of Sufis, and a great many of Islam's preeminent philosophers and orthodox jurists, such as al-Ghazali, were supporters—if not practitioners themselves—of Sufism. As we will see in the next chapter, major figures associated with modern Islamist movements have also been heavily influenced by Sufi thought and practice. Of further sociological significance is the fact that in many settings Sufism attracted mass followings among Muslims in search of spirituality but less inclined to inculcate themselves in the more formal normativity of the shari'ah. Certain manifestations of Sufi populism, such as the celebration of saintly birthdays and the visitation of graves, eventually attracted the ire of more conservative jurists, particularly modernist exponents of the Hanbali school of jurisprudence, who regarded these practices as quasi-idolatrous. And yet figures such as Ibn Taymiyyah, an early fourteenth-century Hanbali jurist much admired by today's most conservatively orthodox scholars, was himself a member of at least two tariqat—a fact that exemplifies the extent to which Sufism was embedded within the Islamic social order and thoroughly intertwined with orthodox normativity. Sufi networks remain politically influential to this day, and as we will see in Chapter 8, many have used the infrastructures and technologies of globalization to expand their capacity and effective reach.

We have spent some time outlining and clarifying these various aspects of Muslim political society and religious authority not because they have come down to us unaltered since the Middle Ages. Rather, it is important for the reader to understand the genesis and evolution of religious authority in Islam—and its relationship to the state—in order to better appreciate the various elements of transformation and continuity that we see today. The caliphate may no longer exist, but we do find today a number of political authorities that stake their legitimacy on religious foundations (i.e. the Saudi royal family and the Islamic Republic of Iran). The ulama certainly continue to function as important intermediaries between the state and Muslim society. In the age of satellite TV, as we will see, their constituencies are potentially global. Sufi brotherhoods are thriving in the era of globalization, and debates regarding the role of shari'ah, and the permissibility of ijtihad continue to be part of contemporary Muslim discourse. The politics may be different today, as may the structure of the political systems in which they play out, but many of the actors and key reference points remain the same.

The Sunni-Shi'i divide in Islam

While the roots of the schism between Sunnis and Shi'a go back to the death of the Prophet Muhammad, the emergence of a fully formed political identity among Shi'a ("Partisans" of Ali and the Prophet's family) is more accurately associated with the early Umayyad period. The martyrdom of Ali's son Hussain at the Battle of Kerbala in 680, an event commemorated by Shi'a each year on the Day of Ashura (the tenth of Muharram), is generally recognized as the event that crystallized a sense of dispossession among those whose political loyalties lay with the Prophet's family. What is generally called Sunni Islam also did not emerge until later. Sunni ("orthodox") Islam refers to followers of the consensus that developed among the early, great legal scholars—meaning that one could only meaningfully speak of such a thing as Sunni Islam after the middle of the ninth century.

Over the decades and centuries following the rise of dynastic politics in Islam, Shi'i theology and jurisprudence took on certain unique characteristics, while continuing to share a great deal with the Sunni core (including the Qur'an and many of the most important collections of hadith). The Ja'fari legal school, for example, emerged in the eighth century as the central jurisprudential reference point for the Shi'i tradition, and a strong Sufi ("mystical") path also developed within Shi'ism. Members of the community, however, found themselves viewed with increasing suspicion and tended to live apart from Sunnis or to hide their religious identities (*taqiya*) in order to avoid being persecuted for holding "heterodox" views. Certain Shi'i political groups did eventually enjoy better fortunes, going on to found a number of important regional empires such as the *Fatimids* in Egypt (910–1171) and the *Safavids* in Persia (1501–1736), the precursor to modern Iran.

The Shi'i tradition operates with a conception of religious authority that differs significantly from the Sunni variant—and this can be seen to have important political implications. In terms of the overall leadership of the community, Shi'a do not recognize the institution of the caliphate. For them, the *imamate*, a line of spiritual leaders that traces back through Ali, serves an analogous but distinct function. This reflects a Shi'a belief that the qualities of spiritual leadership are vested in the descendents of the Prophet. Where Sunnis tend to regard authority as residing within a canonical textual tradition (hence the emphasis on legal orthodoxy), Shi'a have tended to emphasize the embodied authority of a living spiritual guide. Hence the presence in Shi'i Islam of something more closely resembling a formal clergy and the tendency for many observant Shi'a to choose and follow the jurisprudential practice of a particular living cleric.

Within Shi'i Islam, one finds multiple subdivisions. The vast majority (approximately 80 percent) of the world's Shi'a belong to the "Twelver" branch, so-called because they recognize twelve imams. The twelfth or "Hidden Imam" is believed to be in a state of spiritual occultation, destined to return one day in the form of the Mahdi—a redeemer figure. Other important branches are the "Seveners" or Ismailis and the "Fiver" Zaidis. The Druze and Alawis, religious communities found in Syria and Lebanon, regard themselves as rooted in Shi'ism, but some followers of mainstream Shi'i branches dispute this.

Shi'a today constitute approximately 10 to 15 percent of the world's Muslim population, or 130 to 195 million. Over half are to be found in two countries, Iran (90 percent of the population) and Iraq (around 60 percent of the population), with other significant communities to be found in Lebanon, India, Pakistan, Bangladesh, Afghanistan, Azerbaijan, and many of the Arab Gulf Sheikhdoms (Bahrain, Saudi Arabia, Kuwait, Qatar, and the UAE). Significant pockets also exist throughout the Central Asian states of the Former Soviet Union, Turkey, and Yemen.

While Sunni-Shi'i tensions have been part of the politics of state formation in the Middle East for many decades now (see, for example, the case of Saudi Arabia in Chapter 5), the upsurge in sectarian tensions in Iraq in the aftermath of the U.S.-led war to topple Saddam Hussein has led some to speculate about the possibility of a widespread "Shi'a revival" throughout the region.

The gunpowder empires and Europe's rise

While one might be tempted to consider Islam down for the count with the fall of the Abbasid empire in 1258, to do so would be to ignore the extent to which the Islamic world had by then far exceeded the political boundaries of any sovereign entity. This can be nicely illustrated by shifting our lens southward for a moment. While the weak central state was being plundered by foreign invaders, the Indian Ocean was emerging as a vibrant space of commercial and intellectual exchange. Although not all of the countries and ports involved were part of a centralized Islamic empire, Muslim traders and itinerant scholars were the animating force behind a cosmopolitan system stretching from East Africa to Southern Arabia and then across to India, China, and the Malay peninsula. The next three centuries would see the rise of new Muslim empires in Persia, India, and—via South Asian and Yemeni traders—the spread of Islam and the creation of Muslim kingdoms throughout the archipelagoes of Southeast Asia. From the early fourteenth century, Islam also began to find new lands in sub-Saharan Africa, reaching into Mali and down into modern day Nigeria. Centralized political control may have vanished, but the umma, the "community of believers," had never been more expansive.

Three dynasties from this period are of particular significance. Commonly referred to as the Islamic "gunpowder empires" due to the role military technology played in ensuring their preeminence, these are the polities via which the Muslim world eventually encountered political modernity in the form of European imperialism.[5] These are the Safavid Empire (1501–1736), roughly coterminous with—and an important precursor to—modern Iran, the Mughal Empire in the Indian subcontinent (1526–1857), and lastly, one that we will consider in some detail, the Ottoman Empire (1300–1922), which, at the height of its power ruled Asia Minor, Southeastern Europe from the Balkans across to the Caucuses, the North African coast, Iraq and the Levant, and the western coast of Arabia.

A case study, for the most part, in the successful integration and administration of a highly diverse population, the Ottoman Empire had rather humble beginnings. Born from several Anatolian tribal cantons sandwiched between the Seljuqs and Mongols, the ethnically Turkic Ottomans (named for the dynasty's founder, Osman—a Turkic rendering of the Arabic name Uthman) proved themselves highly adept at managing rapid expansion through the creation of a governmental system capable of matching pace with the empire's growth. In 1453 the Ottomans under Mehmet II conquered Constantinople from the Byzantines, renamed it Istanbul and made it their capital for almost the next half millennium. Making extensive use of foreign and non-Muslim administrative expertise, the Ottomans created a bureaucracy unlike any other the Muslim world had ever seen. As a military state, the empire relied heavily on janissaries and the *devshirmeh*, a slave-soldier institution reminiscent of the Mamluks under the Abbasids, whose ranks tended to be recruited from non-Muslim lands, particularly Southeastern Europe.

From 1517, Ottoman sultans began to claim for themselves the title of caliph and by the time the empire reached its zenith in the late seventeenth century, Istanbul's sovereign had generally come to be recognized as the preeminent political authority in the Muslim world. Using a form of subsidiary governance, the Ottomans relied on a system of provincial governors to rule their territories. These local vassals were granted significant autonomy so long as they remained loyal to Istanbul and remitted sufficient tax revenues. The peoples of the Ottoman empires generally enjoyed high levels of religious freedom, although those who accepted Islam certainly possessed privileges unavailable to non-Muslim subjects. Non-Muslims were organized into religious communities known as millets, each of which was ruled according to its own law. Muslim subjects were generally subject to shari'ah provisions according to the Hanafi rite—the official Ottoman jurisprudential school—regarding matters of personal status, although the state also made wide-ranging use of a parallel body of administrative law, the qanun statutes, which enjoyed their own court institutions (cf. the mazalim courts of the earlier Arab caliphs).

Ottoman growth is generally regarded to have reached its apex with the second siege of Vienna in 1683. From that point onward the empire grew increasingly entwined with Europe's emergent imperial ambitions. Sensing first stagnation and, later, evident decline in their fortunes as European powers began to encroach (France occupied Egypt in 1798), the Ottomans agreed during the nineteenth century to institute sweeping political reforms to modernize all aspects of the state bureaucracy and military. Known as the *tanzimat* ("reorganization") period, these efforts did little to check the empire's rapid decline. Well aware of the republican sentiments now emerging as predominant in Europe, the highly educated, cosmopolitan core population of the Ottoman empire began to take on a proto-nationalist consciousness. In response to widespread popular discontent, Sultan Abdulhamid II introduced a short-lived constitution and Basic Law. Ottoman treaty obligations brought the empire into World War I on the side of the Germans, but even before this, internal political forces in the form of the Committee of Union and Progress—an organization of young, nationalist-minded military officers—had already succeeded in forcing a second round of constitutional concessions from Abdulhamid II. After several politically turbulent years and a resounding defeat in WWI, the final Sultan, Mehmet VI, was removed from power in 1922 as the Ottoman Empire dissolved upon establishment of the modern Turkish Republic.

Islamic responses to imperialism: revival and reform

The Ottomans were not the only world power on the rise from the sixteenth century. Europe, now fully emerged from the cocoon of Medievalism, was rapidly gaining in political, economic, and technological strength. 1492 marked both the date of Columbus' landing in the New World, and the Spanish crown's reconquest of the Iberian peninsula with the fall of the last Muslim rulers in Granada. Over the next 300 years, the Spanish would be joined by the Portuguese, the Dutch, the French and the British as seafaring powers in search of new lands for crown and market. Britain developed extensive interests in the New World from as early as the fifteenth century, but did not undertake significant colonial expansion in the Muslim world until representatives of the British East India Company tangled with Mughal rulers in the mid-1700s on their way to establishing British imperial suzerainty over the entire subcontinent. A brief and ultimately unsuccessful foray by the French into Egypt at the end of that century marked the beginning of French interest in the Muslim heartland, culminating in French rule in Algeria and significant colonies and commercial interests in both West Africa and the Levant. The British occupied Egypt from 1882, and by the time her overseas holdings reached their zenith, fully one quarter of the world's population lived under British colonial rule.

How did Muslim thinkers and activists respond to the growing encroachment on their lands by foreign powers? In order to understand the Muslim response to Europe's rise, we need to gain an understanding of two central currents prevalent in Islamic thought from the second half of the eighteenth century, the movements commonly known as *revivalism* and *reformism*. While it is fair to say that the first of these was inwardly focused and the latter more oriented toward external challenges, they can be read collectively as an evolving Muslim response to Islam's perceived decline and the rise of Europe.

Islamic revivalism

Manifestations of what came to be known as the revivalist or renewalist (*tajdidi*) trend were visible from the mid-eighteenth century in settings as diverse as India, Nigeria, Sudan, and central Arabia. We will focus here on revivalism in the last of these contexts since the figure with whom it is most commonly identified continues to animate Islamist thought and Muslim politics today. Muhammad Ibn Abdul Wahhab (1703–92) was a pious religious reformer active in the central heartland of the Arabian peninsula in the middle of the eighteenth century. While it would be a stretch to describe Ibn Abdul Wahhab as a cosmopolitan in terms of the breadth of his engagement with the world beyond central Arabia, he was certainly keenly aware of the predicament facing Muslims throughout the umma and also had some very clear ideas about what was to be done about it. He developed a reputation for preaching a fairly austere Islam premised on the need to return to the model and practices of the Prophet Muhammad and the immediate generations that followed him. This emphasis on the early pious companions, the *salaf al-salih*, has led later movements modeled on this aspect of Ibn Abdul Wahhab's teachings to be labeled *salafi*—the standard orientation of much of the religious establishment in present day Saudi Arabia.

Such prescriptions were hence reflective of how Ibn Abdul Wahhab viewed the ills of Islam. To his thinking, the Muslim world had fallen into decline because Muslims had strayed away from the core teachings and practices of the faith. Ibn Abdul Wahhab had particular concern about the prevalence of what he saw as deviant practices associated with Sufi mysticism. Labeling these activities, such as the worshiping of saints, as dangerous forms of *bid'a* ("innovation"), Ibn Abdul Wahhab sought to purify Islam and return it to its original essence through an intense and often very literal engagement with the original sources and the early companions of the Prophet. It is this approach that later came to be called Islamic Revivalism.

The central concept in his teaching was that of tawhid, referring to monotheism or the oneness of God, a theme elaborated in his key work *Kitab al-Tawhid* ("The Book of Divine Unity"). To Ibn Abdul Wahhab, praying for saintly intercession and visiting graves seemed too close to idolatry and these actions represented everything that was wrong with Islam. The rejuvenation of Islam was to be achieved through a return to the universal core teachings, free from the distorting influences of sociocultural innovation. We know that Ibn Abdul Wahhab spent some time in Basra in present day Iraq where he encountered and debated other leading religious scholars. It is here that translation of his ideas into a political program began in earnest. Returning to Arabia he formed an alliance with Muhammad Ibn Saud (the direct forebear of Saudi Arabia's present kings), and with the military support of the latter undertook a campaign to spread the message of pious reform across the Arabian peninsula. Although Ibn Abdul Wahhab's teachings did not initially find widespread purchase beyond the frontiers of Arabia, his ideas have formed an important reference point for successive generations of the Islamist political project—not least of all among contemporary advocates of Islamic radicalism such as Usama Bin Laden and Ayman al-Zawahiri.

Islamic reformism

In contrast to Ibn Abdul Wahhab, Jamal al-Din al-Afghani (1839–97) was thoroughly in tune with the latest trends emanating from a wide variety of intellectual milieu. Where the former's worldview was shaped somewhat in the abstract in the relatively isolated setting of central Arabia (an area not under Ottoman or any other kind of foreign rule), Afghani theorized the Muslim condition through a direct engagement with the reality of colonial occupation. His biography is particularly telling in this regard. Afghani was born in Persia and lived at various points throughout his life in India, Egypt, Turkey, and even Europe. An itinerant scholar-activist par excellence, Afghani moved from setting to setting, seeking each time to identify and rally a new generation of socially mobile Muslims around the cause of religious reform. In order to understand how the notion of Islamic reform figured in Afghani's analysis, it is necessary to look first at how he viewed the current state of the Muslim world vis-à-vis the West. The most concise statement of his thinking in this regard is contained in a famous essay entitled "An Islamic Response to Imperialism."

Afghani begins by seeking to decouple the direct agents of foreign occupation (e.g. Britain, France) from that which he understands to be the enabling force behind imperial power, namely superior military technology. He refutes the notion that any given country or culture can meaningfully lay exclusive claim to scientific capacity. Afghani implies instead that at different historical junctures, the center of world scientific production has varied, noting that science "is continually changing capitals." For him, the Muslim world in the tenth to twelfth centuries constituted the hub of global scientific innovation. This setting, for him, has simply changed with time, and with it, the locus of geopolitical hegemony. He is not however a technological determinist. Science and technology are only so good as the *philosophy* that underpins them, for "community without the spirit of philosophy [can]not deduce conclusions from ... sciences." Indeed, for Afghani, philosophy must precede and lead to science in order for the significance of the latter to be properly understood and responsibly deployed:

> The first Muslims had no science, but, thanks to the Islamic religion, a philosophic spirit arose among them, and owing to that philosophic spirit they began to discuss the general affairs of the world and human necessities. This was why they acquired in a short time all the sciences with particular subjects that they translated from the Syriac, Persian, and Greek into the Arabic language ... [6]

He goes on to decry the present state of intellectual output in the Muslim world, and herein lies the crux of his internal critique of Islam. Afghani is concerned that the early philosophic spirit of Islam had been abandoned over the centuries as the moral principles of the religion became codified as rigidly dogmatic jurisprudence. Present day scholars of Islam, in his view, had become intellectually stagnant through their unreflective and uncritical use of medieval models and frameworks of moral philosophy. He elaborates:

> The science of principles consists of the philosophy of the *Shari'a*, or *philosophy of law*. In it are explained the truth regarding right and wrong, benefit and loss, and the cause for the promulgation of laws. Certainly, a person who studies this science should be capable of establishing laws and enforcing civilization. However, we see that those who study this science among the Muslims are deprived of understanding of the benefits of laws, the rules of civilization, and the reform of the world. [7]

It is here that Afghani reveals himself to be most sharply at odds with Ibn Abdul Wahhab. Where the latter seeks to rescue Islam from its doldrums by emphasizing a literalist reading of a specific and narrow range of religious sources, Afghani equates civilizational strength with having a dynamic orientation towards knowledge. We should note, however, that his prescription is not simply one that exhorts Muslims to expend more energy studying science and technology. He notes in the essay, for example, that while the Khedive (the Ottoman governor) of Egypt had undertaken considerable educational reform and placed an emphasis on the empirical sciences, the lack of philosophical inquiry within the educational system had rendered pointless the mere acquisition of technical knowledge. Afghani's goal then is to reform Islamic thought and scholarship so as to reinfuse it with what he sees as an originary spirit of philosophical inquiry. According to Afghani, it is not the case that Muslims were engaged in deviant behaviors that distracted from the core teachings of their religion (as per Ibn Abdul Wahhab), but rather that they had lost the will and capacity to engage in original inquiry and critical thinking.

Also crucial to bear in mind is that for Afghani this project of Islamic intellectual reinvigoration possessed a distinctly political valence insofar as it was understood to constitute a path out of colonial rule. The political program to which it was attached went under the mantle of "Pan-Islam" and deliberately invoked notions such as the umma rather than narrower, nationalist sentiments. Through appeals to Muslim unity, Afghani hoped to mobilize the best and brightest of his day around a vision of Islamic emancipation—but emancipation both from foreign rule and from internal religious stagnation. Afghani's political activities took him to all of the major Muslim metropoles, and he was perhaps the first modern Islamic activist to use Europe as a base for publishing and distributing propaganda materials. Indeed, it was the increased literacy rates in Muslim lands from the early nineteenth century that had, in part, made Afghani's mode of activism and social mobilization even possible. His tenure in several settings was short since more often than not he quickly fell out of favor with local rulers who tended to perceive his ideas as potentially threatening to their authority. This happened in Egypt, Iran, and, eventually, within the court of the Ottoman sultan himself.

During his time in Egypt, Afghani exerted considerable influence on the intellectual formation and social consciousness of several figures that would later figure prominently in reformist circles. Perhaps the most important of these was Muhammad Abduh (1849–1905), one of the founders of the modernist movement in Islam. His was a varied career that included political activism, journalism, educational reform and jurisprudence—eventually rising to the rank of Egypt's Grand Mufti. Abduh is strongly associated with social innovations such as the introduction of universal education for all Egyptians irrespective of gender. As a religious intellectual, he argued for the contemporary relevance of ijtihad (Afghani's influence was clear here) and the importance of returning to the spirit of the salaf, the Prophet's earliest companions. Abduh was actually the founder of the modern Salafiyya movement, but his understanding of what this entailed differed considerably from the approaches of both Ibn Abdul Wahhab a century and a half before him and of later exponents of salafism from Hassan al-Banna onward. For Abduh, the salaf provided a model for how to make Qur'anic normativity—to which the pious companions had had direct access, unadulterated by centuries of distortion and corruption— relevant to contemporary social challenges through the creative and judicious exercise of reason and human ingenuity. It was an approach that would also inspire later proponents of reformist thought, such as the Pakistani scholar Fazlur Rahman who drew a sharp distinction between the purity of "normative Islam" and the miscegenation of "historical Islam."[8]

Despite his wide-reaching influence, Afghani's Pan-Islamic vision never came to fruition. The parallel and competing project of nationalism captured the popular imagination far more effectively. The emergent middle classes of Alexandria and Cairo, for example, found it far easier to rally around the banner of Egyptian national self-determination than to define their political identities in concert with distant co-religionists in India, West Africa, and Southeast Asia: a politically independent Egypt was a tangible goal, the *umma* less so. Although the United States president had not intended it for the colonized world, the climate of post-World War I Wilsonian international liberalism—and the notion of national self-determination in particular—drifted over to the Middle East and India. It animated anti-colonial movements that now began increasingly to define themselves in nationalist terms: Sa'ad Zaghlul and the Wafd Party in Egypt, for example, or the Indian National Congress (and, later, Muhammad Ali Jinnah's All India Muslim League)—and, of course, the Young Turks at the very core of the Ottoman Empire.

Aspirations for a pan-ethnic state in the Arab territories of the Ottoman Empire dissipated when it became clear after World War I that Britain and France continued to harbor designs in the central Middle East. The British put nominally independent rulers on the thrones of Egypt and Iraq, but in effective terms their political control in these countries continued through the World War II, and similarly in the mandate territories (established by the new League of Nations) of Palestine and Transjordan alongside renewed French influence in Syria and Lebanon. The one entirely new polity to appear in the Middle East at this time—aside from the new Turkish Republic—was Saudi Arabia (see Chapter 5), founded in 1932 by the Nejdi (central Arabian) prince Abdul Aziz Ibn Saud who managed to unify disparate tribal provinces into a minimally cohesive kingdom. With the abolition of the caliphate in 1924, Islamic political thought was plunged into a crisis. This period represented the first time since the Prophet's death that the Muslim world was without a symbolic religio-political figurehead. The crisis of the caliphate prompted considerable debate among Muslim intellectuals (see Chapter 3). Some argued for the necessity of this institution, whereas others found it largely superfluous to the modern world. Although various forms of pro-caliphate activism occurred during the interwar years—such as the emergence of the Khilafa Movement in India and the various Islamic Congresses sponsored by Egypt—it never gathered sufficient political momentum against the rising tide of nationalism.

In the next chapter we will examine the process of state formation in the Muslim world and the emergence of Islamism as a political project in the context of the modern system of nation-states. Of particular interest to us will be the interplay between societal forces, political elites and ideologies, and the question of wider geopolitical impacts on contemporary Muslim politics.

3 State formation and the making of Islamism

With the collapse of the Ottoman Empire, and a rising tide of anti-colonial sentiment throughout most Muslim-majority lands under European control (see Map 2) the stage was set for a debate between two (seemingly) distinct and incompatible approaches to Muslim political independence: a system of Islamic political universalism, represented by a renewed caliphate, or the nationalist option, which held language, territory, and shared history as the proper foundations of a political order. Various leading scholars and activists debated the merits of these two options, and some also proposed models that sought to combine elements of each. Read together, the ideas of these thinkers—figures such as Rashid Rida, Ali Abd al-Raziq, Abu'l-A'la Mawdudi, and Hassan al-Banna—provide us with a clear sense of how Islamic response to the Western liberal order evolved over the first half of the twentieth century. Understanding the complex interplay of Islam and secular-nationalism in three core Muslim states, Turkey, Egypt, and Pakistan, also helps to set the stage for explaining later instances of Islamic revivalism. This is the period that saw the establishment of the prototypical modern Islamist movement in the form of the Muslim Brotherhood in Egypt. Highly influential in terms of later developments, its formation, evolution, ideology, and political role are worth considering in some detail before sketching out the general course of Islamism over the remainder of the twentieth century.

Modern states in the Muslim world

The shape of the international order changed significantly in the half century following World War I. With European empires dissolving into constituent nation-states and new states forming in previously colonized territories, the international system of sovereign states expanded considerably—particularly once the process of decolonization gathered pace after World War II. In the early twentieth century there were only 50 or so sovereign states in the world. By the end of decolonization that number had more than tripled. The formation of modern states in the Muslim world must be understood as part and parcel of this transformation. In the first

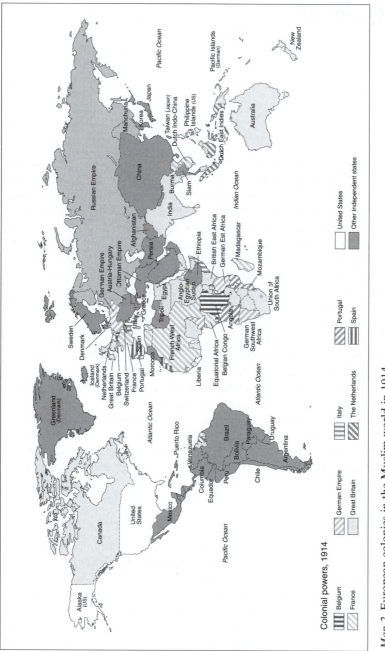

Map 2 European colonies in the Muslim world in 1914

instance, this shift represented a phenomenal rise in popular support for the doctrine of nationalism, a project that was soon co-opted by political elites in much of what came to be known as the Third World or the developing world.

The debate over nationalism took on various forms in different parts of the Muslim world, reflecting the diverse political conditions, histories, and power arrangements under which Muslim communities were living at the time. In the Turkish Republic, the successor state to the Ottoman Empire, Mustapha Kemal Ataturk instituted a veritable cultural revolution, seeking as much as possible to distance the new republic from its Ottoman heritage through an emphasis on rapid modernization and intensely secular norms. In the Arab Middle East, however, this shift played out initially as an exchange between advocates of political futures based on Islam, and those advocating the primacy of nationalist arrangements. As nation-states consolidated in the Arab world, this evolved into a debate between political forces seeking to establish an Islamic version of the nation-state, and those—mainly social and political elites—who grounded their legitimacy in discourses of Arab nationalism. In the Indian subcontinent, which at the time was the most populous Muslim country in the world—initial concerns about the un-Islamic character of nationalism gave way to more pressing worries about the community's future in a Hindu-dominated India. This resulted in calls for the establishment of a separate homeland for Muslims, with Islam itself transformed into a form of nationalism.

Theorists of the post-caliphate order: Rashid Rida and Ali Abd al-Raziq

The Arab response to the abolition of the caliphate is best illustrated through the contrasting approaches of Rashid Rida and Ali Abd al-Raziq, two leading intellectuals working in Egypt during the inter-war years. These two offer an interesting comparison because they also represent figures whose early thinking was strongly influenced by Jamal al-Din al-Afghani and the Salafiyya movement of Muhammad Abduh. As we will see, however, each of them took this project in rather different directions as regards Islam's political priorities. Hailing originally from Tripoli in modern day Lebanon, Rashid Rida (1865–1935) was strongly influenced by Muhammad Abduh's reformist ideas, to which he was exposed while studying a combination of modern subjects alongside the traditional course of Islamic sciences. He later moved to Cairo and worked with Abduh to begin publishing what would become the Salafiyya movement's primary print forum, *Al-Manar* ("the beacon"). Rida is best known for a major work of political theory, *The Caliphate, or the Supreme Imamate* (1923), published just before the crisis prompted by the abolition of the caliphate by Mustapha Kemal in 1924. After making a case for the necessity of the caliphate through his reading of the classical sources, Rida goes on in his text to outline the role of this institution throughout Islamic history. While *The Caliphate* is framed as an argument for the desirability, in theory, of a renewed caliphate, it ultimately proves itself to be a work of political realism by recognizing that prevailing conditions simply did not permit its rejuvenation. Instead, Rida reconciled himself to the notion of an Islamic order within the framework of the nation-state.[1] Rida remained convinced, however, of the importance of a strong relationship between the ulama—as keepers of the tradition and the law—and the political authorities. As the forces of secular modernism became more firmly entrenched amongst Egyptian political elites between the wars, Rashid Rida became increasingly conservative and literalist in terms of his understanding of the central impulse behind the Salafiyya movement. Where Abduh had advocated a general spirit of intellectual rejuvenation inspired by the model of the Prophet's early companions, Rida veered in his later life towards a more constrained normativity based exclusively on the Qur'an and the traditions of the Prophet and his companions. In this regard, his eventual orientation is closer to the approach espoused by contemporary groups that go under the mantle of salafism (see Chapters 5 and 7).

The stance taken by Ali Abd al-Raziq in this debate could not have been more different from that of Rashid Rida, despite the fact that they both considered themselves followers of Afghani and Abduh. Abd al-Raziq, interestingly enough, had undergone an even more traditional religious education than Rida. As a graduate of Cairo's Al-Azhar, the preeminent institution of Sunni learning in the Arab world and a bastion of the traditional ulama, his formal credentials as a scholar of Islamic law and tradition were unquestionable. Imagine then the sensation created by the publication of his 1925 text *Al-Islam wa usul al-hukm* ("Islam and the Principles of Governance")—partly a response to Rashid Rida—whose core point was to deny not only the necessity but even the authorization for a caliphate in the canonical sources of Islam. Abd al-Raziq's case was built on two key points—first, that nowhere in the Qur'an or hadith is anything like an institutionalized caliphate mentioned; and second, that throughout history, the caliphate, more often than not, was maintained and legitimized primarily through force and by threat of discord should it fall, rather than in terms of its intrinsic good. So unconventional a view, which flew in the face of centuries of scholarly consensus, would already have been enough to ensure Abd al-Raziq's notoriety within the religious establishment. He might have denied the need for a caliph but then gone on to argue for the necessity of a national state organized according to Islamic law. Instead, he went even further and suggested that while a government of some sort is indeed necessary, there is nothing in Islamic sources that requires the state to conform to any particular model. For Abd al-Raziq, any form of government that did not violate the core principles of Islam was acceptable.[2] There was for him no intrinsic relationship between religion and state. In the eyes of many, Abd al-Raziq had placed himself, with this last position, firmly within the realm of the secular and in that regard had strayed into territory where even the most reform-minded religious scholars could not follow. Indeed, in the wake of *Al-Islam wa usul al-hukm*, Ali Abd al-Raziq was removed from his position as a judge. It is clear that for him the reformist impulse behind the Salafiyya movement was iconoclastic in nature. It made possible the calling into question of even some of the most taken-for-granted elements of Islamic political thought and history. If one is tempted to wonder who, Rida or Abd al-Raziq, was closer to the ideals of the Salafiyya as originally promulgated by Muhammad Abduh, it is probably safe to say that both of them ended up espousing extremes with which the movement's founder would likely have been uncomfortable. For Abduh the model of the salaf was meant to provide a set of ideational resources and inspiration rather than, as Rida ended up arguing, the sole correct source of social morality. On the other hand, Abduh was not a revolutionary in terms of his political theory, and Abd al-Raziq's denial of the caliphate would likely have struck his mentor as a step too far in this direction.

The intellectual foment in the wake of the abolished caliphate also saw some analogous political organization in the form of a number of Muslim Congresses that were convened between 1924 and 1931.[3] Ostensibly attempts by senior Muslim scholars and leaders from across the umma to discuss Islamic issues and determine a solution to the predicament of Muslim leadership, these meetings were mostly opportunities for political aspirants to jockey for position. After Kemal abolished the caliphate in 1924, the Hashemite emir of western Arabia, Sharif Hussein Ibn Ali, had proclaimed himself caliph—a claim that was never widely recognized. On the Indian subcontinent a Caliphate Movement and Indian Caliphate Committee were formed as responses to perceived threats to Islam by Western powers, but both proved short lived. By the outbreak of World War II, little intellectual or political activity around the caliphate remained.

Nationalist thought and state formation

Despite the intensity of deliberations within the religious camp, the audience for these various arguments remained relatively small. For most Muslims, the public—or political—dimensions of their religion did not seem to be of paramount importance. The primary goal in this arena was the achievement of independence from European colonial rule, and nationalism was certainly proving itself a far more attractive prospect in this regard. In the Middle East, a parallel cadre of intellectuals arose within the nationalist camp, arguing that post-colonial political futures should be built around an Arab identity that mined a rich heritage of language, culture, and history tracing back to well before the founding of Islam.[4] Some of the key figures in the intellectual formation of Arab nationalism included the Egyptians Lutfi al-Sayyid and Taha Hussein, Shakib Arslan from Lebanon, and the Iraqi lawyer Abd al-Rahman al-Bazzaz. While certainly aligned with a contrasting set of sociopolitical sentiments, it is worth noting that many of these writers actually had extensive contact, and were even friends, with central figures in the Salafiyya movement. Rather, their worldviews and cultural compasses were calibrated differently. For figures such as Sati al-Husri (1880–1967), the modern German and Italian nationalist experiences were inspirational. For him, nationalism was a perfect space for the formation of enduring political identities, providing as it did an ideal middle ground between local communalist tendencies and the excessive abstraction of religious universalism.[5] Husri, from a family of Syrian origin, traveled extensively throughout his career. In many regards the pan-Arabist counterpart to Afghani's itinerant pan-Islamism, Husri spent time in Yemen, the Balkans, Syria, and Egypt before emerging as a central figure in the formation of modern Iraqi nationalism and eventually retiring as a senior figure within, fittingly, the League of Arab States. One of the political currents with which Husri had come into contact early in his life (in Macedonia, interestingly enough) would go on to emerge as the driving force behind the formation of the modern Turkish Republic. The Committee of Union and Progress (CUP), an organized manifestation of the Young Turk movement comprising Ottoman military officers of a modernizing disposition, was the group that eventually managed to force major political concessions from Abdulhamid II, the last significant Ottoman Sultan. It is via the CUP that a certain Mustapha Kemal (later known by the honorific Ataturk, "father of the Turks") began his rise to prominence. Following a record of distinguished military service and a rapid rise through the ranks during World War I, Mustapha Kemal emerged as one of the leaders of the Turkish Independence movements following the war. Consolidating his position in Ankara, in the heart of Anatolia, Kemal in 1920 was proclaimed president by the National Assembly of a new Turkish Republic.

The state ideology of the Republic, commonly known as Kemalism, represents a paradigmatic form of modern nationalism in the Muslim world. Over the next 10 years, Ataturk instituted a sweeping set of cultural, bureaucratic, economic, and military reforms that sought to fundamentally reorient the social basis and worldview of modern Turkey. Almost no sector of life was left untouched by these reforms. In the realm of language, a new system for rendering Turkish in Latin (rather than Arabic) script was introduced and enforced. Elements of "oriental" and Islamic dress, such as the Fez, were banned and the wearing of Western clothes encouraged. In terms of history, Turkey's Ottoman and Islamic past was de-emphasized in favor of a new emphasis on the glories of Anatolia's pre-Islamic civilizations. Schoolbooks, based on an exclusively modernist curriculum, sought to inculcate a particular self-image on the part of a new generation of Turks. The children depicted in these texts, distinctly Caucasian in complexion and dress, demonstrated a mastery of Ataturk's modernist program and encouraged their readers to do the same. As part and parcel of a conscious process of Europeanization, Turkey under Ataturk also looked to the

West for new models of military and bureaucratic organization, and also sought to lay the groundwork of a new industrial-based economy.

And what of religion in the new Turkish Republic? Perhaps not surprisingly, Ataturk viewed Islam as a vestige of the Ottoman past he was seeking to eradicate. Islam for him was backwards, anti-modernist, and an obstacle to the Westernizing future he dreamed of for Turkey. While he knew it would be impossible to eradicate the influences of religion altogether (Sufism was also particularly strong in Turkey), he sought as much as possible to bring it under the control of the state and to deploy it in the service of his modernist project. The Kemalist variant of secularism, which emerged over several decades, eventually evolved into a degree of alienation between religion and state that is almost unprecedented in the modern world. For example, the wearing of "Islamic" clothing—such as a headscarf by women—came to be legally proscribed in all public (i.e. state-run) spaces such as government ministries, state universities, and the National Assembly. Furthermore, the government established a directorate of religious affairs (the *Diyanet Isleri Baskanligi*, or "Diyanet") to organize and oversee all institutions—such as mosques and Qur'anic schools—providing religious services in Turkey. It established a network of religious educational facilities, the *Imam-hatip* schools, through which all state-licensed imams were required to pass. The curriculum in these schools was designed to emphasize the essentially private nature of religion and focused exclusively on matters of individual piety and workship (*ibadat*)—which nicely expressed the Republic's definition of the boundaries of Islam. All mosques were to be registered with the Diyanet, and on each Friday this central directorate would also provide the text for a common sermon (*khutba*) to be delivered during *juma'a* (Friday) prayer at all Turkish mosques. A social role for religion, much less any political aspiration, was out of the question. The intensity of this secularizing trend, combined with a quarter century of one-party rule, certainly had implications for later manifestations of Muslim politics in Turkey (see Chapter 4). It undoubtedly represents the most extreme form of secular-nationalism to appear in the Muslim world during the early period of modern state formation.

The case of Egypt provides a model of nationalist politics that parallels aspects of the Turkish example while also diverging from it in significant ways. Although it had been under nominal Ottoman control since 1517, Egypt—since the mid-nineteenth century, and after a dangerous challenge to Istanbul from the modernizing pasha Muhammad Ali—had operated with a great deal of political autonomy. In 1882, the British were led to directly occupy Egypt in order to protect their interests in the Suez Canal and at that point all Ottoman suzerainty effectively ended. British rule, which in theory was exercised jointly with an Egyptian monarch, continued even after formal independence in 1922. Ongoing British involvement in the run-up to, and during, World War II ensured that Egypt's early experiment with democratic nationalism did not consolidate. The country's true political independence had to wait until the emergence of the Free Officer's Movement, a group of secular-nationalist-minded military officers who instigated a coup d'état in 1952 to depose the ineffectual and unpopular monarch Farouk I, a last vestige of Egypt's Ottoman-affiliated dynasties. Out of this revolution arose perhaps the paramount figure of Arab nationalism—and a major world leader—Gamal Abdel Nasser. A key figure not only in the Pan-Arabist movement which bore his name ("Nasserism"—which fused elements of nationalism, socialism, and nonalignment in Cold War geopolitics), Nasser was also at the center of various geopolitical intrigues during his 16-year tenure, including the nationalization of the Suez Canal in 1956 and the formation of the Nonaligned Movement in 1961. A highly adept statesman, Nasser managed to play both sides of the Cold War to Egypt's advantage—a feat that only increased his stature as a symbol of relative Arab independence in what was experienced by many countries in the developing world as a new era of bipolar imperialism.

Nasser's leadership during the Suez Crisis, from which he emerged as the Arab hero who had thwarted a direct threat from Britain, France, and Israel, helped to consolidate his stature as the paradigmatic figurehead of Pan-Arabism—an ideology that traced back to the World War I machinations of Sharif Hussein, the Hashemite emir of the Hijaz in Arabia, and which would later figure in the program of the Ba'ath Party in Syria and Iraq. The zenith of Pan-Arabism in symbolic terms was undoubtedly the ambitious and ultimately short-lived political union of Egypt and Syria into a single country, the United Arab Republic, from 1958 to 1961. Although not nearly as aggressively secularizing as Kemalism, Pan-Arabism—particularly in its Ba'athist variant—eschewed Islam in favor of ethnolinguistic nationalism. Nasser certainly respected but downplayed the importance of religion. After initially seeking alliances with religious forces such as the Muslim Brothers, he turned against them when it became clear that they could not be brought into the fold to buttress and lend religious legitimacy to Egypt's post-1952 secular nationalist order.

Moving over to Pakistan, we find Muslims facing a rather different set of political circumstances and, consequently, engaging the Islam/nationalism debate in a unique way. Muslim Mughals had been in power in India until the Mutiny of 1857, at which point Britain imposed direct rule and deposed them. Despite the concerns of some traditional religious scholars, who either stayed completely apart from politics or advocated more extreme responses such as departing India or enjoining jihad, most Muslims in India developed an anti-colonial, pro-independence stance alongside Hindus. This sentiment found political expression in 1906 with the founding of the Muslim League, an organization that in its early years worked very closely with the broader Indian National Congress towards a common goal of political independence from Britain. A series of events over the next 20 years—including British threats to Muslim property, rising inter-communal violence between Muslims and Hindus, and increased Hindu control of the

Indian National Congress—prompted a reassessment by Muslims of their prospects in India. From the 1930s, momentum began to gather around a new Muslim League orientation in favor of the establishment of a separate Muslim homeland on the subcontinent. While earlier Muslim intellectuals, such as Abul Kalam Azad, held fast to the idea of a multi-religious Indian nationalism, other prominent Muslim figures such as the celebrated philosopher-poet Muhammad Iqbal had become increasingly skeptical about the desirability or viability of such arrangements. Muhammad Ali Jinnah, the political architect of Indian partition, provided the clearest articulation of this new stance in his "Two Nations Theory." According to this thesis, Islam and Hinduism represent two separate moral and social orders that, while they may manage some minimal coexistence, will never successfully integrate. Jinnah's manifesto was in effect a statement on religious nationalism. Its inevitable conclusion was to argue that Muslims and Hindus should pursue separate political futures. Most of India's senior ulama, however, were not initially on board with this position, arguing that nationalism represented an ideology foreign to, and incompatible with, Islam. Nevertheless, in 1940 the Muslim League formally resolved to seek the creation of a separate homeland for Indian Muslims (the "Lahore Resolution") and within two years of World War II, Indian partition occurred and the new state of Pakistan was born. Explicitly styled as an "Islamic state," the precise implications of this were a matter of some controversy and confusion during the early years of Pakistan's political history. Was it primarily a homeland for Muslims with some nominal recognition of Islam as the primary source of public morality, or was it an Islamic state in the sense of a political system based on religious law? As we will see, this question has been central to various debates about Pakistani identity and politics.

The emergence of Islamism

It is at this point, in the aftermath of the establishment of nation-states in the Muslim world that we can begin to speak of the emergence of *Islamism* as a distinctive form of Muslim politics. The term Islamism, as it is used here and throughout this book, refers to forms of political theory and practice that have as their goal the establishment of an Islamic political order in the sense of a state whose governmental principles, institutions, and legal system derive directly from the shari'ah. In the eyes of those who advocate Islamist solutions, religion is generally viewed as a holistic, totalizing system whose prescriptions permeate every aspect of daily life. Islamists, as we will see, often differ in their methods and priorities. Some advocate gradualist approaches while others are more revolutionary. Certain Islamist parties pursue the "shari'ah-ization" of only limited areas of law, whereas others insist on a completely Islamized system. Despite these differences, they share a common commitment to the idea that Islam and public life—and politics more particularly—are not independent domains but rather inextricably intertwined. While earlier advocates of caliphate systems might accurately be seen as Islamists of a sort, our usage of the term here refers specifically to the pursuit of Islamic public normativity within the context of modern nation-states. There is however another vitally important qualifier to be made before we look more closely at Islamism. This is to remind the reader that not all political actors who articulate their motivations or goals in terms of Islam, or who make use of religious symbols, qualify as Islamists. As we will see throughout this book, many of the actors involved in Muslim politics have little interest in pursuing totalizing political orders that conform to shari'ah. Many of them have very different attitudes about the relationship between Islam, society, and politics. Indeed, some avowedly reject the Islamist approach while still defining their own visions as authentic expressions of Islam.

It is commonplace, particularly in Western analysis, to associate the emergence of Islamism with an "Islamic revival" that began to gather force in the 1970s, reaching its zenith with the 1979 Islamic Revolution in Iran. While it is certainly the case that we can identify a significant upsurge in the number and prominence of Islamist groups during this period, to identify Islamism primarily with a period of supposed Islamic revival would be to neglect important continuities. Islamism, it can be argued, has been a feature of Muslim politics since shortly after nation-states began to take root in Muslim lands. Its political fortunes have ebbed and flowed over the past century, but Islamism in one form or another has been a consistent feature of Muslim politics. How and under what conditions did Islamism first emerge and what forms did it take in different contexts?

Early Islamist activists and intellectuals: Hassan al-Banna and Sayyid Abu'l-A'la Mawdudi

To understand the genesis of Islamism in thought and practice, it will be useful to examine the ideas of two figures generally identified as the progenitors of modern Islamism. Hassan al-Banna (1906–49), founder of the Muslim Brotherhood in Egypt, and Sayyid Abu'l-A'la Mawdudi (1903–79), creator in Pakistan of the Jama'at-i Islami party, are widely regarded—along with Sayyid Qutb, whose ideas we will examine in a subsequent section—as having provided important initial formulations of the meaning and nature of Islamist politics. Each played a crucial role not only in the national contexts in which they worked, but also as key reference points for later generations of Islamists across the Muslim world.

Hassan al-Banna was born into a religious family in a village in the Nile Delta north of Cairo.[6] A number of events and factors affected his religious and political consciousness while growing up. These included early contact with and experience of the anti-colonial movement, his affiliation from a relatively young age with a Sufi order, and a keen awareness, no doubt amplified by his father, a local imam, of the declining religiosity associated with modernization in Egypt. Eventually choosing to train as a teacher in Cairo, he accepted a position at a government school in Isma'iliyya, a town in the Suez Canal Zone. Banna's interest in teaching as a vocation had developed as something considerably more than a desire to impart knowledge in a narrow sense. For him, education implied something closer to the religiously inflected notion of *tarbiya*, implying a more holistic sense of human growth and development that accrues through knowledge of religion. The religious knowledge Banna sought to emphasize, however, was not the formal and often abstract methods of jurisprudence and theology. He had no credentials, nor did he seek to act, as an alim. Banna's initial efforts were more oriented towards helping adults and children in Egypt to exercise greater consciousness and awareness of religion in their daily lives. If anything, Banna had become rather skeptical of the apparent social and political apathy displayed by the formal religious establishment. In this he followed Muhammad Abduh and Rashid Rida. Although his father had inculcated in him a deeply seated respect for religious learning, Banna found the scholars of Al-Azhar insufficiently concerned about the creeping secularization of Egyptian society.

Banna's early efforts took the form of lectures and classes taught in his spare time at local mosques, meeting halls, and coffee houses. As his reputation as a public speaker grew he found himself invited into private homes to address small groups. His message combined elements of anti-colonialism and rejection of Western influence with *da'wa* ("calling" to Islam) and appeals for greater religiosity. It was a platform that resonated particularly well in Isma'iliyya, where outward signs of foreign influence were particularly visible. As it became clear that there was a demand for the approach he advocated, Banna decided to create an organization to carry the mission forward. In 1928 he founded the Muslim Brotherhood (hereafter "MB") as a social movement dedicated to religious education and advocating a greater role for Islam in public life. Given its central importance within contemporary Islamism, we will examine the development of the MB in much greater detail in a subsequent section.

In one sense, we might view Banna's efforts as an attempt to embody in daily life the ethos of the Salafiyya movement, with its emphasis on "true" Islam and the model of the Prophet's early companions. Moving to Cairo in 1932, Banna significantly expanded the Brotherhood's bureaucratic framework over the next few years, establishing a central secretariat in addition to numerous local branches throughout the country. Many commentators have emphasized the influence of Sufism's teacher-disciple model on how Banna chose to organize the MB in its early days. He prescribed a daily regimen of worshipful activities designed to maximize religious consciousness, including in this the practice of dhikr (the Sufi ritual of "remembrance"). It should be pointed out that the Sufi order with which Banna had been affiliated, the Hasafiya, was relatively orthodox in terms of its emphasis on living in accordance with shari'ah. In addition to his emphasis on ritual observance, Hassan al-Banna encouraged members of the MB to adopt certain attitudes and demeanors he regarded as enjoined by Islam. These included everything from personal hygiene and exercise to the importance of a strong work ethic and professional growth. Banna wanted to emphasize the possibility of "being modern" while remaining true to Islam. The adoption of Western ways, he taught, was not the only path to social mobility and personal growth.

While the MB had been founded initially as a social movement, its phenomenal growth through the 1930s and 40s, combined with its founder's holistic approach, almost ensured that it would take on a more political demeanor. Hassan al-Banna was not primarily a public intellectual and certainly not a political theorist. In this regard, his views on issues such as the Islamic state were not articulated as systematically or thoroughly as some of his contemporaries (such as Mawdudi, see below). Banna emphasized the practical side of lived Islamism, and in this regard is much better viewed as an instigator, organizer, and activist rather than as a theorist-intellectual. Through his description of the Brotherhood as "a Salafi movement, an orthodox way, a Sufi reality, a political body, an athletic group, a scientific and cultural society, an economic company and a social idea"[7] we can see that Banna envisaged membership in the MB as an all-encompassing experience. But what were his views regarding the proper Islamic political system and the role of the Brotherhood within it?

It should be said at the outset that Hassan al-Banna's primary emphasis was never on the establishment of an Islamic state, nor did he view the government as the primary agent of Islamization—although later MB thinkers certainly would go this route. Rather, Banna sought to reform the existing state through an emphasis on what we might term "social Islam." His focus was on creating a properly Islamic society, and this for him was something that would come about primarily through individual Muslims embracing truly Islamic ways. There is certainly a utopian dimension to his thinking insofar as, according to Banna, the properly constituted Islamic society would have no need for political parties or labor unions since all sources of social tension and cleavage would be eliminated. On the issue of the caliphate, Banna's position was that ultimately such an institution was desirable, although he was perfectly comfortable with the idea of pursuing an Islamic social order within the framework of the nationalist state. Banna's stance towards nationalism was rather ambivalent. On the one hand, he agreed with many traditional religious thinkers of the day that, in essence, the idea of national ties as the primary basis of social affiliation was in conflict with Islamic teachings. At the same time, however, he admired the anti-colonial potential within nationalism and the social mobilizing power of patriotism. Thus, knowing that nationalism was the popular flavor of the day, Banna would often incorporate elements of nationalist rhetoric within his own political discourse—emphasizing, for example, love for one's country as a Muslim duty (so long, of course, as it didn't interfere with one's primary commitment to Islam).

On the more specific issue of the state, we should reiterate that Banna's initial position was one that sought to reform that state from the outside. He was not particularly sanguine about the idea of the Brotherhood, in its early iterations, acting as a political party or taking any active role in government. His main hope was to influence the existing state and help lead it towards proper Islamic conduct. While he certainly did see a role for the state in terms of encouraging public morality (e.g. enforcing bans on certain kinds of social behavior and "un-Islamic" ceremonies), Banna's preferred mode of Islamizing the state in the early days focused on encouraging the state to integrate greater attention to religion and spirituality across all sectors of public life, to hire more graduates of religious schools, and to encourage greater religiosity on the part of the populace. Much of his early political discourse focused on issues of socioeconomic inequality and Banna certainly saw a role for the state in pursuing social justice via the redistribution of resources accruing from zakat (Islam's obligatory income-based tithe). Certainly one of Banna's major complaints with the Egyptian state during the post-independence constitutional period (1922–36) was its emulation of Western liberalism, and he was highly vocal in condemning the state's adoption of un-Islamic models. Indeed, Banna was keenly aware that during this important period of political transition, his Islamic model was competing within a market of ideologies, many of which were of foreign origin. He sought to position Islam as an approach that embodied the best features of all other options while avoiding their contradictions and negative aspects. To understand his populist characterization of competing political ideologies and the Islamic alternative, it is worth quoting Banna at some length:

> In a whimsical moment, I happened to say to my audience at a meeting—which, thanks to God, was a complete success—that this Islamic prayer which we perform five time a day is nothing but a daily training in practical social organization uniting the features of the Communist regime with those of the dictatorial and democratic regimes. Astonished, my questioners demanded an explanation. "The Greatest value of the Communist regime," I said, "is the reinforcement of the notion of equality, the condemnation of class distinction, and the struggle against the claim to property, source of these differences." Now this lesson is present in the mind of the Muslim; he is perfectly conscious of it and his spirit is filled with it the moment he enters the mosque; yes, the moment he enters, he realizes that the mosque belongs to God and not anyone of his creatures; he knows himself to be the equal of all those who are there, whoever they may be; here there are no great, no small, no high, no low, no more groups or classes. And when the muezzin calls, "Now is the hour of prayer," they form an equal mass, a compact

block, behind the imam. None bows unless the imam bows, none prostrates himself unless the imam prostrates himself, none moves or remains motionless unless following the imam's example. That is the principal merit of the dictatorial regime: unity and order in the will under the appearance of equality. The imam himself is in any case limited by the teachings and rules of the prayer, and if he stumbles or makes a mistake in his reading or in his actions, all those behind him— young boys, old men, or women at prayer—have the imperative duty to tell him of his error in order to put him back on the right road during the prayer, and the imam himself is bound absolutely to accept this good advice and, forsaking his error, return to reason and truth. That is what is most appealing in democracy. How, therefore, can these regimes be superior to Islam, which astonishingly unites all their merits and avoids all their sins?[8]

Despite Banna's convictions regarding the self-evident superiority of the Islamic system, this does not mean that in his mind there was no role for the MB in terms of more direct political engagement. As the 1930s wore on into the 40s, MB activism took on a more overly political tenor. Within a few years of founding the Brotherhood, Banna had established a special wing within the movement whose members were trained in the use of coercive and even violent tactics. For his own part, Banna began in the late 1930s to issue open and direct calls to the palace to initiate Islamizing reforms. Tensions between the MB and various hostile political factions within Egypt intensified, culminating in the assassination of the Prime Minister in 1948 by a member of the Brotherhood. A year later, Hassan al-Banna himself was on the receiving end of the government's successful reprisal.

A second figure whose ideas were of central importance to the making of modern Islamism was Sayyid Abu'l-A'la Mawdudi, a contemporary of Hassan al-Banna who worked primarily in the South Asian context. Although Mawdudi's political activities are most closely associated with Pakistan and the Jama'at-i Islami party—which he founded and presided over for 30 years—many of his writings on Islamic political theory are cast in universalist terms and have been highly influential across the Muslim world. An avowed intellectual, his ideas were generally far more systematic, consistent, and better elaborated than those of Hassan al-Banna. It is for this reason that Mawdudi is generally considered to be one of the leading ideologues, rather than primarily a practitioner, of modern Islamism.

Born and raised in southern India, Mawdudi was from a family of Muslim notables with a long record of service to the Mughal emperors and with strong Sufi ties.[9] The family had left Delhi after the Mughal reign came to an end, but Mawdudi's father sought to remind his children of their lineage by steeping them in the classics of Islamic civilization. While studying Arabic and Persian at home, Mawdudi also acquired familiarity with modern subjects such as science from the local school he attended. While his formal education was quite short, Mawdudi was an avid and disciplined autodidact, and he read widely throughout his life in a variety of languages including English. Given the controversial nature of many of his religious views, there has been some debate as to his level of training in religious scholarship. While many observers of Mawdudi—and certainly his religious detractors—have portrayed him as wholly self taught in matters of Islam, at least two biographers report that while living in Delhi in the 1920s, Mawdudi completed the curriculum at a Deobandi seminary and received certification as an alim.[10] One thing that is certain, however, is that Mawdudi did not publicly acknowledge his status as a religious scholar or use it to endow his ideas with greater authority. Like many of the Islamic modernists such as Afghani, Rida and Banna, Mawdudi was critical of most ulama, seeing them as disengaged from society and lacking in political consciousness at a time of crisis. He may therefore have wanted to avoid being associated with their ranks or perceived in any way as a product of their system as opposed to the Islamist alternative his life's work would offer.

Working initially as a journalist, Mawdudi became associated with a wide range of pro-nationalist, anti-colonialist movements and publications. His early output was not communalist in orientation, and he was generally very supportive of the Congress movement and many of the key Hindu nationalist figures such as Gandhi. A distinctly Muslim political consciousness began to form in the young Mawdudi when he became associated with the Society of Indian Ulama. With the collapse of the Caliphate Movement, with which he had been associated, Mawdudi found himself reconsidering his position on nationalism, and also at odds with the religious establishment. Where most ulama in India tended to back the Congress party's nationalist agenda, Mawdudi was becoming increasingly skeptical about nationalism's compatibility with Islam and its implications for Muslim interests in India. Over the next decade and a half, Mawdudi—with a renewed and highly politicized religious consciousness—devoted himself to the cause of reinvigorating the heritage and status of India's Muslims. He authored a number of texts that offered, for the South Asian context, a variant of Afghani's diagnosis regarding Islam's decline. Muslims had strayed from the true path of Islam and allowed local distortions, innovations, and undue reliance on stagnant scholarship to corrupt their faith. His prescription, like that of the Arab Salafiyya, was for a return to "true" Islam—although it should be said that he emphasized the path of revival more than the model of the salaf. By the late 1930s, he was squarely in the center of the political debates regarding the future of Muslims in India. On the one hand, he rejected the Congress Party as a route to further Muslim marginalization in a Hindu-dominated independent India. At the same time, he also spurned the Muslim League's agitation for a separate national homeland for Muslims. With regard to the latter, he could not countenance nationalist ideology within his Islamic framework and also harbored suspicions regarding the secularist tendencies of the League's leadership, Muhammad Ali Jinnah in particular.

When, in 1940, the Muslim League adopted the cause of Pakistan as the core of its platform, Mawdudi was prompted to establish a rival entity through which his alternative political vision could be pursued. In 1941 he set up the Jama'at-i Islami as an advocacy organization and political party seeking Muslim autonomy and rights within India, as well as the propagation of Mawdudi's message of Islamic revivalism. Mawdudi's pragmatic streak was evident when, at the time of partition in 1947, he elected to remain in the part of India that had become Pakistan, moving the Jama'at's headquarters to Lahore. His new cause would be the proper Islamization of Pakistan, and to work to ensure that the new country's status as an Islamic state was reflected in the adoption of a properly Islamic system and political order rather than in a more mundane sense of Muslim nationalism. He remained a controversial figure in Pakistani political life for the next three decades, until his death in 1979, finding himself at odds with the authorities and imprisoned on more than one occasion. Indeed, one reason Mawdudi was admired by so many Islamists living under hostile regimes is because he remained so steadfast in his convictions, even when he knew they were likely to land him in hot water with subsequent secular and military-dominated governments. Mawdudi's status as a major intellectual figure in the eyes of Islamists the world over—he was one of the few non-Arab Islamist thinkers whose works were translated into Arabic—was confirmed during this period, and he spent considerable time traveling and speaking internationally.

What about the content of Mawdudi's political thinking? As we have already seen, his intellectual formation took place within the crucible of anti-colonial sentiment. While a great supporter of Indian independence from Britain, he was certainly no fan of nationalism. Not only was this ideology, in Mawdudi's view, contrary to the universalist ethos of Islam, but it also enabled ethnic chauvinism and served as a handmaiden to aggressive colonialism, arguing that "[even] if [a nationalist] upholds any world ideology, that ideology would necessarily the form of imperialism or world domination."[11] From quite early in his career, then, Mawdudi's primary task came to be the elaboration of the political theory of Islam. Authoring several full-length books on the subject, Mawdudi's conceptualizations in this area were clearly far more extensive and systematic than those of Hassan al-Banna. While their methods may have differed, Banna and Mawdudi occupied essentially the same ideological terrain. Both understood Islam as a totalizing way of life, and the shari'ah as more than just a legal corpus. Rather, the shari'ah was better regarded as a moral system than provider for an entire social order. No political authority could possibly stand apart from this order, and therefore the state must work to install and enforce the Islamic system within society.

The fundamental building block of Mawdudi's political theory is the idea that sovereignty belongs exclusively to God. No worldly political power, therefore, can be truly sovereign. The nature and purpose of human political agency, it then follows, is to bring about a social order reflective of divine ordinance. Mawdudi argued that this representation—or vice-regency—of God's will on earth is the responsibility of all people, or as he termed it, a "democratic caliphate." Although the particular arrangements of a given social setting may invest certain individuals (kings, sultans, presidents) with political authority, they are never sovereign over the people. The responsibility for maintaining God's viceregency always falls to society:

> The position of a man who is selected to conduct the affairs of the state is no more than this; that all Muslims (or, technically speaking, all caliphs of God) delegate their caliphate to him for administrative purposes. *He is answerable to God on the one hand and on the other to his fellow "caliphs" who have delegated their authority to him.*[12]

It is within the context of this notion of collective viceregency that Mawdudi understood the role of the caliphate, and through which he sought to emphasize the essentially democratic nature of the Islamic system—although, as we will see, his understanding of democracy is rather different from the Western liberal variant. He spoke of the importance of ongoing consultation (*shura*) between state and society, but did not place excessive importance on ideas such as power sharing between parties or on processes that produce turnover in terms of who holds the reigns of governments (e.g. elections). So long as a society was properly Islamic and shura was ongoing, Mawdudi argued, the sorts of societal tensions that lead people to demand new rulers would not be a major concern:

> If I were permitted to coin a new term, I would describe this system of government as a "theo-democracy," that is to say a divine democratic government, because under it the Muslims have been given a limited popular sovereignty under the suzerainty of God. The executive under this system of government is constituted by the general will of the Muslims who have also the right to depose it.[13]

Thus Mawdudi's conception of democracy is premised not upon notions of individual liberty and political pluralism, but rather on the notion of a body politic as the repository of divine viceregency. For him, democracy properly achieved also seems, at least in part, to involve a sense of solidarity and an absence of social divisions and tension. We should note that for Mawdudi, the desired absence of social division was understood to fall primarily along the horizontal rather than the vertical axis of society. In other words, it was not a call for egalitarianism. Inequalities between people, he posited, were part of the natural order of things. People have equal rights and should expect to be treated as such, but the Islamic system was not one that sought primarily to place everyone on an equal footing in terms of their material resources or position within social hierarchies. It was, however, incumbent upon the state to make sure that these naturally occurring inequalities were not exploited in ways that violated Islamic normativity. Hence, for example, the Islamic proscription against usury (excessive interest charged on loans).

As we can see in the final passage of the quote above, Mawdudi's theo-democracy also permitted Muslims to depose any political authority that abuses or fails to carry out their duties as deputized caliphs. It is in this area that we encounter some of Mawdudi's more controversial reinterpretations of core Islamic jurisprudential concepts—or at least choices of terminology. Mawdudi describes the method according to which individual Muslims are to assess the policies of the state as a form of ijtihad—that is, independent legal reasoning. As we will recall from the previous chapter, most orthodox jurists hold that ijtihad effectively ceased to constitute a viable legal methodology in the tenth century—and, moreover, that even it were permissible, it could only be carried out by properly trained jurists. Mawdudi states his case as follows:

> All administrative matters and all questions about which no explicit injunction is to be found in the Shari'ah are settled by the consensus of opinion among the Muslims. Every Muslim who is capable and qualified to give a sound opinion on matters of Islamic law, is entitled to interpret the law of God when such interpretation become necessary.[14]

The point turns perhaps on what one understands by "capable and qualified." This could be interpreted to mean that only formally trained experts in shari'ah (i.e. ulama) are permitted to carry out ijtihad with regard to administrative matters, or it might mean that any well-educated Muslim within the "democratic caliphate" has the right to exercise this kind of judgment. Regardless of how we interpret this ambiguity, it is certainly the case that Mawdudi courted controversy here simply by framing his implementation of Islamic democracy in terms of ijtihad.

In terms of political practice, Mawdudi is, in essence, a theorist of Islamic revolution. In his schema, however—and in contrast with later theorists of revolution such as Iran's Khomeini (see Chapter 5)—this does not necessarily involve a fundamental change in the political order. Mawdudi's preference was to reform the existing political order such that the state could become a central agent for the Islamization of society. Here we also find a point of contrast with Banna. The latter had not envisaged a principal role for the state in Islamizing the people, emphasizing instead a primarily societal locus for the desired transformation. Mawdudi on the other hand, realizing the state's enormous capacity and resource base, hoped to see the government initiate large-scale Islamizing reforms, but only once it comes under the stewardship of those who are appropriately educated:

The state is an instrument of reform and must act likewise. It is a dictate of this very nature of the Islamic state that such a state should be run only by those who believe in the ideology on which it is based and in the Divine Law which it is assigned to administer. The administrators of the Islamic state must be those whose whole life is devoted to the observance and enforcement of this Law, who not only agree with its reformatory programme and fully believe in it but thoroughly comprehend its spirit and are acquainted with its details.[15]

Mawdudi's revolution was certainly not an exclusively top-down affair, however. He comes back towards Banna in his thinking when expressing a preference for the Islamization of society before the Islamization of the state. In this view the political order is subsidiary to, rather than constitutive of, the social order. An Islamic state that seeks to enforce shari'ah upon a society that has itself not yet sufficiently internalized Islamic normativity is bound to resort to coercive and authoritarian methods. A sustainable Islamic order will arise when there is a natural symbiosis of purpose between society and state. Mawdudi's revolution was hence processual in nature. Reflecting this view in his political activism, Mawdudi did not form the Jama'at with a view to acquiring state power. Although the party did contest political elections at various points, most of its career under Mawdudi was spent in more of a watchdog and advocacy role rather than aspiring to govern. In Mawdudi's view the state essentially reflects the character of its population, and therefore societal progress towards true Islam was of paramount importance in achieving a lasting revolution. In this, as some commentators have noted, we can see a certain idealism in Mawdudi's thinking—a point that crystallizes when we examine his views on issues such as the *hudud*, the shari'ah's code of punishment for serious crimes. Mawdudi's position maintained the veracity and the necessity of the hudud, but argued that it could only be implemented in a properly Islamized society, one in which the normative parameters it enforces have already been internalized. Under such conditions, Mawdudi reasoned, there would in practice be no need to actually apply this penal code since the behaviors that invoke it would not occur.

Given that he was read and cited appreciatively by a number of later Islamists (including Sayyid Qutb, see below) who advocated a more militant path toward Islamic revolution, Mawdudi's views on jihad have been of particular interest and also a matter of some debate amongst contemporary analysts. The text that ostensibly constitutes Mawdudi's major statement on the theme, *Jihad in Islam*, was written while he was very young and also as a reaction (some have said as an apologetic) in the wake of a media controversy that was critical of Islam's supposedly violent nature. The major thrust of the book is towards decoupling the notion of jihad from an exclusively martial connotation and refiguring it as a more generic sense of "struggle" towards the realization of the Islamic way. Mawdudi does indicate that it may sometimes be necessary, and is permissible, to use violence as part of this process, although he gets caught up over the issue of defensive versus offensive jihad. He makes it clear, however, that education or tarbiya is his preferred method for achieving social change and Islamization and in this sense it would not be accurate to label him a jihadi in today's sense of the term (see Chapter 7).

Looking at Mawdudi's complete body of work, one is certainly struck by the intellectual consistency and fierceness of logic that runs through it. His ideas are simultaneously conservative—in terms of the social values they espouse, including a very limited social role for women—and revolutionary, both in the sense of seeking fundamental social change, and in terms of how he interprets and deploys central concepts of Islamic sociopolitical thought to this end. Hassan al-Banna and Abu'l-A'la Mawdudi both regarded Islam as a total system encompassing all aspects of life—and, furthermore, one from which the state cannot possibly be separated. To realize this system, an Islamic revival was required at the level of society, particularly in the face of what both figures saw in their day as the advancing threat of secularism. Through a return to "true" Islam and the achievement of the social order it prescribes, Banna and Mawdudi aspired to be the harbingers, in L. Carl Brown's assessment, of something like an Islamic "End of History"—that is, a human order in which all existing contradictions and tensions are resolved through the realization of a universal normativity.[16] While they diverged in terms of certain priorities, methods, and choice of personal vocation (one essentially a social activist, the other a public intellectual), the formulations of Mawdudi and Banna went on to inspire the theory and practice of Islamism across several generations and a wide variety of settings.

"Islam is the solution": the evolution and expansion of the MB

As the original and, arguably, most influential Islamist movement of the twentieth century, the MB merits closer examination. We learned something of the circumstances surrounding its founding while discussing Hassan al-Banna above, but given its rapid growth and the central role it came to play not only in Egyptian politics but in a number of countries throughout the Muslim world, it is worth looking more closely at how it evolved and expanded as an organization both during and after Banna's tenure as leader. In this section we will survey the development of the MB in Egypt, looking particularly at its transformation from a social and educational movement into an avowedly political, and eventually even militant, group. Sayyid Qutb, chief ideologue of the MB during the height of its militancy in the 1960s, went on to become one of the most influential Islamist thinkers across the Muslim world, affecting many of the groups and movements we examine in later chapters, so we will want to gain some understanding of his thinking on Islam and politics. Examining developments with the MB since the 1970s, particularly in terms of its changing relationship with the

Egyptian government, will help to lay the groundwork for our analysis of Islam in state and society relations in later chapters. As branches of the MB were established in other Arab countries (and later even beyond the Middle East)—each of them adjusting the model and methodology to suit local circumstances and priorities—it became possible to identify a distinction between the MB as an organizational entity (particularly the original Egyptian group) and something like "Muslim Brotherhoodness"—which describes a broad tendency within contemporary Islamism, the core tenants and methods of which are shared by all manner of group and movements regardless of whether they have any affiliation with the official MB. Drawing this distinction between the MB as a formal group and the Brotherhood as a broad ideological current will help us to better appreciate the complex nature of the MB today. A brief look at the diverse paths followed by some of its various branches outside Egypt will also allow us to understand how local conditions and political imperatives can serve to inflect models originally developed elsewhere.

The MB founded by Hassan al-Banna in 1928 sought primarily to offset the corrosive effects of Westernization and secularism by educating Egyptian society about the importance of religion in public life and by advocating a return to "true" Islam. An important precursor to the Brotherhood can be found in the Young Men's Muslim Association (YMMA), founded the year before Banna's organization. Its similarity to the well-known Christian group of the same name is certainly no coincidence. The YMCA had been present in Egypt since around the turn of the century and those within Banna's circle perceived it as an aggressive missionary force whose influence needed to be countered. Many of the YMMA's teachings regarding proper Islamic lifestyle, and even some of its more public and political positions, were later incorporated into the platform of the MB.

During the first few years of its existence, the Brotherhood worked primarily to consolidate a committed membership in Isma'iliyya and the immediate environs of the Suez. Funds were secured to build a mosque, to which were also attached schools for both boys and girls. It is interesting to note that even during these earliest days Banna attracted attention and suspicion from Cairo, where the palace was unsure what to make of him—communist, nationalist, disgruntled royalist, petty racketeer?[17] "Islamist" was not on the radar yet as a form of opposition politics. It was with the MB's move to Cairo in 1932 that the establishment of the Brotherhood's institutional infrastructure began in earnest. After quickly merging with or assimilating a number of other Islamic groups in the capital, the MB began a period of growth which, over the next decade, would see its base grow to some half million active members across 2,000 branches. More impressive than the size of its following, perhaps, was the fact that the Brotherhood had succeeded in finding supporters across a considerable range of social milieu and professional sectors. Its potential political influence hence also increased over this period, with Banna taking a more direct influence in politics from the mid-1930s. Much of this activity was focused on anti-missionary, anti-colonial, and anti-Zionist efforts. Banna also wrote a number of letters to the king in which he related concerns regarding the socially divisive political climate in the country as well as the importance of establishing an Islamic order. By this time there had also already emerged within the Brotherhood itself certain tensions between the gradualist approach to social change espoused by Banna and a small faction of Brothers—the "hasty and the anxious," as the leader labeled them—seeking to adopt more directly confrontational methods.[18] This particular division within the movement is one that would repeat itself on several occasions later in the Brotherhood's history, and one that also shows up in a number of other Islamist groups.

There are a number of interesting observations to make about the nature of MB ideology and its reflection in the movement's social organization. First of all, although religious in nature, the Brotherhood needs to be seen as a thoroughly *modern* entity. This can be seen in terms of its systematic organization, its methods and locations of recruitment, its division into cadres of professional classes, and its appreciation of the nature of bureaucratic politics. In its rhetoric we find an acknowledgment of modern domains of thought (e.g. sciences vs. humanities), categories of social division (e.g. social classes and the interplay of various forms of social authority), and a distinction between fields such as culture, politics, economics, and society. All these reflect Banna's modern education and the appreciation he gained from studying recent forms of mass social mobilization. While he was certainly at odds with the fascists of Italy and Nazi Germany—both on moral grounds and because of their exclusively nationalist focus—he certainly admired the mobilizing potential, totalizing politics, and intense discipline that these movements represented. Another area in which the MB shows its modernist colors relates to issues of theology and jurisprudence. Rather than adopting an official school of jurisprudential thought (one of the four Sunni madhahib), Banna and the MB instead disavowed these as unnecessary obstacles to the singularity of true Islam. This stance, often identified with the Salafiyya movement, is generally recognized as "modernist" in its rejection of the "traditional" practice of *taqlid*—that is, the emulation of precedent within a particular school of juristic practice. That said, it is also possible to identify certain traces of traditional practice in the MB—holdovers, perhaps, from Banna's extended affiliation with the Hasaniya Sufi brotherhood. This is most clearly present in the emphasis he placed on the student-teacher relationship within the MB and the crucial importance of obedience to the movement's leader. Combining these various elements, some observers have seen in Banna and the MB a "reconstruction of modernity according to Islamic models and motifs."[19]

What of the Brotherhood's organizational structure? This is worth covering to some extent so that we can see how the Brotherhood ethos came to be reflected internally through the various divisions and structures Banna

interests in Egypt's political future. They became central interlocutors with successive governments from the 1920s forward and, at times, among their most vociferous critics. Although not part of the milieu of the political elite *per se,* the effendiyya came to occupy an important mediating layer between the government and broader national sentiment. The Egyptian economy in the early twentieth century was most heavily dependent on cotton exports. A decline in world commodity prices from the 1920s, associated with the global depression, spelled significant hardship for Egypt's agricultural sector and put the new constitutional government under considerable pressure. As writers such as Moaddel (2005, 203) have observed, however, widespread discontent regarding the socioeconomic effects of the policies pursued by political elites and their allies are insufficient to explain why Islamism emerges as a viable alternative political discourse. In order to understand this, we need to understand how the politics of state formation in the Arab world, or, in this case, in Egypt, became simultaneously enmeshed within a broader set of cultural debates about modernity, values, and social authority.

The modernizing state, with its emphasis on economic and bureaucratic rationalization, came to be identified with a shift away from Arab-Islamic heritage. As it came to identify "traditionalist" institutions such as the pious foundations (*awqaf,* sing. *waqf*) and shari'ah courts, increasingly, as obstacles in the path of modernization, the question of the cultural authenticity of this approach became a feature of political discourse. As Moaddel observes:

> To a disinterested observer, the Egyptian version of liberal nationalism would not have appeared to be simply a discourse to resolve the problem of politics in a constitutional direction. It would rather have appeared to be an all-encompassing and comprehensive ideology, dictating a world-view that ranged from a philosophy of history to a style of dress. To a Muslim observer, in particular, the feature of this ideology was defined less in terms of the necessity of liberating Egypt from the vestiges of foreign domination than in terms of opposition to an Islam that was, in the nationalist perception, deleterious to the construction of modern Egypt.[22]

The path chosen by the MB proved uniquely powerful in this context. The MB was not a "nativist" organization, advocating a return to a traditional Arab-Islamic utopia in which modernity in all its forms was rejected. Indeed, as we will see in greater detail below, the MB, and most other subsequent Islamist organizations, was wholly modern in its organization and outlook. By combining an appreciation of modern education, science and technology with a rejection of blind emulation of the West (initially framed in anti-colonial, but then increasingly geoculturalist, terms), the Brotherhood was able to tap into a vein of growing concern across numerous sectors of Egyptian society: how does one partake in modernity's potential for social mobility and national development while avoiding becoming (or continuing to be) beholden to both its culturally and morally eroding effects, and the pervasive influence of its foreign agents? As Moaddel argues, "changes in class relations and the dynamics of interelite political rivalries undeniably shaped the resources and opportunity structures from which the MB drew in its contention for political power and cultural supremacy."[23]

As successive waves of political elites—particularly those, such as the Wafdists, whose early legitimacy was based on an agenda of popular emancipation—came to pursue policies that served their narrow interests and even to allow their own co-option by the British, widespread suspicions towards the dominant political tendencies grew—as did support for the MB "alternative." That this wasn't a political alternative in the conventional sense of a full-developed political party is significant here. By sitting back from the political order of the day and building a broad base of social support, Hassan al-Banna ensured that his group's support was widely courted, at various points, by more or less every significant political party and institution and Egypt, while managing to remain untainted—at least up until the post-World War II period—by direct involvement in the machinations of the day. Neither did the MB become a "client" for any particular political faction. Even though Banna, by the late 1940s, appeared to be accelerating his plan for the direct politicization of MB activity in light of contemporary events, we can say that the legitimacy of the Brotherhood during this first phase lay in its capacity to serve as a repository of spiritual and cultural authenticity in a time of great turbulence.

The Brotherhood's main priority in the years following Banna's death was to rehabilitate its reputation in the eyes of the government so that it could once again operate openly. The decision was hence made to choose a successor to Banna not from the existing ranks of deputies and senior leaders—many of whom were tainted in the eyes of the authorities—but by looking outside the ranks of the Brothers to appoint a new "general guide" (as the head of the movement had been known since 1945). After two years of interim leadership by Salih Ashmawi, who had been Banna's deputy, the decision was made to appoint Hasan al-Hudaybi, a well-respected judge, as the MB's new general guide. Hudaybi was not formally a member of the Brotherhood, merely a sympathetic figure of some official standing who had developed tremendous admiration for Hassan al-Banna and his ideas. In the eyes of the MB's senior deputies, Hudaybi's appointment was intended as a temporary measure to help cleanse the organization's reputation after the violence and unrest of 1946–49. Almost immediately tensions emerged between Hudaybi and amongst certain former lieutenants of Banna. The latter had expected Hudaybi to be little more than a rubber-stamp figurehead, a public persona whose reputation was beyond official reproach. Hudaybi, however, was intent on affecting a genuine transformation in the movement, seeking to return it more clearly to the status of a religious organization and to get away from politics. One of his first acts, in addition to appointing a new cadre of loyal deputies, was to abolish the MB's Secret Apparatus. When it soon became clear that the militant wing continued to operate under a leadership pillar outside Hudaybi's control, he threatened to resign.

This internal dispute temporarily took second fiddle to seismic events happening on the national political landscape, more specifically the Free Officer Revolution of 1952, which led to the king's deposal and also sounded the real end to British control of Egypt. While the MB played no direct role in these events, close contact and coordination between the Brothers and the Free Officers movement is well documented. Indeed, the military conspirators envisaged important roles for the MB in terms of preserving order on the streets at the time of the coup d'état, and also within their contingency planning should things not have proceeded according to plan.[24] Although the Free Officers were diametrically opposed to the MB in terms of ideology, a fact that would be made all too clear very shortly, there was a history of contact between them dating back to the time of Hassan al-Banna. What brought the two together, it seemed, was a shared sense of dissatisfaction about the state of politics in Egypt and a common conviction that none of the existing parties could successfully rid the nation of its endemic corruption. Clearly, each of these two groups hoped to make tactical and strategic use of the other: for the Free Officers, the MB represented a potential source of widespread popular legitimacy and "spiritual" endorsement of the otherwise highly secular revolution they were plotting. Indeed, the precursors to the Free Officers in the 1940s had even entrusted to the Brotherhood the keeping of several stores of armaments in case they might be needed in the struggle to come. To the MB, on the other hand, the Free Officers represented a possible vehicle upon which, in the context of genuine political revolution, an Islamic system could be institutionalized at the level of the state. In the immediate aftermath of the revolution in the summer of 1952, the Brotherhood was generally supportive, but the relationship between the new government, first under Muhammad Naguib and then later under the iconic Gamal Abdel Nasser, and the MB quickly soured.

The Free Officers, now institutionalized as the Revolutionary Command Council (RCC), banned in 1953 all political parties except the Brotherhood, which it labeled—for tactical reasons, rather than through ignorance—a social welfare group. Once it became apparent to the MB that the government was not going to heed its calls for instituting an Islamic order or to allow the Brotherhood any significant public influence, their support quickly disappeared and animosity between the two began to grow. It is here that the emerging schism within the movement came to take on increased importance. As tensions grew between Hudaybi's vision of the Brotherhood's mission and those who supported the existence of the special apparatus and a more confrontational approach, the RCC exploited the rift to discredit Hudaybi's leadership. After an attempt on Nasser's life in 1954, the government banned the organization for seditious activity and imprisoned or put to death a number of its key leaders. Since this time the MB, while certainly very active in Egypt over the next 50 years, has never operated openly as a legal political organization. Over the next 12 years, the Brotherhood—now firmly controlled by the militants and more convinced than ever of the necessity of direct, armed confrontation in the wake of the government's crackdown—continued to operate as an underground opposition movement. While many of its leaders had been imprisoned, killed, or gone into exile abroad, a new generation of ideologues emerged during this more militant phase of the movement's existence. Of these none was more important than Sayyid Qutb. Qutb, who did not even join the Brothers as an active member until 1952, provided the theoretical basis for the evolution of Hassan al-Banna's mission of social transformation into an approach to Islamic politics whose only possible course of action under the prevailing order was armed struggle, or jihad. Qutb served as the chief ideologue of the Brothers during the underground period, and was imprisoned during much of it. Finally hanged in 1966 in connection with a plot to overthrow the government, Qutb garnered a reputation around the Muslim world as a major theorist of Islamism and jihad. Like Mawdudi, his importance transcends the immediate national context of his efforts. Indeed, in the case of Qutb we can say, arguably, that no other modern Islamist thinker has had quite the same influence in terms of giving voice to the revolutionary and jihadi worldview within modern Islamism. His thinking will be apparent in the formulations of several groups we examine later in the book (see Chapter 7), and so Qutb—the last individual Islamist thinker we will address in this chapter—is hence worth looking at in some greater detail.

Sayyid Qutb: hakimiyyah, jahiliyya, and jihad

Sayyid Qutb (1906–66) was born and raised in Upper Egypt (the south of the country), and like Hassan al-Banna before him eventually traveled to Cairo to attend teaching college.[25] Unlike Banna, however, his early work did not reflect immediate Islamist convictions. In Cairo he fell primarily into literary rather than social activist circles, and much of his writing during this period—when they did involve religion—were concerned with the aesthetics (rather than sociopolitical imperatives) of the Qur'an. He also seemed to be searching for a worldview at this early point, uncertain as to the preeminence of the Egyptian, Arab or Islamic frames of identity. The hierarchy of moral obligation was also a concern for the young Qutb, and his work from the 1940s shows him working through some of the central predicaments in modern normative theory such as the balance of obligation between individual rights and those of the community—a theme to which he would return in his later "Islamic" writing. Eventually taking a job as a teacher and then later as an inspector and official within the Ministry of

Education, Qutb did not show any early interest in transforming the social order of his day, although he certainly participated in the key debates and, like most public intellectuals of the time, held broadly anti-colonial views. It was not until the late 1940s that his intellectual output came to settle within a predominantly Islamic frame. His first major work in this vein was *Social Justice in Islam* (1948), a text that seeks to work through questions of social obligation and to establish the superiority of the Islamic paradigm of equity and justice in the face of both liberal individualism and socialist egalitarianism—the two competing models of the day.

From 1949 to 1950, Qutb was dispatched to the United States by the Ministry of Education to study American educational administration methods. His stay there seems to have had a major impact on his worldview and the development of his thinking with regard to Islam. While certainly impressed with the material achievements of American society, he felt that these had been obtained at an unacceptable cost. His account of American culture focused on what he saw as the devastating erosion of capitalist individualism on the moral character of that society. This experience appears to have shifted his understanding of the threat from the West such that it came to be about much more than just colonial occupation. Rather, the West represented a pervasive system of values and beliefs that would undermine any society that chose its path. For Qutb, as Charles Tripp argues, "British Imperialism was characterized merely as one aspect of a more wide-ranging and sinister form of collective enmity—that of the secular, materialist, individualist and capitalist West."[26] Qutb was perhaps that much more interested in the United States because it was a relatively young nation, having been formed when the British Empire was already ascendant. In this regard it represented for him a case study in what happens when a primarily agricultural nation rapidly industrializes and embraces secular modernity—trends that were dominant in Egypt at his time. If America were Egypt's future, he reasoned, then the crisis at hand was perhaps more severe than he had originally imagined, and required urgent redress.

Upon Qutb's return to Egypt it is therefore not surprising that he began to take a greater interest in those groups which, beyond writing about the need for social reform, were actually trying to enact it in practice. Quite naturally he was led towards the MB in this regard, although it does not seem that he actually joined the group until around 1952. Upon becoming an active member, Qutb was immediately placed in charge of the MB's public outreach section. Like many of his Brotherhood contemporaries, Qutb had high hopes for Egypt when the Free Officers Revolution of 1952 occurred. Indeed, reports suggest that he worked quite closely and enthusiastically with the new regime in an effort to integrate a stronger dimension of Islamization into their reform agenda. As Nasser rose to prominence within the RCC and consolidated his power base, however, it became clear that an Islamic social order was nowhere on the agenda, and Qutb soon found himself among the ranks of disillusioned Brothers. Imprisoned briefly during the first round-up of MB activists in 1953, Qutb's more concerted confrontation with the regime begins in 1954 when he was sentenced to 15 years in jail for his role in encouraging subversive activities. Writing and publishing from prison (a privilege afforded him seemingly due to his early support for the Free Officers), the next decade was the most prolific in Qutb's career. During this time he produced *Fi Zilal al-Qur'an* ("In the Shade of the Qur'an"), a major tafsir work that he had actually started in 1952 and which would not be completed until 1965 shortly before his death, and most importantly for our purposes, the seminal *Ma'alim fi al-Tariq* ("Signposts on the Road"; hereafter *Signposts*). The latter text represents his most strident and polemical statement regarding the need to eliminate, by force if necessary, the infidel order that currently dominated Egypt. It is also a text whose core ideas have continued to animate the discourse of Islamist thinkers activists, particularly those of a more jihadi persuasion, up to today. Initially cleared for publication, *Signposts* was soon banned by the state when it became clear that it was circulating widely as an inspirational text for MB followers meeting clandestinely. In 1964 Qutb was released from prison and immediately approached by the Brotherhood's underground leadership to serve as their spiritual guide. It appears that Qutb agreed to take on this role, with the strident, activist tenor of his recent writings clearly representing a dominant trend within the MB. The following year, Qutb was arrested along with several other MB activists and accused of reconstituting the Secret Apparatus with the aim of overthrowing the Egyptian government and killing the president. All involved were given the death penalty and these sentences, including Qutb's, were carried out in 1966.

Sayyid Qutb's social and political thought reflected a wide range of influences over the course of its development. We can find elements of both mysticism and rationalism. Where one might think that his eventual focus on pure shari'ah would lead Qutb to eschew Sufi thought entirely, there is also a sense in which the all-encompassing nature of Sufi devotion comes very close to the Qutbian ideal. Indeed, some of the aesthetic and almost emotive dimensions of direct, individual access to the divine present in his early thinking transferred over into his later thoughts albeit with a rather different set of worldly priorities. As someone who engaged most key debates of the day during the period of his own intellectual formation, it is perhaps inevitable that the path towards Qutb's Islamism occurs in stages. During the first phase in which he begins to combine social and religious thinking, in the late 1940s, Qutb is primarily seeking to situate his understanding of Islam amongst competing ideologies of the day. Charles Tripp has observed that at this point Qutb seems to be trying to reconcile and balance within Islam aspects of liberalism, such as the emphasis on individual rights, with the requirements of the community.[27] An illustrative quote from *Social Justice in Islam* reflects these efforts:

So the [Islamic] regulations lay down the rights of the community over the powers and abilities of the individual; they also establish limiting boundaries to the freedom, the desires, and the wants of the individual, but they must also be ever mindful of the rights of the individual, to give him freedom in his desires and inclinations; and over all there must be the limits which the community must not overstep, and which the individual on his side must not transgress.[28]

By the time he produced *Signposts* in the mid-1960s, as we will see, any interest and concern about the rights of the individual had been wholly subjugated to the higher necessity of the Islamic order.

Qutb's return from the United States in 1950 marks the beginning of the next clear phase in his intellectual development. This begins with his new found conviction that Islam was far more than just a matter of personal spirituality, piety, or moralism, but rather that it prescribed and necessitated the active pursuit of an entire social order. It was this shift that prompted his interest in the activities of the MB and the programmatic ideas of the recently deceased Hassan al-Banna. Qutb began to emphasize the value of organized movements in the pursuit of social change as a vital counterpart to preaching. As he would later write in *Signposts*:

If "preaching" sets right the beliefs and concepts, "movement" removes from the path other material obstacles, foremost of which is the political power that it established on intricate and complex but interrelated ideological, racial, class, social, and economic foundations. And these two—preaching and movements—jointly collaborate in influencing the established system from all four directions, and are conducive to bringing about the new system ... [29]

It was also around this time that Qutb's long-held suspicions regarding the social irrelevance of the ulama and traditional religious orthodoxy seem to have been consolidated. Qutb had been critical in earlier writings about the apparent apathy of the religious establishment, represented by institutions such as Al-Azhar, towards the downtrodden masses of Egyptian society. Qutb's writing began now to increasingly emphasize the importance of direct engagement by individual believers with the truth of the shari'ah, bypassing the mediating influence of the established canon as transmitted by religious authorities—a mode of religious knowledge production which Qutb understood to have been tainted by centuries of un-Islamic innovation (bid'a). As Tripp observes, Qutb appeared to be calling for no less than the creation of a new "Qur'anic generation," modeled on the example of the Prophet's companions who were forced to rely on their direct experience and first-hand knowledge of revelation rather than on blind taqlid (emulation) of figures claiming religious authority.[30] It is in this sense that we can also regard Qutb's thinking as yet another discrepan take on the Salafiyya project instigated by Muhammad Abduh half a century before.

Qutb was also influenced by other emerging currents in Islamist thought during this time. We know, for instance, that from the early 1950s he read and quoted the works of Abu'l-A'la Mawdudi, which by that time had been translated into Arabic. Like Mawdudi and in contrast with Banna, Qutb was primarily an intellectual and theorist. He would have appreciated the comprehensive and systematic reasoning to be found in the work of the former, and it is clear that he drew from Mawdudi in developing his own exposition of Islamic politics. It is perhaps to Mawdudi that we can attribute Qutb's initial discussions of the notion of *jahiliyya*, a concept that would later develop into a central foundation in Qutb's religio-political worldview. Jahiliyya is a term that, in its most common usage, refers to the period of "ignorance" prior to the coming of Islam. Mawdudi's modernist interpretation began to equate jahiliyya with contemporary social orders that fail to institute the Islamic system—in other words, which proceed as if they were ignorant of Islam's truth. In Sayyid Qutb's thought, jahiliyya comes to represent his fundamental diagnosis of the malaise—cultural, moral, political—gripping his society. More than just a metaphor for slack morals, jahiliyya in the Qutbian context came to figure as one half of a thoroughly Manichean worldview. For Qutb there were only two possible routes. One could embrace true Islam and its shari'ah as a total way of life, or one could live in jahiliyya. His later thinking allowed no middle ground, no "almost" or "mostly" Islamic way of life; it was one or the other. Jahiliyya, he reasoned, named the order of the day in Egypt and in other Muslim countries run by secular regimes or corrupt, "pseudo-religious" monarchs. Jahiliyya was also the catch all term that allowed him to thematize all those Western values (secularism, materialism, individualism, capitalism) which threatened to colonize anew—even worse, to colonize the hearts and minds—of Muslims.

But jahiliyya for Qutb was more than just a moral category. In his later work it became an integral component of his theorization of the necessity of jihad. Several observers have noted that Qutb's analysis of what was implied by the condition of jahiliyya, or in this case the presence of unjust Muslim rulers, was a major departure from conventional Islamic political thought. The general consensus up to that point had been that when faced with a Muslim ruler who did not properly enforce the shari'ah, Muslims should make the ruler aware of his shortcomings, but should not actively seek to resist or overthrow the political authorities for fear of bringing about social disorder and strife (fitna). That is to say, it is not the responsibility of the believer to sit in judgment of a ruler's conduct vis-à-vis the shari'ah. This is a moral account that the ruler would eventually settle directly with God.[31] In stark contrast to this norm, Qutb argued—working off precedents found in the fourteenth century jurist Ibn Taymiyya—that it is incumbent upon the believer who knows his Muslim ruler to be delinquent in upholding shari'ah to actively resist that regime and take action to bring about the proper Islamic order. In effect, this meant that it became the responsibility of Muslims to decide whether those around them were infidels (*kaffirun*; sing. *kafir*), or if they were true Muslims upholding the shari'ah. This emphasis on takfir ("excommunication," or declaring someone to be a kafir) and its prominence within the discourse of many jihadi Islamists today is seen by some as evidence of Qutb's direct influence. This is particularly evident in the emphasis today in the discourse of certain Islamists on what they see as fighting the "near enemy" (see Chapter 7).

Qutb's decade of imprisonment and reported torture at the hands of Nasser's regime seems to have crystallized his conviction that it was no longer possible to pursue the reform of jahiliyya social orders through methods of dialogue and persuasion: tarbiya (education) and da'wa (calling to true Islam) were, for him, insufficient in the face of so totalizing a threat. At this point direct resistance and jihad were the only possible—indeed, the obligatory—methods. *Signposts* represented Qutb's manifesto for the pursuit of this goal and is the best textual embodiment of the final phase of his thinking. Most observers have tended to read *Signposts* as a text intended for an audience already most of the way there in terms of embracing Qutb's worldview—in this case, Brotherhood members severely suppressed by the regime and gathering in secret. Rather than being a gentle introduction for the lay reader designed to persuade one of a political role for Islam, *Signposts* assumes an activist stance and then proceeds to elaborate an account of what is required of those who have already embarked "on the path of God" (fi sabil Allah). Those who argue against this course of action, even from a position of religious authority (e.g. ulama), are themselves complicit in the jahiliyya order. As Tripp has observed, Qutb urged his followers to have confidence in their "direct, non-philosophical apprehension of the truth," arguing that as the activist harbingers of a divinely sanctioned order, their interpretation and understanding of shari'ah was intrinsically superior.[32]

This brings us to the issue of jihad and how this concept figured in Sayyid Qutb's thought. That it was present and quite central to his later writing is undeniable. Where commentators have differed, however, is in their analysis of how important violent jihad was to the Qutbian project. Some, such as Sayyid's brother Muhammad Qutb, have argued that invocations of this term in the work of the former should be understood to be referring primarily to the overall struggle to achieve the Islamic order in the literal sense of jihad as "struggle." On the other extreme, there are those who see Qutb's significance to lay exclusively in his theorization and advocacy of violent jihad.[33] As is usually the case with such issues, the truth probably lies somewhere in between. Qutb, certainly in his early and middle periods, would have generally eschewed violence in favor of reform via persuasive and deliberative methods. That said, he also recognized that there were more material dimensions to the struggle that may at times call for militant tactics. Even in his very late writings, however, Qutb is not operating exclusively within the framework of violent jihad. To quote from *Signposts*:

> This movement does not confine itself to mere preaching and persuasion while confronting the physical power, nor does it deem it proper to utilize force and coercion for converting the ideas and thoughts of the common man. Both of these principles are of equal importance in the application of the method of this religion. The very purpose of this movement is to set human beings free from the yoke of human enslavement and make them serve the One and Only God.[34]

His focus here on the "common man" as an inappropriate target for coercive jihad is significant in that Qutb wants to make clear that he holds those political regimes which bring about and sustain jahili orders as most culpable in sin and therefore the proper object of active resistance.

Looking at Qutb's later writings, those in which the discourse of jihad is most prevalent, it is possible to identify two distinct trajectories for this concept, and it seems that each of the two camps seeking to interpret the jihadist import of Qutb's thought has simply chosen to emphasize one over the other. The section of *Signposts* in which Qutb elaborates his understanding of jihad begins with an emphasis on the more holistic sense of that term. Qutb argues that the struggle called for by Islam "is a practical [jihad], which progresses stage by stage and at every stage provides parallel and proper resources according to its practical needs and requirements." It is therefore not inherently violent, but, depending on contingencies, it certainly may need to take on this character. The goal of the jihad is to achieve a total Islamic order, and coercion may or may not be required to get there. Qutb's discussion also takes issue with the prevailing attitude of the ulama of his day towards jihad. For them, generally, the only legitimate jihad was one that sought to defend Muslim lands against direct threats from outside. Qutb denies this territorial conception of Islam ("a creation of the modern age")[35] and seeks to replace it with an understanding of Islam as a moral system whose manifestation in social order must be sought through active struggle:

> From the Islamic point of view, the real justification for declaring Jihad is the defense of the Islamic faith, or the defense of that way of life that presents the practical exposition of faith or the defense of that society in which that way of life is operative. As regards the soil of the country, it is itself of no significance in the eyes of Islam nor does it hold any weight. If anything can impart the respectability and greatness to the soil of the country under the Islamic concept, it is exclusively the establishment of God's rule there and the implementation of the way of life required by God.[36]

Qutb's writing does not lay great emphasis on the need for a caliphate. His concern lies primarily with achieving the proper Islamic order. In this view, any specific political system or form of government that conforms to the normativity of the shari'ah would therefore be acceptable.

Much has certainly been made of the influence of Sayyid Qutb's thinking on subsequent generations of jihadi-oriented Islamists. Some of these have been labeled "Qutbists," indicating the centrality of his prescriptions in their thought and practice. While many of these groups—such as Gemaa Isla-miyya or Islamic Jihad in Egypt (see below), or the transnational Al-Qaeda network (Chapter 7)—do indeed embrace the use of violence, it may be a misinterpretation to identify this as Qutb's primary legacy to them. Of equal if not greater importance is the dualistic worldview (Islam vs. Jahi-liyya) according to which Qutb and many of these latter day movements organize their understanding of particular nations and societies. While "Qutbism"—if such a thing really exists—certainly would potentially repre-sent a highly militant form of Islamism, its distinctiveness obtains primarily in its mapping and categorization of sociopolitical normativity and the obligations concomitant on Muslims seeking to follow the path of God.

The MB revitalized: Sadat and beyond

There was something of a revival in the MB's public fortunes and reputa-tion under Gamal Abdel Nasser's successor, Anwar al-Sadat, who assumed the presidency upon the former's death in 1970. While Nasser had certainly never hesitated to make rhetorical use of religion when it seemed politically expedient to do so, Sadat, the self-styled "believer-president," systematically integrated religion into his public discourse and went much further than his predecessor in terms of reaching out to the religious sector. Sadat built thousands of new mosques and reinvigorated the government's relationship with Al-Azhar University. Numerous Muslim Brothers, imprisoned since the mid-1960s were released and significant latitude was granted to the organization in terms of resuming its publications and some of its social welfare activities. We should note, however, that the Brotherhood still was not legally recognized as a political party. The re-emergent MB was cau-tious in its efforts, a pale shadow of the Qutbian zeal that defined the early 1960s. While it did not hesitate to criticize the government when it disagreed with policies—such as Sadat's move to liberalize certain aspects of Muslim family law—the MB of the 1970s resembled its 1930s incarnation far more than it did the group's confrontational manifestation of the 1950s and 60s.

It is fair to say that by the late 1970s, Sadat's Islamization efforts had begun to backfire. It became clear to the religious organizations that had gained a new lease on life during his early tenure that Sadat was not ready to push for meaningful Islamic reform as they understood it in the sense of more shari'ah across multiple sectors of Egyptian society. Furthermore, a number of his foreign policy initiatives had made him progressively unpopular with important segments of Egypt's population. From the *infitah* ("open door") economic policy, a liberalizing gesture that brought significant instability to Egypt's economy, to his condemnation of the Islamic revolution in Iran, Sadat appeared more and more to be aligning Egypt with the West. The final straw here was undoubtedly his signing of a peace agreement with Israel in 1979, the Camp David Accords. In 1981, Sadat was assassinated by associates of Islamic Jihad, one of a number of militant organizations that had emerged in Egypt over the course of the 1970s. Islamic Jihad, along with groups such as Takfir w'al-Hijra and Muhammad's Youth, emerged from the early 1970s as hardline Islamist alternatives for those drawn to the jihadist impulse of Sayyid Qutb but disillusioned with the moderate stance of the MB. Both Takfir and Muhammad's Youth were involved in various attacks and kidnappings during Sadat's period in power, drawing a strong response from the government and leading to both groups having large numbers of their followers imprisoned or killed. That these were very small extremist groups is certainly not in doubt, but there was a sense in which they represented the fringe of a broader re-Islamization of Egyptian public consciousness. While the methods of Islamic Jihad in killing Sadat were extreme, the nature of their critique of his government—whom they depicted as a despotic "Pharaoh"—certainly was not isolated from certain more mainstream sentiments.

Under Sadat's successor, Hosni Mubarak, the government's cat and mouse game with the Islamists has continued. While the extremist groups that formed in the 1970s have been mostly shut down or exiled, new challenges to the Egyptian government have cropped up on both the militant and moderate fronts. From the mid-1980s, a group known as Gemaa Islamiyya emerged as an umbrella organization to coordinate the efforts of a number of small but highly militant groups operating across Egypt. Composed primarily of extremist student activists from the 1970s, these groups carried out a number of attacks on foreign tourists and other targets that symbolize Western culture. Some have viewed Gemaa Islamiyya as another example of "Qutbism" in action.[37] The Egyptian government's response to these operations has been very aggressive, making full use of the special powers permitted under the special "state of emergency" regulations that were put into effect at the time of Sadat's assassination and then never rescinded. Two developments of note regarding mainstream Islamist movements in Egypt under Mubarak will be looked at in considerable detail in the following chapter. The first of these relates to a noticeable shift in the MB's sociopolitical strategy. This has involved a greater emphasis on seeking social influence via the attainment of leadership roles in the increasingly important professional associations or "syndicates" to be found in major Egyptian cities. The Brotherhood, while still formally banned as a political party, has sought political office by running candidates with no formal party affiliations—including women and Christians—and seeking alliances with former political foes including the new Wafd party. Second, there has also been an attempt to establish a new religiously based "centrist" party, the Hizb al-Wasat. This group, which has so far failed to obtain official recognition from the government and has also been subject to considerable discrimination, embraces the moral guidance of religion as a path to good governance and a solution to corruption, but does not currently include an emphasis on shari'ah or the pursuit of an Islamic state as part of its platform.

But the Brotherhood's political fortunes are not to be traced exclusively within the Egyptian context. Less than a decade after its founding, the movement was already branching out, establishing chapters in Syria and Palestine. Over the next few decades MB parties would become political actors of central importance in countries such as Tunisia, Sudan, and Jordan. HAMAS in Palestine today began life as an offshoot of the Brotherhood. In numerous other countries outside the Arab World such as Turkey, Pakistan, and Malaysia, groups and parties sharing the Brotherhood's core values and basic operational method would emerge. Some of the international and transnational dimensions of the MB movement will be dealt with more fully in Chapter 8, but suffice it for now to reiterate the point made above about the distinction to be drawn between the MB as an organizational entity (particularly in Egypt, but also throughout the Arab world) and the MB "way" as representing a broad tendency within contemporary Islamism that refers to a basic worldview and a general mode of political organization. As we will see, the specific methods and political priorities adopted by MB national chapters and MB-inspired groups vary considerably depending on local circumstances (there is, arguably, little to nothing by way of centralized control within the movement globally—more on this in Chapter 8). Nonetheless, insofar as the MB represented the first sustained and successful articulation of a modern Islamist method, all of these groups owe a debt to the project Hassan al-Banna initiated in 1928.

The MB as a proto-typical Islamist movement

Our analysis of the MB has permitted us to gain some understanding of how and why Islamism—as an intellectual and political project—emerged in the context of secular nationalist state formation in certain parts of the Muslim world. We have seen the discursive and mobilization strategies employed by Hassan al-Banna to reach out to wary and increasingly disenfranchised segments of Egyptian society. Likewise an analysis of Sayyid Qutb's theorization of Islamic social order and jihad permitted us to track the intellectual evolution of the Islamist project through a particularly turbulent militant phase and to better understand some of the antecedents of ideas and approaches employed by contemporary Islamists.

In summary, there are three key points to take away from our analysis of the MB—one of which is particular to this movement, the other two pertaining to Islamism more generally:

(1) *Islamism as a thoroughly modern phenomenon* whose establishment and growth depended on the existence of ideas and social structures typical of modernizing society. Its organizational structure and methods of recruitment and indoctrination likewise represented this orientation. Those drawn to Islamist movements generally have little interest in the "traditional" bastions of Islamic knowledge such as Al-Azhar and the ranks of the ulama. Theirs is rather a direct, active, and living engagement with religious knowledge that speaks to the political imperatives of the day. It is worth quoting Sami Zubaida at length in his characterization of the typical Islamist social profile:

> [W]e are talking about urban populations in the major cities ... plus layers of rural or provincial migrants who arrived at various stages, mostly over the last few decades, first into the old quarters then further out into the sprawling suburbs and shanty towns ...
>
> ... The most active, as we have seen, are the new intelligentsia, the products of modern educational systems facing grim prospects of employment in a society and state which cannot absorb the mass of intellectual proletariat which they produce and where the prizes go to those who have access ... [38]

(2) *Material and ideational factors are both crucial to understanding the emergence of modern Islamism.* It is insufficient to focus exclusively on socioeconomic disenfranchisement as the basis of Islamist mobilization, but neither is the phenomenon of Islamism explained solely by reference to concerns regarding the rise of political systems premised on secular-national values and Western cultural hegemony.

(3) The *distinction between the MB as an organizational entity and the MB "tendency"* as a more generic current within contemporary Islamic thought and social activism. Even groups not formally affiliated with the Brotherhood have been strongly influenced by its analysis and solution for social reform. Likewise, official branches of the Brotherhood outside Egypt are almost wholly autonomous and pursue political agendas based on the specific conditions of their national settings.

Islam and politics through the twentieth century

While the MB is certainly the original and still paradigmatic case of modern Islamism, it represents only a single instance of one particular form of Muslim politics. Over the course of the twentieth century, and particularly in its second half, the world witnessed all manner of Muslim politics, Islamist, and otherwise. In some cases these were state-led efforts to establish governmental systems based on Islam, or to co-opt Islam in the name of the state's national development agenda, or to provide religious legitimacy for ruling monarchies. In other cases we find groups defining themselves in religious terms emerging in the context of war, civil conflict or failed states either to defend the nation or a Muslim subgroup within it in the name of Islam, or to provide social services in situations where a vanquished or absent state lacks that capacity. Others are manifestations of Islamism similar although by no means identical to the circumstances that produced the MB. These for the most part are cases where political parties based on Islam have sought to challenge the legitimacy and effectiveness of (usually) secular national regimes. In some instances we have seen the formation of social movements or religious groups—organized around a particular understanding of Islam—which are not, on the face of it, particularly political in nature. Some of the Muslim mass movements or student groups in Southeast Asia come to mind, as do predominantly quietistic da'wa groups such as the Tablighi Jamaat or the Sufi brotherhoods of West Africa. Through their use of Islamic symbols and the nature and location of their social mobilization, however, it can be argued that groups of this sort are actually key participants in what we have termed Muslim politics. The late twentieth century saw the emergence of various new forms of Muslim transnationalism in the form of diasporic and migrant communities, worldwide Internet forums, and, of course, radical networks—such as Al-Qaeda—pursuing global jihad and a new caliphate. In subsequent chapters this book will look in greater detail at many of these cases and more. For now, we will want to round off our survey of state formation and Islam by looking briefly at several other key countries where Islam and politics were particularly important in the second half of the twentieth century. These cases—some of which will be examined more closely in later chapters—allow us to track some of the other major trajectories of Muslim politics in the modern era.

Saudi Arabia and Pakistan: the new Islamic states

Founded as "Islamic states" prior to or just after World War II, Saudi Arabia and Pakistan represent two countries whose geopolitical significance increased enormously over the subsequent decades—the former because of its enormous oil reserves, the latter because of its strategic location in South-Central Asia. Saudi Arabia was consolidated as a state in 1932 when Abdul Aziz al-Saud secured the allegiance of all major tribes in the Arabian Peninsula and proclaimed a kingdom in his family's name. As in the case of his eighteenth-century ancestor, an alliance with religious forces was crucial to Saud's political aspirations and much of the new state's legitimacy lay in the claims of its namesake family to conduct itself as righteous Islamic rulers. In declaring the Qur'an to be the law of his land, Saud set his country on a path that would distinguish it from many of the secular national regimes soon to appear alongside it in the Arab world. The conservative religious ideology at the foundation of this new state would also, at times, place Saudi Arabia seemingly at odds with emergent global normative agendas such as human and women's rights. For example, when the Universal Declaration of Human Rights (UDHR) came before the United Nations in 1948, Saudi Arabia was one of the few countries to abstain in the vote for its adoption. It did so in protest of the provision in the UDHR (Article 18) that guaranteed an individual the right to change his or her religion. According to the Saudi interpretation of Islam, individuals do not enjoy the freedom to enter and exit religion at will. The Kingdom developed close relations with the West over the next decades as the United States, in particular, cultivated—both geologically and politically—the Saudi potential to ensure America's energy needs during the Cold War and beyond. Relations between the royal family, the Saudi bureaucracy and the religious establishment would ebb and flow, but have remained a key dynamic in terms of the country's internal division of power. Long regarded as the home of a particularly austere and hardcore brand of Islam—commonly known as "Wahhabism"—Saudi Arabia actually contains considerable religious diversity. From the late 1970s onwards, but gathering strong momentum after the 1991 Gulf War, groups of dissident ulama and political activists have mounted a series of challenges to the Saudi regime, questioning its Islamic legitimacy (see Chapter 5). Saudi Arabia has also been one of the chief sponsors of various Islamic causes abroad, at times deploying its considerable material assets and distributive capacity towards the cause of propagating its own variant of Islam (see Chapter 8). In recent years, a gradual and still tentative process of political and religious reform has begun, and is certain to prove vitally important in terms of determining the future course—indeed, the viability—of the Saudi nation.

Pakistan represents another Islamic state founded in the first half of the twentieth century, but under a very different set of circumstances than that of the Saudi kingdom. As we will recall, Pakistan emerged out of the partition of India in 1947 as a homeland for the Muslims of the subcontinent. The early years of Pakistani politics and political discourse were characterized by debates about what it meant to be an "Islamic state"—the two basic positions being, on the one hand, a relatively secular understanding of the Islamic state in Pakistan as representing the nationalist claims of Indian Muslims for their political independence, and on the other hand, a firm belief in the need to organize the political system in Pakistan according to the requirements of Islam. Over the next several decades, political regimes of various sorts—both military and civilian—would exploit this ambiguity by appealing to and seeking to appropriate Islamic symbols and institutions in the pursuit of their particular visions of Pakistan's "Islamic state." Waves of Islamization, such as that pursued from 1977 by Zia ul-Haq, would prompt numerous debates regarding the proper role of shari'ah in Pakistani society. Pakistan's security services would also become embroiled in various regional conflicts through their sponsorship of Islamic causes in neighboring countries, while simultaneously seeking to protect the Pakistani state from internal forms of Islamism they found distasteful.

The new "Islamic revival"

Most analyses of Islamic politics in the later twentieth century are couched in terms of an "Islamic revival" that supposedly began in the wake of the 1967 Arab-Israeli war. The immediate impetus for this movement is generally understood to be the disillusionment of former Arab nationalists after the resounding defeat of Arab armies during the Six Day War. With Nasserism well on the decline, question marks had begun to appear over the Pan-Arabist project, and the secular-nationalist political order at its foundation. Over the next 10–15 years, culminating in the Islamic Revolution in Iran in 1979 and the 1981 assassination of Anwar Sadat by followers of Islamic Jihad, analysts point to an upswing in popular support for Islamist causes throughout much of the Muslim world. The appropriateness of the term "revival" to describe this phenomenon has been much debated. It is certainly the case that segments of Middle Eastern and other Muslim-majority societies not previously interested in religious alternatives to the secular national state did indeed begin gathering behind Islamist causes during this period. However, it would be wrong to regard this rejuvenation of Muslim politics as *sui generis*. Neither was it indicative of an end to Islamist dormancy. Its advocates and their approaches consciously drew on the thought and practice of earlier Islamists and, indeed, in many cases represented the continuation and recatalyzation of those very same movements once the political field had opened up somewhat. In other words, there was nothing wholly new about the Muslim politics that defined the Islamic revival. Some of the groups involved, such as Takfir w'al-Hijra and Muhammad's Youth in Egypt, were composed of former Muslim Brothers seeking new forms of confrontational activism. One moment within this broader revival, however, did represent some thing significantly new. Iran's Islamic Revolution, whose significance and implications we will look at more closely in Chapter 5, marked the first time that a nominally Islamic political order had been achieved by means of a popular Islamic revolution.

Iran's Islamic revolution

Becoming the third significant Islamic state after Saudi Arabia and Pakistan, the revolution that created the Islamic Republic of Iran in 1979 makes for a fascinating case study both of modern social mobilization and the revisionist interpretation of classical Islamic political theory. Although the ulama had been frequent participants in Iranian political debate since the first constitutional agitations late in the nineteenth century, Khomeini's doctrine of *vilayat-i faqih*—establishing the obligation of religious scholars to govern the country—represented a major departure from the traditional social role assigned to the ulama. Shi'i political theory in particular (Shi'a make up 90% of Iran's population) had historically been associated with a tendency toward political quietism. Riding a wave of popular discontent aimed squarely at the pro-Western Pahlavi dynasty—successors to the Qajar dynasty, which itself took over from the Safavid empire—Khomeini leveraged political forces of all persuasions (including communists and liberals) to depose the Shah's ruling regime. While regular elections have been held in Iran since the revolution (and their results generally respected), the preponderance of power held by the country's Supreme Leader has meant that the religious establishment maintains strict control of the country's security services and all forms of media—rendering serious political dissent all but impossible. Iran's population has grown increasingly frustrated at the restrictions enforced by the clerical authorities, but reformist politicians, even when occupying the highest levels of executive power, have been unable to find sufficient latitude to enact meaningful change. Iran has also been active abroad, sponsoring various Shi'i organizations, such as Hizbullah in Lebanon (see Chapter 6 and, briefly, below) and competing with Saudi Arabia for leadership in the Muslim world. It is also worthwhile noting that Iran's Islamic revolution had important implications beyond the world of Islam, occurring as it did in the midst of the Cold War. In some parts of the developing world, Iran's transformation was viewed as a victorious form of "Third Worldism" in which the popular voices had risen up to get rid of a pro-Western, neo-imperialist regime in the name of an alternative "indigenous" system.

Islam and politics beyond the Cold War

This last point about the broader reception of Iran's Islamic revolution points to the importance of considering the wider geopolitical context in which various forms of Muslim politics occur. While all politics may indeed be local (a formulation which today is not at all at odds with a declaration that all politics are simultaneously global), the nature of political power in an interconnected and interdependent world has meant that for some time now—and certainly in the wake of decolonization after World War II—the political orders to be found within many countries in the Muslim world have been strongly affected by the prevailing geopolitical order. In most cases this has meant a shift in the source or location, but not the general nature of the threat identified by Islamists. Where the late colonial and early decolonization periods were about Islamism as an alternative to direct colonial rule and then later the Westernizing erosion of the secular-national order, the onset of the Cold War meant that nationalist regimes were engaged from within based, in part, on how they positioned themselves vis-à-vis the two global hegemons, the United States and the Soviet Union. In time, liberal nationalism and socialism both came to be defined as foreign ideologies, particularly when their adoption by ruling regimes seemed to have little or no positive impact on the daily lives of the masses. From the 1960s, the rhetoric of Pan-Arabism, often with strong socialist overtones, rang hollow, particularly in the wake of 1967 and the Arab defeat at the hands of Israel. For many it was the blind adoption of, or even co-option by, Western methods and politics by these governments that were understood to be the source of their inefficacy and rising internal socioeconomic disparities. It is in this context that we have to understand how inspirational Iran's Islamic revolution might have first appeared to many in the developing world. It appeared to represent a success story of a country "opting out" of the geopolitics of superpower patronage in the name of a wholly different and non-Western order.

Other instances of Islamism, however, were directly implicated in these Cold War machinations. The Soviet invasion of Afghanistan in late 1979 led to the emergence of an Islamic resistance in the form of the Afghan Mujahideen that was enthusiastically supported by the United States. Tribally organized resistance fighters, mobilizing under the banner of Islam, fought an eight-year war of attrition with the far better armed and equipped military superpower that was the USSR and seemingly emerged victorious when Moscow withdrew its troops in 1989. This set the stage, however, for a civil war between regional warlords in Afghanistan (see Chapter 6) and the emergence of a newly confident form of transnational jihadism which took as its goal the elimination of infidel powers worldwide (see Chapter 7). The end of the Cold War, in turn, prompted the emergence of Muslim politics in areas where Islam had been strongly suppressed for generations. In the new Muslim-majority states of the former Soviet Union, for example, Islam was suddenly available as a political vocabulary and various social forces—governments, oppositions, and regional militias alike—sought to mobilize in its name (see "Central Asia: 'Official Islam' and its many alternatives" in Chapter 8). Likewise, Muslim countries outside the immediate region, but also some close Muslims neighbors (ethnically and geographically) sought to exert new influence in Central Asia in part through religion.

Other forms of Islamism during this period had more to do with regional politics, civil wars, and territorial conflicts. The emergence of groups such as Hizbullah and AMAL in the 1980s in the context of the Lebanese Civil War is a good case in point, as is the establishment of HAMAS at the outset of the first *intifada* ("uprising") in the Palestinian territories in 1987. Both are examples of groups that emerged during times of conflict to combat the presence of foreign armies through militant means while simultaneously mobilizing popular support and providing social services to disenfranchised populations (the Shi'a of Lebanon and Palestinians in the Occupied Territories, respectively). As we will see, both have also since gone on to play an active role in their country's political process and even to form governments (see Chapter 6). In other contexts the rise of Islamism has been strongly linked to internal ethno-religious cleavages and regionalism. This is how we can best understand Sudan's self-designation as an Islamic state since 1989 (see "Sudan: Hassan al-Turabi and the Islamic state" in Chapter 5) and also the declaration of Islamic law in certain states of Nigeria in 2000 (see "Nigeria: Shari'a law and the politics of federalism" in Chapter 4).

Perhaps most interesting to observe, however, have been those cases where Islamist movements have entered the political process and sought to contest elections as political parties. The participation of Islamists in elections has been one of the lynchpin issues within the debate over Islam and politics. Some, claiming that Islamists represent a "one man, one vote, one time" approach, argue that any Islamist party elected to power would seek to eradicate the democratic system through which they came into office so as to ensure that they cannot be voted out. Others argue that Islamist parties will see it as serving their long-term interests to adhere to the norms of pluralistic, participatory politics, citing various instances where Islamist parties have entered and exited legislative bodies as the results of elections demand.[39] There is also an ongoing debate, as we will see in the next chapter, as to the very nature of contemporary Islamist movements and their political goals. Part of the problem, of course, is that there is no real precedent that allows us to know what happens when an Islamist party comes to power under relatively normal circumstances since this has never happened—or, at least, never been allowed to happen. In some cases, such as the MTI/Nahda party in Tunisia or the Hizb al-Wasat (see Chapter 4) in Egypt, the government has denied political party status to Islamist groups who seek to enter the political process. In the case of the Refah Party in Turkey (see Chapter 4)—which was briefly in power as part of a coalition government—extra-political forces (in this case the military and the Kemalist courts) have severely circumscribed their latitude of action. The 2006 election of HAMAS to lead the Palestinian Authority is a difficult case to assess given that it occurred in the context of ongoing political occupation and conflict and without the existence of a meaningful state.

The closest we have come to an Islamist party achieving state power through legitimate means and under relatively normal political conditions is Algeria in late 1991 when the Islamic Salvation Front (FIS—"Front Islamique du Salut") contested and won the national elections. With FIS poised to set up a new government, the Algerian military stepped in to annul the results of the elections, impose martial law and ban the FIS from further political activity—setting off an eight-year period of near civil war and untold loss of life (see "Algeria: The Islamist victory that almost was" after this chapter). While the Algerian test case of Islamism in power never came to pass, it prompted an important debate about the implications of Islamist groups entering the political process. Some have pointed to this example as evidence in support of the "repression leads to radicalization" thesis. It is clear that the Algerian example points ahead to a key issue we will engage in considerable detail in the next chapter: the question of where and how Islamist groups have sought to enter the political process and the implications and effects of their doing so on the orientation, agenda and modes of political activism employed by the movements.

Algeria: the Islamist victory that almost was

Algeria is crucially important to the study of Muslim politics and Islamism in several respects. First, the Algerian national elections of late 1991 represented the first time an Islamist party had ever been on the verge of being brought into government through a popular ballot. Had the FIS been allowed to come to power, it would have provided us with a unique opportunity to see what government by Islamists looks like in practice. Second, the Algerian Islamic movement in the form of the FIS was itself a study in the diversity of Islamism and Islamist agendas. Under the Front's umbrella was to be found at least two quite distinct factions, one whose sociopolitical vision was broadly in line with that of the Egyptian MB during the time it sought to work within the framework of the Egyptian system, and another with strongly militant tendencies that questioned the legitimacy of the existing Algerian political order. Finally, the violence and instability that engulfed Algeria in the 1990s provided several catalyzing forces—in the form of movements, ideologues, and experiential knowledge—that would later become crucially important to the global jihadist movement (see Chapter 7).

Algeria gained its independence in 1962 after a long war that gradually wore down the political will of its former colonial power, France. Religion figured as a marker of national identity during this conflict through, for example, the use by pro-independence forces of the slogan *Algérie musulmane* ("Algeria for the Muslims") rather than an ethnolinguistic referent. Behind this rhetoric, however, lay a cultural rift that soon emerged as a defining feature of Algerian politics once the country gained its independence. In broad terms, this cleavage took the form of tensions that emerged between a French-speaking political and economic urban elite and the rural masses, generally oriented towards identity formations emphasizing Arab linguistic, cultural and religious heritage. Aside from the obvious socioeconomic divide represented by this bifurcation, there was a further ideological aspect to bear in mind here in that Algeria's French speakers had a greater tendency to gravitate towards forms of leftist, that is, secular, thought.

Economic tensions in the late 1980s (tied to a sharp decline in oil prices) led to widespread protests against unemployment, government corruption, and shortages of housing and foodstuffs. It is this context that gave rise to the FIS as a political movement. A FIS precursor can be found in the Al-Qiyam Society, a cultural heritage organization founded in the late 1960s by a group of highly educated Algerians seeking to preserve Arabo-Islamic heritage in the face of what they perceived as an increasingly dominant Francophone trend. The early FIS drew from this movement, and built up its influence via voluntary associations, mosque networks, schools, and factory floors. While the Francophone-Arabophone divide was certainly one factor driving the formation of the Islamist movement, membership in the latter did not so easily split along such simplistic cultural lines. The failure of the political left in Algeria to provide socialist solutions to encroaching impoverishment further emboldened the Islamists and swelled their ranks. While the ruling Front de la Liberation National (FLN) sought to introduce liberalizing reforms as an emergency measure, this gesture turned out to be much too little, far too late.

Rather than a single, unified political party, the FIS designation actually referred to something that was more of an "umbrella" organization under which were to be found two quite distinctive factions. The first of these, led by Abbasi Madani (b. 1931) was strongly influenced by the basic model of the MB. It opposed the secularizing trend and sought to establish a basis in public life and law for Islamic norms and legal codes. The second faction, around the younger Ali Belhadj (b. 1956), represented a more confrontational and even militant tendency, seeking to fundamentally reshape the Algerian political order along Islamic lines. The latter group drew energy from the support of Algerian veterans of the Afghan war against the Soviet occupation (see Chapter 7). While these two groups within the FIS were clearly at odds in terms of their core agenda and methods, the advantages of working together during the early years of the Islamist opposition were sufficient to achieve minimal cohesion within the movement.

The FIS had its first electoral venture in the summer of 1990, when it participated in municipal elections just a year after being formed. Its sweeping victory prompted the government, led by the secular-nationalist FLN, to crack down on the movement, arresting key figures, cutting off its funding, redrawing electoral districts to the disadvantage of the Islamists, and postponing parliamentary elections in the face of what was perceived as a popular tide of Islamist support. Despite these blocking maneuvers, the FIS still fared relatively well once national elections finally took place in late 1991. With the Islamists poised to win a parliamentary majority in the second round of voting scheduled for early 1992, the Algerian military intervened in January of that year to annul the elections, impose martial law, and ban the FIS as a political party.

Once it was declared illegal and driven underground, the FIS "coalition" splintered into its constituent pieces. With Madani and Belhadj both in prison, followers of the latter took the opportunity of the military intervention to argue that it was impossible to pursue their aims via the political process. This faction split from the main movement to form the Armed Islamic Group (GIA)—which soon subdivided further along class lines—and proceeded to commence a militant campaign against the Algerian state and even certain civilian targets (journalists, etc.) that it regarded as agents of the secular order. During much of the 1990s, Algeria was in a state of virtual civil war, with casualty levels topping 100,000. Most of the violence in this conflict can be attributed to the GIA and other, sometimes even more militant offshoots. Some of the killing, however, was also linked to groups of paramilitary special forces commonly known as the *eradicateurs*, accused of carrying out attacks on various population centers and then trying to pass them off as the work of the radical Islamists.

Some semblance of order began to return to Algeria from the time of the 1997 elections and a simultaneous ceasefire agreement. The shift towards reconciliation served to further marginalize the radical Islamist factions, who refused to participate in this process. The most extreme among these, the Salafist Group for Preaching and Combat (GSPC) began to form connections with the global jihadist movement, while the capacity of the GIA to wage armed conflict quickly began to dwindle after the turn of the millennium. Under the leadership of Abdelaziz Bouteflika, a veteran politician with roots in the FLN, Algeria worked toward the nearly unanimous popular adoption of a Charter for National Peace and Reconciliation, whose provisions became law in 2006.

4   Islam in the system: the evolution of Islamism as political strategy

In the previous chapter we examined the process of state formation in the Muslim world and the emergence of Islamism as an intellectual and political movement in response to the perceived Westernization of modern regimes and their failure to deliver on the promises of modernization. Through the ideas and work of figures such as Hassan al-Banna, Abu'l-A'la Mawdudi and Sayyid Qutb, we came to understand how Islamism also represented a new approach to the creation of a "living Islam" as lay activists and intellectuals rather than classically trained ulama emerged as the vanguard class of public religiosity understood as the pursuit of a "true" Islamic social and political order. National-secular regimes were perceived as overly secular and concerned primarily with furthering the interests of existing political elites. Likewise, the religious scholars had either been co-opted by the state, or had their heads buried in medieval texts—rendering them, in both cases, ineffectual in terms of pursuing meaningful social transformation along Islamic lines.

The following chapter will look more closely at the evolution of Islamism as a political strategy from, roughly, the 1960s up to the present day. Our main focus will be on the question of how the shifting terrain of internal politics and external geopolitics has impacted how groups pursue social and political activity in the name of Islam. In particular, we will pick up a theme first mentioned in Chapter 1—that of globalization—and try to come to some better understanding of how this disparate set of macro level forces has reconfigured the nature of Islamism over several decades. As will quickly become clear, it is impossible to read Islamism as an atavistic response to modernization that seeks a wholesale return to pre-modern Islamic society. Islamism as a political strategy, we will argue, is thoroughly modern in terms of its ideology and organization; embraces many of the core precepts of modernity; and, in strategic terms, only makes sense as an approach to politics under conditions of political modernity. In other words, modernity constitutes the very preconditions for the emergence of Islamism as a distinct political strategy. As globalization—as a particular stage in the evolution of the modern political economy—has systematically reached into Muslim societies and restructured social life, so has Islamism itself changed with the times.

This chapter will begin by providing a more thorough analysis of the political sociology of classic Islamism as represented by groups such as the Muslim Brotherhood (MB). We will look in greater detail at their bases of social support and try to connect the social location of Islamism with prevailing political economies within certain key states in the Muslim world. Next we will examine the emergence of a new generation of pragmatic Islamists, sometime referred to as "New Islamists" or moderate Islamists, who have sought to pursue religiously oriented political change through participation in elections and by entering into broad coalitions with non-Islamist groups and parties similarly committed to overthrowing authoritarian regimes. We will then look briefly at an emerging trend identified by several observers that sometimes goes by the name of "Muslim democracy." This refers to groups that do not seek to directly institute a political order defined by religion (e.g. through the introduction of shari'ah laws), but which instead works towards secular and pluralistic goals in cooperation with a wide variety of political groups while taking their general moral cues from religious norms. The chapter then goes on to illustrate how these different strategies have evolved in different settings by presenting a series of case studies. First, we will look at how Egypt's MB, formally banned as a political party for decades, has changed its strategy in recent years in response to new political realities and the rise of a new generation of would-be activists. The emergence of the Hizb al-Wasat ("Party of the Center") as an offshoot of the Brotherhood will help us to better understand this generational shift. We move on to the case of Turkey to examine the shift from classic Islamism as defined by parties such as Necmettin Erbakan's Refah (Welfare) Party to the apparent "Muslim democracy" approach of the current ruling AK Party—all of this within the context of a political order defined by the highly secular ideology of Kemalism as enforced by a strong military. In Jordan, finally, we will look at the case of a MB-affiliated party, the Islamic Action Front (IAF), participating in national elections and pursuing a diverse and pragmatic political platform partly defined in response to a rapidly changing political field.

The shifting social profile of Islamism

We will begin with a point made several times in the previous chapter about the social profile of those drawn to Islamist movements such as the MB. We noted that Islamism was neither primarily a rural phenomenon nor were its main activists and advocates to be found among the uneducated poor. Those active within the Brotherhood have traditionally been urban-based, educated in secular institutions, and often employed within modern professional fields such as medicine, engineering, or government bureaucracy. But why should this social group be drawn to a political movement defined in religious terms? In order to understand this seeming incongruence, we need to delve somewhat deeper into the nature of the political economy in the

Arab world during the 1960s and 70s and its interaction with shifting conceptions of Arab and Muslim identity.

The political sociology of classic Islamism

Within a generation of the emergence of modern states in much of the Muslim world, and particularly in the Middle East, it had become clear that the promises of secular nationalism (independence, prosperity, and a proud national or even Pan-Arab identity) were unlikely to become fulfilled. While no longer directly occupied by foreign colonizing powers, it appeared to most Arabs that much of their fate was still decided by the machinations of superpower geopolitics and the intricacies of the Cold War. The failure of Egypt's experimental union with Syria between 1958 and 1962, the defeat of Arab armies by Israel in 1967, and the opening up of the Egyptian economy to world markets during the "Open Door" policy under Sadat all provided Arabs with a sense of growing inefficacy over their political fate. In terms of local politics, it also became clear quite quickly that behind the façade of modern republican states lay a political system still governed by all manner of patronage ties, clan and tribal allegiances, and an alliance between political and economic elites intent on maintaining their grip on power at any costs.

The various programs and schemes through which the government initially sought to provide some form of participation for the newly educated masses very quickly came to be out of synch with the pace of societal development. So, for example, while universities were churning out thousands of graduates in modern fields such as engineering, chemistry, and medicine, there were not enough job opportunities to employ this aspiring middle class. For many, the government bureaucracy became the standard fallback when no other job was available, but even the ranks of the technocrats were soon swollen to a point where the government could no longer take on any new employees. The few and much-coveted positions available within the private sector tended to be reserved for those elites whose patronage propped up the state. Far from opening up new paths for participation and social mobility, the new system seemed to have done no more than to re-entrench existing patterns of social influence behind a new "modern" façade. In many cases the gap between rich and poor actually widened, with meaningful political enfranchisement completely nonexistent outside the few perks offered to members of pro-regime parties. What we witnessed during this period was a classic case of "relative deprivation" caused by rapidly rising economic and political expectations that were not being met by material conditions.[1] While relatively well off compared to those living in the abject poverty of rural areas, the members of this aspiring middle class had come to calibrate its social identity in relation to those of the political elite. By moving to the city and seeking out education they had expected to benefit from the modernizing economy. Alienated from its affluence and unable to gain real access to positions of power, this modernizing generation soon began to explore other vectors and discourses of social action. A number of political sociologists have shown how volatile and prone to various forms of "contentious politics" and the rise of oppositional social movements this kind of environment can be.[2]

We have already noted, but it is worth saying a few more words about the primarily urban nature of modern Islamism. Olivier Roy has written on the importance of the reconfiguration of urban space for the organization and mobilization of Islamist sentiment.[3] As rural families flocked to rapidly expanding cities in the 1950s and 60s, the very landscape of urban space in the Middle East was transformed. Sprawling suburbs and peri-urban zones sprang up around the traditional centers of cities—spaces the state found increasingly difficult to control and where other modern forms of social organization (workers groups, trade unions) also found little purchase due to the absence of regular employment.[4] The population of these new urban areas was composed of a mixture of the semi-enfranchised, such as low-level bureaucrats who would commute to government offices while also holding down part-time jobs at night, but also a new younger generation of the wholly disenfranchised. This is the generation that was born in the city and which, unlike their parents, were unable to gain entrance to university or saw it as pointless to do so given the lack of job prospects afterwards. The advent of Sadat's Open Door (infitah) policies of 1970s disproportionately subjected the lower middle classes to the disruptive effects of exposure to free markets and neoliberal reform—further exacerbating among this group the alienating effects of modernization described above.

It was these spaces and this generation that the Islamists made their own from the late 1960s. With Arab socialism revealed as a chimera, and the advent of an identity crisis prompted by events such as the massive Arab defeat and loss of huge territories including Jerusalem during the Arab-Israeli war of 1967, the situation was ripe for a new ideological basis for sociopolitical mobilization to emerge. This space was increasingly filled by the Islamists when support for Pan-Arabism and Marxism began to sharply decline. The attraction of Islamism as an ideology can be understood in roughly the following terms: modernity, in the form of techno-scientific knowledge, industrialization, and urbanization, is a positive force that should be embraced. Political and economic elites—old and new—had, however, become so thoroughly corrupted and seduced by the excesses of Westernization that they could no longer be trusted to pursue the interests of the nation as a whole. The pervasive spread of Western modes of consumption and the "worship" of status symbols (jeans, automobiles, girl-friends/boyfriends) was akin to a new form of shirk ("idolatry"). The alternative, then, was to turn away from Western modernity and internalize instead the idea that "Islam is the solution"—a standard slogan of the MB. According to this approach, the technical trappings of modernity should be maintained (e.g. science, industry, techniques of management, and social organization) but within an identity and normative framework that took Islam as the exclusive source of all morality. As Roy saw it, this was about turning to the values of Islam and refiguring them not as symbols of backwardness, but rather as a new source of dignity.[5] The West may have science and capitalism, but Islam possesses the far more important and powerful force of morality. Groups did different things with, and mobilized around, this vision in different ways. The MB's "Islam is the solution," combining modernity and piety, represented the most pervasive form of mainstream Islamism. Others took the logic to a more radical extreme. Radical groups such as Takfir w'al-Hijra sought to separate from what they saw as a society irreparably corrupted and—taking a cue from Sayyid Qutb—mired in un-Islamic ignorance (jahiliyya) so as to work for the eradication of the prevailing order, through jihad if necessary.

The urban masses in cities such as Cairo developed new forms of social organization that, for the greater part, escaped most attempts at state regulation. Informal networks of voluntary associations and neighborhood groups became the new norm. If the state and the "modern economy" could not provide, then neighborhoods and urban quarters would become largely self sufficient, constructing their own informal sector economies to trade goods and services and creating alternative "avenues of participation," to use Diane Singerman's language.[6] The MB proved masterful at socializing these new spaces, building strong relationships with various local associations and defining their normative essence in terms of an Islamic framework. Piety and mutual welfare became wholly intertwined. In sociological terms, we can understand the networks and conduits of Islamist activism as crucial sites for the production of what scholars such as Pierre Bourdieu has called "social capital."[7] Variously defined in the literature, the notion of social capital here refers to the value gained (in terms of enhanced personal capacity, pluralized opportunity structures and so forth) from membership and participation in social networks characterized by mutual trust, reciprocity, and a shared normative framework. Urban clubs, reading rooms, and night classes became spaces in which one could pursue self-betterment, but the Brotherhood, through its neighborhood cell structure (the so-called "family" system) also made sure these were also spaces of da'wa and tarbiya—that is, religious education and the propagation of sacred consciousness. Social mobility and piety were constructed as mutually constitutive. One naturally flowed from the other. And with the state almost wholly absent from these spaces, the Islamists had no meaningful competitors.

What were the political implications of this trend? We will remember that in the paradigmatic case of popular Islamist mobilization, that of the MB in Egypt, the group remained formally banned as a political party since the mid-1950s. While the Brotherhood enjoyed a brief upswing in its fortunes under Sadat (see Chapter 3), it was still not able to openly and independently contest elections. As we will see, this political reality has led the Brotherhood in Egypt to shift its political strategy considerably over the past two decades, exploring a wide range of alternative routes to political influence and also new alliances—resembling, in many ways, the "new Islamism" or second generation Islamism described below. Perhaps the best case we have to look at in terms of understanding Islamism as a political strategy is that of Algeria (see "Algeria: The Islamist victory that almost was" after Chapter 3). The Front Islamique du Salut (FIS; "Islamic Salvation Front"), responding to a growing sense of disenfranchisement among Algeria's Arab-oriented masses (urban and rural based), leveraged their support within local neighborhoods and associations into sweeping electoral success at the municipal level. When poised to win national elections in 1991 and form the region's first Islamist government, however, the military stepped in to prevent this from happening. When their counterparts in neighboring Tunisia, the Mouvement de Tendance Islamique (MTI)—which changed its name in the early 90s to Al-Nahda ("Renaissance") to avoid direct reference to Islam—sought to enter politics directly, the highly secular regime of Zein Abedine Ben Ali outlawed the party and its leadership went into exile abroad.

The standard complaint leveled against Islamist parties by incumbent regimes and external stakeholders is that their participation in democratic processes is purely instrumental. It is often said that their ostensible embrace of individual political rights—the "one citizen, one vote" principle—should actually be understood as "one citizen, one vote, one time"— implying that once in power they would quickly work to eradicate democracy and political pluralism, institute shari'ah, and structure the political process such that they could never be removed from office by a popular plebiscite. In other words, those wary of political participation by Islamists, are seeking to characterize Islamism as inherently autocratic and anti-democratic. Despite assurances by most Islamists that they would govern according to constitutional norms and leave government if and when they were voted out, the Muslim world has yet to experience elected Islamist governance in a nation-state setting. How do we assess these claims and counterclaims? To what extent is anti-Islamist alarmism simply a strategy by various regimes, many highly authoritarian themselves, to raise suspicions about a social force by which they feel threatened? On the other hand, to what extent is it possible to embrace the democratic rhetoric of Islamist movements when the specifics of their stated intention to introduce shari'ah remain vague and the limits of their political pluralism (regarding women, non-Muslims, and secular parties) equally ambiguous?[8]

The next generation of "new Islamists" and "Muslim democrats"

The persistent persecution of conventional Islamist parties along with certain demographic changes within the Islamists' traditional bases of social support, have led some Islamist groups from the mid-1990s onwards to pursue new political strategies. Observers have variously described this

Table 4.1 Islamists in legislative elections (1990–2006) for selected countries

Country	Election year	Party/movement	Results	
			Seats won	Total seats in assembly
Algeria	2002	MSP	38	360
		IRM	1	
	1997	MSP	69	231
		IRM	341	
	1991	FIS	188[a]	231
Egypt	2005	Muslim Brotherhood[b]	88	444
	2000		17	444
	1995[c]		1	444
Jordan	2003	IAF	17	104
	1997[d]		–	–
	1993		16	80
Lebanon	2005	Hizbullah	14	128
		AMAL	15	
	2000	Hizbullah	8	128
		AMAL	19	
	1996	Hizbullah	9	128
		AMAL	13	
	1992	Hizbullah	12	128
		AMAL	15	
Malaysia	2004	PAS/PMIP	7	219
	1999		27	219
	1995		7	219
	1990		7	219
Morocco	2002	PJD	42	325
Pakistan	2002	MMA	53	242
	1997	JUI[e]	2	237
	1993	JI	3[f]	237
Palestine	2006	HAMAS	74	132
Turkey	2002	AKP[h]	363	550
	1999	Fazilet[i]	111	550
	1995	Refah	158[h]	550
	1991	Refah	62	550

Notes: a. Algerian military annulled election results. b. The Muslim Brotherhood is banned as a political party in Egypt. Islamist candidates run as independents, although their affiliations are widely known. c. Muslim Brotherhood candidates faced mass arrests and intimidation in the run-up to the 1995 election. d. The Islamic Action Front boycotted the 1997 elections. e. JI boycotted the 1997 elections; shown instead are the election results for the JUI, a longtime political ally of the Jamaat. f. In 1993, JI participated in an alliance with the socialist PPP. g. AKP is not a conventional Islamist party, but much of its leadership and membership base is drawn from Fazilet and Refah. h. Fazilet is the reconstituted Refah party (see Note i.) i. Refah formed a coalition government but was forced out by the military in 1997.

group as "New Islamists"[9] or "moderate Islamists,"[10] but the analysis of
their emergence is essentially the same. Throughout the 1980s and 90s, several regimes in the Muslim world had developed into what Daniel Brumberg calls "liberalized autocracies."[11] Such governments hold regular
elections, tend to allow some semblance of multi-party pluralism, profess
support for global human rights norms, and enthusiastically embrace for-
eign-funded anti-corruption and democracy capacity-building programs. All
the while, however, these processes are carefully stage-managed in a "theater
of democratization" to give the impression of far more power-sharing and
pluralism than actually exists.[12] While various parties may be able to gain
access to state-controlled legislative bodies and to express their views
through relatively open medias, the regime makes sure that they are never
actually able to become meaningful political threats.[13]

The "new Islamists" are essentially those groups that have chosen to
participate in this system in the hope of one day bringing about meaningful
change. While some of these groups have their origins, and in some cases
are still closely affiliated with, classic Islamist parties as described above, the
shakers and movers behind this new ethos of active participation tend to be
of the younger generation. As a generation that grew up during the height
of the ban on Islamist political participation, and with a climate of relatively authoritarian decision-making within Islamist movements themselves,
these younger Islamists grew impatient at their elders' skepticism about
open political participation and began to pursue new strategies. Not only
did they express a new willingness to compete as regular political parties on
the same terms as other political groups, but they also expressed a preference for more participatory deliberations within the movement as a
whole—in contrast to the intensely hierarchical model that characterized
first generation Islamist movements.[14] While their ultimate aims are still
defined in terms of classic Islamism, their "goal horizons"—and certainly
their political methodology—have shifted somewhat. First, we might say
that this shift represents a new embrace of political gradualism over rapid
political reform. Where first generation Islamists sought political power to
reform the social order along Islamic lines, the new Islamists hold out a
longer-term vision for reform. They are more content to contest elections,
take up whatever seats or offices they may win and use their period of
incumbency to gradually introduce elements of the Islamist platform—only
to leave power when voted out and prepare to campaign again. The hope is
that through this approach they will be able to introduce piecemeal reforms
and gradually build up support, enabling the party to enjoy longer and
more frequent tenures in legislatures and governments.

The adoption of the "new Islamist" participatory approach has also
meant a shift in political platforms and electoral strategy. Most of these
groups now emphasize the importance of concepts such as democracy,
human rights, and rule of law far more than their first generation forebears.[15] It has also, at times, meant entering into alliances and coalitions

with non-Islamist parties similarly committed to democratic reform. Where first generation Islamists would have seen such cooperation as politically impossible, the new Islamists have embraced a pragmatic approach which understands it as more important to be actively shaping the campaign for reform, rather than sitting on the sidelines. So although it may at times require certain compromises, the new Islamists have actively sought part-nerships not only with other religiously based groups, but even secular and leftist alliances. They tend to place less emphasis on, or even to drop alto-gether, the rhetoric of shari'ah. Sometimes they will emphasize the values they see accruing from shari'ah (e.g. social justice, individual rights) rather than the goal of shari'ah itself. Even though much of their platform seems to be compatible with, or even to lead towards, a largely secular order, they still realize that this is a lightning rod term and would prefer to speak in terms of political pluralism or civility.[16]

So who are these new Islamists, and how to they relate to other conven-tional Islamist parties? Several of them, such as Egypt's Hizb al-Wasat and the IAF in Jordan will be profiled in greater detail below. The Wasat party broke away from the MB in order to pursue a less narrowly defined and rigid form of Islamism. Their centrist approach (*wasat* meaning "center" in Arabic) reaches out to non-Muslim groups and emphasizes the socially mobile and economically modernist dimension of Islam over literal adher-ence to the shari'ah. In some regards, the Wasat party actually straddles the spectrum between new Islamism and the "Muslim democrat" approach outlined below. The Wasat, which still has not managed to gain official recognition from the government as a political party, counts a number of Coptic Christians within its guiding council, and emphasizes the importance of cross-sectarian values and interests. The MB, with its overtly religious identity, has found itself far more constrained in terms of being able to reach out to non-Muslims. This does not mean, however, that the central Brotherhood movement has been untouched by this second generation. As we will see below, it is possible to detect signs of a generational split even within the core of the MB structure. Hizb al-Wasat's name has sometimes been applied generically to the "new Islamist" movement as a whole. Var-iants of the *Wasatiyya* ("Centrist") approach can also be found in groups such as the IAF, the Justice and Development Party (PJD) in Morocco, and the Yemeni Reformist Union. Some of these groups were founded wholly independent of any existing social movements whereas others, such as the IAF in Jordan, have ties to local branches of the MB but have established themselves as independent political entities in order to shed some of the first generation baggage.[17]

Where some new Islamist groups have encountered difficulties—such as those of the Hizb al-Wasat's mentioned above—others have enjoyed con-siderable electoral success. Morocco's PJD, which in some respects also resembles the Muslim democracy approach detailed below, recently tripled its representation in Parliament (see "Morocco: Islamism in the shadow of the palace" after this chapter). In 2003, the IAF—more clearly identifiable with the MB tendency—won nearly a quarter of all seats in parliament. That same year the Yemeni Reformist Union won a quarter of the popular vote and a sixth of the legislative positions. Assessments as to the significance of the new Islamist movement vary considerably. Some see it as an approach that will force Islamists to "normalize" their political platforms and bring them closer in tune with emerging pluralist norms in order to gain a seat at the electoral table. They emphasize the generational split between old and new Islamists as something genuine and substantive, seeing in the younger generation a tendency to interpret Islamism in a more inclusive manner. Others continue to harbor fears about instrumentalism, fearing that the Islamists' apparent newly found willingness to cooperate with non-Islamists is nothing other than a convenient route to power. So far there is little evidence to support this latter view, but it will take some time for the full political implications of this shift to become manifest.

Another and even more recent political current that some authors have identified in the Muslim world is one that commonly goes under the rubric of "Muslim Democracy."[18] Muslim democrats are commonly compared to the "Christian democratic" parties that emerged in Europe from the late nineteenth century. Described by one prominent theorist as "Islamic-oriented (but not Islamist),"[19] the Muslim democracy movement is typified by several parties whose social base tends to be religiously conservative and to derive their political values from religion, but without seeking to reform the political order in terms of Islam. Turkey's Justice and Development Party (AKP) has been cited as perhaps the clearest example of a Muslim democratic party, but one also finds similar groups in countries such as Indonesia and Pakistan. Vali Nasr characterizes the approach thusly:

> Muslim democrats view political life with a pragmatic eye. They reject or at least discount the classic Islamist claim that Islam commands the pursuit of a shari'ah state, and their main goal tends to be the more mundane one of crafting viable electoral platforms and stable governing coalitions to serve individual and collective interests—Islamic as well as secular—within a democratic arena whose bounds they respect, win or lose.[20]

It may seem difficult, based on this description, to differentiate Muslim democrats from some of the new Islamist groups described above. Indeed, there are sometimes significant areas of overlap between the two. Likewise, and looking towards the more secular side of the spectrum, it is difficult to differentiate Muslim democrats from wholly secular political parties who happen to represent somewhat rightist or conservative values. In the first instance, perhaps the best way of telling Muslim democrats apart from Islamists relates to the relative importance of shari'ah in the political platform and rhetoric of the two groups. Even second generation Islamists who do not make much of religious law in their public profile will still frame their overall platform in terms of closer adherence to the shari'ah. "Muslim Democracts, by contrast," writes Nasr, "do not seek to enshrine Islam in politics."[21] As regards the differentiation of Muslim democrats from other parties of the right, perhaps the best way to do this is to look to the social bases of membership, recruitment, and mobilization. The AKP in Turkey, for example, has a number of active members who joined the group from the remnants of the more conventionally Islamist Refah party, and also draws heavily on the Sufi-oriented Nurçu movement in Turkey.

Nasr draws our attention to several distinct features of the Muslim Democracy approach. First of all, he notes that unlike classic Islamism, which has a rich intellectual tradition, Muslim democracy looks more like an electoral strategy rather than an ideology. This speaks to the pragmatic nature of the approach, and the fact that its fortunes are subject to the exigencies of interest group politics rather than theoretical prescriptions. While certainly leveraging the increase in public religiosity or religious consciousness found today in many parts of the Muslim world, Muslim Democracy seeks to channel this energy into support for a political platform that emphasizes prosperity and economic growth. It is not then surprising, as Nasr notes, that these movements tend to be stronger in contexts characterized by a strong and economically significantly private sector. A pluralistic political field is also seen as likely to push religiously oriented groups towards centrist politics, a fact noted by both Brumberg and Nasr. The latter also emphasizes the important role of the military in pushing together Islamists and non-Islamists who share common concerns about the army's threat to democracy—something we can see in both Turkey and Pakistan, where in each country the military has intervened on more than one occasion in the name of securing the state against forces that threaten public order.

In assessing the prospects of Muslim Democrats, Daniel Brumberg points out that the political conditions in those countries where they have seen some success, such as Turkey and Indonesia, are quite unique and difficult to replicate in the wider Muslim—and particularly Arab—world. Picking up on Nasr's point regarding the importance of both a vibrant private sector business class and a relatively pluralistic political field, he suggests that Morocco might be the one country in the Middle East in which Muslim Democrats could succeed.[22] We have already noted the resemblance between the PJD in that country and Turkey's Justice and Development Party—not only in name, but also in terms of their electoral strategy and the core constituency targeted in their platforms. In summarizing this approach, let us turn again to Vali Nasr:

> The rise of Muslim Democracy suggests that the values of Muslims—which are not to be confused with the demands of Islamists—can interact with practical election strategies to play the main role in shap-

ing political ideas and driving voter behavior. In the end, Muslim Democracy represents the triumph of practice over theory, and perhaps of the political over the Islamic. The future of Muslim politics is likely to belong to those who can speak to Muslim values and ethics, but within the framework of political platforms fit to thrive in democratic settings.[23]

Another analytical value-added that hence accrues from an emphasis on Muslim Democracy is the way it leads us to pay attention to actors in Muslim contexts whose preferences, values, and political behavior derive at least in part from their religion, but who do not view Islamist parties as the only ballot choice permitting the expression of that worldview.

Perhaps the best way to understand the complicated contrasts, points of convergence, and interrelationship between the various approaches to religious politics outlined above—classic Islamism, the new Islamism, and Muslim Democracy—would be to examine their evolution and staging in several country-specific settings. So we will move on now to case studies of Egypt, Jordan, and Turkey in order to more fully explore and contextualize these various shifts in Islamist political strategy. An accompanying textbox analysis of Indonesia will provide us with some points of comparison from a large and important Muslim country outside the Middle East.

Egypt: from the MB to "new Islamists"

The MB in Egypt is synonymous with the modern Islamist movement. Since its founding in 1928, the Brotherhood has provided both the intellectual foundations and the core methodology for many similar groups across the Muslim world. As we saw in Chapter 3, the MB has gone through several phases, each characterized by varying levels of social, political, and even militant activism—and often as a function of its continually changing relationship with the Egyptian state during a turbulent period in that country's history. After several decades underground, the Brotherhood gradually re-entered public life from the mid-1970s and even electoral politics. Banned from forming a political party, the MB instead occupied a whole host of civil and associational spaces at the level of society. Having socialized a well-educated and socially mobile generation of Egyptians in the ways of the Islamist current (*al-tayar al-islami*), the coming of age of this generation within the movement has led it to begin developing its own distinct political vision and, moreover, one that resonates with wider intellectual currents also circulating in Islamic circles. In this section we will trace the emergence of the Wasatiyya (Centrist) trend in Islamic thought and its political manifestation in the form of the Hizb al-Wasat party. We will begin by describing how, from the 1970s onwards, the MB progressively socialized almost every available voluntary and associational space in Egypt, creating significant networks of social influence that granted considerable power despite the limitations placed on them in the formal political sphere. We will then review the relationship between the Islamist movement and the Egyptian state under Hosni Mubarak up until the mid-1990s, focusing on the shift from a policy of limited engagement on the part of the state in the 1980s, to an all out offensive against the Islamists in the following decade. It is at this point that we will take up the theme of the generational divide and the emergence of the Wasatiyya movement, both intellectually and politically. We conclude with the Brotherhood's phenomenal electoral successes at the beginning of the twenty-first century and offer some reflections as to the disparate trends evolving within the movement.

Our coverage of Egypt in Chapter 3 briefly touched on the Sadat and Mubarak presidencies. We will recall that Anwar al-Sadat inherited the presidency from the iconic Gamal Abdel Nasser upon the latter's death in 1970. Rather than simply emulating the policies of his predecessor, Sadat undertook a broad realignment of Egypt's international and domestic posture. More specifically, the Open Door, or *infitah*, policies sought to pursue a course of greater economic liberalization and to open Egypt up to world markets. Domestically, Sadat allowed space for a "rehabilitated" MB—banned since the 1950s—to come back into Egyptian life. After formally renouncing violence in the 1970s, many regard the Brotherhood as having been co-opted by Sadat's regime. This led to factionalization within the Islamist movement when several radical splinter groups, rejecting what they saw as the MB's accommodationist stance, emerged to pursue more militant forms of activism. This culminated in the assassination of Anwar al-Sadat in 1981 after he signed a peace agreement with Israel. Sadat was succeeded by his vice president, Hosni Mubarak, who has continued to rule without appointing a vice president, or rescinding the "state of emergency" declared at the time of Sadat's death that, under the constitution, grants him extended executive powers. Mubarak's party political instrument, the National Democratic Party (NDP), is a non-ideological group whose sole purpose is to retain power. In this regard the NDP has generally had to rely on co-opting various social forces and ideas in order to lend it vision and legitimacy.

The Islamization of the social sphere

The growth of the Islamist presence within civil society and associational life needs to be understood against the backdrop of the economic reform process that began in Egypt under Sadat in the 1970s, and continued apace once Mubarak was in office. Its chief goal was to dismantle the Nasserist welfare state where the public sector had been the sole provider of all basic services and the major source of employment. Through various job-guarantee programs, for example, university graduates could count on government employment once they had completed university. The state provided free medical care to all citizens. The reform process that started under Sadat initially aimed at building up the private sector after years of flirting with socialism under Nasser. Once the international community became involved, and particularly the International Monetary Fund (IMF) after 1987, the economic reforms took on the flavor of a full-fledged structural adjustment process. Egypt was put under pressure to downsize its enormous public sector by, for example, privatizing a number of government-owned companies. The ranks of its bloated bureaucracy were also regarded as being in need of trimming. Loans and external debt reduction became tied to reductions in import duties and the reduction of subsidies on basic goods. Egyptians hence saw the price of bread and electricity increase substantially during the late 80s and early 90s. As is commonly the case with this kind of systemic economic "shock therapy" the initial effects on society did not feel good. The ending of government job guarantees led to massive unemployment; affordable housing became difficult to find; young couples delayed marriage because they and their families could not bear the expense; and many—including civil servants and doctors—found themselves having to work a second job to make ends meet.[24] University completion rates soon far outgrew job creation in both the public and private sectors, forcing highly skilled and professional graduates who had viewed higher education as a path to prosperity to live on small service wages or even agricultural labor. In overall terms, the disparities between Egypt's upper and upper-middle classes and the lower-middle and lower classes increased substantially during this period. Bribery and corruption was rife.

This "retreat of the state" opened up substantial space for other social forces to flourish within neighborhood and civil society spaces, and the MB soon proved itself most adept at leveraging these opportunities. Realizing the potential to create an "Islamic sector" for the provision of basic welfare and charity services, the Brotherhood decided from the late 1970s to make Egyptian society—rather than state political institutions—the target of its reform and mobilization efforts. Soon Islamic social organizations were springing up everywhere: charities, hospitals, schools, mosque organizations—all providing a combination of basic services and a source of new jobs that were not forthcoming from either the state or the private sector. Mosques, the vast majority of which were privately run and financially independent of the state, once under Brotherhood control set themselves up as purveyors of redistributive social justice. Some of the more entrepreneurial beneficiaries of economic liberalization established a system of "Islamic investment companies" during the 1980s. Wholly unregulated and bypassing official banks, these local and "authentic" institutions promised investors enormous rates of return (often double that available in the formal banking sector) alongside a commitment—tapping into the upsurge of popular religiosity—that all funds were handled according to shari'ah requirements.[25] The Islamic investment companies also contributed substantially to Brotherhood political candidates and other of their causes, until a financial meltdown led the sector to be investigated and shut down by the government at the end of the decade. Opponents claimed the companies were little more than elaborate pyramid schemes at best, or, worse, that they were profiting off criminal activities—in either case, hardly "Islamic." Advocates of the practice cited their strong local character ("investment in Egypt by Egyptians") and claimed that the government intervened because they feared the strength of a vibrant economic sector outside their control—particularly one contributing substantial sums to opposition causes.[26] This was not the only segment of the "Islamic sector" that had been enjoying success at the expense of the government, however. Islamic charities had become pervasive and highly efficient by the end of the 1980s. So much so, in fact, that when Cairo suffered a devastating earthquake in 1992, the Islamic relief services were on the scene and dispensing aid hours before the state was able to mobilize its own emergency services—prompting one government official to voice concerns that the Islamists had created a "state within a state."[27] All in all, Islamic social organizations increased from representing a quarter of the voluntary sector in the early 1970s to more than 75% by the end of the 1980s.

In addition to the "Islamic sector" composed of service organizations owned or operated by the Brotherhood, Islamists also became a major force in other key civil society spaces throughout the 1980s. From the mid-1970s, the MB began to establish themselves on student councils and unions in all Egyptian universities, particularly in science and engineering faculties. They quickly became the dominant voice on nearly every campus, completing a rout of secular and leftist rivals. Soon the Brotherhood also began to contest elections within the influential professional syndicates. From the mid-1980s, the Brotherhood progressively took over the engineering, pharmaceutical, and medical associations, culminating with a 1992 victory in the Egyptian Bar Association, long regarded as the last bastion of secularism within the professional classes.[28] Although less successful in the workers unions, which were still heavily influenced by leftist thought, even here the Islamists saw an upswing in their fortunes during the 1980s.[29] The Brotherhood's socialization of associational space in Egypt is highly significant not only because it allowed them to build enormous social capital in some of the most influential and upwardly mobile segments of the country's population, but also because it permitted them to use civil society groups for oppositional politics by proxy. With the MB banned as a political organization, and political party culture generally weak in Egypt, the Brotherhood's enormous footprint in society allowed them to wield considerable clout without getting directly involved in political processes.[30] Indeed, one could even argue that far from being a form of protest against its exclusion from the political sphere, the Brotherhood actually preferred to operate this way. By exercising their normative discipline at the level of society, the Islamists could enjoy considerable influence but without having to be formally accountable (or targetable) within the political system. As Esposito and Voll put it:

The fact that Islamists are specific in their indictment of the government but general in terms of their own programs tends to work in their favor. They are able to criticize the failings of the government, from employment and housing to corruption and maldistribution of wealth, without having to offer their own specific solutions to seemingly intractable problems. They employ Islamic rhetoric and symbols, call for an Islamic solution and the implementation of the Sharia, but do not delineate precisely what these would mean in terms of specific policies. Moreover, although at the macro level, they often only offer general prescriptions and promises, the source of their credibility and success is that at the micro level. Their educational and social programs demonstrate to ordinary people the concrete, tangible meaning and impact of an Islamic order.[31]

The Brotherhood's strategy also had two other significant dimensions. The first of these is related to their deliberate targeting of youth spaces—not only through universities as mentioned above, but also via religious outreach (da'wa) to young people active in mosque organizations. This revealed the MB to have a long-term sociopolitical vision based on the idea of instilling in the younger generation the idea that societal reform along religiously prescribed lines is an obligation that should be pursued through civic activism.[32] The Brotherhood was, in effect, "staging" young people towards the Islamist movement, and seeking to calibrate their horizons of public normativity in terms of religion. "You raise Muslim Brother students in the university," one observer put it, "then five years later you have an electoral base for the professional associations. It's like planting seeds on a farm."[33] The second dimension concerns the Brotherhood's ability to capture and harness the upsurge in religiosity that emerged in Egypt from the 1970s. By tapping into veins of popular piety, the Islamists were able to channel this force towards their social organizations and causes in ways that leftists, nationalists—and certainly not the "empty shell" of the NDP or the secularists—simply could not. By framing its various social welfare activities in terms of "being a better Muslim" the Brotherhood leveraged this swelling religiosity into a privileged role as society's normative arbiter.[34] As Azzam puts it:

> They have been able to foster and direct this [religious] current through their organizational ability and dedication, and there is no rival opposition group to match them. The stress on devotional practice and cultural purification from all that is "un-Islamic" ... provides a framework of action for their followers and has contributed to the Islamization process. ... This emphasis has borne fruit, insofar as the basic belief and practice of Islam have been reasserted and spread among a new generation and throughout a cross-section of society.[35]

The Islamists and the Egyptian state (1981–95)

But Islamist activity was not confined exclusively to the social sphere during this period. Although banned since 1954 from forming a political party, the MB has contested elections in Egypt since 1984 either by running independent candidates or through alliances with other political parties. Although constrained by a state as pervasively present in the political sphere as the Brotherhood is in society, their relative electoral success and subsequent pressure on the regime prompted a crackdown on their activities from the early 1990s and significant public scrutiny of the Islamist trend as a whole. When Mubarak came to power in the wake of the trauma of Sadat's assassination, he immediately pursued a course of limited social and political liberalization in the name of national unity. This was manifested in greater press freedoms, an expansion of civil, associational and political party rights, and an invitation to all political currents (Islamists, secularists, leftists and so forth) to participate in the public sphere.[36] Certainly not unaware of the upsurge in popular religiosity mentioned above, Mubarak initially hoped to co-opt this energy by emphasizing those aspects of religion that were in tune with his ongoing efforts at economic liberalization. This naturally led him to pursue a policy of limited engagement with the social force most clearly identified with this trend, the MB. For its own part, the MB decided to use this opportunity to re-enter politics. In 1984 they formed an unlikely alliance with the Wafd party, whose own political fortunes had been in severe decline. Both parties were victims of the post-1952 Nasserist order and both saw tactical value in the partnership. Egypt's election law required a party to receive more than 8% of the popular vote in order to take parliamentary seats, and by running under the Wafd banner, the Brotherhood permitted them to cross this threshold. This marriage of convenience fell apart rather quickly, however, and the Islamists were forced to look elsewhere. In 1987, the MB entered into a partnership with the Liberal and Labor parties—where key figures had been leaning towards a form of "Islamic socialism"—and formed the "Islamic Alliance." Although it enjoyed some political success in both cases, gaining a number of seats in parliament, it was near impossible for the Brotherhood to pursue its reform agenda via political means since the overwhelming control of parliament by the government party, the NDP, blocked them at every juncture. Since its inception the NDP has held more than a two-thirds majority in every parliament, allowing all "presidential legislation" to pass easily, and even permitting the party to change the constitution.

Despite its stranglehold over the political system, the regime became increasingly wary of the Islamists from the late 1980s. The MB was using the parliament as a public forum to pressure the government to bring all Egyptian laws into accordance with the shari'ah as specified in article two of the constitution. More alarming from the government's point of view, however, was an upsurge in violence associated with several of the radical groups—such as Gemaa Islamiyya and Islamic Jihad—that had emerged during and just after the Sadat years. From the late 80s, Egypt experienced a spate of attacks by militant groups who were no longer targeting only instruments of the state. The geographic scope of their activities also broadened beyond Cairo to include various towns in Upper Egypt (the southern part of the country). Foreign tourists, police officers, and even members of Egypt's Coptic Christian community were killed by the radicals. The Copts, representing about 10% of the country, became the target of widespread discontent on the part of disenfranchised Muslims who resented their relative prosperity in comparison with the wider population. This was hence also a period of heightened interfaith tension. In addition to the violence, radical groups also sought to coercively enforce "public virtue" in various towns and villages by forcing women to wear veils and by carrying out Islamic punishments (hudud) as self-appointed judiciaries. The government's response was swift and strong, with key radical Islamists imprisoned or killed—leading to a tit-for-tat cycle of violence between the regime and the radicals during the early 1990s.

But the radicals were not the only Islamists targeted by the regime. Wary of the MB's enormous influence within the social sphere and dissatisfied by their unwillingness to unequivocally condemn the radical violence, the government began moving against the MB in the late 1980s. They sought to forge a link in the public's mind between the MB as an Islamist organization and the radical Islamism of the militant groups. Many of those in the radical groups had at one time or another been members of the MB but had left the movement after it rejected violence in the mid-70s. They found the Brotherhood's unwillingness to engage in direct jihad to be un-Islamic and a betrayal of the movement's activist forebears (e.g. figures such as Sayyid Qutb). So in the eyes of the regime, the MB was guilty of providing the intellectual foundations and religious justifications for the violence of the radicals. The government's initial efforts were geared towards rolling back the Brotherhood's influence within civil society organizations. Their actions amounted to a "securitization" of various social sectors, such as education and mosques. Suspected Islamists were purged from schools, and new regulations introduced whereby the deans of university faculties were to be appointed by the institution's rectors rather than elected by faculty.[37] Efforts were also made to bring private mosques—regarded as recruiting and mobilizing grounds for radicalism—under government control. Given that over 80 percent of Egypt's approximately 200,000 mosques were privately controlled, however, it soon became clear that this would be logistically and financially impossible. Plans to have all Friday sermons (khutba) vetted by the Ministry of Religious Affairs were soon shelved. The government moved against the Islamist presence in professional and student associations as well, blocking the election of MB candidates to student union councils. In 1993 they also changed the regulations governing elections in professional syndicates. These were now subject to strict quota requirements that demanded the presence of a large percentage of the organization's membership for any election to be valid. If these were not met, then the leaderships of the professional associations were to be appointed directly by the government.[38] What these actions amounted to was an attempt by the regime to shut down or tightly control any space in society where popular elections occurred. In the eyes of the government, unregulated social space came to be viewed as dangerous since the Islamists always seemed to win.

Finally, from 1994 to 1995, the government moved against the MB directly. Scores of Brotherhood activists were arrested and accused of illegal political activities, providing the regime with an opportunity to make a dramatic case against, and attempt to undermine the legitimacy of, the Islamist movement. Many members were put on trial, convicted and sentenced to jail terms of varying lengths. Most significantly from the point of view of the government's attempts to curb MB influence, those convicted of even relatively light crimes were subsequently disbarred from standing as candidates in associational elections (according to syndicate regulations, no one with a criminal record is permitted to stand).[39] Some have subsequently interpreted these actions as a tactic to keep the Brotherhood out of civil society by legally disbarring their participation since other attempts to sideline them had failed. Under this withering pressure from the state, the MB retreated from the social and political spheres, keeping a very low profile through the rest of the 1990s.[40]

Islamic intellectual centrism: the Wasatiyya movement

Before moving on to look at the Egyptian MB over the past decade, we should spend some time examining an intellectual trend that emerged out of the Islamist current from the 1980s and which has been influential in terms of subsequent developments within the Brotherhood mainstream. To say that this trend developed "out" of the Islamist mainstream is significant insofar as the relevant thinkers and activists, while many of them have been influenced by and even affiliated with the MB at one time, should be considered neither part of the Brotherhood nor under its control. The emergence of this group can be linked to the distinction made above between "classic Islamism" and "new Islamism." One writer, Ray Baker, has used the term "new Islamists" to describe this particular group of intellectuals.[41] For our purposes, however, the "new Islamists" will connote a broader generational and strategic shift identifiable in Muslim movements across several settings today. We will refer to the intellectual trend more descriptively as the Wasatiyya (Centrist) movement—as do, it should be noted, several members of the group itself, in addition to other observers.

Identifiable, for Baker, more in terms of tendencies and "family resemblances" rather than a clearly delineated ideology or program, Wasatiyya thinkers nevertheless share a common set of general intellectual trajectories. This is also a relatively heterogeneous group in terms of its professional composition. Journalists, social activists, academics, and religious scholars can all be counted among its numbers. Baker identifies three core groups from which Wasatiyya members are drawn: (1) former leftists who adopted a more Islamist orientation from the 1980s, including figures around the opposition (and at times quite radical) newspaper *al-Shaab*, such as Adel Hussain and Ibrahim Shukry; (2) figures whose social consciousness was formed through participation in civic and charitable associations run by the MB, but who chose not to become affiliated with the MB; and (3) a group of religious scholars emphasizing the relevance of traditional Islamic knowledge to contemporary issues and problems, and seeking to provide non-authoritarian guidance for their solution.[42] Many proponents of the Wasatiyya current are and were already quite famous in their own right—such as historian Tariq al-Bishri and the well-known religious scholar Yusuf al-Qaradawi (see Chapter 9)—before becoming associated with this movement. Indeed, the "manifesto" of the Wasatiyya trend, *Towards a Contemporary Islamic Vision* should be regarded as an aggregate text composed of ideas contributed by a wide range of thinkers over a decade. First sketched out by Kamal Abul Magd in the early 1980s, it was finally published for the public in 1992 after circulating and evolving for a decade within various Islamic circles. Variants of Wasatiyya thinking have been visible in the Egyptian public sphere for well over a decade now, including a famous debate on "Secularism vs. Islam" between Farag Foda (who was assassinated by Islamic Jihad shortly afterward) and one of the key figures in the Wasatiyya movement, Sheikh Muhammad al-Ghazzali. A separate but related effort to establish a political party inspired by elements of Wasatiyya thought emerged from 1996 in the form of Hizb al-Wasat ("Party of the Center"—see below).

What is the nature and character of Wasatiyya thinking? We might summarize its core values in terms of holism, inclusivity, and dialogue. These are all clearly "progressive" sounding terms, a fact that has led many observers, particularly in the West, to take an interest in the movement. But what is meant by them, particularly in the context of Egypt? First and foremost the Wasatiyya needs to be regarded as an intellectual movement with a social consciousness, and moreover one that seeks reform and social transformation. Its thinkers express considerable concern about the plight and poverty of Egypt—materially and culturally—but they diagnose this in terms of both internal and external causes. The movement takes its inspiration from the notion of social justice found in Islam and seeks to achieve a social order that embraces the spirit of the shari'ah. There would be some variation within the group as to what exactly this last part means. Some would want to understand the Qur'an as the source of general principles for good society where others would tend towards actually legislating based on the shari'ah. While the roots of the Wasatiyya are clearly in the Islamist current, their holism lies in how they depart from the common Brotherhood slogan "Islam is the solution." For them, religion is just one part of the solution, and needs to be regarded in conjunction with national interests, economic realities, and cultural traditions. In this sense, we can begin to view the Wasatiyya approach as essentially pragmatic rather than ideological. While embracing religiously inspired reform, Muslims are not seen by the Wasatiyya as the sole agents of that process—another contrast with the Brotherhood. This is where the element of inclusivity comes in. Viewing Egyptian reform as a national project, the Wasatiyya emphasize the need to include those embracing disparate political tendencies and also non-Muslims as equal partners. Active participation by women in processes of social change is seen as particularly important by many within the movement. Finally the Wasatiyya trend highlights the importance of dialogue and collective deliberation—rather than coercion or violence—as the only possible way to achieve sustainable social reform.

Looking at these principles, some observers, such as Baker, have been led to draw parallels between the Wasatiyya and what are commonly known as "new social movements" or NSMs.[43] While this is correct in terms of the social location of NSMs (the middle class), it could give the impression that the values of the Wasatiyya are closely in tune with the kinds of progressive causes generally associated with new social movements, such as the environmental agenda and global feminism. Some figures within the Wasatiyya current, such as Sheikh Yusuf al-Qaradawi, while relatively centrist and modern for a religious scholar, nevertheless still hold views regarding, for example, the status of women and the permissibility of suicide bombing, that many progressives would find difficult to accept. The "progressivist" label is a little more on target when we consider Baker's characterization of the Wasatiyya as a form of "Islam without fear." By this he means that those within the movement are not using Islam as part of a defensive discourse, or as a form of "cultural coercion"—such as by making sweeping statements to the effect that "Islam is under attack" or "as Muslims you must defend your religion" that achieve little other than to tarnish Islam and instill fear in believers and non-Muslims alike. Rather, they seek to figure Islam as a discourse of positive change in tune with emerging norms of pluralism, freedom, and human rights.[44] In other words, one asserts one's "Muslimness" not because it is vulnerable and under attack, but rather as a call to improve society. In this dimension of the Wasatiyya phenomenon we can see several common NSM traits such as an emphasis on post-material concerns and the attempt to challenge dominant cultural codes.[45] Some observers have noticed that as an intellectual trend, this approach is not unprecedented in the Muslim world. In the reformist thought of Muhammad Abduh (see Chapter 2), for example, one can identify clear precursors of Wasatiyya ideas.[46] Indeed, in some regards it might be seen as an approach seeking to recover the heritage of Muhammad Abduh and to take the Islamist movement in a direction obsessed less with the achievement of the correct "Islamic political order" and more focused on the common (and not necessarily an exclusively Muslim or Islamic) public good. It is, in other words, Islam as civilizational potential rather than religious difference.[47]

MB generations and the emergence of Hizb al-Wasat

The "re-entrenchment" of the MB in the mid to late 1990s corresponded to the emergence within its ranks of a clear generational divide. This pitted an "old guard," many of whom had joined the group while Hassan al-Banna (1906–49) was still alive, against a "middle generation" that had joined the movement from the late 1970s. The younger generation, many of whom had been socialized into the movement via various student and professional associations, were interested in exploring new avenues of political participation for the Brotherhood. They resented what they saw as the authoritarian control of a small group of septa- and octo-genarians largely out of touch with modern society.[48] For the middle generation, the priorities of the Islamist movement should be understood in pragmatic terms and as adaptable to changing social realities rather than simply being judged on how faithfully they followed the classic program and method of the Brotherhood. Their influence had already been felt somewhat in 1995 when the MB declared its support for the principle of multiparty politics, a significant departure from the teachings of Hassan al-Banna who had always maintained that in a truly Islamic society political parties would not only be unnecessary but were inherently divisive.[49] In short, this younger group was looking for a more inclusive Islamic politics outside the exclusive confines of the Brotherhood. By refusing to cooperate and form alliances with other political trends, the leaders of the middle generation argued, the Brotherhood would remain marginal in terms of its political influence.[50] Carrie Wickham points out, importantly, that these differences of vision did not break down solely along generational lines, but that the leaders of the modernist, pragmatist trend were clearly to be found within the middle generation.[51]

Out of this divide there emerged in 1996 an attempt by several key figures within the younger generation to set up a political party known as Hizb al-Wasat (Party of the Center; HW). Several of the founding figures were quickly arrested and charged with seeking to form an illegal political organization. It eventually became clear to the government that HW was not simply an attempt by the MB to surreptitiously establish a political party. Indeed, the Wasat founders were widely condemned for having betrayed the Islamist cause. HW applied twice, in 1996 and 1998, for a license to operate as a legal political party and was twice denied with subsequent appeals also failing. The MB itself registered formal opposition to the formation of HW during the application process.[52] Several dozen Brotherhood members who had joined the Wasat founders quickly returned to the MB once the new party began to experience difficulties—a fact cited by the Brotherhood leadership as evidence that many early Wasat followers realized the new party would hurt the Islamist cause, and by the government as evidence that

Wasat was simply the MB under a different name.[53] We should also note that the formation of Wasat did not in any way represent an exodus from the MB by the middle generation. Several of the most prominent figures within this wing remained behind and have since risen to senior positions within the Brotherhood. Some have suggested that they share the same overall vision as those who left to form Wasat, but did not agree with the decision to break with the mother group, while others cite this as evidence for a potential reconciliation between the two groups—a point born out by recent communications from the MB leadership.[54]

Despite the shared emphasis on "centrism," HW and its membership is by no means identical with that of the broader Wasatiyya intellectual movement—although lines of communication and cooperation certainly did exist, with many in the latter expressing support for the upstart politicians. In HW's subsequent legal battles with the state, one of the central Wasatiyya figures, lawyer Selim al-Awa, did work on behalf of the political group. Furthermore, several Wasat figures and Wasatiyya intellectuals collaborated successfully in 2000 to petition for a license to establish, along with a number of prominent secular figures, a Center for Culture and Dialogue. In the absence of both Wasatiyya institutions and a legal space for the discussion and further refinement of the Wasat platform, this association has served as a proxy.

The HW's political platform, which was issued in several iterations from 1996 to 1998, emphasizes democratic reform, government accountability, human rights and—more significantly—support for participation by non-Muslims, secular activists, and women in its activities. Several Coptic Christians were included as members, and a Protestant served on the party's executive council and also played a lead role in authoring one version of the party platform. This is in sharp contrast to the MB which, while generally allowing for the idea that Christian citizens should participate in the political process, would not accept Christians as members of the movement. In another significant break from the MB, the Wasat platform sees sovereignty as vested in the citizens rather than the standard Islamist formulation to the effect the sovereignty belongs to God alone.[55] Some have observed that while mentioning the important role of women in social transformation, the parameters of their activity are still seen in largely traditional terms, with women assigned primarily to the domestic sphere.[56] While shari'ah is conceptualized as an inclusive and participatory process, there still remain certain ambiguities as to its place within the Wasat program.[57]

In the 2000 parliamentary elections the MB faired relatively well, taking advantage of new rules that required independent judicial oversight of all polling activities. They took 17 seats in parliament and also regained control of the law syndicate. More significantly, in 2005, Egypt had its first presidential election featuring more than one candidate. Although Hosni Mubarak won by a wide margin, the precedent was important. In the face of considerable external pressure, particularly from the United States, to make greater efforts towards democracy, Egypt also permitted a longer and more liberal campaigning period in the run-up to the legislative elections that same year. We also saw the emergence of Kifaya ("Enough"), a popular movement demanding political reform that held large demonstrations in the spring. Although the Islamists were not a large part of this contingent (some even rumor that the MB struck a deal with the state to boycott the protests), those in the Wasatiyya movement have expressed general sympathy with their aims. Most importantly, however, the MB in 2005 achieved its best ever electoral showing in the parliament despite an intimidation campaign by the government as voting began. In total, Brotherhood-affiliated candidates won 88 out of 454 seats, creating an opposition bloc composed of 20 percent of the parliament—the largest ever seen in the assembly. While the NDP still has its two-thirds majority, it has had to be considerably more vigilant than in the past in terms of how it handles parliamentary procedure given the disciplined presence of a large Islamist bloc.[58] Some prominent figures within the Brotherhood have now started to talk about the division of the movement into two distinct organizations, one a political party and the other a religious organization—holding out the possibility of either reconciliation (i.e. an "official" split) or direct competition with the Wasat group.[59]

How to assess the significance of what appears to be an emerging "new Islamist" movement in Egypt? Given that it is a relatively young phenomenon whose level of popular support is very difficult to gauge, it might be tempting on the one hand to dismiss the Wasat as a fringe splinter group from the MB that happens to have swung to the left rather than to the right as did the radical groups of the 1970s.[60] Even greater skeptics might insist that at the end of the day the Wasat represent nothing more than a new variant of old school Islamism employing pluralistic rhetoric instrumentally to forge alliances of political convenience. Viewed, sociologically, however, the Wasatiyya trend emerges as something potentially far more significant. While the extent of their popular influence is currently nothing like that of the MB, the fact remains that the Wasat emerged out of spaces initially socialized by the MB. This suggests that within that younger generation there is likely a critical mass of support for a more inclusive form of moderate Islamism. Likewise, the broader Wasatiyya current was first forged by non-MB intellectuals and activists, and this perhaps indicates a wider basis of social support for a trend outside the conventional Islamist movement. In net terms, then, the potential would seem to exist for an explosion of popular support for "new Islamism" in the next decade. This does not mean, however, that "traditional" Islamist movements will be excluded. Some researchers have already indicated that classic Islamist groups are evolving to suit the times—a process that political scientist Carrie Wickham refers to as "Islamist auto-reform."[61] These developments all combine to make the question of who speaks for Islam—or, rather, who speaks for Islam*ism*— that much more relevant for us to consider, as we will in Chapter 9.

Turkey: religion, secular nationalist ideology and the rise of "Muslim democracy"

From a non-ideological ruling party in the case of Egypt, we move now to examine the course of Islamism in a highly ideological state. Turkey provides us with another—and even more extreme—case of Islamists vying for influence in a politically hostile environment. In Egypt the MB was kept out of politics altogether by an NDP determined to stay in power by sidelining any potential rival. In the case of Turkey, however, Islamism has been viewed by the dominant forces of the military and judiciary not so much as a rival to any particular political party, but to the highly secular official state ideology of Kemalism. Unlike in Egypt, Turkish Islamist parties have been permitted to contest elections, and to serve in coalition governments. In 2002 a political party with strong Islamist roots swept a full two-thirds of the Turkish parliament. As the self-appointed guardians of the secular order, however, the Turkish army has always lurked just behind the political stage. On four occasions in 1960, 1971, 1980, and 1997, the army has intervened to suspend or alter the course of popular politics in the name of protecting the Republic. In this section our goal is to understand the evolution of the Turkish Islamic movement in the context of an ideologically rigid state. As we will see, the recent history of Islamism in Turkey has never been a simple case of religion vs. nationalism. Rather, Islamist parties have always had a complex and multifaceted relationship with Turkish nationalism and the Kemalist legacy. Some of the most successful and deeply rooted manifestations of Muslim politics in Turkey also have strong nationalist leanings. In recent years we have also seen the emergence of a new kind of "pietistic politics" with strong roots in the widespread popularity of Sufi movements in Turkey. Some have also associated this with a shift or evolution in the nature of Turkish Islamism, citing the recent political success of the AKP as evidence. Analysts such as Vali Nasr see in the AKP the harbinger of a new form of "Muslim Democracy."[62] We might also be tempted to draw certain parallels here with the divisions that emerged in the Egyptian MB in the mid-1990s and which went on to produce the HW as a political alternative to a self-marginalized and rigid Islamism.

We will begin by briefly reviewing the political legacy of Mustafa Kemal and the concomitant ideology that forms the foundation of the modern Turkish Republic. We will then trace the emergence and evolution of Turkey's Islamist movement from the introduction of multiparty politics in 1956, but with primary emphasis on the period following the Refah Party's strong electoral success in 1994. In order to understand the complex nature of Turkish Islam in terms of its social roots, we will also touch on several of the most important Sufi-based movements whose followers had an increasingly important role in shaping the nature of Islamist politics from the 1990s. After explaining the crackdown on the Refah Party and its various successors, we will analyze the split within the Islamic movement that led to formation of the AKP in 2001 and its almost immediate electoral triumph the following year. Finally, the question of the AKP as a form of "new Islamism" or Muslim Democracy will be considered.

As we will recall from the previous chapter, the modern Turkish Republic was founded by Mustapha Kemal Ataturk in 1922 out of the embers of the Ottoman Empire. He immediately set in motion a comprehensive program of modernization and secularization, seeking to eradicate all vestiges of Ottoman and Islamic "traditionalism" in the name of a Europeanized future. For Kemal, Islam was one of the greatest obstacles to the achievement of this vision and he undertook to comprehensively remove its influence from public life. In 1924 the caliphate was abolished. All court ulama and qadis were removed from their posts. Pious endowments (awqaf) were seized by the state. A government agency, the Diyanet, was charged with the strict regulation of all religious activity in the country, and all mosques came under its jurisdiction. Religion, in the Kemalist view, needed to be molded and disciplined so as to become not only compatible with, but also a conduit for, the process of modernization. The state thus claimed for itself the authority to define religion and also the boundaries of the sacred.

Kemal's Republican People's Party (RPP) effectively ran the country as a single party state until the early 1950s. The "Young Turk" movement that gave birth to the republican movement had its base within the military, and the army of the Turkish Republic quickly established itself—alongside the powerful Constitutional Court—as the chief guardian of the Kemalist legacy. As mentioned above, it has not hesitated on several occasions to intervene directly in politics when the Kemalist order is perceived to be under threat—and in two cases it has even suspended democracy for short periods of martial rule. Intense secularism has been a hallmark characteristic of the state ideology, and in Turkey it has been taken to levels almost unparalleled in other countries. For example, the wearing of headscarves is strictly banned in any government space and in many universities, and all religious institutions are closely and comprehensively regulated by the state. While some see this as a dangerous limitation on religious freedom, others consider it to be an essential component of social stability, fearing potentially destabilizing effects if too much religion were to merge into public life.

Ninety-nine percent of Turkey's population is nominally Muslim—the vast majority of them Sunni (but with some ethnic variation within that sectarian group), and also a considerable *Alevi* (a Shi'i offshoot regarded by many Sunnis as heterodox and ultra-liberal) minority and even some Shi'a. We should also note up front the pervasive and highly influential presence of Sufism in Turkish Islam. As we will see later, Sufi movements have played a major role in the evolution of contemporary ideas about the role of religion in society and politics. Despite the intense secularization program introduced by Kemal, clearly Turks were not simply going to put religion aside. The influence of religion, particularly in provincial and rural areas, remained strong at the societal level even as people accommodated themselves to the absence of religion in public life and "official" space. It is therefore not surprising that once the political system was finally opened up to meaningful multiparty politics in 1950, a party perceived as allowing more space for religion, the Demokrat Party (DP), defeated the RPP and ruled the country until 1960 when they were removed by the military. When first faced with the DP threat, one of the RPP's responses was to try to appear more "religion friendly" itself. From the late 1940s, for example, they began a process of upgrading the system of Imam-hatip (religious training) schools.[63]

As in Egypt, it is important for understanding Muslim politics in Turkey to get a sense of what Islam looks like at the societal level—but for a different reason. In the case of the Egyptian MB, we saw the systematic socialization of civil societal spaces by an Islamist movement pursuing the establishment of a shari'ah-based social and political order. This has not been the pattern of social Islam in Turkey, and nor does one find a similar influence of "neo-corporatist" politics on the state. In the case of Turkey, the most important manifestations of Islam at the societal level are to be found in various Sufi and modern reformist groups. The strongest Sufi order in Turkey are the Naqshbandiyya, a relatively orthodox, or "sober" tariqa founded in the fourteenth century, known for its emphasis on piety and discipline. The other important figure here is the early twentieth-century reformer and activist Said Nursi (1876–1960). Nursi, whose intellectual trajectory can be understood in parallel to that of other Islamic Reformists of the day, such as Muhammad Abduh, sought in his work to emphasize the compatibility of religion and modernity. Strongly influenced by both Naqshbandi Sufism and modern ideologies of national liberation, Nursi's major publication, the *Risale-i Nur* ("Epistle of Light"), is read widely by a large variety of grassroots religious groups in Turkey to this day. The direct inheritors of his thinking are known as the Nurçu movement. Nurçu followers are to be found throughout Turkey, and are often associated with a wide variety of social organizations (charities, schools, clubs, etc.)—but unlike the MB activists inhabiting the same spaces in Egypt, theirs is not primarily a political impulse. One of the best-known and most common Nurçu social formations is the *dershane*, or reading group. These "textual communities," as Hakan Yavuz calls them, are usually organized at the neighborhood level and involve meetings in apartment buildings or dormitories where readings from the *Risale-i Nur* are discussed and prayers said, followed by socializing.[64] The Nurçu meetings are, in effect, spaces for the building of like-minded social capital. Direct political influence has generally been difficult to discern, although, as we will see later, their support for the recently established AKP seems to provide an important base for that party in society. As Serif Mardin has put it:

The influence of the Nurçu sect is ... a diffuse one: while the sect's newspaper disseminates the correct stand to take on current political, social, and economic issues, the effectiveness of the Nurçu is that of a freemasonry, of persons who establish social linkages and personal ties with each other, who support and promote people who think like themselves. But this diffuseness ... is an element to reckon with in the intellectual climate of contemporary Turkey.[65]

The dershane meetings hence represent a combination of Rotary Club-style social capital infused with Sufi piety and self-discipline. Yavuz sees in them a form of "counterpublic" in which new forms of Muslim subjectivity are created in relation to state policies and market practices.[66]

Another key Naqshbandi influence can be seen in the circle around Mehmed Zahid Kotku (sometimes called "Zahid Efendi"), the leader or sheikh of the tariqa in Turkey from the early 1950s until his death in 1980. Kotku pursued a multifaceted strategy as regards religion and politics and clearly sought a more direct and active religious influence. He established circles across the country, set up publications, and even invested in manufacturing. Subsequent analysis of his writings reveal him to have had clear Islamist inclinations, but via an approach that combined elements of religious activism with a nationalist identity.[67] He also played a role in encouraging the formation of the first Islamist political party in Turkey, and in choosing its leader.[68] In Serif Mardin's analysis, the power of the various Sufi-influenced movements lay in their ability to provide a sense of meaning and a normative framework at the level of everyday life. Kemalism, as the state ideology, was a rather abstract body of enforced public norms sitting on an official and closely guarded pedestal. The Sufi way, on the other hand, allowed followers to understand personal piety as part of a much broader experience that invested everyday practice with spiritual meaning and significance. As its influence grew within Turkey's provincial middle classes, and eventually among intellectuals and urban populations, the broad Nurçu movement emerged as a significant repository of upwardly mobile social capital waiting to be channeled into a political project.

A more recent Nurçu-related group that has attracted considerable attention of late is the movement associated with Fethullah Gülen (see Chapter 8), a religious teacher whose work emphasizes an "Islamic ethic of education."[69] Gülen has established a network of schools whose curriculum is wholly modern and secular, but whose teachers are all members of the religious movement. Through dormitory dershanes and supplemental classes, they seek to create parallel spaces for religious education to occur alongside high-quality secular study. Some have interpreted Gülen as providing a form of religiously inflected nationalism that allows him to safely operate within the Kemalist framework. His schools, which also exist in the Balkans and Central Asia, can be seen as institutions seeking to provide the credentials required for participation in modern life (as engineers, lawyers, etc.) while also inculcating a sense of religious consciousness. The idea is hence to create a generation of Turkish elites who will be more comfortable with the idea of leaving greater space for religion in public life.

These, then, are some of the groups that collectively compose the Islamic movement in Turkey. It does not become possible to talk about the formation of a discernible Islamist (that is, overtly political) movement, by contrast, until the emergence in the late 1960s of the National Outlook Movement, or Milli Gorus. In part a product of the rapidly changing economic environment of the time, this group's primary concerns related to (1) the decline of morality associated with the rapid modernization and industrialization of Turkish society; and (2) the threat posed to Turkey's independence by its growing ties to the European Community and the wider global economy. Out of this broad movement, Turkey's first Islamist political party, the National Order Party (soon renamed the National Salvation Party, or NSP) was founded in 1970 under the leadership of Necmettin Erbakan. NSP established itself as the party of the urban poor and the provincial middle class, becoming a permanent although by no means dominant fixture within the parliament during the 1970s.[70] Caught up in the military coup of 1980, the NSP found itself accused by the military of using religion for political purposes. Some observers have noted that alongside the NSP's parliamentary efforts, a less organized and socially based Islamic movement had arisen in parallel. Operating through associational channels in much the same way as the MB in Egypt, many within these groups held to more radical views that had no place in the parliamentary discourse of the NSP. This is a development of which the military would no doubt have been aware.[71] The flexibility of the Islamist discourse is demonstrated by the course pursued by the Refah Party, NSP's successor, during the course of the 1980s. Moving away from the "defensive" Islamism of the 1970s (anti-global capitalism), Refah sought now to emphasize the idea of Turkey's integration into the world economy through leveraging its own resources. Refah, still under Erbakan, used religion partly as a tool to discredit the Turkish Left, arguing that religious leaders and local associations needed to be integrated into the program of national development.[72] This allowed the Islamists to buy into the so-called "Turkish-Islamic Synthesis" favored by the military as a way to marginalize the socialists. Fethullah Gülen's movement also found favor in this same climate.[73] The 1980s can hence be thought of as a period where the Islamists sought to realign their base. Many NSP conservatives, in any case, had departed for Turgut Ozal's conservative Motherland party once the NSP fell on hard times around the time of the coup. Ozal had been a disciple of Kotku, and was generally more open to religion. It was even rumored that he was receiving political advice from the Sufis, leading some to label members of the party as "crypto-Naqshbandis."

The 1990s marked a significant upswing in the electoral fortunes of the Refah Party. Growing popular religiosity combined with the ill effects of economic liberalization reforms (compare with Egypt during roughly the same period) created a climate ripe for Erbakan's Islamist discourse. First in municipal elections during 1994 and then in parliamentary polls the following year, Refah scored big—emerging as the single largest party in the assembly. Their bloc was not large enough to enable them to form a government alone, so Refah was forced into an awkward coalition with Tansu Ciller's "True Path" party and Mesut Yilmaz of Motherland, the premiership rotating between all three of them. Turkish politics soon descended into a mud-slinging match with Yilmaz and Ciller trying to undermine each other, convinced that the Kemalists would keep Refah in check. Within Refah itself, tensions began to emerge between the conservative faction led by Erbakan and a "reformist" bloc that wanted to remake the party in the image of Europe's Christian Democratic parties—a divide that would become highly significant around the time of AKP's formation. The former group wanted to pursue issues like lifting the ban on veils and the realignment of Turkey's foreign policy with other leading Muslim countries—both of which, of course, greatly disturbed the Kemalist establishment. Matters came to a head in early 1997 when a pro-Hizbullah speech by the Iranian ambassador that had been sponsored by the Refah mayor of a provincial town snowballed into a national event after the military sent tanks into the town and arrested the mayor. The Refah government's subsequent show of support for their party member prompted the government to reprioritize politicized religion as the country's number one security threat and to issue a set of secularizing demands to Refah for immediate implementation. When this was not forthcoming, the military—in what has been described as a "postmodern coup"—compelled the government to resign.[74]

Within a year the Constitutional Court also forced the Refah Party to disband. After a few weeks, however, it had been reconstituted as the Virtue Party, with much the same membership and Erbakan still in control from behind the scenes. Over the next four years the military and judiciary hounded several iterations of the Islamist party. Virtue soon found itself out of favor when, after the 1999 elections, one of their female members of parliament tried to take the oath of allegiance wearing a headscarf. By 2000 the courts deemed Virtue beyond the pale and shut it down as well.

This latest legal setback was the final straw for some within the Islamist party. In a move that in some ways looks remarkably similar to the process through which HW emerged from the MB in Egypt, the reformist bloc within the now-banned Virtue Party broke with Erbakan's conservatives to form a new party called Justice and Development (AKP). The conservatives reconstituted themselves as the Saadet ("Felicity") Party. Two points of comparison with the Egyptian case are particularly relevant here. First, one of the major concerns voiced by the reformist bloc—who also tended to be of the younger generation—was that Erbakan's tight circle of loyalists had been running the party in a highly authoritarian manner. Governance was seen as out of step with a rapidly growing provincial middle class base that

wanted to expand the party's platform beyond the more conventional Islamist agenda that Erbakan had been pursuing since the early 1970s. Second,
the reformists were fed up with what they perceived as Erbakan's obsession
with lightning rod issues such as veiling. Where the reformists wanted to
pursue a mainstream national development agenda, Erbakan kept wandering into territory certain to bring the party into disrepute with the Kemalist
establishment. In much the same way that the Wasat group in Egypt resented the MB old guard's unwillingness to pursue a mainstream platform that
would allow for sustained political participation, so the founders of the
AKP sought a centrist synthesis that would allow them more access across
the sociopolitical spectrum—and, likewise, to become more accessible to the
masses. The reformist wing had "concluded that Turkey's military would
never allow an overtly Islamist party back into power, and—still more
importantly—that the ban on Islamic parties was helping other right-of-
center parties ... "[75] The AKP was founded in 2001 and one year later, in
the November 2002 national elections, the party shocked the world with a
landslide victory, gaining two-thirds of all seats in parliament and over 34
percent of the popular vote.

Who were these voters? How and why did the AKP receive such a strong
mandate for so relatively immature a party and political vision? A wide
variety of factors deserve mention here. For those whose sense of public
normativity was derived from religion, but who had little interest in the idea
of an Islamic political order, it made great sense to desert Erbakan's "old
school" Islamism for the more moderate and inclusive shores of the new
party. The AKP victory, then, represented "a clear mandate to redefine the
political center in terms of societal values" under a political party that was
"promising to create a space within which Muslim values can express
themselves, but [without] pushing an Islamist legislative agenda."[76] The
social conduits of this victory had been in the making for some time, with
the aforementioned Nurçu networks and groups such as the Fethullah
Gülen movement playing key roles. Gülen, for example, had sponsored a
series of annual seminars since 1998 known as the "Abant meetings" where
elites and intellectuals from both Islamic and secular backgrounds would
gather to discuss—and usually find themselves in agreement—on issues of
mutual concern.[77] A number of prominent Naqshbandi intellectuals were
also integral members of the new party.[78] But this was not just purely about
an opportunity for more religion in public life. In explaining and understanding the formation of a social base for the AKP's political discourse it
is crucial to understand how notions of everyday "popular" piety interacted
with the Turkish political economy during the 1980s and 90s. For many the
AKP represented the possibility of reconciling economic liberalism with the
traditional values of provincial populations who had been drifting into cities
as urbanization and economic liberalization proceeded apace—a normative
framework that had been gradually evolving within the upwardly mobile
context of Nurçu networks over a decade or more. As Hakan Yavuz puts it:

In the transformation of the Islamic movement in general, and the electoral victory of the AKP in particular, a "new" urban class, consisting of horizontally connected solidarity-based groups with rural origins and shared Islamic ethos, played an important role. This "new" urban class has been excluded culturally and economically by the Kemalist elite. The excluded segment of the population utilized Islamic idioms and networks to overcome their exclusion. Thus Islamic networks both facilitated this group's integration into modern opportunity spaces and offered it a hope for social mobilization.[79]

Hence the tremendous speed of the AKP's electoral success. It was not necessary for the party to socialize a constituency into its political framework—rather, a primed collective of communities or networks more or less "mobilized themselves" when they finally saw in the AKP the centrist synthesis they had been waiting for.[80] Also, in a climate of intense corruption and fiscal mismanagement, such as was to be found in Turkey in 1999–2002, *not* voting for the incumbent parties was very easy.

Also important is the fact that the AKP possessed built-in credibility in the form of its leadership. The party chief, Recep Tayyip Erdoğan was an immensely popular former mayor of Istanbul whose tenure was remembered for the efficient provision of services and also for its fiscal responsibility. In terms of personal style, the contrast with Erbakan could not have been greater. Erbakan was the paternalistic, authoritarian overlord who informed the party faithful what needed to be done. Erdoğan, on the other hand, came across as someone who dwelled among the people—the neighbor, "the guy next door."[81] His was an emphasis on horizontal ties of solidarity rather than vertical ties of obligation. Erdoğan had also clearly been a victim of the Kemalist order. In the 1990s, he was arrested and jailed for several months for having read a poem with religious metaphors at a public rally. Since his criminal record barred him from standing as a candidate for parliament in 2002, he was initially unable to take up the premiership until a constitutional amendment made this possible in 2003. Erdoğan also consciously tapped into a nostalgia for Turgut Özal's brand of 1980s centrist conservatism. "In many ways," Vali Nasr has argued, "the AKP is less an extension of Welfare and Virtue than a reconstruction of the center-right, economically liberal Motherland Party ... "[82]

Finally, there is also a sense in which the phenomenal rise of the AKP can be interpreted not simply as an endorsement of its specific platform, but as a symbolic renegotiation of the Turkish social contract. By voting in overwhelming numbers for a party certain not to be to the liking of the Kemalist establishment, the Turkish electorate—and particularly a newly educated and enfranchised generation of provincial or formerly provincial voters—sent a message to the effect that they, and not the military or the

Kemalists, were in control of the country's political future. This might be regarded as a direct retort to the "postmodern coup" of 1997.[83]

It is still too early to assess the full impact of the new party since, as Vali Nasr puts it, "the AKP is still an electoral strategy in search of a governing agenda."[84] There has been a tendency for the AKP to try to be everything to everyone under the rubric of what Erdoğan calls "conservative democracy"—an attempt to reconcile Islamic values with the legacy of Kemalism.[85] As Yavuz points out, the AKP is "simultaneously Turkish, Muslim, and Western."[86] One can certainly see how early on in an electoral career this kind of flexibility would be a political asset. But as its governmental tenure wears on, this kind of polyglot identity could cause more confusion than dialogue across political currents. Some observers have pointed out that certain tensions are already starting to emerge. The lack of intra-party democracy that caused the initial split with Refah seems in some regards to be reconstituting itself within the AKP.[87] The party also seems unsure of itself—perhaps somewhat understandably—when it comes to controversial religious issues such as the veil. Part of the agenda to differentiate themselves from those of Erbakan's ilk involved less emphasis on these issues in favor of topics and challenges in the mainstream. Of course, the fact of the matter is that in Turkey, the question of the boundaries of public religiosity is an issue that will not go away. And there is a segment of the core AKP constituency that expects them to give it some priority. The AKP, however, which has emerged as perhaps the most pro-European of all political actors in Turkey, has shown greater near-term interest in shoring up its support from the private sector by focusing on economic development and anti-corruption.

Some will see in the AKP a new form of "Muslim democracy" that understands religion as a source of morality that can be brought to bear in the conduct of public administration, but which does not entail the pursuit of a shari'ah-based legislative agenda. Others harbor fear that the AKP is full of "crypto-Islamists" waiting to pounce once the populace has been lulled into complacency. As in the case of the Wasatiyya movement in Egypt, however, political sociology seems to be strongly on the side of the former interpretation. Below the level of Kemalist and corporate elites, the secular-nationalist and provincial-religious currents of Turkish society have been inching towards each other for over a generation, and it makes sense that they should find their political synthesis in the AKP. Trends in a number of other countries, as we have already seen in the case of Egypt, suggest that "Muslim Democracy" may represent a movement on the rise. As we have also seen, however, it is one whose advent is premised on a certain configuration of social, political, and economic factors. As our next and final example, Jordan, will show, Muslim Democracy per se may not be a universal trend within the modern Islamist movement, but generational evolution in Islamist strategy in the context of shifting political economies certainly seems to be.

Indonesia: a paradigmatic "Muslim democracy"?

Although it is the largest Muslim country in the world in terms of population (245 million, some 90 percent of whom profess Islam), conventional Islamism has not been a standard feature of Indonesian politics. At the same time, it is fair to say that Indonesia has more "Islamic" or Muslim-oriented political parties than any country in the Muslim world today. How to explain this apparent enigma? Part of the answer lies in the nature of Indonesian Islam, but we also need to look at the role played by the official national ideology, *Pancasila* ("The Five Principles") and its use by the state as a political tool over several decades.

Indonesian Islam is noteworthy for its generally tolerant and pluralistic character. As Islam settled alongside existing Hindu and Buddhist

culture from the fifteenth century, Indonesian Muslims internalized norms of religious pluralism. While several waves of orthodox modernism from the early twentieth century certainly created a constituency for a more conventionally Islamist approach, Islamist parties in the early post-independence period (best represented by the Masyumi) were not particularly strong. Rather, a central government under Sukarno and later Suharto was already pushing the state ideology as the key organizing principle for Indonesian politics. While a strong endorsement of monotheism is central to the Pancasila, it is not specified in terms of Islam, nor is Islam declared to be the official religion of state. For many Indonesians participation in social Islam took the form of membership in one of the country's two mass Islamic movements, Nahdlatul Ulama (NU) or Muhammadiyah, each of which claims over 30 million members.

In 1973, President Suharto's New Order regime "rationalized" the Islamic party political structure in Indonesia, forcing all of the religious parties under a single umbrella, the Partai Persatuan Pembangunan (PPP) and insisting that it adopt Pancasila as the basis of its political platform. In the 1990s, as support for his regime dwindled in the face of widespread nepotism, Suharto sought to buttress his religious credentials by creating a new association for Muslim intellectuals and technocrats, the Ikatan Cendikiawan Muslim se-Indonesia (ICMI). Certain key religious figures, sensing another attempt by the state to co-opt Islam, stayed away. Among them was Abdurrahman Wahid, who emerged in 1999 as the compromise candidate for president in the wake of Suharto's fall from power. A former head of NU, Wahid focused on questions of democratic reform and inter-communal tolerance rather than shari'ah or the creation of an Islamic state. He was found wanting, as a head of state however, and his tenure in government short-lived. It is clear, however, as Robert Hefner has argued in

Civil Islam (Princeton: Princeton University Press, 2000), that Islamic parties in Indonesia provided much of the core energy driving the movement for political reform in the 1990s.

Indonesia did experience a period of limited radical Islamist upheaval in the early years of the new millennium, with groups such as Laskar Jihad appointing themselves as purveyors of public morality à la the *mutawwa* of Saudi Arabia (see Chapter 5). Other groups sought to stoke intercommunal fires, leading to renewed Muslim-Christian violence in outlying islands. Even a salafi-jihadi strain was to be found in the form of the Jemaah Islamiyah and its leader Abu Bakar Ba'syir. Most notoriously, this group perpetrated the October 2002 Bali bombing, killing over 200. But such activities and tendencies remained in the distinct minority when looking at the broad picture of Muslim politics in Indonesia.

Today, a handful of parties can be regarded as open or responsive to Muslim concerns. These groups do not espouse an Islamic state or a literal application of shari'ah. Rather, they tend to pursue agendas and policies guided by the principles of shari'ah—another example, perhaps, of what Vali Nasr calls the "Muslim Democracy" approach. This leads to an emphasis on accountability in public life rather than direct application of Qur'anic rule. This is perhaps best illustrated by looking at a seemingly contradictory finding of the *Pew Global Attitudes Survey* from 2003. Seventy-three percent of Indonesians indicated that religion is something that should be kept separate from government policy; at the same time, however, 82 percent of Indonesians said that Islam should play a large or fairly large role in the political life of their country. Essentially, what is being expressed here is an understanding of and desire for a distinction to be drawn between religious morality as a source of appropriate public conduct and the direct application of Islamic law in policy.

Jordan: Islamism as loyal opposition in an emerging liberal autocracy?

From two cases of relative hostility towards Islamists on the part of ruling regimes, we turn now to one where the relationship between the state and the Islamists has worked rather differently. The case of the Royal Hashemite Kingdom of Jordan presents us with yet another mode of Islamist participation in the political system. Unlike the Egyptian MB which, as we have seen, went so far during certain phases of its activism as to openly challenge the legitimacy of the state order, the Jordanian branch of the Brotherhood has for the greater part of its existence enjoyed a considerably more cooperative and mutually supportive relationship with the regime. Since the inception of a gradual and at times wavering process of political liberalization in 1989, the Brotherhood's direct involvement in politics has placed certain strains on this relationship, and also led to considerable soul-searching within the Jordanian Islamist movement more broadly. In this section we will survey the involvement of the MB in Jordanian politics from 1989—and in the guise of the Islamic Action Front (IAF) after 1993—with the aim of understanding how Jordan's shifting political environment has impacted Islamist strategies and self-understandings. As we will see, the case of Jordan does not allow us to view the evolution of Islamism as a "staging" process with classic Islamism giving way to the pragmatism of a new Islamism or Muslim Democracy (as per the cases of Egypt and Turkey above). Rather, mainstream Jordanian Islamism in some ways works in exactly the reverse direction, with an older generation of generally pro-regime pragmatists challenged by a younger generation of hardline activists harboring strong grievances towards key government policies.

The Jordanian branch of the MB was established in 1945, and the presence of King Abdullah I at its opening set the tone for the generally close and cooperative rapport between the palace and the Islamists that would endure for nearly half a century. While this relationship certainly experienced its share of turbulence over the years—such as when the regime appeared to lean too pro-Western or to not pay sufficient attention to Palestinian causes—the persistence of a critical mass of common interests tended to see it through these rough spots. Islamist support for King Hussein's 1970 violent crackdown on Palestinian groups operating out of Jordan (commonly known as "Black September"), for example, constituted a key moment in the alliance. In terms of the domestic political field, the regime and the Islamists generally found that they had a vested interest in working together to marginalize the influence of nationalist and leftist movements—ideological forces that both of them found distasteful and potentially threatening. Thus, until entering politics in 1989, the MB worked primarily at the social level as a charitable and da'wa organization. It advocated greater religious awareness and practice, but in a framework that did not at all challenge, and, indeed, even lent support to the royal regime. Even in 1957, when a royal decree banned all political activity, the Brotherhood was considered exempt due to its special status. In this regard, it is difficult to view the MB as wholly "owned" or co-opted by the state—their symbiosis does not necessarily mean the two sides always saw eye to eye. Rather the palace left the Brotherhood to get on with its work so long as it did not interfere with regime policies.

King Hussein embarked on a program of political reform and liberalization in 1989 for several reasons. The kingdom had recently experienced a period of social unrest and protests connected with the harsh effects of IMF-mandated austerity that were part of efforts to introduce greater economic liberalization. Popular discontent about increasing levels of government corruption was also an important factor. The cautious political liberalization process initiated by the king can certainly be understood as an attempt to rebuild national morale and support for the regime. But we can also observe, as has Beverly Milton-Edwards, that King Hussein was well aware of the political support the MB had garnered over the years and felt that it might be safer to bring the Brotherhood into a political system whose rules were dictated by the palace rather than to have it potentially working against the regime at the level of society.[88] Given their popularity, it was therefore not surprising that in 1989 the Islamists did particularly well in Jordan's first parliamentary poll for nearly a quarter century. Since the electoral system at this time did not permit the formation of actual political parties, the Islamists were all technically running as individual, independent candidates. Still, their affiliations were widely known and it was possible for some modicum of a party platform to come through during the short period of campaigning. All in all, MB-affiliated candidates won 20 out of the 80 seats in the assembly, with truly independent Islamists gaining another dozen spots. This made the "Islamist bloc" the single largest political faction within the new parliament.

It became clear very quickly that the direct involvement of the MB in politics would produce new strains on the Islamists' relationship with the regime. Although several of the MB politicians were brought directly into the government, the king's ability to rule by decree and bypass—not to mention dissolve—parliament at will meant that it was difficult for the Islamic bloc to accomplish very much that was meaningful in the way of Islamic reform. Although the regime and the Islamists saw more or less eye to eye on the issue of the 1991 Gulf War (with both supporting Saddam Hussein in the face of what they perceived as anti-Arab and anti-Islamic aggression by the United States), this "temporary alliance" quickly gave way to new conflicts.[89] For example, the government repeatedly struck down Islamist-led attempts to introduce an education bill mandating the segregation of schools by gender, and one of the most well-known and charismatic independent Islamists in parliament, Laith al-Shubailat, undertook an investigation into alleged corruption on the part of a former prime minister.[90] The Islamic bloc was uniformly critical of the regime for its support of the U.S.-sponsored Madrid peace process in late 1991, which they took as evidence of Jordan reaching out to Israel in the vein of Anwar Sadat in the 1970s—not to mention the fact that the king postponed the third session of parliament until after the Madrid talks had concluded in order to deny the Islamists an oppositional forum on the topic.

Late 1991 and 1992 saw a series of trials in which radical Islamist elements were accused of activities against the state. The government sought to link groups such as Muhammad's Army (Jaysh Muhammad), composed of Arabs who had joined the mujahideen in Afghanistan during the 1980s (see Chapters 6 and 7), with Islamism in the popular imagination, prompting accusations by mainstream Islamists that the government was out to slander them. The government even tried and convicted the aforementioned Laith al-Shubailat in connection with membership in a seditious movement. When this brought widespread condemnation from all sides of the political spectrum, the regime backed down, with the king rapidly granting clemency to many of those imprisoned. The government, however, continued in its efforts to sideline Islamist influence. In the run-up to the 1993 parliamentary poll, for example, they suddenly changed the election law, replacing a bloc or slate system of voting with a "one person, one vote scheme." Previously, voters had been able to cast as many votes as their districts held seats in parliament. This permitted them to distribute their political patronage among both local tribal leaders and Islamist groups—a system that favored a strong showing by the Islamists. In response to a new Political Party Law, the MB reorganized itself for the 1993 elections. In order to avoid being subject to provisions of the new law that required all parties to publicly disclose their financial sources and which disallowed parties with ties to any political groups abroad (the Brotherhood in Jordan could still be seen as loosely affiliated with the central party in Egypt), the MB decided not to register as a political party. Instead, it formed a new "umbrella party," the IAF, in which it played a leading—and in the eyes of some partners, a disproportionately powerful—role alongside several other Islamist groups and independents.

Immediately perceiving the new one person-one vote system as a deliberate attempt to decrease their parliamentary representation (as did most other political observers and parties), the IAF considered but quickly dropped the idea of boycotting the elections. As predicted, voters cast their choices primarily along tribal lines in 1993, with the result that the size of the Islamist bloc in the assembly was cut in half. The IAF immediately voiced calls for the election law to be changed. Their opposition to the government reached a fever pitch in 1995 with the signing of a peace agreement between Jordan and Israel. The following year, in response to new protests following the reduction of food subsidies (again stemming from an IMF economic recovery plan that the Islamists had opposed in 1992), the government undertook several initiatives widely regarded as a rollback of the political liberalization that had been introduced in 1989. A new restrictive press law was introduced that required higher capital outlays on the part of media outlets and which made criticism of certain regime-friendly figures illegal. Furthermore, despite consistent and increasingly vociferous calls by the IAF to change the electoral system, the law was left untouched. This prompted the Islamists to organize a boycott of the 1997 elections, stating their opposition to the government's renewed authoritarianism and to the peace deal with Israel. This proved to be a miscalculation on their part since they had hoped this appeal to populist sentiment would pay off in terms of support in the polls. Instead it produced a parliament composed almost exclusively of pro-regime elements. The Islamists were effectively closed out of the political system from 1997.

We might wonder what had led the regime, which had previously enjoyed such strong relations with the MB, to turn against it so strongly in the mid-1990s. In considering this question, Glenn Robinson has offered an explanation focusing on three key factors. First, with leftists and secular-nationalists now sidelined in the political system, there was no longer any "common enemy" to unite the Islamists and the regime; second, the climate of relative political openness after 1989 had encouraged the MB to go further than the government would have liked in terms of criticism—in short, the Islamists had become too difficult to control, and the regime needed to send a signal that they, rather than the opposition, would decide the timing and extent of political reform; and finally, certain demographic shifts (which we will look at in greater detail below) were afoot within the Islamic bloc.[91] More specifically, the "old guard" of the MB, who had tended to be residents of the East Bank or of the former Transjordan, and largely pro-regime in orientation were beginning to be replaced by a younger generation that was more adamantly pro-Palestinian and more likely to push the regime on this question.[92] In summary, a series of developments both internal and exogenous to the Islamist movement in Jordan had at least temporarily strained the symbiotic relationship with the regime beyond the point of continued mutual benefit and the government was now actively looking to restrain the political influence of the MB.

After nearly half a century on the throne of Jordan, King Hussein passed away in 1999 and was succeeded by his son Abdullah. The new king's consolidation of power also coincided with the outbreak of the second intifada in the Palestinian territories in 2000, resulting in considerable tensions within Jordan. Citing the unavailability of new magnetic voting cards but more likely driven by regional security concerns, the king in the summer of 2001 exercised his power to postpone that year's scheduled parliamentary elections after having earlier dissolved parliament. Over the next two years the palace ran the country by decree, issuing over 200 temporary laws that would not be subject to public review until the parliament was reconstituted. At the same time as he postponed elections, Abdullah also promulgated a new election law. This increased the number of seats in parliament, initially up to 104, and later by six more when it was decided to reserve a bloc for women candidates. Most of the new seats came about as a result of redistricting efforts that sought to increase the representation of particular areas, but most of these went to districts likely to return pro-regime representatives.

Despite expressing considerable regret at what they perceived as a complete reversal of the process of democratization and ongoing reservations about the electoral system, the IAF did contest the postponed parliamentary elections when they were finally held in the summer of 2003. While over half the seats were won by pro-regime candidates, the Islamists did manage to take 17 places in the assembly and, more importantly, to regain a presence within the political system. Interestingly, on a number of key issues, the Islamists now found themselves allied with leftist and secular parties also disgruntled with the heavy-handedness of the government during and after the pro-regime parliament.[93] While the new assembly did overturn several of the temporary laws passed by the king, there was no immediate standoff with the regime while the new multi-party assembly settled into place. Continuing to exert pressure to reform the electoral law and emboldened by Islamist electoral successes in Egypt and Palestine, the IAF looked forward to the parliamentary elections of 2007.

Morocco: Islamism in the shadow of the palace

Political participation by Islamists in Morocco is a relatively recent phenomenon, with the first organized electoral effort by a religious opposition movement coming only in 1997. In that year, the Party for Justice and Development (PJD) gained nine parliamentary seats. Five years later they more than quadrupled their representation, sending 42 deputies to the 2002 assembly. Observers of Morocco are unsure what to make of the new Islamist phenomenon. Some see in it the best hope of achieving meaningful political reform, a new source of political energy—not to mention a model of intra-party governance and transparency—that will force the other, larger and longer established opposition parties out of ossified doldrums. Others fear the PJD's rhetoric of openness and their seeming lack of interest in pursuing shari'ah would give way to a traditional Islamist stance once in power.

An assessment of Islamism—or any form of political opposition, for that matter—in Morocco must take into consideration the overwhelming power of the palace. While Mohamed VI has continued the modest reform process undertaken by his father Hassan II, this has focused primarily on issues such as human rights, reforming marriage and divorce law, and greater openness about and discussion of corruption. In terms of fundamental political reform, little has happened since Mohamed's accession in 1999, with the king retaining the power to veto or amend any piece of legislation with no option for parliamentary remedy.

Several aspects of Morocco's political environment are important to bear in mind when considering the role of Islamism, and when comparing it to other countries we have examined in this chapter. First while the two larger opposition parties in front of the PJD are "secular" parties, this term has a rather different connotation in the Moroccan context. Even these two parties—Istiqlal and the Union Socialistes des Forces Populaires, former leftists—would emphasize the importance of religion. What distinguishes the Islamists, then, is their emphasis on the idea that legislation and policy-making in Morocco should proceed with reference to an Islamic framework. Unlike Egypt, where Islamists constitute the only well-organized political opposition, the Moroccan system is replete with political parties—no less than 22 won seats in the 2002 legislative elections. This makes for a very different political calculus than the one faced by the MB in Egypt, where their candidates face little in the way of organized competition. While Moroccan Islamists certainly do not face the same challenges as similar parties in the highly secular Kemalist order of Turkey (indeed, the Moroccan king claims religious leadership credentials via the title of *Amir al-Muiminin*, Commander of the Faithful), they do have to tread carefully in terms of not directly questioning the legitimacy of the crown. And at the end of the day, the king ultimately has power over parliament.

Who are the Islamists in Morocco? There are two main groups today, one a conventional party that participates in the political and legislative processes, and the other a more hardline movement that questions the legitimacy of the monarchy.

The PJD (*Hizb al-Adala w'al-Tanmiya*) – formed in 1996 out of the religious movement Unity and Reform (*Al-Tawhid w'al-Islah*). Socially conservative and strongly identified with an anti-corruption platform, PJD seeks reform within an "Islamic framework" rather than the establishment of a shari'ah-based state. Their support for the monarchy is crucial to ensuring an ongoing political role, although they try to keep a critical distance from the palace. PJD initially campaigned against the liberalization of Moroccan family law, but eventually accepted passage of the new legislation.

Justice and Charity (*Al-Adl w'al-Ihsan*) – an anti-regime religious movement founded in 1974 and strongly identified with its mystical leader, Ahmed Yassine. The latter has been a vocal critical of the royal family and questions the legitimacy of Morocco's monarchy. In and out of jail over the past decades, Al-Adl's leader has consistently refused to take part in what he regards as the kingdom's corrupt and un-Islamic political system. With strong roots in the Sufi orders, Al-Adl's revolutionary mysticism has prompted frequent run-ins with Morocco's security forces.

The palace has watched the rise of PJD warily, and, for their part, the Islamists have been somewhat wary of their own success. Both have the experience of Algeria's FIS in mind (see "Algeria: the Islamist victory that almost was" in Chapter 3), where the rapid rise of an Islamist tide led to a strong backlash from the state and a dissolution of the political and internal security order. Where the palace has at times moved to block the influence of the Islamists, PJD seems to have voluntarily chosen a gradualist approach. For example, in the 2002 elections they deliberately did not field candidates in as many districts as they might have so as to avoid setting off alarm bells. Much of their potential success will depend on avoiding the perception that their willingness to cooperate with the prevailing order is not tantamount to having been co-opted by it. Much of what is noteworthy about PJD lies in their democratic management of internal party governance and their emphasis on transparency and integrity—leading the electorate to identify them as a force for anti-corruption. As parliamentary elections loom in 2007, observers will wonder if PJD's platform will take on a more explicitly Islamist flavor, and whether the party's dynamism and energy will prompt their larger and more established competitors to undertake much-needed internal reforms to keep up.

To better understand the development of Islamist political strategy in Jordan since 1989, we need to look more closely at how and where Islamists are located across Jordanian society, and to better appreciate the roles played by informal associations and networks in Islamic "public life." To begin with, we know that the demographic profile of MB/IAF members in Jordan parallels that of Islamist parties in other parts of the Muslim world—namely, that middle class and professional occupations represent the bulk of the group's membership.[94] Most importantly we need to take account of the rich web of sociality that links the "political" MB in the form of the IAF to the wider activities of the "social" MB as a charitable and da'wa organization. In short, the Islamists were able to operate as a formal political organization while simultaneously staying active in the social realm.[95] While both spaces are subject to considerable state regulation, enterprising Islamic groups are able to "socialize" non-religious spaces (such as professional associations, hospitals, etc.) and also use informal social groups and connections to wield normative influence less easily regulated by the state. As Quintan Wiktorowicz puts it:

> In Jordan, formal organization is more a mechanism of state control than an instrument of collective empowerment. Despite political liberalization, the Jordanian state utilizes an array of administrative techniques to limit the scope and content of civil society organizations. While the most overt forms of pressure have been removed, authoritarian tendencies are embedded in bureaucratic processes, procedures, and regulations, which are used to shape the content of social interactions in civil society ... To escape this form of state control, Islamic groups that challenge the regime retreat to personal networks based upon individuals with shared beliefs and do not reply upon organizations to achieve goals.[96]

While he makes this point primarily with regard to informal networks of salafi-oriented groups not strongly tied to the mainstream MB, Wiktorowicz's insight holds true when referring to the social and political capital

that can accrue from the socialization by Islamists of spaces not conventionally associated with religion (e.g. service providers), and not subject
to the heaviest state regulation (see Egypt above for comparison). "Seemingly apolitical activities such as education and health care provision
become political," write Wiktorowicz and Taji Farouki, "when they challenge other cultural codes and institutions."[97] The vast array of nongovernmental organizations and social service networks operated by the
Muslim Brotherhood emerges as a crucial component of the movement's
efforts to define public normativity—as well as a second terrain of struggle
with the regime. But it is also a space in which the cooperative compact
between the regime and the Islamists becomes relevant insofar as the MB
aids the government at the level of the social by providing alternatives to
more radical strains of Islamism.

How can we best understand the evolution of Islamist strategy in Jordan,
and its interaction with the wider reform process in that country? To begin
with, it is important to note that the IAF, the MB and Jordan's wider Islamist movement are not monolithic entities. In addition to the state-society
dynamic as a force shaping the course of Islamist political participation,
this relationship was also modulated by considerable and ongoing internal
politics within the movement. While the decision by the MB to contest the
1989 elections reflected, perhaps, an emerging consensus among that generation of the Brotherhood about the desirability of Islamists participating
in democratic elections, there certainly were voices within the movement
who did not want to get involved in politics. Some cited concerns that
entering the political field would distract from the movement's focus on
Islamic reform by forcing members to worry about campaigning and building alliances—in short, doing democratic politics.[98] Some Islamists were
reluctant about being forced to debate and compromise on issues which—as
derived from God and His shari'ah—were simply not open for discussion,
as was likely to happen when Islamists worked alongside leftists and secular
parties as co-legislators.[99] It was evident, however, that the vast majority of
the Brotherhood's members did want to enter the political fray. Ishaq
Farhan, a senior Brotherhood figure and eventual Secretary-General of the
IAF, expressed the group's general approach to politics in the following way:

> We believe that Islam offers general guidelines on how political deci-
> sions are to be made. It instructs Muslims to consult with each other.
> But the form or mechanism of consultation has not been specified in
> the Quran. It is left to the believers to design such a form within its
> proper historical context. We believe that democracy is the proper form,
> and Islam is wholly compatible with parliamentary democracy. For sure
> the Quran and Sunna are sacred to us. We make laws according to
> social context and exigencies. Fatwas are not obligatory. We make
> decisions not based on this or that fatwa, but based on the consensus of
> our shura. This consensus should be respected. A general consensus

such as that in the parliament is more important than the views of the ulama. I hesitate to consider those who disagree with us as being out of the bounds of Islam.[100]

The core dividing issue, then, was perhaps not so much one of whether or not to participate, but rather how to think about political participation in relation to the movement's ultimate goals. The party's statement following the successful 1989 elections emphasized its commitment to democracy, pluralism and constitutionalism while simultaneously stating an intention to bring Jordanian law into conformity with the shari'ah. Likewise, the economic content of their electoral platform had also been a mixed bag of fiscal conservatism and support for private property alongside calls for elements of protectionism and a non-interest-based banking sector.[101] Islamists worked alongside fellow parliamentarians of very different political persuasion in, for example, drafting a new National Charter outlining political rights and freedoms—and in the process of doing so they signed off on certain provisions regarding the status of shari'ah (as being one among several sources of legitimacy and legislation) whose wording was probably not ideal in the eyes of the Brotherhood.[102]

This certainly does not mean, however, that once they entered the parliament, internal dissent within the MB disappeared completely. Particularly after tensions with the regime emerged in the early 90s, the presence of factions within the Islamist camp became evident—but as Clark and Schwedler have argued, the alignment of these factions was not fixed and often changed based on the issue at hand.[103] This was evident, for example, in 1995 when some within the IAF considered joining the government, a move that to others in the coalition would have been anathema at a time when the regime was actively pursuing a peace agreement with Israel.[104] At other times, Islamist independents within the IAF umbrella complained of MB hegemony within the movement and some even resigned over this. If pressed to identify somewhat more persistent groupings within the Jordanian Islamist movement, we might perhaps turn to Glenn Robinson's distinction between "cultural" and "political" Islamists. The former camp, composed primarily of East Bank Jordanians, has tended to be more reliably pro-Hashemite over the years and understands Islamism as a political project primarily in relation to social issues such as education, gender segregation, and public virtue. The "political" Islamists, on the other hand, will often be of Palestinian background (West Bankers) and more concerned with issues relating to social justice and political imposition by external powers—the United States, Israel, the IMF—than with matters of cultural practice.[105] Indeed, the importance of the Palestinian issue within the Jordanian Islamist movement is difficult to overestimate. In many ways, the IAF has served as a proxy party for Palestinian interests due to its staunch and vocal opposition to the peace process. It also provides a space for Jordanians of Palestinian background to participate en masse without having to form a separate "Palestinian" party and risk condemnation as an ethnic faction seeking to undermine national unity.[106]

It is also possible to identify a distinct evolution in the Brotherhood's public discourse and internal deliberations after entering the political process. Jillian Schwedler, for example, points out that by 1993, the issue of whether participation in democracy was Islamically permissible had completely disappeared, with the discussion within the Islamist movement commonly structured around the more political question of whether it was worth continuing to contest elections given the regime's attempt to sideline its influence.[107] Others note a marked shift in the nature of IAF discourse from shari'ah-based explanations to a form of public reason grounded in the pragmatics of national interest.[108] From stating general principles in 1989, the Islamists' tangling with other parties and ideologies in the public sphere led them by 1993 to articulate their concerns with far greater specificity. They began, for instance, to advocate a more publicly prominent role for women (albeit still within an Islamically prescribed framework) in order to stave off attempts by other parties—notably leftists and secular liberals— to monopolize this issue.[109] When their parliamentary fortunes declined from 1993, the IAF reached out to non-Islamist parties to pursue those aspects of their program shared by other parties, and also sought to leverage their strong presence in various social and professional organizations (e.g. student associations, trade unions—see above) as alternative venues for politics.[110] In evaluating the development of Islamist political platforms and practices in the years following their incorporation into participatory politics, several analysts have come to the conclusion that their embrace of democratic principles—even if initially strategic and instrumental—has led to the internalization of values that have shifted the Islamists' normative horizons.[111] As Schwedler puts it:

> This does not necessarily mean that the group had evolved to such an extent that it could no longer be considered Islamist, or that Islam was no longer central to the group's diagnosis of the problems faced by contemporary Jordanian society and the group's prognosis for solutions. But gradually ... the Muslim Brotherhood and later the IAF came to explore and accept practices that seemed unthinkable just a few years earlier. Strategies that once triggered considerable debate no longer required any justification at all ... [T]he continued participation of the party illustrated more than an accommodation of democratic practices for strategic reasons. Rather, the internal party debates and particularly its practices illustrate that the group had seriously incorporated elements of a democracy narrative that effectively redrew the boundaries of what practices and strategies the group could justify.[112]

We might want to see in this evidence of the phenomenon that Carry Wickham has referred to as Islamist "auto-reform," referring to the tendency of various Islamist movements (cf. Egypt and Turkey above) to modify not only their political tactics, but also to recalibrate their strategies and public reasoning in response to changing political realities and the internalization of new normative frameworks.[113] In the case of the Jordanian Islamist movement, we see evidence of this not only in the aforementioned evolution of the IAF discourse, but also in the emergence on the political scene of new groups such as the Islamic Center Party (Hizb al-Wasat al-Islami), modeled on the similarly named Egyptian movement.

The case of Jordan thus presents us with the opportunity to gain an understanding of how a reformist rather than revolutionary breed of mainstream Islamism has responded to the onset of a gradual liberalization process that soon began to display many of the characteristics that Daniel Brumberg associates with "liberal autocracy."[114] We would want to stress the essentially symbiotic nature between the Islamists and the regime that has allowed their relationship, despite its ups and downs, to remain within the boundaries of normal politics. As Quintan Wiktorowicz summarizes it:

> Though the [Islamists] may disagree with policies or articulate opposition, [they] continue to act through the institutions of the political system without challenging the raison d'être of state or Hashemite power. The regime and the Muslim Brotherhood share an interest in maintaining the system since both benefit from its continuance. The regime benefits from the Muslim Brotherhood because the movement checks other more confrontational social movements and channels Islamic activism into a nonviolent agenda. The Muslim Brotherhood, on its part, has benefited from organizational opportunities produced by the incumbent regime. State support has allowed the movement to extend its reach in society and had enabled the Brotherhood to more effectively deliver its religious message.[115]

Despite the general persistence of this accommodation over the years, there are those who see the potential for greater tensions between the Islamists and the state in the years to come. This is not so much concern that the core of the Islamist movement will become radicalized, but rather that a younger generation of activists—many of them Palestinian, many of them carefully watching wider regional trends—will break with the moderate Islamist center and turn towards more confrontational tactics. There was considerable outcry in 2006, for example, when several Islamist members of parliament went to pay their respects to the family of the Jordanian leader of Al-Qaeda in Iraq, Abu Musab Zarqawi, after he had been killed by U.S. forces. For others the concern lies with formerly "cultural" Islamists deciding to more aggressively politicize their public virtue agenda should the process of liberalization in Jordan appears to tend towards the adoption of Western values and greater secularism.

The future of Islamist participation: issues and challenges

This chapter has highlighted several key issues and challenges relating to the question of Islamist participation in political systems. As our case studies have made clear, Islamists often represent the only politically organized alternative to discredited authoritarian regimes. Furthermore, much of their influence is to be found within the social sphere, and it flows through a wide variety of associational spaces including civil society groups, informal neighborhood associations, and solidarity networks. We have noted a marked tendency within some Islamist movements, particularly among the middle and young generations, toward finding new avenues of mainstream political participation. In some cases this has also occurred alongside the emergence of new intellectual and social currents that emphasize Islam's compatibility with the norms of political pluralism and inclusivity.

It is clear that in Egypt and Jordan (although markedly less so in Turkey), the Islamists represent the sole form of political opposition with any kind of organized presence in society. By default, oppositional energy is channeled their way because they are the only political force with the wherewithal to effectively capture and deploy it. Their success at the polls therefore tells us just as much about how skilled they are at mobilizing this base and tapping into veins of discontent as it does about the extent to which people actually embrace their normative vision. As Daniel Brumberg puts it:

> Although Islamists have emerged as one of the strongest, if not the strongest, opposition force wherever reasonably competitive elections have been held, these "facts" do not support the seductive conclusion that, given a free choice among alternative ideologies, most Muslims will always embrace an Islamist agenda. The real problem is that, in the Arab world, the fundamentalist agenda has an organized constituency while the non-Islamist agenda is either controlled by a discredited authoritarian regime and/or has little organized basis in society itself.[116]

This same pattern is to be found in a number of other settings, particularly in the Arab world, such as Yemen and Kuwait—and in both of those countries we have also seen the same shift towards a more participatory posture of late. Islamist or pro-Islamic parties also constitute the largest oppositional bloc in Malaysia. It is also evident that in all of the contexts we examined, the ability of Islamists to gain access to, socialize, and build social capital in various civil society and associational spaces has been crucial to their success. This phenomenon came about as a result of Islamists learning very quickly that many regimes would either heavily regulate or try to co-opt their political activities, or go to great lengths to keep them out of the political sphere altogether. Under these conditions, social spaces and voluntary, often informal, networks emerge as important *politicized* spaces for the contestation of policy, morality, and the social order. Islamist activity within the social sphere, as we have seen, is something far more complicated than just proselytizing and persuasion. Rather, these movements seek to redefine peoples' understanding of everyday practices—work, study, shopping, leisure, neighborly chatting—such that they are understood within an Islamic framework. "By providing goods and services," Wiktorowicz and Taji Farouki argue, "Islamists hope to expand networks of shared meaning so that individuals will organize their lives in accordance with Islamic precepts, rather than Western values and norms."[117] But are these precepts inherently incompatible with Western values and norms? This is a vital question to consider when it comes to the issue of the nature and goals of Islamist participation in democratic politics.

In noting the recent inclination toward political participation, we can see that Islamists have understood that if societal reform and transformation are the goals, then confining one's activism to the social sphere only gets you so far. They are well aware that the financial and legal resources associated with the policy-making arena are often the best way to effect large-scale change, and that this space constitutes a vital complement to the work they are doing in terms of recalibrating normative horizons at the grass-roots level. But this raises crucial questions about the nature and ends of Islamist political participation. What are their goals? What impact does democratic activity have on how they think about the meaning and nature of participatory politics? First, there are those who continue to express concerns that Islamist willingness to enter democratic politics is primarily instrumental. They fear that once in office, the Islamists would implement a highly undemocratic legislative agenda and seek to alter the political system so as to make their future removal from power impossible. Others cite concerns that Islamists who suffer political defeat or repression at the hands of the state could potentially turn radical. The example of Algeria, where the banning of the FIS in 1991 became the precursor to years of militancy and bloodshed, is often held up as evidence here. Or there is the possibility that even if an Islamist party, or some faction within it, was willing to play by democratic rules, a radical splinter group could emerge to ruin the show. Likewise, could not the vast network of social organizations these groups have cultivated not also be easily turned toward violent ends?

There are several arguments to be made in response to these concerns. First, the social bases of Islamist support—the networks and associations—are not simply "neutral conduits" into which any kind of ideas and activism can flow and expect to find enthusiastic support. They are normatively grounded and strongly socialized spaces, and, moreover, they tend in a direction that does not lend itself to easy or widespread adoption of radicalism. Their power comes precisely from the fact that people have learned to understand the banal, the mundane, the everyday in terms of Islamic experience—that they identify in these practices forms of stakeholding and stability that would make little sense to disrupt through militant activism. There certainly *do* exist networks that have been socialized in the direction of Islamic radicalism (see Chapter 7), but these are not the same as the spaces occupied today by mainstream Islamism.

Second, regarding the "Algeria scenario," it is important to note that the FIS was not typical of most Islamist movements today. From the time of that group's founding there were already marked tensions present within the group between moderate and highly radical factions. This is simply not the case with most Islamists parties in the Muslim world today. While there are certainly different tendencies present within these groups, as we have seen, their differences tend to be limited to issues of participation vs. non-participation, or how willing they are to cooperate with other parties rather than over questions of radicalism vs. political moderation. With regard to the wider issue of the impact of political repression on Islamist groups, both Wickham and White have noted that in the cases of the MB after the 1970s and of the Refah Party, repression by the state did not lead them to turn radical.[118] Given past experiences that some of these groups have had (e.g. the MB in Egypt during the 1960s), it makes sense that they would come to see it as in their interest to pursue solely legitimate means of participation. Even where blocked by the state, most of them have been able to find alternative avenues by which to pursue programs of moderate politicking; kicked out of the political sphere, they dust themselves off and regroup— witness the various iterations of Refah between 1998 and 2001, or the MB's response to the Mubarak crackdown of the early 1990s.

Indeed, there are those who have argued that becoming subject to institutional constraints and being forced to interact with, listen to, and consider a plurality of views can actually have a moderating effect on the ideology and conduct of political movements. This is the argument that participation leads to moderation.[119] As groups discover that genuine cooperation (and occasional compromise) often allows them to have a greater impact, they come to see this kind of pluralistic politics to be in their interest. In a recent study, Carrie Wickham goes even further, suggesting that we can see at work today something that she terms "Islamist auto-reform."[120] By this she is referring to various learning processes that occur over time as political groups come to internalize the norms of pluralistic politics and then to change their own internal norms, political party culture, and political behaviors. Citing some of the same movements we have looked at above, Wickham draws attention to the fact that this "auto reform" seems to be occurring primarily among the middle and younger generations who do not share the classic Islamist vision wherein party politics compromises Islam. In their understanding, Islamic norms are wholly compatible with, and even encourage, deliberation and discussion between a multiplicity of views. In many ways, the issue comes down—as Daniel Brumberg points out—to whether Islamists are willing to share power. As he puts it:

... [T]he challenge is not to figure out whether Islamism is "essentially" democratic versus autocratic, or liberal versus illiberal. Instead it is to see whether this or that Islamist group is acting within a hegemonic political arena where the game is to shut out alternative approaches, or else within a competitive—let's call it *dissonant*—arena where Islamists, like other players, find themselves pushed to accommodate the logic of power sharing.[121]

It is also the case, as Brumberg also points out, that the "political dissonance" referred to above is most likely to be present in those settings where Islamists contest elections and public debates alongside several other political viewpoints and not just in strict opposition to an authoritarian state. In this view, "Muslim democracy" only becomes democratic when there are other actors present making it difficult for one to play politics exclusively in a populist mode. This point bodes well in terms of the consolidation of Muslim democracy in, say, Pakistan, Turkey, or Indonesia—but perhaps less so in many countries in the Arab world where other, non-Islamic viewpoints lack an organized social base and/or are kept out of the political realm by autocratic regimes. This would lead us to speculate that one needs to take into consideration not only the question of whether Islamist movements are evolving towards pro-democracy stances, but also whether other political tendencies are seeking to become better organized, and regimes allowing more space for "dissonance."

In the end, perhaps it comes down to a question of what Islamists will do with the social capital they have accumulated. Political sociologists have drawn a distinction between "bonding" social capital and "bridging" social capital.[122] The first seeks to create forms of solidarity and trust premised on a shared exclusionary identity. The second, "bridging" kind of social capital, on the other hand, is one characterized by its ability to establish and sustain connections across disparate frameworks of norm and identity. Perhaps we might see the evolution from the classic mode of modern Islamism to new Islamism as, in part, a shift from movements defined primarily in terms of their ability to create and deploy bonding social capital to an approach that emphasizes the primacy—or at least the complementarity—of the bridging mode. But Islamists face distinct challenges when it comes to making this shift. How, for example, does one refigure the commitment to a shari'ah-based order—the very thing that often defines one as Islamist—in ways that allow for partnerships and political investment on the part of non-Islamist and certainly non-Muslim groups? Many of the "new Islamists" emphasize the necessity of a new ijtihad, but without specifying the content or boundaries of that activity.[123] Who gets to develop these approaches (see Chapter 9)? Is it possible to have democratic deliberation regarding points of shari'ah? Views on this question differ considerably across the Muslim world. The very idea of Western liberal secularism is still a non-starter for many Muslims, but this does not in and of itself mean that pluralism and power sharing are impossible—just distinct challenges that require creative thinking.[124]

It is clear that the meaning and nature of Islamist participation in political systems has been evolving over the past generation. There are real signs afoot that younger activists and supporters of these movements are drifting towards the political center in terms of both ideology and method. Furthermore, sociological analysis of their popular bases of support suggest that there is something far more complicated present here than mere political instrumentalism. That said, it is also clear that manifestations of centrist Islam are still very young and few in number. Far more research is required to gauge the level of popular support for this approach and also to better understand the circumstances that both promote and discourage its wider adoption. As we can see, it is clearly impossible to view Islamism in monolithic terms. Likewise we must not isolate it or assume that it will remain unaffected by ambient social, economic, and political transformations. Islamism has always sought to be an active, lived manifestation of Islam. As worldviews and modes of living evolve, therefore, so must Islamism as well.

5 Islam as the system: Islamic states and "Islamization" from above

In the previous chapter we looked comparatively at some of the ways Islamist movements have sought to enter the political process in a variety of countries, how these strategies have evolved over time, and how Islamism itself may be undergoing certain transformations today. Our analytic perspective was predominantly "bottom up" in the sense that we focused on how political parties and movements within society sought to challenge and compete with the authority of national-secular states and varying governmental responses to the attempts by Islamists to enter the political field. The present chapter will reverse the analytic lens to focus instead on those states that have sought to define themselves in terms of Islam, or to pursue strategies of Islamization as a form of political development or as a means for assuming and retaining power. While the governments in some of the countries we looked at in the previous chapter have certainly sought at times to co-opt Islamists (such as Egypt in the 1970s under Sadat) or to appropriate Islamic symbols when politically expedient (such as Nasser's claims that Pan-Arabism represented a form of "Islamic socialism" or Saddam Hussein's description of the 1991 Gulf War as a jihad), our primary interest in the present chapter will be on those nations that have actually declared themselves to be Islamic states, or where broad, pervasive, and systematic "Islamization" programs have been implemented. In this sense, our focus here is on the politics of "Islam from above."

But to make this distinction should not lead us to assume the existence of a real and meaningful dichotomy between "Islam from above" vs. "Islam from below." We would never suggest that in the examples covered in this chapter the state is the sole agent of Islamization, or possesses exclusive authority to define Islam. As will quickly become evident, there are many non-state actors involved in the religious politics of so-called Islamic states. By calling this chapter "Islam as the system," we are rather pointing out that when operating within a political environment characterized as "officially" Islamic or where there is understood to be a privileged relationship between state institutions and Islam, Muslim politics at all levels play out differently. The opportunity structures encountered by Islamist actors, not to mention their choice of religious symbols, the likely impact of these symbols, and the state's response to them will vary considerably when the political system is defined in religious terms. This is the primary dynamic we are seeking to capture when focusing on the idea of Islam as the system.

But no Islamic state is a monolith, either in the sense of there being only a single path or course by which a country becomes one, or in the sense of an Islamic government being capable of excluding other forms of politics— Muslim or otherwise—and challenges to its authority. Each of the countries we focus on in this chapter represents a different model and experience of state-led Islamization. Some, such as Saudi Arabia or Pakistan, were established as Islamic states, although this has meant rather different things in practice in each of their cases. In the case of Iran, an Islamic political order came about through a form of popular revolution, although the political system that has since evolved from it is based on a unique (and not necessarily very popular) interpretation of Islam's role in government. In the case of Sudan (see "Sudan: Hassan al-Turabi and the Islamic state" below), Islamization was an "experiment" associated with a change in regime, while the Malaysian state's embrace of Islam was part of a national development strategy (see "Malaysia: Islamization and national development" below). Even in a country such as Pakistan, established as we have already noted, as an Islamic state, successive regimes have related to and used Islam in very different ways, and we can hence point to something more like a series of Islamizing waves over the course of that country's political history.

The various cases we will examine below will provide us with an understanding of the diverse range of approaches to and experiences of "official" Islamization in the Muslim world. We will come to appreciate that the theory and practice of the Islamic state has meant very different things in different settings, and that we can therefore assume very little about the likely behavior of a given state simply because it has declared itself to be "Islamic." Likewise we will also examine the circumstances that might lead a particular state to pursue Islamization as a strategy and, again, the diverse range of goals they hope to achieve by doing so. As we will see, most Islamic states face various forms of internal challenge to their legitimacy, mostly by actors who question whether the government's embrace of Islam is genuine, or the correctness and authenticity of the Islamic order represented by the state. That is to say that even within Islamic states it is not uncommon to find Islamist opposition groups. The state's monopolization of Islamic normativity is never complete. So while this chapter will concentrate mainly on state-led Islamization efforts, it will be important to also give some attention to the counter-responses of various groups and parties—Islamic and otherwise— in order to appreciate the full political impact of Islamization from above.

Defining the Islamic state in theory and practice

Just what is an Islamic state and wherein lies its "Islamic-ness"? Let us begin by clarifying certain definitional confusions that often and easily arise when talking about Islamic states. The term "Islamic state" is sometimes mistakenly used to refer to any country with a predominantly Muslim population. While more than two dozen countries in the world fit this description, very few of them can be described as Islamic states according to the more specific sense in which we are using the term. They would more accurately be termed Muslim-majority countries or Muslim nations—two terms we have been using frequently throughout this book. In many cases the governments in question are highly secular in nature, and many of them actively seek to suppress the political ambitions of Islamically based groups and parties (as we saw in Chapter 4).

When we talk about "Islamic states" we are talking about a rather different situation, one in which the nature of the state and the political order is defined in Islamic terms. Again, there is room here for confusion. While the constitutions of a number of countries (among them Egypt and Tunisia) mention Islam as the religion of state or as the official religion, this does not in and of itself qualify these nations as having an Islamic state. Those very few countries that do style themselves as Islamic states tend to include further stipulations to the effect that the Qur'an or shari'ah is the primary (or exclusive) source of all legislation in the country, and that the nature and form of the governmental system is derived from Islam. So which are these countries and what, in theory, qualifies them as Islamic states? In order of their founding or transition to Islamic status, they are:

The Kingdom of Saudi Arabia (founded 1932) – whose Basic Law (adopted in 1992) stipulates the Qur'an as the constitution of the country, the authority of the ruling regime as derived from the Qur'an, and the legal system to be based on shari'ah.

The Islamic Republic of Pakistan (founded 1947) – established as a homeland for the Muslims of India, Pakistan's initial draft constitution spoke more of the state's responsibility to promote Islamic teaching and foster conditions that would allow its Muslim citizens to pursue their lives in accordance with the Qur'an and sunna; later versions included causes stipulating that all laws should be "brought into conformity with the injunctions of Islam as laid down by the Qur'an and Sunna."

Iran, known as the *Islamic Republic of Iran* (since 1979) – the constitution of which requires that all laws and policies be in accordance with Islam; mandates a political leadership role for the religious jurist (faqih); and derives most of the document's General Principles directly from Qur'anic sources.

These are the three major Islamic states to be examined in greater detail below. Two other countries representing rather different approaches to the Islamic state—Sudan and Malaysia—are covered in accompanying text boxes. We should note that in addition to these shari'ah-based states, there are a number of other countries that maintain parallel court systems in which certain issues—usually limited to matters of personal status and inheritance—are dealt with according to Islamic regulations, but they have not been included here since the role of shari'ah is carefully controlled by what are in other regards often very secular states. Afghanistan under the rule of the Taliban (1996–2001) would also certainly have counted as an Islamic state, but this case will be dealt with in the next chapter that looks at the role of Islam in weak or transitional states.

We should also bear in mind that the Islamic state in theory and the Islamic state in practice will often mean quite different things. Beyond the constitutional stipulations and titular trappings that allow the states above to lay claim to Islamic status, the role of Islam in day-to-day governance and in the shaping of things such as political institutions, legislative processes, and foreign policy is very difficult to identify with any certainty. In some cases, for example when we see hudud-prescribed criminal punishments being carried out in Saudi Arabia, or an institutionalized role for the clergy in Iran's government, it is easier to recognize the presence of norms and social roles explicitly associated with Islam. In other situations, this will be more difficult. We should remember that our main challenge as analysts is not to pronounce upon whether Sudan is "really" an Islamic state or whether Iran's revolution was "genuinely" Islamic. Rather, what we should be focusing on are the ways in which actors in a variety of social and political situations have sought to mobilize peoples and legitimize institutions on the basis of appeals to Islamic norms and symbols. In the case of the present chapter, we are most concerned with the question of how those actors associated with the structural capacities and institutional legitimacy of the state have included Islam in their politics—but also in the ways in which other political actors in society have responded to the state's claims regarding religious authority. Our inquiries about the state and Islam are hence primarily framed in terms of "why" and "how" questions rather than in terms of trying to gauge the veracity or authenticity of the state's claims vis-à-vis Islam.

Given that we are dealing with Islamic states, our discussions in this chapter will inevitably call to mind some of the deliberations we examined in earlier chapters—most notably Chapter 3—regarding the correct nature and form of the Islamic political order. As we may recall, various Islamic thinkers working during the period when modern states were being established in the Muslim world put forward widely differing views regarding the question of whether Islam was compatible with the modern nation-state. Even amongst those who stated a preference for an Islamic model of the state, we find quite different opinions as to what, exactly, this meant. For some, any form of government was permissible so long as it did not contravene Qur'anic requirements. Others preferred a more active and explicit application of shari'ah to legislative processes and outcomes. As we will see, the practice of Islamic statehood and Islamization has not led to a resolution of these issues, but rather provides us with a rich space in which to explore how these theoretical questions have played out in various efforts by state authorities to implement Islam in politics and policy.

Saudi Arabia: religious legitimacy cuts both ways

For many people the Kingdom of Saudi Arabia represents the Islamic state par excellence. Home to Islam's two holiest cities, Saudi Arabia for many evokes images of strict adherence to Islamic law, deeply conservative social values, oppressive attitudes towards women, and hostility to non-Muslims— all of which are generally taken to be characteristic of "Wahhabism," the form of Islam most associated with the Kingdom. Islam lies at the very foundation of the Saudi state, and the legitimacy of the country's royal family has long rested on its claims to uphold the shari'ah and to rule according to the precepts of the Qur'an. But one would be very wrong to think that after claiming this status for themselves at the time of the Kingdom's founding, the religious legitimacy of the Saud family's rule has been taken for granted. The relationship between the royal family and the religious establishment whose support enabled the former to justify its political ambitions in Islamic terms has always been complex. Indeed, the evolving and at times highly ambivalent relationship between the palace and the ulama has long been a key factor in determining the course of Saudi politics. As we will see, the very same claims used by the Saud to legitimize their rule have also opened them to considerable criticism, from the religious establishment certainly, but also from political elements within society. This has led in recent years to the emergence of various forms of Islamism even within this most conservative of Islamic states.

Our analysis of Saudi Arabia will begin by briefly discussing the historical circumstances surrounding the establishment of three waves of Saudi state building over 200 years, beginning in the mid-eighteenth century and culminating in the modern Kingdom of Saudi Arabia in 1932. The evolving historical relationship between, as one author has put it, the "political ambition" of the Saud family and the "spiritual vision" of their allies among the religious scholars is the key to understanding the complex and multifaceted relationship that obtains between the crown and the religious establishment in the Kingdom today.[1] We will then move on to look at the formation of the modern Saudi state, again paying particular attention to questions relating to the division of competences and powers between the royal family, the government bureaucracy, and religious scholars. The question of how Islam has figured in the foreign policy of the Kingdom will be taken up, and we will also give some consideration here to the much-discussed issue of Saudi Arabia's role in propagating and supporting Wahhabism beyond its borders. Some further details regarding the nature of Saudi society in terms of religious demographics and socioeconomic composition will then be provided, and with this background in place, we will be prepared to look more closely at the development of religious opposition to the Saudi royal family in the Kingdom today. Beginning with the takeover of the Grand Mosque in Mecca in 1979, we will track the development of several distinctive undercurrents of Islamism within Saudi Arabia, focusing particularly on the period following the Gulf War of 1991. This context will also draw our attention to the question of where Saudi Arabia fits into the growth and development of transnational radical Islam of the sort represented by Al-Qaeda (see Chapter 7). The various reform initiatives introduced by the palace during this same period—such as the establishment in 1992 of the Consultative Council—will also be considered in light of various emergent social tensions and ongoing pressures from dissident religious elements. Finally, we will conclude by offering some reflections on recent political developments such as the Kingdom's first ever elections (for municipal councils) and the future course of Islamism in Saudi Arabia.

But before we delve into this account of modern religious politics in Saudi Arabia, it would be worthwhile to spend a few moments discussing and coming to some better understanding of what is meant by "Wahhabism"—particularly since Saudi Islam is generally understood to be coterminous with this concept. This eponymous current of Islamic theology and jurisprudence derives from the thinking of the eighteenth-century religious reformer Muhammad Ibn Abd al-Wahhab (whose ideas we briefly examined in Chapter 2). As we may recall, Ibn Abd al-Wahhab's discourse of religious purification sought to cleanse Islam of the many forms of "innovation" (bid'a) that had been introduced over the centuries, diverting the religion from its true practice as embodied in the traditions of the Prophet and the example offered by those companions who were his contemporaries or near contemporaries by a couple of generations—known as the salaf, or pious ancestors. In this regard, we can say that Wahhabism is a subset of, but not synonymous with, salafism—an approach to Islam we will look at more closely in Chapter 7.

The foundational concept from which all Wahhabi thought derives is that of tawhid, a term that refers to the "oneness" and uniqueness of God, and also the unicity of all things within the divine. It is the emphasis on tawhid—often and variously translated as "monotheism" or "unitarianism"—that led Ibn Abd al-Wahhab to repudiate any and all religious practices that involved even a semblance of worshipping anything other than God. This included various Sufi practices such as the visitation of graves associated with mystical saints, or the celebration of their birthdays. In his major work, the *Kitab al-Tawhid* ("The Book of Divine Unity"), Ibn Abd al-Wahhab cites favorably the ideas of the early fourteenth-century jurist Ibn Taymiyya, a proponent of the salaf and an ardent foe of what was taken to be Sufi heresy regarding matters of worship. Ibn Taymiyya is also regarded as one of the greatest legal minds within the Hanbali school of Sunni jurisprudence, an approach also closely identified with Wahhabism and the Saudi religious establishment. While the substance of Hanbali views on many issues are deeply conservative and often quite literalist, it is important to note that this particular legal school is, in a certain sense, rather less conservative when it comes to matters of legal methodology. Unlike other schools that place considerable emphasis on respecting the opinions and precedents of other jurists, Hanbalism prefers direct reliance on Qur'an and hadith and encourages scholars to exercise ijtihad (independent judgment) based on these sources. This legal approach matched well Ibn Abd al-Wahhab's desire to achieve a pure Islam that reflected as closely as possible the model of normativity found in the Qur'an and sunna.

Aside from the emphasis on tawhid, the ideals of the salaf, and the importance of Hanbali jurisprudence, there is one further aspect of Wahhabism that deserves particular mention. This concerns certain aspects of Wahhabi normative discourse that evolved as a function of how the doctrine was put into practice in political terms. As we will explore more fully below, Ibn Abd al-Wahhab entered into an alliance with a powerful Arabian tribal family, the Saud, in the hope that this partnership would allow the theory of tawhid to be achieved in practice through a political order. This political movement advanced by conquering and gaining oaths of allegiance from various tribes across the Arabian peninsula—often at the point of the sword. In order to legitimize attacks against other clans who were also Muslim, Ibn Abd al-Wahhab had to be able to make the case that the non-Islamic practices followed by these groups had effectively placed them outside the remit of the religion—in other words, that by their incorrect religious practice they had made themselves into infidels (in which case the strictures against Muslims using violence on fellow Muslims no longer applied). Because of this early history of needing to differentiate between true Muslims and religious "others"—one which would be repeated at the time of the founding of the modern Saudi state—Wahhabi discourse today is often characterized by a tendency to establish and legislate moral categories that strongly differentiate various groups of people, and usually in very stark terms (e.g. believers vs. infidels). It is this feature of Wahhabism that has gained it a reputation for intolerance, particularly as regards other religious groups and sects within Islam. Thus the considerable religious pluralism to be found in modern Saudi Arabia (e.g. Shi'a, Sufis, followers of other Sunni legal schools) has very little public profile due to the hostility of the religious establishment. Indeed, an overtly anti-Shi'i stance has long been an integral part of the Saudi state's self conception. One final but important point to make concerns use of the term "Wahhabi" itself. Generally speaking, those who hold these views will never refer to themselves as Wahhabi. Rather, with the exception of certain moments in the early history of the modern Kingdom, the terms "Wahhabi" or "Wahhabism" have been used (and usually in a derogatory manner) only by Muslims of other persuasions, or by non-Muslims. Those who do follow this tendency have historically been more likely to refer to themselves as muwahhidun ("monotheists" or "unitarians"), ahl al-tawhid ("people of oneness"), or sometimes just as salafis. In summary then, Wahhabism is a variety of salafi thought that evolved historically via the social and political experience of state formation and consolidation in Saudi Arabia. Its defining traits are an overwhelming emphasis on the doctrinal essence of tawhid, a marked but not exclusive reliance on Hanbali jurisprudence, and a tendency to draw strong normative distinctions between different categories of peoples.

Religion, the royal family, and the Saudi state

The original antecedent for the modern Kingdom of Saudi Arabia can be traced to an alliance made in 1744 between Muhammad Ibn Saud, a tribal prince in the Nejd region of central Arabia, and the religious reformer Muhammad Ibn Abdul Wahhab. The former saw in Ibn Abd al-Wahhab's purifying zeal the inspirational ideology and religious justification that would permit him to fulfill his political ambition of uniting the various tribes of Arabia, while Ibn Abd al-Wahhab saw Ibn Saud's tribal base as a formidable political vehicle that would permit the message of tawhid to be reflected in a living social order. While it would be wrong to assume that the two saw each other only in instrumentalist terms, both undoubtedly appreciated the great potential of the symbiosis. Ibn Saud implemented this state-building project by establishing a coalition of tribal units loyal to him that could act as the movement's army. Emphasizing their brotherhood in religion, Ibn Saud and Ibn Abd al-Wahhab called them the Ikhwan ("brotherhood"), and over the next 50 years these forces were able to secure more and more territory for the nascent Saudi polity, their numbers growing with each success. The resemblance between Ibn Saud's methods and the early community-building efforts associated with the Prophet Muhammad was certainly not lost on anyone and, indeed, there was a conscious effort to cultivate these kinds of parallels in the minds of potential supporters. The effort reached its symbolic zenith in 1802 when Ibn Saud conquered Mecca and Medina, bringing the two holiest cities of Islam under his control. It was at this point that Ibn Saud attracted the attention and concern of the Ottoman sultan who otherwise tended to have little interest in the tribal intrigues of inner Arabia. With Ottoman control of the holy cities and the pilgrimage now under threat, Istanbul mobilized its Egyptian army—commanded by Muhammad Ali—to expel the Ikhwan from the Hijaz and crush the Saudi state. In 1819, Ibn Saud's capital near Riyadh was sacked, sending both the Saud and the al-Sheikh (the family of Ibn Abd al-Wahhab) into exile. The former managed to re-establish themselves near Riyadh by 1824 and preside over a "second" Saudi state—far more limited and less ambitious in scope—until the end of the nineteenth century. At this point, ongoing pressure from the Ottomans, increased British interest in Arabia, and challenges from other major tribes led the Saud to once again abandon their capital and flee, this time into Kuwait—a favor that would be returned exactly a hundred years later when that country's ruling family would take refuge in Saudi Arabia from Saddam Hussein's invading armies in 1991.

The establishment of the modern Kingdom of Saudi Arabia began with the efforts of Abdul Aziz Ibn Saud to reclaim his family's territories in the first decade of the twentieth century. In a sequence of events that closely

mirrored the efforts of his family's forebear just a little over a century earlier, Abdul Aziz progressively reconquered all of the same territories that
Muhammad Ibn Saud had held, and more beyond. His methods were also
similar and involved reconstituting the Ikhwan and animating them with
the same religious fervor. The organization of the Ikhwan "v2.0" again
echoed the early period of Islam, with Abdul Aziz establishing separate
communities for his religio-political armies that evoked the Prophet's hijra
from the jahiliyya of Mecca into true Islam. In 1926, after taking the Hijaz
from the Hashemite dynasty of Sharif Hussein, Abdul Aziz's forces defeated
the Rashid dynasty occupying Riyadh and declared this the capital of his
new state. His efforts had attracted the patronage of Britain by this time,
and he had frequent dealings with both the British military and London's
political representative for the region. These foreign dealings, but also the
enthusiasm with which he adopted Western technologies and entertained
business propositions from abroad soon brought Abdul Aziz into conflict
with the Ikhwan, however. It is important to remember that just as in the
case of his ancestor, Abdul Aziz's legitimacy in the eyes of the Ikhwan was
based on his credentials as an agent of piety and the advancement of Islam.
Once it began to seem to them that Abdul Aziz was facilitating foreign
interests in Arabia, and particularly when he started to prevent the Ikhwan
from raiding certain tribes outside the Saudi confederation, they mounted a
revolt against him. Abdul Aziz spent the next few years quelling this rebellion, and once this had been accomplished he sought and obtained oaths of
allegiance from the peninsula's remaining holdout tribes. This enabled him
in 1932 to proclaim the birth of the new Kingdom of Saudi Arabia in the
form in which we know it today.

Abdul Aziz's quest for foreign economic partnerships was evidence of a
deep pragmatic streak in his leadership style. He suddenly found himself
ruling over an enormous, peninsula-wide state whose only meaningful
source of public income were the modest revenues associated with custo-
dianship of the hajj pilgrimage. From the early 1930s Abdul Aziz had
received expressions of interest from a number of British and American
companies interested in pursuing the possibility that there might be significant and commercially exploitable hydrocarbon resources under the
Saudi soil. He granted an exclusive concession to Standard Oil of California
(the forerunner to Exxon). In 1938, Dammam Well #7 in the Eastern Province, immediately adjacent to the Gulf coast, struck oil in commercial
quantities. The emergence of Saudi Arabia as a world energy giant, and
moreover one closely allied with U.S. commercial and later political interests, had now begun. The Saudi government gradually acquired greater
ownership of the resulting oil company—the Arabian American Oil Company (ARAMCO) from its American partners—until 1980 when it became
a wholly state-owned entity. In 1988, the company's name was changed to
Saudi Aramco to reflect this and to reflect ongoing attempts to "Saudi-ize"
the country's skilled workforce instead of relying so heavily on imported

expertise—an issue that would prove sensitive later in terms of religious politics.

Let us make a few observations regarding the establishment of the Saudi state and the triangle of linkages that define the relationship between the royal family, the religious establishment, and wider Saudi society. The legitimacy of the Saudi state, as has already been mentioned, rests on the twin pillars of the royal family and the support they receive from the ulama. We can thus speak of the existence of something like a "contract" between the palace and ulama whereby the latter provides for the legitimacy of the former so long as the royal family upholds the shari'ah, while the crown ensures a privileged institutional role for the religious scholars. Also relevant is a second covenant or tacit "social contract" between the royal family and wider Saudi society in which the Saud provide for the protection and welfare of the people in return for their allegiance and political quiescence. Both of these structures of legitimacy and authority are important to understand and to bear in mind later when we move on to examine the emergence of Islamist opposition in Saudi Arabia and various popular voices seeking reform and greater political openness. Institutionally separate from the royal family and the religious establishment (but subject in various ways to the authority of both) is the Saudi government itself and its associated bureaucracy. Initially only a minor player in the governance of the Kingdom, the government bureaucracy comes into its own once the influx of significant oil revenues necessitated the creation of ever more ministries and administrative capacities to oversee the rapidly growing and modernizing Saudi state.

The Islamic character of the Saudi state is to be found in several aspects. First among these is the idea of the Qur'an as the highest law of the land and the Saudi dynasty as the guardian and enforcer of Qur'anic law within the Kingdom. All laws in Saudi Arabia are made in accordance with the shari'ah and all legal processes, overseen by a Ministry of Justice, must conform to its requirements. While Saudi Arabia has no formal constitution, the Basic Law, promulgated in 1992, identifies the Qur'an as the basis for all public affairs. The second defining element of the Saudi model of the Islamic state is to be found in the special status granted to the religious establishment. Overseen by the Higher Council of Ulama, religious scholars have played a major role in buttressing the authority of the royal family by providing fatwas endorsing their policies. It would be inaccurate, however, to view the "official" ulama as rubber-stampers for the Saud. On numerous occasions throughout the history of modern Saudi Arabia, the ulama have not seen eye to eye with the royal family, and the latter has taken steps to circumvent their authority. The third component of the religious state is the *mutawwa* or religious police, a semi-autonomous institution with some connection to (but also at times operating quite independently of) the religious establishment. Charged with the maintenance of public virtue, it is the mutawwa that are responsible for what many in the West perceive as the excesses of Saudi religiosity, such as the harassment of women deemed to be in violation of religiously mandated dress codes. Their pervasive presence throughout the Kingdom is also designed to enforce requirements related to the closing of businesses during appointed prayer times, and they have reserved to themselves the right to administer justice "on the spot" in the form of canings and other types of punishment. Although a quasi-official corps, mutawwa activities have often been at odds with the policies and desires of the royal family, government ministries, and even the religious establishment. In 2002, for example, there were widespread calls from all quarters of Saudi society to reign in their influence when they prevented the evacuation of a girls school during a fire because the students were not sufficiently covered. Fifteen primary school-age girls lost their lives in that incident, and 50 more were injured.

How has the relationship between the Saud, the government, and the religious establishment evolved over the years? Granted broad jurisdiction by the royal family in terms of overseeing functions such as religious education and the annual pilgrimage, the ulama in Saudi Arabia have certainly played a more pervasive role than the "official" religious establishments found in several other Muslim countries. As we have already noted, they have also tended to play a prominent role in lending legitimacy to a wide range of political actions undertaken by the government and the ruling house. For example, the second monarch of Saudi Arabia, Abdul Aziz's son Saud, was widely viewed as incompetent by his own family and the religious establishment played a key role in providing the Islamic justification behind the family's decision to remove him from the throne in 1964 in favor of his brother Faisal. But the influence of the religious scholars has by no means been absolute, witnessing considerable ebb and flow depending on which monarch has been on the Saudi throne and his vision of national priorities. Under King Faisal, for example, certain differences arose between the modernizing tendencies of the palace and the religious establishment which made for a period during which the influence of the ulama were somewhat curtailed. In the wake of Faisal's assassination and the ensuing period of political and economic instability, however, the religious establishment was able to reassert itself under the new king in return for its support in maintaining social order.

The royal family has also employed certain measures and created institutions that have allowed them to exercise some degree of autonomy from the ulama in terms of introducing new laws. A number of legal regimes relating to labor and insurance were introduced in the early 1970s, for example, and the exercise of "administrative discretion"—a version of the qanun courts for customary law used by the Abbasids and the Ottomans—has also featured heavily. The ulama staff and perform a wide range of functions within the country's shari'ah court system, but they do so within the highly bureaucratic environment of the Ministry of Justice (rather than via a separate religious judiciary attached to the Councils of Ulama). The court system itself has also been amended on various occasions, adding layers of appeal beyond the qadi, and also establishing a special Board of Grievances that permits Saudi citizens some course of potential remedy in situations where they believe themselves to have suffered an injustice at the hands of the bureaucracy.

It is important to bear in mind that the negotiation and evolution of these relationships were taking place against a backdrop of tremendous and rapid modernization in terms of the Saudi economy, industry, infrastructure, military, and bureaucracy. Once serious oil revenues came on stream from the mid-1950s, the pace of change was frenetic. Inevitably the rapid modernization of a society just one generation removed from a very traditional and conservative nomadic lifestyle would prove to be the source of considerable social tension—not only in terms of the compact between palace and ulama, but also in terms of the relationship between the royal family and a newly emerging, well-educated professional middle class. Of particular importance to the course of this development process, of course, were Saudi Arabia's relationships with the outside world, not least of all the United States. The idea of a "special relationship" between the Kingdom and Washington D.C. is best captured in the images of the iconic meeting between King Abdul Aziz and President Franklin Roosevelt in 1945. It was during this summit that the United States exchanged guaranteed access to Saudi oil for promises by the new global superpower to protect the sovereignty of the Kingdom and its royal family. While this covenant would represent the crux of the broad arc of U.S.-Saudi relations for the next half century and more, it was not always a smooth road. The Saudis raised objections in the mid-50s, for example, to the extent of U.S. military support going to Israel. The Palestine issue would rear its head again in the wake of the 1973 Arab-Israeli war when Washington's crucial airlift of military supplies to Israel prompted a backlash from a number of Arab and Muslim oil-producing countries who realized that their influence over world oil prices could be used as a foreign policy weapon (not to mention an easy route to huge cash windfalls). Saudi oil revenues more than quadrupled over the single year from 1973 ($4.3 billion) to 1974 ($22.6 billion) and continued to climb precipitously to a high in 1980 of $102 billion.[2]

The role of Islam in Saudi foreign policy has also varied over the years. Although general support for Muslim causes abroad was a pillar of the Kingdom's foreign relations from very early on, Islam only became a political issue in Saudi diplomacy once the power balance in the Middle East region began to shift decisively in the mid to late 1950s. The rise of Gamal Abdel Nasser in Egypt and his socialism-inflected brand of Pan-Arabism emerged as the dominant political current in the Arab world, and Cairo sought to exert influence over other countries in the region. Riyadh's response was to offer an alternative model of Pan-Islamic solidarity, leveraging its symbolic power as the home of the two holy cities to challenge

Egypt's efforts at establishing regional hegemony. The Kingdom would respond similarly to other instances of what it saw as imported Western ideology, such as Ba'athism in Syria and Iraq, and various experiments with Marxist thought throughout the region. Saudi-Egyptian rivalry continued for several years, nearly resulting in war when Egyptian troops entered Saudi Arabia's southern neighbor Yemen in 1962 to back the newly established republican government that was facing a strong challenge from Saudi-backed royalist forces. Also during this period, several of the more hardline activist leaders in the Egyptian Muslim Brotherhood (MB)—facing considerable persecution at the hands of Nasser's government—took refuge within the Saudi religious establishment. This would prove to be a significant development, as we will see, for the later development of Islamist opposition groups within the Kingdom. From the 1960s onwards, and particularly under King Faisal, Saudi Arabia played an instrumental role in establishing, funding, and providing leadership (both officially and unofficially) within a wide range of intergovernmental and nongovernmental Islamic organizations. It was the driving force, for example, behind the establishment of the Organization of the Islamic Conference, and also set up organizations such as the Muslim World League and the World Assembly of Muslim Youth as organs through which to express its preeminence within the Muslim world and to export aspects of Saudi-style Islam (see Chapter 9). Following the defeat of the Arab forces by Israel and the loss of Jerusalem during the Six Day War in 1967, Saudi Arabia saw an opportunity to package this to the rest of the Muslim world as the culmination of Nasser's failed secular nationalist project. In the wake of 1967, Riyadh became increasingly active in pro-Palestinian causes and began for the first time to directly support the Palestine Liberation Organization (PLO). Saudi Arabia would also at various times provide support to Islamist parties abroad such as the MB in both Syria and Egypt, and also the Jama'at-i Islami in Pakistan. Riyadh also cultivated a strong relationships with other prominent Sunni Muslim countries—with Pakistan, during the Islamization years of Zia ul-Haq, emerging as a particularly important ally in Riyadh's efforts to check Iran's growing influence in the Muslim world in the wake of that country's Islamic revolution.

The making of Islamist dissent in Saudi Arabia

Beginning with a major incident in 1979, but gathering significant and sustained force in the wake of the Gulf War of 1991, the Saudi establishment has faced various forms of internal political opposition. Most of this has been articulated in terms of questioning the religious credentials of the royal family and has manifested itself as Islamism in various guises. In this section we will chronicle the emergence and evolution of Islamism in the Kingdom, and situate this within the wider context of ongoing Saudi political development and world affairs.

It is certainly not the case that political opposition to the Saudi royal family was wholly absent until the late 1970s. Rather, the regime had proven itself particularly adept at co-opting dissent and maintaining the status quo in their already very conservative society. In order to better contextualize the emergence of overt discord during this period, we need to relate it to lingering tribal resentments dating back to the period when the first king, Abdul Aziz, turned against various elements within the Ikhwan forces that had enabled him to seize power. The religious establishment—and certainly the effected tribes—had long felt a sense of unease with the way Abdul Aziz had handled the Ikhwan revolt. Their suspicions increased when, in the years following the discovery of oil, more and more foreign workers and non-Muslims poured into the Kingdom to develop its industrial infra-structure. Abdul Aziz was even challenged by the ulama on this last point. Sheikh Bin Baz, who would later rise to the rank of chief mufti within the official establishment, issued a fatwa in 1940s based on a hadith of the Prophet indicating that it was illegal to employ non-Muslims servants in Arabia. Bin Baz eventually backed down with reluctance but the incident identified him as autonomous minded thinker and over the years these cre-dentials enabled him to play an important intermediary role between the royal family and the most hardline of scholars—even once King Faisal tapped him to head up the ulama establishment. One figure influenced and impressed by Bin Baz's early stance toward the regime was a young student at the University of Medina in the early 1970s named Juaiman al-Utaibi, who also happened to hail from the tribal areas connected with Abdul Aziz's crackdown on the Ikhwan. It seems to have been during his time at Medina—the institutional bedrock of Wahhabi thought—that Juaiman came to be convinced of the illegitimate nature of the Saud's rule. His complaints, however, were not just based on lingering soreness over Abdul Aziz's mistreatment of the Ikhwan. In the years following the latter's reign, and particular under the second king, Saud, the royal family had earned itself a considerable reputation for decadence and profligacy, even within the highest echelons of senior princes. Stories of immoral behavior by senior members of the royal family while vacationing abroad were rife, as were accounts of their lavish and excessive lifestyle. With some estimates claiming that 5% of all oil revenues went immediately into the private coffers of the Saud even before reaching the public treasury, it became clear how the family was able to sustain the enormous allowances paid to hundreds (if not thousands) of princes. Even the king at the time, Faisal, who did not have the same reputation for excess as his brothers, came in for suspicion due to his perceived Westernizing tendencies.

Certain that the Saud had abandoned all responsibility as proper Islamic leaders, Juaiman—who had served in the National Guard before entering university—moved onto an activist footing and spent several years con-stituting a small force modeled on the original Ikhwan. In November 1979, during the hajj season, Juaiman's forces dramatically seized control of the

Grand Mosque in Mecca and held it for two weeks. His chief accomplice in this was Muhammad al-Qahtani, who claimed for himself the status of *Mahdi*—Islam's messianic figure. The regime secured a fatwa from the ulama to permit the use of force to expel the rebels, but Saudi Arabia's own national guard was unable to do this. Their initial failed attempt led to the death of over a hundred and it is reported that some of them even decided to join Juaiman's forces. The siege ended after a fortnight when French and Pakistani special forces were finally brought in to subdue the rebels. Juaiman and his conspirators were jailed and most them eventually executed. In addition to the public spectacle of the dissent itself, the regime's botched handling of the incident only served to confirm its inefficacy in the eyes of many.

The years following the Grand Mosque siege witnessed a relative upswing in the political fortunes of the ulama. Faisal's rather weak and short-lived successor, Khaled, did not undertake any meaningful reform in response to the events of 1979 but instead funneled ever more money to the religious establishment in return for their assistance in maintaining stability and the status quo. Saudi society had been shaken not only by the Mecca debacle but by waves of riots that had broken out at the very same time within the Kingdom's Shi'a community (approximately 10% of total population, concentrated in the oil-rich Eastern Province), newly emboldened by the recent success of their co-religionists' Islamic revolution in Iran. The ulama used their new found influence to pressure the royal family and government on issues such as tightly enforced dress codes and various other measures relating to public virtue and proper religious observance. This climate also gave latitude to and encouraged the growth of a tendency that had been developing within the ranks of the religious scholars since the late 1960s. Commonly referred to as the Sahwa ("awakening") movement, this current can be described as a hybrid combination of Wahhabi theology with the political activism of the MB. Various influential thinkers from the more revolutionary wing of the MB had left Egypt for Saudi Arabia in the early 1970s. Among them, for example, was Muhammad Qutb, the brother of Sayyid Qutb (see Chapter 3), who eventually held various teaching positions within the Kingdom's religious university system. This ideological fusion led to the rise of a trend that might be thought of as a form of "activist Wahhabism" in contrast to the pietistic moralism traditionally associated with Saudi salafism. As Gilles Kepel puts it, "Muhammad Qutb's reputation and his family's famous name attracted young readers who sought a confrontation between Islam and jahiliyya and yearned for invigorating, modern ideas for their battle against secularism, socialism, and the West."[3] It is worth noting here that in the eyes of these young would-be activists, attraction to modern ideas and dislike of the West were not understood to be contradictory. This was a generation that had watched with a combination of wonder and ambivalence as their society was rapidly transformed. Their disillusion at what they saw as the culturally eroding effects of

Western modernization led them to engage much more enthusiastically with approaches to political modernity developed by Islamic thinkers such as Hassan al-Banna and Sayyid Qutb. They were similarly disappointed by the religious establishment, which they viewed as too well co-opted by the Saudi regime to ever become an agent of meaningful Islamist reform.

During this same period, a major decline in world oil prices led to significant revenue shortfalls. From a high in 1980 of $102 billion, inflows dropped by some 80 percent over the next six years, putting a tight squeeze on the public budget and forcing the government to begin reducing or abolishing outright a number of social welfare programs. Food and petrol subsidies declined, and the government was also forced to curb certain customary practices such as the promise of a job within the bureaucracy for every (male) Saudi who successfully completed university. The ranks of government positions by this point had swollen to such a point of redundancy that it was unable to sustain salaries, much less take in thousands of new employees each year.

This combination of factors made for a particularly volatile societal climate within the Kingdom in the late 1980s and 90s. With the royal family's severe financial mismanagement more obvious than ever, the Gulf War of 1991 proved to be the major catalyzing event for the development of a concerted and sustained Islamist opposition. This was the case in several regards. First, although the Saudi government had spent an average of nearly $20 billion per year over the previous two decades to purchase from the United States and other Western countries the latest and most advanced weaponry systems (such as F-15 and Tornado jets), it became clear within days of Saddam Hussein's invasion of Kuwait that the Kingdom felt ill-prepared to defend itself against any Iraqi aggression. Instead, Riyadh was advised to accept U.S. military support and within weeks the first of an eventual 500,000 foreign troops arrived in Saudi Arabia. Apart from the political disaster surrounding the Kingdom's inability to defend itself after so much military expenditure and foreign training, there was also the crisis associated with bringing hundreds of thousands of non-Muslim soldiers onto Saudi soil. If there had already been religious sensitivities surrounding the presence of purely civilian technical experts in the oil industry, it is easy to imagine the Wahhabi establishment's reaction to the stationing of a full-scale "infidel" army in the land of the two Holy Cities. Anti-Saud sentiment increased considerably, particularly among non-establishment ulama associated with the Sahwa movement. The final cost of the war was so high as to actually push the public budget temporarily into deficit, necessitating further austerity measures. In November 1990, in the midst of the uncertainty surrounding possible war with Iraq and the arrival of thousands of Western troops in Saudi Arabia, several dozen women drove into downtown Riyadh to stage a protest against the Saudi ban on women driving. While symbolically important in terms of the struggle for women's rights in the Kingdom, it is likely that this action at that time served mainly to embolden the religious sector. "This incident," Madawi al-Rasheed writes, "confirmed the fears of the Islamists, who thought that Saudi Arabia, its tradition and morality were now under greater threat than ever before."[4]

It was in this climate that Saudi Arabia saw the emergence in the 1990s of several political opposition movements. While various forms of Islamism certainly constituted the bulk of this activity, we should note that other political tendencies were present as well. One noteworthy instance of this is to be found in the petition presented to the king in early 1991. Signed by a group of commercial figures, writers, academic and former bureaucrats, this document requested the king to undertake a number of liberalizing reforms and to bring about a modicum of popular political participation through the establishment of a Consultative Council—something that almost every Saudi king had announced as an intention (particularly during times of popular discontent) but without ever following through on the commitment. Tighter restrictions on the power of the religious police were also suggested. It is worth noting that these early requests were not framed in terms of overt criticism of the Saud or their religious legitimacy; in fact, the tone is highly respectful and the signatories clearly emphasized their loyalty to the royal family. This document was followed several months later by a second petition, this one featuring the names of more than 50 religious scholars, with the Sahwa tendency particularly strongly represented. In stark contrast to the first petition, this text sought increased "Islamization" in all aspects of Saudi public life—with a particular emphasis on the conduct of government ministries—and a wider role for the ulama and mutawwa.

Two dissident ulama associated with the Sahwa movement emerged during the next few years as the figureheads of Saudi Arabia's new Islamism. The first of these, Safar al-Hawali, who hailed from the western Arabian town of Hawla, had been a former student of Muhammad Qutb's. The second and slightly younger of the two, Salman al-Awdah, was from the town of Buraida in the Nejdi heartland of both the Saud and Wahhabism. In the late summer of 1992, these two figures were the masterminds behind a much more expansive protest document known the "Memorandum of Advice." The use of the term "advice" (*nasiha*) is significant insofar as various classical Islamic sources cite the offering of advice by Muslim citizens to their rulers as an obligation. The title was hence a political claim in its own right, testifying that not only was this action permissible under the shari'ah, but actually *required*. This document was for more accusatory in tone, suggesting that the government and royal family had failed in their duty to uphold the shari'ah, and detailing a wide range of reforms to be carried out in nearly every sector of society. As "non-official" ulama who had developed something of a reputation as dissidents, the public lectures of Hawali and Awdah had already been subject to restriction. The nasiha document attracted increased scrutiny of their activities and both were subsequently arrested over the next two years as part of a large government crackdown on anti-establishment preachers. Significantly, the royal family looked to the official religious sector to condemn the document, but were left wanting in the response they received. While Bin Baz did offer a fatwa that warned against the threat of fitna (civil disorder) stemming from publishing the nasiha in such a public way, he did not pass judgment on any of its content.[5] Over the next two years, several protests calling for the release of Hawali and Awdah and the enactment of the nasiha demands took place in areas such as the Nejd—particularly in and around the latter's strong hold in Buraida—necessitating further arrests and governmental restrictions. More militant tendencies were also at work in the Kingdom, and both 1995 and 1996 saw bomb attacks on U.S. military facilities. It became clear that in addition to the conventional Islamism of the Sahwa, there were elements of Usama Bin Laden's jihadist networks at work on the peninsula in the guise of the so-called Advice and Reform Committee.[6] Usama Bin Laden, son of one of the Kingdom's great industrial and commercial families, had gone to Afghanistan to fight alongside that country's mujahideen against the Soviets in the 1980s. Here he linked up with militant Islamists of varying national origins and began to assemble the network that would eventually become Al-Qaeda (see Chapter 7). Repulsed by a royal family that he perceived as having sold out to the West, he developed strong anti-regime views and was eventually stripped of his Saudi citizenship in the early 1990s. Strong condemnation of the Saud's rule and associated policies such as the continued presence of foreign troops in Arabia have been mainstays of the Bin Laden worldview for over a decade.

In the face of such unprecedented activist pressure, the king announced in 1992 the establishment of a national scale *Majlis al-Shura* (Consultative Council) in addition to the promulgation of a new Basic Law—the closest Saudi Arabia had ever come to having a constitution. The Majlis, it should be noted, is not a legislative institution, but rather a representative body charged with the task of providing guidance to the king on various matters of state and public interest. Its religious legitimacy derives from the Qur'anic injunction to the effect that all matters of concern to the community should be decided through consultation (shura) amongst stakeholders. King Abdul Aziz set up a consultative body of sorts in the 1920s, but it never became more than a small and marginal presence. The new body set up in 1992, while hardly a potent institution in terms of its political power, was significant in a number of respects. Initially composed of 60 members, the size of the Majlis was later expanded to 120. All are appointed by the king, and charged with the review of laws and other matters brought before it, or issues of concern adopted by the Council itself. Although it possesses little in the way of formal power (legislative or executive oversight), the Majlis al-Shura has evolved into an important component of the Saudi political system. While the king is not in any way required to act on its guidance, he cannot simply ignore the view of the Majlis. The professional composition of its membership is also significant in that, unlike many other political bodies in the Kingdom that pronounce on matters of public good, the members of the Council are not primarily religious scholars. Instead they are mainly former bureaucrats and ministers, prominent commercial figures, and intellectuals. In this regard it can be argued that the Majlis provides some modicum of check against the monopoly of the ulama in public life. Particularly in recent years as the imperatives for genuine reform have become clearer, the Council's growing influence as an institutionalized voice of managed change has consolidated somewhat.

The next phase of Islamist opposition, from late 1994, saw several of the key activist figures relocating to the relative safety of countries outside the Kingdom. The most important of these groups, the Committee for the Defense of Legitimate Rights (CDLR), set up shop in London and managed to garner considerable media attention for itself. A partnership between two scientists with Sahwa sympathies, Muhammad al-Mass'ari and Sa'ad al-Faqih, the CDLR waged a public relations campaign with the Saudi regime by distributing literature and sending thousands of faxes each day to government offices in the Kingdom. When Riyadh raised concerns with the British government about their activities and requested that they be shut down (with the tacit threat of jeopardizing future Saudi arms purchases), Al-Mass'ari won an injunction in the high court granting him indefinite leave to remain in the UK. This only served to draw more attention to the group, and they were at the height of their notoriety when a dispute between the movement's leaders led to a split and a significant loss of reputation within the Kingdom itself. Mass'ari, who kept the name CDLR, insinuated that Faqih may have been co-opted by the regime, while Faqih criticized Mass'ari—a highly flamboyant public personality—for allying the CDLR with globally oriented Islamist movements such as Omar Bakri Muhammad, Hizb ut-Tahrir and al-Muhajiroun (see Chapter 7). Faqih, wanting to maintain a strict Saudi focus to their work, initiated a successor group, the Movement for Islamic Reform in Arabia (MIRA), but never managed to regain quite the momentum CDLR had in its early days. MIRA has continued to publish materials and publicize otherwise unreported events in the Kingdom.

Within Saudi Arabia itself, the regime successfully weathered the difficult period of the early and mid-90s and managed to reassert itself by the end of the decade. King Fahd's failing health after a stroke in 1995 led to a frenzy of speculation amongst Saudi watchers as to the regime's stability. The Crown Prince, Abdullah, as a half-brother to the other senior princes (the so-called "Sudeiri Seven") was considered to be in a weak position with the possibility that another of Abdul Aziz's sons might claim the throne on Fahd's death—or even that the succession might skip a generation. Abdullah was also known to be highly religious and had made remarks in the past critical of certain aspects of the Kingdom's relations with the United States—and this had led some to conclude that he might have been significantly less pro-Western, or might once again use oil as a geopolitical tool. By the late 1990s, it became clear that the family had rallied around Abdullah, who was now effectively in day-to-day control of the Kingdom. Most of the dissident activists had been co-opted or imprisoned, and even figures such as Safar al-Hawali and Salman al-Awdah had been released from prison. Al-Awdah even regained some public prominence—but without the anti-establishment rhetoric—starting a website (www.islamtoday.net) and even a television program. Inevitably, there has been considerable speculation in the wake of his "rehabilitation" as to whether he has been co-opted by the establishment, or has decided that toning down the activism in favor of gradualism is more likely to produce meaningful pro-Islamic reform. Of course these two views are not necessarily mutually exclusive. Some of the former Sahwa ulama also appear to have moderated their discourse even more thoroughly, advocating an unlikely fusion of Islamism and liberalism.[7]

The most recent phase of Saudi Islamism can be dated to the aftermath of the 9/11 attacks on the United States. Fifteen of the 19 hijackers who flew planes into American targets that day were Saudi citizens, placing new strain on U.S.-Saudi relations amidst calls for Riyadh to crack down on militant currents within the Kingdom. During 2002 and several times again in 2003 after the U.S. invasion of Iraq (which occurred with more Saudi support than was publicly acknowledged by either side), various targets in Saudi Arabia were struck by militants claiming affiliation with Usama Bin Laden. In 2005 and 2006 officials became even more alarmed when attacks moved into the strategic Eastern Province—including an attempted bombing at Abqaiq, one of the nerve centers of the Kingdom's oil industry.

The confusing landscape of Islamist opposition in Saudi Arabia can thus be said to consist today of three main strands which function together as an ecosystem of sorts. The first of these would be the Sahwa movement, representing the fusion of Wahhabi thought with MB-style activism. The vanguard of the opposition in the early 1990s, this group has now apparently moved towards a more gradualist orientation, with some members almost holding "quasi-official" status. With greater pressure for liberalizing reform in the wake of 9/11, the Sahwa seeks to reject this path in favor of Islamizing reform, but from an avowedly moderate and—by Saudi standards—relatively centrist stance. The second, and as yet still rather nascent, current would be the one represented by the new Islamic liberals. Many of the relevant figures here, such as Mansur al-Nuqaidan and Hasan al-Maliki were formerly associated with the Sahwa movement or even more radical groups. Having become disillusioned with Wahhabism, but still eager to maintain their Islamic credentials, they have sought to offer a religious critique of the salafi-jihadi tendency and to keep the focus of their efforts on reform at the societal rather than political level. Their argument is essentially that Saudi society is not yet ready to deal with political openness and to bring this now would only entrench the Wahhabi establishment further since this is the only normative discourse that most Saudis can recognize at this point.[8] The final Islamist tendency is to be found in the umbrella group Al-Qaeda on the Arabian Peninsula, the inheritors of the legacy of the Bin Laden-oriented Advice and Reform Committee and a direct offshoot of his early efforts in Afghanistan. Most of the regime's anti-Islamist efforts in recent years have been aimed primarily at identifying cells and affiliates of this group since it is generally viewed as representing the greatest threat of violence in the short term. It is unlikely that this group's operations are coordinated by its more global namesake, but given the centrality of Arabia and the holy cities of Mecca and Medina within the discourse of Bin Laden and Ayman al-Zawahiri, it is likely that some channels of communication still exist.[9]

How is Saudi Islamism likely to evolve in the coming years? This will most likely turn out to be a function of how the regime balances competing social, political, and religious forces during this very sensitive and volatile period of reform and transition. While the royal family seems now to have understood that undertaking genuine reform is necessary in order to permit the Kingdom in its present form to last into the next century, the challenge will be to make this happen quickly enough to stave off rapidly escalating social tensions but not so quickly as to bring about instability and the collapse of social cohesion. Since the death of Fahd in 2005, the new king, Abdullah, has shown himself above all to be a pragmatist. The path to reform may also turn out to be something of a personal race for Abdullah since, like most of the other princes in direct line to the throne, he is nearly an octogenarian. Soon the royal succession will have to move down a generation and for the most part this bodes well since the Western-educated grandchildren of Abdul Aziz tend to be more sensitive to the need for reform and to the exigencies of a global world than their fathers have been. There have been a few signs that the Kingdom is moving slowly in this direction. In 2005, Saudi (male) citizens voted in the Kingdom's first-ever national scale elections to choose the members of new municipal councils. While the role and powers of these councils are still unclear, and the winners tended to be those candidates who had received a nod of approval from the religious establishment, many observers have suggested that in a society as closed as Saudi Arabia's, any participatory process of this sort is a salutary step. The regime has promised that for the next round of elections women will also be allowed to vote, and in late 2005, for the first time, women were elected onto the influential Chamber of Commerce in Jeddah, the country's largest commercial city.

Abdullah's credentials to steward such a reform process are relatively strong. He is not tainted by the same penchant for decadence and excess associated with his siblings. His religious credentials and personal piety are beyond reproach, and he has always maintained strong relations with the tribally organized national guard—which means that his power base is relatively secure. Fears in the West about an anti-American bias have so far proved unfounded with pragmatism tending to guide his foreign relations and energy policy. In the wake of 9/11 and the Iraq War, surging oil prices have brought Saudi revenues back up to levels not seen since the late 1970s. But the successful management of this much-needed transition will still depend on Abdullah—and his successors—carrying the center-right bulk of Saudi society along with him. The considerable cultural, economic—and, increasingly, political—tensions present in the Kingdom today will not easily be assuaged, nor will the influence of the Wahhabi religious establishment (either at home or abroad) be easily contained. Most Saudis, as we have seen, still define their social and political identities in religious terms, and public discourse will continue for some time to be animated primarily by Islamic idioms and symbols.

Pakistan: politics and religion in an ambiguously Islamic state

Created as a homeland for Muslims of the subcontinent at the time of India's independence and partition in 1947, Pakistan's subsequent political history has reflected the fact that in this particular context the question of just what it means to be an Islamic state has never been definitively settled. Secularizing and Islamizing paths have been pursued by military and civilian regimes alike, with different actors advancing a wide range of claims about the meaning and nature of religion in Pakistani public life. This section will first briefly review the circumstances surrounding Pakistan's foundation and will then move on to examine the changing course of the debate about Islam and the state through a short survey of the country's political and constitutional history up to 1999. Next we will consider the place of Islam in the contemporary political landscape under President Pervez Musharraf. The main emphasis here will be on his attempts to co-opt certain forms of Islamism while simultaneously keeping other currents of politicized religion at bay in a complex regional security environment. We then go on to look more closely at the main groups within Pakistani society agitating for a greater political role for Islam, focusing specifically on the Jama'at-i Islami and its evolving relationship with the state. The section concludes by drawing out several key analytical themes that will help us to compare and contrast Pakistan not only with the Saudi case surveyed above, but also with the subsequent and final example of the Islamic state to be included in this chapter, that of Iran.

As we will recall, the idea of Pakistan was first advanced as a political cause by the Muslim League of India and Muhammad Ali Jinnah when Muslims came to be increasingly concerned about their fate in a Hindu-dominated India in the run-up to that country's independence after World War II. Jinnah's famous "Two Nations Theory" advanced the claim that due to their religious differences, India's Muslims and Hindus were effectively two different national peoples, with their own unique histories and cultures. According to his logic, separate national homelands for each was the only possible political solution. To the highly Westernized and secular

Jinnah, there did not appear to be any tension between this form of nationalist discourse and Islam. For those of a more religious, and particularly Islamist, persuasion, however, nationalism was anathema to Islam, leading them to reject the cause of a separate Pakistan. The leading voice in this camp was undoubtedly Abu'l-A'la Mawdudi, whose general approach to Islamism we have looked at in some detail in Chapter 3. The traditional religious scholars, such as those associated with major seminaries such as Deoband near Delhi, did not intervene directly in these debates and tended to default to a position that would have kept Muslims as part of India—perhaps with some measure of communal autonomy as regards the application of personal status law. In the wake of widespread violence between Muslims and Hindus from 1946, the Indian Congress Party consented to the idea of partition and Pakistan was founded in August 1947 with Jinnah as its first Governor-General and effective head of government. The new country was composed of two distinct regions separated by over a thousand miles of Indian territory. "West Pakistan" was composed primarily of the Punjab, Sindh, and Balochistan. "East Pakistan," which would later become Bangladesh in 1971, consisted of most of the former Indian province of Bengal. The mountainous northern region of Kashmir has been claimed by both India and Pakistan and has been the subject of several wars between the two since as far back as 1948.

The first years of Pakistan's existence were occupied primarily with the settlement of ongoing violence and the establishment of basic state institutions. Given the immediate territorial dispute and subsequent war with India over Kashmir, the military quickly became one of the most important prominent and influential institutions within Pakistani politics—a point whose importance will become clear below. Mawdudi and the Jama'at-i Islami (JI) elected to remain in Pakistan and set themselves up as the leading voices advocating for a thoroughly Islamic political order in the new Muslim state. As regards the role of religion and politics, these early years were characterized by considerable debate between the secularizing tendencies of Jinnah (who died very shortly after the country's founding) and his followers, and the Islamism of Mawdudi and the JI. For the former group, Pakistan's status as an Islamic state was not meant to imply much more beyond the idea of a national homeland for Muslims. For Mawdudi and his JI followers, however, the creation of an Islamic social and political order was incumbent upon the new country's rulers. The impasse that arose between these two distinctive visions is illustrated by the fact that it took almost 10 years to negotiate the country's first constitution. In the mean time a temporary "Objectives Resolution" (1949) offered a minimal sense of state legitimacy. It opened with a statement to the effect that sovereignty belongs to God alone, and stated a desire for Muslims in Pakistan to be "enabled" to live their lives according to the prescriptions of the Qur'an and sunna.

Two further events that occurred during Pakistan's first decade also help to illustrate the tensions between these two approaches to the Islamic state.

During the process of negotiations leading up to the first constitution, those from the religious sector (mainly Islamists and ulama) requested that the government declare members of the *Ahmadiyya* sect to be non-Muslims. The Ahmadis are named after Mirza Ghulam Ahmad, a religious reformer from the late nineteenth century. They are controversial because one subset of the movement regards Mirza Ghulam Ahmad as a prophet, raising the ire of orthodox Muslims—such as those represented by the Deoband establishment in Pakistan—who recognize no prophets after Muhammad. These views have made Pakistan's Ahmadi community the target of consistent persecution and violence since the country's founding. In the early 1950s, the Islamists—Mawdudi among them—argued that followers of the Ahmadiyya movement could not hold prominent government positions since they did not qualify as "true" Muslims. The ensuing public debate led to widespread rioting and violence against Ahmadis in the Punjab. In the wake of the investigation that followed, Mawdudi himself was convicted of inciting religious hatred and violence, jailed and eventually even condemned to death—a sentence that was later abrogated. The Ahmadiyya controversy is important because it forced the Pakistani state for the first time to confront certain basic questions regarding who counted as a Muslim and how an Islamic state should behave towards Muslims and non-Muslims alike.[10] The second notable event was the adoption in 1956 of the country's first constitution. This document, for the most part, seemed to represent a vindication of the Muhammad Ali Jinnah vision. The bulk of it was devoted to outlining a modern parliamentary republic and to spelling out the division of competences between various institutions of state. Several components of this first constitution also mentioned religion, but in many cases these were largely symbolic or left considerable room for interpretation: the name of the country was specified as the "Islamic Republic of Pakistan"; the state was based on "Islamic principles" (without explaining what these might be); the head of state was to be a Muslim; and there was to be created a research institution charged with drawing up guidelines relating to the Islamization of society. Finally, this first constitution also contained the so-called "Repugnancy Clause" which specified that no law could be adopted in contradiction to Islam.

The years between 1958 and 1977 represented a relative decline in the influence of the religious sector in Pakistan, but certainly not the disappearance of Islam from political discourse. Following the imposition of martial law and Muhammad Ayub Khan's coup in 1958, the government began to pursue a new course of Islamic modernization. Ayub Khan sought to implement an intensely secularizing approach to national development, looking to models such as modern Turkey under Mustapha Kemal. Westernization and rapid economic development were his core goals, and he sought to reform and tame the religious establishment so as to bring it in line with this project. Part of this involved revising the constitution in 1962, but Ayub Khan's attempts to remove many of the Islamic provision of the

1956 document were soon rebuffed by a subsequent amendment. The 1962 version included a new section on "Islamic Institutions" which called for the creation of an Islamic Council to offer advice regarding the Islamic character of legislation. This body had relatively little real power, however, due to its advisory nature. Unlike, for example, the Guardianship Council in Iran, which is required to scrutinize every law adopted by parliament, legislators in Pakistan were free to bypass or ignore the Islamic Council. To head up the Islamic research council mandated by both versions of the constitution, Ayub Khan appointed Fazlur Rahman, a Western-trained intellectual, and charged him with assisting the government to promulgate a modernist interpretation of Islam compatible with the regime's national priorities. So not only did Ayub Khan pursue a secular path but he also began to stake a claim by the state to speak on behalf of and to define the meaning of Islam for society. Perhaps unsurprisingly, this brought him into direct confrontation with the religious establishment, particularly when he sought to reform family law—an area the ulama regarded as their core turf—along modernist lines. The differing arguments presented by the modernist and ulama members of the Commission on Marriage and Family Laws also serve to illustrate once again the clear divide over the two approaches to Pakistan as an Islamic state alluded to above. The modernists, for their part, advanced the claim that because it would be impossible for the classic Islamic sources to comprehensively imagine the full range of circumstances and issues that would face humanity in the course of its development, it was necessary to leave considerable space for independent and innovative interpretation of religion within the "broad framework" of the Qur'an and sunna. The religious establishment, incensed by what it perceived as a frontal assault on its authority, accused the Commission of ignoring centuries of settled jurisprudential precedent and questioned their authority to make any pronouncements regarding matters of religion.[11]

The next phase of the evolving dance between the state and Islam is associated with Zulfikar Ali Bhutto's tenure as President and Prime Minister (1971–77). In the late 1960s, East Pakistan's sense of marginalization within the republic had grown to a point where its population elected advocates of political separatism to almost all of East Pakistan's parliamentary seats in the 1970 elections. Widespread violence broke out when Yahya Khan (Ayub's successor) arrested the leader of this movement and sent the military into the East to suppress Bengali opposition. The leaders of East Pakistan declared independence as the new state of Bangladesh and a full-blown war developed over the ensuing months—ending quickly and decisively in favor of Bangladesh soon after India entered the conflict against Pakistan. The collapse of Yahya Khan's regime in the wake of this loss brought Bhutto to power. His party, the Pakistan People's Party (PPP), represented a largely socialist orientation and drew its support primarily from rural areas and the urban poor. Economic nationalism and agrarian reform were his initial priorities, as was to be expected, but Bhutto soon

found himself having to adopt more and more religious rhetoric and symbolism in his policy-making, particularly in the face of rising government
corruption and the failure of his economic initiatives. The religious establishment had been suspicious as to whether a committed socialist could ever
be a Muslim, and were almost immediately hostile to his government.
Bhutto sought to paint an Islamic face on much of his political platform,
describing his policies as the pursuit of Qur'anic social justice in the name
of, for example, Musawat-i-Muhammadi ("Muhammad's egalitarianism").
A new constitution in 1973 redistributed the balance of power between
Pakistan's constituent provinces and its two senior government positions, in
addition to enshrining Islam as the religion of state. In order to placate the
ulama, he also compromised in terms of several issues long on their agenda.
The weekly holiday was changed from Sunday to Friday, the Muslim holy
day, and in 1974 he settled the Ahmadiyya issue by amending the oath of
office taken by Pakistan's leaders to include a statement recognizing the
final prophethood of Muhammad.[12] In terms of international relations,
Bhutto sought after the loss of Bangladesh to emphasize Pakistan's affi-
nities with the Arab world, securing new development funding for the
country in the name of Islamic solidarity and establishing a prominent role
for Pakistan in the emerging bloc of Islamic nations whose geopolitical role
had been enhanced in the wake of the oil shock of 1973.

The religious sector remained unconvinced, however, and in the run-up to
the 1977 elections they formed a political umbrella called the Pakistan
National Alliance (PNA) to challenge Bhutto's PPP. This coalition was
driven by the JI, but also contained other religious parties and groups,
including those representing the traditional ulama. Their basic complaint
related to the intense corruption associated with Bhutto's regime, and they
held out "true Islamization" as the antidote. Demographically it is significant to note that their base of support was to be found primarily among
the middle and lower-middle classes, as opposed to the PPP, which depended on the seeming unlikely combination of hardcore support among the
political elite and rural poor. Although Bhutto handily won the elections in
1977, the PNA refused to end its campaign against him, alleging pole fraud
and undertaking a widespread national effort to discredit his leadership. It
was the ongoing conflict between these two forces—the state and the religious sector—that was used by army chief Zia ul-Haq in July 1977 to
undertake a coup d'état and declare martial law in the name of both Islam
and national unity.

Zia's 11-year rule (1977–88) is particularly interesting for our purposes
given the centrality of Islamization to his endeavors. To begin with, his coup
had been justified as necessary for the establishment in Pakistan of the
"System of the Prophet." Zia immediately reached out to the PNA alliance,
and particularly the JI, to be his partners in this project. They responded
enthusiastically, hearing Zia's proposals—such as the introduction of an
Islamic criminal code (hudud) and an interest-free economy—the closest

any regime had come to the comprehensive Islamization of society that they had been seeking since Pakistan's founding. Not only were members of the JI appointed to cabinet positions (marking the first time they had ever served in government), but the Islamic Council created by the 1962 constitution was revamped to act as a direct advisory body to the executive. Significantly, however, Zia maintained martial law for eight years (after promising elections within 90 days of taking power) and also suspended certain democratic provisions in the constitution so that, he claimed, they could be reviewed to ensure their compatibility with the shari'ah.

Much of the Islamist enthusiasm for Zia's Islamization program was due to the fact that it was enacted across a wide range of social sectors. He created a system of Shari'ah Courts charged with ensuring that all laws in Pakistan were in accordance with Islam (although the martial law provisions and national taxation practices were exempt) and also legalized state enforcement of public virtue (e.g. no public consumption of food or drink during daylight hours in Ramadan). Other areas of social practice derived from religion that had previously been informally or privately regulated were also brought within the purview of the state. So, for example, with regard to the zakat system of alms (one of the five pillars of the religion) the government instituted a system whereby a 2.5% tax was levied annually on all bank accounts. This produced considerable discontent among both the country's Shi'a population whose traditions handle the payment of zakat differently, and some segments of the urban populations who, as the only holders of bank accounts, felt unfairly targeted by this system of enforced direct tithing. Islamic studies became a mandatory at all levels of education, and a new International Islamic University was established in Islamabad. The diplomas issued by the country's *madrasas* (religious schools) were also deemed to be the equivalent of secular university degrees, meaning the madrasa graduates would be eligible for positions in the government bureaucracy.[13] Under Zia and with the resounding approval of the conservative ulama a number of measures that particularly affected women were undertaken—most notably a provision to create universities separated by sex and to revise the Law of Evidence Act to reflect the view that evidence presented by a woman is worth only half that presented by a man.[14]

Although much of this would clearly be to the liking of the ulama and the Islamists, it was not long before they began to have concerns about Zia's regime. It became clear to them after several years that there were distinct limitations as to how much political influence he would allow the Islamists to have. So long as their interests and input were confined to matters of religion, Zia was happy to listen. Once the Islamists began to pursue a wider political role for themselves in the wake of their first taste of real power, they suddenly found doors closing in their faces. As Husain Haqqani puts it, Zia "realized that he had overestimated the Jama'at-i Islami's ability to run a modern Islamic state."[15] Consequently he widened the breadth of his consultation on Islamic issues such that the Jama'at became one of many voices—from Pakistan and from abroad—contributing to Zia's Islamization project, including traditionally apolitical groups such as the Tablighi Jama'at (see Chapter 8). Zia cultivated close ties with Muslim allies such as Saudi Arabia, where remittances from thousands of Pakistani migrant laborers provided an economic boost. As Pakistan's strategic importance to United States Cold War interests in the region grew, financial support from Washington for Zia's regime increased nearly threefold to $4.2 billion in combined development and military aid.[16] Much of this was linked to Pakistan's strong support for anti-Soviet forces across the border in Afghanistan and contributed to the development and consolidation in northern parts of the country of a militant strain of Islamism (see Chapters 6 and 7).

As their discontent with Zia increased, the JI found itself in the predicament of trying to direct credible criticism toward a regime whose legitimacy they had done so much to build in its early years.[17] Initially this dispute led to some seemingly contradictory policies on the part of the Jama'at. For example, it began to publicly criticize the regime for continuing martial law and refusing to hold elections, but did not join the Movement for the Restoration of Democracy (MRD)—a coalition of various social and political forces advocating a return to civilian rule. At the same time, it became an avid fan of Zia's new support for Islamic forces in neighboring Afghanistan, the mujahideen, who were fighting a Soviet invasion.[18] However, as the marginalization of Islamists—who, as Zia by now realized, constituted only a narrow segment of Pakistani society—continued during the mid-80s, the Jama'at even began reaching out to non-religious parties.[19] When martial law did eventually end in 1985, Zia took measures to ensure his position until the end of the decade through a referendum tying approval of Islamization to his continued rule.[20] The culmination of the broad project was cut short in 1988 when Zia was killed in a suspicious plane crash.

How to assess the motivations and meaning behind Zia's Islamization? At first glance it might be tempting to dismiss it as a very sophisticated form of religious co-option by the government—or, more accurately, the military. One might also suggest that Zia stepped in as he did in 1977 not so much to create space for Islam, but rather to "recontain" it after Bhutto had lost control of the religious sector.[21] Something considerably more complex was afoot here, though. Zia had long held a reputation for religiosity and personal piety, often making special provisions within the battalions under his command for religious observance.[22] Indeed, some have speculated that Bhutto put him in charge of the army specifically because he expected a pious military officer to harbor little in the way of political ambition.[23] It is likely, then, that much of his Islamization program was genuine in terms of intent, but over ambitious in terms of the political role he initially envisaged for the Islamists and the ulama. Finding them lacking as public administrators, he began to include a wider range of voices in his policy-making deliberations. Once in power, he also likely discovered that the challenges of running a complex and fragile state—particularly one that became a frontline nation in the Cold War after Iran's revolution and the Soviet invasion of Afghanistan, not to mention ongoing tension with India—meant that Islamic idealism would have to give way to certain political realities.

Malaysia: Islamization and national development

Malaysia provides an interesting example of state-led Islamization as an integral component of national economic development policy. While a small majority of Malaysia's population is ethnically Malay (or *bumiputra*—"sons of the soil"), much of the country's wealth has historically been concentrated in the hands of its minority communities: ethnic Indians, and particularly the Chinese. From the 1970s, with the announcement of the National Economic Policy (NEP), the government introduced a number of measures to effect a transfer of wealth into the hands of the ethnic Malays. At the same time, however, the ruling United Malays National Organization (UMNO) sought a unifying identity discourse that would stimulate Malay participation in the national development process and ensure a key economic role for the country's indigenous population. In choosing Islam to play this role, the state was able to accomplish two tasks simultaneously. By seizing for itself the banner of Islamization, UMNO was able to marginalize radical Islamists for whom dissent expressed in religious terms was a way to challenge the prevailing political order. Second, by introducing a sweeping Islamization program—with particular emphasis on public morality, work ethic, and Islamic finance—the state was able to use religion to socialize Malays into its vision for national development.

During the 1980s and 90s, the two key players here were the Prime Minister Mahathir Mohamed and his deputy and protégé Anwar Ibrahim. Anwar had previously been the leader of an Islamist youth movement, ABIM, that had played a key role in instigating the Islamization trend at the grassroots level in the 1970s. Mahathir calculated that by bringing the charismatic and skilled Anwar into the UMNO fold he would be able to harness the energy of the Islamic movement in the name of state policy. Anwar, having been officially anointed from on high, rose quickly through the UMNO ranks, eventually attaining the rank of Deputy Prime Minister in the mid-1990s. Mahathir realized by the end of the decade that Anwar's popularity and ambition were likely a threat to his own political fortunes, and in 1998 Anwar was fired and jailed on charges of sexual deviance.

Shortly afterward, Mahathir and UMNO faced a temporary challenge from another source of Islamism, the Parti Islam Se-Malaysia (PAS). This political party, developed in the mold of the MB, had been around since the time of Malaysian independence from Britain in the mid-1950s and had even served as part of a coalition government in the

1970s. Despite Mahathir's declaration that Malaysia was an Islamic state, the PAS platform was based on the complete shari'ah-tization of the Malaysian system—including hudud penalties. Although PAS had traditionally enjoyed electoral support in a few of Malaysia's northern conservative states, the party was able in 1999 to take advantage of a wave of popular discontent over the mistreatment of Anwar Ibrahim. In the parliamentary elections that year PAS won control of a second state, Terrenganu, alongside Kelantan, and a total of 27 seats in the assembly. Their fortunes proved to be short-lived, however, when five years later the ruling UMNO party—now under the leadership of the new Prime Minister Abdullah Badawi—increased its majority. PAS saw the loss of most of its parliamentary seats and only managed to maintain control of one state. Anwar Ibrahim was released from prison in 2004, promising a return to politics.

The years from 1988 to 1999 were turbulent ones in Pakistani politics. While arguably more democratic once elections resumed, this decade was marked by considerable instability with governments changing every 2–3 years to reflect power struggles between the leaders of various parties and also the fact that massive corruption had become a mainstay of Pakistani politics, regardless of who happened to be in power. The two major figures in Pakistani politics throughout the 1990s were Benazir Bhutto, the daughter of Zulfikar who had inherited the PPP mantle upon her return from abroad, and Nawaz Sharif, leader of the Pakistan Muslim League within the Islamic Democratic Alliance (IDA), a coalition of mostly religious parties that sought to claim Zia's legacy. The two exchanged the prime ministership twice over 10 years, with Bhutto's tenure marking the first ever for a woman in the Muslim world. Even Nawaz Sharif's support for a Shariah Bill that would subjugate all Pakistani civil law to religion did not placate his JI partners as corruption grew and the latter were increasingly squeezed out of any meaningful policy-making role. Their relationship soon revealed itself for what it was: an alliance of convenience based on shared animosity toward Benazir Bhutto's PPP, and the Jama'at then broke with Nawaz in 1993 in order to directly contest elections. Despite the PPP's victory, the success of Nawaz's Pakistan Muslim League (PML) in drawing pro-religious votes away from the Islamists is cited by Vali Nasr as an early indication of the political potential inherent in the "Muslim Democracy" approach we examined in the previous chapter.[24] Nawaz Sharif's last years in power were characterized by an attempt to appropriate Islamic symbols in the course of pursuing rapid economic development à la Mahathir Mohamed in Malaysia and populist nationalism—the height of which was Pakistan's first official nuclear test in 1998, in response to a similar move by India.[25] Nawaz's increasingly autocratic rule and dismal economic record during the final years of his tenure led to tensions with the army and he was replaced in a 1999 military coup d'état by General Pervez Musharraf.

Initial indications suggested that Musharraf was likely to go the secular and modernizing route espoused by Ayub Khan in the 1960s. The September 11, 2001 attacks on the United States proved to be a turning point in his tenure, however. Faced with choosing between active support for the United States and a more passive stance that risked American hostility towards his regime, Musharraf took the former course. Unable to form a meaningful alliance with the grassroots of the PPP, Musharraf came to depend instead on a flank of the PML to serve as a "president's party"—but also on an unlikely alliance with the new Islamist bloc. The Mutahida Majlis Amal (MMA), led by the JI, was ostensibly formed in opposition to Musharraf ruling as a military officer and also his willingness to promote American strategic interests in the region. In actual fact he was able to strike a deal with them whereby greater Islamist participation in parliament, achieved via electoral redistricting, was exchanged for support by the latter in Musharraf's efforts to amend the constitution so that his period of rule could be extended. As part of this he also promised to resign from the military two years after the elections of 2002. The Islamists did indeed see electoral gains, although they only polled 11 percent of the vote—a figure that provides a sense of how correct Zia had been to regard the Islamists as a niche force, politically. When Musharraf apparently reneged on his promise to put the army behind him, he lost—perhaps irrevocably—any willingness to work with him on the part of the Jamaat. Musharraf is aware that the real political threat, particularly if he is pressured to ease back the political chokehold, would come from the PPP, the party which actually won the greatest number of votes in the 2002 elections. As of 2006, Benazir Bhutto remained abroad, although—sporting an alliance-in-exile with Nawaz Sharif—she vowed to return to fight the next election.

As we have seen from the preceding account, the role of Islam in Pakistani politics is a complex and multifaceted affair. With religion such an intrinsic and yet ambiguous part of public life in Pakistan, it becomes difficult to identify any single or main source of religio-political discourse. The traditional ulama, particularly those alumni of the Deoband tradition, have a significant role to play—not least of all through the thousands of madrasas (estimates range from 10,000 to 40,000) they have founded across the country. These are particularly important in the rural, mountainous, and isolated Northwest Frontier Province, where for many madrasas remain the only feasible source of education of any sort. The much-discussed linkages between the madrasas and militant extremism will be discussed in Chapters 6 and 7, but they have played little direct role in mainstream Islamist politics except to provide a base for certain of the parties within the religious blocs—most particularly the ulama party, the Jamaat Ulama-i-Islam (JUI). Musharraf has sought, with considerable pressure from the West, to curb the influence of the more radical Kashmiri-based Islamist groups such as the Lashkar-i-Toiba, but he has been far more circumspect when dealing with associated humanitarian groups such as Lashkar's Jamaat-ud-Dawa.[26]

Without any doubt, the most significant force in Pakistan in terms of conventional Islamism has been the JI, although its role has evolved considerably over the years. Founded initially as more of an advocacy group seeking to ensure that an Islamic social order would be implemented in Pakistan, it developed into a voice for direct political dissent, and then finally into a bona fide political party pursuing power like any other. It also demonstrates many of the hallmark features we have come to associate with conventional Islamism through our coverage in Chapters 3 and 4. The Jama'at's social base, for example, is not to be found in madrasas or mosques, but rather in modern associations and professional organizations.[27] Its student affiliate, the Islami Jamiat-i-Talaba (IJT) has been a major resource in terms of mass mobilization when necessary.[28] While it has certainly cooperated with traditional ulama by forming religious coalitions (e.g. the PNA and MMA) to challenge "un-Islamic" rulers, the JI has at other times sought to keep its distance from religious scholars whom they often view as insufficiently interested in comprehensive and active sociopolitical reform—an approach comparable to that of the MB in Egypt (see Chapter 3). While its electoral appeal has never been enormous, Jama'at supporters are to be found in some of the most socially mobile and influential segments of Pakistani society, ensuring a political influence disproportionate to their relatively small active membership and polling base.

In summary, we can make the following broad points relating to Islam and politics in Pakistan. It becomes clear when looking at the country's political history that the initial ambiguity surrounding Pakistan's status as an Islamic state established the question of religion's public role as a primary political currency. As Vali Nasr puts it:

> ... [A] state built in the name of Islam and as a Muslim homeland, confronted with insurmountable ethnic, linguistic, and class conflicts, quickly succumbed to the temptation of mobilizing Islamic symbols in the service of state formation. This tendency has only been reinforced over the years as the state has failed to address fundamental socio-economic issues, carry out meaningful land reform, and consolidate power in the center. This has opened the door for Islamic parties to enter the fray. The incremental sacralization of the national political discourse has clearly favored a political role for those who claimed to speak for Islam and who advocate Islamization. Their activism, in turn, strengthened the impetus for Islamization.[29]

We have seen both in successive regimes and the multiple iterations of Pakistan's constitution the ongoing efforts of different political actors to define the parameters of the state-religion relationship. This brings us to the second point, which deals with the question of who gets to speak on behalf of or to define Islam for Pakistani society. We will recall that Ayub Khan initially found himself in trouble with the religious sector (both the ulama and the Jama'at) due to his attempts to claim for the state the right to make authoritative claims about religion—and a particularly liberal modernist vision of Islam at that. This approach, also favored by Zulfikar Bhutto, involved the state mobilizing Islamic symbols in the name of its preferred policies while simultaneously marginalizing the ulama and Islamists. Zia ul-Haq's alternative model, which initially fared rather better, ceded the space of Islam to the religious specialists and brought them into a limited position of direct public authority while still carefully controlling their access to meaningful political power. We can recall the argument about Zia's seizure of power representing not only a desire for Islamic reform, but also an outflanking maneuver to ensure the Islamists did not become too powerful vis-à-vis the state once Zulfikar Bhutto had lost the ability to assert meaningful authority over them. Finally, the case of Pakistan leads us to reassess certain assumptions we might have about how the militaries within Muslim-majority states view Islam. While the case of Turkey and the Kemalists might lead us to assume that the secular-nationalist and bureaucratic tendencies of modern militaries predispose them to reject Islamism, the Pakistani example refocuses our analysis of the military's priorities more on social and political *order*. The army of Pakistan—which certainly does have Islamists within it—has not pursued a straightforward policy of seeking to marginalize and reduce the societal influence of religion. Rather, their main concern has been the preservation of public order, state authority, and the general course of national development. When striking up alliances with Islamists— as Zia ul-Haq did in the late 1970s or like Pervez Musharraf after 2001— have proven useful in pursuing these goals, they have not hesitated to do so.

Iran: revolutionary Islam and the clerical state

The third and final model of the contemporary Islamic state that we will examine in some detail is that of Iran. Iran is significant for several reasons. It is the one example of an Islamic state that has come about through popular revolution, rather than being declared as such at the time of its founding (e.g. Saudi Arabia, Pakistan), or through a regime change in the wake of sustained internal conflict (Sudan, Afghanistan). The Islamic Revolution of 1979, for many observers, represented the zenith of modern Islamic revival, and a source for propagating revolutionary Islam to other national settings. For others it provided a test case of what Islam in power would look like. Subsequently, the example of Iran has been pointed to by those wary of Islamists participating in politics. As we will, see, however, the doctrinal bases of the Islamic Republic of Iran are unique (many would argue wholly innovative), and certainly quite distinct from mainstream Islamist thinking as represented by the MB. There are parallels to be drawn, however, to the socioeconomic and political conditions that prompted popular mobilization toward Iran's revolution and the circumstances that have led to growing support for Islamists in other countries.

In this section we will briefly review Iran's modern political history, focusing on the role of the ulama in politics under the late Qajar shahs and the Pahlavi dynasty through the 1970s. Next we will examine the ideological basis for Islamic revolution in the thought of Ayatollah Khomeini, and more specifically in his doctrine of vilayat-i faqih. The contributions of other notable intellectuals, particularly those such as Ali Shariati who reached a mass audience, will also be assessed. We will examine the course and events of the 1979 revolution itself and then offer an account of politics within the Islamic Republic and the implementation of the clerical state. The rise and fall of the reform movement under president Mohammad Khatami (1997–2005) will be analyzed, as will the socioeconomic circumstances leading to popular support for electing a relative hardliner, Mahmoud Ahmadinejad, as his successor. We will conclude by drawing out the major analytic themes that emerge from Iran's experience of the Islamic state.

As we will recall from Chapter 2, the modern Iranian state evolved via the Shi'i nationalism of the Safavid dynasty (1501–1736), and their successors the Qajars (1781–1925). During the late Qajar period, where our account begins, the ulama of Iran enjoyed a prominent role within society and widespread legitimacy as deputies of the occulted twelfth imam, and as guardians of the spiritual legacy of the Prophet's family. While not directly involved in statist politics, they could claim pervasive social influence and also played an important advisory role in certain matters of official policy. The rising autocracy that characterized late Qajar rule, however, led the ulama to adopt a more defensive stance vis-à-vis the regime, and they soon found their interests largely in line with those of the nascent nationalist movement that has arisen in response to both Qajar arrogance and creeping Western influence in the country's affairs. Two events in particular during this period help to illustrate the political role of the ulama and allow us to understand why it is that many Iranians understood the religious scholars to be a key player in popular agitations for social change—a point that will become important later when we look at the sociology of the 1979 Islamic Revolution.

During the Tobacco Protest of 1891, leading ulama openly opposed Nasser al-Din Shah's granting of a concession for the sale and export of Tobacco to a British commercialist. Their fatwa led to a widespread boycott of tobacco products in Iran and their allies in the merchant class shut down major bazaars throughout the country, prompting the palace to eventually back off. These same ties with Iran's merchants, in addition to the mobilizing potential inherent in the country's mosque networks, also allowed the religious scholars to play a key role during the country's first Constitutional Revolution in 1906. As the palace began in the early twentieth century to cede more and more access to Iranian territory to Western powers and commercial interests, popular demands for curbs on their authority and the introduction of the rule of law grew. Widespread protests organized by religious scholars and merchants led to a five-year period of significant internal unrest as a constitution and parliament were repeatedly established and then abolished in the wake of direct interventions by Britain and Russia. After the country was occupied during World War I, a coup d'état by the head of a provincial military family, Reza Shah, brought an end to Qajar rule.

Essentially secular modernizers, the new ruling family sought to define and legitimize themselves in terms of Iran's ancient heritage, taking the name "Pahlavi," a language spoken in pre-Islamic Persia. Both Islam and Zoroastrianism were made the religions of state, and royal pageantry heavily on symbols from Iran's pre-Islamic past. If Reza Shah had a model, it was probably Mustapha Kemal Ataturk, who we will recall also de-emphasized the modern Turkish Republic's links with Ottoman Islam in the name of a broader Turkish civilization. Unlike their Turkish cognate, however, the Pahlavis did not seek to fundamentally and pervasively restructure Iranian culture and society. The religious establishment, for example, was left intact, but brought under state control—particularly when Muhammad Reza took over from his father in 1941.[30] With the advent of the Cold War, Western powers courted the Pahlavi Shah for privileged access to Iranian oil and he was only too happy to oblige. This pro-Western stance gave rise to considerable political opposition, exemplified by Mohammed Mosaddeq's National Front movement. The National Front, which enjoyed the support of the usual merchant-ulama coalition, initially supported Mosaddeq's nationalization of Iranian oil upon assuming the prime ministership in 1951. As he proceeded to introduce a number of liberalizing reforms—such as political rights for women—he quickly lost the support of the clergy. Fleeing the country after a popular revolt in the wake of his efforts to dismiss the Prime Minister, Muhammad Reza quickly returned to the throne when a CIA-orchestrated coup unseated Mosaddeq in 1953. Some scholars have speculated that had Mosaddeq still had the support of the ulama and their mobilizing capacity, the coup may not have succeeded.[31] Having perhaps come to the same conclusion and realizing the importance of ulama support for his political legitimacy, Muhammad Reza reached out to the religious sector with enhanced funding for their seminaries and various other causes. This period of relative détente was shattered in 1959, however, with the Shah's efforts to pass a new Land Reform Bill. The provisions in this legislation would have redistributed large quantities of land controlled by the ulama in the form of awqaf, the pious endowments from which much of their income—and hence their independence from the state—depended. While this particular dispute ended in an impasse (the bill was passed but never implemented), it was the harbinger of considerable tensions soon to arise.

Muhammad Reza's suspension of the parliament in 1961 prompted protests by a coalition of both secular and religious social forces, which eventually turned violent. The Shah's deepening dependence on the West led to increasingly vociferous public critique of his policies, and no figure was more ardent in this than Ruhollah Khomeini, a cleric from the seminary city of Qom. Despite being arrested and then released by way of warning, Khomeini did not tone down his rhetoric and his success in mobilizing popular opposition sentiment led the government to violently suppress anti-government forces in a 1963 action that killed, by many estimates, several thousand. Khomeini himself was expelled from the country, going first to Turkey and eventually settling in the Iraqi Shi'i university city of Najaf. Throughout the rest of the 1960s and 70s, the Shah turned Iran into a police state, relying heavily on the climate of fear instilled by his secret security service (SAVAK) to maintain order and quell opposition. Half-hearted attempts at reform in the 1970s produced nothing but a growing sense of socioeconomic disparity between political elites and the masses, and endemic hatred of the Shah by the latter.

Before moving on to look at the events of Iran's Islamic revolution, it may be helpful to spend some time considering the evolution of Ayatollah Khomeini's political thought. This will enable us to better understand the doctrinal and ideological foundations of 1979's political earthquake. Khomeini's religious education, which saw him studying under several of Iran's leading ulama, introduced him to a wide range of religious disciplines. He developed a particularly keen interest in philosophy and mystical thought, continuing to study and teach these subjects in private after coming under pressure from traditional scholars to remove them from his public lectures. Some have even speculated that Khomeini's intense engagement with mystical thought may have given him an early sense of being predestined to play a special role in public affairs.[32] Khomeini's first sustained reflections on politics are to be found in the 1942 text *Kashf al-Asrar* ("The Unveiling of Secrets"). Primarily a critique of "comprador" ulama unable to gain any critical distance from the Shah, the *Kashf* also reserves a few choice barbs for the Pahlavis themselves. Regarding matters of government, Khomeini is not yet at a point where he argues for the state to be led by religious scholars. Rather, he points out that since all law comes from God, any legitimate government must implement the shari'ah and remove any laws incompatible with it. No particular form of government is un-Islamic in and of itself, but if a monarchical model was to be followed then it would be best for the king to be appointed by the leading religious leaders in order to ensure the "government of God."[33] He did hold out the possibility, however, that ulama might serve as members of parliament or have a privileged advisory role to the monarch.[34]

Khomeini's major statement on Islamic political theory is contained in *Hukumat-i Islami* ("Islamic Government"), first delivered as a set of lectures in Najaf during 1969–70, and later collected and published in book form. It is in this text that Khomeini provides the fullest explanation and justification of the doctrine of vilayat-i faqih ("guardianship of the jurist"). As a principle arguing that political authority should be vested in religious scholars, vilayati-i faqih is the basis for Khomeini's distinctive model of the

Islamic state. *Hukumat* unfolds methodically, beginning with a lengthy proof of the necessity for government based on Qur'anic, Prophetic, and Shi'i tradition. Even in this first section of the book, it becomes clear that Khomeini has not only a theoretical purpose, but also a political intent. It is not just that an Islamic government is required, he argues, but that true Muslims also have the obligation to remove from power those forces that actively seek to prevent the establishment of such a government:

> Both law and reason require that we do not permit governments to retain this non-Islamic or anti-Islamic character ... In order to assure the unity of the Islamic umma, in order to liberate the Islamic home-land from occupation and penetration by the imperialists and their puppet governments, it is imperative that we establish a government. In order to attain the unity and freedom of the Muslim peoples, we must overthrow the oppressive governments installed by the imperialists and bring into existence an Islamic government of justice that will be in the service of the people.[35]

Beyond the establishment of an Islamic government, Khomeini is clearly starting to lay the groundwork for an activist orientation toward political change. His criticism of obscurantist ulama disconnected from con-temporary political challenges continued in his public lectures during this time, and he urged his students to prepare for the obligations of establishing (and running) a true Islamic order.[36]

The next section of *Hukumat-i Islami* is the most innovative for it is here that Khomeini seeks to make a case for the direct political authority of religious scholars—to say, in effect, that the state should be in the hands of the ulama. The groundwork for the argument is based on the idea of the ulama as the trustees of the authority of the imams, themselves the vice-regents of God. While Khomeini was by no means the first Shi'i scholar to put forward a version of this argument, his was certainly the most compre-hensive treatment of the subject in the context of the modern nation-state. Until this time, the most direct exposition of the subject was to be found in the work of the early nineteenth-century scholar Mulla Ahmad Naraqi, who had argued for a unique and privileged governmental role for the ulama in the absence of the Imam.[37] Khomeini opens this section of his work by making a case for the unique nature of the political order he has in mind:

> Islamic government does not correspond to any of the existing forms of government ... Islamic government is neither tyrannical nor absolute, but constitutional. It is not constitutional in the current sense of the word, i.e., based on the approval of laws in accordance with the opinion of the majority. It is constitutional in the sense that the rulers are sub-ject to a certain set of conditions that are set forth in the Noble Qur'an and the Sunna of the Most Noble Messenger.[38]

Since the capacity to legislate is vested exclusively in God, Khomeini reasoned, it would be necessary for anyone charged with implementing and enforcing God's law to be an expert in the shari'ah. "Since Islamic government is a government of law," he argued, "knowledge of the law is necessary for the ruler, as has been laid down in tradition. Indeed, such knowledge is necessary not only for the ruler, but also for anyone holding a post or exercising some government function."[39] Khomeini reaches the culmination of his argument by arguing that if a ruler does not know the shari'ah (i.e. if he is a secular monarch) then he will have to rely on the guidance of those who do and his authority will be undermined; and yet, if he does not accept such counsel from the experts than it is impossible for him to rule justly. The natural conclusion of this line of argument is to remove the mediating layer of the non-jurist sovereign, and replace him with religious scholars. Hence Khomeini's assertion that " ... the true rulers are the fuqaha themselves, and rulership ought officially to be theirs, to apply to them, not to those who are obliged to follow the guidance of the fuqaha on account of their own ignorance of the law."[40] In the most straightforward terms, vilayati-i faqih as a doctrine argues that in an Islamic state the highest authority should be vested in those who have the greatest knowledge of the divine law upon which the political order is based. It therefore follows that the state should be in the hands of the religious scholars.

We should note that the lectures comprising *Hukumat-i Islami* were formulated for and delivered in a seminary setting to religious scholars. Its method of argumentation and evidence reflect the very particular discourse of the ulama and hence would not be persuasive to those outside this tradition. If Khomeini wanted to lay the basis for a popular revolution, he would need to find a mediator who could frame his ideas and imperatives for a wider audience. Two such figures played this role in Iran during the years of his absence—one of them as something of an official surrogate and the other as an independent public intellectual whose transformational worldview made it possible for an entire generation to see their aspirations reflected in Khomeini's project. As a Khomeini student of longstanding, Murtaza Mutahhari became the Ayatollah's proxy during his years in exile. Unlike his teacher, however, he had studied contemporary Western ideology and philosophy and was conversant in the Marxism that so many young Iranians found attractive. While drawn to aspects of the anti-capitalism present in socialist thought, he found Marxism's lack of attention to spiritualism and morality to be a fundamental flaw. He was hence able to engage such ideas, but then to provide a comprehensive Islamic critique, aimed squarely at religiously inclined members of the educated, lower middle class.

His lay counterpart, and eventual competitor, was a young intellectual named Ali Shariati. Shariati had studied in Paris for several years, eagerly imbibing all the latest currents in Western philosophy and social critique. Through Frantz Fanon he developed a sense of Third World consciousness, and via Ché Guevara the impetus to do something about it.[41] While skeptical about the material reductionism to be found in Marxism, he was enthralled by the emancipatory dimensions of socialist thought. He argued that Islam—and Shi'i Islam in particular—possessed the same critical edge and capacity to liberate the oppressed. What else was Shi'i history, he argued, if not an account of righteous struggle in the face of hegemony? "To Shariati," argues Vanessa Martin, "the imperialists and capitalists were enemies, and the Marxists were competitors. To Mutahhari, all were enemies."[42] We can see in his claims that Islam already contained all the best that was to be found in various Western ideologies echoes of other modern Islamist activist-intellectuals such as Hassan al-Banna. We also find here traces of figures such as Jamal ad-Din al-Afghani and a foreshadowing of Fazlur Rahman in his distinction between "Alid" and "Safavid" Shi'ism— the conceptual device through which Shariati served up his own critique of the ulama. The "Alid" formulation referred to the core doctrine and experience of the Prophet's family, while "Safavidism" came to be a symbol for the corruption and undermining of this living tradition by the ulama. Where Mutahhari had first cooperated with Shariati because he thought the latter might be helpful in building support for the ulama among the educated middle classes, he soon began to see Shariati's immense popularity and anti-clerical stance as major threats. Far more than any figures within the clerical establishment, Shariati, who died in London in 1977 under suspicious circumstances, had found a tenor that successfully married religious discourse with the political aspirations of Iran's young, educated middle class. In this regard he played a major role in priming society so that they could comfortably get behind the major political transformation that was shortly to follow. It is therefore not surprising that as the Islamic Revolution later unfolded, it was Shariati's formulations that worked their way into Khomeini's rhetoric and populism.

With the Shah's regime increasingly beholden to the United States, popular discontent with his rule became endemic. The accusation of *gharbzadegi* ("Westoxification"), coined by the intellectual Jalal al-Ahmad in the 1960s, seemed to perfectly capture the popular perception that the regime had by now wholly subordinated Iran to Western interests. Emboldened by the new U.S. president Jimmy Carter's emphasis on human rights, a group of secular intellectuals called for the Pahlavis to institute greater democracy and constitutionally guaranteed freedoms. Under Washington's wary eye, the Shah did not seek to suppress the movement and this emboldened student groups who subsequently took to the streets. When in early 1978 these protests were joined by the ulama and bazaar merchants, however, the government cracked down, killing several dozen people. This set in motion a cycle that would continue over much of the rest of the year: mourning rituals would turn into political protests, police would arrive, violence would ensure, protestors would be killed, and the cycle would restart.[43] In September 1978 the Shah declared martial law and on the following day—

known as "Black Friday"—at least several hundred people were killed in Tehran's Jaleh Square. The sheer shock of this massacre prompted certain groups that until now had refrained from joining the protests, such as the secular-national middle class and many blue-collar workers, to get involved. Worried about Khomeini's growing symbolic influence, the Shah petitioned Iraq to kick the cleric out of the country and in October 1978 he set up new headquarters in Neauphle-le-Chateau outside Paris, France. Ironically, this enabled his voice in Iran to grow even louder as he now had free reign to say whatever he wanted where his public discourse in Iraq had been circumscribed. Not only did the Persian service of the foreign media broadcast his statements into Iran, but thousands of cassette recordings of his speeches were smuggled into the country and circulated widely, prompting some to regard Iran as the first "media revolution."[44] As Henry Munson puts it, "the technology and political freedom of the West brought Khomeini closer to Iran in France than he had been in Iraq."[45]

The brewing revolution reached its climax when a crowd of over 2 million—Islamists, ulama, communists, secular modernists, students, workers, professionals, and bazaaris alike—all turned out for protests on the Shi'i holiday of Ashura in December 1978. The following month, the Shah fled the country and on February 1, 1979 the Ayatollah Khomeini made a triumphant return to Tehran. Over the next few months revolutionary forces attacked various hold-outs from the Shah's regime and soon all remaining army and police units had either been defeated or switched their loyalty to the clergy-led forces. Khomeini appointed Mehdi Bazargan, a scientist with strong but moderate Islamist credentials, to head up a new cabinet. The real power, as it quickly transpired however, lay with Khomeini's Islamic Revolutionary Council. When a group of militant students stormed the U.S. Embassy, holding several dozen American hostages for over a year, Bazar-

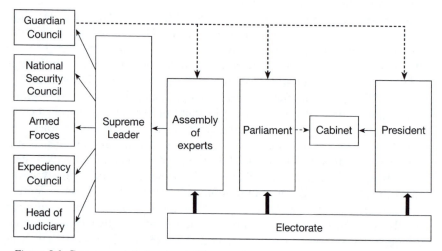

Figure 5.1 Governmental structure of Iran

gan found himself powerless to intervene due to the clergy's tacit support for the students. He and his cabinet resigned after only nine months in office, leaving the political field wide open for Khomeini's supporters. Over the previous months, the coalition of diverse political forces united in their opposition to the Shah fell apart as their disparate interests took over. The Tudeh (communist) party, the secular nationalists, and the Khomeinist clerics—all intrinsic components of the revolutionary forces—discovered very quickly that they had mutually incompatible visions of the post-Shah, constitutional order. Those outside the Khomeini camp were surprised at the vehemence with which the cleric pushed his revolutionary Islamic agenda. It was not the outcome that most of the non-religious groups who participated in the revolution had expected, and there were several reasons for this. The first point to make relates to historical precedent. The population at large would not have found it at all strange to see the ulama at the forefront of a popular reform movement given their role in similar efforts throughout Iranian history such as the Tobacco Protest of 1891, the first Constitutional Revolution in 1906, and the protests in the early 1960s where religious and secular forces worked together to oppose the Shah's suspension of parliament. In short, Iranians had no reason to think there might be anything to fear from a revolution led by the clergy since things had generally turned out fine in the past. Second, many of them had not read Khomeini's writings directly, and certainly not his work on the doctrine and practice of vilayat-i faqih. The speeches he made from abroad in the run-up to the revolution had not provided much detail about the specifics of the post-revolutionary order, and most people were happy to rally behind his Islamism as a surrogate form of anti-Pahlavi discourse. Khomeini's public relations handlers had also been careful to package the clerical agenda in a way that would appeal to mixed audiences. Finally, even those, such as the secular-nationalists, who were aware of Khomeini's intentions, were under the impression that they would be able to outflank him after the revolution and to co-opt the religious sector. Underestimating the organization and capacity of Khomeini's supporters, they were largely blindsided when in the month following the revolution he systematically cracked down on any and all groups within the revolutionary network who questioned his authority or seemed likely to do so in the future. This led to mass arrests, "disappearances" and many killings, particularly among communists, secular-nationalists, and Islamist elements not aligned with Khomeini. The Islamic left, best represented by the Mojahiden-i-Khalq movement, was outlawed and subsequently operated as an underground opposition group. The Ayatollah's loyalists usurped the *komiteh* worker's organizations that had been used to organize strikes and protests during the revolution and through this network they enforced order and conformity with the new order. Not even the ulama escaped this purge. The majority of religious scholars—while certainly opposed to the Shah and only too happy to make common cause alongside one of their own—did not agree with Khomeini's doctrine on religious grounds, and even less with his political aspirations. Many of them simply chose to keep quiet, but those who did speak out—such as the senior Ayatollah Shariatmadari—were silenced, placed under house arrest, or worse. The dust had hardly settled from the revolution when, in September 1980, Iraq invaded Iran in the hope of catching the latter off guard and pre-occupied with internal matters. Instead, the occasion of war with an Arab neighbor led by a highly secular regime provided Khomeini with a new source of national unity and a rallying cry to defend and perhaps even to spread the impulse of his recent revolution.

Khomeini held a national referendum in early 1979 asking the population to endorse the idea of an Islamic Republic, and based on this mandate he proceeded to draft a constitution. The first draft of this was rather more secular than he had hoped and so it was handed over to an assembly of clerical experts for revision, resulting in the present version (subsequently amended in 1989). It is this document that defines the framework and institutions of Iran's new Islamic government—or the Islamic Republic of Iran as it was henceforth to be called. In addition to affirming the principle of divine sovereignty (Article 2), the "General Principles" section of the constitution also stipulates that all laws and regulations in the Islamic Republic are to conform to the shari'ah (Article 4). Khomeini's doctrine of vilayat-i faqih is also enshrined here (Article 5) through a statement confirming that in the absence of the hidden Imam, leadership of the community falls to the Islamic legal specialist (faqih). It then goes on to link this specifically to the office of the Supreme Leader or Guide described below.

In addition to the familiar tripartite division of executive, legislative, and judiciary branches of government, the Iranian constitution also provides for several unique institutions and organs that have a major impact on the distribution of political power within the system—most of which are staffed by and under the control of the clerics. The most important of these is the office of the Leader (*rahbar*), or Guardian-Jurist (*valiy-i faqih*)—commonly known as the Supreme Leader. In addition to setting national priorities and overseeing the "general policies of the Islamic Republic," the Supreme Leader also possesses a number of unique powers and competences that make his office far and away the most powerful within the political system. The armed forces (especially the elite Islamic Revolutionary Guards Corps), police and security apparatus of the Republic all answer directly to the Supreme Leader and he also appoints the head of the Judiciary and regulates the country's media and information services. In short, all of the instruments associated with the exercise of power in a modern state are reserved for the Supreme Leader. While the country does have a separate President, many of the powers commonly associated with the executive branch of a government are reserved for the Supreme Leader in the Iranian system. The president of the republic has the power to appoint ministers, although two of these (Defense and Intelligence) are customarily agreed in consultation with the Supreme Leader.

A further instrument of the Supreme Leader's control is to be found in the Guardianship Council. Its main task is to oversee legislation enacted by the country's parliament (the Islamic Consultative Assembly), ensuring that all laws passed are compatible with the shari'ah. The Guardianship Council also vets all candidates for the parliament, presidency, and the Assembly of Experts (see below). Of the Council's 12 members, half are appointed directly by the Supreme Leader and the other six proposed by the Judiciary and then approved by the parliament. Should an irreconcilable dispute arise between the parliament and the Guardianship Council, the matter is referred to the Expediency Council. Created by a 1989 constitutional amendment, this Council—all of whose members are appointed by the Supreme Leader—is charged with settling the aforementioned disputes and also with offering ad hoc advice to the Supreme Leader on matters of his choosing. The final body unique to the Islamic Republic is the Assembly of Experts, which in theory supervises the office of the Supreme Leader. The Assembly, whose 86 members are popularly elected every eight years, is charged with selecting the Supreme Leader (who serves for life) and also has the power to dismiss him, although the body has never publicly challenged its appointee. In Iran the president and members of parliament are all popularly elected, with both serving terms of four years. While the system is clearly grossly stacked in favor of the Supreme Leader who, through his lifetime appointment, is not regularly accountable to the populace, it is worth noting that Iran's record of holding regular elections for both parliament and the presidency—and respecting their outcomes, even when they do not turn out to the Supreme Leader's liking—is one of the better in the Muslim world. Of course the Supreme Leader possesses such a preponderance of power that he has nothing to fear in terms of day-to-day institutional politics should a president or parliament ever oppose him. It is also interesting to note that within the Iranian system membership in one of the aforementioned bodies or councils does not preclude one from serving on another at the same time. For example, former president Ali Akbar Hashemi Rafsanjani has served simultaneously as chairman of the Expediency Council and deputy chair of the Assembly of Experts.

Iran became an increasingly closed society from 1980, as new regulations promulgated by conservative clerics began to affect various aspects of daily life. Women, in particular, bore the brunt of these changes. Veiling was made mandatory from 1983, and family laws were revised to permit polygamy, child and temporary marriages, and the progressive gender segregation of more and more public space. Politics in the country was dominated by a single party, the pro-Khomeini Islamic Republican Party (IRP), but even within this group a number of clear factions had started to emerge after a few years. Conservatives favored a privileged political role for the clergy, and strict adherence to traditional social norms. They were the inheritors of the ulama's historical alliance with the bazaari merchants, and so their economic views tended to favor private enterprise and property.

Indeed, much of their wealth was to be found in the awqaf ("pious endowments") system—technically a form of private asset. The hardline revolutionary faction, on the other hand, was not happy with this status quo. They sought a radical redistribution of wealth in the name of social justice and the nationalization of industry. This impasse made it particularly difficult for the much-needed land reform process to make significant headway during the 1980s. By 1984, with inflation high, money in short supply, and oil prices low, there arose a sub-faction of "pragmatic realists" from amongst the conservatives who realized that significant economic liberalization was the only way to ease Iran's fiscal pressures—a trend that was reinforced when Rafsanjani assumed the presidency. In terms of foreign policy, the hardliners were stridently anti-Western (and anti-American in particular; this was the faction that had orchestrated the U.S. Embassy siege) in their orientation, and sought to export the revolution to other Muslim countries. The conservatives on the other hand, emphasized relations with other Muslim countries, but—although certainly not pro-American—were less unequivocal in their condemnation of the West or the possibility of Iran normalizing its relations with the rest of the world.[46]

That rest of the world, and particularly Iran's neighbors, had certainly taken note of the 1979 upheaval in Tehran. Third World revolutionary movements were emboldened by Khomeini's success and the regimes they opposed expressed new fears that the Iranian model might spread to other settings in the developing world. Closer to home, Arab countries with significant Shi'i populations—notably Saudi Arabia, Bahrain, and Kuwait—all experienced various levels of unrest in the wake of the revolution. Iran also reached out to their oppressed co-religionists in Lebanon, providing vital support for the founding and evolution of Hizbullah (see Chapter 6)—patronage that continues to this day. Likewise, Khomeini provided support for Shi'i opposition movements in neighboring Iraq, a factor that continues to be important today in post-Saddam Iraq (see Chapter 6). The Iran-Iraq War (1980–88) enacted an enormous toll on both countries, but Iran's use of "human wave" tactics—whereby members of the paramilitary Basij Corps would repeatedly throw themselves at enemy lines, or clear minefields with their bodies—created an entire generation of "martyrs" for the revolution and provided a sense of national unity that distracted from domestic political woes. Iran's hopes for the rehabilitation of its international image were not helped in 1989 when Khomeini issued a statement condemning the British novelist Salman Rushdie to death. In Khomeini's estimation, Rushdie's novel *The Satanic Verses*, contained blasphemies that made its author an apostate from Islam, and hence subject to death.[47]

By the late 1980s, voices of dissent began to be heard from within the clerical establishment itself. Some, such as Khomeini's former right hand man Hossein Ali Montazeri, found themselves subject to public rebuke after requesting that the government consider the consequences of some of its failures. Montazeri, who had been selected in 1985 by the Assembly of

Experts to succeed Khomeini as the Supreme Leader found himself stripped of this office-in-waiting, and was later even placed under house arrest. When Khomeini eventually died in 1989, the power struggle between conservatives and hardliners anticipated by some observers never materialized. The Supreme Leadership passed to the former president Ali Khameini and parliamentary speaker Ali Akbar Hashemi Rafsanjani was elected president. A series of constitutional amendments in 1989 had abolished the position of prime minister and afforded the president new powers. The choice of Khameini as Supreme Leader, it should be noted, was somewhat controversial because as a religious scholar he was relatively junior. He was quickly given a "field promotion" from the rank of Hujjat al-Islam to Ayatollah, but even this could not smooth over the fact that his credentials were more political and administrative than religious. For some this marked something of a reconceptualization of the Supreme Leader's role after Khomeini's passing. The constitutional revisions had also defined the Guide's role more clearly, laying stronger emphasis on his political qualifications.

The period of Rafsanjani's presidency (1989–97) is generally identified with the rise of a third significant force in Iranian politics, that of the pragmatists. This group, who tended to draw from the ranks of the conservatives, sought to cautiously introduce certain liberalizing reforms. With Rafsanjani as their figurehead, the main task facing them was to put Iran's economic affairs in order and to reconstruct the country after the indecisive but costly war with Iraq. A number of five-year development plans were introduced, coupled with the introduction of economic policies that would make it easier for Iran to qualify for loans from international financial institutions (the International Monetary Fund (IMF), World Bank) that could permit the country's infrastructure to be rebuilt. This became all the more challenging when, in 1995, the United States introduced a comprehensive ban on business dealings with the Islamic Republic. Rafsanjani also permitted considerably more debate within both the media and parliament, and it became commonplace to hear executive policies and initiatives criticized openly. While this period saw a relative decline in the influence of the hardliners (particularly after the Iraq War), this did not mean that the pragmatists had a free hand. The 1992 parliamentary elections brought the assembly firmly into the hands of the conservatives, and this created certain constraints on Rafsanjani's latitude to maneuver and to pursue grand national developmental schemes—meaning that his efforts to reform the economy brought mixed results.

While Rafsanjani's rule was characterized by certain shifts of power within the existing order and a modicum of carefully controlled openness, it was not until the election of Mohammad Khatami as president in 1997 that the landscape of Iranian politics was significantly reconfigured. Khatami, a philosopher and former culture minister who had been somewhat sidelined by the establishment for his liberal views, was one of three figures going up against the clergy's "official" candidate, parliamentary speaker Ali Akbar

Nateq Nuri. The latter had received Khameini's endorsement, and the commander of the Revolutionary Guard issued orders to vote for him—prompting many observers to assume that his victory was a foregone conclusion.[48] The pragmatists, for their part, quietly endorsed Khatami's candidacy. Against all expectations, Khatami won an overwhelming victory, taking 69 percent of the vote. He had campaigned on a platform of reform and openness, messages that resonated with Iran's younger voters—and particularly with women, whose support was shown by subsequent analysis to have been decisive in his victory. The conservative clergy were rather taken aback by the scale of Khatami's triumph, with some immediately posing questions as to his suitability to serve in the executive. He was likened by them to ulama involved in leading the 1906 Constitutional Revolution, and conservatives were reminded that this process had resulted in a secular constitution—implying, in effect, that Khatami was a threat to the post-revolutionary order. Seeking to stay above the factional fray, as had Khomeini before him, Khameini as Supreme Leader welcomed Khatami's victory and endorsed the idea of debating the values and meaning of the revolution. Daniel Brumberg, arguing that Khatami's thinking reveals him to be opposed to the very idea of clerical dominance, because "they lack adequate knowledge of matters extrinsic to Islam" noted that he was nevertheless "always careful to reach this conclusion through Khomeini"—and thereby to remain onside in the eyes of the conservatives.[49] Some had expressed surprise that, with his liberal record, Khatami had been permitted by the Guardianship Council to even stand as a candidate. It may have been that, having regarded Nateq Nuri's as a sure thing for the presidency, Khatami was selected by the Council in order to give the impression of greater pluralism in terms of the range of views represented in the election. Khatami's new cabinet, once formed, certainly reflected his reformist orientation, but he was still constrained by the Supreme Leader in terms of his appointments to the key security posts. Significantly, he appointed a woman to serve as one of the Republic's vice presidents—the first time since the revolution that a woman had held a high executive office.

Khatami came to embody a generation's hopes for liberalization in Iran. In the months following his election, expectations for the enactment of meaningful reform by his government grew tremendously—but the political space afforded him to pursue this agenda certainly did not. Khatami also won great admiration overseas, where many saw him as the harbinger of a pro-Western counter-revolution. In this regard, there are certain parallels to be drawn between the rise to power of Mohammad Khatami in Iran and that of Mikhail Gorbachev in the Soviet Union. Gorbachev's *glasnost* and perestroika projects were seen by many observers outside the Soviet Union as an attempt by its premier to roll back communism altogether. In fact, Gorbachev was still firmly committed to the basic Soviet model and to socialism—he only wanted to reform them. Similarly, Khatami was perceived by some outside Iran as a force working to undo the Islamic

Revolution and re-Westernize Iran. Khatami, however, remained committed to the ideals of the Islamic Revolution and sought rather to make it more sustainable through reform and greater openness. Khatami will have been well aware, given the balance of power between the presidency and the various bodies controlled by the conservative clerics, that he would face an uphill battle all the way.

While Khatami's ability to directly enact significant reform was limited by restrictions incumbent upon his office, his election emboldened a nascent grassroots reform movement within Iran. Over the next few years it grew rapidly to become the largest popular political faction within the country, culminating in a reformist sweep (71 percent of seats) in the 2000 parliamentary poll. Led by the Islamic Iran Participation Front (IIPF), the reformists commanded strong support across the universities and the middle classes. Their emergence was associated with enormous growth in the number of nongovernmental organizations and civil society organizations—particularly newspapers and other media forums—with strong support for these initiatives coming from Khatami's office. Unsurprisingly, it was not long before tensions between the reformists and the conservative clergy came into the open. In 1998, legal action against Tehran's pro-reform mayor brought students onto the street, and soon the government began to close down reformist publishing houses on a regular basis. Most of these simply reopened immediately under a different name, but these actions demonstrated Khatami's inefficacy in the face of press and censorship laws shaped entirely by the Supreme Leader's judiciary. An even more oppressive press bill passed in 1999 prompted even wider demonstrations and a police crackdown. Khatami initially supported these protests, but he was later pressured by conservatives to denounce the students' defiance. The conservatives were also able to rely on at least two other forces within Iranian society to add to their own pressure on the reformists. The bazaari merchants, for example, were keen to continue the special economic favors they enjoyed under the status quo, and so worked where possible to undermine reformist influence. More worrying were various pro-clerical vigilante groups who showed up and attacked student protests. While it is not entirely clear whether these were actually controlled by the clerics it is certain that at the very least, little was done to curb their activities.

By 1999, however, the reformists were making considerable inroads into the political system. Local and municipal elections were held in Iran for the first time, and reformist groups scored a strong victory. Since these seats were not subject to review by the Guardianship Council, most councils ended up with at least one woman member. The height of the reformists' electoral success came during the 2000 national parliamentary elections when almost three-quarters of the seats were won by IIPF-oriented candidates. By way of protest against conservative interference in reform efforts, Khatami prevaricated about whether to run for re-election in 2001. In the end he chose to stand and was returned with an even larger majority than in

1997. The reformist parliament mounted a legislative counter-attack on the conservatives the following year, seeking expanded powers for the president and a reduction in the purview of the Guardianship Council. Despite a few concessions on the part of the clerical establishment, such as Ayatollah's Montazeri's release from house arrest in 2003, the conservatives began a concerted and systematic crackdown on the reform movement. Press censorship increased dramatically, with a number of reformist outlets shut down permanently. In the run-up to the 2004 parliamentary elections the Guardianship Council deemed a great many of the reformist candidates ineligible to stand, and conservatives ended up winning a little over half the seats. Without a viable candidate for the 2005 presidential elections (Khatami was ineligible to stand for a third consecutive term), the best the reformists could hope for was a strong showing by the conservative pragmatist Ali Akbar Rafsanjani. After two rounds of voting, however, Rafsanjani was defeated by his hardline opponent, Mahmoud Ahmadinejad. This seemed to spell an end to the reform movement as all political offices sympathetic to their position were now firmly back under clerical control.

It is difficult to make an evaluation of Khatami's presidency. Clearly he was not able to achieve much in the way of sustained liberalizing reform. Many observers concluded that he would not have been able to do this without forcing a direct and likely very violent confrontation with the forces of the regime—and clearly he was not prepared to go this far. While he may have disappointed many of those who put faith in him, Khatami opened sufficient space for the reformist aspirations of Iran's educated youth generation to be seen around the world. That said, this same generation still faces socioeconomic challenges in addition to a lack of political freedom. Of the 1.5 million applicants to Iranian universities in 2001, spaces were only available for 10 percent of these. Less than 1 percent of university graduates are able to immediately enter employment. Khatami's fortunes were also not helped when the United States, while recognizing the existence of strong reformist sentiment in Iran, named the Islamic Republic as part of an international "axis of evil" alongside Iraq and North Korea in the wake of the September 11, 2001 attacks. This action was all the more bewildering to the Iranians after the assistance they had provided in helping to stabilize Afghanistan in the wake of the fall of the Taliban. This new hostility from Washington allowed the conservatives to reclaim the mantle of anti-Americanism, and to portray the reformists as allies of U.S. imperial designs in the region. In the end, it became clear that the logical conclusions of Khatami's thinking simply could not be contemplated in the contemporary environment. He was not, however, the sole ideologue of the reformist movement. Figures such as the philosopher Abdolkarim Soroush, combining "neo-Marxist sociology and mystical individualism," emerged as a major critic of the clerical state after having initially served the revolution and helping to institutionalize it.[50] He argues, for example, that Islam and state need to be kept apart not because religion corrupts politics, but rather the converse—that politics, with its base and immoral pursuit of power, poses a threat to the purity of religion. His writings have earned a considerable following both in Iran and abroad, and he has tended to spend large periods of time outside Iran lecturing at Western universities. From within the clerical establishment itself reformist voices have arisen, such as Mohsen Kadivar, whose reformist-oriented political theories earned him a prison sentence in the late 1990s.

The election of Mahmoud Ahmadinejad in 2005 marked the rise of a hardline neo-Khomeinism in Iranian politics. While highly conservative, his political base was not the religious scholars or their merchant allies. Ahmadinejad, a former mayor of Tehran, was above all a populist and his rhetoric was aimed squarely at the socioeconomically dispossessed of Iran. Where Khatami had reached out to the educated young middle and lower-middle classes, Ahmadinejad packaged himself for the country's poor. The largely uneducated generation that had grown up with, and often fought in, the Iran-Iraq war formed the heart of his constituency. These former *basijis*, the volunteer martyrdom forces composed mainly of untrained teenagers that would throw themselves at Iraqi positions to clear the way for the regular army, took heart in Ahmadinejad's populist revolutionary nationalism and his promises to improve their standard of living. True to form, since taking office his rhetoric has been extremely hardline, calling for the eradication of Israel and calling into question the truth of the Holocaust as a historical event. Anti-Americanism was also a strong component of his election platform and he raised tensions with the United States and the international community by reopening Iran's nuclear program in 2006.

Three aspects relating to the role of Islam in Iranian politics emerge from our survey as particularly noteworthy. First there is the fact that the religious scholars were no strangers to the political landscape, having played an important role in anti-monarchical politics several times throughout modern Iranian history. In this sense, they encountered very little in the way of social barriers when seeking to enter mass popular politics in the lead up to the Islamic Revolution in the 1970s; indeed, it was the clerics who provided the only viable mobilizing framework. Second, and somewhat related, is the fact that while this was an Islamic revolution in name, it was actually a highly heterogeneous affair in terms of who actually took part. Without the support of a broad range of social classes, sectors, and political orientations, it is unlikely that the religious leaders would have had the human resources necessary to successfully mount such an upheaval in the social order. Finally, although the ruling religious regime is often thought of in monolithic terms, it becomes very easy to identify a broad spectrum of interests, policies, and political visions that define several clear factions within the clerical establishment itself.

As this chapter has shown, the "Islamic state" varies considerably from context to context depending on the circumstances of its establishment and the configuration of social and political forces within the various national

settings in which such polities exist. "Islam as the system" does not necessarily tell us much about how much or what kind of politics we are likely to
find in such a state. In the case of Saudi Arabia, the royal family managed
until fairly recently to keep a tight lid on political opposition of any sort,
while in Pakistan—an Islamic state with a very different source of legitimacy—we find political history defined in terms of the ebbs and flows of
different visions of Islamic polity. Iran, as a revolutionary state based on an
innovative doctrine of direct clerical rule, seems to have gone furthest of all
in terms of institutionalizing within the state social actors and discursive
forms defined almost exclusively in religious terms. But as former Iranian
president Mohammad Khatami once wrote:

> If we limit ourselves to the appearances of and have a narrow view of
> religion, then the concept of "Islamic Republic" itself will mean
> separation from Islam. Where did you ever have anything called a
> republic in Islam? Where in Islam—the beginnings of Islam—do you
> find anything called a parliament?[51]

His point here is that it is impossible to understand the meaning, nature,
and form of the Islamic state today without reference to the discourse of
political modernity that inevitably frames its very formation. For him the
religious nature of the state is not achieved by placing the world "Islamic"
in front of the word "republic," but rather in assessing the normative
implications inherent in various arrangements of power and social order.
On this reading, certain institutions in avowedly non-Islamic settings could
still qualify as "Islamic," and also vice versa.

Common to all three cases we have examined in detail above is the idea of
embracing an Islamic state as part of transition from one social order to
another—but not generally in the context of a prior dissolution of order or
an extended conflict that has tended to prevent the establishment of societal
stability. In the next chapter we will move on to examine several cases where
Islam has sought to fill the vacuum of an absent state or social authority, or
has emerged as a mobilizing (and sometimes competing) discourse in situations of protracted violent conflict—Islam, in other words, for lack of a
system.

Sudan: Hassan al-Turabi and the Islamic state

In 1989, a military coup d'état brought General Omar al-Bashir to power
in Sudan. It soon became clear, however, that the main beneficiary (and
likely instigator) of this turn of events was the National Islamic Front
(NIF), Sudan's MB affiliate. The NIF was led by Hassan al-Turabi, an
inveterate Islamist politician and intellectual trained in Europe. Turabi's party presided over what he termed an "Islamic experiment,"
seeking to broaden and deepen existing shari'ah laws while consolidating

their grip on power by filling key government posts. Political parties were outlawed and Islamic law declared throughout the country: Sudan had seemingly joined the ranks of the "Islamic states" alongside Pakistan, Iran, and Saudi Arabia. Over the course of the 1990s the situation evolved into a power struggle between Turabi and Bashir as the latter saw the military's influence eroded by various NIF (now renamed the National Congress) power plays. Turabi, who had since risen to become Speaker of the Parliament, fell foul of Bashir by signing unauthorized agreements with separatist movements in the country's south and found himself jailed or under house arrest from 2001 to 2005.

Turabi's efforts to implement a model of the Islamic state in Sudan must be understood against the backdrop of that country's ethno-religious demographics, multiple ongoing conflicts, and Turabi's own unique approach to political pragmatism and public messaging. Sudanese politics have long been plagued by sectarian and tribal rivalries, overlayed by a major civil war pitting the Arab Muslim government of the north against the mostly sub-Saharan African population (mostly Christian or animist) of the south. Despite repeated assurances by Turabi to the effect that Islamic law would only apply to Muslims, the continued persecution of non-Muslim citizens throughout Sudan has left many suspicious of the "Islamic experiment." In 2005, a Comprehensive Peace Accord was signed between the southern Sudanese People's Liberation Movement (SPLM) and Bashir's government. It creates a largely autonomous region in the south, with provisions for security and resource sharing, as well as a referendum on full independence in 2011.

Many observers have pointed to a certain ambiguity—some say duplicity—in Turabi's conduct as both ideologue and politician. While many of his writings, particularly those aimed at Western audiences, seem to advance relatively liberal and progressive interpretations of Islam (e.g. women are not required to wear veils, should be fully employed and can act as imams; alcohol should be tolerated in the privacy of the home), Turabi seems to have done little to bring about the implementation of these ideals in the context of the Islamic state in Sudan. His positions on issues such as the proper means for transitioning to an Islamic political order also seem to have shifted and swayed over the years depending on the state of Sudanese politics and relative political fortunes of his party at any given time. While extolling the virtues of democracy and political pluralism in his writings, Turabi has played a key role in maintaining Sudan's authoritarian system after 1989. In the early 1990s, he served as coordinator-in-chief of a new international network of Islamist movements, hosting several conferences attended by leading MB parties and movements. Turabi also invited Usama Bin Laden to Sudan in 1991, providing him refuge and support after the latter had been forced out of his native Saudi Arabia.

6 Islam for lack of a system: Islamism in weak and failed states

This chapter represents the last in a series of three thematically organized accounts of contemporary Muslim politics under various political circumstances. We have looked already at the evolution of Islamism as a political strategy where groups and parties seek to enter the political system (Chapter 4). We then went on to examine how Muslim politics play out in three countries where the state is, to some degree, defined in terms of Islam. In this chapter we will be looking at several cases of Islam and politics in settings where a state has collapsed, or due to ongoing military occupation and violent conflict, is functionally absent or, at best, very weak. As we will see, many of the same discursive and mobilizing mechanisms are at work in these situations. The political environment of a weak or absent state, however, often presents Muslim actors with a very different set of opportunity structures.

In the case of a failed state, Islamist actors generally do not need to worry about the problem of defining themselves vis-à-vis an existing (and potentially hostile) political authority, or about devising a strategy to challenge or confront the ruling state. But neither will they enjoy the relatively luxurious circumstances of political opposition where one can sit back and cast barbs at the state without being required to implement alternatives, or be held to account. Once in power, on the other hand, any legitimacy or support they may derive from their religious identity will quickly be put to the test once faced with the realities of actually running a country. In cases of state failure, the relevant exigencies are much more demanding since it will often be necessary to recreate (or create anew, in some cases) the foundations of government and public administration. In a situation of military occupation, on the other hand, many of the same constraints associated with a hostile state may bear on the activities of Islamist groups. As we will see, however, under circumstances characterized by the presence of multiple currents of liberation discourse (nationalist, leftist, religious), Islamists and occupying authorities may find themselves entering into odd constellations of alliance or quietism in the pursuit of various short- and medium-term goals. In political climates defined primarily in terms of liberation from an external power, the repertoire of political symbols available to Islamic actors, and their articulation in terms of religion, will also differ from situations of straightforward opposition to an existing state. Finally, where state capacity is weak, Islamist actors that are well organized, funded, and managed may emerge as parallel service providers or, in some areas, may even begin to resemble "shadow governments" in terms of how deeply they become entrenched as legitimate guarantors of welfare and public order as well as promulgators of resistance to foreign enemies.

We should clarify how the cases we will be examining in this chapter differ from certain others we have already looked at and which, at first glance, may represent political climates that seem to display many of the same features we have detailed above. In looking at Egypt, for example, we emphasized the "retreat of the state" as a provider of social welfare in the context of economic liberalization and public sector reform. As we saw, Islamist actors at the societal and even local neighborhood level worked to fill the void left by the absent state, and so built for themselves an enormous pool of social capital and popular legitimacy. While we will also be looking in this chapter at situations where Islamists offer social services that a central state is unable or unwilling to provide, the crucial difference rests in the fact that in these cases the state is missing altogether, or is so weak as to be wholly absent from people's considerations regarding alternative sources of welfare or political identity. In other words, unlike in Egypt where the state, despite its "retreat" from the realm of the social, was still a dominant presence in terms of its public order and security capacities, we are dealing here with situations where it is dubious as to whether the existing political authorities would even meet the bare minimum requirements to qualify as a state—such as Max Weber's conception of the state as possessing a monopoly over the capacity to use violence. In short, in this chapter, we are dealing with situations where Islamists operate in settings in which political sovereignty and national legitimacy are ambiguous at best, and potentially up for grabs.

Nigeria: shari'ah law and the politics of federalism

Between 1999 and 2003 12 states in northern Nigeria passed legislation implementing varying degrees of shari'ah law. In the wake of this development, certain areas of the north have seen instances of violence associated with "vigilante justice" and several high-profile human rights cases—most notably that of Amina Lawal who, in 2002, was sentenced to death (eventually overturned on appeal) by a shari'ah court on charges of adultery.

What drove the enforcement of shari'ah in the north and how can we understand it as an example of Muslim politics? Rather than representing an upswing in the fortunes of conservative Islamists, the emergence of the shari'ah legislation is first and foremost a regional response to Nigeria's return to civilian rule in 1998 after 15 years of martial law and several army coups. There were concerns in the north that a civilian government would be weak on law and order, promoting certain northern leaders to search for solutions couched in idioms— such as Islam—with local appeal. A second and related issue concerns the division of power between the central government and the various constituent states of the Nigerian federation. Here we see Islamic language and symbols being mobilized as part of a politics that asserts strong regional and cultural identities vis-à-vis a federal state still seeking to consolidate its position under civilian rule.

Nigeria's population of 132 million is believed to be 50 percent Muslim, with the majority of those professing Islam living in the north of the country. Various ethnic, linguistic, tribal, and sectarian cleavages and tensions have been endemic to Nigerian politics since independence from Britain in 1960.

We also looked at Iran, which, having experienced a revolution may appear to be subject to some of the same considerations regarding the reconstruction of state institutions. Iran, however, was neither a classic failed state nor the victim of a protracted conflict or civil war. It was certainly a state that had lost popular legitimacy, but that is very different from a state that fails in the sense of comprehensive institutional decay. Its revolution was also a relatively short-lived affair, meaning that a new political authority was able to set about the business of governing relatively quickly, and was also able to tap into some level of continuity in terms of existing institutions and human resources—while, of course, adding some unique institutions of its own. The core point is that in setting up the Islamic Republic of Iran in the wake of the 1979 revolution, Khomeini faced a very different set of political and structural challenges than those confronting the Taliban in 1996 as they went about the business of converting their country into the Islamic Emirate of Afghanistan.

Our exploration of Muslim politics in weak, failed, and conflict states will occur through two main case studies, with supplementary coverage of two further examples. First, we will examine the rise of HAMAS in the occupied territories of Palestine. After a brief overview of its origins and the basic course of its political career to date, the evolution of its political and military strategy in a complex and constantly changing political environment will be analyzed. We will have two main areas of focus with regard to HAMAS. First we will consider the enormous social base the movement developed for itself (particularly in Gaza) through a comprehensive network of social services. This will be examined in terms of popular legitimacy and capacity to mobilize for political and military operations. Second, we will consider its relations with the PLO and, later, the Palestinian Authority, in terms of competing for national legitimacy. How, we will ask, did HAMAS adapt the Islamist project to a political setting defined in terms of resistance to occupation and national liberation? Finally we will look at HAMAS' decision to enter politics, its 2006 landslide electoral victory, and the challenges posed by its taking over the reins of power in the Palestinian Authority.

Our second case study will be the Taliban of Afghanistan. We will look at the circumstances that permitted them to come to power in the aftermath of the civil war that broke out in Afghanistan following the withdrawal of Soviet forces. Of particular interest to us will be the interaction between the Taliban's form of austere public religious normativity and prevailing religious norms in Afghanistan. While it is clear that the people of Afghanistan welcomed the Taliban, not only because of their promise to restore order, but also because of their religious basis, it emerges that the popular Afghan conception of what a religious state means and looks like did not correspond to the literal Islamism of the Taliban *mullahs*. This fact, complicated by persistent ethno-sectarian rivalries and the new regime's utter lack of administrative experience, meant that the Islamic Emirate of Afghanistan was fatally crippled from the very outset. A failed state gave way to what was, at best, a "quasi-state."[1] Supplementary textboxes will give us some insight into two other recent examples of post-conflict countries where Islamism has been an important political factor. We will look at Hizbullah in Lebanon and its fraught conversion from an armed resistance movement during that country's civil war (1975–90) to, in its aftermath, an Islamist social movement and political party—albeit one that still possesses a heavily armed militia that serves as Lebanon's de facto army on its southern flank. We will also look at the role of religious actors in Iraq after Saddam Hussein and the emergence of sectarian tensions as the fault lines of the new Iraqi political landscape. All of this in the context of an ongoing insurgency, partly led by foreign elements, and the continued presence of U.S. troops—a "quasi-occupation."

Islamism in Palestine: nationalism, charity, and violence

HAMAS is a complex and controversial entity. It has been variously described as a political movement, a terrorist group, and a social welfare organization. The difficulty in analyzing HAMAS arises from the fact that it is, in fact, all three of these things—but not reducible to any one of them. The highly politicized and often polarized environment in which all of these manifestations of HAMAS operate also poses significant challenges to the would-be analyst. To those convinced of Israel's legitimacy and concerned for its security, HAMAS is clearly first and foremost a terrorist group. To those, on the other hand, who see Israel's occupation of Palestine as illegal and dehumanizing, HAMAS represents a legitimate form of resistance. The account offered here will not try to make the case for one or the other of these two positions, but will seek instead to explore the circumstances under which the discourse and ideology of HAMAS have evolved, and also how and why, at given times, it has made particular choices from among the various strategic and tactical options available to it. In a climate in which "terrorism" has become such a loaded term, its association with a particular group runs the risk of obscuring the fact that terrorism is a tactic rather than an ideology. To characterize (or dismiss) a movement solely in reference to its use of a particular tactic does not help us, as political analysts, to explain how it mobilizes people and symbols in the pursuit of its political goals. Glenn Robinson puts it well when he writes:

> ... [B]y labeling Hamas a terrorist group, [we] ignore most of what Hamas actually does. Hamas is a social movement with thousands of activists and hundreds of thousands (perhaps millions) of Palestinian sympathizers, and it engages in extensive political and social activities far removed from suicide bombers. Second, it is always problematic to speak of terrorist groups (or states), as opposed to groups (or states) that periodically use acts of terror for tactical political reasons. By understanding terrorism in tactical terms rather than as a generic group attribute, rational responses become potentially more effective and less obviously politically hypocritical.

HAMAS is particularly difficult to assess in this regard since, while much of its charitable activity is indeed "far removed" from its suicide bombers, there is also significant evidence to suggest that some within the political bureau of HAMAS have direct control over the activities of its military wing. And yet we cannot understand why the movement enjoys such widespread support among Palestinians, even those who eschew violence and/or have little interest in an Islamic state, unless we look at HAMAS in its totality. Likewise, without a holistic analysis, we will achieve little understanding of the internal dynamics of the movement and hence be unable to identify where it may be headed in the future.

Our coverage of HAMAS will be divided into two main sections. In the first we will examine the origins of the movement and provide a brief overview of its activities from the time of the first intifada in 1987 up to the 2006 electoral victory that brought it to power in the Palestinian Authority. The second section will provide an analytical focus on several major topics and themes relating to HAMAS. We will look at its social base, structure and funding; its ambivalent and constantly changing relationship with the Palestine Liberation Organization (PLO, particularly the dominant Fateh faction); the evolution of HAMAS' discourse, strategy and topics from the time of its founding; and, finally, various aspects of the internal HAMAS sociology (factions, generational differences, etc.) that may indicate the group's political future. Finally, we will analyze the circumstances that brought HAMAS to power in 2006 and the various challenges posed by its control of the Palestinian Authority and the Palestinian Legislative Council.

HAMAS: origins, evolution, and political career

HAMAS as a distinct political movement was born in December 1987 at the inception of the first Palestinian intifada ("shaking off"), or uprising, against the Israeli occupation of the West Bank and Gaza. HAMAS is an acronym for *Harakat al-Muqawama al-Islamiyya* ("Islamic Resistance Movement") and the word *hamas* also means "enthusiasm" or "zeal" in Arabic. While formally constituted in the late 1980s, the social roots of HAMAS go back much further and can be found in the Palestinian branch of the Muslim Brotherhood (MB) which was established during Hasan al-Banna's lifetime. During much of the MB's history in Palestine, control of its operations was divided between Egypt and Jordan, with the Gaza region falling to the former and the West Bank to the latter—particularly after the West Bank was annexed to Jordan in 1950. After 1967, when Gaza and the West Bank both came under Israeli control, the Gaza branch in particular was increasingly isolated from both the central MB organization as well as its other Palestinian affiliates. Where before 1967 the MB had been politically active against Israel—even sending Brotherhood volunteers to fight in Palestine in the late 1940s and early 50s—it confined itself almost exclusively to religious and social affairs for the next 20 years.[2]

In the late 1960s, the leadership of the MB in Gaza fell to a young activist, Ahmed al-Yassin. Sheikh Yassin, as he commonly came to be known, was a schoolteacher and mufti who had studied at Al-Azhar in Cairo, and also undergone teacher training. Before taking over the reins of the MB, he had served as the imam in several mosques and also as a teacher in schools run by the United Nations Relief Works Agency (UNRWA).[3] From the 1970s, Yassin oversaw the creation of a rapidly expanding network of charities and social services in Gaza. The central institution in this endeavor was the Mujamma al-Islami ("Islamic Center"), founded by Yassin in 1973. This body became the core of the MB's activities in Gaza and its influence grew rapidly as it came to encompass dozens and then hundreds of autonomous social organizations. Many religious institutions in Gaza also came under its control. An influx of funding from Saudi Arabia during the 70s also allowed it to build more places of worship and by 1986, 40 percent of all mosques in the area were run by the MB.[4] Israel, seeking to curry favor with the Islamists as a check on the growing influence of the Palestinian left, also provided funds for the endowment of awqaf—a tactic they would try to use again at the founding of HAMAS. In 1978, the Islamic University of Gaza was founded and also began to work closely with the Mujamma. Much of the HAMAS intellectual leadership would eventually emerge from the faculty and administrative ranks of this institution. We should note that while the MB also established similar associations in the West Bank, they were not as closely integrated and many were still controlled from Jordan—unlike the Gaza institutions, which were almost entirely home grown and managed.[5]

The path leading to the formation of HAMAS out of the MB begins in the 1980s, when certain tensions regarding the Brotherhood's overall socio-political strategy began to emerge. As the occupation wore on, a faction of MB radicals—dissatisfied with the organization's confinement to the religious and social spheres—broke away to form Islamic Jihad. This armed group, whose formation can in some regards be compared to the violent MB splinter groups that appeared in Egypt in the 1970s such as Takfir w'al Hijra and the Gemaa Islamiyya, proceeded to undertake various militant acts against the Israeli occupation forces. Their activities, while confined to a very small group, served to raise tensions considerably and to prime the Occupied Territories for a more active form of resistance.[6] In this climate, certain tensions brewing within the MB became more pronounced. Essentially this broke down as a division between a younger generation, unassociated with the MB before 1967, who wanted to take a more politically active stance towards the Occupation, and the older, Jordanian-linked faction that preferred to continue focusing on religious and social activity. The intifada became the wedge that separated the two.[7] For the younger generation the idea of waiting until society has become properly Islamized before moving to political action—the classic Brotherhood gradualist approach—was not suited to conditions of direct military occupation by a foreign power, in this case Israel.[8] Turning to the notion of jihad they sought to invest the Brotherhood in Palestine with a new "doctrinal conviction" and to find in Islam a theology of liberation.[9]

On December 8, 1987 an Israeli truck crashed into two Palestinian taxis, killing their occupants. Seeing this as a deliberate act of aggression, Palestinians took to the streets in several days of protests that were fanned and sustained by a number of preceding and subsequent acts of violence. The evening after the bus incident, Sheikh Yassin held a meeting with several other MB leaders in Gaza—most notably Abd al-Aziz al-Rantisi, who would later become a key figure in HAMAS—at which they determined to establish a political movement to coordinate and lead an active resistance in the name of Islam. The formation of HAMAS was formally announced in February as the level and intensity of protests and street violence grew, much of it organized out of Gaza by the new group. This uprising, which became known as the intifada, was a complex affair. It was led primarily by the Palestinian youths (*shabab*), but found active participation from all walks of life and political persuasions. Its coordination was by no means confined to the ranks of the Islamists. The PLO, the leading nationalist force, was another major player and this group—whose top file leadership was living in exile in Tunisia at the time—formed a coordinating body of its own (the Unified National Leadership) to organize protests and general strikes. It both complemented and competed with HAMAS in this regard (see below). Where the activities of Islamic Jihad served as the "accelerant" toward the intifada's ignition during the 1980s, the uprising itself was conducted by ranks mobilized by both nationalists and Islamists.[10] The MB in

Palestine initially kept some distance from HAMAS in case it failed and prompted an Israeli crackdown on the Brotherhood's religious activities. However, several months into the intifada, when it was clear that HAMAS had staying power (and, interestingly, once the MB saw merchants and bazaaris joining in the uprising), they proudly declared HAMAS to be their "strong arm."[11] Over the next few months, the Palestinian MB merged itself, and its institutions, completely into HAMAS—becoming, effectively, the same organization.[12] Even Israel initially handled HAMAS very gently, hoping that its presence would split the Palestinian population between Islamist and nationalists—leading to greater political disunity within the Occupied Territories.[13] As the frequency and intensity of the protests grew, so did HAMAS' profile and popular reputation. When the foreign-based PLO leadership made a bid for political normalcy by recognizing Israel and renouncing violence, HAMAS was well positioned to claim that it was now the only Palestinian force still willing and able to pursue active resistance in the name of national liberation.[14] Not only that, but, for the time being at least, its leadership was based in Palestine and actually living through the Occupation, unlike the PLO's seniors abroad.

In 1989, the intifada—which until this point had consisted almost exclusively of strikes, street protests and low-level violence involving rock-throwing youths and burning tires—took a new turn. HAMAS began for the first time to use firearms and explosives against Israeli forces, prompting a swift response by the Israeli Defense Forces (IDF) who arrested and imprisoned Sheikh Yassin. In this power vacuum, control of HAMAS for the next two years (until Yassin was released in a prisoner swap), shifted to the group's expatriate leadership—most notably Musa Abou Marzouk in the United States.[15] In 1991, in order to protect its military forces from the IDF and clarify the group's command structure, HAMAS formally established a separate military wing, the Izza al-Din al-Qassam Brigades—named after a MB resistance fighter from the 1930s who had led operations against the British and Zionist Jews.[16] Over the next decade, as HAMAS began to make increasing use of violent tactics, the Brigades would become for much of the outside world the public face of Palestinian Islamism. During this same period HAMAS broke completely with the PLO in terms of cooperation due to the latter's willingness to participate in the U.S.-sponsored Madrid peace process. Even before the talks began the Islamists dismissed this as a form of capitulation, in effect, to Israel's terms for resolving the conflict.

As HAMAS attacks against the IDF expanded from 1991 and grew to also encompass civilian targets inside Israel itself, the Israeli government attempted in late 1992 to undertake what it regarded as a comprehensive "house cleaning" of Palestinian religious radicalism by deporting over 400 Islamist intellectuals and leaders to a remote mountain top village in southern Lebanon. The Islamists managed to convert this into a major public relations coup, however, when the world's media arriving to interview these exiles found a group of highly articulate intellectuals and professionals shivering in the cold rather than cadre of crazed militants.[17] By this time the intifada had stalemated around a war of attrition that was highly costly to the Israelis in military and political terms, and to the Palestinians for both economic and political reasons. In 1993, after months of secret discussions—during which both the Israelis and Palestinians swore publicly that they would never sit down together around a negotiating table—it was announced that Israel and the PLO had devised and were ready to sign a Declaration of Principles (DOP) providing for mutual recognition and security guarantees, as well as the first phase of a gradual handover of political autonomy to a new Palestinian Authority. Hopes for a rapid settlement, with significant political and economic dividends for the Palestinian population, increased exponentially in the aftermath of the signing of what became known as the "Oslo Agreement"—named for the Norwegian capital where most of the content had been negotiated. Oslo also permitted Yasser Arafat to stage a triumphant return from exile and to reclaim the mantle of Palestinian national leadership. For its part, HAMAS found the Oslo agreement very worrying from both a normative and political point of view. It regarded the piecemeal approach to Palestinian autonomy contained in the treaty to be highly problematic. It seemed to them, and to many other Palestinians, that Arafat had given away much in return for very little in that the core issues of the conflict (final status, Jerusalem, Palestinian right of return) were all left untouched. They also feared the political boost this would give to the PLO and particularly Arafat's Fateh faction, which looked set to take over the newly established Palestinian Authority. HAMAS joined the PFA, an Oslo-rejectionist coalition comprised of various groups who feared the agreement would turn Palestine into a series of Arab "Bantustans" (as per the South African model)—that is, enclaves of Palestinians surrounded on all sides by Israel.[18] The Islamists demonstrated they still had some basis of popular support in late 1993 by winning the student council elections at Bir Zeit University, the first time in 20 years that Fateh had not been victorious there.[19]

As the first elections for the new Palestinian Authority (PA) approached, HAMAS found itself considerably divided over how to respond. The rejectionists wanted nothing whatsoever to do with the PA and the radicals wanted to combine this with renewed aggression against Israel to try and scuttle the agreement altogether. The pragmatists and moderates within HAMAS felt the organization would be able to have more impact from within the PA and advocated full participation.[20] Sheikh Yassin, back in prison (with a life sentence) by this time, hesitantly endorsed the group's participation. In the end, the hardliners won out and the Islamists boycotted the elections. Even after the victory of the rejectionists it was still unclear to them how best to proceed. While hoping to see the peace deal unravel over time, they were very aware that a hopeful Palestinian population still endorsed the terms of Oslo for the most part, and they were wary of damaging this support through a new campaign of violence aimed at destroying the fragile entente. When the peace process began to go awry after the assassination of Israeli Prime Minister Yitzhak Rabin by a Jewish militant in late 1995, HAMAS escalated the pace of a series of post-Oslo attacks that had started the previous year. In the run-up to Israel's 1996 election, HAMAS carried out numerous attacks on civilian targets in Israel, ensuring a victory for the right wing candidate Benjamin Netanyahu. Over the next several years, HAMAS suffered a range of setbacks. Arafat and the PA were strongly pressured by Israel to contain HAMAS and to this end the PA police forces rounded up and imprisoned a large number of the movement's operatives. Its latitude of maneuver on the home front was severely curtailed as the PA also took over control of a number of its institutions and mosques—regarded by HAMAS, effectively, as a declaration of civil war. Indeed, clashes between forces loyal to HAMAS and PA police occurred in the summer of 1996. In 1999 Jordan moved against the Palestinian Islamists' political bureau in Amman, forcing its leadership into exile in Syria.[21] One positive development for HAMAS during this period was that Sheikh Yassin was released from prison in 1997 in another prisoner swap, this time with Jordan after the authorities in Amman captured two Israeli agents who had attempted to assassinate Abd al-Aziz al-Rantisi, the head of the HAMAS political bureau.

By 2000, HAMAS' political influence and operational space had been significantly curtailed as Arafat consolidated his increasingly autocratic rule over the Occupied Territories. As the Americans sponsored a last-ditch round of comprehensive peace negotiations between Arafat and Israel's Labor government that fall, the far right wing Israeli opposition leader Ariel Sharon paid a provocative visit to the *Haram al-Sharif* in Jerusalem's Old City, the third holiest site in Islam. This was the catalyst for the release of a wide range of Palestinian frustrations and as regular protests and clashes settled in over the next few months, a second intifada was declared. Arafat hoped to seize the new intifada as an opportunity to distract from the dismal state of his government and reunify the population around his leadership of a new resistance effort. However, he found the ranks of his own Fateh faction highly divided, with the younger generation of leaders who had been inside Palestine during the first intifada (rather than living relatively comfortably in exile abroad) fed up with Arafat's authoritarian system of cronyism and patronage that denied them any effective role in the PA. The second intifada, which saw the PA headquarters placed under Israeli quarantine, hence served only to emphasize Arafat's inefficacy and to increase the popularity of both the younger Fateh leaders and HAMAS. Where stone-throwing youths had been the iconic image of the first intifada, HAMAS raised the stakes considerably from 2001 with frequent suicide bombings causing large numbers of civilian and military casualties in Israel. Once Sharon came to power in Israel, the crackdown on all forms of Palestinian resistance, but HAMAS in particular, kicked into high gear. In

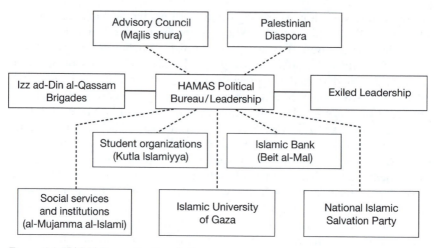

Figure 6.1 HAMAS organizational diagram
Source: Adapted from Shaul Mishal and Avraham Sela, *The Palestinian Hamas*, New York: Columbia University Press, 2006.

2004, in a show of force and to emphasize a new zero tolerance policy, the IDF assassinated Sheikh Yassin with a helicopter gunship, and several weeks later also killed his replacement Abd al-Aziz al-Rantisi. While this "decapitation" attack certainly initially left HAMAS in political disarray, the symbolism involved led to an enormous upswing in popular support for HAMAS among Palestinians—even within the majority that did not share their Islamist vision. Yasser Arafat, seeking to stem the by now constant barrage of criticism aimed at him from all sides, reluctantly introduced a division of powers within the PA that created a new prime ministership. Behind the scenes, however, he worked to keep power concentrated in his own hands. When he died in late 2004, the PA—and the Fateh old guard in particular—were bitterly despised by the population of the Occupied Territories.

When the 2006 elections for the Palestine Legislative Council (the Palestinian parliament) came around, HAMAS this time announced that they would participate. While opinion polls showed that Fateh was severely handicapped and everyone expected HAMAS to do well, the result that finally transpired was not widely anticipated: the Islamists won a landslide, taking enough seats to allow them to form the PA government. While Fateh's Mahmoud Abbas had won the presidency after Arafat's death, ensuring that the PLO would still have a key role in government, the day-to-day administration of the Palestinian territories was to be in the hands of HAMAS. With the world still shocked and wondering how this as-yet politically untested organization would reconcile its record of militancy with the responsibilities of holding official office, HAMAS conferred within itself as to several political options—including setting up a government of national unity by inviting non-HAMAS politicians into its cabinet. In the end it decided to go it alone and appointed Ismail Haniyeh, a relatively young moderate who had led the faction arguing for HAMAS' participation in the first elections in 1996, as the new Prime Minister. Questions linger as to the HAMAS legislative agenda, and to the ambiguous role of its political bureau based in Damascus—accused by many of having a monopoly of control over the movement's militant wing. As HAMAS has refused to recognize Israel or renounce violence altogether (it initially declared a truce upon winning election), much of the foreign aid to the PA and associated social organizations has been withheld—providing us with a wide array of challenges to explore below.

Explaining and understanding HAMAS

Before we consider the fascinating case of HAMAS as a potential example of Islamism in power, we need to gain a better understanding of HAMAS as a social movement. To this end we will spend some time analyzing the group's social base, structure, and funding in an effort to explain the foundations of its popular legitimacy. Looking at how the relationship between HAMAS and the PLO evolved over the years since the founding of the former will provide insight into how HAMAS has responded to a shifting political field. Both of these will then allow us to consider the overall trajectory in the Islamists' discourse and tactics in recent years before finally exploring the internal sociology of the movement for clues as to where HAMAS may be going in the future.

As we have already noted above, HAMAS draws much of its popular support and legitimacy from the vast network of social services it has established over the years. This is not something that HAMAS created from scratch when it was established in 1987, but rather these various social organizations were inherited from its parent organization, the MB, which had been cultivating them for two decades before HAMAS even appeared on the scene.[22] In this connection, it is worth observing that the MB's recruitment patterns in Palestine during the 1980s shifted to include a much larger proportion of middle class and well-educated supporters. Not only did they bring with them the technical skills and managerial know-how required to run a vast and closely integrated network of associations, but they also brought to the MB a political consciousness that was increasingly impatient with the Brotherhood's exclusive focus on religious and social activity. This was indeed important to them, but they were ready for more political activism alongside their social work.[23] The MB's only real Islamist competitor, Islamic Jihad, while more active in terms of armed resistance, was unable to establish itself as a mass movement at the social level in the way the MB had. Islamic Jihad hence had very little to draw upon in terms of social capital, and only a very narrow base of popular support.[24] In addition to the social welfare services provided by Sheikh Yassin's network, the Mujamma al-Islami gained further local legitimacy through the provision of various mediation and arbitration services.[25] By combining both social services *and* social authority in this way, we can see how by the time HAMAS was created, the foundations of its political legitimacy were already well established.

The structure of HAMAS is complicated and intricate (see Figure 6.1). Its central decision-making body is the Political Bureau (*al-maktab al-siyasi*), currently based in Damascus, which is composed of the central leadership and various ministerial-like organs. The exact relationship of the military wing—the Izza al-Din al-Qassam Brigades—to the Political Bureau is the subject of considerable controversy (see below), but it seems to operate with some degree of autonomy (within broad parameters prescribed by the political office) while also sometimes acting on specific taskings from the political wing. Within the brigades are to be found a number of specialized units focusing on weapons development, internal security, and so forth. HAMAS also runs a recruitment program within Israeli jails. In terms of the organization's social wing, we are talking about an enormous network of social organizations and services, many of which are formally autonomous but coordinated via the Mujamma al-Islami. They are not directly under the control of the Political Bureau, but maintain close affiliations with it, and some of their directors have a role in the political office, or have done in the past.

The sources of funding for HAMAS' social services and military operations are many, divers
e, and frequently overlapping. Ziad Abu-Amr has identified six major sources for the HAMAS budget: direct donations from the Occupied Territories; support from sympathetic Islamist movements in other countries (particularly the MB, but some have also cited Al-Qaeda in this regard); donations from HAMAS-run foundations and private individuals abroad; foreign governments sympathetic to the movement's causes (particularly Saudi Arabia and Iran); relatively small amounts from the PLO; and, finally, various investment instruments established by HAMAS.[26] To this list we can also add, somewhat ironically, the Israeli government, which during the 1980s, as we have noted, provided funding for some of the social organizations that eventually became the basis of Islamist popular support as a means to undermine the growth of leftist influences within the mainstream national resistance movement. It took a little bit of time for HAMAS to gain the confidence of regional governments sympathetic to the Palestinian cause since it was initially assumed that the movement was just a newly politicized wing of the MB—a group that many of these states (Egypt and Syria in particular) had had problems with in the past. But this did not prove to be an impediment for long.[27]

Next we will want to look more closely at the HAMAS activists and supporters. The movement's leadership and its intelligentsia, much like other movements we have looked at such as the MB and Jama'at-i Islami, is drawn primarily from members of the professional and technocratic class.[28]

During the 1980s and 90s the MB and later HAMAS made considerable inroads in terms of their representation within professional associations and syndicates. Before regular elections were held under the PA, university councils were often regarded as the best way to gauge the relative support for various Palestinian political factions. During the first intifada, HAMAS made an impressive dent here, rivaling Fateh at many schools and gaining outright control of several student councils. The leadership of HAMAS has often cited universities as more important to them as political spaces than mosques. The latter are often tied to awqaf controlled by Israel or Jordan, while the educational settings enjoy relative autonomy.[29]

The social base of HAMAS support is generally highly conservative, and skeptical of secularism, which it equates with the inefficacy and corruption of the PLO.[30] The rank and file supporters of HAMAS tend to come from lower middle and working class backgrounds and tend to be socialized into the movement's values through exposure to its social services network. To better understand the appeal and popularity of HAMAS' welfare services, it will be useful to consider certain demographic aspects of the Occupied Territories. A full 70 percent of the Palestinian population is under the age of 30, 50 percent of it under the age of 15. The availability of skilled and professional employment is scarce, with fewer than 20 percent of secondary school and university graduates finding regular work upon completing their educations.[31] When Israel closes its borders to Palestinian day laborers, the unemployment rate for the population as a whole can surge as high as 75 percent. Given the corruption and inefficacy of the PLO and the PA, the HAMAS welfare charities are sometimes the only option people have.

This network of organizations is so diverse as to cover almost every sphere of social activity. Just to provide a sense of the array of what HAMAS has on offer, we might consider the following aggregate list, compiled from the various services cited by a selection of leading researchers:

Charitable societies
Hospitals
Dispensaries
Kindergartens and schools (religious and secular)
Sporting clubs
Elderly homes
Tithing (zakat) committees
Computing centers
Libraries
Scholarships
Legal aid
Summer camps
Recreation facilities

HAMAS does not require users of these services to join the movement, although there are certainly special benefits reserved for activists, as well as a "Martyr's Fund" that supports the families of those who die in the course of militant operations. It has been estimated that some 95 percent of the HAMAS budget goes to support this network of services, and they are by far the most well-known face of Islamism throughout the Occupied Territories.[32] Many, as has been pointed out, use them not because they identify with the religious basis (although for many this is indeed a factor), but because they are the only ones available, or the only services that can be trusted. For a long time, HAMAS was the only organization the UNRWA in Palestine trusted to deliver and distribute food donations.[33] Some observers have noted that even Palestinian political opponents of HAMAS who want to make humanitarian donations will do so via the Islamists' social organizations since they are the only ones they feel they can trust—unlike Fateh—not to embezzle the funds.[34] Quite simply, the Palestinian public has come to trust HAMAS-provided social services, but not their PLO counterparts.[35] We should emphasize again that many if not most users of the HAMAS services network are not active supporters of the Political Bureau, and nor do they share the movement's vision for an Islamic state in Palestine. Some researchers have cited evidence, admittedly limited in scope, suggesting that many of those who make use of Mujamma al-Islami facilities and services do not participate in other Islamist activities—or that they are even aware of the Islamist linkages.[36] This last claim is perhaps somewhat over-stated given that most of the Islamist facilities feature subtle (and sometimes quite overt) elements of evangelism, such as posters and other media.

Hizbullah's multifaceted Islamism: militia, political party, service provider

While its origins lie in a loose alliance of Shi'i clerics in the early years of Lebanon's Civil War, Hizbullah's dramatic rise to prominence as a revolutionary militia is linked to Israel's invasion of Lebanon in the early 1980s. The group made a name for itself through a concerted campaign of suicide bombings and other attacks on Israeli forces and their proxies, emerging as a rival to AMAL, Lebanon's other major Shi'i militia and political movement. During this time, Hizbullah's stated aims were the removal of Israeli and Western forces, and the achievement of a revolutionary Islamic state in Lebanon. Its chief ally and benefactor in this was Iran, still fresh from its own Islamic Revolution (1979) and seeking to export the model to other Shi'i settings. Much of Hizbullah's activism was directly bankrolled by Tehran, with crucial political support also coming from Syria.

Hizbullah reluctantly accommodated itself to the political realities of the 1989 Taif Agreement that effectively ended the Civil War. Unlike other militia groups, however, Hizbullah managed to keep hold of its weapons—arguing that so long as Israel continued to occupy southern Lebanon (which it did until 2000), its armed stance was required to guarantee the safety of Shi'a in the south and also the territorial integrity of Lebanon. For its part, the weak central government (under strong Syrian influence until 2005) was only too happy to "outsource" the defense of the country's southern flank to a much better trained (thanks to Iran) and experienced army. Throughout much of the 1990s, Hizbullah forces were engaged in exchanges with Israeli forces along the southern border.

In a major change of tactics associated with a new secretary-general, the young cleric Sayyid Hassan Nasrallah, Hizbullah decided to contest the 1992 parliamentary elections. It was helped along in this decision by its sponsor Iran, which by the early 1990s was ruled by a faction of conservative pragmatists (see Chapter 5) more concerned with Iran's economy than the export of revolution. Hizbullah won a clear majority of those seats reserved for Shi'i candidates and began the process of creating a full political party structure. Taking a cue from HAMAS in the Palestinian territories, Nasrallah also oversaw the creation of a vast infrastructure for the provision of social services (some free, others for payment) in Shi'i areas, essentially filling gaps in e.g. education, healthcare, garbage collection, electricity and water provision, where the state was absent. Since 1991, Hizbullah has run its own TV station, Al-Manar ("The Beacon"), which has a large following among Palestinians in addition to being highly popular with Lebanese Shi'a. While Hizbullah has become somewhat less financially dependent on Iran in recent years, a great deal of its social service work and military arsenal are still funded in whole or in part by Tehran and other Iranian-controlled foundations (generally estimated at $100 million per year).

Political tensions with Hizbullah emerged in 2005 in the aftermath of the assassination of ex-Prime Minister Rafiq Hariri, an act believed by many to have been coordinated by Syria. In the face of widespread anti-Syrian demonstrations, Hizbullah mounted its own mass counter-protests. The movement's political wing entered the government that formed after the 2005 parliamentary elections, holding two cabinet seats and controlling a third. In the summer of 2006, Hizbullah fought a month-long war with Israel ("The July War") involving massive Israeli airstrikes against Lebanese infrastructure in retaliation for Hizbullah's kidnapping of two Israeli soldiers (which Hassan Nasrallah claims the organization intended to use as bargaining chips to gain the release of several Hizbullah supporters still held by Israel in contravention of a prisoner swap agreement). The intensity of the short war shocked the world, even those who were its main protagonists. Hizbullah emerged from this conflict with significantly increased stature albeit mixed reviews from the Lebanese population. As of late 2006, it was mired in a standoff with the Lebanese government, seeking to gain increased representation in the cabinet.

As an analyst of Muslim politics, trying to discern which of Hizbullah's many roles—militia, political party, or provider of social services—represents its true identity is not particularly helpful. Rather, it is important to recognize that Hizbullah is all of these things. Its leadership is able to spread their social and political capital across the full breadth of these activities, pragmatically emphasizing whatever role is most useful at a given political juncture. What we should be trying to figure out, however, is how the organization's political choices and responses to particular situations narrow or expand its range of options over time. In other words, even as Hizbullah tries to maintain all three modes of operation, might not political realities and changing circumstances on the ground force them to evolve in particular directions? Also worthy of note is the way that Hizbullah manages to combine a Shi'i identity with elements of Lebanese nationalism, enabling it lay claim to constituencies beyond is sectarian base.

But just how much support does HAMAS have among the Palestinian population? If we were to use the results of the 2006 Palestine Legislative Council elections as an indicator, we would be talking about somewhere in the neighborhood of 45 percent—which is in line with the figure that the HAMAS leadership has traditionally claimed (40–50 percent). But there is reason to believe that this figure reflects a relatively large protest vote against Fateh rather than active endorsement of the HAMAS vision. Various observers have tried to estimate the base level of active political support for HAMAS among Palestinians and have come up with widely varying figures. A polling agency in the Occupied Territories came up with the figure of 18 percent, although its methodology is disputed.[37] A study by a HAMAS-affiliated academic of the professional syndicate elections in the West Bank suggested an aggregate tally for the Islamists of 45 percent and, for the PLO and its affiliates, 50 percent.[38] Khaled Hroub, author of *HAMAS: Political Thought and Practice*, estimated based on his own observations and anecdotal evidence that the Islamists' core political support in 2000 was around 30%.[39]

Participation in Islamist social activities or use of their facilities also should not be regarded as a zero sum game in terms of representing a choice of HAMAS at the expense of the PLO. As a member of an Islamist football club, quoted in Michael Jensen's research, put it:

> I liked the PLO very much; I liked [Yasser Arafat]. During the Intifada we suffered very much at the hands of the Israelis. They shot at us. They killed many of us. I wanted a change, I wanted to do something to

redress this injustice and suffering. So then Hamas did something. During that time, when people were hurting daily, they sought comfort in religion. People went to religion to pray to God to help us during the Intifada.[40]

This statement provides us with some insight as to why Arafat's position on HAMAS social services was a version of "can't live with them, can't live without them."[41] It is not that Palestinians choose HAMAS to the exclusion of other political options, but rather that the Islamists have developed a reputation for themselves of "walking the talk." In addition to their armed resistance to Israeli occupation, they also provide the Palestinian people with services that help to alleviate the worst effects of the Occupation—and they do so far more effectively than any other social or political force in the territories. The Islamist welfare network is effective, dependable, and—particularly today, in comparison with Fateh—free of corruption. For many, it is worth reiterating, it has been the only available source of welfare under very difficult socioeconomic circumstances. It is therefore not surprising that people rally around HAMAS when it is under threat or criticized. In some cases this may just be an instrumental "don't bite the hand that feeds you" response, but for the most part, the organization genuinely has the respect of the Palestinian people—respect, moreover, that the secular nationalist alternative in Fateh sorely lacks. In 2006, they were clearly able to turn this into an electoral advantage. By the same token, however, if the ability and willingness of HAMAS to engage in active resistance is a source of their popularity, this means they require the ongoing presence of something to resist in order to keep that support and legitimize their continued existence. For this reason, along with the fact that it is ideologically opposed to peace with Israel, HAMAS is less predisposed than other political forces to contemplate a negotiated settlement. This prompts some to point out that while they may be skilled at alleviating the symptoms of Palestinian suffering, they are less apt to directly and realistically confront the political conflict at the root of that suffering.

We can now move on to examine how the HAMAS ideology, discourse, and political strategy has evolved since its founding. Crucial to this, of course, has been the issue of its relationship with the PLO. Despite the phenomenal support the Islamists garnered for themselves during the course of the intifada, we need to bear in mind that in absolute terms, their popularity never eclipsed that of Yasser Arafat and the PLO. HAMAS was never in a position to actually challenge Fateh's leadership of the Palestinian cause—until, that is, the 2006 PLC elections. If we look at the text of the HAMAS Charter, we find the Islamists going to great lengths to emphasize their efforts as a complement to those of the nationalists. The PLO is referred to as "closest to us" and as being "like a father or brother." That said, the Charter does go on to point out that the secular approach espoused by the PLO is not acceptable to HAMAS.[42] In 1988, the Palestine

National Council, along with its renunciation of violence and recognition of Israel, declared the existence of a Palestinian state. Interestingly, HAMAS—still very young as an organization—begins here to display its independence from the main MB organization in terms of how it responds to this declaration. While the Cairo-based mother organization welcomed the newly declared Palestinian state, Sheikh Yassin—from within the Occupied Territories—asked skeptically how it would be possible to have such a state when no Palestinian territory had yet been liberated.[43] Over the next few years, HAMAS and the PLO—while in theory partners in the intifada, also competed with each other for control of the popular uprising. For example, the PLO's Unified National Leadership and HAMAS maintained separate and uncoordinated calendars for calling general strikes.[44] They also differed in terms of their priorities. For example, on the days of general strikes, the PLO issued orders for schools under its control to be let out in order to maximize the size of the protests. HAMAS, by contrast, kept students in the classroom on its strike days arguing that their education would prove to be more important in the long run.[45] There are also, of course, any number of political, tactical, and security reasons why it would have made sense for the two organizations to institute various forms of "traffic control" around the protests.

Tensions between the two factions became more pronounced in 1992 when a new Labor government came to power in Israel promising—or, in the eyes of the HAMAS rejectionists, threatening—to make peace with the Palestinians within a year.[46] The PLO's willingness to entertain concerted peacemaking, particularly in the wake of the Madrid process which HAMAS had bitterly opposed, led to open clashes between the Islamists and Fateh, an act which some observers have suggested led HAMAS to temporarily "lose the streets" given the PLO's majority support and the gathering hopes around the possibility of a negotiated settlement.[47] But HAMAS revealed themselves to be highly attuned to the realities of this shifting political balance. At the very same time the two sides were fighting it out on the streets of Gaza, there was an internal document circulating within the HAMAS political bureau that outlined the pros and cons of a full range of possible approaches to the PLO, from a complete boycott to a demand for full participation in any political process.[48]

HAMAS was just as taken aback as the rest of the world when the Oslo agreement was announced in September 1993. Indeed, it is also likely that the PLO leadership would have gone out of its way to deny the existence of the secret negotiation channel that produced it for fear of prompting a strong HAMAS backlash. In the spring of 1994 the PLO and HAMAS signed a political truce of sorts in an act that angered Israel. Yitzhak Rabin, the Israeli Prime Minister, had clearly been looking to Arafat to begin treating the Islamists as criminals rather than to make new declarations of solidarity with them.[49] HAMAS was soon caught in a bind since, as noted above, although it was strenuously opposed to the Oslo Accords and the peace process more generally, it did not want to risk alienating itself from a newly hopeful Palestinian population that had decided to put its faith in Arafat and the exchange of peace for land. Hence its offer of a "ceasefire" with the Occupation in early 1994 (see below) in order to demonstrate that even it was willing to consider a possible future alongside an Israel whose name it still would not utter publicly. HAMAS decided to lay low for the time being and wait for the peace process to fall apart—even going so far as to enter into another rapprochement with Arafat in the run-up to the 1996 elections that the Islamists had decided to boycott.[50] When Rabin was assassinated in late 1995, throwing off a warming relationship between Israel and Syria (a peace agreement had already been signed with Jordan earlier that year), HAMAS decided it was the right moment to go on the offensive against the peace process. There ensued over the next few months an acceleration of attacks on Israeli civilian targets, with the result that the right-wing Likud party in the form of Prime Minister Benjamin Netanyahu came to power in Israel. Relations with the PLO and the PA reached their nadir when Arafat sent his new police forces against the Islamists in the face of Israeli threats to withdraw from future peace talks unless the PA put an end to Islamist violence.

The political and popular fortunes of HAMAS did not revive until the outbreak of the second intifada when it once again found itself at the forefront of widespread discontent at not only continued Israeli occupation and oppression, but also the failure of the peace process to pay out any of the dividend that had been promised, and the growing authoritarianism within the PA. While Arafat had hoped to turn the new protests to his advantage, the only credible Fateh faces on the streets were figures themselves opposed to the PLO autocracy. These were generally younger Fateh activists, such as Marwan Barghouti, who had entered politics during the first intifada while the PLO old guard was in Tunis. When Arafat set up his PA executive, these younger figures were all but shut out from any meaningful positions of political influence.[51]

Aside from the difficult "antagonistic co-operation" that generally defined the HAMAS relationship with Fateh, how did the Islamist strategy evolve over the years in other respects?[52] Mishal and Sela have pointed out that in some respects the founding of HAMAS was as much about ensuring the survival of the MB in Palestine as it was about seizing an opportune moment to "go political." As the scale of violence and general unrest in the Occupied Territories grew in the run-up to 1987, the MB's Mujamma al-Islami began to fear that either Islamic Jihad or the PLO would turn the new climate to its advantage.[53] HAMAS did have an immediate and major impact on the ideological terrain of Palestinian resistance, however, because it developed a political discourse that permitted Islam and nationalism to become entwined in the popular imagination. And more than just Islam as religion, this was an approach that turned Islam into a discourse of active resistance, a jihad against the illegitimate occupation of Palestine—itself a divinely ordained endowment (waqf) to be protected by whatever means necessary. But they were also able to tap into and mobilize the existing MB social base, not only in terms of it network and facilities, but also in terms of its socializing and mobilizing capacity. In the vision of Sheikh Yassin and HAMAS, only a "fortified society" (educated, employed, healthy) would be able to engage in the jihad. Therefore, it was vitally important for social development work to occur alongside and in parallel with active, armed resistance.[54] HAMAS political activism and the MB's socialization and welfare efforts were hence wholly symbiotic. In explaining its worldview and seeking to mobilize the Palestinian masses, HAMAS relied on a series of cultural framings that combined elements of the classic MB program with a number of idioms specific to the Palestinian condition in order to create a "more authentic nationalism."[55] These included, in addition to the idea of Palestine as a sacred territory or waqf, the Islamist standard bearer, "Islam is the solution"; the notion of a larger Jewish conspiracy; and (especially after 1993) the virtue of patience on the part of the Palestinian people, who should not settle for a compromised peace agreement that was bound to fail.[56]

Sheikh Ahmed Yassin was himself notoriously ambiguous when it came to the idea of whether a negotiated settlement with Israel would ever be possible. We have already noted the Islamists' tendency to avoid taking completely obstructionist positions at times when it seemed a negotiated settlement might be possible—although they would always refrain from opening up an ideological can of worms for themselves by refusing to recognize the legitimacy of Israel outright. Consider the following excerpt from an interview with Sheikh Yassin quoted by Ziad Abu-Amr:

> *Question*: Do you recognize Israel?
> *Answer*: If I recognized Israel, the problem would be finished, and we would have no right left as Palestinians.
> *Question*: But if Israel withdrew from the West Bank and the Gaza Strip, would you recognize it?
> *Answer*: When it withdraws, I will say.
> *Question*: But at that time, should it be recognized?
> *Answer*: I leave this matter to the representatives of the Palestinian people.
> *Question*: Who are they?
> *Answer*: Those whom the Palestinian people will elect.[57]

Yassin reveals here a distinctly pragmatic streak, one that—as in the case of the HAMAS 1994 offer of a "ceasefire with the occupation"—not only implicitly recognizes the existence of Israel, but also the possibility of Palestinian coexistence with it, and the permissibility of the Palestinian people (rather than a *fatwa*) determining the nature of their future relations with Israel. On other occasions, when asked about the compatibility of

Islamism with democracy in Palestine, Yassin had insisted that he would
need to respect the will of the Palestinian people to choose their own political system, even if they opted for communism. While some have declared
this to be nothing more than instrumentalism, others have cited consistent
evidence that much of the HAMAS leadership is wholly pragmatic when it
comes to political issues.[58] The Islamists appeared to demonstrate an affi-
nity for *realpolitik* in the wake of the Oslo Accords, seeking primarily to
delay implementation of the agreement rather than to destroy it.[59] Some
within HAMAS even claimed that several of the bomb attacks committed
in its name between 1994 and 1997 were not officially sanctioned by the
movement.[60]

Indeed, the issue of the HAMAS military wing and who controls it is a
complex one. Some observers claim that it operates almost wholly autonomously of the Political Bureau, citing the authority of the latter over the
brigades as "more symbolic than concrete."[61] Others argue strongly that
there is persuasive evidence of a link between the external headquarters and
the military wing—or even that military operations are carried out under
the direct and unique orders of the political office.[62] What is most likely to
be the case, however, is that the relationship has varied over the course of
HAMAS' political career. There have been periods where Izza al-Din al-
Qassam has been left to operate autonomously, attacking at the time and
with the means of its own choosing, so long as it does not stray outside
certain broadly prescribed boundaries. At other times, however, it is likely
that hardliners within the overseas Political Bureau have exercised direct
planning and operational control over HAMAS attacks. In this regard it
would also be worthwhile to give some consideration to the decision by
HAMAS, in 1994, to extend its tactics to encompass attacks on Israeli
civilian targets. Before this date, HAMAS had only targeted elements of the
Israeli security apparatus. Various spokesmen for HAMAS have sought to
justify this move in different ways. Some have argued that attacks on Israeli
settlers in the West Bank and Gaza are justified because they are themselves
armed and have attacked Palestinians in the past. Others have employed
somewhat labored logic to point out that because Israel's army has a policy
of universal conscription for the Israeli population, then all of its citizens
are potential or former members of the IDF. The mainstream justification
used by HAMAS for attacking civilians, Khaled Hroub argues, is essentially
the same as the one previously used by the PLO before its renunciation of
violence.[63] Namely, that because the Palestinians do not have the power and
military wherewithal to defend themselves in conventional warfare, they
have no choice but to seek to create in the minds and national psyche of
their occupiers, military and civilian alike, a sense of insecurity that will
ultimately lead them to withdraw from the disputed territories—in other
words, to induce fear as a political weapon. While HAMAS has come under
widespread criticism for its policy of targeting civilians, there is evidence of
a debate within the organization as to whether such attacks are indeed

justifiable—one that generally breaks down along the lines of a broader sociological divide, and this is what we will turn to now.

Since the time of the first intifada, there have been pronounced differences within HAMAS between those—mostly of a longer MB pedigree—who have been cautious about the pace and extent of Islamist political activism, and those—many of whom joined HAMAS directly without any prior MB experience—who viewed the movement as a vehicle for active and immediate radicalism.[64] This difference between the HAMAS pragmatists or moderates and the HAMAS radicals has often broken down along the lines of the distinction between the movement's external leadership abroad, and the leaders within the Occupied Territories. Jean-Francois Legrain, for example, points out that at the time of the 1991 Gulf War, the group's leaders in Amman sided with the Jordanian MB and supported Saddam Hussein whereas HAMAS leaders in Gaza mostly kept quiet.[65] We see this divide again in 1996 at the time of the first elections for the PA where moderate "insiders," such as Ismail Haniyeh, the Palestinian Prime Minister after the 2006 elections, wanted to participate but were over-ruled by the external leadership. Indeed, there ensued a complicated debate during which a wide variety of political options was considered, ranging from a campaign of violence to undermine the peace agreement, to open participation in PA politics, to disbanding the movement and returning to exclusively religious and social activity.[66] Sheikh Yassin himself drifted back and forth between the pragmatist and radical camps, and his capacity to do so is part of what made him such an effective and popular leader. As regards the 1996 elections, for example, he offered in a letter from his jail cell a cautious recommendation for HAMAS to participate:

> Holding elections is now an issue for the Palestinians; the Islamists are divided between supporting participation and those opposing it; as far as I am concerned, but only God knows, I consider it is better to participate than to abstain, providing that the Council be empowered with legislative privileges (*tashri*); as a matter of fact we are opposed to what is happening in the streets, so why not express our opposition within the legislative institution which will de jure become in the future the authority representing that Palestinian people? [This participation] will reassert the strength of the Islamic presence on the arena and will prevent it from losing ground because of its isolation.[67]

From the late 1990s, then, it became clear that the division between the HAMAS internal and external leadership, which had been evolving since as early as Sheikh Yassin's arrest in 1989, has solidified along the lines of clear difference in strategic vision. The radicals within the external political bureau—young, skilled, adept at fundraising abroad—wanted to impose Islam from above, and sought to use their control of the group's military brigades to achieve this. The internal leaders, those based within the

Occupied Territories, were mainly older MB stalwarts who preferred to Islamize from the societal level up.[68] But there is also some evidence that within the internal leadership are to be found younger moderates whose political vision shares something in common with the "new Islamists" we examined earlier (see Chapter 4)—insofar as they are at least convinced that political participation within a democratic framework is the way forward, even if, we should note, their vision of the politics that should flow from that participation is not entirely in keeping with liberal norms. This division within HAMAS most likely represents the fault line that will determine the range of possible political futures available to it as a social movement.

HAMAS in power ... and beyond

In the Palestine Legislative Council elections of January 2006, HAMAS, campaigning under the name "Change and Reform," won 74 out of 132 seats, giving it a 56 percent controlling majority of the assembly and the opportunity to form the first non-Fateh-dominated PA government. The level of corruption and autocracy within Fateh had reached new heights and they were widely seen as a discredited political force. Nonetheless, it was assumed they would still win at least a plurality of seats and be forced into a coalition government. HAMAS was expected to do well, but very few—perhaps not even HAMAS itself—anticipated an outright majority victory. How can their phenomenal electoral success be explained and, more importantly, what are its implications for the future of the peace process, Palestinian political society, and HAMAS as a social movement?

The HAMAS victory can essentially be explained in terms of three factors:

(1) A protest vote, at least in part, against Fateh's corruption and a swing towards HAMAS as the only alternative political force with any credibility as a provider of effective governance and societal welfare.
(2) The superiority of the HAMAS political mobilization machinery and its sheer ability to turn out voters through its vast infrastructure of organizations and informal networks.
(3) The fact that HAMAS had shown itself in recent years to be the most consistent and committed advocate of active resistance against the ongoing Israeli occupation.

Western powers were shocked by the Islamist victory and moved quickly to cut off financial aid to the PA, refusing to allow their funds to be used by a political party that would not publicly recognize the legitimacy of Israel, and which had used terrorism in the past. The HAMAS military wing declared a truce when the party was elected, but refused to disband as the United States and Europe insisted. The weeks following the election provided worrying images of HAMAS' own security forces patrolling the streets and occasionally confronting regular PA police, most of whom are drawn from the ranks of Fateh.

The newly appointed Prime Minister, Ismail Haniyeh, is the leader of the movement's moderate-pragmatist faction, and has been very cautious in his rhetoric since taking office. Most of the concern centers on the HAMAS political bureau, presently located in Damascus, and overseen by the hard-liner Khaled Meshal. If its immediate financial crisis is not resolved, the PA will likely collapse or wither away. While some, particularly in the West, support shutting down a HAMAS-led PA, others—including some voices from Israel—have warned that a collapse of the PA could lead to wide-spread instability and violence in the West Bank and Gaza. In this view, it is in no one's interest for the PA to become a failed quasi-state. Some have also argued that given recent American pressure for democratization in the Arab world, it must respect and live with the results of legitimate elections even if it finds the results distasteful. Others raise questions about the effects on HAMAS of actually having to govern, citing arguments along the lines of the "participation leads to moderation" thesis (see Chapter 4). Much will likely depend on whether the new HAMAS government is willing to recognize Israel, and come to some arrangement regarding the future of the party's military wing.

The Taliban in Afghanistan: deobandism, ethnicity and geopolitics

Afghanistan offers us an example of "Islam for lack of a system" that differs in significant ways from the case of Palestine above. The period of the Taliban's rule in Afghanistan (1996–2001) was characterized by the imposition, on a society ravaged by nearly two decades of continual warfare, of a highly austere and literal interpretation of Islam. Initially welcomed by the Afghan populace in the hope that they would be able to restore some semblance of peace and order, the Taliban's model of an Islamic political order soon revealed itself to be at sharp odds with many Afghan religious and society norms. In this section we will provide a brief overview of the immediate domestic and geopolitical background that preceded the emergence of the Taliban as a political force in 1994. We will then examine the major features and events of the Taliban's five years in power, including their approach to governance and relations with the outside world. Particular attention is given to the impact of the Taliban's rule on women in Afghanistan. In the analytical section that follows, we will explore the political sociology of the Taliban as a movement. Who were they? What shaped and animated their religious and political consciousness? We will also consider the various factors that led to their stunning success and rapid takeover of most of the country. This is followed by an examination of the Taliban's ideology and religio-political worldview, and we make a number of observations about the Taliban-style Islam and prevailing religious norms in Afghanistan.

Background: Afghan resistance, civil war, and the geopolitics of energy

Essentially a valley between two formidable mountain ranges, Afghanistan has figured heavily in the geostrategic considerations of regional and world powers for many years. As an ethnolinguistically diverse society with strong regional and tribal traditions, Afghan national identity has been premised on the common religion, Islam, that unites these disparate groups, and also on a strong sense of commitment to Afghan territorial integrity. Afghanistan was the focus of a considerable strategic rivalry between Britain and Russia in the early twentieth century known as the "Great Game," or, to the Russians, "the Tournament of Shadows." A version of this same contest would repeat itself nearly a hundred years later when Afghanistan became the subject of Cold War contention between the United States and the Soviet Union.

In the early 1970s, Afghanistan was still under the rule of King Zahir Shah from an ethnically Pashtun family, the Durrani, that had figured prominently in Afghan history for centuries. Various political tensions were beginning to emerge at this time, with Zahir Shah's Prime Minister, Muhammad Daud Khan, looking to embark on an ambitious modernization plan. At Kabul University, however, Marxists opposed to both the Daud Khan and the royalists were beginning to make their voices heard. In 1973 Daud Khan overthrew Zahir Shah and declared a new republic. Now president, Daud Khan faced continual pressure from leftist forces over the next five years. In 1978 he was himself toppled in a communist coup that brought the People's Democratic Party of Afghanistan (PDPA) to power.[69] The latter's socialist program did not prove particularly popular when they tried to export it beyond the comparatively cosmopolitan confines of Kabul, with the PDPA meeting significant resistance in the provinces of the country. Using the now endangered PDPA regime as pretense, the Soviet Union invaded Afghanistan in December 1979.

Over the next nine years, the Soviet forces fought a war of attrition against an Afghan resistance force commonly known as the mujahideen. Despite their superior armaments and military technology, the Soviets could not decisively win what quickly turned into a guerilla war in unfamiliar and highly inhospitable terrain. For their part, the mujahideen regarded the war as a jihad, and their religiously inspired persistence and superior knowledge of the land played major roles in allowing them to hold off their far better armed foes. Several other factors were instrumental in the mujahideen's eventual victory. Paramount among these is the fact that they were receiving massive amounts of financial and military aid from the United States and Pakistan, mostly coordinated through the Inter-Services Intelligence directorate of the latter, but with considerable CIA involvement as well. This comprised the supply of money, training, and weapons to mujahideen forces, as well as logistical and medical support from just over the border. One particularly decisive element here was the U.S. decision to supply the mujahideen with shoulder-mounted Stinger missile systems that permitted them to "snipe" Soviet helicopter gunships. Although American military assistance officially started after the Soviet invasion, subsequent historical evidence suggests the United States was aiding the mujahideen a full half year before the USSR intervention in the hope of coaxing the latter into what U.S. National Security Advisor Zbigniew Brezinski was quite rightly convinced would become the Soviet "Vietnam."

Pakistan had many reasons to become an active supporter of the mujahideen. It had been wanting for some time to cultivate a strong strategic relationship with the United States, and the Soviet war in Afghanistan provided the perfect opportunity. By sponsoring the mujahideen, much of whose leadership drew from the ethnically dominant Pashtun areas of southern Afghanistan on the Pakistani border, Pakistan was also able to ensure its influence over those tribal elements that might try to make common cause with Pakistani Pashtuns inside its own rather tenuous northern border. Furthermore, it was distinctly in Pakistan's interest to maintain Afghanistan as a "buffer state" between itself and the Muslim regions of the USSR to the north. Another important aspect of the Soviet war was the presence in Afghanistan, from the early 1980s, of a relatively large number of foreign Muslim fighters who traveled to the region to fight in solidarity with the mujahideen. These "Arab-Afghans," as they came to be known, will be discussed in greater detail in Chapter 7. Among them was one Usama Bin Laden who would later go on to found the Al-Qaeda global jihadi network, and to play a decisive role in the future of the Taliban.

In 1988 the Soviet Union decided to cut its losses and began to withdraw troops from Afghanistan, a process completed by 1989. Much to everyone's surprise, the communist government, led by Najibullah, managed to stay in power until 1992 by striking a number of deals with provincial power brokers. When the government did eventually fall, however, Afghanistan entered a dark period of civil war between rival mujahideen factions. Once their common enemy was gone from the scene, rivalries old and new emerged within the ranks of the mujahideen. These groups—which broke down largely along ethnic and regional lines—were well armed and still had access to considerable resources left over from the generous funding they received during the resistance. The key figures here were ethno-regional warlords, such as Hikmatyar and Rabbani, each of whom also headed a nominally Islamist political party. During the mujahideen period, all Pakistani financial aid was funneled through these party structures, so in some regards the "re-ethnicization" of Afghan politics in the wake of the Soviet withdrawal can be seen as a byproduct of the resource clusters associated with various mujahideen warlords.[70] In some regards, it was also just a scramble for power between heavily armed political rivals. As Thomas Barfield puts it, "each faction leader realized that if he did not obtain power now, he never would."[71] For the next four years these clans fought it out, with the civilian population caught in between them and often bearing the brunt of the effects of this conflict. After nearly a decade of fighting a war forced on them by an external power, the people of Afghanistan were now suffering at the hands of their own leaders. Exchanges of rocket attacks, for example, killed hundreds, and many population areas were cut off from basic resources. After a long war with the Soviets, things just seemed to get worse during what came to be known as *topakeyano daurai*, the "time of the gunmen."[72]

Before we go on to examine the direct circumstances leading to the formation of the Taliban, it would be helpful to say something briefly about the new geopolitical context in which the future of Afghanistan was playing out. The dissolution of the Soviet Union prompted various regional and world powers to reassess their strategic postures. The United States, in particular, was interested in the energy resources to be found around the basin of the Caspian Sea and began to assess various routes by which oil and gas might be transported to seaports for onward shipping. In the early 1990s, one possible route that would allow it to bypass Iran involved pipelines through Afghanistan and Pakistan. For this reason, Washington D.C. was keeping a careful eye on the situation in Afghanistan and continuing its cooperation with Pakistan (whose strategic calculus remained basically the same) with the aim of achieving stability in the latter's northern neighbor. Iran, for its part, would have preferred to cash in on pipelines flowing through its territory, When the Taliban emerged, then, seeming to promise a new sense of stability and order for Afghanistan, Iran found itself opposing the new movement both ideologically and strategically. Ideologically because it was led by radical Sunnis who were vehemently anti-Shi'i in their outlook, and strategically because the Taliban risked creating conditions that would allow precious energy supplies to bypass Iran altogether.[73]

The rise and political career of the Taliban, 1994–2001

The Taliban (meaning "students") emerged as an organized movement in the summer of 1994 out of the southwestern city of Qandahar. Its leader, Mullah Omar, had fought in the Afghan resistance against the Soviets, but was not considered a major (or even minor) figure in the Afghan political scene. More of a local notable, the popular story surrounding the Taliban's formation has it that Mullah Omar led a small group of young Qandahari men (most of whom had studied at madrasas in Pakistan—hence "Taliban") against a gang of local criminals who had been raping and pillaging in the area. From here the movement grew very quickly, spurred on it would seem from various forces on the other side of the Pakistani border. Over the next two years, the Taliban assumed control of more and more of the predominantly Pashtun areas of the south, earning a reputation among locals for putting an end to clan rivalries, petty crime, and enforcing public order and safety—the first time any social force had been able to do so for two decades. It is clear that even from this early stage that the Taliban were receiving considerable support from Pakistani intelligence, and it appeared that they had been chosen by the latter to serve as Islamabad's new "client" up north in replacement of Gulbuddin Hikmatyar's Hizb-i Islami faction which had proved ineffectual in implementing Pakistan's agenda.[74] As they grew in numbers and confidence and began to move into the north of the country, several of the rival warlord factions sought to establish a temporary alliance to counter the threat from this new and unexpected force.[75] This was to little avail, however, as the Taliban proceeded apace through the provinces, taking Qandahar in late 1994, the western city of Herat in the late summer of 1995 and, finally, the capital itself, Kabul, exactly a year later. Resistance to the Taliban was pushed further and further into the north of the country, and it was in this area, around cities such as Mazar-i-Sharif—which changed hands twice in 1997—that the Northern Alliance under Ahmed Shah Massoud would make its stand against Mullah Omar's forces.

Perceptions of the Taliban among Afghanis varied considerably. Some within the civilian population associated them with a return to royalism since many of the Taliban leaders were from the same Pashtun Durrani tribe as the king. Among the various warlord clans, however—particularly the non-Pashtuns—they were seen as agents of Pakistan or Pashtun nationalists.[76] We have already mentioned Iran's fears that the rise of the Taliban represented a new source of American strategic influence, a concern also shared by many within Afghanistan itself. It is indeed true that during its early period, the United States essentially pursued a "hands off" policy, generally trusting the Pakistanis to serve as stewards of their mutual interests in the region.[77] In some ways, the Taliban served to unite various forces in Pakistan usually at odds with each other but who had a common interest in seeing the Taliban succeed—although for very different reasons. The political party of the religious scholars, the JUI, supported them on religious grounds, whereas the secular government of Benazir Bhutto appreciated their strategic utility.

Iraq after Saddam: sectarianism and Muslim politics

Given the demographics of Iraq, it was inevitable that religion would emerge as a major political issue in the aftermath of the 2003 U.S.-led war that toppled the regime of Saddam Hussein. For the country's majority Shi'i population, in particular, an end to minority Sunni rule represented an unprecedented political opportunity. As the security situation remained fundamentally unstable over the next few years, however, and with foreign militant Islamists fanning the flames of sectarian dissent, religion became much more than just a form of symbolic currency in Iraq. Rather, the Shi'i-Sunni cleavage quickly emerged as the organizing principle of post-Saddam politics, with many Iraqis seeking refuge in sectarian formations that felt safer and more reliable than a weak central government still largely beholden to the United States and its ongoing military occupation. While national religious figures such as the senior Shi'i cleric Grand Ayatullah Ali Sistani urged moderation and refrained from direct involvement in politics, other sectarian leaders, such as the young activist Muqtada al-Sadr and his militia, positioned themselves as defenders of the Shi'a against Sunni attacks—emerging as major new players on the Iraqi political landscape.

Iraqi parliamentary politics is also dominated by religion, with both of the leading non-Kurdish coalitions organized along sectarian lines. Islamist parties play prominent roles in both, such as the Shi'i Islamic Dawa Party and Supreme Council for the Islamic Revolution in Iraq (SCIRI) and the Sunni Iraqi Islamic Party—which represents the MB tendency in Iraq.

The issue of Islam's role in legislation proved divisive during early negotiations over the country's new constitution, and there have been persistent concerns raised about the extent to which the Iranian model of clerical rule might prove attractive to some of the more revolutionary Shi'i factions. In addition to concern about Iran's influence over the Shi'a and the possibility of region-wide ignition of sectarian tensions, some have wondered about neighboring Saudi Arabia's likely response to a major Shi'i power play in Iraq.

Once in power, the Taliban as a movement more or less ceased to exist as Mullah Omar and his associates went about the business of trying to build a functioning government.[78] Much of this was pure trial and error since many of the group's top leaders had very little experience in public administration. Furthermore, after almost 20 years of conflict and civil war, the country's existing governmental institutions were in tatters. Mullah Omar established a central consultative council, or shura, as the executive branch of government, and under it a number of regional shuras associated with the main provincial population centers. One of the early missteps they made was to appoint as the leaders of these provincial shuras—some of which were located in areas where the population still harbored considerable suspicion towards the Taliban—individuals with little or no ties to the local area.[79] In 1997 Mullah Omar announced to the world that the name of the country was being changed to the "Islamic Emirate of Afghanistan," its former identity as a republic having been deemed Western and un-Islamic. In terms of international recognition, the Taliban only managed to gain official endorsement from three countries: Pakistan (for obvious reasons), Saudi Arabia (who saw in its austere version of Islam the influences of Wahhabism), and the United Arab Emirates (which had considerable economic interests in the country).

Gilles Kepel characterizes Taliban governance as being confined to three core areas: morality, commerce, and war.[80] We will want to dwell more extensively on the question of public morality under the Taliban, but would also do well to briefly consider the second two aspects. With regard to war, Mullah Omar established a command hierarchy for the movement's forces, with the goal of continuing their efforts to bring more of the country under Taliban control. These forces fought throughout the entire period of the Taliban's tenure in government, and, by the time of their demise in the fall of 2001, had managed eventually to bring all but a pocket of far north-eastern Afghanistan that was being held by Ahmed Shah Massoud's forces under their control. In terms of commerce, the Taliban did very little for the country's almost exclusively agricultural economy. With very little going on in the way of state regulation in many areas, Afghanistan soon became a throughput haven for smuggled and counterfeit goods, many of them emanating from new duty free ports in the Gulf.[81] By taking a cut from this trafficking, the regime was able to establish a source of income to supplement the aid it was receiving, at least in the early days, from Pakistan and Saudi Arabia. Both of these countries came under considerable pressure from the United States to cut back on their support for the Taliban once it became clear that they were systematically abusing human rights and allowing elements of the global jihadi network (see Chapter 7) to operate with impunity in Afghanistan.

The Taliban were particularly notorious for the strict moral code they implemented and enforced on the population of Afghanistan. The sources of this are to be found in the particularly conservative variant of Islam that many of their leaders had been taught at madrasas in Pakistan. Most of these schools are affiliated with the Deobandi movement, named after a seminary established in India in the nineteenth century that became the center of a movement seeking to reform and purify Islam along lines that closely resembled the teachings of Muhammad Ibn Abdul Wahhab, founder of the austere Wahhabi school. The Wahhabi tendencies of the Taliban were most clearly on display in the form of the "vice and virtue squads" they established to roam around towns enforcing public morality—much like the mutawwa police in Saudi Arabia. Some of the policies they implemented included a total ban on music, movies, dancing, and television, a requirement that men grow beards, the enforcement of daily prayers, and the introduction of hudud justice—the Qur'anically prescribed penal code mandating capital punishment for murder and adultery, and limb amputation for theft.[82] Likewise, anyone converting to Christianity was threatened with a death sentence.[83]

Afghan women suffered particularly harshly under the Taliban, with the rigid Deobandi legal code serving to reinforce the highly conservative gender norms that already characterized Pashtun customary law. Women were forced to cover themselves from head to toe in a *burqa*, a practice that already existed in some parts of the country, but one that had never been enforced. The structure of this garment was so comprehensively concealing as to leave only a small grill for air in front of the mouth. Women were also required to bring a male relative with them anytime they ventured out in public. For the most part, however, the Taliban's policies were actually designed to eliminate women from public space as much as possible. Girls were initially forbidden from attending schools since separate schools for them had not yet been established and the education of boys was considered more important (girls were later allowed to attend school). Women were also banned from the workplace, creating significant new economic hardships for already impoverished families. In many cases these were widows whose husbands had been killed during the Soviet war, and they were now forced to take desperate measures—begging, drug trafficking, prostitution—to provide for their families. Obviously, many of these opened them up to the risk of harsh punishment at the hands of the Taliban if caught. Perhaps most worrying is the fact that for the first two years of Taliban rule, women had no practical access to healthcare. As women they could not be treated by male doctors, and since women doctors were banned from the workplace, there was nowhere for them to go. As in the case of their position on schooling for girls, the Taliban eventually amended this policy.

Governance under the Taliban was wholly ineffectual. By trying to directly implement what they had been taught out of dusty medieval tomes in madrasas—and, moreover, by implementing *only* what they had been taught and not being willing to think or act outside those boundaries—the Taliban quickly brought an already decimated Afghan state closer to the brink of collapse. Most of its ministries were wholly inoperative, and the more effective of its civil servants turned out on the streets because their association with the bureaucracy rendered them "too modern." As Gilles Kepel put it:

> The summary exercise of [governmental] functions did not make the Islamic Emirate of Afghanistan anything like a modern state: in fact it was more a community organized according to Deobandi norms but merely "swollen" to the dimensions of a country subjected to moral coercion on the inside and jihad on the edges.[84]

As they became increasingly alienated from both Afghan society and the international community, the Taliban only seemed to become more radical. In 2001, for example, they used infantry units to destroy the famed statues of the Buddha at Bamyam, claiming their presence to be incompatible with the strictly monotheistic ethos of Islam. When a coalition of renowned Islamic scholars from the Middle East issued a fatwa indicating that such monuments should be left intact, it was summarily dismissed by Mullah Omar.[85] Coming under increased harassment from the Taliban and accused of Christian proselytizing, many international NGOs withdrew their programs and services from Afghanistan at about this same time. As far as Mullah Omar was concerned, sovereignty and the capacity to legislate normativity were invested exclusively in God. If these values happened to conflict with international ethics, there was no contest: Islam overrules any human normative construct.[86] Several observers have noted that this further radicalization of the Taliban occurred in conjunction with, and can perhaps be partly explained by two other developments. First, the last remaining senior moderate within the Taliban executive shura, Muhammad Rabbani, died in the spring of 2001. Second, Pakistan and Saudi Arabia had cut off much of their support for the Taliban in response both to international pressure (in the case of Pakistan) and, in the case of Saudi Arabia, extreme displeasure at the fact that the Taliban were providing sanctuary for Usama Bin Laden—a sworn enemy of the Kingdom.[87] The Taliban by this point were coming to rely increasingly on Bin Laden's financial largesse and were hence more susceptible to his influence. It was clear—and highly displeasing—to many Afghans that Arabs and other foreigners associated with Bin Laden were playing a large role in Mullah Omar's military operations against the Northern Alliance.[88] In October 2001, within weeks of an American assault in reprisal for the September 11, 2001 attacks on the United States, the Taliban government of Afghanistan fell swiftly from power. Many of its key leaders, including Mullah Omar escaped, and melted into the complex mountainous terrain along the Pakistani border. Most Afghans rejoiced at the downfall of the harsh regime and hardly blinked an eye as thousands of American troops poured into their country. After all, in their minds the Taliban had effectively just spent several years allowing Pakistanis and Arabs run the country.

Explaining and understanding the Taliban

One thing that is particularly remarkable about the Taliban is that very few in Afghanistan had heard of them or their leaders before they took over the country. There seemed almost to be something spontaneous about their formation. The political mobilization of student movements was nothing new in Afghanistan, however, and neither was it surprising that the Taliban were able to generate human resources so quickly once we understand how they recruited. In historical terms, there is a tradition of student-led political movements that dates back to the period of British rule in the nineteenth century.[89] More recently, madrasas in both Afghanistan and Pakistan had proven to be fertile recruiting grounds for the ranks of the mujahideen during the war with the Soviets.[90] In the case of the Taliban, Mullah Omar only needed to send word to some of the leading madrasas in the Northwest Frontier Province (NWFP) of Pakistan, such as the famed Dar ul-Uloom Haqqania, for them to shut down the schools and send the students north to fight. The Taliban also had Pakistani intelligence actively recruiting, training, and sending soldiers north.

So we can make the following observations about the social composition of the Taliban forces. In ethnic terms, they were overwhelmingly Pashtun—indeed, prompting many beyond the southern provinces to fear a

"Pashtunization" of Afghanistan once they appeared. They are Sunni Muslims with strong roots in the vast network of Deobandi madrasas that dot the landscape of southern Afghanistan and northern Pakistan.[91] We should also note that many within their ranks were refugees from Afghanistan who had fled to, or been born in, Pakistan during the Soviet occupation. Many of them had never even been to Pakistan, or had only just returned during the civil war following the Soviet withdrawal. The Pakistani madrasas had played a vital role in the lives of refugees during the war. Where the modernist Islamist Jama'at-i Islami in Pakistan, associated with the thinking of Abu'l-A'la Mawdudi had sought to cultivate mainly an educated, middle class following, the Deobandis fashioned themselves into the champions of the rural poor.[92] Madrasas such as Samiul Haq's Dar ul-Uloom Haqqania in northern Pakistan provided free education, food, and for orphans or those who had nowhere to live, free housing as well. These schools also held out the hope of some sort of social mobility.[93] The NWPF capital of Peshawar was essentially a "war economy" town during the conflict with the Soviets, with all manner of logistics, recruitment, and procurement being managed from its center. The madrasas became the conduits of choice for rapid movements into lucrative positions with the mujahideen organizations. Many of the Taliban leaders were exactly of this background, having schooled in Pakistan and then joined the ranks of the mujahideen fighters. Also interspersed within the Taliban forces were a fairly large number of Pakistanis who had been recruited out of madrasas or trained directly by Pakistani military intelligence—leading some to label Taliban an Afghan-Pakistani "hybrid."[94] Many in Afghanistan and around the world marveled at the Taliban's rapid military success, wondering how a group of young, inexperienced students could prove so adept at defeating battle-hardened warlord forces. The answer, of course, lies in the fact that their leaders were all experienced mujahideen, and they were receiving all manner of assistance from Pakistan.

In order to understand the worldview of the Taliban rank and file, it is vital to understand the world of the Deobandi madrasa. Life in these institutions revolved around rote memorization of the Qur'an and other religious texts for hours on end, usually interspersed only with breaks for religious observance. They were very insular spaces—often in highly remote areas—and generally cut off from the world.[95] Students came to know and conceive of the world mainly through the teachings and texts they encountered between the walls of the classroom, and through the attitudes that prevailed among the teachers. The version of the Deobandi curriculum taught in these schools shared much in common with salafi and Wahhabi doctrine. It was highly conservative, very literalist, and quite categorical in its moral logic. In short, these were not spaces to learn critical thinking skills; they were settings in which knowledge defining the boundaries of the permissible and the forbidden was imparted. In the madrasa, it was also quite easy to imagine the Islamic utopia—a textual polity—without ever having to consider how the exigencies and realities of human culture and society might disrupt its realization. In other words these were, in keeping with Olivier Roy's characterization of the "neo-fundamentalist" trend in Islam, "deculturing" spaces.[96] This was an Islam stripped of local cultural, ethnic, or tribal custom. The socialization of these students, religious and otherwise, was hence fundamentally different from what they would have experienced back home in Afghanistan, where ethnic and tribal identity is everything. These were somehow de-Pashtunized Pashtuns whose sole sense of public identity derived from a very puritanical breed of Islam.

The Taliban were able to use this worldview to their advantage in terms of recruiting from the ranks of ex-madrasa students. Many of these refugee students had returned home in the early 1990s and were shocked at what they encountered upon visiting their home country for the first time.[97] In their minds a victory by the righteous mujahideen over the forces of atheism could only mean that Afghanistan would now be the model Islamic society—just like the mullahs taught back in the schools. What they found however was a country torn asunder by ethnic rivalry and greedy, power-grabbing warlords. Violence and crime ruled the streets. Thus, when the call came for them to put the Islam they had learned into practice and join the ranks of a new mujahideen—one that would rid Afghanistan not of infidel communists, but of un-Islamic thought and practice—they responded enthusiastically.

We have already described the rapid success enjoyed by the Taliban, with most of Afghanistan falling under their control in a very short period—and all accomplished by a movement with no history and no formal social base to speak of. How can this be explained? One leading analyst of Afghanistan, Larry Goodson, attributes the Taliban's success to five factors:[98]

(1) Ethnicity – they were able to make quick progress and gather considerable momentum in the southern part of the country around Qandahar where fellow Pashtuns were in the majority and readily accepted them.
(2) Religiosity – as an Islamist movement who "walked the talk" when it came to implementing shari'ah and enforcing public order, the Taliban's emphasis on piety and virtue won them many admirers. Their religious practice was also very close to the prevailing Pashtun tribal customs, which made its acceptance less of a reach in the south than in other, religiously heterogeneous parts of the country.
(3) Fatigue and attrition – after nearly 20 years of constant war, the populace was willing to accept anyone who held out the hope of restoring peace, order, and some semblance of normal life. "War weariness" had set in.[99] The various clans and factions that could have opposed the Taliban had spent the last few years wearing each other down and were in no position to resist the sweeping rise of the new movement.

(4) Money – significant foreign assistance and various internal revenue streams allowed the Taliban to buy off the leadership of any would-be opponents.

(5) Pakistan – in addition to the recruitment, training, logistics, and weapons support provided from south of the border, various madrasas associated with the Deobandi network in Pakistan and its political party counterpart, the JUI, provided the Taliban with thousands of students.

The rise of the Taliban can be seen to represent a range of continuities and discontinuities in terms of local religious norms and the relationship of religion to politics. In terms of continuities, it represents, as Thomas Barfield has pointed out, the latest phase in a debate that has ensued for a century in Afghanistan between traditionalists and modernizers.[100] In the former camp we would find, for example, royalists and clerics, and in the latter faction republicans and communists. In this particular iteration, we find the Taliban trying to effect a moral "ruralization" of the comparatively modern, cosmopolitan (a dangerous quality in their minds), urban space of Kabul.[101] David Edwards sees this as a return to "village identity" through a rejection of the institutions of modernity (e.g. universities, government bureaucracy—hence the decline of the Afghan civil service under the Taliban).[102]

The discontinuities represented by the Taliban are, however, far more numerous. Barry Rubin notes that within the Taliban project are to be found both elements of regionalism and ideology.[103] While their ethnic composition certainly allowed the Taliban to benefit from the dominant Pashtun character of their southern stronghold around Qandahar, they were—by the very same token—perceived as purveyors of "Pashtun extremism" by the inhabitants of disparate ethnosectarian regions in Afghanistan. Indeed, it is fair to say, as several observers have pointed out, that under the Taliban, sectarian polarization and the "ethnic stakes" both became considerably more pronounced in Afghanistan.[104] There was nothing in their religious ideology, however, that should, or did, predispose them to any particular systematic political strategy or agenda. As Barbara Metcalf puts it:

> None of the Deobandi movements has a theoretical stance in relation to political life. They either expediently embrace the political culture of their time and place, or withdraw from politics completely. For the Taliban, that meant engaging with the emerging ethnic polarities in the country and seeking allies wherever they could find them.[105]

And yet certain distinct attributes of the Taliban's political tactics can indeed be discerned—particularly during the early phase of their activity. For the most part these were correctives to recent trends in Afghan political life that they found distasteful. The emergence of strong cults of personality around particular warlords during the recent civil war, for example, led them to pursue an "anti-charismatic" approach that sought as much as possible to downplay the role and profile of individual leaders in favor of the morality embodied in the practices of their social movement.[106] Similarly they also worked to transcend the factional and political party lines that had taken root within the various mujahideen factions and the religious classes during the Soviet period. These parties represented modern forms of bid'a (innovation) that threatened the solidarity and unity of the umma. In a properly Islamic society, political parties would be superfluous and would only produce strife and the pursuit of narrow interests at the expense of piety.[107]

It has also been noted that in some respects the Taliban introduced innovations of their own in terms of reconfiguring the alignment of forces between religion, tribe, and the state in Afghanistan.[108] Where religion had previously played a mediating role between tribe and government—unifying the former where necessary, and likewise reigning in the latter—the Taliban now sought to define and occupy the state. This represented a fundamental shift in the traditional role of religion. And the transformation was by no means confined to the functional dimensions of religion in Afghan society. The very form and content of the religion seemed alien to many outside the more conservative Pashtun areas in the south. Afghan Islam has traditionally been very flexible in terms of dealing with sectarian differences and multiple interpretations of Islam. Many Afghans, for example, were tolerant of, and embraced, Sufi teachings and practices. The Taliban, on the other hand, "instituted an uncompromising moral severity and inflexibility that ... [did] not mesh well with Afghan sensibilities."[109] Islamic scholars viewing the Taliban from outside Afghanistan saw something that appeared as retrograde Pashtun tribal custom masquerading as religion. Even some radical salafi sheikhs were led to characterize the Taliban's ulama as "half-scholars."[110] From within Afghanistan, however—particularly outside the south—the problem appeared to be just the reverse: the Taliban had apparently abandoned local traditions of religious tolerance for a strict and ruthless Islam, something quite foreign, imported from Saudi Arabia and Pakistan.[111]

What has become of the Taliban since they were removed from power by the United States, and Hamid Karzai's democratic government installed in their place? Are they likely to remain a political force in the region? We will recall that back in October 2001, many of the key leaders in the movement, including Mullah Omar, escaped into the mountains bordering Pakistan. From as early as 2002 there were signs that elements of the Taliban were regrouping, although as a far less centralized entity. They have engaged in a number of attacks on foreign aid workers in the south of the country, and seem to be touting themselves primarily as a Pashtun nationalist force to maintain pressure on Karzai's attempts at unifying the nation.[112] It is likely that they have made contact with and may be working in coordination with whatever remains in the area of Bin Laden's Al-Qaeda network. In addition to these militant activities, there is also evidence that Taliban-connected forces have continued to enforce Islamic justice and public virtue in pockets of southeastern Afghanistan.[113] Despite pressure from the U.S. on Pakistani President Pervez Musharraf to close down the madrasas that have supplied their fighters in the past, most remain open—meaning that Peshawar and its environs are still open to the Taliban as a mobilization zone.[114] The notion of a "decentralized" Taliban, as mentioned above, is important to bear in mind as we consider the likely short- to medium-term future of the movement. The question is whether "Taliban" as a term will continue to refer to an organized movement, or whether it will become instead a general ideology of resistance and a symbol of Deobandi-influenced Islamization in Afghanistan around which a wide range of political and militant elements can mobilize.

Islam for lack of ... or instead of a system?

This chapter has surveyed several cases, two of them in considerable depth, where Muslim political actors have sought to fill public voids left by weak, failed, or failing states. As we have seen, this dynamic is particularly prevalent in conflict and post-conflict settings. Clear contrasts have emerged with the various other cases of Islamism and Islam-state relations that we have examined in earlier chapters. Unlike the "Islamic authoritarianism" of Iran or Sudan, none of the Islamist forces examined above were able (or, in at least one case—that of Afghanistan—even had any desire) to rely on complex, modern bureaucracies to promulgate and enforce their vision of an Islamic political order. Similarly, and unlike Islamist movements and political parties in countries such as Egypt, Turkey, Jordan, and Pakistan, the efforts of groups examined above have not primarily been based around devising strategies to challenge a well-established, entrenched, and stable state, or to infiltrate a political sphere denied to them. Rather, the Islamists featured here have tended to develop capacities and competences that allow them to operate in situations of political uncertainty, instability, unpredictability, and furthermore, ones defined by an absence—or a newly emerging sense—of institutionalized political process.

Looking across the range of cases we have surveyed in this chapter, several common points or patterns present themselves:

(1) Islamist and Muslim social movements as providers of services that weak, failed, or surrogate states lack the capacity to deliver on their own (e.g. HAMAS, Hizbullah, Deobandi madrasas). This represents a mode of Islamism defined not in terms of instituting a formal political order based on Islam, but rather Islam as a social consciousness seeking to "fortify society" to a point where it can itself become the source of a popular political impulse in search of Islamic public normativity.

(2) Islamism that develops in the context, and at the vanguard, of a popular resistance movement against foreign occupation (e.g. HAMAS, Hizbullah, Afghan mujahideen, Iraq). Islam functions as a form of nationalist discourse that derives its legitimacy from religion, or competes with other forms of organized resistance for the nationalist mantle.

(3) In the absence of a state capable of articulating a viable or unified national project or imaginary, the conflation of Islamism with a variety of sub-national identity formations (ethnicity, sectarianism, etc.). Contrary to the Islamism as nationalism model described just above, this is a situation that can work against the consolidation of a stable, nationally unified state in the aftermath of conflict (e.g. Iraq, Lebanon, Afghanistan).

It should be emphasized again that "Islam for lack of a system" does not represent a rigid category of analysis with a thick set of structural determinants. Rather, much like the idea of "Islam as the system," it suggests in metaphorical terms some of the broad outlines of a certain political environment. Just as the analyses offered in the previous chapter did not in any way suggest that the dynamics of Muslim politics in countries such as Saudi Arabia and Iran can only be understood by reference to the fact these are, nominally, Islamic states, neither has the present chapter sought to imply that Islamism in Palestine and Afghanistan is to be understood exclusively in relation to the relative absence of strong, centralized political authority. Rather, as in the earlier chapters, the goal here has been to help the reader understand the variety of political opportunity structures, mechanisms of social mobilization, and symbolic resources available to Muslim actors in those situations where a recent or ongoing conflict (or failed state) has opened spaces for Islam to reach into, renegotiate, and articulate anew the meaning and practice of public normativity.

Having now, over the course of six chapters, explored the historical evolution of Islam and politics, the theory and early development of Islamism as a political project, and numerous case studies illustrating various Islamist modes and strategies across a variety of political environments, we will now move on to examine the interaction of Muslim politics and globalization through three chapters focused on key contemporary issues. The next chapter will address the rise of Usama Bin Laden's Al-Qaeda and the global jihadi movement. This will be followed by a survey of the full range of contemporary Muslim transnational social and political activity to assist us in better calibrating our understanding of the spectrum of global Islam, moderate and radical alike. We then move on to address the all-important question of who speaks for Islam today when it comes to issues of political identity, social activism, and public norms.

7   Radical Islamism and jihad beyond the nation-state

> The life of the Muslim umma is solely dependent on the ink of its scholars and the blood of its martyrs. What is more beautiful than the writing of the umma's history with both the ink of a scholar and his blood, such that the map of Islamic history becomes colored with two lines: one of them black—that is, what the scholar wrote with the ink of his pen—and the other one red—what the martyr wrote with his blood.
>
> Abdullah Azzam

Since the early 1990s, numerous acts of violence around the world have been committed in the name of Islam—perhaps none so dramatic or far-reaching in its global effects as the September 11, 2001 attacks on New York and Washington D.C. by militants associated with Usama Bin Laden's Al-Qaeda network. This act led to a renewed debate about the meaning and place of violence and jihad in Islam. What does Islam say about violence and the conditions under which it is permissible? How widespread is support for this kind of violence among Muslims? What leads one to become a religious militant? What is Al-Qaeda and how did it come about? These are all questions that we will explore in the present chapter, with a view to achieving a more nuanced understanding of contemporary Islamic radicalism. We first need to explain how the ideology and methods of radical Islamists differ from mainstream Islamism. While the point is often made—correctly—that violent Islamists represent a small fringe minority of Muslims, and even of Islamists, there are important points of connection and intersection to be drawn with other forms of politicized Islam, and also with various intellectual and theological debates that have been ongoing for some time within the Islamic tradition. We also need to explain the geopolitical circumstances that led to the genesis and evolution of the contemporary global jihadist movement. To this end we will examine the phenomenon of the so-called "Afghan-Arabs"—citizens of Arab countries who traveled to Afghanistan during the Soviet occupation (1980–88) to fight with the mujahideen against the USSR (see Chapter 6). Simultaneous and subsequent developments in Egypt and Algeria will also turn out to be salient in terms of the emergence of a Jihadi movement global in scope.

One of the major themes that will emerge over the course of this chapter is a shift in the nature of jihadi activity from an emphasis on the governments of Arab and Muslim countries to a new focus on targeting foreign forces that occupy Islamic lands or persecute Muslims—in other words, the United States and those allied with it. This development has produced a new kind of "transnational" or "nomadic" jihadi fighter whose senses of political identity and aspiration are not defined in terms of effecting change in the country whose citizenship he happens to hold. Unlike groups that we looked at in the previous chapter such as HAMAS and Hizbullah (whose goals are primarily if not exclusively national in orientation), for these new militants, the terrain of the jihad is truly global in scope—and likewise the geography of their activism. It is for this reason that this chapter is defined in terms of Islamic radicalism "beyond the nation-state." Today even several violent Islamist groups whose efforts are primarily local or regional in nature have become affiliates (some on a purely ad-hoc basis, others more enduringly) of the global jihadi network. Thus, for us to focus our analysis purely on Al-Qaeda as an organizational entity would be to miss the central impulse of the transnational jihad movement.

In terms of theology and ideology, we will spend some time discussing salafi Islam—the doctrinal orientation most commonly associated with intellectuals and leaders of the contemporary jihad movement. We will look at several variants of salafi thought and activism and explain the major differences between them. This will lead us to consider the concept of jihad in terms of both its classical meaning in Islamic learning and key debates among various doctrinal factions as to its contemporary relevance and permissibility. We will then move on to look at the sociology and infrastructure of contemporary jihadi and radical Islamist groups through case studies of two groups: Al-Qaeda and Hizb ut-Tahrir. Who joins these radical movements and for what reasons? What kinds of backgrounds and biographies predispose someone to membership in a jihadi group? Through what mechanisms are potential activists recruited, acculturated and "radicalized" into the movement and its mindset? Why do these militants subscribe to the authority of religious leaders whose formal credentials are often dubious and whose views are so out of step with mainstream Muslim sentiment and scholarship? After considering these various issues we will address some of the logistical dimensions of radical networks, including their methods of organization, communication, and finance. In the case of both of these—sociology and infrastructure—it will emerge that the jihadi movement not only takes advantage of various aspects of contemporary globalization, but, it will be argued, can only be understood by reference to globalizing processes and their social effects. Globalization, in other words, was a prerequisite condition for the emergence of this particular Islamic worldview. Al-Qaeda, as Peter Bergen puts it, "is as much a creation of globalization as a response to it."[1]

Defining and conceptualizing radical Islamism

This chapter is structured around an analysis of what we are calling "radical Islamism." What does this term connote, and how does it differ from other forms of Islamism that we looked at in earlier chapters? We will recall that Islamism was defined in terms of an aspiration to institute a political order that reflects the norms of Islam, and the shari'ah more specifically. For the most part the Islamist groups we have dealt with to this point, such as the Muslim Brotherhood (MB) in Egypt or Jama'at-i Islami in Pakistan—have taken the form of political parties or social movements. In the previous chapter we also looked at several movements emphasizing violent resistance in the name of Islam—namely the Afghan mujahideen, HAMAS in Palestine, and Hizbullah in Lebanon. We also noted, however, that the militant agendas of these groups have been geared toward political goals defined in terms of national liberation and Islamism within a single state. HAMAS and Hizbullah, as we saw, also have political wings and engage in broader social service and charity activities. The radical Islamists that constitute the focus of the present chapter are markedly different in terms of their goals and methods. Like the Islamists we studied in Chapters 4 and 5, they seek to implement an Islamic political order, and like the Islamic resistance movements of Chapter 6, they are willing to use violence to achieve these ends. Their understanding of these concepts and tactics is significantly different from mainstream Islamism, however. Radical Islamism, as defined here, is characterized by:

(1) A vision of Islamic political order that rejects the legitimacy of the modern sovereign nation-state and seeks to establish a pan-Islamic polity or renewed caliphate;
    and/or
(2) An emphasis on violent struggle (jihad) as the primary or even the exclusively legitimate method for the pursuit of political change

This political orientation is hence radical in two senses—its politics and its methods. It is politically radical insofar as it rejects the contemporary system of territorially defined sovereign nation-states as illegitimate and seeks to replace it with a shari'ah-based, pan-national Muslim polity—usually defined in terms of a re-established caliphate (see Chapter 2). It is also radical in that most of the groups pursuing this political worldview advocate jihad as a legitimate—indeed, often a required—method for bringing about desired political change. Unlike the radicals, the Islamists we looked at in Chapters 4 and 5 have generally sought to make progress toward an Islamic political order via political (electoral, legislative, power-sharing) or social (civil society, informal networking) means. Those that have employed violence have done so only on a national scale and, according to their account, only after other means of achieving change had been exhausted.

Groups differ among themselves—often quite substantially—in terms of how much emphasis and priority they lend each of these two dimensions of radicalism. Usama Bin Laden's jihad, for example, focuses more on the removal of foreign forces from Muslim territories than on the establishment of a new caliphate. The Hizb ut-Tahrir ("Party of Liberation") movement, on the other hand, puts much greater emphasis on the need for a caliphate, and prefers to pursue this as much as possible via non-violent means. And even among those who focus primarily on jihad, as we will see, there is considerable debate as to timing, targets, and the legitimate boundaries of violent activism. In this regard it is important to note that an individual's participation in or support for Islamic radicalism should not be viewed as synonymous with their having abandoned all sense of morality or adopting an "any and all means are justified" approach to the conduct of political violence. Most decisions to use violence of this sort are made in the context of a complex normative matrix whose terms and boundaries are continually in dispute among the scholars and leaders of these movements. Members of some jihadi groups have sometimes criticized and broken off connections with members of other movements whom they deem to have transgressed certain lines of legitimate conduct—such as, for example, targeting non-combatants ("innocents") or making disproportionate use of violence. Radicalism cannot therefore be conceived as a monolithic category. Rather, like all political orientations, it has within it a spectrum of thought and action, and debates and tension are ongoing between the various points along that spectrum. The methods employed by some Islamic radicals are so extreme and shocking that many observers have difficulty differentiating between the disparate ideologies and worldviews that drive jihadi activists—tending to lump them all together into a single category. To do so is, however, an analytical mistake as it papers over important differences that would allow us to acquire a more thorough understanding of the forces that shape the political worldviews of these various groups.

We have already mentioned that the extreme politics and methods of these groups clearly distinguish them from mainstream Islamists, many of whom strongly and consistently condemn their activities. While it is certainly important to emphasize the extent to which the jihadis represent a clear break from the Islamist center and to point out that they represent the extreme end of the spectrum of Muslim politics, it would also be a mistake to assume they emerged *sui generis* with no basis in pre-existing Islamic political ideologies. Important lines of connection and continuity with major Islamist thinkers and movements do exist and are hence important to emphasize alongside the more innovative and aberrational aspects of the global jihadi movement. What is the nature of these linkages? The first thing to note is that they are not in any sense current lines of cooperation or coordination. As we have already noted, mainstream Islamists, for the most part, strongly repudiate the jihadis, and vice versa. In order to understand these relationships we need to go back to Egypt in the late 1960s and early 1970s, during the time that the MB had been driven underground and its key ideologues, such as Sayyid Qutb (see Chapter 3), captured, exiled, or killed. Qutb is in many respects the key figure here. His particular understanding of jihad and radical Islamic activism are central to the thinking of contemporary jihadi leaders and scholars. We will also recall from earlier discussions that when the MB was "rehabilitated" and co-opted by Anwar Sadat during the 1970s, its leadership renounced violence altogether. This prompted several more militant factions of the brotherhood to break away and form groups such as Takfir w'al-Hijra, Gemaa Islamiyya, and Islamic Jihad—the latter of which was responsible for Sadat's assassination in 1981. Mohammad Farag, a chief activist in the Jihad group, provided a manifesto—"*The Neglected Duty*," a reference to jihad—that would become the standard reference point for a new generation of Egyptian jihadis. In it, he made the case that jihad should be carried out wherever Muslim lands were under the control of unbelievers (secularists, nationalists)—even if, crucially, these leaders claimed to be Muslim (the so-called "near enemy"). This view was echoed in scholarly discourse by a young, blind dissident alim, Sheikh Omar Abdel Rahman, who would later go on to serve as the spiritual guide to Gemaa Islamiyya and to be convicted in the planning of the first World Trade Center bombing in 1993.

This doctrine constituted not only a major departure from classic theories of jihad (see below), but also proved to herald a new era of Islamist violence committed against and within Muslim states. In the eyes of Farag, and many jihadis to follow, the MB's commitment to political quietism had betrayed the spirit of its greatest martyr, Sayyid Qutb. By abandoning active resistance to the Egyptian state, in their view, the Brotherhood was willfully neglecting an obligation that Qutb had come to discern through his own suffering and eventual death at the hands of Nasser's regime. The Egyptian jihadis of the 1970s and 80s hence understood themselves to be the inheritors of Sayyid Qutb's legacy of active struggle. They also saw themselves as a righteous movement in contrast to the MB, which in their view had effectively thrown its lot in with that of the infidel regime. During the 1980s and 90s their trajectory would intersect in important ways with that of a group whose jihadi worldview was shaped by different but not less influential experiences.

Geopolitics and the making of the global jihadi movement

The emergence of the contemporary global jihad movement can only be explained within the context of late Cold War geopolitics. The watershed event here was undoubtedly the 10-year Soviet war in Afghanistan (1979–89). After Moscow seized Kabul—ostensibly to prop up a failing socialist regime, but primarily to secure a strategic foothold near South Asia and the Middle East—local mujahideen fighters (as the Afghan resistance, organized along tribal lines, was known) fought a decade-long guerilla war of attrition against Soviet troops. Hailed as a jihad against atheist forces, the persistence and commitment of the Afghan fighters earned them considerable attention from the rest of the Muslim world—and particularly within Islamist circles. Soon a number of radical Arab Islamists whose efforts had previously been confined to resistance against states and occupiers in their home countries began to find their way to Afghanistan to join the struggle. They formed the vanguard of a generation of "Arab-Afghans" who, over the next decade, would find in Afghanistan the vision and human resources that would allow them to begin constituting a new pan-Islamic network of jihadi activism. These fighters—or, in most cases would-be fighters (very few of them had any military experience)—came from all over the Muslim and Arab world. Estimates of their numbers vary from 5,000 to 50,000, but it is likely to have been in the tens of thousands.[2] Nearly every country in the Middle East was represented, but with particularly large contingents from Egypt, Algeria and the Gulf. Volunteers from non-Arab countries could also be found. This diversity provided an umma-oriented esprit de corps among the itinerant militants, giving them a sense of being part of something much larger than the liberation of an occupied country. Indeed, for many of them, Afghanistan was a relatively foreign concept and not really one in which they had any personal investment. The symbolism of fighting for a "real" Muslim cause was what counted. Others came in search of training and recruits that could later be used against regimes at home. This was not quite yet a vision of global jihad, but it began to provide the raw ingredients for shaping just such a consciousness.[3] As David Cook puts it:

> For many, this equation of jihad with the war in Afghanistan was powerful and liberating. Although the largely Arab Muslim volunteers probably played only a small part in the eventual defeat of the Soviet forces in Afghanistan, the campaign was the first time in centuries that people from all over the Muslim world had gathered together—irrespective of their ethnic and sometimes doctrinal differences—to fight exclusively *for the sake of Islam.* Thus, the battlefield of Afghanistan was the religious and social incubator for global radical Islam in that it established contacts among a wide variety of radicals from Muslim antigovernmenal and resistance movements and fused them together.[4]

One of the most important founding figures within this movement was Abdullah Azzam, a Palestinian and a member of the MB who moved to Afghanistan shortly after the Soviet invasion. Azzam, who would later play a major role in cultivating the thinking of Usama Bin Laden, established the so-called Maktab al-Khadamat ("Services Bureau") as a way station and guest-house for Arab fighters. One of his publications, *Ilhaq bi-l-qafila* ("Join the Caravan") circulated in the Arab world and became an important early recruiting tool for the Afghan jihad. Azzam's thinking was along the same lines as that of Sayyid Qutb and Muhammad Farag, but he went even further in stressing the obligation of all Muslims to wage jihad in the occupied lands of Palestine and Afghanistan. We should note that at this point, the focus of jihadi theory on the part of these ideologues was still very much on the liberation of Muslim territories rather than on the idea of a general global effort against the enemies of Islam.[5] Some saw Afghanistan as an opportunity to gain some jihad experience without having to worry about repressive state security services, as were to be found in most Arab countries. This was a relatively "open" environment where volunteers could receive training and gain some battlefield experience before heading back to tackle the "near enemy" at home. Some of the leaders also hoped that success in Afghanistan might serve as a "trophy Jihad" that would inspire a new generation of activists to take up arms against infidel regimes back home. Azzam played a major role in creating the culture and lore of the Arab-Afghans. He authored, for example, numerous martyrologies—descriptions of the feats and miracles associated with jihadis who had made the ultimate sacrifice.[6] Through these, the Arab-Afghan experience came to have an associated mythology that aided both in recruitment and the inculcation of discipline and commitment on the part of those already in the field. Abdullah Azzam played an instrumental role in shaping Usama Bin Laden's worldview and convincing him that in the Afghan war he had found his calling.[7] Had Azzam not been assassinated in 1989, some speculate, he rather than Bin Laden might have served as Al-Qaeda's chief since the core concept for the organization was really Azzam's.[8]

Arab-Afghans were not the only ones hoping to derive benefit from the Afghan situation. Three other external players exerted a particularly important influence over the course of the Afghan war of resistance, and—both directly and indirectly—over the efforts of the Arab jihadi forces. First, there was the United States that saw in assistance to Afghanistan an opportunity not only to block communist expansion but also to wear down Soviet forces in a manner similar to what had befallen its own military in Vietnam. To this end they provided training and weaponry to the mujahideen forces, generally via the CIA or local proxies. While there is no evidence to suggest that the Arab-Afghans were ever directly aided by the United States, it is certainly the case that the Americans were aware of their presence and saw no harm in it. Afghanistan's neighbor, Pakistan, seized the chance to strengthen its relationship with the United States by supporting anti-Soviet forces and simultaneously boost its Muslim credentials. Not only were all manner of pro-mujahideen forces—including the Arab-Afghans—permitted to use Pakistani territory as a staging ground, but additional direct assistance was provided by Pakistan's Inter-Services Intelligence (ISI). A post-Soviet, pro-Pakistan regime in Afghanistan also would have permitted Islamabad access to the Muslim states of the USSR, as well as "strategic depth" in terms of its ongoing rivalry with India.[9] Finally, Saudi Arabia, increasingly vying with Iran for leadership of the Muslim world in the wake of the latter's 1979 Islamic revolution (see Chapter 5), saw Afghanistan as an opportunity to demonstrate its commitment to a Muslim struggle while simultaneously pushing its Wahhabi variant of Sunni Islam. We should note that while Al-Qaeda has claimed that it never accepted financial assistance from any of these three governments—claiming instead that its activities were bankrolled by donations from private charities and the Muslim masses—there is considerable evidence to suggest that cash from the Gulf did make up a sizeable proportion of their operating capital.[10]

Turning back to the Arab-Afghans, it is important to note that very few of them stayed in Afghanistan for the full decade of the war with the Soviets. Many traveled just on short "tours" to get a taste of jihad, others rotated in and out, and many stayed for a few years before returning to their countries of origin or proceeding elsewhere. Those who returned home often played important roles in terms of changing or challenging the course of Islamism in their countries. Returning Algerians, for example, became central players in Ali Belhadj's radical wing of the Front Islamique du Salut (FIS) and later in the Armed Islamic Group (see "Algeria: The Islamist victory that almost was" in Chapter 3). In Jordan ex-Afghans formed the short-lived Muhammad's Army as a challenge to the political methods of the MB. And in Egypt, many of the militants in Gemaa Islamiyya and Islamic Jihad who took part in the 1990s campaign of violence in that country were alumni of the Afghan Jihad. Thousands of students from Pakistani madrasas on the Afghan border had played an active role, and many of these went on to join the insurgency in Kashmir. After the Soviet withdrawal and Afghanistan's descent into civil war (see Chapter 6), there was a general dispersion of the Arab-Afghans, but some stayed in the country. Most notably, a small but loyal contingent developed around the person of Usama Bin Laden, a Saudi citizen who had come to Afghanistan and fallen under the tutelage of Abdullah Azzam. Bin Laden, whose family was among the Kingdom's leading industrialists, quickly developed a reputation as a dedicated fighter and a superb logistician. He also had considerable monetary resources at his disposal, at least initially, although analysts differ as to how much of this he actually directed towards jihadi causes versus how much he raised through connections and networking. Also in Afghanistan from the very early days and soon closely tied to Bin Laden was Ayman al-Zawahiri, a medical doctor and the leader of Egypt's Islamic Jihad who would eventually fold his group into Bin Laden's network.

The founding of Al-Qaeda ("The Base") dates to this period around the end of the Afghan war, and can be associated with Bin Laden's efforts to constitute a network of jihadis prepared to continue the jihad in an itinerant, transnational mode. This move actually reflected a crucially important evolution in the contemporary doctrine and scope of jihad that we will discuss further below. Bin Laden spent a short period back in Saudi Arabia but quickly fell foul of the authorities over his stringent critique of their willingness to permit U.S. forces to defend the Kingdom against a possible attack by Saddam Hussein's forces instead of his Muslim network. Bin Laden and his cadres relocated to Sudan in the early 1990s at the invitation of Islamist ideologue Hassan al-Turabi (see Chapter 5) and he was stripped of his Saudi citizenship shortly thereafter. In Sudan, Bin Laden set about developing a number of business interests connected to infrastructure development (presumably to raise capital for future jihad efforts), but as his rhetoric and politics turned increasingly anti-Western, Sudan came under increasing pressure from the West to kick him out. Bin Laden's forces, for example, had confronted and targeted American troops during the latter's intervention in Somalia in 1992, and he was a suspect in the 1995 bombing of U.S. troop barracks in the Eastern Province of Saudi Arabia. In 1996, Turabi finally capitulated and, with U.S. consent, Bin Laden returned to Afghanistan where he took up residence under the protection of the newly established Taliban regime (see Chapter 6)—a development that had itself been facilitated by Pakistan, again with apparent U.S. compliance.[11] It was at this time that Bin Laden's Al-Qaeda network entered into the active phase that would soon earn it a worldwide reputation.

Salafism and jihad: core concepts

Before we move on to look more closely at Al-Qaeda and the sociology of contemporary Islamic radicalism, it is important to gain an understanding of two key terms that surround debates about authority and activism in militant circles. Many radical Islamists today are described today as "salafis," or as influenced by salafi teachings. What is salafi Islam in doctrinal terms and in practice, and how does it relate to violent radicalism? The term "jihad" is also frequently invoked both to describe and to justify violence in the name of Islam. What does jihad actually mean and how have debates about its purpose and permissibility evolved in the modern era?

Salafis and salafism: multiple legacies of the righteous predecessors

The term "salafi" refers to the *salaf al-salih*, or "pious ancestors"—a designation for the companions of the Prophet Muhammad (the *sahaba*) and the first three generations of Muslim scholars. In one sense, this is a generic term, while in quite another it describes a more specific approach to jurisprudence and the core tenants of faith. So one may well encounter Muslims who express their admiration for and a desire to emulate the model of the *salaf*, without actually themselves being "salafis." Salafis proper, or practitioners of "salafism," are defined by their exclusive reliance on sources and evidence from this earliest period of Islam. Later generations of Muslims and Islamic scholars are believed to have introduced various innovations that diverge from and dilute the purity of Islam. Strictly speaking, salafism is a *manhaj*, or method, that describes a particular way of relating textual sources and religious knowledge to one's life. Following, but also supplementing Quintan Wiktorowicz's scheme, we can identify six key features of the salafi approach:

(1) An emphasis on tawhid (divine oneness, monotheism) as the core and defining doctrine of Islam; tawhid should be reflected in every aspect of a Muslim's thought and practice—and most crucially with regard to worship. Even to give the appearance of worshipping anything or anyone other than God is tantamount to shirk (idolatry) and a grave sin.
(2) A strict reliance on Qur'an and, with regard to sunna, on those hadiths whose authenticity is unquestioned. The various sahih (authentic) collections of hadith are the preferred source, and particularly those reports whose chain of transmission (isnad) are the strongest.
(3) Rejection of sectarianism and jurisprudential pluralism. For salafis there is no such thing as different groups of Muslims or different interpretations of the religion. One either is or is not a true Muslim based on one's adherence to the salafi path. Likewise, there is only Islam, and from it flows a single, true method. Therefore, the idea of the various schools of jurisprudence (madhhabs) in Sunni Islam is also rejected. In practice, however, much salafi jurisprudence looks similar to the highly literalist Hanbali school.
(4) Following closely from this, a rejection of the jurisprudential practice of taqlid—or blind emulation of legal precedents. For a religious scholar simply to follow, in an unexamined manner, the lead of an earlier jurist is to avoid the obligation of making sure that a given ruling is in accordance with evidence and has been arrived at through the proper methodology. Salafi legal methodology can therefore be described as a form of constant ijtihad (independent judgment), but not in the sense of permitting individual or subjective interpretation. Rather, this sense of ijtihad refers to the scholar's obligation to perform due diligence by going directly to the sources.
(5) Rejection of bid'a, or "innovations" that distort the purity of the message and the method. Salafis believe that after the salaf generations, subsequent Muslims and Islamic scholars have adopted various forms of bid'a that caused them to stray from the proper path. Examples would include various Sufi rituals such as the visitation of graves or veneration of saint—both practices that salafis would see as contravening the regulations of workship (ibadat) that stipulate God as the only object of worship. For scholars to engage in taqlid (see above) is seen as dangerous because it may lead them to reproduce some bid'a from an earlier precedent—hence the need to go directly to the sources.
(6) With regard to religious epistemology, salafis reject those forms of philosophy, such as the Mutazilites and Asharites (see Chapter 2) who permit the exercise of reason in determining the outward meaning of religion. Rather, one must rely exclusively on a strict and literal reading

of direct revelation (Qur'an) and the direct example of the Prophet (sunna). To permit individual reason to enter the picture, salafis believe, would be to introduce unconscious desires into one's understanding of Islam. Matters of *aqeeda* (creed or core tenants of faith) are therefore of great importance to salafis.[12]

Despite the strong aversion to emulation, there are a number of scholars who contemporary salafis hold in particularly high regard in terms of their contributions to the development of the salafi method. These include figures such as the early fourteenth-century jurist Ibn Taymiyya whom they laud for his contributions in terms of reorienting Islamic legal practice towards the earliest sources and for his efforts to expunge from Islam various forms of bid'a—particularly practices associated with Sufism. Today one will also often see the terms "salafi" and "Wahhabi" used interchangeably. While this is understandable since the two approaches share much in common, there are also important reasons to differentiate them. Wahhabism—which can be considered a variant of salafism—takes its name from the eighteenth-century Arabian religious revivalist Muhammad Ibn Abdul Wahhab. Much influenced by the ideas of Ibn Taymiyya, Wahhab's main concerns related to the centrality of tawhid and the dangers posed to Islam by bid'a. His political alliance with the Saud family and the fact that the Saudi religious establishment is founded on his teachings have led Wahhabism to be strongly identified with the Saudi practice (and projection) of Islam. While sharing, as we have noted, much of the same doctrinal orientation as salafis, Wahhabis have tended to emphasize and prioritize certain dimensions over others (tawhid and bid'a). The public and social implications of salafism have also been interpreted in very particular ways by Wahhabis. The social structure of Arabia, for example, led Wahhabi scholars to lay great emphasis on differentiating true believers from infidels in the name of justifying political expansion and the use of violence against other Muslims. This has led to an emphasis among Wahhabis on the practice of takfir—that is, declaring someone to be an infidel or an apostate from Islam. As we will soon see, the concept of takfir has also been central to contemporary debates about jihad.

Another common source of confusion regarding salafism, particularly when it comes to social and political movements, is the fact that the line of nineteenth-century religious reformers beginning with Jamal ad-Din al-Afghani, and which includes figures such as Muhammad Abduh and Rashid Rida, are often described as the progenitors of the modern salafi movement. If one looks at their ideas, particularly those of Abduh, who was the first to refer to his movement as Salafiyya, they seem anything but highly conservative and literalist—indeed, in many respects they appear relatively progressive. Abduh's idiom of salafism, however, was rather different from that of those who we today call salafis. For him, the salaf symbolized the individual's effort to understand and practice Islam according to a living, active model and without resorting to the cloistered and arcane teachings of religious scholars. It was an injunction to bypass centuries of crusty tradition in the name of discerning religion's direct relevance to modern issues and predicaments. The salaf, for Abduh, were more of a metaphor for the idea that Muslims should have confidence in taking religion into their own hands—much the same way the Prophet's early companions were forced to do. A genealogy of today's salafism does indeed lead back to Muhammad Abduh's movement, but only via several mediating figures who reoriented its trajectory in crucial ways. Rashid Rida (see Chapter 3), an Islamic political theorist and discipline of Abduh, is generally credited for outlining the idea of the modern Islamic state after the abolition of the caliphate in 1924—initially, interestingly, emphasizing the compatibility of the shari'ah with modern political norms. As he watched the growing and, to his mind, morally corrosive influence of secular nationalism take hold across Arab society, however, Rida sought refuge in the security of a highly conservative and literalist understanding of religion—adjusting the meaning and thrust of the Salafiyya movement accordingly. His ideas were taken up, developed, and further disseminated by figures such as Abu Ala Mawdudi and—most importantly—Sayyid Qutb. The latter, in particular, played a signal role in making the final conversion of salafism into a doctrine of political activism and violent struggle.

It is important to note that salafi religious doctrine does not, in and of itself, lead to radical politics as defined above. There are, in fact, many salafis today who eschew politics altogether and deem it wholly inappropriate for religious scholars to become involved in activism, much less jihad. Thus while all salafis are intensely conservative and strict literalists in terms of their understanding of religion, they do not all espouse the active pursuit of Islamic political orders or encourage violence. Rather, salafism represents a spectrum of thought and practice, with several distinctly identifiable positions within it. With regard to issues of social and political activism, we might postulate the existence of three forms of salafism:

(1) *Salafi quietists* – emphasize the importance of individual adherence to proper thought, practice, and shari'ah, but reject the idea of actively pursuing an Islamic political order as a distinct religious duty (or even Islamically permissible) unto itself; to do so, in their mind, would lead one to emphasize the pursuit of worldly power at the expense of piety and religious obligation. The correct Islamic society will emerge when, through tarbiya (education), Muslims have collectively adopted the correct method. Most salafis today fall into this category, and it is a tendency whose influence is growing in many Muslim settings, particularly those, such as in the West, where Muslims feel their religious identity to be under threat.

(2) *Salafi Islamists* – believe in the active pursuit of an Islamic political order defined in terms of the salafi method. Violence may be a necessary

part of this, but only under very specific conditions. This approach to salafism developed in Saudi Arabia from the 1960s when a number of intellectuals and scholars associated with the MB in Egypt (mostly followers of Sayyid Qutb) came to Saudi Arabia and began to teach in Saudi universities. It might therefore be regarded as a fusion of Wahhabi theology and the activist method of the MB. It became influential among a small but dedicated group of scholars and future activists who studied in the Kingdom. This was in stark contrast to the Saudi religious establishment, most of whose members were firmly in the quietist camp.

(3) *Salafi jihadis* – combine the political imperatives of the salafi Islamists with a conviction that contemporary circumstances make violent struggle an individual duty incumbent upon all Muslims (see section below on jihad). Quietism or the pursuit of societal transformation via political participation are both regarded as illegitimate—the former because it ignores what salafi jihadis and Islamists see as a Qur'anic requirement for Muslims to actively and immediately implement the shari'ah by whatever means possible, and the latter because the willingness of Islamists to work within political systems defined and controlled by infidels is tantamount to recognizing the legitimacy of those regimes.

Much of the current focus on salafi Islam has actually centered on the activities of a narrow group of salafi jihadis and, to a lesser extent, salafi Islamists. Thus it becomes important to differentiate between what we might see as mainstream salafi religious doctrine—conservative and literalist in its religious orientation but not particularly active politically—and a thoroughly "political salafism" wherein the doctrinal dimensions of the salafi manhaj become vested with an activist impulse that seeks, through violence or otherwise, to replace infidel political orders with shari'ah-based models. The rest of our discussion in this chapter will therefore be focused on political salafism, and, more particularly, its jihadi variant.

Jihad: struggle and violence in the name of Islam

Like salafi, the term "jihad" has various meanings in Islam and these are often a source of considerable confusion for the casual observer. Literally, the verbal root of the word in Arabic refers to notions of struggle or exertion. Classical Islamic scholars differentiated between two primary idioms of jihad: the Greater Jihad (*jihad al-akbar*) and the Lesser Jihad (*jihad al-asghar*). The Greater Jihad refers to one's spiritual or inner struggle to overcome the self (*nafs*) in the course of submitting fully to the path of God. It is about the effort one expends to live one's life in accordance with the shari'ah and to affirm the core tenants of faith. The Lesser Jihad—conceived as such because it is never an end in itself, but only a means towards achieving the Greater Jihad—refers to the outward struggle to implement or defend Islam, which can be physical or violent in nature. Over the centuries, religious scholars have sub-speciated these general categories in various ways, differentiating, for example, between *jihad al-qalb* ("struggle of the heart"), *jihad b'il-lisan* ("struggle by the tongue"), *jihad bil-qalam* ("struggle by the pen"), and *jihad bil-sayf* ("struggle by the sword"). It is not therefore a matter of trying to discern which is the "real" meaning of jihad, but rather understanding how and why different senses of the term have come into play. Sufis, for example, have tended to lay great emphasis on the notion of spiritual struggle. Islamists, on the other hand, have emphasized the outward dimension—but not necessarily always in reference to warfare. The idea of *jihad bil-yad* ("struggle by the hand"), for instance, can refer to non-violent political activism or expending financial resources. While the inward and outward senses of jihad are both widely used in the classic literature of Islam, it should also be pointed out that occurrences of the term jihad in historical and political texts have generally carried a martial connotation. It is for this reason that the term "jihad" is frequently, but incorrectly, translated as "holy war."

To understand the discourse on jihad as a form of warfare, it is first important to gain some insight into classical Islamic conceptions of "moral geography" and just war theory. Classical scholars divided the world into two primary "zones": *dar al-islam* (the domain of Islam) and *dar al-harb* (the domain of war). The first of these refers to lands under the control of Muslim rulers and where the laws and regulations of Islam are implemented. It is permissible to use force to defend dar al-islam if it is attacked. Dar al-harb, on the other hand, refers to those lands ruled by non-Muslims and, more particularly, where Muslims are being prevented from living according to Islam. Classical doctrine held it permissible to wage offensive jihad against these territories. As the doctrine of jihad evolved, it came to emphasize an almost exclusively defensive concept of jihad—particularly once the various wars of conquest had achieved a considerable expansion of Muslim territorial holdings (see Chapter 2). During Ottoman times, a third zone, that of *dar al-ahd* (domain of treaty) was created to cover Christian territories in southeastern Europe with whom the Ottomans had made tributary arrangements. Some recent theorists have also used this term to describe the arrangements by which Muslim and non-Muslims live together in non-Muslim states.[13] We can say then that the general consensus among scholars, prevalent until quite recently, was that jihad was only permitted in order to defend Muslim lands that come under attack from outside. Moreover, on this understanding, jihad could only be declared by the proper authorities. As an inherently political practice, it made no sense outside of the framework of the Islamic caliphate or a Muslim sultanate. To accompany the core principles, there was also developed a detailed *fiqh al-jihad* (jurisprudence of warfare) that detailed the regulations and norms pertaining to the use of force. This covered much the same ground as the rules relating to *jus in bello* in Western Just War Theory—for example the doctrine of proportional force, distinctions between combatants and non-combatants, and so forth.

The modern transformation in jihad doctrine closely parallels the development of the Wahhabi and salafi approaches discussed above. Again we begin with Muhammad Ibn Abdul Wahhab in the eighteenth century. We have already discussed the political alliance with Muhammad Ibn Saud that allowed him to propagate his zealously puritanical understanding of Islam (see Chapter 5). One of the obstacles to Wahhabism's expansion beyond the confines of central Arabia was the unwillingness of other Muslim tribes and clans—many of which subscribed to various forms of sufi practice—to adopt its norms. Abdul Wahhab was hence led to reinterpret classical Islamic doctrines regarding the boundaries of belief such that these non-Wahhabi Muslims could be declared infidels—that is, subjected to takfir. The lands they occupied could therefore be regarded as dar al-harb and hence legitimately attacked. This piece of ijtihad represented a major revision to one of the most enduring principles of jurisprudential consensus, that Muslims do not wage war against other Muslims. Moreover, as the tribal leader of a desert province with highly porous frontiers, it was not at all clear that Muhammad Ibn Saud even possessed the necessary political authority to declare a legitimate jihad. Several generations later, as one might expect, the interpretation of jihad by those in the Reformist tradition (Afghani, Abduh, Rida, etc.) sought a return not only to the meaning found in the classical approach, but even introduced ijtihad that went in quite the opposite direction of Abdul Wahhab's—that is, taking Qur'anic verses that seemed quite unambiguously to enjoin violence against particular groups and reinterpreting them to de-emphasize the martial dimension or the necessity of using physical force.[14]

For the purposes of understanding contemporary salafi-jihadi violence, however, we need to move forward another couple of generations to consider once again the contributions of Sayyid Qutb, ideologue of the MB during its radical phase. Qutb's conception of jihad needs to be understood within the framework of the other core concept that animates his thinking, namely the idea of the modern world as a world of jahiliyya, or pre-/un-Islamic ignorance (see Chapter 3). Qutb's overall worldview, of which his idiom of jihad forms an intrinsic part, is itself a comprehensive and revolutionary reinterpretation of the social and political implications of Qur'anic normativity. In a world dominated by secularism, capitalism, atheism, imperialism, and immorality—a world where even nominally Muslim rulers have abandoned Islam in pursuit of these vices—distinctions such as dar al-islam and dar al-harb no longer make sense. All the world is in need of repair, and there are no meaningful borders of dar al-islam to defend.[15] This does not mean however, that jihad is forbidden; rather, these are the very conditions that instill it as a duty. The capacity of Muslims to freely choose and practice their religion is everywhere denied, and revolutionary jihad is required to remedy this state of affairs. Anyone who prevents the realization of Islam is therefore a legitimate target of jihad. Jihad, for Qutb, cannot be understood in relation to notions of "proper legal authority" or "offensive versus defensive war." Jihad is about reclaiming for God a sovereignty that has been usurped. It is about making space in the world for His order and making sure that no earthly power is in a position to block the choice by Muslims to live according to that order.[16] To be clear, though: the aim is not to compel people to accept Islam for this must be an individual choice, freely made. Rather, it is about Qutb's reinterpretation of the conditions under which that choice can be made. Where jahiliyya reigns, no Muslim, or potential Muslim, is in a position to truly make that choice.[17] Who, then, are the agents of jihad? We have already noted that for Qutb, all Muslims must accept the obligation to struggle towards the realization of Islam. More particularly, however, he lays great emphasis on the hope that a "Qur'anic generation" will arise—one that will, to use a computing metaphor, hit the reset button or "reboot" Islam into a basic installation or safe mode. This "Qur'anic generation" will have no need for the apparatus of classical Islamic learning since its sources, like Qutb's, will be none other than, and exclusively, the literal word of God as found in the Qur'an.[18]

It is not surprising that Qutb's revolutionary worldview found considerable purchase among the radical breakaways from the Egyptian MB a decade after his death. His ideas confirmed their suspicion that the Brotherhood as a movement had effectively abandoned Islam to become part of the jahiliyya order. A number of subsequent thinkers and activists made contributions or added new areas of emphasis to Qutb's ideas on jihad. We may recall Muhammad Farag's notion of jihad against the "near enemy"— that is the governments of states in the Muslim world that had adopted secularism and nationalism, and had circumscribed the practice of Islam— an idea that was already present in Qutb's work. In the mind of latter day interpreters, to quote Wiktorowicz, "Western influence over Arab governments through foreign assistance, International Monetary Fund loans, military connections and political alignments renders these governments 'puppets' of the West and its Zionist allies in the Middle East. Arab regimes are thus considered the functional equivalent of foreign occupiers."[19] This is a principle that Farag made operational via the assassination of Anwar Sadat in 1981. Later, Abdallah Azzam, whom we have mentioned above, channeled and inflected Qutb's thinking in the Afghan context by laying out an explanation as to why jihad was a duty impingent on all believers. Offensive jihad against unbelievers was indeed, as Qutb argued, a duty—but one that was to be regarded as *fard kifaya*, that is, as a collective obligation. This means that so long as some group of Muslims is undertaking the effort (classically, an "official" Muslim army) then no individual action need be taken. If, however, a Muslim land comes under attack by infidels, then jihad becomes a matter of *fard ayn*, or individual obligation. Every Muslim is expected to join the fight to re-establish the integrity of Muslim borders, with the highest obligation falling on those closest to the incursion—hence Azzam's appeal to the "Arab-Afghans."[20]

From "near enemy" to "far enemy": the new global jihad and its discontents

In the decade following the conclusion of the Afghanistan war, the doctrine of jihad among radical Islamists underwent a significant evolution. To begin exploring this, we need to start with the immediate aftermath of the conflict. The vast majority of Afghan Arabs at this point returned to their home countries and, as we have noted, many of them became involved in various forms of Islamic radicalism on the home front. Much of the intensity of the Islamic violence in countries such as Algeria and Egypt during the 1990s, for example, can be understood as a direct result of the injection into national settings of battle-hardened Arab-Afghans keen to continue the fight. But, as Fawaz Gerges notes, most of these eventually "met their Waterloo on homefront battlefields."[21] Others preferred to continue operating in the expatriate mode and to look for other Muslim causes to defend. Thus, during the 1990s, we saw contingents of Afghan Arabs fighting in settings such as Bosnia, Chechnya, and Kashmir. In many cases their hardline and highly militant Islam did not mesh at all well with local religious norms, such as the strong Sufi tradition in the Balkans and the Caucasus. There to fight on behalf of Muslim populations, they were not necessarily regarded as a welcome addition by the forces they had supposedly come to defend. In both cases—homeland struggles and new Muslim defensive jihads—the main point to make is that even when the Afghan war ended, radical Islamists found themselves with plenty of other opportunities to continue the fight.

We have already covered the movements of Usama Bin Laden's group during much of the 1990s, but have said less about how notions of jihad were evolving within his camp. Ayman al-Zawahiri, the leader of Egyptian Islamic Jihad, had been drawing closer and closer to Bin Laden. By the mid-1990s his authority in the circle was second only to the Saudis and he soon folded the Islamic Jihad group into Bin Laden's—hoping, some have argued, to displace Bin Laden's leadership and gain control of what he hoped were considerable and much needed funds for his own program. From the mid-1990s, Zawahiri developed an alternative vision for the jihadi movement. Having noted the failure of the homeland radicals to succeed in bringing about revolution, he began to argue that the movement's failure lay in its inability to mobilize the umma as a whole against a common enemy.[22] Emboldened by the fall of the Soviet Union, some within Bin Laden's circle were beginning to come around to the idea that Muslims should be taking the fight against jahiliyya directly to the source—namely, the Crusaders (the United States and its Western allies) and the Zionists (Israel, as backed by the United States). This new emphasis on the "far enemy" was a major

254   *Radical Islamism & jihad*

departure for Zawahiri who, throughout most of his time in Afghanistan, had viewed the mujahideen's mountains as a training zone for later battles on the home front.[23] In some regards, the doctrine that Zawahiri now began to promulgate was Sayyid Qutb and Abdullah Azzam pushed to their logical extreme. If all the world is jahiliyya and Muslims are under duress or assault everywhere, then the jihad must be fought in all places by all Muslims—a violent reinterpretation, in some regards, of Jamal ad-Din al-Afghani's Pan-Islamist ideology (see Chapter 2). We should also note that globalization is, in some respects, a crucial enabling dimension to this vision. Previously, on Azzam's account, one was relieved from the obligation of jihad if one was not near enough to or could not travel to the battlefield.[24] With a worldwide theater of operations, and given the relative ease of transnational travel and communication, the idea of "global jihad" began to take on real meaning.

The small movement soon began to adapt its organizational structure to the new vision. In the late 1980s, as the Afghan war wound down, Bin Laden had formed a loose organization called Qaedat al-Jihad ("The Jihad Base"), or Al-Qaeda for short. Its purpose was to allow for ongoing communication and coordination between a core grouping of Arab-Afghans with shared views of the movement's priorities. Al-Qaeda now became Bin Laden's primary operational unit, with its ideology increasingly defined in terms of striking at the "far enemy" (the United States)—a new idiom, in other words, of global jihad. In 1998, the World Islamic Front for Jihad was formed as a loose coalition of radical groups (several of them splinter factions from radical groups with a more domestic orientation) willing to wage jihad on a global scale. Connections also began to be forged with various other local and regional groups with radical tendencies. Thus, from the very beginning, Al-Qaeda was as much a network or "umbrella organization" as it was a discrete entity unto itself.

Al-Qaeda and its affiliates have carried out or been involved in numerous attacks against American interests since the mid-1990s. These include the Khobar Towers bombing of 1995, the bombing of the U.S. embassies in Kenya and Tanzania in 1996, the attack on the USS Cole in 2000, the September 11, 2001 attacks on the World Trade Center in New York City and the Pentagon in Washington D.C., the Bali bombing of 2002, bombings in Morocco and Turkey in 2003, the Madrid bombings of 2003, the assassination of U.S. foreign service personnel in Jordan in 2005, and the July 7 bomb attacks in London. This track record would suggest that Al-Qaeda has been largely successful in redefining the doctrine and methodology of jihad in favor of its preferred focus on the "far enemy." In fact, there has been considerable infighting within the jihadi movement since the mid-1990s and Al-Qaeda now finds itself in a rather embattled position on the fringes of this current rather than in a front-and-center, defining leadership role. The point here is that while the methods employed by Al-Qaeda and the spectacles they create have done much to define the jihadi movement, in the popular imagination, according to Bin Laden's vision, the global jihadists have actually come under considerable criticism in recent years from other jihadi leaders who see them as having over-stepped important boundaries.

Criticism of the new transnational jihad has come from a variety of sources and has been prompted by numerous factors. Some of the key figures here are former scholars and leaders associated with groups such as Egypt's Gemaa Islamiyya—such as Karam Zuhdi and Nageh Ibrahim—who appear to have changed their views after having been imprisoned.[25] Likewise a number of former Saudi dissident ulama such as Safir al-Hawali and Salman al-Awda (see Chapter 5). In some cases, the views now articulated by these figures have come under considerable suspicion since their circumstances give the appearance of them having been co-opted by the respective regimes. Aspects of their core critique, however, appear to be accepted by many jihadis still operating outside the reach of the authorities. Jihadi intellectuals living in exile in Europe, such as Hani al-Sibai and Omar Rushdi, have also come out against Bin Laden and the global jihadis.[26] As Mohammed Derbala, a Gemaa Islamiyya strategician, has put it with regard to Bin Laden, "their hearts are with [him], but their swords are against [him]."[27] Needless to say, a great number of quietist salafis, such as the late Muhammad Nasir al-Din al-Bani and Saudi figures such as Abdel Nasser al-Obeikan, who have been against jihad all along, have come out against Al-Qaeda along with leading conservative ulama linked to the MB and Azhari sheikhs such as Yusuf al-Qaradawi (see Chapter 9) and Muhammad Hussein Tantawi.

We are of course most interested in the debate *within* the jihadi movement since this offers us the clearest sense of how the internal debate among those who favor jihad is shaping up. While different critics of Al-Qaeda from within the jihadi camp have their own areas of primary complaint, we can summarize the range of issues generally regarded as problematic in the following way:

(1) The shift of emphasis from the "near enemy" to the "far enemy" was a strategic mistake, and, moreover, not sufficiently grounded in religious evidence. This shift suited Bin Laden's circumstances and was facilitated by his resources—but it did not represent the general will of the jihadi movement.

(2) Al-Qaeda's "successes" have led regimes to crack down on Islamist movements and particularly jihadis all over the Muslim world—making it increasingly difficult today for them to carry out operations against the near enemy.

(3) The act of takfir—that is, declaring Muslims to be infidels in order to justify one's disagreement with them, or in order to carry out operations against Muslim civilians—was being used far too freely and without regard or respect for proper authority in doing so.

(4) Disproportionate use of force, both in terms of the scale of killing and destruction and in terms of the targets selected. This had in fact been an ongoing issue within the broader jihadi movement since the intense GIA operations in Algeria during the 1990s in which thousands of civilians were killed.

There are signs that these various lines of critique have been having an impact on Al-Qaeda's ability to find and retain quality recruits. The further critiques offered by mainstream scholars and intellectuals, whom Muslims are far more likely to listen to than the jihadis, have also severely discredited Bin Laden and his ilk—a fact borne out by recent opinion poll surveys in the Muslim world. In the Arab world in particular, the number of people expressing any degree of confidence in the Al-Qaeda leader has fallen significantly in recent years.[28] This apparent trend against Bin Laden and global jihadism will be taken up again in the conclusion to this chapter.

Al-Qaeda: shadow empire of jihad

What is Al-Qaeda and what are its aims? How is the group organized, where does its financing come from, and what does its membership look like? This section will offer a description of Al-Qaeda and some of its basic features. We will then proceed to look more specifically at the sociology of the movement. In particular, we will look at the two distinct generations of Al-Qaeda activists who differ greatly in terms of both their origins and professional backgrounds, and in terms of how and why they are drawn into the network. Issues of mobilization and radicalization will also get some attention, and we will return to the question of salafism and its role in shaping the worldviews of radical activists. Finally, some aspects of Al-Qaeda as a social movement will be examined.

Al-Qaeda ("the base") evolved in Afghanistan during the final years of the 1980s. The basic rubric for the group was devised by Abdullah Azzam, who had in mind to create a mobile fighting force that could be dispatched anywhere in the world to assist Muslim fighters—"an Islamic rapid reaction force," in the words of one observer.[29] After Azzam's death, Bin Laden took over the nascent organization, which at this point was more of a verbal memorandum of understanding between a small group of like-minded individuals, albeit one backed by an impressive network of logistics and transnational activist contacts. As Bin Laden and Zawahiri shaped their new jihadi vision over the next decade, Al-Qaeda's importance among the many nominal entities under their control rose significantly. By the late 1990s, Al-Qaeda was firmly established as Bin Laden's primary operational unit. It was to be the militant vanguard of a new jihadi vision aimed at combating the "far enemy." Bin Laden's main goal after the Gulf War of 1991 came to be the removal of American forces from Saudi Arabia—or, as he, refusing to recognize the legitimacy of the Saudi royal family, preferred to refer to it, the "Land of the Two Holy Mosques." While he certainly paid lip service to other Muslim causes, particularly Palestine, where Israeli occupation in his mind was a function of American support for Zionism, it is clear from his statements at this time that Bin Laden's focus was on the United States. The general tenor of his vision can be gauged from two documents produced in 1996 and 1998, the "Declaration of Jihad" and the statement on the "World Islamic Front."

Al-Qaeda's structure and organization also evolved exponentially during these same years. Bin Laden systematically built up a vast global network of political affiliations, financial interests, logistical handlers, and—of course—activist cells. All of these were tightly integrated, functionally differentiated, and organized into a clear division of labor, all designed to feed and sustain Al-Qaeda's capacity to wage jihad. This infrastructure was so complex and had so many layers—often with multiple "firewalls" between them—that many of the entities enmeshed within it were not even aware they were part of a giant jihadi operation. Rohan Gunaratna summarizes is thusly:

> Al-Qaeda is ... characterized by a broad-based ideology, a novel structure, a robust capacity for regeneration and a very diverse membership that cuts across ethnic, class and national boundaries. It is neither a single group nor a coalition of groups: it comprises a core base or bases in Afghanistan, satellite terrorist cells worldwide, a conglomerate of Islamist political parties, and other largely independent terrorist groups that it draws on for offensive actions and other responsibilities. Leaders of all the above are co-opted as and when necessary to serve as an integral part of Al-Qaeda's high command, which is run via a vertical leadership structure that provides strategic direction and tactical support to its horizontal network of compartmentalized cells and associate organizations.[30]

In many respects, then, at the height of its operations, Al-Qaeda was best characterized as a "holding company," which—in addition to its own cells—could directly tap into a wide range of otherwise autonomous organizations to leverage their particular skills and capabilities for a given operation.

Al-Qaeda's cell structure is particularly important in terms of understanding its ability to operate a vast network of activists and yet remain undetected. Composed generally of 2–15 members, these cells—based mainly in Western countries—operated via their leaders through an exclusively vertical chain of authority. The lack of horizontal ties between them meant that cells were never aware of each other's existence or whereabouts—and sometimes not even all the members of a given cell knew each other. This cell model has been widely used by clandestine activist groups of all sorts. Most widely associated with various Marxist-Leninist groups, it was also extensively employed by the MB in its early phases (see Chapter 3).

Al-Qaeda's ability to forge ad hoc or affiliate relationships with other Islamist and radical entities was also key to its operational capacity. Sometimes these were regional or even local groups that had built up a strong presence in an area of interest to Al-Qaeda, but where the network had limited capacity. This is the best way to think of Al-Qaeda's relationship with the Jemah Islamiah group in Southeast Asia, a radical group seeking to establish a caliphate in that region. Although many of Jemah's key figures, such as Hambali, its chief tactician, have been described as members of Al-Qaeda, they are actually best thought of as local "subcontractors" to whom Bin Laden's network have outsourced a particular operation such as the Bali bombing of 2002. Al-Qaeda seems to have been wholly pragmatic in forming these relationships. Network affiliates are not universally salafi-jihadi, some are Shi'i, and some—it appears—are not even Muslim. Rather, these are groups that share a desire to attack the United Sates and are happy to enter into cooperative relationships with capable partners. In return for rendering services to Al-Qaeda, its contractors could expect not only financial reward, but also to gain access to Bin Laden's networked resources (logistics, training) to aid in the pursuit of their own goals—not to mention the prestige that accrues in activist circles from working with Al-Qaeda.

Bin Laden, trained in economics and management rather than religion and Islamic jurisprudence, built a robust network of financial interests that permitted Al-Qaeda to sustain its operations and to bankroll allies and affiliates. While many popular accounts suggest that much of this work was directly funded by his own personal fortune, the reality is that Bin Laden was not sitting on billions that could simply be channeled into militant activities. Rather, most of the money he did have was used to create a system of investments and business interests that would provide a source of continual funding for Al-Qaeda's shadow empire of jihad. During the early Afghan period, Bin Laden could count on generous funding from Pakistan and various states in the Gulf (Saudi Arabia, Kuwait), but once the war was over, this mostly dried up in terms of direct government contributions. He had, however, managed to build up a significant base of contacts and relationships with private foundations, charities, and wealthy individuals who would prove to be a crucial source of funding as Al-Qaeda's operational portfolio developed. Bin Laden found it necessary to make cash payments to various groups and governments, not only to directly assist his operations, but also to buy him breathing space or connivance. His generous support of the Taliban government in Afghanistan is one clear example of this.[31] The finance network was funded through an array of investment schemes and small businesses, with all revenues to Al-Qaeda funneled through a careful money-laundering system involving hundreds if not thousands of bank accounts all over the world. The globalization of finance was hence key to the globalization of Al-Qaeda. The organization possessed a special council charged with ensuring that all of its financial operations were conducted in accordance with the shari'ah.[32] Bin Laden also made use of the informal *hawala* system to transfer money. This method, initially developed in South Asia, permits sums to be sent from one town—or even one country—to another based on relationships of trust that link the various parties involved in the process. There is no record of the transaction and no means by which to track it. Many of the same conduits and contacts were also part of Al-Qaeda's logistics capacity, which enabled the group to move personnel and materials around the world very quickly. Gunaratna suggests that Bin Laden devised "the most complex, robust and resilient money-generating and money-moving network yet seen" and one is indeed led to speculate as to whether Al-Qaeda might better be thought of as a finance and logistics operation first, and as a terrorist group second.[33]

Al-Qaeda made extensive use of communications, both strategically and tactically. On the strategic front, Bin Laden demonstrated a mastery of the modern global media through a series of high-profile statements and interviews released to major networks (CNN, Al-Jazeera). He could be assured, through careful timing, his choice of topic, and even language, to gather an instant worldwide audience. His statements were usually passed to networks and websites through several orders of separation. Partly this was the operational security for which the group had become renowned, but it also helped to heighten the sense of mystery surrounding communications from Al-Qaeda. Western media and government analysts would spend subsequent days pouring over, dissecting, and interpreting these messages. It is interesting to note, as some observers have, that Bin Laden's target audiences for these communications were chosen very strategically. In particular messages he employs symbology and message framings that are aimed at very particular, sometimes niche, audiences. Sometimes he is addressing the world as a whole, or the United States more specifically. Other times a message that gets a worldwide airing, however, was intended primarily for a very specific Islamist or jihadi group. On the tactical side, Al-Qaeda became well known for its extensive use of satellite telephones, information technology, encryption, and steganography. From the late 1990s, once it became clear to Bin Laden that he was being closely monitored by various intelligence agencies, he stopped making widespread use of electronic forms of communication and began to rely instead on direct person-to-person contacts.

Much has also been made of Al-Qaeda's network of training facilities, centered primarily in Afghanistan. Not only were the group's own operatives trained here, but Bin Laden would make it possible for other jihadi groups to send personnel to these camps. Many of the recruitment videos produced by Al-Qaeda feature the training sites, which Bin Laden was clearly keen to show off. They were also among the highest priority targets of the U.S.'s counter-offensive against Al-Qaeda beginning with the 1998 bombings of camps in Afghanistan and a suspected weapons production facility in Sudan. The group also produced training manuals and guide-books that provided copious details about how to operate in a wide variety of environments and to undertake various sorts of attacks from manu-facturing explosives to the use of various weapons systems. The most famous of these is probably the *Encyclopedia of the Afghan Jihad*, a book which compiled and synthesized thousands of accounts of mujahideen and Arab-Afghan operations, serving as an invaluable "institutional memory" of the war that could be used by later jihadis.[34] There is also evidence that in its operations Al-Qaeda utilized aspects of modern management science, including post-attack assessment and evaluation reports to enable the improvement of future operations.[35]

Al-Qaeda's active membership was diverse and varied considerably in terms of its size and composition over the years. Initially made up, as we will see below, almost exclusively of Arab-Afghan alumni, it began from the 1990s to attract Muslim fighters from all over the world, including a number of converts from the West. The training camps, at any given time, would be populated by jihadis from the Philippines, Libya, Somalia, Bangladesh, and northern California. There is evidence to suggest that all positions of administrative consequence and certainly those with any mili-tary command responsibility were firmly in the hands of Arabs—with Arabic also serving as the movement's *lingua franca*.[36]

Perhaps one useful metaphor for thinking about Al-Qaeda, particularly in terms of its resilience and regenerative capacities, is to compare it to the Internet. Like the Internet, Al-Qaeda is in many ways a "network of net-works." The technology behind the Internet was designed in the late 1960s by researchers working for the U.S. Department of Defense who sought to create a system for exchanging data that would be impervious to a nuclear strike by the Soviet Union. To this end, they created various forms of redundancy into the core data transfer technology that would permit mes-sages to continue to be sent across the network even if entire sections of it were destroyed. The Internet is also decentralized in terms of its structure, meaning that there is no single choke point or control unit on which other operations depend. Al-Qaeda certainly possesses this redundant capacity insofar as its tightly integrated network of operations can continue to function even if part of it is closed down or destroyed. Al-Qaeda does, however, possess a more centralized control mechanism in the form of its top leadership—but even this had proven to be remarkably resilient and capable of becoming portable very quickly in the face of threats, as wit-nessed in Bin Laden's ability to evade capture when the United States invaded Afghanistan in 2001. Even if Al-Qaeda's ability to centrally com-mand and control militant operations has been severely degraded—as both military and law enforcement operations against its finance network seem to have done—there is evidence to suggest that its influence and capacities have been channeled into other manifestations and modes of operation, despite declining popular support.

The sociology of radical Islam: mobilization, identity, and authority

Now that we have a basic understanding of Al-Qaeda's aims and structure, we can move on to look in greater depth at those who choose to associate with it and work on its behalf. This section will investigate various dimensions of the sociology of radical Islam. We will focus more specifically on shifting trends across two generations of jihadi activists and also on the question of how salafism as a form of religious discourse interacts with processes of identity formation to shape the worldviews of would-be activists in particular ways. How does radicalization occur and what is it about particular forms of religious authority that attracts and holds the loyalty of followers? We will also discuss some of the ways in which radical Islamist groups can be thought of in terms of social movements more broadly conceptualized.

As Olivier Roy has noted in his book *Globalized Islam*, it is possible to identify two distinct generations of Al-Qaeda activists. The comparative sociology of these groups is telling in terms of what it allows us to discern about the evolving nature of the jihadi discourse and movement. The first generation of Al-Qaeda operatives, those who constituted the bulk of the organization in the late 1980s and very early 1990s, were generally citizens of Muslim countries and had direct prior experience of political or militant activism either in their home countries, as Arab-Afghans, or—most commonly—both. They generally had very little experience of the West and their axis of movement was generally confined to Afghanistan, Muslim conflicts in neighboring countries, and their countries of origin.[37] The second wave of Al-Qaeda personnel, from the 1990s, by contrast, tended to have strong connections to the West. Many were recruited in Europe (and to some extent North America) or were citizens of Muslim countries who had spent some time living, studying or training in the West as expatriates. Important to note about this second generation, Roy tells us, is the "deterritorialized" nature of its Muslim identity. Where the original Al-Qaeda activists were firmly socialized in a nation-state environment and had developed their Islamist consciousness primarily in terms of its circumstances, this new generation of jihadis often had weak senses of national and religious identity. For many in the first wave, transnationalism was something of a reach, an idea they needed to get their heads around; for the second generation, however, it was a natural way of life—the "jihadi jet set."[38]

In order to better understand this new mode of malignant cosmopolitanism, we need to look more closely at how and why radical religious discourse resonated with these deterritorialized identities. We will discuss these processes primarily in the context of the recruitment and socialization of young Muslims in Western contexts since Al-Qaeda and other radical groups seem to have relied heavily on these settings to provide many of the foot soldiers for their second generation operations. In terms of the first wave, the socialization into jihad occurred primarily through existing radical Islamist structures whose activities and leaderships became increasingly transnational from the 1980s. When looking at the second wave, however, we are confronted with a situation in which ideologues and recruiters are often handed a *tabula rasa* Muslim identity (in the form of a new convert or an immigrant Muslim experiencing new-found sense of religiosity) upon which they employ a range of discursive and disciplining techniques to inculcate certain worldviews and activist tendencies. This may sound like we are referring to something akin to brainwashing, but at work here is actually a much more sophisticated process of socialization that leverages existing cognitive, ideational, and identity formations to sculpt a very particular form of global Muslim subjectivity.

Several observers have already noted the "deculturing" or "universalizing" dimensions of salafi Islam.[39] These two terms refer, respectively, to the analytical and normative aspects of a similar phenomenon. Salafism, with its hostility toward religious innovation (bid'a) aims to rid Islam of anything that has entered the faith through contact with various local, "cultural" beliefs and practices. Syncretism, in the salafi view, is the enemy. Its anti-madhhab stance is further evidence of this. There are no schools of jurisprudence to debate between, salafis insist—there is only Islam. In a normative sense this has proven very appealing to many young Muslims living in the West who feel alienated by their parents' understanding of Islam (see Chapter 8). Their parents seem trapped in an understanding of Islam as it was practiced in, for example, the village in Bangladesh from which they migrated 20 years ago. They seem obsessed with details relating to how one should hold one's hands while praying, saints days, various festivals—but nothing to do with religion and modern life. Rejecting the "village Islam" of their parents they go in search of a form of Islam that speaks to the issues and challenges of living as a Muslim in a global world—and, moreover, a Muslim caught between two senses of identity. The second and third immigrant generations have generally been born and raised in the West and are well versed (and often comfortable with) its cultural patterns and norms. At the same time, they are aware of belonging to a different and at times disparate identify formation, that of Islam. They search for a universal form of religion that will help them to reconcile what they are (Muslims) with where they are (the West), and that will also help to provide them with some sense of meaning and purpose.

This search for a universal idiom of Islam can lead in two general directions. In some cases it prompts young Muslims in the West to emphasize those aspects of their religion that reflect global human rights norms, democracy, and political and cultural pluralism: the umma as an integral part of a common global humanity. But this same search for universal Islam can also lead towards a universalism defined, religiously, in salafi terms—and, politically, in terms of Muslim struggles the world over: the umma as a righteous community under assault. While there is no sure way of determining which of these two general currents will prevail when it comes to a given individual, it is possible to make observations about how and why the salafi discourse in particular may seem appealing under certain circumstances. It is also important to note that only a very tiny minority of those drawn to salafi Islamist circles in the West ever get anywhere near the battlefield of jihad. For many, political salafism is a "phase" they go through before either slipping into a conservative but non-Islamist mode of religious practice, or, in some cases, becoming so disillusioned with the movement that they begin to question the very basis of salafism or even Islam. We have already referred above to the deculturing nature of salafi Islam. Several other aspects of the radical discourse merit our attention in terms of their interaction with identity and shifting religious norms in Western contexts.

Meaning-making and identity constitutive worldviews

For those Western Muslims who experience their dual identities as confusing and destabilizing, radical Islamic discourses can provide a matrix of meaning that permits them to derive a clearer sense of purpose and worldview. By shifting the focus of their identity away from the apparent tension between being, for example, simultaneously British and South Asian, and orienting it instead toward a resolution of this tension in a universal, salafi Islam and membership in the global umma, radical ideologues help culturally disoriented Muslims (or recent converts, as yet unsure of their way in Islam) to experience their lack of clear identity foothold not as a weakness or an absence, but rather as something empowering that invests them with the ability to be a "real" Muslim—and, moreover, to prove it by becoming politically engaged on behalf of the embattled umma. Describing the appeal of the radical Islamist group Hizb ut-Tahrir (see below), one former member put it this way:

> They had a very profound analysis of why the Islamic world is in such an abysmal state, how it declined and most importantly how we can elevate ourselves from this position, and break free. The group was not allied to any political regime, it was not operating on the basis of personal or financial motivation, it didn't have a sectarian approach. As long as you are a Muslim and are committed to its beliefs and its causes, you are welcome to join the party.[40]

A previously liminal identity thus rediscovers itself as part of the vanguard of a new global movement. Radical salafism accomplishes a gradual "desocietization" whereby adherents withdraw further and further from the ambient mainstream community, associating exclusively with other "real Muslims" and gradually detaching themselves from the national-societal contexts in which they live.

"Sheikhly" charisma and the ethics of care

Another dimension of Muslims' attraction to radical movements relates to the personal charisma associated with the scholars and leaders of these movements. Various observers have noted that within Al-Qaeda's second wave, a great many of those recruited in the West have been living on the margins of society—often coming from broken homes and families, unemployed, involved in petty crime and so forth. The leaders of the radical groups, as one analyst has documented, tend to display a genuine sense of care for those who come into their circle.[41] For many young Muslims living in the margins, frequently subject to racism and discrimination, this will represent the first time someone has ever seemed to take a genuine interest in them and the direction of their lives. The personal charisma of radical ideologues hence seems vitally important in terms of creating an emotional bond with members of the group.[42]

Salafism and techno-scientific cognitive style

Many drawn to the radical movements are not by any means marginalized members of society. Rather, they often have very high levels of education, are employed, and even have families in some cases (compare with the demographics of mainstream Islamist groups such as the MB). Theirs is not a lack of social integration, but rather a seemingly successful integration process that has gone awry. Elements of the identity and worldview crises alluded to above begin to enter the picture and they come to the radical circles in search of a clearer sense of meaning. Well aware of the educational background of these potential recruits—many of whom will have graduated from top scientific and engineering schools—the religious scholars and intellectuals will often articulate radical Islamist ideology in a form that fits comfortably with the "cognitive style" and methods of analysis to which their students are accustomed. Salafi Islam is particularly conducive to this approach. The grammar of salafism suits the structure of modern scientific knowledge production. When teaching salafi Islam to such a group, for example, a sheikh can diagram it on a board such that it closely resembles problem-solving methods or engineering flowcharts. Given that much of the salafi discourse can be explained in terms of discrete categories of analysis, it becomes a relatively straightforward matter to communicate its teachings in a way that allows a follower with a techno-scientific education to work methodically through a given situation (framed in terms of religiously given normative categories) and to eventually achieve—just as science does—a single, correct answer at the end of that process. This answer, it should be noted is not subjective and nor is it open to interpretation. It is the end result, again, just like science, of an "objective" method whose infallibility is beyond reproach. Faith in science as a technical method becomes faith in salafism as a religious method.

Activism, violence and "instinctual" religious knowledge

Observers and analysts of radical Islam have speculated as to the process that leads an individual to become willing to engage in violence, or other forms of "high-risk" activism.[43] Is it the religion itself that "radicalizes" them? Is it the teachings of a senior religious scholar who eventually convinces them that violence in the name of Islam is not only permitted, but required of them? Limited anecdotal evidence actually suggests that many individuals come into radical circles having already decided that they want to undertake violent jihad. Some, in fact, may only very recently have become Muslim, or "reactivated" a previously dormant sense of religiosity.[44] Thus it is not salafism itself or the authority of religious scholars that serve as the "radicalizing agents," but rather prior life experiences and worldviews that have culminated in a decision to actively seek participation in political violence. The religious authority of salafi sheikhs, in any case, is anything but absolute. While those who engage in jihad do seek religious justification for their actions, they may sometimes do so after having already decided to act. In this regard, given the lack of religious hierarchy in Islam, it becomes easy for them to shop around—via the Internet or personal connections—to find a sheikh who will authorize and, moreover, provide textually grounded (and hence irreproachable) evidence as to why violence is permitted or even required in a given situation. It is also worth recalling here Sayyid Qutb's teachings about how activist interpretations are privileged above those of religious scholars (see Chapter 3). For someone strongly molded in the "Qutbist" worldview, there is the potential that they may even untether themselves from formal sources of religious authority altogether. This phenomenon is illustrated in testimony given by the widow of a jihadi accused of planning the 2002 Madrid train bombings: "Sometime we received texts [by religious scholars] from the Internet, but my husband did not read them, his relationship to jihad was instinctual."[45] Thus while activists may operate in frameworks whose general normative parameters are defined by a given religious authority, their willingness to engage in violence is not necessarily a learned behavior accruing exclusively from their participation in this network. Moreover, it seems that under certain circumstances they may disconnect from, or simply ignore, those aspects and teachings emanating from formally trained religious scholars that are dissonant with the activist orientation to which they have committed.

Hizb ut-Tahrir and *khilafah*: a non-violent radical Islamism?

Al-Qaeda has understandably been the focus of considerable attention and analysis in recent years, but are there not to be found today other radical Islamist movements not already affiliated with Al-Qaeda and which espouse a different approach to revolutionary politics? One such group that we will examine below is Hizb ut-Tahrir. It is a radical group in that its primary goal is the re-establishment of a global caliphate. It prefers to do so on a gradual basis, however—one country at a time—and without the use of violence (despite claims by others to the contrary—see below). Where Al-Qaeda can clearly be labeled a jihadi organization, Hizb ut-Tahrir's emphasis on the caliphate leads us to regard it as a *khilafist* group.

Hizb ut-Tahrir al-Islami (the "Islamic Liberation Party"—hereafter HT) significantly predates Al-Qaeda. Founded in Jerusalem in 1952 by Taqi ud-Din al-Nabhani, HT emphasized from the beginning the importance of establishing a single party (*hizb*) through which Muslims could work for the re-establishment of the caliphate (*khilafah*). In the eyes of Nabhani and his followers, it was only through revolutionary action in concert that the world's Muslims could restore themselves to a position of global power. In this sense, the founding of Nabhani's movement marks a reincarnation of certain elements found in earlier discourses on Pan-Islam, yet with a stronger emphasis on the importance of a single Muslim polity. Nabhani faced considerable opposition from the Jordanian state (which still controlled Jerusalem at that time), and also found it difficult to develop a mass following for his party. With Arab nationalism gathering strength as the dominant political ideology of the day, appeals for a new caliphate fell largely on deaf ears. HT found itself moving underground at the same time as it began to establish small footholds in other Arab countries. Noted to be particularly strong in Turkey, where memory of the Ottoman caliphate still endures to some extent, the group's activities in the Middle East and Asia (outside the reach of anti-HT propaganda in the Arab world) have been well documented during the first decades of its existence.[46]

The structure of HT, while highly fluid in practice, is organized around a series of hierarchical committees. The party maintains a worldwide central leadership committee headed by an *amir* (leader), currently Ata Ibnu Khaleel Abu Rashta. The group does not disclose the location of the central committee, but it is variously reported as being based in Lebanon, Jordan, or Syria. Each nation (or "province" since the party does not recognize the validity of the nation-state model) in which HT operates possesses a 5–10-member committee headed by a *mu'tamad* (regional leader). These national leadership councils subdivide into smaller local (usually urban) committees under a *naqib* (local head) and neighborhood study circles guided by a *mushrif* (study circle guide). In countries where it has been subject to persecution by authorities, HT has been known to adopt a rigorously enforced cell structure. Much of the activities—and even the identities—of the group's leadership are highly secretive. Sometimes even senior country leaders know very little about the opaque global leadership structure. It is reported that there are certain issues and topics on which country branches are required to consult the central leadership before speaking or acting, and some have noted the presence of central leadership representatives observing and advising "field" offices in other countries.

Sporadic references to crackdowns on HT branches in North Africa and Turkey can be found throughout the 1970s and 80s, and the group resurfaced to a torrent of negative publicity in Britain in the early to mid-1990s. Having engaged in a heavy recruiting drive at UK universities, HT found itself banned from British higher education campuses by the National Union of Students following accusations of anti-semitic activities. The group's mu'tamad in the UK at the time, Sheikh Omar Bakri Muhammad, emerged during this time as a controversial public figure, challenging all Muslims in the UK to adopt the pursuit of khilafah as the only possible course of Islamically authentic political action available to Muslims. Although its beliefs and program remained a minority tendency, the radical political position adopted by the group managed to effectively polarize the British Muslim community for a short period.[47] Seeking to label all who rejected the caliphate as Western collaborators—or in Bakri's terms, "chocolate Muslims"—HT prompted a vigorous debate about the political imperatives of Islam as a minority community. In 1996, after significant disagreements arose within the UK leadership of HT as to the theological basis for the group's political activities and the scope of its work, Bakri left the group to found the al-Muhajiroun movement. This latter organization, which Bakri styled as salafi (he sees HT as Ash'ari in its *aqeeda*) and closer in orientation to the jihadi worldview of Bin Laden, lasted until 2004 when it was abruptly closed down by its leader who later fled the country when Islamists began attracting increased attention from British law enforcement in the wake of the July 7, 2005 bombings in London. Severely discredited in the eyes of Muslims and non-Muslims alike, HT retreated from the public eye for several years, leaving the limelight in the UK to groups such as al-Muhajiroun. Attention to HT's activities increased again in the summer of 2001, but this time centered on Central Asia where reports had emerged of active cells organized out of Uzbekistan that authorities were trying to link with Al-Qaeda.[48] A vigorous debate ensued, particularly in Washington D.C. policy-making circles, as to whether HT members in Central Asia were involved in violence. Amongst sporadic but rarely corroborated reports to this effect, the International Crisis Group in 2003 issued a report indicating that there was no evidence to suggest that HT member had committed violent acts in the region. Although London remains an important site of fundraising, recruitment, and coordination for the group, HT's political activism seems increasingly to be focused elsewhere, with Pakistan, Indonesia, Jordan, and Palestine claimed as major areas of focus at the present time. The movement seems to be growing particularly quickly in Indonesia, where its leader Ismail Yusanto, has been active in organizing rallies. HT was banned in Germany in 2003 on account of engaging in anti-semitic activities.

Sources of support for HT vary considerably from context to context, and in this sense it is difficult to produce something like a profile of a "typical" party member. It has proven itself skilful in adapting its discourse to local conditions and at appealing to a wide range of particular grievances. In the early 1990s, for example, it was successful in recruiting among second and third generation South Asian immigrants in the UK, many of whom had been raised with a form of Islam they regarded as disengaged from worldly issues and political imperatives. Alienated by their parents' "culturally distorted" Islam (see above) and socially adrift in a society into which mainstream integration proved difficult, the discourse of radical resistance offered by HT appeared highly attractive. By placing khilafah—a marginal ideal at best in mainstream Muslim political thought—firmly at the center of its religious discourse, HT was able to take advantage of a relative lack of religious knowledge on the part of its young recruits. When asked about the extent of desire in the umma for a new caliphate, group members often give a general answer about Muslims desiring greater unity. When it is put to them that such a desire does not necessarily translate into support for khilafah, and that those seeking a political order based on Islam might prefer groups such as the MB (the most popular Islamist tendency in the Arab world), HT supporters tend to explain that Muslims will eventually realize that the correct political implementation of Islam must necessarily lead to khilafah.

So how, in HT's view, will this new caliphate come about? The party's political discourse begins by recognizing the lack of any "executive structure" in the Muslim world as a major problem and one that must, according to a shari'ah obligation impingent upon all Muslims, be rectified. In terms of its methods, it seeks to style itself as non-derivative in the sense that it does not study and emulate the approaches taken by previous Islamist movements. Instead, it seeks to go back to the basic legislative sources of the religion—the Qur'an, hadith, and usul al-fiqh. The correct method for establishing khilafah is fixed and can, it claims, be found in the shari'ah, but this should be distinguished from "means and style," which is necessarily specific to place and time. HT, at least in the UK, explains that its work is intellectual and political, and in this regard they reject militant methods. Realizing the close relationship between force and power, however, HT does speak of actively seeking *nussrah*—support from the armed forces or those responsible for security and public order—in countries where it operates, but claims that this is a form of activity controlled exclusively by the party's central leadership. While appealing to a young and generally well-educated audience, the group finds support for its program by simultaneously adopting a populist rhetoric designed to link socioeconomic disenfranchisement to religiosity. For example, HT's publicity literature in the UK defines capitalism as "the detachment of religion from life." Regarding the geographic scope of its activities, the group expresses a willingness to work anywhere and everywhere, but suggests that the caliphate has the best chance of being re-established in those lands where a precedent already exists (i.e. the Middle East and former Ottoman territories). While global khilafah remains the party's ultimate goal, it espouses a gradualist approach.

HT describes three general phases to its work. During the first of these, the "culturing" phase, the basic structure of the party is assembled and members are socialized into its beliefs, agenda, and worldview. Once it is on firm footing, the party can then move on to phase two, "interaction," which involves going out into society to explain the necessity of khilafah and call Muslims to support or join the party. The third and final phase, "seeking power," is where the most concerted use of nussrah is made in order to actually establish khilafah. HT formally rejects violence as a means to achieve political change and is committed—publicly at least—to pursue power exclusively through peaceful means. Privately, some members will indicate that at the very final stages of phase three, a "push" might be required to bring about an actual change in power, but they see this is something akin to a coup d'état (its impulse having arisen, presumably in the military via HT's nussrah) rather than any kind of jihad.

Widespread suspicion still obtains as to HT's involvement in or willingness to use violence, despite its claims to the contrary and the fact that no solid evidence exists to suggest that the party has ever employed militant tactics. There is, however, some evidence that points to former members of the party becoming involved in violence after leaving HT. For example, two former students of Omar Bakri Muhammad were recruited by HAMAS to carry out suicide attacks in Israel in 2003. This has led some to claim that regardless of whether HT itself espouses violence, its ideology and radical program constitute "waypoints" on the way to violence. Their fear is that members of the party more inclined toward immediate radical activism may become disillusioned with the party's "gradualist" approach and desert it in favor of the jihadi ranks.

HT's potential to evolve into a mass movement, which Al-Qaeda never did, is difficult to assess. There have been signs recently, however, that it is trying to broaden its appeal, particularly in the wake of 9/11 when it began to come back out into the open in the UK after a half-decade of relative quiet. There are signs that the movement has been on an active recruitment drive, trying to bring into its fold those Muslims who share Usama Bin Laden's critique of Western secular imperialism, but who reject his violent methods. HT, on this account, becomes the non-jihadi alternative route to world Islamic revolution. One of the obstacles to HT growing its membership beyond the young and overwhelmingly male "hotheads" who attended its angry rallies on British university campuses in the 1990s is the fact that for most Muslims (and certainly those in Europe), the caliphate was simply an issue to which they could not relate. They wanted an Islamic movement that would address the issues and problems they faced in their day-to-day lives rather than one that seemed to be narrowly obsessed with a vision of Islamic political utopia. To this end, after 9/11, HT in the UK seemed to change its tune considerably, at least in terms of its public image. It began participating in meetings and forums with other Muslim groups, including ones that HT in the 1990s under Omar Bakri Muhammad would never have considered communicating or collaborating with. There was also a short-lived effort to publish an Islamic lifestyle magazine, *Salam*, which folded after several issues. The name of the party never appeared on this publication and the caliphate was never covered in its pages. Rather it was trying to find new markets for HT by addressing issues such as multicultural marriage. In the reasoning of the leadership, the party—still trapped somewhere between phases 2 and 3 of its work plan—needed to find a voice and vision that would get people listening. Once people saw that the party was addressing issues they cared about, it stood to reason, they might become more interested in its political priorities. Many observers of British Muslim politics have dismissed this facelift and the appearance of a "kindler, gentler" HT as pure instrumentalism, claiming that the same old radical ideas lurk just below the surface.[49] Like many of the more radical movements operating in the UK, HT reduced its public profile considerably after the July 2005 London bombings.

How should we think about HT's breed of radicalism in comparison to that of Al-Qaeda? Bringing in a metaphor from the Bolshevik Revolution, we might think of HT as the advocates of "khilafah in one country" in contrast to the more "Trotskyite" Al-Qaeda, which favors continual world-wide jihad. Some among the leadership of these movements have also traveled ideologically over the course of their careers. HT's (and later al-Muhajiroun's) Omar Bakri Muhammad—a former member of the MB—has been fairly comfortably involved, it would seem, with a diverse range of political movements and doctrinal orientations. Looking at their overall political goals, however, certain common themes clearly arise. It can be said that both groups seek to render the worldviews of local Muslims more global, but not in a cosmopolitan, tolerant sense. Promulgating Islam as a higher order identity, would-be supporters are asked to de-emphasize national affiliations in the name of the umma and to understand the suffering of Muslims in other lands as their own—and as circumstances into which they are obliged by their religion to intervene. In this sense, the khilafist-jihadi agenda might be said to hold the greatest appeal for those whose sense of belonging is already in flux—those disjunct from mainstream society and somehow adrift. Radical Islamist discourses structured around a strong antagonism to prevailing social orders hence serve to crystallize political identities and affiliations. The clarity of vision and moral certainty of salafi Islam become more attractive to some than the indeterminacy and relativism of more moderate, pluralist approaches.

The political discourse of both groups also makes frequent use of the notion of kuffar ("unbelievers"; infidels) as a technique of moral othering. This is where the obsession with normative categories begins to take on a social reality. Non-Muslim others are figured as those beyond the pale of social responsibility. Although, contrary to popular belief, salafi discourse does not require Muslims to engage in armed conflict with kuffar wherever they may be found (unless they are themselves laying siege to Muslims—

which, today, in the view of many salafi groups they are); unbelievers are understood to be located outside the normative remit of social relations. By placing the unbeliever in a category of radical difference, the possibility of coexistence premised on cultural pluralism and political civility is precluded.

Looking ahead: future formations of radical Islam

Examined from a sociological perspective, as this chapter has shown, radical Islamist movements such as Al-Qaeda and HT do not appear to be that different from other organized social movements who participate in "contentious politics."[50] The same collectivization of discontent combined with processes of mobilization around opportunity structures and resource capabilities are clearly present here. The "micromobilization" of social capital as concentrated in small cells of like-minded individuals permits relationships of solidarity to be converted into mutually supporting activist units as "sentiment pools" coalesce around a more rigid and deployable political framework.[51] Some analysts have emphasized the sense in which salafi jihadis display some of the same characteristics as "new social movements." This label refers to "post-materialist" groups organized primarily around a common set of values or normative commitment—that is, a particular sense of "the good."[52] As Quintan Wiktorowicz puts it:

> Similar to many new social movements, the Salafis are attempting to build new identities and alternative norms that challenge dominant cultural codes, and in so doing they create an "imagined community" and networks of activists determined to reproduce and expand a particular interpretation of Islam. Such networks ... bypass traditional rule-making institutions, such as tribes or states, by creating endogenously produced sets of understandings about individual behavior and social interactions.[53]

Thus the Islamist radicals can be thought of as one example of a much broader category of "anti-systemic" social movement seeking to challenge the normative premises of the current world system, a point also made by Olivier Roy.[54] Where some groups focus on the socioeconomic dimensions of uneven resource distribution as a byproduct of the modern capitalist system, the radical Islamists associate the latter with an imperializing secularism that contravenes a social and political order they believe to be divinely sanctioned. This does not mean that Bin Laden and his ilk share the views or goals of, for example, various anti-globalization movements. Indeed, in many if not most regards, their views on social norms, permissible forms of activism and end goals are quite diametrically opposed. Rather we want to make the point that Al-Qaeda represents a highly extreme form of the more generally recognizable phenomenon of contemporary anti-systemic social activism.

What directions might radical Islam take in the future? Is it possible to discern today any new patterns in its organization and methods? How will its fortunes fare? Beginning with the last question, there are those such as Fawaz Gerges who argue based on considerable research that Al-Qaeda's fortunes as a social movement are on the decline. We have already discussed various negative reactions to Bin Laden's approach within the jihadi movement itself and the precipitous decline in recent years in popular support being expressed for the Al-Qaeda leader. Gerges contends that due to a number of factors, the international campaign against terrorism not withstanding, Al-Qaeda's recruitment pool has dried up severely in recent years. He also senses an ongoing "general realignment within the jihadist current against, not in favor of, Al-Qaeda and global jihad."[55] It seems that Bin Laden has had to rely on jihadi recruits of increasingly inferior quality as those with meaningful skills and experience trend away from the Al-Qaeda model. Some would cite the case of Abu Musab al-Zarqawi in evidence of this. Until killed by U.S. forces in 2006, Zarqawi had been the head of Al-Qaeda's operations in Iraq after the 2003 American invasion. Rather than having been handpicked for this task from among a pool of top candidates, Zarqawi more or less claimed the mantle of Al-Qaeda in Iraq for himself after operating independently for some time—with Bin Laden reluctantly acquiescing to the merger of Zarqawi's organization (al-Tawhid w'al-Jihad) into Al-Qaeda's overall structure. Zarqawi's reputation within jihadi circles was less that of a spiritual warrior and more a criminal thug prone to excessive violence. He became a figure of acclamation for the movement only after the United States cited his presence in Iraq as evidence of a non-existent partnership between Saddam Hussein and Al-Qaeda. Even then, Zarqawi's cult of personality only became a recruiting tool among very young, mainly Western, "wanna-be" jihadis rather than among the hardened activists, most of whom found him highly distasteful. Is the fact that Bin Laden could do no better than Zarqawi to run Al-Qaeda's operations in Iraq evidence that most of the radical activists have now deserted him? Does Bin Laden now rely mainly on amateurs?

It will take some time to discern how fatal the intra-jihadi debates, the U.S.-led war on terror, and the popular rejection of Bin Laden will prove to Al-Qaeda's fortunes. It is clear now, however, that he has not been able to mobilize the Muslim masses around his message. There may be those in the slums of various cities in the global south who wear t-shirts declaring Bin Laden to be a new Ché Guevara, but, as Gilles Kepel puts it, "Bin Laden has been unable to unify poor urban youth, the Muslim middle classes, and the Islamist intelligentsia into a coalition capable of repeating the only triumphant Islamic revolution the world has ever seen: the one that took place in Iran in 1979."[56] But does Bin Laden really need to mobilize the masses in order for the global jihadi movement to be considered successful? In comparison with the MB, Fawaz Gerges points out that Al-Qaeda "has no parallel supporting social, political, or educational institutions." "In comparison with the Brotherhood," he continues, "Al-Qaeda is a skeleton of an organization. Now it has been reduced to an ideological label, a state of mind, and a mobilizational outreach program to incite attacks world-wide."[57] But might we not by the very same token see this shift in Al-Qaeda's role as evidence of its durability albeit in a different form? In looking at global Islamic radicalism today, Olivier Roy sees two new trends emerging. The first he calls "franchising," whereby local groups with no affiliation or connection to Al-Qaeda undertake operations in the name of its general worldview; and the second involves transnational jihadis making common cause with other extreme "new social movements" such as the far-left and other radical anti-globalization groups.[58] It seems more likely however that Al-Qaeda would be more likely to join forces with those that also premise themselves on an exclusionary identity and a rigidly con-servative politics—a "coalition of the intolerant," in other words.

Beyond the scaled back and by now severely disrupted and somewhat disabled network described above, there are perhaps three ways that we might conceptualize Al-Qaeda today:

(1) *Al-Qaeda as ideology*: a worldview or mindset consisting of a general critique of the prevailing world system shared by a wide range of radical Islamist groups (some affiliated with Al-Qaeda, some not), and also a desire to actively strike at the perceived sources of global injustice and enforced secularism—mainly the United States and its allies.

(2) *Al-Qaeda as mythology*: the worldview described above can also be marketed as a legendary status symbol well after Al-Qaeda's own active career (or the life of its leader) has come to an end. The Al-Qaeda "brand name" continues to inspire not only radical Islamists, but all manner of popular anti-systemic movements who now have evidence, based on Al-Qaeda's example, that it is possible to mount successful attacks on the sources of world hegemony.

(3) *Al-Qaeda as technology*: Bin Laden's movement provides a basic model or template for networked organization and activism, aspects of which can be emulated by various "franchises" across various scales—local, national, regional, and global.

As ideology, mythology, and technology, then, it seems likely that some aspect of Al-Qaeda will continue to exert influence in radical Islamist circles even if and when its operational capacity is destroyed or disappears. The popular appeal of radical Islam, particularly in its activist variant, will continue to be limited to a very small and highly extreme minority of Mus-lims. Many of the symbols it champions and aspects of its overall critique, however, will still resonate more widely in the Muslim world. How will these views manifest themselves politically as we enter what some are calling a "post-Islamist" age, and just who in this complex environment speaks for Islam? These are questions that we will take up in the final chapter. In order to do so, however, we need to first realize that Al-Qaeda is not the only form of global Islam currently competing for Muslim hearts and minds. Muslim transnationalism occurs in a wide variety of forms today, and the real impact of Al-Qaeda cannot be understood without first situating it within the wider ecology of contemporary global Islamic networking and social movement.

8 Muslim transnationalism: brotherhoods, networks, diasporas

In the previous chapter we focused on a particular type of "deterritorialized" radical Islamic politics—certain groups whose goals and methods are not tied to any one country, but which seek to effect revolutionary change in multiple countries simultaneously, or in some cases to recover historical models of Muslim polity such as the caliphate. In recent years, and particularly in the aftermath of the attacks in the United States on September 11, 2001, the very notion of "transnational Islam" has tended to be associated with radical and militant agendas of this sort. In actual fact, the violent approach of groups such as Al-Qaeda represents but a very small percentage of Muslim transnational social and political activity. Transnational Islamic radicalism needs to be situated within a much broader ecology of global networking and transborder religious activism in the Muslim world. This chapter will survey the full range of contemporary Muslim transnationalism and will help the reader to better understand how and where various strands of local and global Muslim politics fit together. We begin with a brief historical overview of Muslim transnationalism that will permit us to appreciate how the movement of peoples and ideas across borders and territories has been an intrinsic part of Islamic history. We then move on to sketch a typology of various kinds of transnational actors and activities in the Muslim world and to explain the interplay between them. These include various governmental and nongovernmental organizations (NGOs), scholarly and educational associations, Sufi and pietistic networks, and a variety of diaspora and migrant communities. Several of these are then singled out for closer examination in terms of their significance for contemporary Muslim politics. The chapter ends with an exploration of several analytic themes that arise from our survey of Muslim transnationalism. To what extent does globalization make it possible today to speak in terms of a new umma? What is the nature of transnational Islam in terms of its tendency toward radical or moderate politics? Are we seeing a decline in the ability of the state to organize and control religious activism in Muslim majority countries? Is it possible to speak in terms of a distinctly Muslim approach to globalization? These are some of the questions the concluding section will hope to answer.

Before we begin our account, however, it would perhaps be useful to clarify a matter of terminology. This concerns our usage of the term "transnational." To many readers the terms transnational and international might be largely synonymous, but we are using them here in slightly different ways. For our purposes, "international" refers to interactions between two or more sovereign units in world politics, usually nation-states—hence *inter*-("between") *national*. It is thus primarily about state-to-state politics. Two countries signing a diplomatic treaty or deliberation by the members of the United Nations Security Council would count as examples of "international" relations according to our definition of that term. "Transnational" on the other hand refers to a wider range of social formations and transactions which are structured across the borders and spaces of nations, but which do not necessarily entail a primary role for sovereign governments. Examples of transnationalism include the activities of NGOs such as Amnesty International and Oxfam International which pursue a wide range of advocacy and programmatic work relating to, respectively, strengthening global adherence to human rights norms and the reduction of poverty and hunger worldwide. Transnational activities are not by any means limited to this kind of social change and development work. Profit-making entities— large corporations such as Coca-Cola and Nike—are organized transnationally, as are a wide range of professional associations (e.g. World Federation of Scientists), religious groups (e.g. the Lutheran World Federation), and sporting bodies (e.g. the International Mountain Bicycling Association). For our purposes, however, the distinction is particularly important to bear in mind because of our emphasis on viewing the Muslim world through a global perspective. Insofar as transnationalism provides a better way of understanding social formations organized across or beyond various territorial polities, it also provides a better account of Muslim politics under globalizing conditions.

A brief history of Muslim transnationalism

As Chapter 2 has already made clear, the rapid territorial expansion of Islam in the decades following the death of the Prophet Muhammad means that Muslim transnationalism has a history dating back to the time of the first caliphs. But before touching on various examples of Muslim transnationalism in history, we would do well to dwell for a moment on several aspects of Islamic theology and religious practice which already embody this concept. The first point to make here is that Islam, like Christianity, understands itself in *universalist* terms. This means that the message of, and participation in, Islam are open to all peoples regardless of ethnicity, nationality or race. The ability of Muslim states and empires to accommodate and integrate peoples of diverse cultural and national background was touched up at various points in Chapter 2. Muslims involved in propagating the religion (da'wa) have often emphasized the lack of importance

Islam places on racial and ethnic distinctions and the social hierarchies history has attached to them. Observers also point to various passages in key scriptural sources in emphasizing Islam's openness to lands and peoples beyond its origins in western Arabia. The Qur'an (49:13) itself seems to enjoin transnationalism when pointing out that people "were made into nations and tribes so that you may come to know each other." In praising the virtues of knowledge and education, the Prophet Muhammad in a famous hadith exhorts believers to travel far and wide—"even to China"— in search of learning. There is also an element of transnationalism built into the ritual observances of Islam. As we will recall from Chapter 2, one of the five pillars of Islam is the hajj—requiring all able-bodied Muslims who have it within their means to make the pilgrimage to Mecca once in the course of their lifetimes, regardless of their country of origin. In recent years performance of the hajj has brought some 2.5 million pilgrims to Saudi Arabia per annum. As we will see, there are also important social and political dimensions to hajj-related transnationalism.

Under the first caliphs, Islam, as we have seen, expanded rapidly beyond its relatively humble origins in western Arabia to encompass all of the Middle East and North Africa, Persia, and parts of southern Europe—most notably the Iberian peninsula. Over the coming centuries it would also spread into West and other regions of sub-Saharan Africa, the Indian subcontinent, much of Central Asia and across to the archipelagoes of Southeast Asia. While Islam's multinational empires were nominally united under a single caliph until the end of World War I, the caliph's effective political authority over the broad expanse of Muslim-majority and Muslim-ruled lands had declined significantly by the tenth century. While it became difficult to speak of the umma—that is, the community of believers, potentially global in scope—as a single polity, Muslim transnationalism in the Middle Ages was nonetheless thriving. The worlds of commerce and scholarship had combined by the thirteenth century to create within the Mediterranean Sea and the Indian Ocean a vibrant space of transnational exchange, linking merchant and scholar from Africa to Arabia and across to Persia, India and points further east.[1] This proto-global "world system" was sustained by the exchange of various goods and commodities within inter-regional trade networks.[2] The emergence of various centers of learning and academic excellence across the Muslim world (e.g. Cairo, Damascus, Samarqand) and the circulation of peoples and ideas between them turned the ulama into a sort of transnational "epistemic community," to borrow a term from international relations theory—that is, a professional class that had developed its own specialized methods and languages and, moreover, ones that could be recognized and used by anyone with the correct education and training regardless of nationality. The ulama were not the only social force in the Muslim world to travel across territorial boundaries, however. Many of the Sufi brotherhoods established in the first years of Islam had become thoroughly transnational entities by the fourteenth and fifteenth centuries as the cosmopolitan circuits of the Muslim world led devotees of particular sheikhs and orders to establish branches of the leading brotherhoods such as the Qadiriyya, the Naqshbandiyya, and the Chistiyya in distant lands.

The history of modern Muslim transnationalism begins in the middle of the eighteenth century with two figures whose importance lies not so much in their own transnational activities or provocations, but rather in their renewed emphasis on that which is universal in Islam as opposed to that which had entered the religion as a result of local custom and practice. Shah Walliullah and Muhammad Ibn Abdul Wahhab are both regarded as key figures within the movement commonly known as Islamic Revivalism (see Chapter 2). The essence of Islamic Revivalism lay in a spirit of purification that sought to remove from Islam those forms of innovation (bid'a)— understood by the Revivalists as corrupting distortions—which had entered religious practice by way of various local beliefs, customs and superstitions becoming conflated with "true" Islam. As scholars, and to some degree, as activists, the work of both of these figures was mostly confined to the Indian subcontinent and central Arabia, respectively. Their religious imaginations, however, certainly extended beyond the realms of the theological and spiritual insofar as both figures were directly concerned with aspects of more world affairs. Both were concerned with what they perceived as the decline of Islamic civilization vis-à-vis Europe and the West. Shah Walliullah was also concerned with what he saw to be the potential for the majority Hindus of India to challenge Muslim dominance in the subcontinent. Both saw the solution to Islam malaise as lying in a return to the Islam of the Qur'an and the Prophet's tradition. Shah Wali Ullah is also often cited as an important precursor in the movement to create a movement for pan-Islamic solidarity, although this was not initially conceived of in political terms.

A more avowedly cosmopolitan idiom of pan-Islamic thinking developed in the mid to late nineteenth century within the movement known as Islamic Reformism. The key figure here is Jamal al-Din al-Afghani. Like his Revivalist forebears, Afghani saw in the rise of European imperialism (and particularly in its economic and military prowess) evidence of Islam's decline. Likewise, he diagnosed the problem as one of Muslims turning away from the true essence of their religion. In Afghani's analysis, however, the ulama and traditional religious scholarship more generally was part of the problem. Arguing that Muslims possessed the same capacities for critical and scientific inquiry as the Europeans, and that modernity was wholly compatible with the precepts of their religion, Afghani enjoined Muslims to rediscover the cultural and intellectual dynamism inherent in Islam by reforming their approach to modern life. He saw Muslims and Muslim leaders (especially the ulama) as apolitical and detached from worldly affairs. Afghani argued that it was only through unity in their common Muslim identity that people across the many Muslim lands under European colonial rule would find their liberation—hence the name given to the political movement he founded, Pan-Islam. While Afghani traveled extensively throughout his career, finding followers and undertaking extensive advocacy and publishing activities through the Middle East and even Europe, the Pan-Islam movement never attracted a critical mass. For most Muslims, the idea of a common identity in Islam was too abstract to bridge continents of geographic, cultural, and political separations. Nationalist sentiment, as we have seen in Chapter 3, proved a far more powerful discourse of anti-colonial mobilization. With the abolition of the caliphate in 1924 and the failure during the inter-war years to revive any meaningful form of world Muslim leadership, the idea of transnational Muslim political unity fell into decline until the 1950s when it was revived by fringe political movements such as Hizb ut-Tahrir (HT) (see Chapter 7). Despite short bursts of popular appeal to pan-Islamic sentiment in the wake of events such as the Six Day War in 1967, the oil shock of 1974 and Iran's 1979 Islamic Revolution, transnational Islam during the Cold War has tended to be associated more with intergovernmental bodies (such as the Organization of the Islamic Conference, founded in 1969) and various state-sponsored initiatives (such as the Saudi-led Muslim World League)—both of which will be looked at in greater detail below.

Muslim transnationalism in the contemporary world

If we were simply to enumerate every aspect of Islam today that involved some measure of transnational interaction, we would produce an endless list and very little of analytical value. Given the high levels of interconnectedness across borders and the ease by which peoples and ideas cross large expanses of world-space today, even the most localized idioms of Islam are embedded and, inevitably, affected by broader global trends. So as to maintain the utility of "transnational Islam" as an analytic lens, therefore, this chapter's coverage will limit itself to those *forms of Muslims politics whose primary modes of organization and activism transcend the territorial boundaries of nation-states*—or those that are national or local in nature, but which also encompass an important transnational dimension. An example will help to provide further clarification here. The Tablighi Jama'at (TJ) (see below) is a pietist movement with strong roots in South Asia where it was founded, but maintains a presence in nearly every country with a Muslim population of any significant size. It primarily engages in itinerant da'wa activity and its annual gatherings attract hundreds of thousands from all over the Muslim world. We include it here as a prime example of transnational Islam. A group such as HAMAS (see Chapter 6), while embodying the broad Muslim Brotherhood (MB) ideology and receiving some measure of financial support from abroad, is focused almost exclusively on the Palestinian territories in terms of its organization and activism and therefore would not be regarded as an example of transnational Islam according to our definition.

Before moving on to outline a typology of contemporary transnational Islam, a few explanations and qualifications regarding the range of our coverage are in order. First, because they are of sufficient importance today to merit a chapter of their own (Chapter 7), transnational radical groups such as Al-Qaeda and HT have not been included. That said, some of the other forms of transnational Islam covered below are linked in various ways to global Islamic radicalism and where this is the case it will be indicated. Second, while we will not look in great detail at particular branches of the MB (such as HAMAS in Palestine or al-Nahda in Tunisia), we will look at the transnational dimensions of the MB movement as a whole and how its various layers of organization (national, regional, global) relate to one another, and how they have been evolving in recent years. Third, we should note that several of the examples we examine below, while they may be primarily transnational in terms of their organization, do at times pursue and support Muslim politics that have quite nationally or even locally defined goals. Conversely, a good many of the Muslim social and political movements pursuing national or even local goals do maintain transnational connections for purposes of eliciting support and funding and undertaking advocacy work. So, for example, much of the work of the Organization of the Islamic Conference (OIC) since its inception has been focused on the question of Palestine. And Hizbullah, while first and foremost a Lebanese political group, has also received significant funding from abroad, most notably from Iran and Syria. Fourth, one might reasonably question the inclusion in this chapter of various Muslim diaspora groups and migrant communities in the West since most of these understand their identities and politics in relation to the countries in which they now live, in some cases for several generations. They are included here for several reasons, among them the fact that their very presence in Europe and North America is itself part and parcel of the new transnational flow of peoples associated with globalization. In many cases we can also identify evolving patterns of relationships between diasporas and various groups and governments in their countries of origin. Within the younger generation of Muslims in the West, the search for more universalistic idioms of Islam also brings us close to various transnational themes. Finally, the reader will note that this chapter does not include any coverage of either the various transnational Muslim media forums (e.g. Al-Jazeera satellite TV or prominent websites such as Islam Online) or any of the individual scholars and activists who in recent years have sought to develop global constituencies for their ideas and to establish themselves as transnational authority figures. These two trends are important enough to merit a dedicated analysis and will therefore be taken up in detail in the next chapter.

The multiple forms of contemporary Muslim transnationalism

It would perhaps be useful at this point to provide a typology of contemporary transnational Islam. It is possible to identify perhaps seven distinct, broad categories of Muslim transnationalism today, several of which

subdivide into further types. It should also be noted that in a good number
of cases, broad areas of overlap and intersection between these categories
exist within individual groups and movements.

(a) "Traditional transnationalism": Sufi and pietistic networks

Sufi (mystical) networks, perhaps the most historically durable form of
Muslim transnationalism, have existed since the second century following
the death of the Prophet. These brotherhoods (tariqa; pl. turuq) have constituted important structures of social order in many Muslim societies
throughout various eras and have operated across borders for centuries.
Indeed, the most influential Sufi networks operating today—groups such as
the Naqshbandiyya and the Qadiriyya—have been around for at least five
centuries. Despite a relative decline in the Middle East during the nineteenth and early twentieth centuries in the face of orthodox revivalism,
Sufism has enjoyed a huge resurgence in recent years, most notably among
Muslim communities located in Europe and North America. We should
also note that during this period of relative dormancy in the Arab world,
the brotherhoods were thriving in regions such as Central, South and
Southeast Asia. During the latter part of the twentieth century various
waves of postcolonial migration and transnational labor patterns associated
with increased globalization have transplanted various Sufi orders and their
followers. The Naqshbandiyya order associated with the Cyprus-based
Sheikh Nazim, for example, can claim a widespread global following. A rich
set of transnational practices linking Britain and Pakistan has emerged
around the cult of the living saint Zindapir.[3] It is these more fluid, personal
and informal linkages, then, which provide an entry point for our discussion
of contemporary transnational Islam.

The brotherhoods generally display features associated with traditional
forms of social authority, such as the leadership of a charismatic, hereditary
sheikh who accepts an oath of allegiance and tutelage from a disciple
(murid). Most notable, perhaps, for its sheer social ubiquity, contemporary
Sufism penetrates all walks of life and often transcends class and clan. Its
influence, for example, is to be found in the public administration and private education of Turks via, respectively, the Adalet ve Kalkinma (AK)
Party and the Fethullah Gülen movement (see Chapter 4), the political
economy of Senegal through the Tijaniya brotherhood's ownership of the
peanut industry and the daily devotional and social lives of Muslim immigrant communities in the United Kingdom and the United States via
entrepreneurial Sufi networks looking to keep in step with expanding diasporas. New technologies of communication and travel have permitted the
centralized authority of traditional sheikhs to become thoroughly trans-
continental. It is not uncommon for the leaders of the brotherhoods today
to lead a highly itinerant existence, circulating constantly between global
headquarters, regional offices and the local lodge (zawiya) in many countries.

Another important phenomenon within this category of "traditional" transnationalism is the pietistic groups. These are best exemplified in the contemporary world by the TJ movement, first established in India in 1927.[4] Generally regarded as conservative traditionalists, Tablighis take it as their mission to encourage Muslims across the umma's many sub-communities to observe the tenets of faith and practice appropriate forms of worship. Wandering bands of TJ followers are often dispatched on da'wa missions by regional offices throughout the world—not seeking primarily to make conversions to Islam, but rather to renew the piety and assure the correct devotional practice of existing Muslims.

While the social significance of both Sufi networks and pietistic groups is clear in terms of their breadth of global reach and popularity, scholars differ as to the political significance of such movements. While the influence of Sufism as a socio-religious force has certainly been integrated into politics, economy and education (as alluded to above), the brotherhoods rarely take overtly political stances. Rather, they would be more likely to seek to widen their influence by gaining the interest and eventual membership of local leaders and opinion-makers. The TJ, likewise, describes itself as an apolitical organization whose orientation eschews the machinations of power and wealth. The vast majority of its followers hold to this ethos. There have nonetheless been instances in which followers on the margins of TJ have become involved with political activists organized through the religious seminaries (mainly in South Asia) in which TJ's religious conservatism was initially articulated. Others have argued that while most Tablighi followers may not themselves become involved in politics, the work they perform in terms of heightening religious consciousness can often serve to "prime" the way for Islamists to emerge.[5] The founder of TJ, Muhammad Ilyas, was himself a great admirer of Abu'l-A'la Mawdudi (see Chapter 3) and understood his Tablighi work to complement that of the Islamists.

(b) Broad-based Islamist ideologies

In contrast to the mystical and politically quietist tendencies described above, we can identify several broad intellectual and ideological tendencies that emerged in the Muslim world during the twentieth century and which today continue to animate several of the more activist and politically engaged (hence "Islamist") movements and individuals to follow in subsequent categories. Olivier Roy speaks of two key ideological trends in twentieth-century Islamism: the Jamaat al-Ikhwan al-Muslimin or MB (est. 1928) movement out of Egypt, and the Jama'at-i Islami (JI; est. 1941) trend out of Pakistan (regarding both, see Chapter 3).[6] These differ primarily in terms of the audiences to which they have tended to appeal rather than in their intellectual and programmatic substance—although one can certainly speak about different areas of emphasis in each. The Sunni Arab world has proved most fertile for MB thinking, with branches of Hasan al-Banna's original Egyptian group established throughout the Middle East by the late 1980s. Some of these offshoots—such as HAMAS in Palestine, al-Nahda in Tunisia and the National Islamic Front (al-Jabha al-Islamiya al-Qawmiya) in Sudan went on to become prominent Islamist parties within their respective national settings.

The JI, by contrast, has been most prevalent among South Asians and members of South Asian immigrant and diaspora communities—meaning that its influence is to be found primarily in Pakistan, India, East Africa, the Caribbean, and the United Kingdom. The JI has been very closely associated with the ideas of Abu'l-A'la Mawdudi and it is fair to say that in many cases followers have come to the movement through an encounter with his ideas rather than the other way around. The Islamic Foundation (est. 1973) in Leicester in the UK, for example, began life as a JI publishing offshoot seeking to make Mawdudi's writings available to the rapidly growing South Asian Muslim diaspora in England. Since then it has moved on to embrace themes and approaches outside the JI canon, but still maintains close leadership ties with the central party in Pakistan.

There is an important point to be made about the distinction between, for example, the MB or its various branch chapters as organizational entities and what we might term "Muslim Brotherhoodness" as the description of a broad and prominent intellectual orientation which produces a diverse range of actual political platforms and agendas in the Arab world and beyond. It is possible to look at individual national branches of the Brotherhood and to understand their positions and actions in the context of the domestic political landscape of, say, Jordan or Egypt. The MB does indeed possess an international coordinating body, the Tanzim al-Alami, and it is rumored to have a disproportionate number of Egyptian members on its executive committee. The Tanzim, however, is not a formal centralized control mechanism. Its deliberations reflect the varying priorities of its regional and national affiliates. In Europe, for example, there has been ongoing tension between leadership figures within the Muslim Association of Britain (the UK's MB affiliate) and the Federation of Islamic Organizations in Europe (FIOE), the Brotherhood's regional umbrella for Europe. Where the former has sought to become more directly engaged in politics and protest around U.S. and British foreign policy, the FIOE has sought to advocate more of a public education approach to the MB agenda. So while the Tanzim certainly works to advance the broad cause of the Brotherhood movement across the world, it is not able to impose the will of Cairo on MB branches in other countries. Politics within the Tanzim tend to reflect the diversity of its membership.

"Muslim Brotherhoodness" or the MB "way," on the other hand, is not coterminous with the policies or activities of anyone or even the aggregate of these individual parties. Rather, the intellectual milieu of the MB is a more generic worldview that emphasizes the social distinctiveness of

Muslims, the importance of public religion and a broad model for socio-political mobilization. It does not in and of itself necessarily lead to calls for the establishment of Islamic states or political/legal orders based on religion—although this is certainly a route taken by many of its more prominent exponents over the years.

Likewise, the essentials of the JI program were formulated in the context of Muslims living as minorities in British India and so its initial impulses—like those of the MB—were simultaneously about decrying Western interference in the Muslim world while seeking to define a distinctive public role for religion in society. The distinction between the general tendencies and the organizational manifestations of these two broad approaches is a crucial one to make in order to avoid the assumption that all movements or leaderships that have at one time been influenced by the MB share the goals of Egypt's MB party.

(c) NGOs: charities, da'wa groups, and advocacy networks

Within the Muslim world can be found a broad range of organizations whose nature and purpose correspond very closely to the conventional model of NGOs – that is, non-profit entities formally independent of state control organized around advocacy of a particular issue or agenda. It is also worth mentioning that most NGOs operate according to a formal constitution or a set of by-laws, and do not—unlike various Islamist parties—generally seek to obtain political power. For the sake of clarity, it is most useful to emphasize the issue of advocacy and the formally constituted structure of these groups in order to differentiate them from other manifestations of transnational Islam. Muslim movements that operate under the NGO rubric represent a vast range of interests and normative programs, many of which—as will be seen—are at odds with each other.

Muslim transnational NGOs might be seen to subdivide into four additional categories:

(1) *Humanitarian and charity organizations* such as Islamic Relief Worldwide (IRW) and Muslim Aid, that offer disaster relief and development assistance throughout the world, generally with an emphasis on those areas in which large numbers of Muslims are present. Both organizations have headquarters in the UK, but maintain field offices and engage in programming throughout the Muslim world. Like their Christian counterparts (e.g. Lutheran World Relief), these charities cite a religious basis and inspiration for saving lives and providing humanitarian assistance, but generally operate along the same lines and according to the same standards as "secular" relief organizations such as Save the Children. Both Muslim Aid and IRW, for example, are signatories to the 1994 Code of Conduct for the International Red Cross/Crescent Movement and NGOs in Disaster Relief, and both maintain varying levels of affiliation with relevant United Nations bodies and nongovernmental coordinating agencies in the UK.

(2) *Da'wa and Islamic solidarity organizations* such as the Rabitat al-Alam al-Islami or Muslim World League (MWL, est. 1962) and the Nadwa al-Alamiya lil-Shabab al-Islami or World Assembly of Muslim Youth (WAMY, est. 1972). These groups both maintain offices in a wide range of Muslim-majority countries and also in nations with significant Muslim minorities, such as the United States and Canada. Their emphasis is primarily on da'wa activities, seeking to promote Islamic teachings and provide religious information to Muslims as well as to present the religion to non-Muslims. Some national branches of the MWL have also become involved in the establishment and organization of Islamic schools in various countries. As its name suggests, WAMY's work focuses primarily on global Muslim youth culture and Islamic solidarity amongst young Muslims. To this end they organize regular international football tournaments, educational exchange programs, and Muslim scouting camps. While MWL and WAMY are formally non-governmental entities, most observers cite strong Saudi connections in both cases.[7] The Secretary General of MWL, for example, is always a Saudi and it is believed that the programmatic agendas of both organizations are strongly influenced by the Kingdom—leading some to raise questions about the extent to which the Islamic solidarity they promote is confined to the strongly salafi-Wahhabi variant of Islam found within the Saudi establishment. In this regard, it might be said that these organizations display certain of the characteristics described under the state-sponsorship category below.

(3) *Issue advocacy groups* such as Women Living Under Muslim Law (WLUML). WLUML was founded in 1984 in response to a number of incidents in which women across several countries saw their rights (defined by WLUML primarily according to universal human rights standards) denied in the name of implementing "Muslim law." WLUML uses this latter term to emphasize the extent to which religious jurisprudence in the Islamic world is often derived from multiple human (hence "Muslim") interpretations of divine essence ("Islam"). Although WLUML has no formal secretariat, it maintains an international coordination office in London and major regional outlets in Pakistan and Nigeria. Its model of operations corresponds very closely to what some scholars of international relations have termed "transnational advocacy networks."[8] Like other rights-based organizations such as Amnesty International, WLUML operates an alert and information service to publicize instances of women's rights being denied in the name of religious law. The group's regional affiliate in Nigeria was closely associated, for example, with the international profile that developed around the case of Amina Lawal, a woman sentenced to be stoned to death for adultery in 2002—a conviction that was later overturned. WLUML also produce publications and educational materials in a variety of languages, which aim to provide basic information about rights and advice for women about how to handle situations of legal discrimination. While WLUML does not identify itself as a Muslim organization per se, many of the affiliates within its network certainly do

and, moreover, some of them do articulate their arguments for women's rights using the language of shari'ah and Islamic symbols.

(4) *Scholarly networks* such as the International Institute for Islamic Thought (IIIT) and the faculty and alumni networks associated with institutions such as the International Islamic University Malaysia (IIUM). IIIT was established in 1981 as a transnational Islamic "think-tank" and a forum for encouraging research and scholarly publication in areas relating to the advancement of Islamic thought. With headquarters in Herndon, Virginia outside Washington D.C., IIIT has developed a global intellectual agenda around the "Islamization of knowledge," hosting numerous conferences, mainly in the United States and the Middle East, and publishing a wide variety of books on this theme. The Institute operates branch offices in various Muslim countries, including Egypt, Indonesia, Pakistan, Jordan, and Nigeria, while its headquarters receives delegations of visiting scholars from Central Asia, the Balkans, and the Philippines.

The IIUM was established in 1982 through the sponsorship of eight member countries of the Organization of the Islamic Conference (OIC; see below) as a global resource for tertiary Islamic education. Based just outside Kuala Lumpur, Malaysia, IIUM offers a wide range of degree programs across multiple faculties and disciplines and its faculty and students (including a fair number of non-Muslims) represent the full diversity of the umma. It has evolved into an important site for pan-Islamic networking, and a space in which multiple nationally and culturally mediated interpretations of Islam mingle. That said, the academic programs at IIUM have tended to advance a fairly orthodox agenda in terms of religious knowledge, reflecting a general tendency toward religious conservatism in the university's sponsoring countries and host nation. Similar institutions exist in Pakistan (the International Islamic University in Islamabad), Saudi Arabia (the University of Medina), and—of course—the great forbearer of Islamic educational cosmopolitanism, Al-Azhar University in Cairo, Egypt. Al-Azhar, founded in the late tenth century, is the oldest university in the world still in operation.

One further notable example within this category would be the transnational education network organized around the Turkish populist preacher and religious entrepreneur, Fethullah Gülen (see Chapter 9). The Gülen movement embodies elements of Sufi personal renewal and orthodox pietism combined with an emphasis on modern education and development. Drawing on the teachings of the early twentieth-century reformer Bediüzzaman Said Nursi and the subsequent Nurçu movement, Gülen has sought to combine Islamic ethics with modern (secular) education. His works consist of a number of books that are closely read by his followers and disciples and, more concretely, an attempt to export his distinctive model of the Muslim society via a vast network of schools stretching from Central and Southeastern Europe throughout Central Asia. These schools are based on a secular curriculum of arts, sciences and foreign languages, but the teachers in the schools are generally members of the Gülen movement. The outward persona of the movement (and the curriculum in the schools) is secular and nationalist, but the religious basis upon which it rests consists of a fairly standard and conservative reading of Sunni Islam. The teaching of religion per se is hence not a primary priority for the Gülen movement. Rather it seeks to achieve social reform by offering an alternative track for elite education—taught by Gülen movement members who embody the Islamic model in their personal and professional comport—with the hope that its alumni will end up in positions that enable them to bring about religious reform. Some have seen in this a form of crypto-Islamism, but all evidence to date suggests that Gülen's movement represents an entrepreneurial approach to "grassroots" social reform by way of personal piety in the context of a country in which the public space in which "religious movements" can operate is severely circumscribed.[9]

(d) Intergovernmental organizations

The major Islamic intergovernmental association is the OIC, founded in 1969 as a multilateral forum in which Muslim-majority countries could discuss and find solutions for issues of import to the wider Muslim world. Although often billed as a space of pan-Islamic unity, individual state interests have generally dominated OIC debates whenever issues of geopolitical substance have come before the organization. A notable exception would be the aftermath of the 1973 Arab-Israeli war, where the OIC emerged to speak with a relatively unified voice. The organization is loosely modeled on the United Nations and, indeed, its institutional structure mirrors certain aspects of the latter organization. The OIC, like the UN, possesses a number of specialized agencies and affiliated bodies such as the Islamic Educational, Scientific and Cultural Organization (ISESCO), whose mission is modeled on UNESCO but with an emphasis on issues of Islamic culture. Another specialized organ, the Islamic Development Bank (est. 1975), provides financing for development projects in the Muslim world that adhere to the principles of Islamic banking and economics. The OIC holds regular meetings at a variety of levels up to head-of-state, but has tended over the years to become identified more with the rhetoric rather than the practical implementation of Islamic unity. With many of the organization's key bodies headquartered in Saudi Arabia, the OIC's history has also served as a useful vantage point from which to observe the evolution of relations between the "core" and "periphery" of the Muslim world, and the competition for influence of various Muslim powers (e.g. Iran, Saudi Arabia, and Pakistan).

(e) State sponsorship of Islamist activism and religious propagation

Individual countries in the Muslim world have also been involved in promoting various aspects of transnational Islam in the contemporary period.

Saudi sponsorship of organizations such as the MWL and provision of funds for a wide range of Islamic causes abroad (including groups such as HAMAS) are well known. The Kingdom has also financed the building of mosques and religious schools (madrasas) throughout the Muslim world—with varying levels of strings attached in terms of what kind of Islam gets propagated through these channels. This phenomenon is often cited as evidence that the Saudi state has actively promoted the spread of its own highly literalist and ultra-conservative brand of "Wahhabi" Islam. Often however, the transnational circulation of these funds is more directly tied to a host of relatively autonomous Islamic charities that have operated out of the Kingdom with very little regulatory oversight by the Saudi government. That said, it is indeed the case that some of this money has been channeled under the direct auspices of members of the Saudi royal family. Large amounts of Saudi-sourced funds also end up in the hands of charities and pious foundations (awqaf) whose activities are solely of a humanitarian nature. Iran and Pakistan have also sought to sponsor and channel funding to co-religionists abroad, in the name of both geopolitical interest and sectarian unity. One can think here of Tehran's support for groups such as Hizbullah in Lebanon and various Shi'i entities in Iraq post-2003 and Pakistan's support for insurgent movements in Afghanistan during the 1990s and in Kashmir over several decades.

Central Asia: "Official Islam" and its many alternatives

Since the early 1990s, Islam has emerged—however unevenly—as a potent political force in the Muslim-majority states of the Former Soviet Union (FSU). During the decades of Soviet rule, it is important to note, Islam never disappeared completely, despite the Communist Party's strong aversion to religion. Rather, Moscow sought to reorganize and harness the power of Islam for its own geopolitical purposes—e.g. gaining Cold War support from other Muslim nations in the Middle East and elsewhere. Although most mosques were effectively closed down or diverted to other uses, many aspects of religion continued to be present in the rhythm and culture of everyday life in Central Asia. The social roots of the Sufi brotherhoods were particularly strong in the region, and not easily eradicated—even by the mighty Soviet state.

The post-Soviet period saw an inevitable renewal in Central Asian religious life, but this has assumed many forms. Many of the "official muftis" of the communist period sought similar accommodations with the post-independence political elites, serving as the new conduits of state-sanctioned Islam. Other groups sought a more ambitious social and political role for religion, advocating various forms of Islamism, and some settings—most notably Uzbekistan and Tajikistan—have seen radical Islamists engaged in violent attempts to overthrow regimes. Groups such as the Islamic Renaissance Party (IRP), HT (see Chapter 7), and the Islamic Movement of Uzbekistan (IUM)—represent these various strategies.

Central Asia has also become the target of a wide range of Islamization efforts originating from outside the region. Significant amounts of Saudi money poured in to support mosque-building efforts after the Soviet Union fell in 1991, and various Turkish groups—including representatives of the state *Diyanet* (see Chapter 4)—have also sought influence among their linguistic kin in Central Asia. Most notably, the movement around the popular preacher-teacher Fethullah Gülen (see elsewhere in this chapter) has opened a number of schools throughout Central Asia and these enjoy considerable popularity—prompting some governments in the region to view them with suspicion despite the group's moderate orientation.

(f) Hajj and the politics of pilgrimage

Hajj, the pilgrimage to the holy sites of Mecca, is a religious obligation concomitant upon all Muslims of able body and means once during their lifetimes. Hajj traditionally occurs during the final month of the Islamic calendar, Dhu al-Hijjah, in the run-up to the *Eid al-Adha* ("Feast of the Sacrifice"), one of the two major Muslim holidays. Some Muslims also undertake a pilgrimage to Mecca outside the framework of the hajj rites, and this is known as *umra* (often called the "lesser pilgrimage"). The hajj today brings over two million Muslims to Mecca each year. The number of pilgrim-sending countries involved has grown steadily over the last decades, from 25 nations in the 1950s to 75 countries today. The size of the annual gathering and more specifically the size of individual national contingents has ebbed and flowed depending on the geopolitical (and meteorological) climate. Another important factor has been the state of bilateral relations between pilgrim-sending countries and Saudi Arabia, under whose auspices the hajj takes place. While the importance of the hajj lies primarily in its immense symbolic force, this is also the very reason for its political significance. As we will see, it has played an important role in the course of domestic politics within pilgrim-sending countries, as well as in the international relations between key Muslim nations.

There are perhaps three key areas in which we can identify a clearly political dimension to the hajj, and also a fourth aspect that relates to the wider themes of globalization and commodification. The first of these pertains to the domestic politics of countries that send large number of pilgrims each year. Most of the key nations here—such as Pakistan, Malaysia, Indonesia, Nigeria, and Turkey—have established official state agencies to oversee the hajj process and to enforce relevant national policies relating to the annual gathering. The hajj has also become more overtly politicized through the introduction of various subsidies and regional quota systems by political actors seeking to obtain or maintain positions of power. By offering to absorb part or all of the costs associated with the expensive and often arduous trip to Saudi Arabia, some politicians have been accused of peddling promises of enhanced spirituality for political gain. Likewise, the practice of awarding disproportionate numbers of places in a country's annual pilgrimage quota to politically sensitive regions and constituencies has been seen as an attempt to curry political favor among voters and notables. Another dimension to the domestic politicization of the hajj can be seen in the embrace of hajj symbolism and imagery by the leadership of unpopular or failing regimes seeking to buttress their legitimacy. One of the clearest examples of this can be seen in the case of the former Indonesian president Suharto who, in 1990, seeking to rehabilitate his image and enhance his credentials in the eyes of the more religiously inclined, undertook pilgrimage amongst considerable pageantry and a media blitz. For several weeks, Indonesian television screens were full of images of Suharto wearing the ihram garment and mingling as a simple, humble pilgrim—one Muslim among a million of his equals. This occurred at a time when his government and also his family were both under considerable scrutiny in connections with charges of nepotism. We might interpret the 1999 election year hajj enthusiasm of his fellow Southeast Asian ruler, Malaysia's Mahathir Mohammad, in much the same way. Several other leaders of otherwise highly secular regimes in the Muslim world have also found it politically expedient at times to cloak themselves in the symbolism of pilgrimage when seeking to emphasize their connectedness to the common people or their religious credentials.

A second political dimension of the hajj relates to international politics, and more specifically relations between key nations within the Muslim world. Much of this politicking is centered on Saudi Arabia which, since World War II, has exercised overall managerial authority over the hajj process as the sovereign state in which Mecca and the holy sites are located. Much of the growth in hajj attendance from the 1950s onwards reflected the changing economic fortunes of newly decolonized states—particularly in those oil-producing nations now capable of sending greater number of pilgrims each year. Regional politics did certainly enter into the picture however, such as during the period of increased hostility between Egypt and Saudi Arabia over Yemen in the 1960s.[10] Since two countries neighboring the Kingdom, Egypt and Yemen had traditionally sent a larger proportion of pilgrims each year than many countries further afield, their absence from the hajj was clearly reflected in terms of absolute attendance during these years. During its period of unchallenged authority over the entire hajj system through the 1960s, Saudi Arabia used the annual event of the pilgrimage as a "hosting opportunity" to lobby for its foreign policy objectives among other Muslim states. In 1962, for example, at the height of

Egyptian-Saudi rivalry, King Faisal of Saudi Arabia used the occasion of the pilgrimage to seek a fatwa from the ulama condemning socialism—a central component of Gamal Abdel Nasser's Pan-Arabist ideology.[11] The hajj was also an important forum through which the Kingdom cultivated support for the creation of the OIC.[12] Once the OIC was in place, however, a new regime for hajj management was created within it, and Saudi Arabia found itself having to cede some measure of control over the pilgrimage. In particular, the Saudis found themselves having to rely more and more on the support of other major Sunni powers within the OIC in order to check the influence wielded by Iran in the wake of the Islamic Revolution of 1979.[13] This involved the placement of strict quotas on the number of pilgrims coming from Iran as Riyadh sought to suppress the potential spread of revolutionary Shi'ism to other Muslim countries—particularly after unrest during the 1987 pilgrimage was linked to Tehran.

Which brings us to the third aspect of hajj politics—the potential for increased networking and transnational social mobilization to develop out of contacts made between Muslims from different countries during the hajj. While a number of important public intellectuals and social activists—among them Malcolm X in the United States and Ali Shariati in Iran—have cited the transformative effects performing hajj had on their sociopolitical consciousness, there has been little evidence to suggest that the hajj itself has served as a space for significant transnational political mobilization amongst Muslims. We have seen, however, that the Saudi authorities feared exactly this effect in the wake of Iran's Islamic revolution, which was itself followed very shortly by the seizure of the Grand Mosque in Mecca by internal religious dissidents during the hajj season in 1979 (see Chapter 5). The Saudis expressed similar concerns about potential protests and political activity during the hajj in early 2002 in the context of the highly charged atmosphere created by the September 11, 2001 attacks in the United States. While many participants have expressed a renewed sense of Muslim unity and umma-consciousness after participating in the hajj, others have observed the persistence of strong national and racial divisions during the pilgrimage.[14]

Finally, it is interesting to note some of the ways in which the hajj has evolved into a micro world economy unto itself. Over the last few decades travel services specializing in hajj packages have been established throughout the Muslim world, and a good many of these are subject to strict regulation by the national hajj management agencies in the countries in which they operate. Various levels of service are available, including "first class" packages that include expedited passage through Saudi immigration, deluxe local accommodations, and air-conditioned rest stops throughout the various stages of the pilgrimage rites. Indeed, after oil, the hajj is the second largest source of revenue for Saudi Arabia, bringing in some $10 billion annually. The "hajj economy"—increasingly a perennial rather than a seasonal phenomenon—also represents a significant portion of GDP in other countries such as Nigeria, Malaysia, and Pakistan.

(g) Muslim diaspora and migrant communities in Europe

With a combined Muslim population of over 20 million, Europe is an increasingly important part of the umma.[15] Although significant attention has been paid to Muslim communities in the West only in the last few years, there have been Muslim communities present in Europe for several hundred years—but in particularly large numbers from the 1960s as a result of various waves of postcolonial migration from South Asia, North Africa, and Turkey (representing the regions of origins for the majority of the Muslim populations of Britain, France and Germany, respectively). The first generation of European Muslims tended to live fairly isolated existences, ghettoized in peri-urban neighborhoods around large cities in Northern England, Paris and Marseille in France, and Berlin in Germany. These communities were usually also at the bottom of the labor chain and found themselves subject to considerable racial discrimination. The problem was exacerbated by considerable disunity within the Muslim community as well. Islam was not, at this time, a common focal point of identity. So while in the British context, for example, there were distinct communities of Pakistanis, Bangladeshis (after 1973), Indian Muslims, Yemenis, Lebanese and Iraqis, they tended to socialize only within their own ethno-national and sometimes even provincial circles. Even within the large South Asian community there were at least two distinct Muslim orientations that split the more conservative Deobandis from the more Sufi-influenced *Barelwis*. Mosque services tended to be run by one or another ethno-sectarian group rather than becoming a focal point for the emergence of a common British Muslim identity.

The differentiated composition and diverse experience of Muslims in various European countries makes it difficult to speak about Islam in Europe in monolithic terms. In each of the three major countries (France, Germany, UK) the varying circumstances surrounding the arrival of Muslim communities and the distinct national traditions of secularism and church-state relations have made for varying different experiences. In France, for example, the strong tradition of laïcisme—a form of secularism that stresses a strict division between religion and public life—has created considerable controversy around a number of Muslim practices and beliefs. In 2004 this resulted in the passing of a law banning the wearing of ostentatious religious or proselytizing symbols (the Muslim headscarf being treated here as a religious symbol) in public schools. This can be contrasted with the situation in the UK. While British Muslims have certainly faced their share of challenges, the British version of secularism has tended to focus more on issues of multifaith tolerance and Muslims in the UK have faced relatively little pressure from the government to conform with particular norms. In Germany the Muslim population arrived initially as *gastarbeiter*, with the assumption that they would return to Turkey after several years. This makes the first generation of Muslims in Germany the one European Muslim community that might accurately be described as a diaspora

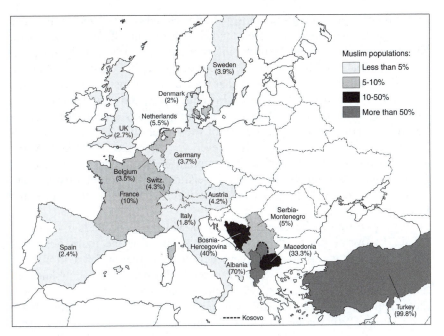

Map 3 Muslim communities in Europe
Source: Courtesy of BBC.

in the sense of a population outside its homeland seeking eventually to return there. Germany's citizenship laws, which have tended to emphasize genetic descent over culture or tenure of residency, have made it difficult for many Turks who arrived as guest workers to acquire full citizenship rights. This can be contrasted with the cases of France and Britain, where the majority of the Muslim population are full citizens.

This last point is important insofar as it reminds us of the fact that for a great many of Europe's Muslims, and particularly within the younger generation, Europe is their home. Many European Muslims understand their identity as much, if not more so, in British, French, or Dutch national terms than in relation to any kind of larger Islamic affiliation. Many have sought to develop distinctively European idioms of Islam, or "hyphenated" identities that encompass their comfort with multiple cultural vernaculars. Generational differences are particularly important within the European context. In Britain, for example, it became possible to identify from the mid-1990s a generation of young Muslims who had become largely disillusioned with what they saw as the introverted and culturally tainted "village Islam" of their parents. This was an approach to religion that, in their eyes, was more interested in abstruse debates about the minutiae of devotional rites than it was concerned with the day-to-day challenges of growing up in a multicultural society. They rejected their parents' tendency to seek religious services from imams and ulama "imported" from their countries of origin rather than from home-grown mosques and scholars—a tendency reinforced by the ghettoized lives they often tended to lead, cut off from mainstream European society. Young Muslims interpreted their parents' religious practice as one that tried to pretend they were still living in Pakistan, or Algeria, or Turkey, rather than recognizing that their new circumstances demanded a new form of religious imagination. In many cases, the younger generation turns away from religion altogether, becoming largely secular. And herein lies an important point—that not all of those identified as European Muslims necessarily identify primarily or even very strongly with Islam. Many are "Muslim" in the sense of having an ethno-national background from a Muslim majority country. To view this segment of the community through the lens of Islam or to project Islam onto them would be quite problematic in analytical terms.

Turning to those who do self-identify as Muslims, one finds a variety of trends. In overall terms we might say that amongst the more observant within the younger generation there developed a search for a more universalist form of Islam that would transcend ethnosectarian squabbling and factionalism. In some regards it might be compared with the reformist movement associated historically with figures such as Afghani and Abduh (see Chapter 2) that sought to make Islam relevant to contemporary social and political exigencies rather than remaining beholden to clerical obscurantism. While on the face of it the search for a new Islamic universalism might seem to point toward a more pluralistic and tolerant form of Islam— and, indeed, this is certainly one important dimension of this movement—it is possible to identify a range of sociopolitical responses within the Muslim communities of Europe to the circumstances they have faced in recent years and how these relate to wider geopolitical and transnational concerns. For some universalism is understood to mean the compatibility of Islam with the common values and norms found in other moral systems and faith traditions—leading to greater pluralism and tolerance. For others, however, the search for Islamic universalism leads to a hardened and literalist emphasis on the core tenants of "true" Islam (often salafi in orientation—see Chapter 7) and, politically, toward global Muslim polities.

These two positions represent the extremes of a much wider spectrum. For purposes of establishing some ideal-type categories, we might more usefully speak of three broad sociopolitical orientations to be found among European Muslims today:

(1) Pluralists: tend to be most comfortable with the co-presence of multiple value systems and faith communities in the same country; also generally more open to the idea of multiple interpretations of Islam. While taking a special interest in "Muslim issues" (broadly defined), this group tends in its politics to vote for and support mainstream political parties. Muslim and European national identities are equally important and wholly compatible; civic duty and active participation as citizens encouraged.

(2) Communitarians: believe that it is possible to achieve accommodations that will allow them to live amongst non-Muslims; multiple interpretations of Islam are possible, but only within certain parameters prescribed by tradition; preference for socializing within Muslim circles and, while sometimes voting for mainstream parties, may pursue what they see as "Muslim rights" (relating to e.g. personal status laws). More adamant communitarians may seek to establish Muslim parties. Muslim identity usually seen as primary.

(3) Radicals: reject the possibility of coexistence with non-Muslims in the same polity and work to bring about a fundamental change (non-violently or violently) to the prevailing political order—either by establishing Islamic states in Europe, or by reviving a global caliphate; narrow and literalist understanding of Islamic sources with little room for multiple interpretation; actively seek to set themselves apart from non-Muslims and even other Muslims who do not share their views. These groups are covered in greater detail in Chapter 7.

The reality of Muslim sociopolitical life in Europe is obviously more complicated than these categories can hope to capture. There are large groups of Muslims who fall between these categories, or who hold views and exhibit behaviors relating to more than just one of them; in short, there is considerable overlap and many shades of grey at work here. As regards how these various orientations are reflected in organizational terms, we once again find a considerable range of activity. Efforts to establish national Muslim organizations in European countries date back to the late 1960s, but very few of these were initially able to gain much traction due to the ethnosectarian divisiveness cited above. In recent years however, participation and support has consolidated around a number of groups, most notably in the British and French contexts. For the most part these are not political groups, but rather representative bodies—although some of them do maintain varying levels of affiliation with particular sectarian or Islamist views. In Germany, for example, where most Muslims are of Turkish origin, we have seen considerable competition in recent years between the Diyanet, representing "official" Turkish secular Islam, and Milli Gorus, strongly influenced by the Islamist current in Turkey (see Chapter 4).

In the UK, the main organization is the Muslim Council of Britain (MCB), founded in 1997. An umbrella body representing some 400 groups, the MCB has served in recent years as the Muslim community's central interlocutor with the British government—leading some Muslims to criticize it as becoming too intimate with officialdom. Other critics, however, view the MCB as too conservative in its views and beholden to an older generation of Deobandi and salafi-influenced leaders. This has prompted attempts to establish more liberal alternatives, such as the British Muslim Forum, established in 2005. Two other important groups in the UK are the Muslim Association of Britain (widely seen as affiliated with the MB and predominantly Arab in terms of its membership), and the Al Khoei Foundation, which serves as a voice for the Shi'a minority among British Muslims. While the MCB has certainly been the government's main point of contact regarding issues relating to Muslims—such as the events of 9/11 and the Iraq War of 2003—this changed somewhat in the wake of the London bombings of July 7, 2005. At this point the government established an advisory council comprised of all four groups mentioned above, a move which represented a decline in the MCB's role as the sole voice of Islam in the UK. One initiative to come out of this consultative process has been the establishment of a body within the Muslim community to set best practice standards for mosques and the training of Imams in the UK—a move that was seen as particularly important in the wake of ongoing issues relating to the Finsbury Park Mosque in north London, widely viewed as a fertile ground for recruitment into some of the radical networks we examined in Chapter 7. The Mosques and Imams National Advisory Board (MINAB) was established in the summer of 2006 to play this role.

In the French context the main national umbrella organization is the Conseil Francais de la Culte Musulman (CFCM—"French Council of the Muslim Faith"), established in 2003 by the government in order to provide a centralized point of entry into and consultation with the French Muslim community. Organized into some 25 regional councils, the dominant voices and trends within the Council have been the other main French Muslim organizations which all also occupy seats on the Council's executive committee. These are the Union des Organizations Islamiques de France (UOIF), a group that is close to the MB in terms of its general orientation; the Council of the Grande Mosquee de Paris (GMP)—generally viewed as moderate and supportive of integrating Muslims into French society, its rector, Dalil Boubakeur was president of the CFCM in its early years; and the Federation National des Musulmans de France (FNMF), generally viewed as having close ties to the Moroccan government. The bodies representing Turkish Muslims in France (the Comite de Coordination des Musulmans Turcs de France—CCMTF) and Muslims of Sub-Saharan background have also played a role within the broader Council. Like the MCB in the UK, the CFCM has also come in for its share of criticism. Some detractors, most notably hardline voices within the Muslim community, view it as a puppet of the French government. On the other side, there are those who criticize the French government for appearing to legitimize the voice of groups such as the MB by giving them a prominent role—via the UIOF—within the Council. One important distinction to be drawn between the CFCM and the MCB is that while the former was established by the French government as a quasi-official body, the formation of the latter was an exclusively civil society initiative that developed within the British Muslim community.

On the broader regional stage we find groups and voices that have sought to advance the agenda of a distinctly European Islam in recent years. On the organizational side, the most influential of these has been the FIOE, coordinated out of London and generally seen as close to the MB. A prominent individual voice representing this broader European approach is that of Tariq Ramadan, the grandson of MB founder Hassan al-Banna and the author of *To Be A European Muslim* and *Western Muslims and the Future of Islam*. Ramadan has been highly influential in terms of inspiring the younger generation of European Muslims to become active participants in mainstream society and to regard their presence in Europe as an opportunity to develop a better understanding of their religion within open societies. A controversial figure who we will look at more closely in Chapter 9, Ramadan represents one of various contemporary Muslim leaders who argue that Muslims in the West—in tune with modern thinking and facing a unique set of challenges—are in the best position to reinvigorate the intellectual tradition of Islam.

With regard to the broad picture, and looking at Europe's Muslim community over the past decade, we see conflicting trends with regard to questions of social integration. Certainly among the more affluent and better-educated segments of the community we can see increased signs of stakeholding and integration: business ownership, participation in civic organizations, active engagement with mainstream politics, etc. At the same time, however, large parts of the Muslim community continue to lead a marginalized existence on the fringes of society with little access to labor markets. In some cases, even those that achieve high levels of education do not see the rewards. For example, the unemployment rate among French university graduates of North African origin is over 25 percent, five times higher than the national average for similarly qualified job seekers. For most Muslims in Europe, higher education is not even in the picture. There is hence a growing disparity between a small number of Muslims in Europe who seem to be "making it" and a mass segment of the community that seems to be stalled in its socioeconomic development, or in some cases, slipping back. It is among this latter alienated and increasingly "de-societized" group that some observers see the potential for increased social unrest (such as the protests outside Paris and several other French cities in late 2005) or even recruitment into radical and militant Islamist groups.

Part of the problem is linked to Europe's overall labor and demographic profile. There is tremendous demand for labor, particularly in the low-skilled segment of the market. Increasingly these positions are filled by immigrants, but in a climate of heightened regulation in this area. At the same time, many immigrant families have been living in Europe for several generations and they or their children are looking to move up the labor chain—often with little real prospect of success. Added to this, Europe's "indigenous" population is aging rapidly. With much higher birth rates among immigrant families, more and more of the youth age bracket is filled by Muslims whose prospects for socioeconomic mobility are not commensurate with their growing position within Europe's population. In some countries, this increased Muslim presence has been a source of considerable tension. The Netherlands is a case in point, where several incidents over the past five years—most notably the killing of the film-maker of "The Van Gogh" by an Arab immigrant—linked to a perceived backlash against immigrants among the notoriously tolerant Dutch population have led some to speculate about a looming "Muslim question" for Europe. The vociferous debate around the Danish Cartoon Affair of early 2006 reflected this heightened sense of cultural crisis. Where one side cites what they perceive as a failure on the part of Europe's Muslims to integrate into the societies in which they now live, Muslims cite feelings of exclusion, discrimination, and racism. Just as the norms relating to secularism and the role of religion in society vary from setting to setting, so do the meanings and expectations connected to the idea of social integration by immigrants. In the French context, for example, integration is understood as meaning the adoption of French values and norms (laïcisme, no differential rights for cultural groups, etc.) whereas in the British context it has tended to mean something more like tolerance of cultural pluralism and participation in civic life.

The dynamics of Islam in Europe have tended to be strongly affected by wider trends in world politics and also subject to the influence of various groups operating from outside the region. This can be seen when we consider the highly polarizing effects of events such as 9/11 and the Iraq war on Muslim communities in Europe. Both became opportunities for Muslims of various political orientations, moderate-integrationist and radical alike, to try to rally others to their various causes. Discourses of Muslim identity once again became framed around debates about who counts as a "real" Muslim. Were the real Muslims the ones who supported Usama Bin Laden and cause of global jihad (as the radicals claimed) or were the real Muslims those who argued for pluralism and Islam's compatibility with European citizenship (as the moderates claimed)? These are issues we will look at more closely when we take up the question of "who speaks for Islam?" in the next chapter.

While the coverage of individual groups and movements within this typology is by no means exhaustive, these seven categories taken together account for the vast majority of contemporary Muslim transnationalism. The categories themselves are ideal types rather than perfect models of social reality. There exist significant examples of transnational Islam that do not fit easily or even predominantly into any single category but which rather embody important aspects of several types found above. As pointed out in the beginning of this chapter, there are also a number of other important types of transnational Islam—most notably various media and Internet forums, and various Muslim authority figures working to build global followings—that have been left out of this chapter because they will be examined in detail in the next chapter on the changing nature of Islamic authority.

Transnationalism, globalization and the Muslim world: key themes

After this descriptive inventory of transnational Islam, it would be useful to conclude by briefly considering the wider significance of these actors. How does increased Muslim transnationalism in the contemporary era interface with other trends in Muslim politics within the wider world? What is the import of this global activity in terms of how it affects traditional Islamic concepts and practices? From the various examples of Muslim transnationalism examined above, four key themes emerge.

First, there is the question of whether the new global consciousness associated with increased Muslim transnationalism may lead some Muslims—invoking Benedict Anderson's well-known idiom of nationalism—to "reimagine the umma."[16] Although the idea of the umma has existed in the Islamic lexicon for centuries, the diversity and political schisms of the Muslim world have made it difficult for the term to refer to the social reality of global Islamic unity. As new technologies of travel and communication bring far-flung corners of the Muslim world into greater contact with each other, however, there is the possibility that world Muslims—many of whom share the experience of living in impoverished conditions and who see their way of life under threat from large-scale social forces—may find it both possible and attractive to understand themselves as part of a single global community. As much as transnationalism makes it possible for Muslims to have a greater sense of the wider umma, it simultaneously makes them more aware of the diversity—and political divisions—that characterize it. In this regard, a new "umma consciousness" does not in and of itself lead to greater Muslim unity. As will be argued in the next chapter, it may sometimes also lead to a new politics *within* Islam as different interpretations and political tendencies compete for followers throughout the umma. For this reason it becomes impossible to characterize the rise of transnational Islam as representing either an inherently radicalizing or pluralizing (in the political sense of those terms) trend. Transnational Islam is about the extension of Muslim social relations and discourses across ever greater expanses of world-space—but the political nature of these interactions is not intrinsically defined by their transnational character. In Chapter 7 we examined some of the factors that permit the global propagation of radical and jihadist discourses, and in Chapter 9 we will undertake a more general analysis of how various experiences of globalization may lead Muslims in quite different directions as they look for "authoritative" Islam.

Second, and following on from this first point, it is nonetheless manifestly clear that Muslim transnationalism has not in any sense eroded the inherent pluralism of Islamic discourse (in a quantitative rather than qualitative sense)—quite the opposite, in fact. Today more than ever, Muslims around the world have access to multiple voices and interpretations of Islam, many of which emanate from settings quite distinct and far removed from their own. This fact has significant implications for the changing nature of religious authority in the Muslim world, a theme we will explore in much greater detail in the next chapter. The barriers to participation in public Islamic discourse have declined significantly over the past decade and traditional ulama have to contend with a growing class of "Islamist new intellectuals" who may not possess formal religious training but nonetheless have access to core texts and the technologies required for engaging in public critique.[17] There is also now at work in the Muslim world a process through which the spatial provenance of religious knowledge becomes relativized in a dualistic—and in some senses seemingly contradictory—fashion. This is perhaps best captured through a term coined by the sociologist Roland Robertson who spoke of globalization being best understood in its cultural aspects as a process of "glocalization."[18] Through this somewhat unwieldy neologism, he seeks to capture the sense in which globalization allows not only the importation into local contexts ideas with universalist pretensions, but also the fact that inevitably such ideas are adapted and mediated to suit the new climates into which they enter—in other words, the global becomes localized. Part and parcel of the same process, of course, is the possibility that highly localized idioms of Islam can more easily find their way into global spaces to be consumed by Muslims in distant and disparate settings.

It might be argued that in the Muslim world today we see a great many examples of "global Islam" in search of local supporters—a theme that we will explore in the next chapter through the activities of Sheikh Yusuf al-Qaradawi, one of the most senior ulama within the Sunni branch of Islam and, through his television shows on Al-Jazeera, a global media phenomenon in his own right. If, as it will be presented, his work represents an attempt to reassert a form of lowest common denominator orthodoxy in the Muslim world, this must in part be seen as a reaction to the fact that Muslim transnationalism has reconfigured the geography of authoritative knowledge in the Muslim world. While the *Sunni* tradition of the Middle East may have constituted the historical centre of gravity in Islamic learning, it can be argued today that a wide range of voices from areas in what have traditionally been seen as the "periphery" of the Muslim world have emerged as innovative challenges to stagnant orthodoxy in the Middle Eastern core. Muslim scholars and activists in, for example, Indonesia, South Africa, Iran, and Switzerland can all claim significant global followings in the wider umma.

Third, the rise and increasing salience of the many nongovernmental actors examined above raises the question of whether the era of state-controlled or "state-patrolled" Islam is coming to an end. While governments in countries such as Egypt, Turkey, and Pakistan have never been able to completely co-opt religious forces through various forms of "state Islam" (see Chapters 4 and 5), it can be argued that the new Muslim transnationalism—combined with the increasing permeability of borders—puts the regulation of religious discourse and activism even further beyond their reach. This trend meshes well with wider arguments about globalization that cite a decline in the structural capacity of the state.[19]

Finally, there is the possibility that the new Muslim transnationalism covered in this chapter represents the opening up of a space in which distinctly Islamic alternatives to globalization—or perhaps *Islamic modes of globalization*—might begin to emerge alongside and in agonistic yet constructive interaction with ongoing processes of economic integration.[20] Rather than constituting a final "clash of civilizations" before the "end of history," it is possible to see "Muslim globalization" as representative of the possibility that any future global culture in the *longue durée* might emerge dialogically rather than dialectically.

9 Who speaks for Islam? Religious authority in the global umma

"Who speaks for Islam?" is one of the most commonly asked questions today among observers of the Muslim world, and one that has no definitive answer. To the casual analyst of world affairs, it will probably seem that the voices of radicals and militants have disproportionate influence among Muslims in the contemporary world, and that discussions of tolerance and moderation are all but absent from Islamic discourse. Aside from the texts and transmissions of global jihadi revolutionaries such as Usama Bin Laden, we are also told that each week in mosques around the world—many of them funded by Saudi Wahhabis—fiery orators preach hatred against non-Muslims, the United States, and the West. While phenomena of this sort are undeniably present in the Muslim world today (and much reported in the media), merely to point out their existence tells us very little about their prevalence and relative influence vis-à-vis other tendencies and currents within the Muslim world. In Chapter 7 we discussed the target audience of global jihadi radicals and sought to contextualize the appeal of their discourse as part of a religio-political consciousness shaped by a particular experience of the relationship between religious identity and political power in a variety of contexts. We emphasized that this jihadi approach has very limited appeal among most Muslims today, but that the few who do act on it have potential for great visibility and spectacle—witness September 11, 2001 or the July 7, 2005 attacks in London.

Some readers may be surprised to learn that there also exists in the Muslim world today a highly pluralistic understanding of Islam, linking liberal interpretations of the Qur'an and sunna with forms of social activism and politics usually associated with progressive causes. The various figures associated with the Progressive Muslims Union are a case in point here. Or one might look to the work of the South African scholar-activist Farid Esack, who reads the Qur'an as a text enjoining him to reach out to those that society has ostracized or left behind—hence his work with HIV communities in Africa.[1] The Sudanese legal specialist Abdullahi An-Na'im, calling for "Islamic reformation," has made enormous strides in showing the commonalities and compatibility between Islamic law and universal human rights.[2] The reader will probably not have heard much about these figures since the work that they do doesn't offer much in the way of media spectacles. Explosions play far better on television than squatter camps or theoretical treatises.

Both of these camps represent the extreme fringes of a much broader Islamic spectrum today. Like any movement on the margins, their numbers are relatively small, and likewise their appeal. If we want to find out who speaks for Islam, then we need to begin with a different set of questions— namely, we need to ask what kinds of Muslims are *listening*, and how do they understand the meaning and role of Islam in their varied lives. To talk of Islamic authority in the abstract would be to reify something that is largely contingent on social relations of culture, power, and history across a wide variety of contexts. Our goal in this chapter is to help the reader understand how various forms of Islamic authority are produced through interaction between individuals and communities embedded in particular sociopolitical contexts, and a wide range of normative traditions and institutions which have themselves evolved considerably over time. The role of globalization will constitute a particular focus in this chapter since many of the sociocultural and technological transformations commonly associated with this idea have had a major effect on the forms and conduct of religious authority. More specifically we will look at globalization's role in creating a wide range of "Muslim public spheres" in which various understandings of Islam are advanced and debated today by new audiences.[3] The circulations and inflections of Islamic authority in these publics, as we will see, have important implications for how people understand and conduct themselves as political actors. Our goal, in the end, is to provide readers with some insight into the social processes through which religious authority is constructed, and also to familiarize them with the intrinsic heterogeneity of Islamic authority today (i.e. the idea that no *one* speaks for Islam). Beyond this we will want to provide some sense of the wider "ecology of authority" in which the various claims to Islam made by a range of actors today are situated. Salafi-jihadis and traditional ulama—radicals and centrists—compete today for the attention of Muslims all over the world in a new global public sphere. Alongside them various entrepreneurial voices are finding new ways to build constituencies among global consumers of religion.[4] The state is also still very much a part of this equation and, as we will see, some of those whose discourses we examine serve to reinforce statist definitions of Islam, while others seek explicitly to transcend political subjectivity defined in terms of national citizenship in pursuit of a Muslim identity defined in terms of the umma. It is this idea of Islamic public normativity understood in terms other than the creation of an Islamic state that will allow us to begin assessing the notion of post-Islamism—a key theme of the next and final chapter.

We will begin here with a few core conceptual issues relating to Islamic authority and then move on to an overview of the traditional structures of authority in Islam and look at certain aspects of their transformation and, in some cases, their fragmentation, from the nineteenth century onward. We then consider some of the ways in which globalization and globalizing processes have affected authoritative discourse in Islam at various levels, from the local, to the national, to the emergent global stage on which claims to religious authority can now be made. The rise of new media and information and communication technologies (ICTs) are considered in terms of their pluralizing effects on Islamic authority and the ways in which they have both opened spaces for new voices of Islam to be heard while simultaneously reinforcing more traditional forms of religious authority. Having sketched out the landscape of Islamic authority in a global world, we then move on to examine several of the most important figures and institutions competing today for followers within the Muslim world. These represent a diverse range of strategies and sociopolitical goals, from a globalization of the Islamist project to grassroots social change achieved through personal piety. These actors vary considerably in terms of their "scale" of operations. Some, such as Aa Gym, a populist preacher in Southeast Asia, is primarily a national voice speaking to middle class Indonesians. Yusuf al-Qaradawi, on the other hand, actively courts a global audience through a network of regional research centers, satellite television and Internet forums, and new transnational associations of ulama. We will compare and contrast three of these approaches, those of Muhammad al-Sha'arawi, Yusuf al-Qaradawi, and Amr Khaled and show how the shift from one to the other allows us to trace the evolution of new religious publics in contemporary Islam. So while we will never be able to answer the question "who speaks for Islam?" in any definitive way, an examination of the multiple approaches to, and voices of, Islamic authority operating in the world today will help us to understand the circumstances under which Muslims in different settings and circum-

Table 9.1 Percentage of Muslim turning to various sources for guidance in religion

Country	Local Imam or sheikh	National religious leaders	Religious leaders on television	Imams and institutions outside	None	DK/Ref
Great Britain	42	4	4	28	16	6=100
France	26	18	6	31	19	1=101
Germany	18	25	3	12	32	10=100
Spain	26	5	4	30	30	6=101
Egypt	29	30	22	16	3	*=100
Turkey	27	37	6	7	16	8=101
Indonesia	60	30	3	4	2	1=100
Pakistan	46	19	6	11	7	11=100
Jordan	25	24	25	26	0	*=100
Nigeria	64	13	3	11	9	*=100

Source: Pew Research Center (2006), "Muslims in Europe: Economic Worries Top Concerns About Religious and Cultural Identity"

stances may find one or another type of Islam more appealing or attractive as he or she seeks political answers to the issues and problems of everyday life in a global world.

Thinking about authority in Islam

In the absence of a formal church there is no "official" voice of Islam in the world. Unlike the Catholic Church, Islam has no pope or centralized governing structure—no single source toward which Muslims can turn in order to know definitively where their religion stands on any given issue. And yet this does not mean that figures of authority are absent from Islam. In many regards the history of Islam is a history of differentiated claims to religious authority, with multiple figures and institutions rising to the fore at different times, and more often than not, existing alongside each other in considerable variety. The impossibility of identifying a single locus of religious authority in the Muslim world also does not mean that it is not possible to discuss religious authority in Islam in considerable detail. There is indeed a commonly recognized set of social actors and institutions associated with Islamic authority, and likewise a rich tradition of discursive resources and styles (see Chapter 2). The ulama (religious scholars), mosque leaders and various educational institutions (madrasas, Al-Azhar university) are examples of the former, while the Qur'an and traditions of the Prophet Muhammad represent textual variants of the latter.

What exactly do we mean by authority in this context, however? Obviously we do not want to think of this term simply as a synonym for power or force; we are not concerned with how various actors compel or coerce people to do things in the name of religion. Rather, we are primarily concerned with the establishment and reproduction of particular forms of social normativity understood to derive from religion. This is a particularly complicated issue in the context of Islam. When it comes to the ulama, for example, much of their status is a function of the fact that they are understood to be the keepers and curators of a divine authority whose nature transcends (or precedes) social relations. As Hamid Dabashi puts it, this is a form of authority (at least in its Sunni form) that is primarily concerned with the "collective routinization" of religious knowledge.[5] The Qur'an, in particular, as the literal word of God, but also the sunna of the Prophet, are regarded as authorities in their own right. Although many generations of Muslim have relied on scholarly commentaries and exegeses of these texts in order to make their meaning fully—and socially—explicit, there is also an important sense in which they are Islam's prime repositories of the authoritative in their own right. It is therefore not surprising that at various points in Islamic history—from the Khawarij in the late seventh century to Takfir w'al Hijra in Egypt in the 1970s—we have seen the rise of political groups premised on the rejection of all worldly or human religious authority in favor of strict and exclusive adherence to the Qur'an and sunna. Even groups who espouse this approach have tended to rely on "scholars of exception" or "hero activists"—such as Sheikh Umar Abdul-Rahman or Usama Bin Laden (see Chapter 7)—to provide inspirational resources and leadership.

For most Muslims today, of course, the quest for the authoritative in Islam is something far more complex and nuanced in that it involves a combination of both direct, personal and reflexive engagement with textual sources ("What does the Qur'an say and where am I in the Qur'an?") and also the consumption of mediated knowledge from various authorities claiming privileged or superior access to Islamic truth. Of course, in a global world—where increased social connectedness across world-space and the availability of new media and information technologies give Muslims access to an unprecedented range of potential religious authorities—the question of who speaks for Islam becomes even more complicated. For example local imams and mosque leaders are able to rely on their direct ties to the community and a sense of legitimacy that derives from their proximity to those they serve, not to mention the power of face-to-face, personalized relations. Yet in many settings today, Muslims are also exposed to new ideas and alternative views emanating from ulama, Islamist intellectuals and religious populists located in other regions, countries and even continents. Under such circumstances it becomes almost impossible to identify any one of these sources as "authoritative." Religious authority, as Olivier Roy has styled it inevitably becomes a form of bricolage, as Muslims incorporate multiple interpretations and traces of a wide variety of discourses into their religious worldviews.[6]

The point about the pluralistic nature of religious authority around the Muslim world becomes clearer when we look at a recent poll by the Pew Research Center that asked Muslims in 10 different countries whom they trust most to offer them guidance as a Muslim. Those polled were asked to choose between local imams, national religious leaders, religious figures on television, imams and institutions outside their country, or none of these. As we can see (Table 9.1), the responses vary considerably from country to country, indicating not only the absence of a single clear pattern to Islamic religious authority, but the fact that the relative strength of these various sources of authority vary considerably between contexts. The only way to really gain a clearer sense of how and why a particular voice is privileged over others within a given national setting is to look sociologically at the particular circumstances surrounding the production, consumption, and politics of religious knowledge in that locale.

Under these conditions it would be tempting, on the one hand, to characterize contemporary Islamic authority as a situation of *heterarchy*—a term from network analysis which implies a system governed collectively by multiple units having roughly the same status or level of authority (as contrasted with a *hierarchical* system). In many respects this term seems to capture the highly pluralistic and formally non-hierarchical nature of religious authority in Islam today. On the other hand, however, it is doubtful whether we are really dealing with a situation of "collective governance" insofar as that term implies a shared sense of common endeavor toward mutually defined goals. As we have already seen throughout the course of this book, and will examine in even greater detail in this chapter, there exist in the Muslim world today widely varying visions of what Islam means socially and politically in the world. States, ulama, social movements and individual "lay" Muslims all lay claim, often in competing and mutually exclusive ways, to religious knowledge, creating a puzzling morass for many Muslims trying to discern what Islam has to say about the issues and questions they face in their everyday lives. It is this predicament that constitutes the focus of the present chapter.

Traditional Islamic authority and its transformation

Throughout Islamic history, religious authority has emanated from a wide variety of social and institutional locations. In Chapter 2 we examined the rise of the ulama as a class of scholars with privileged access to texts, methods, and traditions of knowledge that invested them with the capacity to speak authoritatively on matters of religion and, more particularly for our purposes, the sociopolitical implications of Islam. We also outlined the key forms of textual and methodological authority (Qur'an, sunna, ijma, qiyas, ijtihad). The vast collection and research activity of figures such as Bukhari and Muslim provided the hadith sources for the study of the Prophet's sunna. Other scholars, such as Al-Ashari, al-Ghazali, and Ibn Rushd would make major contributions to the fields of theology and epistemology. The great jurists, Imams Malik, al-Shafi'i, Abu Hanifa and Ibn Hanbal in the Sunni tradition and Jafar al-Sadiq in the shi'i tradition, laid the foundations for a system of legal deliberation that would emerge as a central institution in the definition of Islamic normativity for successive centuries. The public dimensions of scholarly discourse were to be found in the issuing of fatwas on matters of the day and various questions brought before them, and also in the deliberations and rulings of qadis—the judges in the Islamic court system.

But these scholarly figures were by no means the only important forms of Islamic authority to be found within the traditional system. The sheikhs of the various Sufi orders also represent crucially important purveyors of religious insight and experience. While some of these figures also possessed training within the classical disciplines of Islamic learning, the nature of their religious authority is different from that of the ulama in that for the former it is understood to derive from their place within an inherited line of succession rather than through their scholarship. The *baraka* ("blessings," "spiritual wisdom," or "divine charisma") of a Sufi sheikh is understood to be a quality residing within, and particular to, his family line. The enormous prevalence of Sufi orders and activity across most segments of society throughout the greater part of the Muslim world has meant that these brotherhoods came to play—and, indeed, continue to do so today—an enormous and influential role in the lives of their adherents.

There are also, of course, the various caliphs, imams, sultans, and kings to be considered in terms of their religious authority. While most of these figures wielded power as worldly rulers and deployed the usual repertoire of political tools to enforce their authority, it is important to note that many of them—particularly the caliphs—did derive a large measure of their legitimacy from the symbolic power that accrued from their role as protectors of the faith. Many of them also relied on "official" court ulama to lend religious credence to their various policies and undertakings, while portraying themselves as the political enforcer of that religious knowledge. The symbolic importance of the caliphate as an institution is attested to by the fact that its abolition, as we saw in Chapter 3, was considered a moment of crisis for Islamic political theorists. And as we have seen in Chapter 7, there are still a wide range of Islamist movements active today who consider the re-establishment of the caliphate to be a primary goal. The analogous institution to the caliphate within the shi'i tradition is the Imamate, based on descendents of the Prophet's cousin Ali—although the various branches of shi'ism differ as to how many imams they recognize. It is also worth noting that the shi'i imams have not tended to play a direct role in political rule, not least of all because in many Sunni-dominated settings it was dangerous for them to publicly declare their shi'i identity much less make any claim to political authority. In the modern era, we find examples of several states where the political legitimacy of royal families and ruling regimes is intimately linked to their claims to religious authority. In Chapter 5, for example, we noted the close ties between the Saudi royal family and the religious establishment. We also looked at the case of Iran where the most powerful positions of state are occupied by ulama based on Khomeini's doctrine of vilayat-i faqih.

Since we have cited several examples of inherited religious authority above, it would be worth mentioning at least one more example of this in the Islamic tradition. Those who claim direct descent from the Prophet Muhammad have often enjoyed notable status in the societies and communities in which they live. Identified by the honorific Sharif or Sayyid, the Prophet's descendents—sometime referred to collectively as the *shurafa*—have been historically charged with the stewardship of Mecca and Medina and the Hajj process from the early thirteenth century until the founding of modern Saudi Arabia. The leaders of the family have since gone on to become the rulers of Jordan. Given the widespread dispersion of the Prophet's descendents, however, the shurafa are also something of a transnational phenomenon, and in recent years we have even seen international shurafa conferences.

How has the nature and role of the ulama changed in recent years? To fully answer this question it is important to examine the period of modernization that began in the Muslim world during the nineteenth century. Some aspects of this we have already surveyed, such as the successive waves of Islamic revivalist and reformist thought (see Chapter 2)—although without looking more widely at the sociological shift in the production of religious knowledge that this entailed. The reader may recall that the reformists in particular expressed concerns about what they viewed as the stagnation of the ulama and the atavistic tendencies of religious scholars. In their view, religious knowledge needed to be reinvigorated by being made relevant to the pressing sociopolitical challenges of the day. Jamal al-Din al-Afghani—always more an activist than a thinker—took the lead in transforming Islamic modernism into a political and more specifically an anti-colonial agenda, decrying the obscurantist tendencies of the traditional ulama along the way.

Another important point to bear in mind here is the effect of modern mass education in the Muslim world. As modernizing rulers in countries such as Egypt pushed for the education of wider segments of the population from the early 1800s onwards, but particularly in the early twentieth century, literacy rates began to increase, as did the number of people who began to seek and find in modern sources new kinds of knowledge and "tools" with which to think. As awareness of the urgency of contemporary social and political problems began to increase within the populace, the relative disconnectedness and political irrelevance of the religious establishment became more pronounced. Alongside the role played by mass education, we also need to recognize the socially transformative impact of the introduction of the printing press—a development Benedict Anderson cites as particularly important in his seminal account of the formation of national consciousness.[7] We can certainly argue that at some level, the combination of readily available literature—religious and otherwise—had a democratizing effect on religious discourse insofar as it marked a decline in the ulama's monopoly over the production and delivery of religious knowledge. As Francis Robinson puts it:

> Books ... could now be consulted by any Ahmad, Mahmud or Muhammad, who could make what he [would] of them. Increasingly from now on any Ahmad, Mahmud or Muhammad could claim to speak for Islam. No longer was a sheaf of impeccable [religious credentials] the buttress of authority; strong Islamic commitment would be enough.[8]

Robinson's last point here is particularly important. As there arose a generation for whom religious knowledge was intrinsically connected to one's sociopolitical consciousness, the insular and other worldly orientation of the ulama seemed dangerously disengaged. Being a good Muslim was no longer about conforming to the dictates of scholars, but rather about going out into the world to make Islam into a publicly embodied experience. In one sense, then, this transformation of the traditional system—in addition to pluralizing the field of religious knowledge production—also opened up spaces into which discourses such as the Islamism of al-Banna, Mawdudi, and Qutb could arise (see Chapter 3) alongside secular nationalism. We can recall, for example, Sayyid Qutb's statement to the effect that the activist's interpretation of Islam is privileged (see Chapter 3). So we are not talking just about new kinds of people having access to religious knowledge, but also about new ways of *using* Islamic knowledge—a point to which we will return later in the chapter.

One should not infer from the above that the authority and social role of the ulama simply disappeared with the rise of the modern state, however. Nor would it be fair to leave the reader with the idea that the ulama and their discourse represent a static and anachronistic approach to Islam, unable to cope with the exigencies of the modern world. Work by a number of scholars has shown that the ulama have not only adapted their discourse and priorities to suit changing social conditions throughout history, but were also active in positioning themselves strategically within the political field as modern states arrived in the Middle East and elsewhere.[9] The ulama continue to act as major sources of Islamic authority and legitimacy, but they do so today alongside a wide range of other actors, institutions, groups, media sources and individual voices—many of which we will profile in this chapter. Their input also continues to be sought by a wide range of social and political actors—including state governments—seeking religious legitimacy for various actions and policies. But this happens in new and unexpected ways today, such as when the French government in 2004 sought and received—or apparently received (see below)—a fatwa from the Grand Sheikh of Al-Azhar in Cairo to the effect that Muslims living in France should abide by newly passed legislation that forbade the wearing of headscarves in public schools—an act that created considerable controversy within the Egyptian religious establishment.

This last point brings us to the issue of the relationship between the state and the ulama. We looked at this in some detail in Chapter 5 when dealing with Saudi Arabia, but the Saudi case—whereby the legitimacy of the state was premised, and continues to depend, on the public support of religious scholars—is not typical in most of the Muslim world. Far more so has been cases such as those of Egypt and Pakistan where modernizing states sought to co-opt religion and deploy it in the pursuit of nationalist agendas. In the case of Egypt, this is best represented by the Nasser regime's reform of the Al-Azhar institutions from 1961. Rather than eradicate the venerable religious academy, the Free Officers sought instead to bring it into tune with the times. Faculties teaching secular subjects (medicine, engineering, etc.) were added to the university so as to enable it to produce graduates capable of finding work in the modern state and its economy rather than introverted, socially disconnected ulama. Malika Zeghal describes this process as one that "integrated the religious sphere into a 'reforming' project: to control, transform and instrumentalize the religious sphere by retaining the old channels of religious education and re-institutionalizing them under the ideology of 'modernization' (*tahdith*) and 'reform' (*islah*)."[10] This also involved a "resocietization" of the ulama—that is to say a move by the state to remove them as privileged sources of social authority and public normativity and reconfigure them as citizens expected to live according to the rhythms of modern life.[11]

But there was more going on here than just an attempt by the state to co-opt, contain, or "normalize" the ulama. There was also an attempt to divest them of the exclusive authority to define and speak on behalf of Islam— something that was also occurring in other national settings. In the case of Egypt it took the form of the state "putting Islam to work," to use Gregory Starrett's evocative formulation, in the pursuit of national developmental agendas. By advancing a particular vision of Islam through state schools and government social programs, Egypt sought to recalibrate the normative horizons of religion to fit with the Nasserist vision of the modern state.[12] An emasculated Al-Azhar, with its Grand Sheikh as a political appointee, came to be regarded as an instrument of "statist Islam," causing Islamist movements such as the Muslim Brotherhood (MB) to distance themselves even further from the ulama. Realizing that the spaces of their authority were soon to be thoroughly occupied by the state, a number of the more ambitious religious scholars, such as Yusuf al-Qaradawi, left Egypt and ended up in places like Saudi Arabia or other countries in the Arab Gulf.

Friction between the state and the religious scholars arising from attempts by the former to define and speak on behalf of Islam can also be found in a number of other Muslim contexts during roughly this same period. We have seen in Chapter 5, for example, how in Pakistan under Ayub Khan, the state's attempts to define and promulgate a modernist Islam via the Islamic Research Institute led to considerable protest from the religious establishment and closer ties between the ulama and the Jama'at-i Islami. The famous Shah Bono case in India in the 1980s is another case in point. Here the Indian Supreme Court—dominated by Hindus—ruled in favor of a woman claiming financial support from her divorced husband and accompanied this with a modernist reinterpretation of the Qur'an. The ulama and many conservative Muslims regarded this not only as a Hindu power play through interference in Muslim personal status affairs but also as an illegitimate attempt by a secular authority to rule on matters of religion.[13] Extreme and politicized tensions between the state and ulama, we can then say, seem to be a function not so much of the religious scholars merely becoming co-opted by the state (something that has happened to varying degrees throughout Islamic history), but a byproduct of the modern secular state claiming the authority to define, reinterpret, and even issue legal rulings on matters of religion.

In the era of nation-states and globalization, then, it is more appropriate to address the question of how the authority of the ulama has been restructured and relativized rather than simply sidelined. As we will see, traditional ulama have been among the most enthusiastic adopters of information technology in the pursuit of new transnational audiences, reflecting the idea that in some cases globalization actually has the potential to increase the scale of their social influence beyond the prior confines of local and national boundaries. To this end, we see today a number of traditional authority figures that have deliberately sought to calibrate the tenor and coverage of their religious discourse in order to attract as wide an audience as possible across the Muslim world. This means focusing on "universal" issues and challenges facing Muslims the world over rather than on questions specific to particular national and local settings. With the emergence of new forms of transnational radicalism (see Chapter 7), we have also seen a concerted effort on the part of religious authorities representing more moderate forms of Islam (and Islamism) to counter their discourse with an emphasis on Islamic centrism—sometimes with considerable support from state authorities. So while the ulama continue, as one would expect, to represent the voice of a generally conservative Islam, it is not possible to identify them with any one particular political viewpoint or agenda. Among their ranks today we find conservative centrists (probably the majority), global jihadists, supporters of the regime's status quo, and even a few progressives. In what follows, therefore, in addition to considering new actors, we will also look at how ulama in various settings have responded to the challenges of a global world, and adapted their discourse and methods to suit a wide variety of worldviews and political agendas.

Globalization and contemporary Islamic authority

How has globalization affected the nature of Islamic authority? In this section we will examine various dimensions of religious authority in the contemporary Muslim world in relation to processes of globalization. This will include looking at the rise of new voices and claims to Islamic authority and how they relate to the persistence and transformation of traditional sources of religious knowledge. Particular attention will be paid to the emergence of networked models of religious authority and the increasingly transnational relationships upon which they are premised. The role of new media and ICTs will also be examined, and this will lead on to a discussion of how we might be seeing today not only a shift in the location and nature of Islamic authority, but also a transformation in how and why Muslims seek and make use of religious knowledge.

We should begin by briefly reviewing what we mean when talking about globalization as a set of transformational processes. In Chapter 1 we touched on various sociological and economic accounts of globalization, and outlined some of the concrete manifestations of globalization in the world. We associated globalization primarily with the increased interconnectedness and extension of social relations over world-space, and the rise of a world economy premised on neoliberal norms. In terms of how globalization manifests itself in the world, there are three dimensions in particular to be mentioned as a preface to our discussion of Islamic authority:

(1) *Structural interdependence* – the interpenetration of markets, economies, and policy spheres has meant that national and local settings are increasingly implicated in decision-making processes (political, fiscal, etc.) that occur elsewhere. At the individual level this entails a greater level of "exposure" to external risks and outcomes, and a higher level of awareness and sensitivity to the world as a single social, political, and economic space.[14] In the developing world, in particular, this has focused attention on global structures of socioeconomic inequality and power asymmetries.

(2) *Transnational "people flows"* – under globalizing conditions, there has been a distinct increase in the number and frequency of peoples moving across borders. This is primarily for purposes of labor migration, and can involve both guest worker schemes and semi-permanent or permanent settlement. Temporary professional and educational travel is more common today, alongside leisure travel and tourism. The prevalence of civil wars in weak and failing states has also meant an enormous increase in the number of refugees and asylum seekers moving over frontiers and seeking refuge abroad.

(3) *New media and information technologies* – with the advent of long distance and wireless telephony, satellite television, and the Internet, it has become progressively easier and less expensive for greater numbers of people to communicate across borders. Furthermore, a number of these technologies also reduce the barriers associated with reaching mass audiences, such that individuals can more easily "broadcast" and groups with shared interests can create and sustain networks even when geographically dispersed.

It is also important to situate these phenomena within the wider context of global political and economic modernization in order to understand their implications in terms of how people understand their political identities and interests. Particularly in the developing world, where most of the world's Muslims live, modernizing processes and the mixed experience that many populations have had with them have been at the root of much of the politics we looked at in Chapters 4 and 5. As socioeconomic expectations rose within an emerging and newly enfranchised (in educational and economic, if not necessarily political, terms) middle class, a growing sense of frustration at the reproduction of global structures of inequality within their own domestic spheres has been in many cases the hallmark experience of modernization in the developing world. The persistence of relatively high levels of authoritarianism (often operated through traditional and informal structures of social power—e.g. tribes, clans, ruling families) has led to a sense of political inefficacy among populations unable to hold their leaderships accountable for failed policies. This is the backdrop against which we have to consider the three manifestations of globalization outlined above and what they might mean in terms of new opportunities for political activities and a new role for religious authority within these politics.

Authorities old and new: global ulama and new religious intellectuals

Let us turn more specifically to the question of Islamic religious authority in the context of globalization, considering some of the ways transnational people flows, new media, and greater structural interdependence in the world might be having an impact within various spheres of Muslim politics. In the first instance there are a number of fairly straightforward points to be made about a greater sense of awareness amongst Muslims of the issues and challenges facing their co-religionists, and of the multiple interpretations and understandings of their religion. Through media, communication, and travel, a greater consciousness of "Muslim issues" can develop, and this potentially has a tremendous impact on the sorts of politics people take an interest in, and where they turn to for guidance and leadership in addressing these issues—a question we looked at in Chapter 7 with regard to radical movements, and one we will return to again below. Second, the same tripartite combination of media, communication and travel brings Muslims into contact with an increasingly diverse range of interpretations and practices of Islam, and the voices of authority that represent them. This makes it possible for a Muslim living in a particular setting to be exposed simultaneously to certain messages circulating in his or her local mosque community, and a quite different—and perhaps even contradictory—discourse emanating from the ulama of a religious show on satellite TV, or an online religious chat room. Moreover, the new ideas encountered may very well come from outside the ulama or the religious establishment. The Pew survey cited above, for example, found that in Jordan approximately equal percentages of the country's population indicated the local imam, national religious leaders, religious figures on television, and imams and institutions abroad as their primary source of religious guidance.[15]

In discussing the ulama so far we have indicated both a relative decline in their social influence since the early twentieth century and also the phenomenon of secular national states intruding on, and seeking to co-opt, their authority to speak on behalf of Islam. But we have also noted that religious scholars remain a vitally important source of Islamic authority alongside new competing voices. How have the traditional ulama responded to globalization and the rise of new transnational voices—many of them, such as Usama Bin Laden—highly radical and militant? Perhaps the paradigmatic case is to be found in that of Sheikh Yusuf al-Qaradawi. An Egyptian trained at Al-Azhar, Qaradawi was closely associated with the MB in his younger years. As an activist within the academy, he worked to bring his fellow Azharites closer to the Brotherhood in terms of their thinking and goals. Jailed as part of the government's crackdown on the Islamists in 1954, he left Egypt soon after and has since made his career abroad. Based for many years now in the Gulf Sheikhdom of Qatar (where he serves as Dean of the Shari'ah Faculty at Qatar University), Qaradawi has developed a reputation as an independent scholar untainted by association with state power. Although he is no longer formally associated with the MB, many MB members still regard his thinking as the preeminent scholarly manifestation of the Brotherhood tradition today.[16]

Qaradawi rose to regional fame among a mainstream audience in the late 1990s through his program on the Al-Jazeera satellite program, *Shari'ah w'al-Hayat* ("Shariah and Life"). We describe the show in greater detail below, but the important thing to note for now is Qaradawi's ability to discuss and offer opinions on a wide range of contemporary and "modern" issues (science and technology, globalization, health, etc.) while still remaining firmly anchored within the classical traditions of Islamic learning. Qaradawi's appeal, however, is not limited to the Arab world—indeed, in many regards he represents the best example today of a thoroughly global alim. His works have been translated into dozens of languages and can be found on the bestseller shelves of Islamic bookstores from Los Angeles to Cape Town to Jakarta. He has developed a particular following among Muslim communities in the West, especially in Europe. As we have noted in Chapter 8, Muslims living in the West have often sought out ways to find Islamically "authentic" solutions to the uniquely modern issues and problems they sometimes face in the West. Qaradawi's aforementioned ability to bridge these two worlds explains in great measure his appeal to European Muslims.

Interestingly, Qaradawi has actively sought to cater for this and others among his various global publics. Over the past decade he has worked to establish something like a global infrastructure for the dissemination of his particular religious worldview. Actively embracing technologies that would have made Jamal al-Din al-Afghani, his Pan-Islamist forebear, green with envy, Qaradawi has established institutions and research centers such as the European Center for Fatwa and Research (ECFR) in Ireland, designed expressly to provide religiously sanctioned advice on a wide range of matters to Muslims living in Europe. A popular bi-lingual website, Islamonline.net also operates under his general guidance. Most recently he has been involved in efforts to establish an International Union of Muslim Scholars that seeks to unite ulama from a wide range of sectarian backgrounds— Sunni, Shi'i, *Ibadi, Yazidi*, etc.—in the name of global Islamic ecumenism. He also played a prominent role in the 2005 International Islamic Conference held in Amman, Jordan. At this event, a multi-sectarian gathering of religious scholars issued a joint statement that sought to reassert the authority of the ulama to pronounce on matters of religion. More specifically, it emphasized the un-Islamic character of the practice of takfir, that is excommunication or the declaration of other Muslims as infidels. This latter piece was clearly an effort by mainstream ulama to counter the radical discourse of salafi-jihadi voices that seek to apostatize any Muslim who disagrees with their views. It also provides us with a way of reading the overall trajectory of Qaradawi's discourse and worldview.

We can perhaps best think of Qaradawi's overall enterprise as an attempt to "re-center" Islam for a global audience. This is an approach that seeks to pull Muslims back from both of the extremes mentioned at the opening of this chapter, radical militancy and progressive liberalism alike. Qaradawi exhorts Muslims toward moderation, reminding them that the Qur'an figures Muslims as a "community of the middle." Qaradawi is both popular and controversial because he straddles the line between different camps. Salafis and ultra-conservative literalists find him "too modern" and overly willing to engage extensively and borrow ideas from non-Muslims, while liberals find many of his views far too conservative and "traditional." Some of his views have also been politically controversial. While his has been one of the loudest and most consistent voices condemning acts of terrorism such as the 9/11 attacks, he has also stated in the past that Palestinian suicide attacks on Israeli civilians are legitimate—prompting some Western governments, including the United States, to place him beyond the pale. It is undoubtedly the case, however, that figures such as Qaradawi are working to put Usama Bin Laden and his Al-Qaeda ilk out of business. For most Muslims his is a voice of authentic moderation and centrism, and yet it still advocates an Islam (and, moreover, an Islam*ism*) that most secular liberals find repugnant. This has placed many advocates of political liberalism in a significant conundrum when trying to figure out how and whether to engage with Qaradawi. As a figure of undisputed authority representing the views of a great many moderate (in the sense of rejecting violence) Muslims, he would appear to be a prime interlocutor. Many of his more controversial and conservative views, however, make some (in the West, at least) hesitant to do so.

But perhaps it does not make sense to place so much emphasis or importance on a single individual. Indeed, in some ways Qaradawi's greatest influence lies in the political potential inherent within the generation of young Muslims—many of them living in the West—who have internalized his core ideas, but who reject certain of his views. Many of them have primarily read Qaradawi as someone who shows them the possibility of being modern and authentically Islamic at the same time. Their politics is one that is premised primarily on active participation as a citizen of particular nation-states rather than an Islamist project seeking to overturn the political order.

Qaradawi's "engaged alim" approach is not the only form of Islamic authority that has been making waves among modern, educated Muslims. Authors such as Olivier Roy have spoken about the rise of what he calls "new Islamist intellectuals."[17] These are individuals that are often highly educated, but not trained as religious scholars in the traditional sense.

Indeed, they may often be specialists in fields such as science and engineering and capable of formulating a religious discourse that appeals far more effectively to others who share their background than the traditional approach of classically trained ulama. Many of these new religious intellectuals are largely self-taught in terms of their religious knowledge, but manage to find supporters by articulating religion in a vernacular that resonates with the times. Roy distinguishes these figures from both ulama—whose authority is premised on the systematic and methodical exegesis of texts, but rejected by the new religious intellectuals as either too obscure or allied with the state—and also from Westernized Muslim intellectuals who appear to have abandoned the sacredness of the text, treating it as an object readily open to critical inquiry as if it had the same status as any other text. It is worth quoting Roy at length to better understand the political implications of this mode of knowledge production:

> The state has no means by which it can control the new Islamist intellectual in his social function. His thought does not correspond to his social position, he does not live from his profession, the networks of his activities are on the fringe of institutions, when they are not entirely clandestine. He operates in remote places (meeting houses, sites of worship, educational centers) and in spaces outside of the traditional society that the state has not resocialized (the new suburbs).
>
> The new intellectual has an autodidactic relationship to knowledge. Knowledge is acquired in a fragmented (manuals, excerpts, popular brochures), encyclopedic, and immediate manner: everything is discussed without the mediation of an apprenticeship, a method, or a professor ... The new media, such as radio, television, cassettes, and inexpensive offset brochures, make snatches of this content available. The new intellectual is a tinkerer; he creates a montage, as his personal itinerary guides him, of segments of knowledge, using methods that come from a different conceptual universe than the segments he recombines, creating a totality that is more imaginary than theoretical.[18]

Who then are these new Islamist intellectuals? We have already seen many of them in earlier chapters. Hassan al-Banna and, to some extent, Sayyid Qutb (see Chapter 3) from the MB were key progenitors of this mode. Ali Shariati (see Chapter 5), ideologue of Iran's Islamic revolution, is also a prime example here—cobbling together elements of Marxism and Islam across a matrix of modernity's *mustadafin* ("dispossessed"). We might even regard Usama Bin Laden (Chapter 7) as new Islamic intellectualism taken to its most radical extreme.

Where Roy has focused on the role that new Islamist intellectuals have played in building the social base of conventional Islamist movements such as the MB, others have drawn our attention to the role played by a different kind of intellectual in fostering reformist and progressive approaches to

Islam.[19] These are the various "reformist" scholars of contemporary Islam, figures that would usually fall into Roy's category of Westernized intellectual—although such categorizations in this case cannot always be made so quickly or easily, particularly if they are understood to entail an abandonment of faith. A great many of the reformist Muslim scholars working today—figures such as Abdolkarim Soroush in Iran (see Chapter 5), Fatima Mernissi in Morocco, Muhammad Shahrur in Syria, the late Nurcholish Madjid in Indonesia, and Amina Wadud or Ebrahim Moosa in the United States—have developed highly innovative and pluralistic interpretations of Islam that combine a variety of Islamic and Western sources and methods. While many of them have considerable followings in the Western academy (and, sometimes much to their chagrin, Western capitals), the highly intellectualized and theoretically complex style of their academic discourse renders their work largely inaccessible to most Muslims.[20]

Not all of these new religious intellectuals can be defined as clearly "Islamist" or "liberal-modernist" in orientation. Some of them advance a religious discourse that bridges aspects of both approaches. One such "hybrid" figure of particular importance would be the Turkish populist preacher and religious entrepreneur, Fethullah Gülen. The vast social movement structured around Gülen embodies elements of Sufi personal renewal and orthodox pietism combined with an emphasis on modern education, wealth generation, and Turkish nationalism. Drawing on the teachings of the early twentieth-century reformer Bediüzzaman Said Nursi (d. 1960) and the subsequent Nurçu movement, Gülen has sought to combine Islamic ethics with modern (secular) education. His works consist of a number of books that are closely read by his followers and disciples and, more concretely, an attempt to export his distinctive model of the Muslim society via a vast network of schools stretching from Central and Southeastern Europe throughout Central Asia. These schools are based on a secular curriculum of arts, sciences and foreign languages, but the teachers in the schools are all generally members of the Gülen movement. While the Gülen movement is not itself directly involved in politics, there are at least two important political dimensions to their work. The first of these relates to linkages between the ruling AK party in Turkey (see Chapter 4) and the Nurçu movement from which it, like the Gülen group, draws its base. The second aspect relates to a possible interpretation of the Gülen movement's longer-term goals. It has been noted by some observers that Gülen's religious thinking and normative practice is, at root, quite orthodox.[21] In other words, he is not interested in new, liberal interpretations of Islam. There are some who see in his schools and his targeting of possible future elites an attempt to "de-Kemalize" the Turkish establishment by creating a generation of public administrators and business leaders willing to allow more space for public religiosity. By emphasizing secular education, nationalism, and modernity in his schools, he operates in ways the Kemalist state must respect—while still remaining grounded in and offering supplementary education in religion.

Another important figure of this sort is Tariq Ramadan. Born in Switzerland, Ramadan is the grandson of MB founder Hassan al-Banna. Trained in both Western philosophy and traditional Islamic sciences, Ramadan emerged in the mid-1990s as a leading voice among young European Muslims. His core message was one of civic and social engagement, encouraging young Muslims in the West to participate in the mainstream life of their host societies rather than to "ghettoize" themselves, as had their parents during the first generations of Muslim immigration to Europe. While insisting that one's commitments as a Muslim and one's obligations as a citizen of, say, France were not mutually incompatible, Ramadan's work reveals an inevitable debt to his family's MB affiliations when he cites the importance of religion as a normative compass for public life—a position that put him at odds with the intellectual and policy-making establishments in France, and apparently, also the United States when in 2004 Washington D.C. denied him a work visa to take up a university professorship in the U.S. Ramadan has also emphasized the idea that Muslims living in the West are in a position to define the future of Islam by virtue of the freedoms that they enjoy. As a social activist, Ramadan has sought to draw connections between the Islamic emphasis on social justice and the general goals of the anti-globalization/global justice movement. Like Qaradawi, he is viewed by a growing constituency of admirers around the world as a Muslim intellectual who addresses the contemporary, lived experience of Islam in a globalizing world, while remaining "authentically Islamic" by virtue of his family's heritage and his emphasis on the continued importance of tradition and jurisprudence.

But whose religious discourse reigns supreme today, the ulama or the new religious intellectual? Of course there is no single answer here. What we have tried to draw attention to above is the changing nature of the relationship that modern individuals have to religious knowledge—not necessarily abandoning it, but producing and consuming it in new ways (more on this below). Ulama, such as Yusuf al-Qaradawi, have sought to adapt their discourse to these changing circumstances, actively incorporating modern questions and concerns into their scholarly deliberations. Indeed, Qaradawi has even warned in his work against the possible excesses of the new Islamist intellectuals when it comes to politics. While endorsing the idea of an Islamic "awakening" (Sahwa)—his term for the much-needed revival in public religious consciousness—he cautions that unless religious scholars play a role as partners or guides, those working with improvised religious knowledge are likely to get some things wrong at best, and even perhaps to turn violently radical.[22] While this is clearly a warning about "Bin Ladenism," we can also see ulama today seeking to reclaim a role for themselves in mainstream Islamism of the MB variety. Qaradawi, for example, has been working on a book project that takes Hassan al-Banna's teachings and expounds on them from the point of view of Islamic jurisprudence.

But how, we still want to ask, does an individual make sense of these multiple viewpoints and reconcile them with his or her self-understanding

₁ Islam and experience of daily life? How are choices made about which of these several and quite discrepant paths, all of which are apparently prescribed and mandated by Islam, an individual Muslim will follow? These are questions that can be more fully explored by examining various aspects of contemporary Islam's listening publics.

Transnational communities and religious authority

The increase in transnational people flows associated with globalization is directly connected to the establishment of new Muslim immigrant and diaspora communities over the past decade, particularly in Europe and North America (see Chapter 8). These new communities are especially interesting to look at from the point of view of religious authority for a number of reasons. First of all, in the process of moving sometimes thousands of miles from homeland societies into new and unfamiliar sociocultural settings, one is disembedded from an existing order of religious practice and authority and relocated to social spaces in which the structures of religious authority—if they exist at all—might seem quite different and alien. In the case of Muslim communities resettled in the West, it is important to note that we are also often dealing with situations of migration from a society in which Muslims are in the majority to societies where Islam is in the minority—and in many cases little understood as a religion or viewed as strange and incompatible with prevailing sociocultural norms. Under these circumstances it becomes less easy to take one's religion for granted since it is no longer an intrinsic part of the social fabric or the ambient cultural environment. Some studies of Islam among migrant communities suggest that this sudden awareness of one's religious otherness can lead to a greater propensity among some Muslims to "objectify" their religion—that is, to think about it for the first time as something whose meaning and function need to be considered and, in some cases, reformulated.[23] Let us recall that in the case of Muslim communities in Britain, for example, we saw a propensity within the first generation to try as much as possible to reproduce religious practices from the homeland within these new settings. In terms of religious authority, this was manifested in a tendency to stay within and in some cases to even intensify sectarian boundaries, and to "import" imams from their countries of origin in order to provide religious services.[24] This can be contrasted with the second and third generations who have tended to express various degrees of dissatisfaction with their parents' idiom of Islam, finding in it little of use in terms of helping them to navigate their culturally hybrid and hyphenated identities (e.g. British-Muslim). As regards religious authority, the younger generation has often turned away from traditional mosque leaders (particularly those from abroad) and sought instead to develop groups and movements with like-minded peers looking for an Islam that speaks to their specific issues and problems. Hence the popularity of younger, home-grown voices in certain Muslim contexts, such as the Young

Muslims UK movement, or, in the United States, Hamza Yusuf and the San Francisco-based Zaytuna Institute.

That said, the Pew survey mentioned above found that Muslims in Europe are still on average twice or three times more likely to seek religious guidance from imams and institutions abroad than their counterparts in Muslim majority countries.[25] In some cases, also, state authorities actively seek to influence and discipline religious practice within their diaspora populations, as in the case of the Turkish Diyanet's activities within migrant communities in Germany.

Global networks of religious authority

Religious authority in Islam is not exclusively confined to single individuals or institutions. Utilizing the wide range of connective and communicative technologies available in today's global world, it has been possible for some authority figures in Islam to begin building global networks that link like-minded opinion makers and institutions across a wide range of local and national settings. Those with formal training in the classical disciplines of Islamic scholarship are able to speak to counterparts in other countries using a common professional language—leading some to emphasize the "cosmopolitan" nature of ulama discourse.[26] Much like the transnational advocacy networks (TANs) discussed in the previous chapter, these constellations of religious scholars constitute conduits through which particular interpretations of Islam—and juristic activity derived from them in the form of fatwas—can be disseminated to widely dispersed audiences. They represent, in short, a means by which a global constituency for certain approaches to Islam can be created and sustained. One of the clearest examples of this is to be found in the various international fiqh councils that have been established in recent years. While some of these, such as the European Council for Fatwa and Research (ECFR), are closely associated with notable religious scholars such as Yusuf al-Qaradawi, others are connected with the official religious establishments of particular governments, as in the case of Saudi Arabia and the Fiqh Council of the Muslim World League, or the International Islamic Fiqh Academy of the Organization of the Islamic Conference. As with previous examples, the political orientations of these networks run the gamut from highly progressive (such as the Liberal Islam Network in Southeast Asia) to revolutionary jihadism (as represented by various affiliates within the Al-Qaeda network—see Chapter 7). These networks, their members, and the composition of their audiences are particularly important to understand because they act as "force multipliers" for specific interpretations of Islam and allow for the transnational propagation and "translation" of these approaches into a much wider range of societal and political settings. It should be pointed out, however, that the strength of their authority is only as good as Muslims' willingness to pay attention to them. It is not the case, for example, that the establishment of the ECFR in

Jublin sent shockwaves across Europe's Muslim community. Indeed, most Muslims in Europe have probably never heard of it. Rather, the ECFR provides those Muslims already predisposed to a Sunni, MB-oriented Islam with a "local" institution able to bring this perspective to bear on the specific issues they face in the European context.

While many of the examples cited above relate to networks structured around the dissemination of fatwas generated by traditional ulama, it is certainly not the case that today's transnational Muslim networks convey exclusively orthodox discourses. The Progressive Islam movement, for example, seeks to open spaces for liberal and pluralistic interpretations of Islam and its broad network connects regional groups in Southeast Asia, South Africa, Europe and North America.[27] The movement is particularly popular with the younger generation of Muslims living in the West where high levels of education make it possible for them to engage with the intellectualist orientation of the Progressive Islam approach. It is also worth mentioning here the advocacy and solidarity network Women Living Under Muslim Law (WLUML) (see Chapter 8). While it does not primarily self-identify as a Muslim group, WLUML is important to consider for our purposes because much of its work involves providing women in various local settings with resources that will permit them to contest human rights violations committed against them in the name of "authoritative" Islam. Their training and information materials, such as *Great Ancestors: Women Asserting Rights in Muslim Contexts*, are designed to be used by local womens' organizations in a variety of settings to challenge prevailing assumptions about the historical absence of women from public life and processes of social change.[28]

The role of new media and popular Islam: a virtual ummah?

Much has been written about the impact of new media on Islam and politics in recent years, with various observers emphasizing very different aspects of this phenomenon. Some scholarly accounts have emphasized the pluralizing effects of new Muslim media spheres, while popular media coverage tends toward a focus on the Internet as a space of radical Islamist networking or satellite television as a conduit for Islamic terrorism.[29] Our purpose in what follows, however, is not to come to definitive conclusion about whether new media have a pluralizing or radicalizing effect on Muslim politics. We will provide instead an analysis of how new communications technologies have had an impact not only on how and where Muslims seek religious authority, but also on what counts as authoritative Islam and who counts as a legitimate figure of authority. As Charles Hirschkind has argued, the scholarly debate about the impact of modernity and new media on religious practice has generally been framed in terms of two seemingly exclusive processes: (1) media as permitting the extension of religion's disciplining and authoritative properties so as to facilitate conformity with a particular moral order; or (2)

Table 9.2 Internet penetration rates for selected Muslim countries

Country	Internet Penetration Rates (%)
Afghanistan	0.1
Algeria	5.8
Bangladesh	0.2
Egypt	7.0
Indonesia	8.1
Iran	10.8
Iraq	0.1
Jordan	11.9
Kuwait	26.6
Lebanon	15.5
Libya	3.3
Malaysia	40.2
Mali	0.6
Morocco	15.2
Nigeria	3.1
Pakistan	6.4
Palestine	7.5
Qatar	20.7
Saudi Arabia	10.8
Senegal	5.0
Somalia	0.7
Sudan	7.8
Syria	4.2
Tajikistan	0.1
Tunisia	9.3
Turkey	21.4
United Arab Emirates	36.1
Uzbekistan	3.3
Yemen	1.1

Note: Internet penetration rate signifies the percentage of total population with access to Internet communications. Source: Internet World Stats, *Usage and Population Statistics*, 20 December 2006.

media as opening new spaces of deliberation and a concomitant democratization of authority in the religious sphere.[30]

While new arenas of religious discourse have certainly been created, this does not necessarily mean that the messages, values and norms communicated within these spaces are also new. It can be argued that in many cases traditional forms of authority and articulation work very well in new media spaces, and indeed, have used these spaces to reach out to an expanded audience base. In other cases, however, we find that new Muslim public spheres do allow for some level of pluralization in religious discourse, lowering the barriers to participation and permitting new figures to lay claim to Islamic authority. In the end, though, we cannot truly understand the impact of new media on Islamic authority without placing it in the context of changing patterns in terms of how Muslims understand and consume religion, and also the control and ownership of information sources.

Our account of new media and Islam picks up where we left off above when discussing the impact of mass education on the authority of the ulama. The central dynamic here is the same, but potentially even more radical: not just more and more Muslims having direct access to the primary sources of religious authority, but also the possibility that more and more Muslims can now put forward their own views on Islam before a mass audience. But first a few words of clarification regarding what is meant here by "new media." While new technologies are certainly heavily implicated in the two main forms of new media we will be examining below—namely satellite television and the Internet—the impact on religious authority has more to do with changing patterns of access to and ownership of the media than with the technologies themselves. Thus the "newness" of these media lies not just in the fact that they are often enabled by technological advancements, but also in the nature and structure of their social impact. Several dimensions or "effects" of this phenomenon are of particular significance:

(1) *The rise of mass audiences* – a phenomenon that begins with the printing press and the first wide circulation newspapers, the ability of a particular message to reach mass audiences (in the hundreds of thousands if not millions) is today primarily associated with broadcast media such as television and satellite television, but also with new information technologies such as the Internet.
(2) *Reduced production barriers* – not only are ever larger audiences able to receive messages, but new media such as the Internet also make it relatively easy for almost anyone to produce and disseminate information.
(3) *Proliferating spheres of participation* – the combination of the previous two effects makes for considerably increased conversation and deliberation across a multitude of communicative spheres. While not necessarily always democratizing or pluralizing in the sense of making space for disparate views to be heard and considered equally, scales of participation are markedly augmented.
(4) *Changing patterns of ownership and control* – some new media forms make it possible to challenge or transcend prior forms of regulating access to information. Satellite television, for example, provides an alternative to state-owned channels—yet its content still remains subject to certain market considerations. The relatively low cost of setting up a presence on the Internet and the ability to host it beyond the reach of state authorities make it possible for individuals and groups to have a political voice far less susceptible to official censorship.

In several places this book has already mentioned various examples of media becoming an integral part of Muslim politics. In Chapter 2, for example, we saw Jamal al-Din al-Afghani make extensive use of late nineteenth-century "new media" to publish the journal *Al-Urwat al-Wuthqa* ("The Firmest Bond") and circulate it to a transnational Muslim audience out of an office in Paris, France. Later we saw the important role that smuggled audio cassettes of Ayatollah Khomeini's sermons played in preparing the way for the 1979 Islamic Revolution in Iran, and also the "denial of service" tactics employed against Saudi government fax machines by the Islamist opposition in London. Lebanon's Hizbullah has its own satellite TV station, *Al-Manar*, and we have talked about the important role of salafi-jihadi websites in sustaining the transnational radical movement. And clearly a good many of the transnational movements and groups discussed in Chapter 8 make extensive use of new communications technologies.

Looking at more mainstream Internet use among Muslims, there are a number of key points to make. The first of these is that until relatively recently it was only possible to talk about the Internet having an impact on Muslims in the West. This is due to the fact that in most Muslim-majority countries, Internet penetration rates are still very low (see Table 9.2). It was primarily in diasporic contexts that we began to see "Islamic" websites during the second half of the 1990s. These chat rooms, discussion boards, and portals emerged as alternative spaces for the discussion of religion and Muslim identity and as sources of information about the availability of religious services in contexts where access to such resources was often scarce. On the discussion boards associated with these sites could often be found various conversations and debates about the merits and defects of various schools of thought in Islam and their representative scholars. But Muslims would also put forward their own understandings and interpretation of various matters relating to religious practice, and also jurisprudence. In short, some of these forums became new spaces of ijtihad, no doubt greatly assisted by the fact that by the late 1990s it was possible to use a search engine to comb vast online databases of hadith and other key textual sources. Sites sprang up where users could submit by e-mail or online form a request for a fatwa, and a response would be received, also electronically, from a "scholar" of Islam. Given the anonymous nature of Internet communications, however, it was often difficult to discern anything about the credentials of the ulama on the other side of these web portals. In at least one case it turned out that the scholar in question was an enterprising graduate student in engineering at a university in the southern United States who moonlighted as an alim.[31] The important point to be made here is that in formal terms the juridical opinions dispensed on these sites often looked very similar to those produced by scholars with formal training. These lay "experts" had learned to mimic the grammar and forms of juridical discourse and, with a thousand miles between them and their audience, were able to masquerade as bona fide ulama. Certainly there was a market waiting to be tapped: immigrant Muslims generally have less easy access to religious expertise, so it is not surprising that even once online fatwa services and satellite TV call-in shows were established in the Middle East, most of the queries came from Muslims living in the West.

This does not mean, however, that the traditional ulama ignored the advent of information technology. A great many Islamic universities quickly recognized the values of computerized storage as an archival medium and began scanning many of the classical works of Islamic learning. Soon a number of websites associated with prominent ulama came online and it became possible to access a select range of their works and scholarly opinions online. One particularly important development in this area was the establishment of islamonline.net, a site associated with and under the general guidance of Sheikh Yusuf al-Qaradawi. Qaradawi's site, in both English and Arabic, has become very popular with Muslims in the West since they perceive it as affiliated with a renowned figure of indisputable authority. Today, many of the major religious scholars from various sects and schools of thought have a presence on the web, with a particularly strong showing by major Shi'i figures such as Grand Ayatollah Ali Montazeri (www.amontazeri.com), Muhammad Hussein Fadlallah, regarded by many as the spiritual leader of Hizbullah (www.bayynat.org.lb), and Grand Ayatollah Ali Sistani in Iraq (www.sistani.org).

The form of new media that has had the most significance in the wider Muslim world, however, is undoubtedly satellite television. The Qatari-based Pan-Arab channel Al-Jazeera emerged in the late 1990s as the first of several satellite-based news channels (which now include Dubai's Al-Arabiya and Saudi Arabia's al-Ekhbariya) seeking to break the mold of standard state-controlled media in the Arab world. Al-Jazeera sought to define itself as an open, pluralistic and uncensored forum through its slogan "*al-ra'i w'al-ra'i al-akhr*" ("one view, another view"). In addition to its continual news coverage, groundbreaking shows such as "*al-ittija al-muwakis*" ("the opposite direction") quickly won a mass following through their hard-hitting, critical discussion of current affairs. Arab audiences watched while, for the first time, government figures and other public authorities were subjected to no holds barred questioning regarding their policies and forced to defend themselves. Unsurprisingly, the station ruffled some feathers among those governments targeted by its programming, prompting complaints to the Qatari authorities. To Arab audiences, however, this simply proved that a media outlet in their region was finally playing the critical and investigative role they had long hoped for.

It was also Al-Jazeera that first catapulted Sheikh Yusuf al-Qaradawi to widespread regional prominence. On the show "Shari'ah w'al-Hayat" ("Shari'ah and Life"), where he has been a mainstay, Qaradawi discusses all manner of topics, many of which—such as matters relating to medical technology and sex—are not the standard fare of religious television programming in the Arab world. Callers are invited to phone in with questions and Qaradawi dispenses wisdom and guidance live on air for all to see. This program helped him to develop a unique reputation as a classical scholar of impeccable pedigree (he is a graduate of Al-Azhar University) and undisputed authority, but one who was willing to discuss and deliberate on "modern" subject matter and to help Muslims to see Islam as relevant to specific issues of the day. We should note that despite the "interactive" phone-in component of Shari'ah w'al-Hayat, the show is still rather traditional in that it is structured around a revered religious authority dispensing knowledge; it is not a forum for the discussion of different interpretations of religion. As Jakob Skovgaard-Petersen puts it, "Yusuf al-Qaradawi represents the Shari'ah, and everybody else represents life."[32] In more recent years, satellite channels devoted exclusively to religious programming, such as Saudi Arabia's *Iqra*, have been established and launched the careers of a new generation of popular religious figures—not least of all the Islamic "televangelist" Amr Khaled (see below)—who serve up a rather different sort of religious television.

"Popular Islam": piety, consumption, and public religion

The point above about websites as arenas for the discussion of competing interpretations of religion and scriptural sources helps us toward recognizing another important phenomenon associated with the migration of religious discourse and symbolic capital into spaces not formally constituted as "religious." Some scholars have noted how the introduction of religious commodities—posters, games, models, key chains, various talismans—into local economies of meaning have led to novel interpolations of "Muslimness" and modern life.[33] Others have looked more specifically at how the mass circulation and incorporation of certain media forms into everyday life have opened new spaces of public religion. Hirschkind, for example, has studied the impact of audio cassette recordings of sermons in Cairo, pointing out that in many cases the conveyance of authoritative speech from the mosque to the car or into the home does not simply represent a new extension of religion's disciplining power. He argues instead that these cassettes and the conversations they provoke often occasion considerable deliberation and debate regarding the boundaries of religious normativity. In this sense they create new Muslim public "counterpublics" in which listeners turn into active agents for the social production of religious knowledge and public religiosity.[34] Similar to what can be seen on the aforementioned website discussion boards, "reference to authoritative Islamic sources does not close debate. Instead, the lines of argument pivot precisely on the proper interpretation of those sources."[35]

Other examples allow us to take this insight even further and ask questions about how the commodification and repackaging of religiosity may in fact also indicate a shift in how Muslims in certain settings understand and pursue political or socially transformative action in the name of Islam. Among Muslim communities in the West, for example, the commodified commingling of religious symbols and the aesthetics of youth culture has seen the emergence of product lines that might be associated with something like "cool Islam"—hip-hop music, clothes, comedy, etc. The American Muslim hip-hop act Native Deen or the British *nashid* (religious chant or song) singer Sami Yusuf represent this trend, as do various clothing lines such as Muslim Gear. Beyond allowing one to be cool while being Muslim, some of these products also incorporate elements of religiously prescribed normativity, in effect subsuming the fulfillment of religious obligations within practices of consumption. We can cite the rise of "*hijab* fashion" as an example of this, and also the advent of retail schemes that permit Muslims to pay their zakat tithe by purchasing certain products that generate a percentage of their value in charitable donations. Jenny White, writing about Turkey, talks about what she terms the rise of a "Muslimhood" model that involves the use and consumption of objects imbued with religion (books, games, TV shows) in all aspects of everyday life.[36]

Some observers have seen in this a shift in the way Muslims understand the location and nature of doing politics. As Amel Boubekeur has noted:

> [T]he Islamic identity need no longer be represented as political, ideological, and institutional, but as the choice of an individual consumer ...
> Where the traditional Islamist militancy was heavy, expensive, and very framed, the Islamic identity suggested by this new culture sets up mobilizations, identifications, modes of actions, and participation that is less expensive, less stigmatizing. The classical notions of Islamism, such as the sacrifice for the cause and the suffering, weak, and dominated disappear. What is proposed is the revalorization of the personal pleasure of consumption, success, and competitiveness.[37]

This trend is not confined to Muslims in the West. In the Arab world it can be seen, for example, in the meteoric rise of the television preacher Amr Khaled. With a purely secular educational background, Khaled's programs on the Saudi-owned Iqra religious channel owe a considerable debt to the style and discourse of American televangelists such as Billy Graham, or Joel Osteen, and talk show hosts such as Oprah Winfrey. We can best understand the phenomenon by contrasting Amr Khaled with previous idioms of religious television. Egypt's most popular TV sheikh through much of the 1990s had been the venerable Muhammad al-Sha'arawi. Broadcasting from a mosque in the traditional attire of a religious scholar, the aesthetics of his show were austere, sober, reverent—that is, *religious* according to the conventional style. Sha'arawi's discourse represented for the most part the Islam of the Egyptian state. This was an Islam of worship, piety, and morality—an Islam that belonged in the home, in the mosque, and in one's commitment to education, work and family; politics, much less jihad, never entered the picture. With the rise of Al-Jazeera, this mold was broken by Yusuf al-Qaradawi, the former Muslim Brother broadcasting from beyond the reach of the Egyptian state. It is not so much that Qaradawi's discourse represented a direct and overt politicization of religion, but that he would pronounce on any and all topics that happen to be raised. Arabs publics, unsurprisingly, had a lot of questions about the political implications of their religion and issues such as democracy, the legitimacy of various regimes, relations with the West, and the meaning and role of jihad.

If Sha'arawi was state Islam and Qaradawi a voice of mainstream Islamism operating beyond the effective reach of state authority, Amr Khaled represents still a third approach.[38] Gone are the turban and cloak of the alim, replaced instead by a young, clean-shaven man attired in designer Western suits. His set is modern, ergonomic; it looks like *Oprah Winfrey*. The content and style of the program is very different from either of the sheikhs. Khaled does not preach, lecture, or offer religious opinions according to the norms of Islamic scholarly discourse. His speech is not characterized by pronouncements about whether various practices or behaviors are *halal* ("permissible") or *haram* ("forbidden") by the shari'ah. Amr Khaled's Islam is one of hope, prosperity, and the possibility of gaining God's love, favor, and forgiveness. It emphasizes piety not simply as a matter of ritual obligation, but as a way in the world that complements the pursuit of personal success and affluence. As Tammam and Haenni argue:

> The secret of his success [is] that he position[s] himself outside the rivalry between political and official Islam, by offering a religious product compatible with the modern expectations of the urban middle classes: a worldly religion that talks about inner peace and spiritual well-being, and rejects religious observance in which rite is an end in itself. It refuses to see Allah as a God of retribution.[39]

Amr Khaled is not, however, a purveyor of liberal or progressive Islam; this is most certainly not an "Islam is whatever you make of it" approach. He emphasizes, for example, the importance of many traditional social norms associated with religion such as the headscarf. But such observances need not involve renouncing the pleasures of life. Indeed, a good Muslim on his account should seek to acquire wealth and to make others want to emulate their success. This approach has earned Amr Khaled a tremendous following among the young, educated, socially mobile middle classes of Egypt and other Arab countries—particularly among women, who find in his gentleness and openness a refreshing contrast to the dour disposition of traditional ulama. Perhaps not surprisingly, Khaled has come in for considerable criticism from a variety of more traditionally religious camps. Ulama question his credentials and his authority to speak about matters of religion at all. The MB and figures associated with it—perhaps alarmed at the prospect of losing an entire generation to this new trend—dismiss Amr Khaled as a representative of "air-conditioned Islam."[40] Tariq Ramadan, for instance, castigates him for avoiding difficult social and political issues, claiming that once viewers realize the superficiality of his religious discourse they will abandon him in favor of a more socially engaged, activist Islam.

As regards the Egyptian state's attitude toward Amr Khaled, it would appear on the surface that his approach to religion is right in line with their desire to push a modernized and personalized form of Islam compatible with capitalism and economic growth. But the relationship is considerably more complicated than that, as evidenced by the fact that Amr Khaled is currently based outside Egypt and not permitted to give public lectures in the country. What worries the state is not so much the content of his programming, which—as we have seen—would be regarded as wholly innocuous, but rather the fact that his enormous following represents a base of potential social mobilization on a national scale. Some have expressed fears that he is actually working in conjunction with the MB—a wolf in sheep's clothing, so to speak—and that once the moment is ripe, he will turn his followers to the cause of Islamism. Others, taking a warning from Tariq Ramadan's critique of Khaled, fear that a large segment of the latter's supporters will, once they develop a taste for a more activist stance, desert Amr Khaled in favor of the Brotherhood. Whatever his larger intentions, if any, it is clear that Amr Khaled's project is evolving. In his more recent program *Suna'a al-Hayah* ("Lifemakers"), Khaled urges his viewers to channel their piety into social welfare and community development projects, and to send in accounts and video footage of their efforts so that they can be broadcast for all to see. It also provides an opportunity for networking between these "lifemakers" so as to enable them to leverage and scale up the impacts of each other's projects. This "taking Islam into the streets" would of course be viewed as rather problematic by the state, and, in the case of Egypt would look remarkably similar to some of the activities of the early MB under Hassan al-Banna.

All these concerns, however, miss the essentially "post-Islamist" (see Chapter 10) character of Amr Khaled's approach. While transformation and social change are clearly on his agenda, they are pursued in a manner that neither asks fundamental questions about the prevailing political order nor seeks to directly advise or influence the keepers of that order—as the MB did and still does. This is a rather different kind of collective action. Boubekeur puts it thusly:

> The traditional intra-Islamic modes of action and mobilization, such as aggressive street demonstrations and political militancy, make less sense. The new Islamic elites reinterpret their relations ... in terms of networks and partnerships. Notions of partnership will develop according to standards of competence and competitiveness.[41]

... or, in other words, according to free market norms. When translated into politics this approach would likely lead Egyptian voters toward the centrist blend of religion and modern political economy represented by the

Hizb ul-Wasat or other "Muslim democratic" parties (see Chapter 4) rather than to the MB. This orientation is part of a wider trend found in other parts of the Muslim world. In Indonesia, for example, the popular preacher Abdullah Gymnastiar, who commands audiences of up to 80 million, incorporates elements of modern motivational speaking and management strategy into his religious discourse.[42] The Turkish religious entrepreneur Fethullah Gülen (see above) is another figure who emphasizes the Islamic injunction to pursue personal wealth, creating—in Boubekeur's words—a form of "Islamic ethic allied with cultural globalization."[43] In the United Kingdom one can point to the establishment of the Muslim lifestyle magazine *Emel*, specifically targeted at socially mobile young Muslims, and women in particular.

This chapter has sought to survey the heterogeneous and rapidly shifting landscape of contemporary Islamic authority in the context of globalization and the changing nature of public religiosity. We have surveyed both the major actors involved in advancing claims to religious authority, and the diverse range of audiences to which they appeal. Various forms of new media and patterns of consumption emerged as particularly important in the context of a new "post-Islamist" approach to Muslim politics. This leads us to ask questions about how globalization processes might be reconfiguring the very terrain of religious politics in the Muslim world. In the next and final chapter we will draw out several key "meta-issues" that will likely act as key drivers of Muslim politics in the coming years and also consider the debate on "post-Islamism" before offering some reflections on the likely impact of globalization on the future of Muslim politics.

10 Beyond Islamism: globalization and Muslim politics

This book has covered considerable ground in seeking to understand the nature of contemporary Muslim politics. We began by tracing the intellectual and political roots of modern Islamism in the context of state formation in the Muslim world. We then examined various explanatory accounts of Islamism before moving on to the first of several case studies. After working through multiple examples of Islam and politics in the system, as the system, and in the absence of a system, we moved on to analyze the nature of today's transnational Islamic radicalism. An examination of several other major spaces and institutions through which Muslim politics occur today brought us, in the previous chapter, to examine the question of who speaks for Islam in today's globalized world. It has become clear through our wanderings across the many terrains of Muslim politics that we are not dealing with a monolithic phenomenon. Islam and politics commingle in almost infinite variety across a vast range of settings, issues, actors, and levels of analysis.

In seeking to highlight these many and often quite disparate trajectories of contemporary Muslim politics, we find ourselves faced with a considerable challenge in concluding this volume. Ours has primarily been a survey effort, an attempt to reveal to the reader the myriad shapes and forms of Muslim politics across the umma, and less an attempt to assert a discrete thesis or argument. While certainly structured in our approach, we have not sought to impose a single organizing principle on our coverage of Islam and politics. Therefore, to try in this final chapter to force artificial convergence on so diverse a phenomenon in the hope of pithy summary would be to defeat the basic premise of our approach. So rather than seeking to draw together and reconcile the divergent strands of Muslim politics running through this book, we will leave them to run their many and as yet indeterminate courses. Our efforts here will focus instead on three tasks. First we will delve back into the morass of empirical material thus far presented and from it pick out several key themes and cleavages that might be identified as among the drivers of Muslim political futures. These will be presented across three principle domains: Islamist politics, religious knowledge, and Muslim identity. We will then move on to a critical analysis of the debate on post-Islamism—a concept that has been hinted at throughout the volume, but whose full consideration we have deliberately left until the end. The question of post-Islamism, we will argue, has important implications not only for the future of Muslim politics, but also for the methods by which we study both Islam and the political. The final section of this conclusion will then offer some reflections on various aspects of globalization and globalizing processes in terms of how they may inflect the many futures of Muslim politics.

Key themes and tensions: Islamist politics, religious knowledge, Muslim identity

The wealth of empirical and case study material we have explored over the course of this volume suggest that there are three "meta issues" around which we might build a discussion of the major themes and tensions present in today's Muslim politics. These are the changing nature of Islamist politics; the politics of religious knowledge ("who speaks for Islam?"); and then, finally, several issues relating to how Muslims understand their identities—and, in particular, their political identities—in the context of globalization. We will consider each of these in turn.

Islamist politics

As has become clear, particularly through our analysis of Islam "in the system" in Chapter 4, the standard model of Islamist politics seems to be undergoing considerable transformation today in many contexts. We presented this as a shift to a "new Islamism," and located it in the activities of groups such as the Hizb al-Wasat party in Egypt and the AKP in Turkey. Read by some as the harbingers of a new era of "Muslim Democracy," this shift certainly merits some careful consideration in terms of what it reveals about the fault lines present within the Islamist project and the hints it provides as to where it might be going. The first point to be made here relates to the shifting sociology of Islamism. In the cases of both Hizb al-Wasat and AKP we saw breakaway factions from within traditional Islamist movement splitting off to pursue a different course. For the most part, these were younger activists who had concerns about lack of meaningful participation on two fronts. First, internally, they felt as if the stewardship of their "mother" parties, the Egyptian Muslim Brotherhood (MB) and Refah/ Virtue, respectively, was in the hands of an "old guard" who were behind the times in terms of their strategic vision and also unwilling to allow the younger generation any meaningful say in the making of party policy. On the external front, and related to this first point, this new generation felt as if the reactionary policies and practices of the old guard prevented the party from evolving to a point where it would have the opportunity to participate in the discussion and resolution in the political sphere of crucial questions now facing their respective societies. While Hizb al-Wasat has still to gain official recognition as a political party and the AKP rode to power on a powerful wave of popular dissatisfaction with Turkey's corrupt political system, their futures—and that of Islamism more generally—will depend on how the strategic vision of these movements fits in with prevailing public sentiments. An important point here, and one made by several observers such as Ray Baker and Graham Fuller, is that in many respects the discourse of traditional Islamism is an "Islam of fear" or "the Islam that says no."[1] In other words, it is a breed of politics more concerned with delineating between right and wrong, imposing moral strictures, and telling people what they can and cannot do, rather than offering positive and distinctive solutions to pressing problems. The "new Islamists," with their emphasis on pragmatism and policy rather than public virtue, are seeking to redress this by figuring Islam as a discourse of progress and social justice. So we see here a distinct generational divide over vision and strategy. But that may itself be too simple an analysis. As the work of scholars such as Carrie Wickham shows, this is not simply a divide between young and old, with the young Islamists preferring pragmatism and the old Islamists mired in ideological dogma. Rather, she suggests, there has been a far more complicated process of Islamist "auto reform" underway, one that pervades the Islamist movement as a whole.[2] Indeed, it is possible to identify older "new Islamists" and also younger activists who have elected to remain with the Brotherhood—both of who believe that the MB is perfectly capable of accommodating, indeed become the vanguard, of a new Islamist pragmatism.

But the future of Islamism is, of course, not only about internal upheavals. Much of it will depend on the wider political and societal environments in which Islamist actors operate. It is likely that in the next round of parliamentary elections in Turkey, the AKP will have to contend with a political environment that has adjusted to its presence, and has closed down its monopoly on certain issues relating to anti-corruption, good governance, European accession, and political legitimacy. In many ways this will be "Muslim Democracy's" first real test—that is, having its vision and implementation assessed in terms of the value they add to a political marketplace characterized by what Brumberg calls "dissonance" (meaning a multiplicity of distinct and competing political agendas).[3] AKP has, for the most part, stayed away from "religious" issues, and yet it has a party base that is looking for it to address these—and, all the while, the Turkish army (guardians of the Kemalist legacy) watches carefully over its shoulders. In Egypt, too, much hinges on how the existing authorities respond to new popular demands for political openness—best represented, perhaps, in the media spectacle that was the Kifaya movement. Was this perhaps not just an ephemeral moment—the illusion of mass undercurrents of concerted popular discontent made visible in an age where SMS text messaging makes the temporary mobilization of thousands a relatively easy task to accomplish: political protest almost as a form of leisure activity? To dismiss it this way would be unfair and to misread the thrust of popular politics in Egypt today. The question is really about the state and how it will deal with trying to balance the preservation of old guard privileges with the demands of a generation of politically conscious, technologically savvy, and less easily co-opted Egyptians. For the Islamists the question is whether they can make inroads with this generation. Part of the reason why both the MB and the Egyptian state have held back in recognizing the "new Islamists" is that they realize there is a potent force here. In an autocratic environment where the main goal of a government party is simply to hang on to power, "it is not the ideological profile of candidates which is the deciding factor," Francois Burgat argues: "[I]t is the Islamic opposition's estimated political power which determines their fortune for good or for ill."[4] Hizb al-Wasat combined with the popular mobilizing potential of a TV personality such as Amr Khaled (see Chapter 9) could pose a significant threat to both the old Islamists and the state. On this issue, at least, their interests are closely aligned. One wonders, then, whether the Brotherhood might make a deal with the state whereby it negotiates a legal return to the political sphere in return for reintegrating the renegade pragmatists. The tensions between "old" and "new" Islamism—and how their dance plays out in the context of wider political reform processes—will hence be important to watch over the coming years.

But with Egypt and Turkey we are dealing with two Muslim states where issues of social segmentation (tribe, clan, etc.) are less important, and where highly diversified social spheres have evolved over many decades. What of those settings where Islamists, and moreover Islamists of the fairly traditional sort (e.g. Jordan, Kuwait, Yemen), are already participating in politics, and where there is less evidence of an emerging schism within their respective movements? Here we would want to raise two issues in particular—ones that certainly apply to the MB in Egypt (which from 2006 had considerable parliamentary presence) as well as other Islamist movements in that same vein (e.g. Jama'at-i Islami in Pakistan or Malaysia's PAS) should they come to play a more prominent role in electoral politics. We are referring here to the issue of the shari'ah and the question of political power sharing. In many regards, and assuming that the legitimacy of the sovereign, modern nation-state as a political model is accepted, these represent the sole outstanding issues that cause problems with regard to Islamist participation in democratic politics.

The pursuit of a shari'ah-based political order has long been a hallmark—perhaps even the defining or constitutive—feature of Islamism. Within Islamist circles, and amongst interested outside observers, there has always been considerable speculation as to just what exactly this would entail. Practices have also varied. There are a number of countries in the Muslim world today, for example, where otherwise secular states are happy to allow issues of personal status (marriage, inheritance, etc.) to be regulated by shari'ah while reserving for themselves the conduct of other areas of the law (e.g. criminal justice, civil matters). Some aspects of the shari'ah seem rather clear cut if imported wholesale from scriptural and jurisprudential sources (e.g. personal status, hudud punishments). But we can also identify issue areas where the traditional sources have very little to say (e.g. medical ethics, regulatory policy) beyond general principles. And it is on this very question that the debate turns: to what extent does the "shari'ah-tization" of policy and law mean the direct and literal application of prescriptions found in classical Islamic jurisprudence or to what extent does it mean creating a legal code infused with the moral principles found within the teachings of religion? For those within the literalist camp the issue has been one of legislative authority. If sovereignty is God's alone, the authority to legislate rests similarly within the realm of the divine. The idea of the people as legislators is rejected; hence, also, the rejection by early Islamists of legislative democracy (see Chapter 3). The other camp argues that the shari'ah in its ostensible form is already the product of centuries of human interpretation and deliberation by religious scholars. Since revelation proceeds via language and language always involves human interpretation, "the people" are already intrinsically involved in its legal codification. The safest thing would therefore be to identify the general moral standards expressed by these teachings (as found in Qur'an and sunna) and allow these to act as the guiding principles, rather than the direct content, of legislation.

There certainly exist today Islamists who firmly espouse each of these two positions. Most, however, combine elements of both. Just to provide a sampling of some of certain views expressed by Islamist intellectuals and leaders who have sought to find a middle approach.

- Shari'ah can only ever apply in a direct and literal form to Muslim citizens. Non-Muslims can have their affairs regulated by their own personal status tradition, or be subject to a state civil code that might be informed by the "spirit" and "principles" of shari'ah.[5]
- The specific implementation of a given point of shari'ah should be left up to the ijma (consensus) of those governed by it. Therefore the citizens should choose from among a range of possible interpretations of a given legal point.[6]

So here are two positions—ranging from instrumentalism to pragmatism—that illustrate for us the diversity of views on this issue to be found amongst contemporary Islamists. Pushing the defenders of Islamism as shari'ah to substantiate their claims, Graham Fuller asserts that "there is no visible correlation between application of Shari'a law and the attainment of a better society and governance in today's Muslim world."[7] Declaring himself more a fan of the idea that "Islam is the solution" (in the sense of religious as a source of moral guidelines and spiritual resources for the conduct of everyday life) than the claim that "shari'ah is the solution," Fuller goes on to advocate the need to continually reinterpret Islamic principles in order to make them relevant to contemporary conditions and predicaments.[8] There are certainly Islamists who would agree with Fuller, but others who would offer a variety of retorts. Some would claim that the reason shari'ah has not appeared to better society is because there is nowhere today where it is being properly applied. The examples of Saudi Arabia and Afghanistan under the Taliban would likely be dismissed by many contemporary Islamists as too extreme; likewise, in Iran, the idea of clerical rule is still seen as too much of an innovation. Some, of course, would take issue with the way in which Fuller is likely defining "better society and governance"—but others, particularly among the new Islamists, would likely agree with him.

The question of shari'ah becomes particularly important when we come to consider questions relating to the role and rights of women. A political party holding conservative views regarding gender roles is not in and of itself a barrier to democratic participation since such groups are to be found in all societies. The problem here is more one of a potential conflict between the principle of the equality of all citizens, regardless of gender, and legislation that would seek to enshrine the differentiated rights of men and women (as found in the Qur'an and sunna) within a political framework. Again, the positions here vary considerably from context to context. There are conservative Islamists, particularly in countries in which tribal norms run strong, who would prefer a literalist application of Qur'anic strictures with regard to gender. Others argue that those aspects of the Qur'an and sunna should be read as products of their time that were articulated to match with prevailing norms. Rather, what should be extracted from this, in their view, is the idea that men and women have differentiated social roles, but that in legal terms they should be regarded as equals.

This debate is also one that seems, in practice, to break down along the lines of the old and new Islamists mentioned above. The advocates of Muslim democracy, such as the AKP in Turkey, have not included shari'ah in their legislative agenda. Indeed, their core support comes from a movement that understands religion largely in privatized and individualized terms (see Chapter 4). Islam for them is a source of morality, and, moreover, a morality that should guide their conduct within all spheres of life. But this is very different from saying that Islam's morality should be enshrined in law. For many of the "new Islamists," then, Islam is about turning religion into an agenda for anti-corruption, economic justice, and the pursuit of personal prosperity and happiness—hence, in Ray Baker's terms, an "Islam without fear." The divide between old and new Islamists, as we have mentioned, is useful in terms of reading developments within the sociology of the movement. The evolving position of Islamism on the question of shari'ah, however, will serve as an important indicator of where the movement is going in terms of its normative discourse.

The final issue to be considered under Islamist politics is the question of power sharing and political inclusiveness. For many skeptical about Islamism, this has long been the crux of the issue—hence the enduring power of the Islamism as "one man, one vote, one time" discourse; that is, the fear that once Islamists are in power, they would modify the political system to make sure they could never be voted out. It appears that Islamists gave up long ago on the idea of a totalist politics. As we will recall from Chapter 3, early Islamism eschewed the idea of party politics along the lines that it would likely lead to strife and fitna (disorder) within society. In their view, once an Islamic political order had been achieved, there would be no need for party politics. For some years now, Islamist parties in countries such as Jordan, Malaysia, Morocco, and Pakistan have been contesting and respecting the results of elections alongside parties representing a wide range of political orientations. It is true that we have not yet experienced a situation where a traditional or "old" Islamist party has been elected to rule on its own, but there is every reason to believe that Islamists today are becoming increasingly accustomed to the idea of sharing power with other groups and respecting the rules of multiparty democracy.

Through our case studies we have seen numerous examples of Islamist parties who have entered into alliances with secular parties not just because doing so allowed them, instrumentally, to gain access to the political sphere (such as the MB's partnership with the Wafd in Egypt in the 1980s), but because they have identified areas of common interest and realize that cooperation allows them to more effectively pursue their agenda—even if and when this entails some modicum of compromise. Once again, this has been a hallmark feature of what we have termed "new Islamism," but it is also clear that this willingness—even enthusiasm—for competitive political participation was evident even before the younger generations of Islamists began to assert themselves. In several countries, as we have also observed, Islamism represents the only meaningful form of organized political opposition. In other words, they do not yet have to compete with any political forces that rival them in strength or legitimacy. This, as Brumberg, points out, will also be an important indicator: how do Islamist parties conduct themselves in political environments where multiple political tendencies of roughly equal strength are vying for power?[9]

The politics of religious knowledge and authority

It is often remarked that we are witnessing today a struggle within Islam, a battle for Muslim hearts and minds contested among different claimants to true and authentic Islam. We examined many of these dynamics with regard to religious authority in Chapter 9. As became clear to us through that discussion, the crux of the issue is less about who speaks for Islam and more about the Muslims who are listening. Claims to religious authority are never absolute. Neither religious scholars nor "new Islamist intellectuals" nor populist media preachers possess undisputed authority to define and mandate the meaning and social requirements of religion. The important point to bear in mind is that the Muslims who constitute the target audience for these claims are not listening solely "as Muslims." Muslims are also students, mothers, voters, shoppers, sports fans, agricultural laborers, and software developers. As such they pursue multiple lines of social affiliation and understand their public identities in pluralistic terms. Their understandings of and orientations toward religion and its relevance to these various spheres of everyday life vary tremendously. Does this mean that Islam is just one of many prisms through which they engage the world? Yes, but this does not mean that it necesarity has a special or privileged role to play in how those who consider themselves believers engage the issues and problems in their lives. It does mean, however, that it becomes impossible to assume that the content and prescriptions of successful claims to Islamic religious authority articulated before Muslim audiences will determine the political behavior of the latter. Nodding to oneself while the imam rails against the immorality of modern society does necessarily mean joining an Islamist party the very next day.

Many observers of the Muslim world have asked why the reformist, modernist, or liberal variants of contemporary Islamic thought do not seem to have a strong following among Muslims today. Some have taken this to be evidence of Islam's anti-liberal or un-democratic character. But here do we need to ask the same questions about who is listening. Generally, we might postulate, it is not that Muslims outright "reject" the ideas of reformist Islam (see Chapter 9), but more that they have difficulty relating them to the circumstances of their social reality. We have already mentioned in the previous chapter that there is a formal barrier to the wider reception of these ideas in the very language employed for their articulation. But beyond that, there is also the question of the extent to which these reformist ideas correspond to the lived experience and needs of most Muslims. Let us consider an example. Many of the reformists emphasize the compatibility of Islam and democracy, showing very elegantly that at its roots the shari'ah is primarily a discourse of equality and participatory governance. It is also the case, however, that many citizens of Muslim majority countries have lost all faith in the idea that their ruling regimes will ever make space for real democracy. Indeed, many have become jaded regarding the whole notion of politics. "Politics" for them is simply a space in which traditional patterns of elite influence and client patron relationships play out. It has nothing to do with stakeholder citizens deciding collectively on their societies' futures. They have little interest in politics because "being political" or acting politically in the conventional sense of that term does not seem to have any bearing on their lives. Discourses on the democratic essence of Islam, therefore, elicit little more than shrugged shoulders in the lower middle-class suburbs of Cairo and Karachi.

Hardline and radical discourses, on the other hand, at least seem to capture something of the reality of existence in these settings. When Usama Bin Laden rails against the West and new forms of imperialism, it is at least possible for Muslims to see themselves as part of the reality he describes.

The vast majority of them find his solutions and methods to be ridiculous and immoral, *but he is addressing issues to which they can relate.* So while this certainly does not make for, as Bin Laden would wish, a mass mobilization of Muslims in support of Al-Qaeda, it does mean that many Muslims see little reason to invest in counter-discourses of supposed democracy and prosperity. The purveyors of the latter are seen, and are easily portrayed, as agents of Westernization. Not only are their ideas seen as largely irrelevant to the circumstances of most Muslims, but their legitimacy is in question. Under conditions where many Muslims see themselves as subject to the continuing influence of colonialism and imperialism (albeit in new forms), it becomes difficult for promises of socioeconomic and political deliverance to be taken seriously.

Clearly, then, making room for reformist and liberalizing Islamic discourses is much more than making people comfortable with the idea of multiple interpretations of religion (although this is a piece of it). Rather, it is more a case of attending to the geopolitical, domestic political, and socioeconomic realities that make it difficult for people to see anything of relevance to their lives in such ideas. Muslims will not invest in reformist Islam unless they have reasons to buy into the idea that the political and economic realities of their lives can also be reformed. Until then, reformist Islam will still read to many Muslims as an invitation to buy into the very system that maintains the hegemonies they see all around them. Under these circumstances, where no one else appears to be offering realistic alternative solutions, people will continue to be drawn to political discourses that at least narrate to them and reflect the conditions of their disenfranchisement—even as they reject en masse the sometimes radical and militant prescriptions that accompany these claims. Radicals and ultra-conservatives pursue a "politics of authenticity" by questioning whether reformist discourses represent anything more than the corruption of Muslim minds with Western values and ideas. Clearly, as Graham Fuller argues, it makes little sense to speak about the "authenticity" of either Western or Islamic ideas since both bear the traces of so many historical, cultural, and political encounters.[10] Islamism is hardly a rejection of modernity—rather, it affirms the idea of individual political subjectivity and the possibility to achieve positive, progressive change through human agency. These are ideas clearly present in both the Western liberal and Islamic traditions. It is therefore not a matter of making better claims to "true" Islam by reformists, or of finding comprehensive evidence to the effect that reformist values are consonant with the jurisprudential sources of Islam. To play this game is to remain trapped within a discourse of authenticity. Rather, this debate should be reconstituted as a "politics of relevancy" and played out within the realm of the political. Muslims will respond pragmatically to solutions that actually effect their lives much more than they will to assurances that the ideas behind those solutions are Islamic.

Muslim political identity in the shadow of the umma

Olivier Roy has written about the "deterritorialization" of Muslim political identity, while other writers have spoken of "transnational political Islam" or "reimagining the umma."[11] All of these authors are trying to capture the sense today in which Muslims appear sometimes to be caught between the universalizing and particularistic aspects of their identities. Accompanying this is further deliberation and debate as to what holding a Muslim identity means in political terms. As the various case studies we examined have shown us, it is evident that the solution to this question plays out rather differently across disparate contexts. In Western countries, for example, where Muslims (some of them "deterritorialized" in Roy's sense of the term) live as religious minorities under political systems controlled by non-Muslims, this has sometimes produced debates about whether it is permissible for Muslims to participate politically in such systems. How, in other words, should they regard issues related to the rights and duties associated with citizenship in states ruled by non-Muslims (see Chapter 8)? In countries where Muslims are in the majority, the question of Muslim political identity has been engaged rather differently. It is less a question here of whether it is legitimate to participate in governments run by non-Muslims and more a question of whether Muslims have a religiously prescribed duty to pursue the establishment of an Islamic political order through politics. In these contexts, as we have seen, it is the very fact that Muslims hold a wide range of views about what their religion says about politics and public life that accounts for the multiplicity and diversity of Muslim politics that we have seen over the course of this volume.

While some Muslim political actors, particularly those working in the vein of transnational radicalism (see Chapter 7) have sought to mobilize Muslim hearts and minds around global, pan-Islamic agendas, most evidence suggests today that Muslim political identities are oriented primarily towards national or even local concerns. The ideal of the umma is simply far too abstract for most Muslims to relate to their daily lives. This does not mean, however, that globalization is irrelevant in terms of its effects on Muslim political considerations. In addition to Muslim attitudes toward the various political-economic effects commonly associated with globalization (see below), it is also the case that the increased senses of interconnectedness and communication associated with globalization have led to much higher levels of informed awareness about events going on in the world—a phenomenon that is, of course, hardly confined to Muslim settings. This means that geopolitical events and factors have come to play a larger role in Muslim political considerations. Even if Muslim identities remain primarily nationalized, this does not mean that it is not possible for them to make common cause with co-religionists elsewhere, or to sympathize with "Muslim" issues. This relates to the sense in which religion constitutes today an important sense of post-materialist identity and the basis for transnational social movements. In the same way that American and German environmental activists can jointly advocate for curbs on greenhouse gases without German and American political identity becoming one and the same, so can Senegalese and Malaysian Muslims advocate for an end to Israel's occupation of Palestine without this implying anything in particular about the existence of a new, global Muslim identity.

But there is another important point to be made about globalization and Muslim political identity, one that helps to form a bridge into our subsequent discussion of the notion of post-Islamism. This relates to the idea, advanced by various writers, that globalization may be having an impact on the modalities and locations through which politics occur. If globalization is understood to mean the hegemony and pervasive penetration of a particular mode of neoliberal economy, then it would stand to reason that globalization also has some effect on the reconfiguration of subjectivity and personhood. We see this particularly in the idea that globalization gives rise to forms of subjectivity defined and premised primarily in terms of practices relating to consumption. As the expression of particular values and moral systems in the public sphere come increasingly to be intertwined with forms of consumption, these same lifestyle practices begin to take on political connotations. Likewise, as states become primarily the guardians of the neoliberal order in a globally interdependent system of markets rather than politically "neutral" spaces in which competing visions of the good life vie for power, we are witnessing a retreat of the political into the social sphere—where, as we have just pointed out, social identities are increasingly structured by practices of consumption. This is much more complicated than simply a claim to the effect that "we are what we buy." Rather we are trying to indicate here a sense in which consumptive practices come to assume politically normative connotations at the same time that public identities find themselves increasingly figured in terms of consumptive practice. In many of the societies we examined in our case studies, the point was made that Islamist politics have been confined to, and have thoroughly socialized, many aspects of the social sphere. This would suggest that there is considerable potential for unique and innovative idioms of Muslim politics to occur in those settings where religiosity, consumption, and social identity find themselves occupying the same space. It is here that the notion of post-Islamism becomes relevant since some observers have seen in it signs of the privatization or individualization of religious practice. Rather than viewing this simply as evidence of the growing secularization (in the Western sense) of Muslim society under globalization— and hence the end of Islamism as a meaningful political project—we might also want to entertain the possibility that post-Islamism refers to a relocation and transformation of the political in terms of its interaction with Muslim subjectivity.

Post-Islamism and its discontents

The concept of post-Islamism is most commonly associated with the "French School" of Islamist analysis—namely Olivier Roy and Gilles Kepel. Roy initiated the debate in 1992, without yet, however, using the term "post-Islamist," with his book *The Failure of Political Islam*.[12] In this work he claimed that the failure of Islamists to advance their agenda through successfully obtaining state power was evidence that the movement had failed. Furthermore, the fact that some of them had begun to participate within pluralistic political systems as if their candidacy represented just another option among many (rather than God-given, indisputable normativity) was also seen as evidence that Islamism had become "domesticated" and had moved so far away from its initial formulations as to have become irreparably diluted. In a subsequent elaboration, this time framed explicitly in terms of "post-Islamism," Roy cited several additional features of contemporary Islamism that to his mind confirmed its demise.[13] In addition to the failure of Islamists to gain state power and their willingness to participate in political processes, evidence of our entry into the era of post-Islamism was seen by Roy in the following:

(1) Islamist movements are now almost universally *nationalist in orientation* and have mostly dropped the rhetoric of Pan-Islamic solidarity and umma-based identity. In other words, the world system of nation-states is no longer contested.
(2) There is *no geostrategic value* to accrue from pursuing an Islamist path, in the sense that the global system as it is currently configured rewards those who conform to the norms of free markets and democracy rather than the requirements of shari'ah.
(3) Even where they do contest elections, there is *no "Muslim vote"* that Islamists can reliably depend on; Muslims at the polls tend to vote their interests rather than their religious identities.
(4) By emphasizing democracy and civil society while trying to enter the political field, Islamists have contributed to the *inadvertent modernization and secularization* of their societies.
(5) Contemporary *"re-Islamization" is about the privatization of religion* and the triumph of individualistic conceptions of piety and the sacred over collective and socially mobilized Islamist projects. Religion and politics are here redefined as autonomous spheres.

For Roy, then, the utopian vision of the original Islamists has slowly dissolved over the years such that today, Islamism represents little more than a group of socially conservative political parties that are qualitatively indiscernible from any other political current.[14] He sees Islamist parties as having been worn down and more or less oppressed into political integration—to a point that they have actually, in some cases, become more open to democratic ideals than the authoritarian states that seek to control them.[15] The revolutionary edge of Islamism, in his analysis, has given way to accommodation within the existing system and—likewise—the rhetoric of social justice has disappeared from Islamist discourse.[16] Even quasi-revolutionary Islamists have turned on their own project when it appeared to interfere with national interests. Roy sees Sudanese President Bashir's jailing of Islamist ideologue Hassan al-Turabi and his subsequent initiation of peace talks with leaders of the Southern Sudanese People's Liberation Army (SPLA) as evidence of this.[17] Even the Taliban in Afghanistan, he points out, did not bother to create a strong, centralized Islamic state even though they had free reign to do so.[18] With regard to the heightened public religiosity visible in many Muslim countries, Roy sees nothing to favor the fortunes of Islamism. He sees this phenomenon—"re-Islamization" in his terms—primarily as the triumph of privatized, individualistic religion over socially mobilized, political struggle. It is worth quoting him at length on this since we will want to return to some of his specific language when we later move on to a critical discussion of the post-Islamist argument:

> Contemporary re-Islamization is a cluster of individual practices that are used as a means of finding jobs, money, respect, and self-esteem, and bargaining with a marginalized state that has played on conservative re-Islamisation but been unable to control it. The reference to Islam is everywhere and nowhere; it is diluted, pragmatically put forward for any purpose, ostensibly expressed in dress and speech, and instrumentalized in courts. In this sense ... re-Islamisation has nothing to do with state power and could not be labeled "totalitarian" ... The aim [of re-Islamization] is to reconstruct a true Muslim community by starting from the individual. It is based on an individual reappropriation of Islamic symbols, arguments, rhetoric and norms.[19]

Gilles Kepel, arguing essentially along the same lines in an essay entitled "Islamism Reconsidered," points out that Islamists today will frequently deploy the language of universal human rights rather than advancing Islamic alternatives.[20] He points also to the lack of a clear and cohesive program on the part of Islamists, citing the fact that their discourse appears variously and simultaneously to contain elements of reactionary rightist politics (moral structures, shari'ah, veiling), and also an emancipatory progressive agenda (social justice, anti-hegemony).[21] He also echoes Roy's point to the effect that the paths followed by some Islamists appear to have led toward greater secularization. "Paradoxically," Kepel argues, "the Islamist movement may have generated the conditions for its own obsolescence."[22]

There are a range of comments and objections that might be offered in response to Roy's (and, by extension, Kepel's) characterization of the post-Islamist condition. We should begin, however, by asking what their understanding of post-Islamism tells us about how they view Islamism, politics, and religion more generally. It is clear that for Roy, Islamism refers only to projects that seek to achieve an Islamization of the social order by capturing state power. In this regard, and bearing in mind what we learned in Chapter 3, it is tempting to wonder if this is too narrow a conceptualization of Islamism. Certainly there have been in the past, and, indeed, continue to exist today, Islamists who understand their goals primarily in terms of achieving state power. In the early days of the MB and Jama'at-i Islami, however, both of these movements saw themselves as seeking first and foremost the Islamization of society. It is only when, in their view, the state began to interfere with this process and to suppress their activities, that some Islamists movements shifted toward a more conventionally political stance. In short, Islamism has always had within it multiple and sometimes contradictory strands of thought and action. Thus we are led to agree with Salwa Ismail when she suggests that "before declaring the advent of post-Islamism, we should question the assumption that Islamism was ever coherent and homogenous."[23]

Roy is correct to point out that many Islamists have dropped their rhetoric to the effect that it is not possible to compromise with Islam when it comes to participation in the political sphere and are now happy to take what they can get when it comes to finding support from electorates or would-be political partners.[24] Islamists now make a case for their agenda based on the interests of voters rather than simply, as they often did in the past, stating the inherent superiority of their approach because of its basis in Islam. But does this necessarily mean we have entered a post-Islamist phase? Many of these groups continue to call for laws to be made compatible with the shari'ah. Is this still not a gradualist form of power-seeking Islamism? Roy continues to get hung up on the idea that an Islamic order can only come to pass by Islamist movements holding state power. In this regard he misses both non-"political" paths to the Islamization of the social order and also the possibility that in some Islamist visions, the modern state may be viewed not as a goal to capture but as an obstacle to true Islamization. This is why we must question his depiction of the Taliban's lack of enthusiasm for establishing a strong central state as evidence of their post-Islamist character. Could it not be that in the Taliban version of Islamism, modern centralized political power was viewed as un-Islamic? Given that they fired half of the country's civil servants and bureaucrats upon taking power, this would suggest that they harbored considerable contempt for the instruments of modern political power. Some observers have suggested that Roy stops short of recognizing the presence of Islamism when actors and movements stop short of centralized power because his understanding of Islamism is calibrated in terms of a homology with revolutionary movements of the left.[25] What Kepel sees as a lack of clear program within the Islamist movement should not be seen as indicative of its having lost its way, but rather of the fact that Islamism has always been somewhat ambiguous when placed on a traditional spectrum of politics understood in terms of right and left. As we pointed out earlier in this volume it is the fact that elements of both rightist and leftist thought have always sat comfortably within Islamism that, in many ways, permitted it to survive in political landscapes subject to strongly shifting winds. As to Roy's claim that "social justice" has disappeared from the rhetoric of Islamism, one need only to think of those Islamists—such as Tariq Ramadan—who have joined the anti-globalization movement in the name of Islamic social justice, or of the popularity of political parties that emphasize social justice as a form of anti-corruption discourse (e.g. AKP in Turkey and JPD in Morocco). Certainly some of the meanings have changed with the withering of traditional leftist politics, but this does not mean that the symbols have lost their potency. Likewise, simply because an Islamist movement endorses the values contained within "non-Islamic" normative discourses—e.g. human rights or freedom of expression—this does not mean that they have abandoned Islamism. To suggest that this is the case, as Kepel does, would imply the impossibility of any kind of "overlapping consensus" between Islamic values and the morality of other systems.[26] Similarly, when Islamists criticize the positions and policies of other Islamists, they are not necessarily undermining the integrity of Islamism as a whole. Indeed, some have interpreted this ability to engage in "auto-critique" or "auto-reform" to represent a further maturing of the Islamist project rather than its demise.[27]

Salwa Ismail points out that Roy's conceptualization of post-Islamism reveals considerable poverty in his understanding of the political.[28] His dismissal of "morality-based activism," as represented by the re-Islamization trend (private/individualist) suggests that he relies on an overly materialist conception of politics in which political efficacy is understood to equate exclusively with participation in formal, institutionalized structures (legislatures, elections, etc.).[29] Ismail urges us instead to interpret the entry of symbolic and normative contestation into the social realm as the opening of new spaces for the conduct of politics rather than as the abandonment of the political.[30] The Islamist socialization of the civil societal realm, in countries such as Egypt for example, has certainly given rise to the dissemination of normative codes and practices that would not gain the official approval of the state and hence take on a distinctly political character.[31] What we are dealing with, then, is not an absence of the political, but rather a situation of comparative hegemony—with the state totalizing the space of the political, and Islamism reigning in the societal realm.

Ismail's critique of post-Islamism à la Roy also gets us some of the way toward a better understanding of the point made above about how we can read in globalization and everyday practice within Muslim society, the creation of new spaces of the political. Islamism, on this interpretation, does not abandon politics, but rather pursues the political through functionally differentiated spaces, taking advantage of existing and new social practices—often, as we have seen, far more effectively than the state is able to. As Ismail puts it:

The fundamental argument here is that the strategies used by Islamists intertwine with existing forms of social organization. The modalities of constituting power and authority are articulated internally, out of the structural arrangements and the strategic choices of actors. Inasmuch as they are part of the fabric, it is natural that many of the Islamists have adapted strategies that are the same as those pursued by the communities in which they have been active.[32]

Therefore we should not regard the movement of symbols and signs related to Islam into the realm of the social as, in Roy's terms, the "banalization" of Islam. He seems to view the association of religious symbols with everyday practices as representing a movement away from "real" religion—suggesting, as Ismail claims, that he has very particular ideas about what counts as Islamic and un-Islamic practices—or "real Islam."[33] She would rather we view this process not as one where religion becomes subjugated to the logic of the social, or its normative priority de-emphasized in favor of other codes. Rather, "this process must be understood in terms of the interaction of religion with the social as entailed in the mobilization of particular religious traditions and their reworking and re-insertion into new domains."[34]

Other writers respond to Roy from a different angle. Francois Burgat, for example, suggests that the movement of Islam from the political into the social spheres is hardly a "new" finding indicating the advent of a new phase beyond Islamism. He points out that much of the literature on Islamism for the past several decades has been emphasizing the Islamist occupation of the social sphere as a constitutive feature of Islamist practice and a vital aspect of their political strength.[35] Through their domination of society, Burgat argues, "Islamists implacably continue to be both advance guard and main body of mobilized activity."[36] He also argues that it is not possible to say that Islamism has been defeated until we can identify an alternative political ideology and social force possessed of the same mobilizing potential.[37] This last point is perhaps somewhat weaker in that we might counter to the effect that if "liberal autocratic" states such as Egypt have succeeded in thoroughly regulating the practice of democratic politics (and democratic language games in the public sphere), and if the Islamists are now primarily operating in a democratic mode, then the state is, in effect, controlling the Islamists.

Another observer of post-Islamism, Asef Bayat—who was also the first to use the term—argues that we need to differentiate between two versions of this concept.[38] The first of these sees post-Islamism as a condition whereby Islamists come to question the efficacy and legitimacy of their own ideology, and thus begin hemorrhaging support from their core constituency.[39] This is very much the sense in which Roy and Kepel use the term. However, Bayat also sees in post-Islamism the name of a normative project: "a conscious attempt to conceptualize and strategize the rationale and modalities of transcending Islamism in social, political, and intellectual domains. Yet post-Islamism is neither anti-Islamic, un-Islamic, nor is it secular."[40] Bayat first used the term in relation to post-revolutionary Iran during the period of Hashemi Rafsanjani's rule whereby the latter sought to work through some of the apparent contradictions between Islam as implemented in the system of the Islamic Republic and that country's ability to pursue national development (see Chapter 5). In contemporary usage, however, Bayat seems to associate the term more closely with forms of political discourse that look like what we have elsewhere termed "progressive Islam" (see Chapter 9). We see this when Bayat tells us that post-Islamist movements are now about "emphasizing rights instead of duties, plurality in place of a single authoritative voice, historicity rather than fixed scriptures … [they] acknowledge, in other words, ambiguity, multiplicity, inclusion, and compromise in principles and practice."[41] He also makes the important point that Islamism and post-Islamism are not zero sum conditions. It is quite possible, he asserts, for Muslims to simultaneously partake in aspects of both practices.

For our purposes in this volume, the notion of post-Islamism is best understood in reference to the combination of the shift from "old" to "new" Islamism, the bottom-up approach to Islamization, and—particularly—the rise of new forms of religious authority outside the framework of either traditional religious scholarship or conventional Islamist politics. Amr Khaled would be a good example of this (see Chapter 9), as would some of the new discourses of Muslim identity to be found in the West. Where some might be tempted to dismiss the emergence of Muslim hip-hop bands and clothing lines as purely apolitical symptoms of consumer culture, others will see in them new forms of identity politics and new spaces for the contestation of normatively laden signs and symbols. On the fringes of Islamism, then, might we not be seeing the rise of a very different kind of "radical" Islamist politics? Hints of it are to be found in the "punk Islam" novel by Muhammad Michael McKnight, *The Taqwacores,* or in the emergent networks of Sufi-anarchist movements—themselves closely allied with anti-globalization and global justice causes (see below). The post-Islamism we have in mind, then, is not one that describes the demise of efforts to establish an Islamic social order. It is most definitely not, as Roy and Kepel seem to see it, the acceptance by Islamists of Francis Fukuyama's thesis regarding the "end of history"—whereby all competitors to capitalism and liberal democracy (including Islamism) have been vanquished.[42] Rather, this approach to moving "beyond Islamism" is about the transformation of the Islamist project into a strategy whereby the pursuit of Muslim politics occurs across a wide variety of spheres and domains. Post-Islamism, that is, not as the abandonment of Muslim politics, but rather as their reconstitution in forms more suited to a globalized world—a world in which, we might want to suggest, the state is only one among many sites of the political.

Globalization and the future of Muslim politics

By way of concluding this volume, it might be interesting to think a little about some of the various social, economic, and political—including geo-political—trends associated with globalization and how they might play out in terms of their effects on Islamism and Muslim politics. We have suggested above that we are already seeing important effects in this regard in terms of the evolving strategy of traditional Islamist movements as they simultaneously engage democratic politics while continuing to exert influence within the spheres of the social and—increasingly—the individual. What broader transformations might globalization bring to the landscapes of Muslim politics as macro forces—primarily economic ones—play out in the context of specific localities and societies? Moreover, are these trends that favor the growth and consolidation of Islamism in their present forms?

For many analysts, globalization has been associated with a steep rise in urban poverty.[43] On the peripheries of many global cities in the Muslim world—Cairo, Istanbul, etc.—we find enormous slum areas inhabited by millions of people who, by and large, tend not to be integrated into existing social welfare arrangements as provided by the state. In these areas we find vast informal sectors for the conduct of commerce, governance, and jus-tice—forms of social and political life that do not appear on official radars. As we have seen above, particularly in the case of Egypt, these are the environments in which Islamist movements such as the MB have tended to thrive. Their charity services and voluntary associations, many of which operate through informal networks well suited to the social climate of urban peripheries, permit them to build considerable mass constituencies and accumulate social capital through the provision of services beyond the capacity of the state. In this regard, then, we might want to wonder about correlations between increased urban poverty in Muslim-majority countries and the strength of Islamist social influence and mobilizing potential.

What about globalization's economic effects more generally and their impact on Muslim society? Henry and Springborg make the interesting point that some of the best-developed infrastructures for the support of global banking and financial systems are to be found in some of the most "traditional" and conservative Muslim nations today—such as Saudi Arabia.[44] This has much to do with the way the political economies of some of these countries, through energy production, have come to play a crucial and privileged role within the global economy to the exclusion of other Muslim nations lacking hydrocarbon resources. This "semi-peripheral" status, in the terms of world-systems theorists, has permitted them to build strong strategic relationships with powerful client states in the West, and often to avoid the worst effects of global structural adjustment efforts.[45] Some of the smaller states, particularly in the Arab gulf region, have clearly decided to play the globalization game. One can think, in particular, of a country such as the United Arab Emirates (UAE). The emirates of Dubai and Abu Dhabi have sought in recent years to establish themselves as key nodes of globalization in the region, providing duty free logistics, import-export, forwarding services, and quality-of-life residential and leisure facilities. They seek similarly to participate in the culture of global elites through the hosting of major golf and tennis tournaments, and for mass audiences by establishing themselves as major tourism and shopping destinations.

Most of the Muslim world, however, has missed out on globalization and would seriously question whether contained within it are the seeds of Muslim prosperity. For many Muslims, globalization is still associated with Westernization and new forms of hegemony. Some see in this fact the potential for hardline Islamists to benefit. As Brumberg puts it:

> Globalization has reinforced such paranoia [of the West] by expanding the gap between the haves and have-nots. Globalization's losers fill the urban slums of Rabat, Algiers, Cairo, and Amman, creating an enormous pool of potential recruits for illiberal Islamism, whereas the winners are found among the Westernized intelligentsia and small business community.[46]

While globalization certainly could lead many Muslims toward reactionary forms of Islamism, this does not by any means represent the only political trajectory open to them. In countries where anti-globalization movements and networks are well organized, we could well find Muslims joining forces with a wide spectrum of political opinion—green, leftist, luddite—all united by virtue of their opposition to neoliberal economics. The well-known European Muslim intellectual and activist Tariq Ramadan is to be found today as much in global justice circles as he is to be found in front of exclusively Muslim audiences. There is room here, also, for traditional Islamism. The British branch of the MB, for example, recently sent a delegation to the meetings of the World Social Forum in Venezuela. Global Muslim activism should hence not be thought of exclusively in terms of illiberal Islamism or radical jihadism. There is plenty of scope for Muslims dissatisfied with the global systemic status quo to make common cause with a much broader coalition of social and political movements organized around what they perceive as the alienating and disenfranchising effects of neoliberal globalization.

For most Muslims, however, politics will continue to be understood primarily in local and national terms. But this does not mean we should discount globalization or, more particularly, geopolitics from our analytical consideration. Muslim activists and voters, well networked and connected as we have seen, are highly informed and have strong opinions with regard to issues such as state cooperation with international financial institutions. Geopolitics is also vital here. Quite aside from concerns about invasive neoliberalism, most Muslims have serious concerns about a wide range of world issues, from U.S. policy in the Middle East, to Turkish membership in the European Union, to tensions between Pakistan and India, to an American-led "War on Terror" that often appears to Muslims as a war against Islam. While Islamist parties reflect these concerns in their platforms and public messaging, they are by no means exclusively Islamist issues. Such concerns tend also to be adopted by almost all segments of the political spectrum. Where these matters have an impact on the Islamist political field, however, is when it comes to political pluralism and the acceptance by Muslims of approaches and ideas strongly identified with the West. This insight would suggest that the pluralization of the Muslim political field is something that needs to be pursued not exclusively in terms of promoting openness and democracy within Muslim countries, but also by addressing democratic deficits attendant in the conduct of world politics more generally.

The challenge of moving "beyond Islamism," as we have tried to suggest throughout this book, is about widening the boundaries of what counts as Muslim politics. Islamism, in both its "old" and "new" variants, will no doubt continue to be an important feature on the Muslim political land-scape for the foreseeable future. But Islamist actors will increasingly find themselves contending not only with various secular political currents, but also with new forms of Muslim politics that contest their vision of an Isla-mic social order and which seek to propose alternative idioms of Islamiza-tion and public religiosity. But we should not view this, as some proponents of the post-Islamism thesis have suggested, as an unbundling of religion and politics—that is, as a shift toward unconscious secularism. Rather, moving beyond Islamism—like moving beyond the state—means the erasure of the boundaries that supposedly constitute "religion" and "politics" as separate domains in the first place. Only through making this move, we might con-tend, does it become possible to fully appreciate the impact of globalization on the Muslim world and to understand the complex array of forces and relations which enact—and through which are enacted—all manner of Muslim politics.

Appendix

Key economic and political indicators for selected Muslim countries

Country	Total Population	% Muslim	HDI Rank	GDP (Billions of USD)	Inequality Ratio	GDP Growth	Freedom House	Transparency International Ranking	Voice & Accountability	Political Stability	Government Effectiveness	Regulatory Quality	Corruption Control	Rule of Law
									World Bank Institute Governance Indicators (expressed in percentile rank)					
Afghanistan	31,056,997	99	—	7.2	—	—	PF	—	12	2	9	5	3	1
Algeria	32,531,853	99	102	102.3	6.1	0.9	NF	84	25	18	43	26	42	32
Bangladesh	147,365,352	88	137	60.0	4.6	2.5	PF	156	31	7	21	15	8	20
Egypt	77,505,756	91	111	89.3	5.1	2.5	NF	70	18	21	43	35	43	55
Indonesia	241,973,879	88	108	287.2	5.2	1.8	F	130	41	9	37	37	21	20
Iran	68,017,860	99	96	196.3	9.7	2.3	NF	105	10	16	26	7	41	29
Iraq	26,074,906	97	—	12.6	—	—	NF	160	9	0	1	6	5	1
Jordan	5,759,732	95	86	12.8	6.9	0.5	PF	40	28	36	58	58	66	62
Kuwait	2,335,648	85	33	74.7	—	-0.4	PF	46	33	49	66	64	79	69
Lebanon	3,826,018	70	78	22.2	—	3.7	PF	63	29	16	46	44	45	44
Libya	5,765,563	97	64	38.8	—	—	NF	105	24	9	7	4	11	2
Malaysia	23,953,136	60	61	130.1	12.4	3.5	PF	44	1	56	16	7	20	31
Morocco	32,725,847	99	123	51.7	7.2	1.1	PF	79	60	48	38	34	48	51
Nigeria	128,771,988	50	159	90.0	9.7	0.8	PF	142	27	32	48	39	55	52
Pakistan	165,803,560	98	134	110.7	4.3	1.6	NF	142	30	5	20	16	6	6
Palestine	3,761,904	84	100	3.5	—	—	PF	—	13	6	34	28	16	24
Saudi Arabia	26,417,599	99	76	309.8	—	-0.1	NF	70	27	75	70	60	78	80
Senegal	11,126,832	94	156	8.3	7.5	0.9	F	70	4	26	42	53	63	58
Somalia	8,591,629	99	—	—	—	—	NF	156	55	42	50	43	52	47
Sudan	40,187,486	65	141	27.7	—	3.4	NF	156	2	1	0	0	1	0
Syria	18,448,752	88	107	26.3	—	1.5	NF	93	3	3	8	8	2	3
Tajikistan	7,163,506	95	122	2.3	5.2	-4.8	NF	142	6	20	9	10	37	43
Tunisia	10,074,951	99	87	28.7	7.9	3.2	NF	51	16	9	12	16	12	17
Turkey	69,660,559	99	92	363.3	9.3	1.6	PF	60	19	50	67	52	60	59
UAE	2,563,212	76	49	104.2	—	-0.5	NF	31	1	34	3	2	4	5
Uzbekistan	26,851,195	89	113	13.7	4.0	1.3	NF	151	21	65	69	65	83	67
Yemen	20,727,063	99	150	14.5	5.6	1.7	PF	111	4	3	10	4	13	7

Notes: The Human Development Index (HDI) is a UNDP statistical indicator that assigns country rankings on the basis of several quality-of-life factors, with higher rankings corresponding to higher standards of living; the ratio of inequality is the income or expenditure richest 20% to that of the poorest 20% with lower numbers indicating greater equality; GDP growth is average annual growth 1990–2004; the Freedom House rankings designate countries as Free (F), Partially Free (PF) or Not Free (NF) based on an analysis of political rights and civil liberties; the Transparency International rankings measure perceptions of national corruption, with more corrupt countries at the higher end of the scale; the World Bank Institute Worldwide Governance and Anti-Corruption Indicators measure six different aspects of national political life, with higher percentiles corresponding to better governance. Sources: CIA World Factbook (Population data); World Bank World Development Indicators (GDP); UNDP Human Development Report 2006 (HDI, Inequality, GDP growth); Freedom House, "Freedom in the World Report 2006"; Transparency International, "Corruption Perceptions Index 2006"; World Bank Institute, "Worldwide Governance Indicators 2006."

Glossary

alim	Religious scholar (singular of *ulama*)
aqeeda	Creed, or tenets of belief
Ayatollah	Literally, "Sign of God"; High-ranking Shi'a cleric
bid'a	Innovation
dar al-ahd	"Land of Treaty"
dar al-harb	"Land of War"
dar al-islam	"Land of Islam"
da'if	A weak *hadith*
da'wa	Propagation of the religion; "calling" to Islam
din wa dawla	"Religion and state"
faqih	Legal scholar or jurist
fatwa	Opinion or edict of a legal scholar (plural: *fatawa*)
fiqh	Islamic legal science
fitna	Social discord
hadith	Report about the Prophet Muhammad
hajj	Pilgrimage to Mecca
halal	Permissible
haram	Forbidden
hijra	Migration
hizb	Party or group
hudud	Prescribed punishments in Islamic law
Hujjat al-Islam	Literally, "Proof of Islam"; Middle-ranking Shi'a cleric
ijma	Consensus
ijtihad	Independent reasoning or judgment
intifada	"Shaking off"; mass uprising
islah	Reform
isnad	Chain of transmission in reference to *hadith*
hawala	Pre-modern monetary transfer system
jahiliyya	Pre- or non-Islamic ignorance
jihad	Religious struggle; of a spiritual and/or worldly nature
kalam	Scholastic theology
khilafa	The institution of rule by the caliph
madhhab	School of Islamic law (plural: *madhahib*)

madrasa	Religious school
majlis al-shura	Consultative council
mufti	Scholar who issues a *fatwa*
mutawwa	Religious police
mujahideen	Those who perform *jihad*
nasiha	Advice or counsel, as given to a figure in authority
qadi	Judge
qanun	Non-religious law
qiyas	Legal methodology based on analogical deduction
sahih	Sound *hadith*
salaf	Pious ancestors; the first three generations of Muslims
salafism	Movement seeking return to the practices of the *salaf*
Shi'a	Partisans (of Ali); the largest minority sect in Islam
shari'ah	Religious law
shura	Consultation
sira	Biographical literature about the Prophet
sunna	"Orthodox" traditions of the Prophet
Sunni	The people of tradition or orthodoxy; vast majority of Muslims
Sufism	Islamic mysticism
tafsir	Qur'anic exegesis
tahdith	Modernization
tajdid	Renewal
tarbiya	Education/human development
tariqa	Sufi order
tawhid	Divine unity
ulama	Religious scholars (singular: *alim*)
umma	The community of Muslims, potentially global in scope
usul al-fiqh	Principles of legal science
waqf	Charitable endowment (plural: *awqaf*)
wilayat al-faqih	Guardianship of the legal scholar
zakat	tithe

Notes

1 Introduction: thinking about Islam and politics in global perspective

1 T. Asad, *Genealogies of Religion: Disciplines and Reasons of Power in Christianity and Islam*, Baltimore, MD: The Johns Hopkins University Press, 1993.
2 T. Asad, op. cit., p. 1.
3 D. Eickelman, 'Inside the Islamic Reformation', *Wilson Quarterly* 22, no. 1, 1998, 80–89.
4 D. Brumberg, 'Islam is Not the Solution (or the Problem)', *The Washington Quarterly* 29, 2005, 97–116.
5 Asad, op. cit., pp. 200–201.
6 J. Esposito, *Islam and Politics*, 4th edn, Syracuse, NY: Syracuse University Press, 1984, pp. 72–73.
7 A. Sadri, M. Sadri (eds), *Reason, Freedom, and Democracy in Islam: Essential Writings of Abdolkarim Soroush*, New York: Oxford University Press, 2000.
8 M. Fandy, 'Tribe vs. Islam: The Post-colonial Arab State and the Democratic Imperative', *Middle East Policy* 3, 1994; Brumberg, op. cit., 97–116.
9 D. Eickelman, J. Piscatori, *Muslim Politics*, Princeton, NJ: Princeton University Press, 1996.
10 D. Eickelman, J. Anderson (eds), *New Media in the Muslim World: The Emerging Public Sphere*, Bloomington, IN: Indiana University Press, 2003; R. Hefner (ed.), *Remaking Muslim Politics: Pluralism, Contestation, Democratization*, Princeton, NJ: Princeton University Press, 2005.
11 D. Harvey, *The Conditions of Postmodernity: An Enquiry into the Order of Cultural Change*, Malden, MA: Blackwell Publishers, 1990; A. Giddens, *The Consequences of Modernity*, Stanford, CA: Stanford University Press, 1990.
12 J. A. Scholte, *Globalization: A Critical Introduction*, 2nd edn, Basingstoke: Palgrave, 2005.
13 R. Robertson, *Globalization: Social Theory and Global Change*, London: Sage, 1992.
14 A. Appadurai, *Modernity at Large: Cultural Dimensions of Globalization*, Minneapolis, MN: University of Minnesota Press, 1996; S. Croucher, *Globalization and Belonging: The Politics of Identity in a Changing World*, Lanham, MD: Rowman & Littlefield, 2003.
15 P. Mandaville, *Transnational Muslim Politics: Reimagining the umma*, New York: Routledge, 2004.
16 D. Eickelman, J. Anderson, op. cit., *passim*.

2 Islam and politics: history and key concepts

1 Unless otherwise specified, the general treatment of Islamic political history contained in this chapter is based on a synthesis of the following standard sources:

M. Hodgson, *The Venture of Islam: Conscience and History in a World Civiliza-tion*, vol. 1–3, Chicago, IL: The University of Chicago Press, 1974; I. Lapidus, *A History of Islamic Societies*, 2nd edn, Cambridge: Cambridge University Press, 2002; A. Hourani, *A History of the Arab Peoples,* New York: Warner Books, 1991.
2 I. Lapidus, *A History of Islamic Societies*, 2nd edn, Cambridge: Cambridge University Press, 2002, p. 36; W. Mandelung, *The Succession to Muhammad: A Study of the Early Caliphate*, Cambridge: Cambridge University Press, 1997.
3 M. Siddiqi, *Hadith Literature: Its Origins, Development & Special Features,* Cambridge: Islamic Texts Society, 1996, p. 109.
4 W. Hallaq, 'Was the Gate of Ijtihad Closed?', *International Journal of Middle Eastern Studies* 16, 1984.
5 M. Hodgson, *The Venture of Islam: Conscience and History in a World Civiliza-tion*, vol. 1–3, Chicago, IL: The University of Chicago Press, 1974.
6 S. Afghani, 'An Islamic Response to Imperialism', in J. Donahue, J. Esposito (eds), *Islam in Transition: Muslim Perspectives,* New York: Oxford University Press, 1982, p. 18.
7 Ibid.
8 F. Rahman, *Islam & Modernity: The Transformation of an Intellectual Tradition,* Chicago, IL: The University of Chicago Press, 1984.

3 State formation and the making of Islamism

1 H. Enayat, *Modern Islamic Political Thought*, Hong Kong: The Macmillan Press, 1982.
2 H. Enayat, op. cit., pp. 62–68; A. Raziq, 'The Problem of the Caliphate', in M. Moaddel, K. Talattof (eds), *Modernist and Fundamentalist Debates in Islam,* New York: Palgrave Macmillan, 2000, pp. 95–100.
3 M. Kramer, *Islam Assembled*, New York: Columbia University Press, 1985.
4 R. Khalidi, *The Origins of Arab Nationalism,* New York: Columbia University Press, 1991; A. Dawisha, *Arab Nationalism in the Twentieth Century: From Tri-umph to Despair*, Princeton, NJ: Princeton University Press, 2003.
5 W. Cleveland, *The Making of an Arab Nationalist: Ottomanism and Arabism in the Life and Thought of Sati al-Husri*, Princeton, NJ: Princeton University Press, 1972.
6 D. Commins, 'Hasan al-Banna (1906–49)', in A. Rahnema (ed.), *Pioneers of Islamic Revival,* London: Zed Books, 1994; L. C. Brown, *Religion and State: The Muslim Approach to Politics,* New York: Columbia University Press, 2000, pp. 143–148.
7 L. C. Brown, op. cit., p. 146.
8 J. Donahue, J. Esposito (eds), *Islam in Transition: Muslim Perspectives,* New York: Oxford University Press, 1982, pp. 81–82.
9 S. V. R. Nasr, 'Mawdudi and the Jama'at-I Islami: The Origins, Theory and Practice of Islamic Revivalism', in A. Rahnema (ed.), *Pioneers of Islamic Revival,* London: Zed Books, 1994; L. C. Brown, *Religion and State: The Muslim Approach to Politics,* New York: Columbia University Press, 2000, pp. 148–153.
10 Ibid.
11 J. Donahue, J. Esposito (eds), op. cit., p. 95.
12 J. Donahue, J. Esposito (eds), op. cit., p. 259. Emphasis in original.
13 J. Donahue, J. Esposito (eds), op. cit., p. 254.
14 Ibid.
15 J. Donahue, J. Esposito (eds), op. cit., p. 257.
16 L. C. Brown, op. cit., pp. 146, 153.
17 R. Mitchell, *The Society of Muslim Brothers,* New York: Oxford University Press, 1993, p. 9.

18 R. Mitchell, op. cit., p. 18.
19 S. Zubaida, *Islam the People & the State: Political Ideas & Movements in the Middle East*, London: I.B. Tauris & Co, 1993, p. 157.
20 R. Mitchell, op. cit., p. 198.
21 P. Bourdieu, 'Forms of capital', in J. C. Richards (ed.), *Handbook of Theory and Research for the Sociology of Education,* New York: Greenwood Press, 1983; J. Coleman, *Foundations of Social Theory*, Cambridge, MA: Harvard University Press, 1990.
22 M. Moaddel, *Islamic Modernism, Nationalism, and Fundamentalism: Episode and Discourse,* Chicago, IL: The University of Chicago Press, 2005, p. 211.
23 M. Moaddel, op. cit., p. 198.
24 R. Mitchell, op. cit., pp. 103–104.
25 C. Tripp, 'Sayyid Qutb: The Political Vision', in A. Rahnema (ed.), *Pioneers of Islamic Revival,* London: Zed Books, 1994; L. C. Brown, *Religion and State: The Muslim Approach to Politics,* New York: Columbia University Press, 2000, pp. 153–159.
26 C. Tripp, op. cit., p. 158.
27 C. Tripp, op. cit., p. 157.
28 J. Donahue, J. Esposito, op. cit., p. 126.
29 S. Qutb, 'War, Peace, and Islamic Jihad', in M. Moaddel, K. Talattof (eds), *Modernist and Fundamentalist Debates in Islam,* New York: Palgrave Macmillan, 2000, p. 229.
30 C. Tripp, op. cit., p. 179.
31 L. C. Brown, op. cit., p. 158.
32 C. Tripp, op. cit., p. 173.
33 P. Bergen, *The Osama bin Laden I Know: An Oral History of Al-Qaeda's Leader,* New York: Simon & Schuster, 2006, pp. 18–20.
34 S. Qutb, op. cit., pp. 225–226
35 Ibid.
36 S. Qutb, op. cit., p. 241.
37 S. Qutb, op. cit., p. 178.
38 S. Zubaida, op. cit., p. 159.
39 J. Schwedler, *Faith in Moderation: Islamist Parties in Jordan and Yemen,* New York: Cambridge University Press, 2006.

4 Islam in the system: the evolution of Islamism as political strategy

1 T. Gurr, *Why Men Rebel,* Princeton, NJ: Princeton University Press, 1969.
2 C. Tilly, S. Tarrow, *Contentious Politics,* Boulder, CO: Paradigm Publishers, 2006.
3 O. Roy, *The Failure of Political Islam,* London: I.B. Tauris, 1994.
4 Ibid.
5 Ibid.
6 D. Singerman, *Avenues of Participation: Family, Politics, and Networks in Urban Quarters of Cairo*, Princeton, NJ: Princeton University Press, 1995.
7 P. Bourdieu, 'Forms of capital', in J. C. Richards (ed.), *Handbook of Theory and Research for the Sociology of Education,* New York: Greenwood Press, 1983.
8 N. Brown, A. Hamzawy, M. Ottaway, 'Islamist Movements and the Democratic Process in the Arab World', *Carnegie Endowment for International Peace Policy Brief* 67, 2006.
9 R. Baker, *Islam Without Fear: Egypt and the New Islamists,* Cambridge, MA: Harvard University Press, 2003.
10 A. Hamzawy, 'The Key to Arab Reform: Moderate Islamists', *Carnegie Endowment for International Peace Policy Brief* 40, 2005.

11 D. Brumberg, 'The Trap of Liberalized Autocracy', *Journal of Democracy* 13, 2002, pp. 56–68.
12 A. Hamzawy, op. cit., p. 4
13 D. Brumberg, op. cit., pp. 56–68.
14 N. Brown, A. Hamzawy, M. Ottaway, op. cit., pp. 3–19.
15 A. Hamzawy, op. cit., p. 2.
16 Ibid.
17 N. Brown, A. Hamzawy, M. Ottaway, op. cit., pp. 7–8.
18 V. Nasr, 'The Rise of "Muslim Democracy"', *Journal of Democracy* 16, 2005, pp. 13–27.
19 V. Nasr, op. cit., p. 13.
20 Ibid.
21 V. Nasr, op. cit., pp. 13–14.
22 D. Brumberg, 'Islam is Not the Solution (or the Problem)', *The Washington Quarterly* 29, 2005, p. 110.
23 V. Nasr, op. cit., p. 20.
24 M. Hammoud, 'Causes for Fundamentalist Popularity in Egypt', in A. Moussalli (ed.), *Islamic Fundamentalism: Myths & Realities,* Reading: Ithaca Press, 1998, p. 308.
25 Ibid, p. 310–12; M. Azzam, 'Egypt: The Islamists and the State Under Mubarak', in A. S. Sidahmed, A. Ehteshami (eds), *Islamic Fundamentalism,* Boulder, CO: Westview Press, 1996; S. Zubaida, 'Religion, the State, and Democracy: Contrasting Conceptions of Society in Egypt', in J. Beinin, J. Stork (eds), *Political Islam: Essays From Middle East Report,* New York: I.B. Tauris & Co, 1997, pp. 51–63.
26 S. Zubaida, op. cit., pp. 51–63.
27 C. Wickham, 'Islamic Mobilization and Political Change: The Islamist Trend in Egypt's Professional Associations', in J. Beinin, J. Stork (eds), *Political Islam: Essays From Middle East Report,* New York: I.B. Tauris & Co, 1997, p. 130.
28 C. Wickham, op. cit., pp. 126–130.
29 H. Mustafa, 'The Islamist Movements under Mubarak', in L. Guazzone (ed.), *The Islamist Dilemma: The Political Role of Islamist Movements in the Contemporary Arab World,* Berkshire: Ithaca Press, 1995, p. 167.
30 H. Mustafa, op. cit., p. 171.
31 J. Esposito, J. Voll, *Islam and Democracy,* New York: Oxford University Press, 1996, p. 190.
32 C. Wickham, op. cit., p. 124.
33 C. Wickham, op. cit., p.125.
34 M. Azzam, op. cit., p. 119.
35 Ibid.
36 H. Mustafa, op. cit., p. 166.
37 J. Esposito, J. Voll, op. cit., p. 187.
38 J. Esposito, J. Voll, op. cit., p. 185.
39 C. Wickham, *Mobilizing Islam: Religion, Activism, and Political Change in Egypt,* New York: Columbia University Press, 2002, pp. 214–216.
40 C. Wickham, op. cit., p. 217.
41 R. Baker, op. cit., p. 1.
42 Ibid.
43 J. Habermas, 'New Social Movements', *Telos* 49, 1981, 33–37.
44 R. Baker, op. cit., p. 241.
45 Q. Wiktorowicz, 'The Salafi Movement: Violence and the Fragmentation of Community', in M. Cooke, B. Lawrence (eds), *Muslim Networks from Hajj to Hip Hop,* Chapel Hill, NC: The University of North Carolina Press, 2005, p. 211.

46 A. R. Norton, 'Thwarted Politics: The Case of Egypt's Hizb al-Wasat', in R. Hefner (ed.), *Remaking Muslim Politics: Pluralism, Contestation, Democratization*, Princeton, NJ: Princeton University Press, 2005, pp. 133–161.

47 R. Baker, op. cit., p. 193.

48 C. Wickham, op. cit., p. 218.

49 A. R. Norton, op. cit., p. 140.

50 C. Wickham, op. cit., p. 217.

51 Ibid.

52 A. R. Norton, op. cit., p. 142.

53 Ibid.; J. Stacher, 'Post-Islamist Rumblings in Egypt: The Emergence of the Wasat Party', *The Middle East Journal* 56, 2002, p. 422.

54 J. Stacher, op. cit., pp. 419–420; C. Wickham, op. cit., p. 222; S. Otterman, 'Muslim Brotherhood and Egypt's Parliamentary Elections', *Council on Foreign Relations,* 2005, pp. 1–3.

55 J. Stacher, op. cit., p. 424.

56 J. Stacher, op. cit., p. 429.

57 J. Stacher, op. cit., p. 426.

58 D. Williams, 'Egypt's Muslim Brotherhood May Be Model for Islam's Political Adaptation', *Washington Post,* February 3, 2006, A14.

59 S. Otterman, op. cit., pp. 1–3.

60 J. Stacher, p. 430.

61 C. Wickham, 'The Causes and Dynamics of Islamist Auto-Reform', *ICIS International* 6, 2006, pp. 6–7.

62 V. Nasr, op. cit., p. 14.

63 M. H. Yavuz, *Islamic Political Identity in Turkey,* Oxford: Oxford University Press, 2003, p. 60.

64 S. Mardin, 'The Nakshibendi Order of Turkey', in M. Marty, R. S. Appleby (eds), *Fundamentalisms and the State: Remaking Polities, Economies, and Militance,* Chicago, IL: The University of Chicago Press, 1993, p. 220.

65 Ibid.

66 M. H. Yavuz, 'Islam in the Public Sphere: The Case of the Nur Movement', in M. H. Yavuz, J. Esposito (eds), *Turkish Islam and the Secular State: The Gülen Movement,* Syracuse, NY: Syracuse University Press, 2003, p. 14.

67 S. Mardin, op. cit., p. 222.

68 Ibid.

69 B. Agai, 'The Gülen Movement's Islamic Ethic of Education', *Critique* 11, 2002, pp. 27–47.

70 R. Margulies, E. Yildizoğlu, 'The Resurgence of Islam and the Welfare Party in Turkey', in J. Beinin, J. Stork (eds), *Political Islam: Essays from Middle East Report,* New York: I.B. Tauris, 1997, p. 148.

71 Ibid.

72 M. H. Yavuz, *Islamic Political Identity in Turkey,* Oxford: Oxford University Press, 2003.

73 J. White, 'The End of Islamism? Turkey's Muslimhood Model', in R. Hefner (ed.), *Remaking Muslim Politics: Pluralism, Contestation, Democratization,* Princeton, NJ: Princeton University Press, 2005, p. 93.

74 D. Wakin, 'Turkey Military "in Charge"', *Associated Press,* June 21 1997.

75 V. Nasr, op. cit., p. 23.

76 M. H. Yavuz, op. cit., p. 256; V. Nasr, op. cit., p. 24.

77 J. White, op. cit., p. 91.

78 M. H. Yavuz, op. cit., p. 250.

79 M. H. Yavuz, op. cit., p. 257.

80 Ibid.

81   J. White, *Islamist Mobilization in Turkey,* Seattle, WA: University of Washington Press, 2002, p. 138.
82   V. Nasr, op. cit., p. 23.
83   M. H. Yavuz, op. cit., p. 263.
84   V. Nasr, op. cit., p. 23.
85   S. Tepe, 'Turkey's AKP: A Model "Muslim Democratic" Party?', *Journal of Democracy* 16, 2005, p. 76.
86   M. H. Yavuz, op. cit., p. 263.
87   S. Tepe, op. cit., pp. 73–74.
88   B. Milton-Edwards, 'Climate of Change in Jordan's Islamist Movement', in A. S. Sidahmed, A. Ehteshami (eds), *Islamic Fundamentalism,* Boulder, CO: Westview Press, 1996, p. 124.
89   B. Milton-Edwards, 'A Temporary Alliance with the Crown: The Islamic Response in Jordan', in J. Piscatori (ed.), *Islamic Fundamentalisms and the Gulf Crisis,* Chicago, IL: The Fundamentalism Project of the American Academy of Arts and Science, 1991, pp. 88–108.
90   G. Robinson, 'Islamists under Liberalization in Jordan', in A. Moussalli (ed.), *Islamic Fundamentalisms: Myths & Realities,* Reading: Ithaca Press, 1998, pp. 169–196.
91   B. Milton-Edwards, 'Climate of Change in Jordan's Islamist Movement', in A. S. Sidahmed, A. Ehteshami (eds), *Islamic Fundamentalism,* Boulder, CO: Westview Press, 1996, p. 134.
92   G. Robinson, op. cit., pp. 169–196.
93   R. Ryan, J. Schwedler, 'Return to Democratization or New Hybrid Regime? The 2003 Elections in Jordan', *Middle East Policy* 2004, pp. 138–151.
94   M. Moaddel, *Islamic Modernism, Nationalism, and Fundamentalism: Episode and Discourse,* Chicago, IL: The University of Chicago Press, 2005, p. 307.
95   J. Schwedler, *Faith in Moderation: Islamist Parties in Jordan and Yemen,* New York: Cambridge University Press, 2006, p. 169.
96   Q. Wiktorowicz, *The Management of Islamic Activism: Salafis, the Muslim Brotherhood, and State Power in Jordan,* Albany, NY: State University of New York Press, 2001, pp. 3–4.
97   Q. Wiktorowicz, S. T. Farouki, ' Islamic NGO's and Muslim Politics: a Case from Jordan', *Third World Quarterly* 2000, p. 686.
98   J. Schwedler, op. cit., p. 158.
99   J. Schwedler, op. cit., p. 162.
100 M. Moadell, 'Islamic Action Front Party: Interview with Dr. Ishaq A. Farhan', in M. Moaddel, K. Talattof (eds), *Modernist and Fundamentalist Debates in Islam,* New York: Palgrave Macmillan, 2000.
101 G. Robinson, op. cit., p. 176.
102 G. Robinson, op. cit., p. 174; J. Schwedler, op. cit., p. 162.
103 J. Clark, J. Schwedler, 'Who Opened the Window? Women's Struggle for Voice within Islamist Political Parties', *Comparative Politics* 35, 2003, pp. 293–313.
104 G. Robinson, op. cit., p. 188.
105 G. Robinson, op. cit., p. 189.
106 G. Robinson, op. cit., p. 191.
107 J. Schwedler, op. cit., p. 166.
108 M. Moaddel, *Islamic Modernism, Nationalism, and Fundamentalism: Episode and Discourse,* Chicago, IL: The University of Chicago Press, 2005, p. 313.
109 J. Schwedler, op. cit., pp. 164–165; G. Robinson, op. cit., p. 179.
110 J. Schwedler, op. cit., p. 167.
111 J. Schwedler, op. cit., p. 172; G. Robinson, op. cit., p. 178.
112 J. Schwedler, op. cit., pp. 169, 172.
113 C. Wickham, op. cit., pp. 6–7.

114 D. Brumberg, 'The Trap of Liberalized Autocracy', *Journal of Democracy* 13, 2002, pp. 56–68.

115 Q. Wiktorowicz, op. cit., p. 95.

116 D. Brumberg, 'Islam is Not the Solution (or the Problem)', *The Washington Quarterly* 29, 2005, p. 104.

117 Q. Wiktorowicz, S. T. Farouki, op. cit., p. 688.

118 C. Wickham, op. cit., pp. 6–7; J. White, op. cit., p. 138.

119 J. Schwedler, op. cit., p. 172.

120 C. Wickham, op. cit., pp. 6–7.

121 D. Brumberg, 'Islamists and the Politics of Consensus', *Journal of Democracy* 13, 2002, p. 112.

122 R. Hefner, 'Introduction: Modernity and the Remaking of Muslim Politics', in R. Hefner (ed.), *Remaking Muslim Politics: Pluralism, Contestation, Democratization,* Princeton, NJ: Princeton University Press, 2005, p. 17; R. Putnam, *Making Democracy Work: Civic Traditions in Modern Italy,* Princeton, NJ: Princeton University Press, 1993.

123 N. Brown, A. Hamzawy, M. Ottaway, op. cit., pp. 9–10.

124 A. Tamimi (ed.), *Power Sharing Islam?* London: Liberty, 1993.

5 Islam as the system: Islamic states and "Islamization" from above

1 J. Piscatori, 'Ideological Politics in Sa'udi Arabia', in J. Piscatori (ed.), *Islam in the Political Process,* Cambridge: Cambridge University Press, 1983, pp. 56–72.

2 G. Kepel, *The War for Muslim Minds,* Cambridge, MA: Harvard University Press, 2004, p. 164.

3 G. Kepel, op. cit., p. 175.

4 M. Al-Rasheed, *A History of Saudi Arabia,* Cambridge: Cambridge University Press, 2002, p. 167.

5 M. Al-Rasheed, op. cit., p. 171.

6 M. Al-Rasheed, op. cit., p. 183.

7 S. Lacroix, 'Between Islamists and Liberals: Saudi Arabia's New "Islamo-Liberal" Reformists', *Middle East Journal* 58, 2004, pp. 345–365.

8 International Crisis Group, 'Saudi Arabia Backgrounder: Who are the Islamists?' *ICG Middle East Report* 31, 2004, p. 8.

9 International Crisis Group, op. cit., p. 14.

10 J. Esposito, *Islam and Politics,* 4th edn, Syracuse, NY: Syracuse University Press, 1984, p. 119.

11 J. Esposito, op. cit., p. 124.

12 J. Esposito, op. cit., p. 173.

13 H. Haqqani, *Pakistan: Between Mosque and Military,* Washington, DC: Carnegie Endowment for International Peace, 2005, p. 152.

14 J. Esposito, op. cit., p. 185.

15 H. Haqqani, op. cit., p. 138.

16 H. Haqqani, op. cit., p. 152.

17 S. V. R. Nasr, 'Islamic Opposition in the Political Process: Lessons from Pakistan', in J. Esposito (ed.), *Political Islam: Revolution, Radicalism, or Reform?* Boulder, CO: Lynne Rienner, 1997, pp. 148–149.

18 M. Ahmad, 'Islamic Fundamentalism in South Asia: The Jamaat-i-Islami and the Tablighi Jamaat', in M. Marty, R. Appleby (eds), *Fundamentalisms Observed,* Chicago, IL: The University of Chicago Press, 1991, p. 483.

19 H. Haqqani, op. cit., p. 139; S. V. R. Nasr, op. cit., p. 149.

20 J. Esposito, op. cit., p. 185.

21 S. V. R. Nasr, op. cit., p. 146.

22 H. Haqqani, op. cit., p. 113.

23 H. Haqqani, op. cit., p. 112.
24 V. Nasr, 'The Rise of "Muslim Democracy"', *Journal of Democracy* 16, 2005, 14.
25 S. V. R. Nasr, *Islamic Leviathan: Islam and the Making of State Power,* New York: Oxford University Press, 2001, p. 156.
26 'The Future Looks Bearded', *The Economist: Survey of Pakistan,* July 8 2006, p. 8.
27 M. Ahmad, op. cit., p. 485.
28 M. Ahmad, op. cit., p. 492.
29 S. V. R. Nasr, 'Islamic Opposition in the Political Process: Lessons from Pakistan', in J. Esposito (ed.), *Political Islam: Revolution, Radicalism, or Reform?* Boulder, CO: Lynne Rienner, 1997, p. 141.
30 J. Esposito, op. cit., p. 126.
31 H. Munson, *Islam and Revolution in the Middle East,* New Haven, CT: Yale University Press, 1988, p. 53.
32 B. Moin, 'Khomeini's Search for Perfection: Theory and Reality', in A. Rahnema (ed.), *Pioneers of Islamic Revival,* London: Zed Books, 1994, p. 74.
33 B. Moin, op. cit., p. 81.
34 L. C. Brown, *Religion and State: The Muslim Approach to Politics,* New York: Columbia University Press, 2000, p. 165.
35 R. Khomeini, 'The Form of Islamic Government', in H. Algar (trans.), *Islam and Revolution: Writings and Declarations of Imam Khomeini (1941–1980),* Berkeley, CA: Mizan Press, 1981, pp. 48–49
36 B. Moin, op. cit., p. 89.
37 V. Martin, *Creating an Islamic State: Khomeini and the Making of a New Iran,* New York: I. B. Tauris, 2000, p. 117.
38 R. Khomeini, op. cit., p. 55.
39 R. Khomeini, op. cit., p. 59.
40 R. Khomeini, op. cit., p. 60.
41 L. C. Brown, op. cit., p. 169.
42 V. Martin, op. cit., p. 93.
43 H. Munson, *Islam and Revolution in the Middle East,* New Haven, CT: Yale University Press, 1988.
44 A. Sreberny-Mohammadi, A. Mohammadi, *Small Media, Big Revolution: Communication, Culture, and the Iranian Revolution,* Minneapolis, MN: University of Minnesota Press, 1994.
45 H. Munson, op. cit., p. 63.
46 J. Esposito, op. cit., pp. 222–223.
47 J. Piscatori, 'The Rushdie Affair and the Politics of Ambiguity', *International Affairs* 66, 1990, pp. 767–789.
48 N. Keddie, *Modern Iran: Roots and Results of Revolution,* New Haven, CT: Yale University Press, 2003, p. 269.
49 D. Brumberg, *Reinventing Khomeini: The Struggle for Reform in Iran,* Chicago, IL: The University of Chicago Press, 2001, p. 199.
50 D. Brumberg, op. cit., p. 207.
51 'Khatami on Religious Thought Renewal', *Iran Daily,* June 21 1999, cited in B. Bakhtiari, 'Dilemmas of Reform and Democracy in the Islamic Republic of Iran', in R. Hefner (ed.), *Remaking Muslim Politics: Pluralism, Contestation, Democratization,* Princeton, NJ: Princeton University Press, 2005, p. 118.

6 Islam for lack of a system: Islamism in weak and failed states

1 R. Jackson, *Quasi-States: Sovereignty, International Relations and the Third World,* Cambridge: Cambridge University Press, 1990.
2 J. Esposito, *Islam and Politics,* 4th edn, Syracuse, NY: Syracuse University Press, 1984, p. 228.

3 M. Jensen, 'Islamism and Civil Society in the Gaza Strip', in A. Moussalli (ed.), *Islamic Fundamentalism: Myths & Realities,* Reading: Ithaca Press, 1998, p. 200.

4 G. Usher, 'What Kind of Nation? The Rise of Hamas in the Occupied Territories', in J. Beinin, J. Stork (eds), *Political Islam: Essays From Middle East Report,* New York: I.B. Tauris & Co, 1997, p. 340.

5 J. Legrain, 'HAMAS: Legitimate Heir of Palestinian Nationalism?', in J. Esposito (ed.), *Political Islam: Revolution, Radicalism, or Reform?* Boulder, CO: Lynne Rienner Publishers, 1997, p. 163.

6 J. Esposito, op. cit., p. 229.

7 Z. Abu-Amr, *Islamic Fundamentalism in the West Bank and Gaza: Muslim Brotherhood and Islamic Jihad,* Bloomington, IN: Indiana University Press, 1994, p. 83.

8 M. Levitt, *HAMAS: Politics, Charity, and Terrorism in the Service of Jihad,* New Haven, CT: Yale University Press, 2006, p. 30.

9 Z. Abu-Amr, op. cit., p. 85.

10 J. Legrain, op. cit., p. 160.

11 G. Kepel, *Jihad: The Trail of Political Islam,* Cambridge, MA: Harvard University Press, 2002, p. 154.

12 G. Robinson, 'Hamas as Social Movement', in Q. Wiktorowicz (ed.), *Islamic Activism: A Social Movement Theory Approach,* Bloomington, IN: Indiana University Press, 2004, p. 127.

13 G. Usher, op. cit., p. 341.

14 J. Legrain, op. cit., p. 165.

15 S. Mishal, A. Sela, *The Palestinian Hamas: Vision, Violence, and Coexistence,* New York: Columbia University Press, 2000, p. 58.

16 S. Mishal, A. Sela, op. cit., p. 64.

17 G. Kepel, op. cit., p. 327.

18 J. Legrain, op. cit., p. 167; G. Usher, op. cit., p. 344.

19 G. Usher, op. cit., p. 344.

20 J. Legrain, op. cit., p. 172.

21 G. Kepel, op. cit., p. 341.

22 G. Kepel, op. cit., p. 156.

23 G. Robinson, op. cit., p. 121.

24 G. Kepel, op. cit., p. 151.

25 Z. Abu-Amr, op. cit., p. 70.

26 J. Burr, R. Collins, *Alms for Jihad: Charity and Terrorism in the Islamic World,* Cambridge: Cambridge University Press, 2006, pp. 216–221.

27 K. Hroub, *Hamas: Political Thought and Practice,* Washington, DC: Institute for Palestine Studies, 2000, p. 148.

28 J. Esposito, op. cit., p. 229.

29 G. Robinson, op. cit., p. 128; M. Jensen, op. cit., p. 203.

30 G. Usher, op. cit., p. 347.

31 G. Kepel, op. cit., p. 152.

32 G. Robinson, op. cit., p. 127.

33 J. Esposito, op. cit., p. 230.

34 K. Hroub, op. cit., p. 236.

35 K. Hroub, op. cit., p. 235.

36 M. Jensen, op. cit., pp. 214, 210.

37 K. Hroub, op. cit., pp. 229–230.

38 K. Hroub, op. cit., p. 217.

39 K. Hroub, op. cit., p. 233.

40 M. Jensen, op. cit., pp. 213–214.

41 G. Robinson, op. cit., p. 127.

42 Z. Abu-Amr, op. cit., p. 82.
43 Z. Abu-Amr, op. cit., p. 72–73.
44 G. Kepel, op. cit., p. 153.
45 K. Hroub, op. cit., p. 238.
46 S. Mishal, A. Sela, op. cit., p. 121.
47 G. Usher, op. cit., pp. 346–347.
48 S. Mishal, A. Sela, op. cit., p. 121.
49 G. Usher, op. cit., pp. 346–347.
50 G. Kepel, op. cit., p. 330.
51 G. Kepel, op. cit., pp. 323–333; J. Legrain, op. cit., p. 169.
52 S. Mishal, A. Sela, op. cit., p. 96.
53 S. Mishal, A. Sela, op. cit., p. 35.
54 K. Hroub, op. cit., p. 234.
55 G. Robinson, op. cit., p. 134.
56 G. Robinson, op. cit., pp. 130–134.
57 Z. Abu-Amr, op. cit., p. 32.
58 K. Hroub, op. cit., p. 210.
59 G. Usher, op. cit., p. 343.
60 J. Esposito, op. cit., p. 231.
61 Ibid.; J. Legrain, op. cit., p. 171.
62 S. Mishal, A. Sela, op. cit., p. 65; M. Levitt, op. cit., p. 241.
63 K. Hroub, op. cit., pp. 247–248.
64 J. Legrain, op. cit., p. 170.
65 Ibid.
66 J. Esposito, op. cit., p. 232.
67 J. Legrain, op. cit., p. 172.
68 S. Mishal, A. Sela, op. cit., pp. 161–162.
69 T. Barfield, 'An Islamic State Is a State Run by Good Muslims: Religion as a Way of Life and Not an Ideology in Afghanistan', in R. Hefner (ed.), *Remaking Muslim Politics: Pluralism, Contestation, Democratization,* Princeton, NJ: Princeton University Press, 2005, p. 221.
70 T. Barfield, op. cit., p. 223.
71 T. Barfield, op. cit., p. 225.
72 D. Edwards, *Before Taliban: Genealogies of the Afghan Jihad,* Los Angeles, CA: University of California Press, 2002, p. 288.
73 B. Rubin, 'Afghanistan under the Taliban', *Current History* 98, 1999, p. 87.
74 T. Barfield, op. cit., p. 227.
75 D. Edwards, op. cit., p. 289.
76 L. Goodson, *Afghanistan's Endless War: State Failure, Regional Politics, and the Rise of the Taliban,* Seattle, WA: University of Washington Press, 2001, p. 108.
77 B. Rubin, op. cit., p. 88.
78 B. Rubin, op. cit., p. 81.
79 Ibid.
80 G. Kepel, op. cit., p. 229.
81 G. Kepel, op. cit., pp. 230–231.
82 J. Esposito, op. cit., p. 235.
83 T. Barfield, op. cit., p. 233.
84 G. Kepel, op. cit., p. 231.
85 G. Kepel, op. cit., pp. 233–234; T. Barfield, op. cit., p. 232.
86 T. Barfield, op. cit., p. 232.
87 G. Kepel, op. cit., p. 234.
88 T. Barfield, op. cit., p. 233.
89 D. Edwards, op. cit., p. 291.
90 B. Rubin, op. cit., p. 80.

91 B. Rubin, op. cit., p. 85.
92 G. Kepel, op. cit., p. 225.
93 D. Edwards, op. cit., p. 292.
94 D. Edwards, op. cit., p. 293.
95 G. Kepel, op. cit., p. 225.
96 O. Roy, *Globalized Islam: The Search for a New Ummah,* New York: Columbia University Press, 2004, p. 258–265.
97 T. Barfield, op. cit., p. 229.
98 L. Goodson, op. cit., pp. 109–110.
99 D. Edwards, op. cit., p. 295.
100 T. Barfield, op. cit., p. 230.
101 G.Kepel, op. cit., p. 229.
102 D. Edwards, op. cit., p. 294.
103 B. Rubin, op. cit., p. 80.
104 L. Goodson, op. cit., p. 132.
105 B. Metcalf, '"Traditionalist" Islamic Activism: Deoband, Tablighis, and Talibs', *ISIM Papers* 4, Leiden: Institute for the Study of Islam in the Modern World, 2002.
106 D. Edwards, op. cit., p. 294.
107 D. Edwards, op. cit., p. 298.
108 D. Edwards, op. cit., p. 296.
109 D. Edwards, op. cit., p. 300.
110 Sheikh Omar Bakri Muhammad, Personal interview with author, London, July 2002.
111 T. Barfield, op. cit., p. 232.
112 S. Zunes, 'Afghanistan: Five Years Later', *Foreign Policy in Focus Report,* October 2006.
113 E. Rubin, 'In the Land of the Taliban', *New York Times Magazine,* October 22, 2006.
114 S. Zunes, 'Afghanistan: Five Years Later', *Foreign Policy in Focus Report,* October 2006.

7 Radical Islamism and jihad beyond the nation-state

1 P. Bergen, *Holy War, Inc.: Inside the Secret World of Osama Bin Laden,* New York: Touchstone, 2001, p. 200.
2 O. Roy, *Globalized Islam: The Search for a New Ummah,* New York: Columbia University Press, 2004, p. 297.
3 F. Gerges, *The Far Enemy: Why Jihad Went Global,* Cambridge: Cambridge University Press, 2005, p. 12.
4 D. Cook, *Understanding Jihad,* Berkeley, CA: University of California Press, 2005, p. 128.
5 F. Gerges, op. cit., pp. 12–13.
6 D. Cook, op. cit., p. 153.
7 D. Cook, op. cit., p. 131.
8 R. Gunaratna, *Inside Al Qaeda: Global Network of Terror,* New York: Columbia University Press, 2002, p. 86.
9 O. Roy, op. cit.; B. Rubin, 'Afghanistan under the Taliban', *Current History* 98, 1999, p. 84.
10 F. Gerges, op. cit., p. 75.
11 G. Kepel, *The War for Muslim Minds,* Cambridge, MA: Harvard University Press, 2004, p. 121.
12 Q. Wiktorowicz, 'The Salafi Movement: Violence and Fragmentation of Community', in M. Cooke, B. Lawrence (eds), *Muslim Networks from Hajj to Hip*

Hop, Chapel Hill, NC: The University of North Carolina Press, 2005, pp. 211–213.
13 T. Ramadan, *To be a European Muslim,* Leicester: The Islamic Foundation, 1999.
14 D. Cook, op. cit., pp. 96–97.
15 D. Cook, op. cit., p. 105.
16 F. Gerges, op. cit., p. 5.
17 D. Cook, op. cit., p. 106.
18 D. Cook, op. cit., p. 108.
19 Q. Wiktorowicz, 'The New Global Threat', *Middle East Policy* 8, 2001, 26.
20 Q. Wiktorowicz, op. cit., p. 23.
21 F. Gerges, op. cit., p. 27.
22 F. Gerges, op. cit., p. 25.
23 F. Gerges, op. cit., p. 13.
24 Q. Wiktorowicz, op. cit., p. 23.
25 F. Gerges, op. cit., p. 200.
26 F. Gerges, op. cit., pp. 200–228.
27 M. Derbala, quoted in F. Gerges, op. cit., p. 233.
28 Pew Global Attitudes Survey Attitude Reports 2002–6; see http://pewglobal.org/
29 R. Gunaratna, op. cit., p. 21.
30 R. Gunaratna, op. cit., p. 54.
31 R. Gunaratna, op. cit., p. 57.
32 R. Gunaratna, op. cit., p. 59.
33 R. Gunaratna, op. cit., p. 61.
34 R. Gunaratna, op. cit., p. 70.
35 R. Gunaratna, op. cit., p. 75.
36 R. Gunaratna, op. cit., p. 98.
37 O. Roy, op. cit., pp. 257–258.
38 O. Roy, op. cit., p. 302.
39 O. Roy, op. cit., p. 258; P. Mandaville, 'Sufis and Salafis: The Political Discourse of Transnational Islam', in R. Hefner (ed.), *Remaking Muslim Politics: Pluralism, Contestation, Democratization,* Princeton, NJ: Princeton University Press, 2005, pp. 314–315
40 M. Whine, 'Hizb ut-Tahrir in Open Societies', in Z. Baran, *The Challenge of Hizb ut-Tahrir: Deciphering and Combating Radical Islamist Ideology,* Washington, DC: The Nixon Center, 2004.
41 Q. Wiktorowicz, *Radical Islam Rising: Muslim Extremism in the West,* Lanham, MD: Rowman & Littlefield, 2005.
42 F. Gerges, op. cit., p. 34.
43 Q. Wiktorowicz, op. cit., p. 4.
44 M. Sageman, *Understanding Terror Networks,* Philadelphia, PA: University of Pennsylvania Press, 2004.
45 F. Gerges, op. cit., p. 8.
46 S. Taji-Farouki, *A Fundamental Quest: Hizb al-Tahrir and the Search for the Islamic Caliphate,* London: Grey Seal, 1996.
47 P. Mandaville, *Transnational Muslim Politics: Reimagining the Umma,* London: Routledge, 2001, p. 129.
48 A. Rashid, *Jihad: The Rise of Militant Islam in Central Asia,* New York: Penguin Books, 2002, p. 135.
49 Dilwar Hussain, Personal Interview with author, London, June 2006.
50 C. Tilly, S. Tarrow, *Contentious Politics,* Boulder, CO: Paradigm Publishers, 2006.
51 Q. Wiktorowicz, 'The Salafi Movement: Violence and Fragmentation of Community', in M. Cooke, B. Lawrence (eds), *Muslim Networks from Hajj to Hip Hop,* Chapel Hill, NC: The University of North Carolina Press, 2005, p. 210; D. Snow, E. B. Rochford, Jr., S. K. Worden, R. D. Benford, 'Frame Alignment

Processes, Micromobilization, and Movement Participation', *American Socio-logical Review* 51, 1986, pp. 464–481.
52 R. Inglehart, *Culture Shift in Advanced Industrial Society,* Princeton, NJ: Princeton University Press, 1990.
53 Q. Wiktorowicz, op. cit., p. 211.
54 O. Roy, op. cit., p. 317.
55 F. Gerges, op. cit., p. 229.
56 G. Kepel, op. cit., p. 151.
57 F. Gerges, op. cit., p. 40.
58 O. Roy, op. cit., p. 323.

8 Muslim transnationalism: brotherhoods, networks, diasporas

1 P. Risso, *Merchants & Faith: Muslim Commerce and Culture in the Indian Ocean,* Boulder, CO: Westview Press, 1995.
2 J. Abu-Lughod, *Before European Hegemony: The World System AD 1250–1350,* Oxford: Oxford University Press, 1989.
3 P. Werbner, *Pilgrims of Love: The Anthropology of a Global Sufi Cult,* Bloomington, IN: Indiana University Press, 2003.
4 M. Masud, *Travellers in Faith: Studies of the Tablīghī Jamā'at as a Transnational Islamic Movement for Faith Renewal,* Leiden: Brill, 2000.
5 Y. Sikand, 'The Tablighi Jama'at and Politics: A Critical Re-Appraisal', *The Muslim World* 96, 2006, pp. 175–195.
6 O. Roy, *The Failure of Political Islam,* London: I.B. Tauris, 1994, pp. 107–131.
7 R. Schulze, *Islamischer Internationalismus im 20. Jahrhundert: Untersuchungen zur Geschichte der islamischen Weltliga,* Leiden: Brill, 1990.
8 M. Keck, K. Sikkink, *Activists Beyond Borders: Advocacy Networks in International Politics,* Ithaca, NY: Cornell University Press, 1998.
9 M. H. Yavuz, J. Esposito (eds), *Turkish Islam and the Secular State: The Gülen Movement,* Syracuse, NY: Syracuse University Press, 2003.
10 R. Bianchi, *Guests of God: Pilgrimage and Politics in the Islamic World,* Oxford: Oxford University Press, 2004, p. 51.
11 J. Esposito, *Islam and Politics,* 4th edn, Syracuse, NY: Syracuse University Press, 1984, p. 113.
12 R. Bianchi, op. cit., p. 4.
13 R. Bianchi, op. cit., p. 5.
14 R. Bianchi, op. cit., p. 13.
15 J. Nielsen, *Muslims in Western Europe,* 2nd edn, Edinburgh: Edinburgh University Press, 1995; S. Hunter, *Islam, Europe's Second Religion: The New Social, Cultural, and Political Landscape,* Westport, CT: Praeger Publishers, 2002.
16 B. Anderson, *Imagined Communities,* New York: Verso, 1991.
17 O. Roy, op. cit., pp. 89–106.
18 R. Robertson, 'Glocalization: Time-Space and Homogeneity-Heterogeneity', in M. Featherstone, S. Lash, R. Robertson (eds), *Global Modernities,* London: Sage, 1995, pp. 25–44.
19 M. van Creveld, *The Rise and Decline of the State,* Cambridge: Cambridge University Press, 1999.
20 P. Lubeck, 'Islam, Globalization, and State Capacity', Unpublished paper, 2006.

9 Who speaks for Islam? Religious authority in the global umma

1 F. Esack, *Qur'an, Liberation and Pluralism: An Islamic Perspective of Inter-religious Solidarity Against Oppression,* Oxford: Oneworld, 1997.

2 A. An-Na'im, *Towards an Islamic Reformation: Civil Liberties, Human Rights, and International Law,* Syracuse, NY: Syracuse University Press, 1990.

3 D. Eickelman, J. Anderson (eds), *New Media in the Muslim World: The Emerging Public Sphere,* Bloomington, IN: Indiana University Press, 1999; A. Salvatore, D. Eickelman, *Public Islam and the Common Good,* Leiden: Brill, 2006.

4 V. Miller, *Consuming Religion: Christian Faith and Practice in a Consumer Culture,* New York: Continuum, 2005.

5 H. Dabashi, *Authority in Islam: From the Rise of Muhammad to the Establishment of the Umayyads,* Piscataway, NJ: Transaction, 1989.

6 O. Roy, *Globalized Islam,* New York: Columbia University Press, 2004.

7 B. Anderson, *Imagined Communities,* New York: Verso, 1991.

8 F. Robinson, 'Islam and the Impact of Print', *Modern Asian Studies* 27, 1993, p. 245.

9 M. Q. Zaman, *The Ulama in Contemporary Islam: Custodians of Change,* Princeton, NJ: Princeton University Press, 2002; M. Zeghal, 'Gardiens de l'Islam. Les oulémas d'al-Azhar dans l'Egypte contemporaine', Paris: Presses de Sciences Po, 1996.

10 M. Zeghal, 'The "Recentering" of Religious Knowledge and Discourse: The Case of al-Azhar in Twentieth-Century Egypt', in R. Hefner, M. Q. Zaman (eds), *Schooling Islam: The Culture and Politics of Modern Muslim Education,* Princeton, NJ: Princeton University Press.

11 Ibid.

12 G. Starrett, *Putting Islam to Work: Education, Politics, and Religious Transformation in Egypt,* Berkeley, CA: University of California Press, 1998.

13 M. Q. Zaman, 'The Scope and Limits of Islamic Cosmopolitianism and the Discursive Language of the "Ulama"', in M. Cooke, B. Lawrence (eds), *Muslim Networks from Hajj to Hip Hop,* Chapel Hill, NC: The University of North Carolina Press, 2005, pp. 84–106.

14 U. Beck, *Risk Society: Towards a New Modernity,* London: Sage, 1992.

15 Pew Global Attitudes Project, 'Muslims in Europe: Economic Worries Top Concerns About Religious and Cultural Identity', Washington, DC: Pew Research Center, 2006.

16 Azzam Tamimi, Interview with author, London, June 2006.

17 O. Roy, *The Failure of Political Islam,* London: I.B. Tauris, 1994, pp. 89–106.

18 O. Roy, op. cit., pp. 95–97.

19 C. Kurzman (ed.), *Liberal Islam: A Sourcebook,* Oxford: Oxford University Press, 1998.

20 P. Mandaville, 'What Does Progressive Islam Look Like?' *ISIM Newsletter,* June 2003.

21 B. Agai, *Zwischen Netzwerk und Diskurs: Das Bildungsnetzwerk um Fethullah Gülen,* Schenefeld: EB-Verlag, 2004.

22 J. Skovgaard-Petersen, 'The Global Mufti', in B. Schaebler, L. Stenberg (eds), *Globalization and the Muslim World: Culture, Religion, and Modernity,* Syracuse, NY: Syracuse University Press, 2004, pp. 153–165.

23 P. Mandaville, *Transnational Muslim Politics: Reimagining the umma,* London: Routledge, 2001.

24 Ibid.

25 Pew Global Attitudes Project, 'Muslims in Europe: Economic Worries Top Concerns About Religious and Cultural Identity', Washington, DC: Pew Research Center, 2006.

26 M. Q. Zaman, op. cit.

27 O. Safi (ed.), *Progressive Muslims: On Justice, Gender, and Pluralism,* Oxford: Oneworld, 2003.

28 F. Shaheed, A. Shaheed, *Great Ancestors: Women Asserting Rights in Muslim Contexts,* London: Women Living Under Muslim Law, 2005.

29 D. Eickelman, J. Anderson (eds), op. cit.; P. Mandaville, op. cit.; S. Glasser, S. Coll, 'The Web as a Weapon', *The Washington Post,* August 9 2005, A01.

30 C. Hirschkind, 'The Ethics of Listening: Cassette-Sermon Audition in Contemporary Egypt', *American Ethnologist* 28, 2002, 623–649; C. Hirschkind, 'Civic Virtue and Religious Reason: An Islamic Counterpublic', *Cultural Anthropology* 16, 2001, pp. 3–34.

31 P. Mandaville, op. cit.

32 J. Skovgaard-Petersen, op. cit., p. 158.

33 G. Starrett, 'The Political Economy of Religious Commodities in Cairo', *American Anthropologist* 97, 1995, pp. 51–68.

34 C. Hirschkind, 'Civic Virtue and Religious Reason: An Islamic Counterpublic', *Cultural Anthropology* 16, 2001, pp. 3–34.

35 C. Hirschkind, op. cit., p. 9.

36 J. White, 'The End of Islamism? Turkey's Muslimhood Model', in R. Hefner (ed.), *Remaking Muslim Politics: Pluralism, Contestation, Democratization,* Princeton, NJ: Princeton University Press, 2005, pp. 87–111.

37 A. Boubekeur, 'Cool and Competitive: Muslim Culture in the West', *ISIM Review* 16, 2005, p. 13.

38 L. Wise, '"Words from the Heart": New Forms of Islamic Preaching in Egypt', Unpublished M. Phil Thesis, St. Antony's College, Oxford University, 2003.

39 P. Haenni, H. Tammam, 'Egypt's air-conditioned Islam', *Le Monde Diplomatique,* September 2003.

40 Ibid.

41 A. Boubekeur, op. cit., p. 12.

42 C. Watson, 'A Popular Indonesian Preacher: The Significance of AA Gymnastiar', *Journal of the Royal Anthropological Institute* 11, 2005, pp. 773–792.

43 A. Boubekeur, op. cit., p. 12.

10 Beyond Islamism: globalization and Muslim politics

1 R. Baker, *Islam Without Fear: Egypt and the New Islamists,* Cambridge: Harvard University Press, 2003; G. Fuller, *The Future of Political Islam,* New York: Palgrave Macmillan, 2004.

2 C. Wickham, 'The Causes and Dynamics of Islamist Auto-Reform', *ICIS International* 6, 2006, 6–7.

3 D. Brumberg, 'Islamists and the Politics of Consensus', *Journal of Democracy* 13, 2002, p. 112.

4 F. Burgat, *Face to Face with Political Islam,* New York: I.B. Tauris, 2003, p. 167.

5 H. al-Turabi, 'The Islamic State', in J. Esposito (ed.), *Voices of Resurgent Islam,* New York: Oxford University Press, 1983, pp. 241–251.

6 R. Ghannouchi, 'The Participation of Islamists in a non-Islamic Government', in A. Tamimi (ed.), *Power Sharing Islam?,* London: Liberty, 1993, pp. 51–63.

7 G. Fuller, op. cit., p. 198.

8 G. Fuller, op. cit., pp. 200–201.

9 D. Brumberg, 'Islam is Not the Solution (or the Problem)', *The Washington Quarterly* 29, 2005, pp. 97–116.

10 G. Fuller, op. cit., p. 201.

11 O. Roy, *Globalized Islam: The Search for a New Ummah,* New York: Columbia University Press, 2004; P. Mandaville, *Transnational Muslim Politics: Reimagining the Umma,* London: Routledge, 2001.

12 O. Roy, *The Failure of Political Islam,* London: I.B. Tauris, 1994.

13 O. Roy, *Globalized Islam: The Search for a New Ummah,* New York: Columbia University Press, 2004, pp. 58–99.

14 O. Roy, op. cit., p. 75.

15 O. Roy, op. cit., p. 74–75.
16 O. Roy, op. cit., p. 77.
17 O. Roy, op. cit., p. 74.
18 O. Roy, op. cit., p. 98.
19 O. Roy, op. cit., p. 99.
20 G. Kepel, 'Islamism Reconsidered', *Harvard International Review* 22, 2000, p. 26.
21 G. Kepel, op. cit., p. 22.
22 G. Kepel, op. cit., p. 26.
23 S. Ismail, *Rethinking Islamist Politics: Culture, the State, and Islamism,* London: I.B. Tauris, 2003, p. 175.
24 O. Roy, op. cit., pp. 72–75.
25 S. Ismail, op. cit., p. 169.
26 J. Rawls, 'The Idea of an Overlapping Consensus', *Oxford Journal for Legal Studies* 7, 1987, pp. 1–25.
27 S. Ismail, op. cit., p. 163; C. Wickham, op. cit., pp. 6–7.
28 S. Ismail, op. cit., p. 168.
29 S. Ismail, op. cit., p. 160.
30 S. Ismail, op. cit., p. 167.
31 S. Ismail, op. cit., p. 168.
32 S, Ismail, op. cit., p. 171.
33 S. Ismail, op. cit., p. 170.
34 S. Ismail, op. cit., p. 173.
35 F. Burgat, op. cit., p. 180.
36 F. Burgat, op. cit., p. 182.
37 Ibid.
38 A. Bayat, 'The Coming of a Post-Islamist Society', *Critique: Critical Middle East Studies* 9, 1996, 43–52; A. Bayat, 'What is Post-Islamism?', *ISIM Review* 16, 2005, p. 5.
39 A. Bayat, 'What is Post-Islamism?', *ISIM Review* 16, 2005, p. 5.
40 Ibid.
41 Ibid.
42 F. Fukuyama, *The End of History and the Last Man,* New York: Harper, 1993.
43 M. Davis, *Planet of Slums,* London: Verson, 2006; R. Neuwirth, *Shadow Cities: A Billion Squatters, A New Urban World,* New York: Routledge, 2005.
44 C. Henry, R. Springborg, *Globalization and the Politics of Development in the Middle East,* Cambridge: Cambridge University Press, 2001, p. 225.
45 G. Arrighi (ed.), *Semiperipheral Development,* Beverly Hills, CA: Sage, 1985.
46 D. Brumberg, op. cit., p. 102.

Suggestions for further reading

Readers who would like to explore topics and themes covered in this book in greater detail are advised to consult the following works.

Political Islam (general)

J. Beinin, J. Stork (eds), *Political Islam*, London: I.B. Tauris, 1997.

F. Burgat, *Face to Face with Political Islam*, New York: I.B. Tauris, 2003.

J. Clark, *Islam, Charity and Activism: Middle-Class Networks and Social Welfare in Egypt, Jordan, and Yemen*, Bloomington, IN: Indiana University Press, 2004.

D. Eickelman, J. Piscatori, *Muslim Politics*, revised edn, Princeton, NJ: Princeton University Press, 2004.

J. Esposito, *Islam and Politics*, 4th edn, Syracuse, NY: Syracuse University Press, 1998.

G. Fuller, *The Future of Political Islam*, New York: Palgrave, 2003.

R. Hefner (ed.), *Remaking Muslim Politics: Pluralism, Contestation, Democratization*, Princeton, NJ: Princeton University Press, 2005.

S. Ismail, *Rethinking Islamist Politics: Culture, the State, and Islamism*, London: I.B. Tauris, 2003.

G. Kepel, *Jihad: The Trail of Political Islam*, Cambridge, MA: Harvard University Press, 2002.

B. Milton-Edwards, *Islamic Fundamentalism Since 1945*, London: Routledge, 2005.

M. Moaddel, *Islamic Modernism, Nationalism, and Fundamentalism: Episode and Discourse*, Chicago, IL: The University of Chicago Press, 2005.

J. Piscatori, *Islam in a World of Nation-States*, Cambridge: Cambridge University Press, 1986.

O. Roy, *The Failure of Political Islam*, London: I.B. Tauris, 1994.

——, *Globalized Islam: The Search for a New Ummah*, New York: Columbia University Press, 2004.

J. Schwedler, *Faith in Moderation: Islamist Parties in Jordan and Yemen*, New York: Cambridge University Press, 2006.

G. Starrett, *Putting Islam to Work: Education, Politics, and Religious Transformation in Egypt*, Berkeley, CA: University of California Press, 1998.

C. Wickham, *Mobilizing Islam: Religion, Activism, and Political Change in Egypt*, New York: Columbia University Press, 2002.

Q. Wiktorowicz, *The Management of Islamic Activism: Salafis, the Muslim Brotherhood, and State Power in Jordan*, Albany, NY: State University of New York Press, 2001.

Q. Wiktorowicz (ed.), *Islamic Activism: A Social Movement Theory Approach*, Bloomington, IN: Indiana University Press, 2004.

S. Zubaida, *Islam the People & the State: Political Ideas & Movements in the Middle East*, London: I.B. Tauris & Co, 1993.

——, *Law and Power in the Islamic World*, London: I.B. Tauris, 2005.

Primary source readers on Islam and politics

J. Donohue, J. Esposito (ed.), *Islam in Transition: Muslim Perspectives*, 2nd edn, New York: Oxford University Press, 2006.

C. Kurzman (ed.), *Liberal Islam: A Sourcebook*, Oxford: Oxford University Press, 1998.

——, *Modernist Islam, 1840–1940: A Sourcebook*, Oxford: Oxford University Press, 2002.

M. Moaddel, K. Talattof (eds), *Modernist and Fundamentalist Debates in Islam*, New York: Palgrave, 2002.

Islamic history

J. Berkey, *The Formation of Islam: Religion and Society in the Near East, 600–1800*, Cambridge: Cambridge University Press, 2003.

M. Hodgson, *The Venture of Islam: Conscience and History in a World Civilization*, 3 Volumes, Chicago, IL: The University of Chicago Press, 1974.

I. Lapidus, *A History of Islamic Societies*, 2nd edn, Cambridge: Cambridge University Press, 2002.

R. Schulze, *A Modern History of the Islamic World*, London: I.B. Tauris, 2002.

Islamic political thought and thinkers

K. Abou el-Fadl, *And God Knows the Soldiers: The Authoritative and Authoritarian in Islamic Discourses*, Lanham, MD: University Press of America, 2001.

I. Abu-Rabi, *Intellectual Origins of Islamic Resurgence in the Modern Arab World*, New York: SUNY Press, 1995.

A. an-Naim, *Toward an Islamic Reformation: Civil Liberties, Human Rights, and International Law*, Syracuse, NY: Syracuse University Press, 1996.

R. Baker, *Islam Without Fear: Egypt and the New Islamists*, Cambridge, MA: Harvard University Press, 2003.

L. Carl Brown, *Religion and State: The Muslim Approach to Politics*, New York: Columbia University Press, 2000.

H. Enayat, *Modern Islamic Political Thought: the Response of the Shi'a and Sunni Muslims to the Twentieth Century*, London: I.B. Tauris, 2005.

S. Khatab, *The Political Thought of Sayyid Qutb: the Theory of Jahiliyya*, London: Routledge, 2006.

J. Landau, *The Politics of Pan-Islam: Ideology and Organization*, Oxford: Clarendon Press, 1990.

V. Nasr, *Mawdudi and the Making of Islamic Revivalism*, New York: Oxford University Press, 2002.

F. Rahman, *Islam & Modernity: The Transformation of an Intellectual Tradition*, Chicago, IL: The University of Chicago Press, 1984.

A. Rahnema (ed.), *Pioneers of Islamic Revival*, London: Zed Books, 1994.
A. Rahnema, *An Islamic Utopian: A Political Biography of Ali Shari'ati*, London: I.B. Tauris, 2000.
A. Sachedina, *The Islamic Roots of Democratic Pluralism*, New York: Oxford University Press, 2001.

The Islamic state

A. Ali Engineer, *The Islamic State*, New Delhi: Vikas Publishing House, 1994.
A. El-Affendi, *Who Needs an Islamic State?*, London: Grey Seal, 1991.
S. V. R. Nasr, *Islamic Leviathan: Islam and the Making of State Power*, New York: Oxford University Press, 2001.

Sunni-Shi'i politics

M. Momen, *An Introduction to Shi'i Islam*, New Haven, CT: Yale University Press, 1985.
Y. Nakash, *Reaching for Power: The Shi'a in the Modern Arab World*, Princeton, NJ: Princeton University Press, 2006.
V. Nasr, *The Shi'a Revival: How Conflicts Within Islam Will Shape the Future*, New York: Norton, 2006.
Y. Richard, *Shi'ite Islam: Polity Ideology and Creed*, Oxford: Blackwell, 1995.

Jihad

M. Bonner, *Jihad in Islamic History: Doctrines and Practice*, Princeton, NJ: Princeton University Press, 2006.
D. Cook, *Understanding Jihad*, Berkeley, CA: University of California Press, 2005.
R. Peters, *Jihad in Classical and Modern Islam: A Reader*, Princeton, NJ: Markus Wiener, 1996.

Radicalism

M. Hafez, *Why Muslims Rebel: Repression and Resistance in the Islamic World*, Boulder, CO: Lynne Rienner, 2003.
M. Sageman, *Understanding Terror Networks*, Philadelphia, PA: University of Pennsylvania Press, 2004.
Q. Wiktorowicz, *Radical Islam Rising: Muslim Extremism in the West*, Lanham, MD: Rowman & Littlefield, 2005.

Other transnational Islam

J. Benthall, J. Bellion-Jourdan, *The Charitable Crescent: Politics of Aid in the Muslim World*, New York: I.B. Tauris, 2003.
R. Bianchi, *Guests of God: Pilgrimage and Politics in the Islamic World*, Oxford: Oxford University Press, 2004.
J. Burr, R. Collins, *Alms for Jihad: Charity and Terrorism in the Islamic World*, Cambridge: Cambridge University Press, 2006.

M. Cooke, B. Lawrence (eds), *Muslim Networks from Hajj to Hip Hop*, Chapel Hill, NC: The University of North Carolina Press, 2005.

B. DeGorge, *From Piety to Politics: The Evolution of Sufi Brotherhoods*, Washington, DC: New Academia Publishing, 2006.

R. Hefner, M.Q. Zaman (eds), *Schooling Islam: Modern Muslim Education*, Princeton, NJ: Princeton University Press, 2007.

A. Karam (ed.), *Transnational Political Islam: Religion, Ideology, and Power*, London: Pluto Press, 2004.

P. Mandaville, *Transnational Muslim Politics: Reimagining the Umma*, London: Routledge, 2003.

B. Mauer, *Mutual Life, Limited: Islamic Banking, Alternative Currencies, Lateral Reason*, Princeton, NJ: Princeton University Press, 2005.

A.E. Mayer, *Islam and Human Rights: Tradition and Politics*, Boulder, CO: Westview Press, 1999.

Muslims in Europe

S. Allievi, J. Nielsen (eds), *Muslim Networks and Transnational Communities in and Across Europe*, Boston, MA: Brill, 2003.

J. Bowen, *Why The French Don't Like Headscarves: Islam, the State, and Public State*, Princeton, NJ: Princeton University Press, 2006.

J. Cesari, S. McLoughlin (eds), *European Muslim and the Secular State*, Burlington, VT: Ashgate Publishing Company, 2005.

S. Hunter, *Islam, Europe's Second Religion: The New Social, Cultural, and Political Landscape*, Westport, CT: Praeger Publishers, 2002.

J. Laurence, *Integrating Islam: Political and Religious Changes in Contemporary France*, Washington, DC: Brookings Institute Press, 2006.

P. Lewis, *Islamic Britain: Religion, Politics and Identity Among British Muslims*, London: I.B. Tauris, 2002.

J. Nielsen, *Muslims in Western Europe*, Edinburgh: Edinburgh University Press, 2004.

Islam and new media

L. Abu-Lughod, *Local Contexts of Islamism in Popular Media*, Amsterdam: Amsterdam University Press, 2006.

G. Bunt, *Virtually Islamic: Computer-Mediated Communication and Cyber Islamic Environments*, Cardiff: University of Wales Press, 2000.

——, *Islam in the Digital Age: E-Jihad, Online Fatwas, and Cyber-Islamic Environments*, London: Pluto Press, 2003.

D. Eickelman, J. Anderson (eds), *New Media in the Muslim World: The Emerging Public Sphere*, Bloomington, IN: Indiana University Press, 2003.

N. Sakr, *Satellite Realms: Transnational Television, Globalization and the Middle East*, London: I.B. Tauris, 2001.

Globalization and Islam

A. Ahmed, H. Donnan (eds), *Islam and Globalization: Critical Concepts in Islamic Studies*, London: Routledge, 2006.

J. Meuleman (ed.), *Islam in the Era of Globalization: Muslim Attitudes Towards Modernity and Identity*, London: Routledge Curzon, 2002.

A. Mohammadi (ed.), *Islam Encountering Globalization,* London: Routledge Curzon, 2002.

B. Schaebler, L. Stenberg (eds), *Globalization and the Muslim World: Culture, Religion, and Modernity,* Syracuse, NY: Syracuse University Press, 2004.

Islam, gender, and politics

L. Ahmed, *Women and Gender in Islam: Historical Roots of a Modern Debate*, New Haven, CT: Yale University Press, 1992.

A. Barlas, *"Believing Women" in Islam: Unreading Patriarchal Interpretations of the Qur'an*, Austin, TX: University of Texas, 2002.

L. Deeb, *An Enchanted Modern: Gender and Public Piety in Shi'i Lebanon*, Princeton, NJ: Princeton University Press, 2006.

D. Kandiyoti (ed.), *Women, Islam and the State*, Philadelphia, PA: Temple University Press, 1991.

S. Mahmood, *Politics of Piety: The Islamic Revival and the Feminist Subject,* Princeton, NJ: Princeton University Press, 2005.

Z. Mir-Hosseini, *Islam and Gender: The Religious Debate in Contemporary Iran*, Princeton, NJ: Princeton University Press, 1999.

P. van Doorn-Harder, *Women Shaping Islam: Reading the Qur'an in Indonesia*, Champaign, IL: University of Illinois Press, 2006.

Index